# WEST AFRICA

**Geographies for Advanced Study**

Edited by Professor Stanley H. Beaver, M.A., F.R.G.S.

The British Isles: A Geographic and Economic Survey
Central Europe
Concepts in Climatology
East Africa
Eastern Europe
Geography of Population
Geomorphology
The Glaciations of Wales and Adjoining Regions
An Historical Geography of South Africa
An Historical Geography of Western Europe before 1800
Human Geography
Introduction to Climatic Geomorphology
Land, People and Economy in Malaya
The Landforms of the Tropics, Forests and Savannas
Malaya, Indonesia, Borneo and the Philippines
North America
The Polar World
A Regional Geography of Western Europe
The Scandinavian World
The Soviet Union
Statistical Methods and the Geographer
The Tropical World
Urban Essays: Studies in the Geography of Wales
Urban Geography
**West Africa**
The Western Mediterranean World

# WEST AFRICA

## A study of the environment and of man's use of it

R. J. Harrison Church BScEcon PhD

Professor of Geography in the University of London
at the London School of Economics and Political Science.
Sometime French Government Post-graduate British Fellow at the Sorbonne (Paris)

with a chapter on

## Soils and soil management

P. R. Moss BSc PhD

Professor of Biogeography
University of Birmingham

Longman

LONGMAN GROUP LIMITED
London
*Associated companies, branches and representatives*
*throughout the world*

New editions © R. J. Harrison Church
1960, 1961, 1963, 1966, 1968
Seventh edition © Longman Group Ltd. 1974

First published 1957
Second edition 1960
Third edition 1961
Fourth edition 1963
Fifth edition 1966
Sixth edition 1968
Seventh edition 1974

Russian edition 1959

ISBN 0 582 48073 6 Paper
ISBN 0 582 48072 8 Case

*Text filmset in Monophoto Times New Roman by*
*London Filmsetters Limited*
*Printed in Great Britain by*
*J. W. Arrowsmith Ltd., Bristol*

*If this book be of sufficient merit,*
*it is dedicated to the peoples of*
*West Africa and to all who have their*
*welfare at heart*

# Contents

# Contents

*Contents*

*Contents*

*Contents*

# Contents

# List of text figures

# List of plates

# List of plates

# Acknowledgements

For permission to reproduce photographs we are grateful to the following:

*Air Afrique:* Plate 29; Air Ministry: Plate 73; Afrique Photo: Plates 44, 79 (Pichonnier); Ashanti Goldfields Corporation: Plate 90; Azur Ciné Photo: Plate 55; British-American Tobacco Company Ltd: Plate 103; J. Allan Cash: Plate 117; Charter Consolidated: Plates 56, 57; La Cognata: Plate 60; Coopération: Plates 3, 5, 37, 43, 96 (Ledoux), 94 (Billere), 51, 52, 54 (all de Chaitillon); Coopération France (B. Nantet): Plate 35; Coopération (Cᵗe d'Ivoire): Plate 82; Dahomey Information Service: Plate 97; Diamond Corporation (West Africa) Ltd: Plate 75; Documentation Française: Plate 18; R. Doganis; Plate 62; Ghana Information Service: Plates 15, 84, 85, 93; Ghana Ministry of Agriculture: Plate 16; Gränges International Mining: Plates 77, 78; D. Hilling: Plate 25; IFAN: Plates 6, 36 (both G. Labitte); Plate 30 (A. Cocheteux); Institut Géographique National: Plates 42, 46; Miferma; Plate 53; Sierra Leone Selection Trust: Plate 74; Orlando Ribeiro: Plates 67, 68; United Africa Company Ltd: Plates 10, 11, 12; United Africa Company Ltd & Tom Smith London: Plates 87, 89, 98, 99, 105, 111; P. Waeues; Plates 65, 66; West African Photographic Service: Plates 9, 17, 91.

Plates 113–115 are Shell photographs and Plate 116 is a B.P. photograph.

Plates 1, 2, 4, 7, 8, 13, 14, 19–24, 26–28, 31–34, 38–40, 45, 47–50, 58, 59, 61, 64, 69–72, 76, 80, 81, 83, 86, 88, 95, 100–102, 104, 106–110, 112 and 118 are the author's photographs.

# Preface

West Africa has been in contact with the outside world longer than any other part of Africa south of the Sahara. No other area of Africa has undergone such profound political, economic and social changes as have taken place recently in West Africa. The world and West Africa are making a great impact on each other.

No apology is necessary, therefore, for this study of West Africa, based on over thirty-six years of wide reading in scattered literature in several languages, and on very extensive field work throughout the area. While it casts its net widely, it does not necessarily include all that might be regarded by some as geographical; nor is its scope confined to matters exclusively geographical. Nevertheless, material wholly germane to political science, anthropology and economics is not discussed in detail. No person could rightly imagine from the text that such matters are unimportant, but their study requires other specialists and other books.

Part I deals with the natural conditions in West Africa, and with some of the human problems which these present. Part II analyses man's work in agriculture, livestock holding, mining, energy sources and industry, and the provision of transport, as well as the distribution of man himself, which often but not always results from these activities. Part III is an examination of the individual countries, after a general review of the political divisions.

There is some variation in the content of chapters on the several countries, which results from their different natures and the relative availability or reliability of the material. The regional approach has been adopted in almost all chapters because, contrary to widespread belief, there is great regional variety in West Africa, a fact well understood by its peoples. A further reason for the study of regions within the countries of West Africa is that they have been neglected, although they are of major importance in development plans. Development schemes will fail, as many have done, unless they are based on a regional appraisal of the physical, economic and human resources.

The initial idea for this book came from the late Professor Sir Dudley Stamp, a beloved and outstanding teacher with whom I was privileged to work for many years as a colleague. My numerous visits to West Africa have been supported by several foundations, governments, other public and private institutions, not least the London School of Economics and Political Science. To all of them I am profoundly grateful. Nor could I ever forget the patience and hospitality shown me by administrative and technical officers, merchants, missionaries and private people—African, European and Lebanese—on countless occasions.

Many secretaries have at one time or another typed parts of my manuscript, and successive ladies in our Drawing Office have drawn or revised my maps with skill, artistry and patience. Many friends checked the original version of the manuscript, and Professor S. H. Beaver, another former teacher and colleague of mine, was an assiduous and helpful editor.

Chapter 18 on Portuguese Guinea is based on notes originally provided by my student contemporary in Paris, Professor Orlando Ribeiro of the University of Lisbon. Almost all the chapters have been seen by specialists or local residents, who have added greatly to the value of the book.

Considerable time and thought have been expended in finding and arranging suitable illustrations. As the numbers of these must be limited, I have included none of vegetation; excellent photographs of this may be seen in some of the references cited for Chapter 4. I am indeed grateful to those who have provided illustrations without fee, and to authors, editors and publishers who have permitted me to use certain maps.

Every effort has been made by me and my helpers in verifying facts and conclusions but West Africa is changing rapidly. Matters now true may cease to be, and some mistakes may have slipped in. I should be grateful to anyone who takes the trouble to tell me of any errors, for which I take responsibility.

My sincerest wish is that this book will contribute to the knowledge of a delightful part of a fascinating and developing continent. May it be read in the spirit of the dedication.

## Note on the seventh edition

The resetting of this seventh edition has given me a free hand to excise or add material. Professor P. R. Moss has contributed a new chapter on soils, which has greatly enhanced the book. Chapters 8–11 have been very substantially changed and enlarged, whilst the chapters on the individual states have all undergone heavy revision and modification. In particular, much more has been added in Chapter 8 and in the individual state chapters on industry, and references and bibliographies are everywhere updated and strengthened. Photographs are now in the text, and most are new. Almost all maps have been modified or corrected, major roads have been added to country maps, and there are some new ones.

The opportunity has also been taken to metricate the book, non-metric equivalents being supplied in brackets. I am most grateful to my son for undertaking this tedious task. I have rounded some of his precise equivalents where this would make for easier understanding, and where approximations are intended.

The chapters on Fernando Po, São Tomé and Príncipe have been omitted, largely because these islands belong more truly to West-Central Africa. The space gained has facilitated the expansion of Chapters 8 to 11 and of many other chapters.

Consequently, this edition differs much more from its predecessor than has any other. As with good food guides, it is important to use an up-to-date edition.

*May* 1973                                                                                      R.J.H.C.

# Note on Geographical nomenclature

The spelling of African place and tribal names is in a confused state. The early European orthography of African names was often grossly inaccurate. Some names have since been officially changed and improved, while others have persisted in their unsatisfactory form. The author, though wishing to see a name properly recorded, must use the official style, so that the name may be located on a map. At the suggestion of Mr M. Aurousseau, former Secretary of the Permanent Committee on Geographical Names for British Official Use, I have adopted the names used by the map-making authorities of each country, except where long-recognised English equivalents exist, e.g. Timbuktu. For tribal names, I hope that I have succeeded in using the names most widely used and generally accepted by British ethnographers.

Confusion might arise over such terms as Guinea coasts, Guinea coast-lands, Guinea Highlands and Guinea Savanna. Except where these are mentioned in the chapter on Guinea, they should be understood as referring to natural features of wider occurrence. The first two concern fringes of the Gulf of Guinea.

# Introduction

Long usage has given the term 'West Africa' a clear meaning, for it is usage based upon a real separateness. West Africa is the mainland area lying south of the Sahara and west of the boundary between Nigeria and Cameroon, a boundary that is one of Africa's major physical and human divides. Thus, this study of West Africa comprises the nine francophone countries, the four anglophone ones, Liberia and Portuguese Guinea.

The distance between the extremities of West Africa is nearly equal to that between London and Moscow. The total area is 6·2 million sq km (2·4 million sq miles), or five-sixths that of the United States. The population is over 100 million, being about one-half that of the United States, or the same as that of France and the United Kingdom. The francophone republics occupy three-quarters of the area; yet, largely because some of these republics include vast tracts of the Sahara, they have under one-third of the total population. Nigeria, one of the largest and most densely populated countries of the Commonwealth, has a population of about 65 million in an area four times that of the United Kingdom. Moreover, Nigeria has well over one-half the population of West Africa and over twice that of the four times larger area of the francophone republics.

West Africa has for long been divided internally. Relief, climate, vegetation, soils and the responses in agriculture, livestock keeping, ethnic types, societies and religion, all tend to give an arrangement of east–west belts. The greatest and most fundamental division is between the south and the north. The former has a generally heavier rainfall, rather leached soils, was originally most forested, produces the oil palm and other useful tree crops, grows cassava, yams or rice for the main foods, and is inhabited by purer Negroes who were originally animist in religion and organised in small states or tribes. The latter has a lesser but more concentrated rainfall alternating with a long dry season, less leached soils, savanna woodland vegetation, produces guinea corn and millet as the main foodstuffs, is inhabited by fixed agricultural peoples or by nomadic pastoralists (particularly the Fulani), the dominant religion is Islam and the political organisation is often in larger units.

West Africa was possibly reached by Dieppe mariners in 1364; certainly by Portuguese ships from the fifteenth century onwards, particularly by those bound for Asia or Brazil. But the generally surf-bound coast, dense forest, trying climate and disease, all combined to restrict contact to the shipping of gold, slaves and other valuable commodities, such as ivory, pepper and gum.

Attention was concentrated on the 'Gold Coast' (now Ghana), where many huge castle headquarters remain today; on the coast between the Volta and the Niger deltas (long known as the 'Slave Coast'), where Lagos lagoon and the Niger Delta afforded anchorages, and slaves were available from the prisoners of the states of Ashanti, Dahomey, Yorubaland and Benin; and on the coast between the Gambia and Sierra Leone, where estuary anchorages were available. The slave trade provoked such hostility towards Europeans that they were not encouraged to penetrate inland, either by the ordinary Africans or by the slave-trade intermediaries, who were jealous of their position.

Slavery was not introduced to West Africa by Europeans. It had long been the practice of Arab peoples to take Negro slaves—and for African rulers to use their prisoners for this purpose, but it was the Europeans who introduced the large-scale overseas slave trade. This trade took African peoples, their gaiety and culture into the lands of North, Central and South America. In the Caribbean Isles they virtually replaced the indigenous peoples. In the United States the institution of slavery was a main cause of one of the most cruel and costly civil wars of all time; and the political, social and economic problems of the American Negro are still grave. Negroes are also of great importance in Brazil, but there they have been more fully absorbed and prejudice has been largely over-come. The settlement of West Africans in the New World remains one of West Africa's greatest contributions to world affairs.

After the abolition of the slave trade, West Africa declined for a time in economic importance. The Danes withdrew from the Gold Coast in 1850 and the Dutch in 1872. In 1866 the British Parliament gave serious thought to the idea of withdrawal.

There was soon to be quickened interest. France had never lost enthusiasm, especially in Senegal, and, after her defeat in the Franco-Prussian War, she was encouraged by Bismarck to seek compensation in the colonial field. Other powers were also impelled by the prestige which colonial possessions were thought to confer. Rapid industrialisation in Europe and rising populations required tropical raw materials such as palm oil and rubber, as well as markets, which West Africa could supply. The Berlin Conference of 1884–85 enunciated the principle that title to territory could be maintained only by effective occupancy. In the resulting 'scramble for Africa' the political map of West Africa was mostly filled in by 1890 and entirely so by 1904.

Unfortunately, too much 'development', by Africans and others, has been in the nature of a 'robber economy', at the expense of the human and natural resources. This befell peoples and lands which, through earlier excessive isolation, had lagged behind in comparison with many parts of the world.

Recently there has been rather more rational development of mineral resources such as tin, diamonds, manganese, iron, phosphates, mineral oil and bauxite, as well as of gold mining. With this has gone the remarkable development of peasant-grown cash crops, such as cocoa and groundnuts, and of plantation crops in certain countries. Economic development is still uneven, and depends on available transport rather than on utilising the most suitable soils in the best climatic region. West Africa produces about three-quarters of the cocoa, groundnuts and palm kernels entering world trade, and one-quarter of the palm oil. West Africa also produces over 10 per cent by weight of the diamonds, nearly 10 per cent of the iron ore and 5 per cent of the tin.

West Africa's position is also important strategically. During the Second World War the fine harbour of Dakar was denied to the Allies until 1943. The closing of the Mediterranean during much of the period from mid-1940 to 1942, and the long voyage round Africa to provision the British Eighth Army in North Africa, caused Takoradi (Ghana) to be

FIG. 0.1. West Africa and the world
(Based on a map in the author's *Modern Colonisation* by permission of Messrs Hutchinson.)

used to receive supplies. These were then flown across to Egypt, a new network of airfields being built for this purpose in Ghana and Nigeria.

American troops landed in Liberia in October 1942, to establish air bases for Atlantic patrols and to safeguard, on this flank, the landings in North Africa. America later built a harbour at Monrovia and large amounts of American money have been spent in Liberia to develop rubber cultivation, iron mining, communications and other economic and social services. During 1941–42 the French pushed on with their long-discussed project for a trans-Saharan railway. They did not make much progress, but it may again be reconsidered.[1]

European administration cut across the old physical and human divisions of West Africa, creating new political units often incorporating both savanna and forest lands. Europeans also introduced contrasting policies. The French tried to make African Frenchmen or French Africans, and replaced African chiefs by direct rule which by British standards was highly centralised. The British retained and developed African institutions. Instruction was often given in African languages, and conscription was never applied.

In the early days the French policy seemed harsh in its effects on native life and institutions, but it may now prove to have been the means of unifying peoples previously very divided. By contrast, British policy which consistently sought to retain African society, may have been too conservative and may have made more arduous the creation of wider loyalties than those of tribes. But if greater unity can be attained it is likely to arise out of African life itself, rather than by copying European ideals and institutions.

# PART I

# The physical basis of West Africa

*The following chapters relate to the whole of West Africa. Further details concerning matters discussed here may be found in the territorial chapters.*

# 1

# Geology, coasts and shores

## Geology

This account is intended as an outline and aid to the explanation of surface forms, relief, drainage, soils, mineral deposits and the reactions of man.

Geological exploration of West Africa is difficult because of the rarity of fossils and the common masking effect of lateritic and sand formations, overburden or dense vegetation. There are also few geologists in the field for such a large area, most of them have had to be trained outside West Africa, and climatic conditions are unkind to field work.

West Africa, like most of Africa, is largely composed of Pre-Cambrian rocks, which have been folded and are often aligned from northeast to southwest, as is reflected in much of the relief. They are exposed over about one-third of West Africa, or over two-thirds of the area south of 12° N, and are part of the vast continental platform of Africa, which in West Africa has an average elevation of about 400 m (1 300 ft). The oldest rocks may be about 4 000 million years old. Some are metamorphosed sedimentary rocks; others are ancient volcanics and intrusives.

Pre-Cambrian rocks have been variously subdivided, but their ages are uncertain, as radioactive dating methods are not reliable with metamorphic rocks. The oldest, or Lower Pre-Cambrian, probably comprises the Archaean (or Dahomeyan) and, probably, the Birrimian System.

The Archaean consists largely of highly metamorphosed rocks. Prevalent acidic types are mica schists, gneisses and quartzites; most are the product of granitisation and metamorphism of original sediments. Basic rocks are garnetiferous gneisses and amphibolites. Gneisses of similar composition are found in the Kasila Series of Sierra Leone, and others are known in Mauritania and Nigeria.

The Birrimian System occurs in southern Ghana and the Ivory Coast. The Lower Birrimian has folded and steeply dipping alternating greywackes and argillaceous beds, as well as some tuffs and lavas. The Upper Birrimian (Greenstones) consists mainly of volcanic rocks. The Kambui and Marampa schists of Sierra Leone may also be Birrimian.

The Middle Pre-Cambrian probably includes the Akwapimian–Togo–Atacora Systems, and the possibly contemporaneous Tarkwaian System.

3

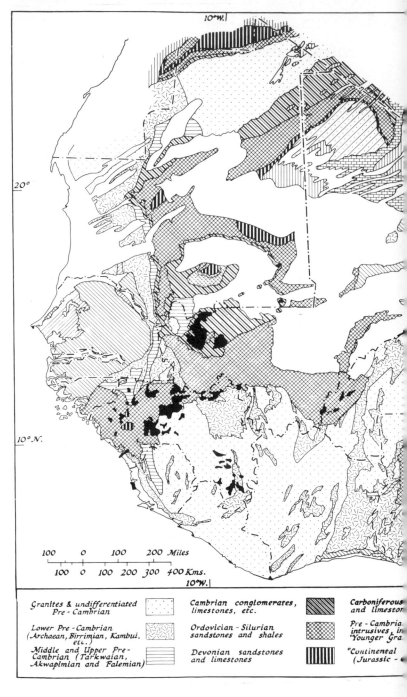

10°W.

20°

10° N.

```
100    0    100   200 Miles
100    0    100  200  300  400 Kms.
```
10°W.

| Granites & undifferentiated Pre - Cambrian | Cambrian conglomerates, limestones, etc. | Carboniferous and limeston |
| Lower Pre - Cambrian (Archaean, Birrimian, Kambui, etc.) | Ordovician - Silurian sandstones and shales | Pre - Cambria intrusives, in "Younger Gra |
| Middle and Upper Pre-Cambrian (Tarkwaian, AkwapImian and Falemian) | Devonian sandstones and limestones | "Continental (Jurassic - |

Fɪɢ. 1.1 Geology

(For place names see Fig. 2.1.)

4

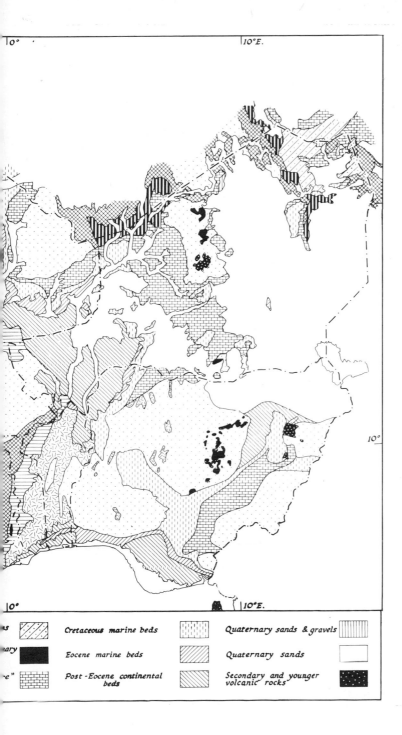

| | Cretaceous marine beds | | Quaternary sands & gravels |
|---|---|---|---|
| | Eocene marine beds | | Quaternary sands |
| | Post-Eocene continental beds | | Secondary and younger volcanic rocks |

Indeed, the Akwapimian may be a facies of the Tarkwaian. The former consists of quartzites, argillaceous sediments and silicified limestones which were probably deposited on a continental shelf. On the other hand, the Tarkwaian System consists of schists, quartzites and conglomerates (including auriferous conglomerates akin to those of the Witwatersrand), but no limestones. The sediments were probably originally deltaic or littoral, derived from nearby Birrimian mountains. Thus, the gold occurs as fossil placers, derived from the destruction of original deposits in the Birrimian.

The Upper Pre-Cambrian probably includes the Falémian of Mauritania and eastern Senegal, the Rokel Series of Sierra Leone and the Buem Series of Ghana, Togo and Dahomey. It consists mainly of quartzites, phyllites and shales.

Diamonds, haematite iron ore, chrome and manganese ore occur in Pre-Cambrian rocks. Granite intrusions of at least three different ages are known, gold and tin being associated with some of them. Ultrabasic and basic intrusions of Pre-Cambrian age are found in the peninsulas behind Conakry and Freetown, and at several points on the Liberian coast (Fig. 21.1).

The trend lines of Pre-Cambrian folds run north-northeast to south-southwest in the interior massifs of Aïr and Adrar des Iforas, and in Ghana, Togo and Dahomey. In Liberia they have an arclike disposition from northwest to southwest; in Sierra Leone and farther north the directions are northwest to southeast, and north to south. There is a close connection between these trend lines and many relief features.

The eroded surface of one or other of the Pre-Cambrian groups provided a fairly level floor for the advance and retreat of shallow Palaeozoic (or Primary) seas. Little is known about the age of most of their deposits in West Africa. Basal-conglomerate beds, dolomitic limestones, sandstones and shales of Cambrian or Cambro-Silurian age are found in the western Sahara, associated with the great Taoudéni syncline (see Fig. 1.1). They outcrop southwestward from Saharan Algeria along the northern and southern sides of the Eglab (or El Hank) anticline, southward to the Tambaoura Scarp and eastward into Mali. They reappear to form the vivid Bandiagara Scarp in the south-centre of the Niger Bend (Plate 63).

Above come Ordovician siliceous sandstones. These are found in the synclines of Tindouf (south of the Anti-Atlas) and Taoudéni. They also cover shield rocks in the Fouta Djallon of Guinea, in Mali (Manding Mountains, Bandiagara and Hombori plateaux), and in the Upper Volta (Banfora).

The Ordovician sea retreated and was followed by the deeper Silurian one, which lay over much of the Sahara and part of Guinea, and into which great rivers brought much mud. Voltaian rocks of east-central Ghana are probably Ordovician or Silurian, but in the absence of fossils their precise age is unknown.

Following the Silurian there were alternating continental and marine phases in the Devonian. Deposits are found in the Tindouf and Taoudéni synclines of Mauritania, around the interior massifs of Adrar des Iforas and Ahaggar, in Guinea, and at Accra in Ghana—where the Devonian is marine in origin.

The Lower Carboniferous (Dinantian) sea succeeded the Devonian era. Its limestones are mainly restricted to the basins of Tindouf and Taoudéni. As this sea withdrew northwards, leaving gulfs and lagoons, it was replaced by continental conditions in Upper Carboniferous (Westphalian) times. Estuarine sediments of Carboniferous (or, perhaps, Upper Devonian) age occur between Cape Coast and Dixcove (Ghana).

In some cases Hercynian movements probably reinforced Pre-Cambrian trends, as in the Akwapim–Togo–Atacora range. Hercynian trends have two main directions: those of wide distribution of northeast to southwest direction; and those from northwest to southeast, which are limited practically to the borders of Senegal–Mali (Tambaoura), the Fouta Djallon of Guinea, and Adrar (Mauritania).

Associated with and also subsequent to these Hercynian movements are many basic eruptive rocks comprising dolerite, basalt, gabbros and serpentine in dykes and sills. These outpourings are very important in the Fouta Djallon, e.g. northwest of Mamou, on Bintimani (Sierra Leone) and many peaks of the Guinea Highlands.

Apart from block faulting, uplifts and downwarps, and volcanic activity, the broad structure of most of western Mali, Guinea, Sierra Leone, Liberia, and almost all of the Ivory Coast and Ghana was determined by the end of Palaeozoic times. For the most part, these lands have almost certainly been above the sea continuously since then.

From Permian to Lower Cretaceous times there was a long period of elevation, denudation and redeposition of the products of subaerial erosion, which Kilian called the 'Continental Intercalaire'. These deposits survive around Adrar des Iforas, Aïr and elsewhere. They consist of sandstones, conglomerates and variegated clays, containing fossilised wood and occasional remains of dinosaurs, reptiles and fishes. Their age is Jurassic to Lower Cretaceous.

Marine transgressions occurred in Cretaceous and Eocene times, entering in the east from the Gulf of Guinea and thence along the Benue, Gongola, Chad and Middle Niger basins. Shallow seas to the west of Adrar des Iforas and between the massifs of Aïr and Tibesti were linked with the Mediterranean, which then covered North Africa. Cenomanian deposits, important from Agadès southwards into Nigeria (where there are also Albian deposits), sometimes consist of thick clays, siliceous and chalky limestones, the latter forming plateaux and minor scarps. On the borders of these seas, the sandstone, shale and coal seams of Enugu (Nigeria) were laid down, and were followed by early Tertiary seas, lagoons, lakes or mudflats.

A Cretaceous–Tertiary gulf occupied Senegal, the Gambia and north-western Portuguese Guinea; another the coastal Ivory Coast and the extreme southwest of Ghana; a third the Volta Delta, Togo, Dahomey and Nigeria. Their deposits include gravels, clayey sands, shales, lime-stone, gypsum-bearing marl, ferruginous sandstone (Gambia and Senegal) and lignites (Nigeria). Phosphates, salt, oil, gas and bituminous sands occur in them.

Continental conditions existed over all West Africa from Eocene or Oligocene times, except for a few places on the coast. In the far north stony wastes or *regs* and sand dunes or *ergs* were formed round the innermost massifs in the western Sahara, and frequently conceal a fossil relief underneath them. In late Tertiary and Quaternary times, the Middle Niger was a series of freshwater lakes, but there was no Quaternary sea.

Volcanic outpourings occurred again in Cretaceous, Eocene, Miocene and Pliocene times, and were, in part, associated with the upward move-ment which also caused the retreat of the Eocene seas.[1] Basement rocks in the Benue valley were folded in with the Cretaceous sediments. They were also often faulted, as in the Jos Plateau, Aïr and in the Fouta Djallon. All this was probably caused by the Alpine earthstorms in the north. Volcanic flows are important on the mainland in Aïr, southwest of and around Jos, in the Cameroon and Bamenda Highlands and west of Biu. In Gorée and Cape Manuel (Dakar) there are Miocene basalt lava flows and volcanic tuffs.

Volcanic activity was renewed in Quaternary times in Aïr and on Cape Verde (Plate 30). South of Kumasi, in Ghana, is Lake Bosumtwi, which occupies what some think is an explosive caldera but others consider a meteoric scar.

There was a maritime gulf in western Mauritania in early Quaternary times, but subsequently lacustrine or continental conditions became more general there and in western Senegal. Freshwater limestones, clays and sands (some of the latter being æolian) remain as evidence of these conditions.

In the interior the main features of Quaternary age have been erosion and deposition caused by the oscillations of sea level, the evolution of the present drainage system, and the formation of sand.

On the left bank of the Middle Niger are many virtually dry river valleys, such as the Tilemsi, Dallol Bosso, Azaouack and Dallol Maouri. Upstream there may have been others, but their courses have been obscured by windborne sands. There are similar relic valleys (Ferlo, Sine and upper Saloum) in Senegal. Urvoy[2] deduced three alternating wet and dry periods during Quaternary times, and considered that the Middle Niger is now in a relatively dry period.

These changes explain the existence of dry valleys and some river terraces; they are also part of the explanation for the drying out of the lakes in the Middle Niger, upward movement of the land being another contributory factor.

During dry Quaternary periods there has been intensive weathering of sandstone formations, and wind has spread great sheets of coarse loose sand over vast areas north of an approximate line through Zaria, Ouagadougou, Bamako and Dakar. In wetter periods the rivers have spread out sheets of finer alluvium. These loose deposits smooth out many irregularities of relief.

West Africa is remarkable for its considerable geological variety— greater than in some other parts of Africa. Nevertheless, there is a great predominance of worn down Pre-Cambrian rock, and widespread masking by sand in the interior and by lateritic material in the south.

## Coasts and shores

The nature of any coast depends mainly on the types and disposition of rocks, earth movements, relief, drainage and climate. The shoreline is more affected by winds, longshore drift, waves and tides. Both the coasts and shores of West Africa are difficult ones, and their natures have profoundly affected West African development.

Southward to Almadi Point, near Dakar, marine trade winds, longshore drift and powerful waves, backed by the greatest fetch of open water of the Atlantic, are smoothing a low shore. The Senegal (Fig. 12.2) and Saloum estuaries are obstructed by variable sandpits. Behind the dunes are relic lagoons (*niayes*), now mere pools or wet depressions.

From the Saloum to Cape St Ann (southern Sierra Leone), the coast and river estuaries have been drowned, thus causing a ria coastline. Though the land has since gained upon the sea, there are few smoothed coasts. The explanation is that the continental shelf is wider, the tidal range is high for West Africa (4–5 m: 13–17 ft), tidal scour is strong, and the southwest or northeast winds agitate the waters of a coast disposed across their path. Mudflats (with mangrove) form readily in the estuaries of Casamance (southern Senegal), Portuguese Guinea, Guinea and Sierra Leone.

Southern Sierra Leonean and Liberian shores are characterised by northwest trending sandspits, which seem to be helped by a smaller tidal range than that found farther north.

The western shore of the Ivory Coast and the central part of Ghana have only moderate coastal accumulation. The change in coastal orientation in relation to waves of maximum fetch results in movement away from Cape Three Points. Both coasts have occasional small but abrupt rocky promontories which, in the case of the Gold Coast, provided a little shelter for slave ships anchored east of them. On some promontories are the massive castles of the slaving and gold-trading era. The western Ivory Coast, however, was not attractive to traders, as there was no gold readily available and the people had a reputation as cannibals, causing the coast to be known as 'la Côte des Mal-Gens'. On the other hand, the relative dryness and low temperatures in July–September were added attractions of the Ghana shores.

From near Fresco (centre of the Ivory Coast shoreline) to Cape Three Points, and again from west of the Volta Delta to east of the Niger one, the coasts have suffered submergence. This may be the consequence of postglacial rise in sea level, but 'the known downwarped character of the coast, as attested by the altitude of sedimentary beds, suggests that the condition of partial drowning may have been repeated on a number of occasions, and that the last downward movement may have combined with the rise in sea level in producing the present appearance'.[3]. These coasts have since been smoothed by continuous longshore drift under the action of heavy surf, and they often excel those of Mauritania and Senegal in sandbar and lagoon formation. Yet erosion is or has been taking place at Assinie (Ivory Coast), Keta (Ghana), Grand Popo (Dahomey) and at Victoria Beach (Lagos).

As an illustration of the forces to be met with along this coast, one may cite the silting, within a few months, of the badly located Abidjan canal of 1904–07. Many years later, on October 4 1933, because of high floodwaters in the lagoon, a metre-wide (3 ft) ditch was cut through the old abandoned canal to release the flood. In three days the ditch had a mouth 100 m (330 ft) wide, which in another five days had become 300 m wide. Yet after a week the flood exit had ceased, and six months later the outlet was fully blocked by the action of the sea. A short way along the coast at Grand Bassam, a high sand-pit at the western side of the Camoé estuary has grown over 3·3 km (2 miles) in fifty years.

The inland edges of lagoons in the Ivory Coast, Togo and Dahomey are often quite steep, and around Abidjan there are considerable cliffs. Gautier[4] considered these to belong to an old shoreline; but though these cliffs are of loose sandy material, easily smoothed by wave action, they show no evidence of it.

West African coasts are mainly low, sandy and without natural harbours, except where a river and tidal range have kept an opening, as at Freetown, Lagos, precariously on certain inlets of the Niger Delta, and at Calabar. Even on the Niger inlets, the Escravos and Forcados bars threatened to kill the ports of Burutu, Warri, Koko and Sapele until a breakwater protecting the Escravos mouth was built (Fig. 26.7). Almost everywhere the shore is dangerous to approach. Ports have been enormously expensive to construct. In only two respects is the West African coast relatively fortunate—in its lack of coral reefs and of violent storms.

# 2

# Relief and drainage

## Relief

West Africa lies generally between about 200 and 500 m (600 to 1 600 ft), and consists mainly of the worn, monotonous and fairy level surfaces of the platform of Pre-Cambrian rocks. Higher relief may occur where trends in the ancient rocks can still be traced, e.g. the north–south hills of the Sierra Leone interior. Residual granite domes are common, and the 'Younger Granites' are responsible for some bold relief, e.g. of the Jos Plateau in Nigeria. Certain series of the Pre-Cambrian give higher relief, e.g. the several Birrimian, Tarkwaian and Akwapim–Togo–Atacora ridges.

Gently folded or unfolded Primary rocks, which have been strongly dissected, are responsible for the impressive relief of much of the Fouta Djallon of Guinea, and for vivid erosion scarps, e.g. those of Mampong and Gambaga (Plate 1) limiting the Voltaian sandstones of Ghana, that of Banfora in southwestern Upper Volta, and of Bandiagara in Mali (Plate 63). Others are partly along fault lines, such as the north–south scarps of the interior of the Fouta Djallon.

The generally low plains on Secondary or later sediments are also monotonous, though they may contain scarps such as the north–south Secondary and Tertiary ones in eastern Nigeria, or the Tertiary one of Thiès in Senegal.

Resistant basic intrusives formed the Freetown mountains, Cape Mount (Liberia), etc. Intrusive dykes give many abrupt features in the Fouta Djallon, at Kakoulima near Conakry, and at Siguiri—all in Guinea. A dolerite capping over granite has preserved Bintimani, 1 948 m (6 390 ft) in northeastern Sierra Leone.

Cretaceous and later volcanic activity has been responsible for part of the highest relief of the Jos Plateau, for the Bamenda and Cameroon Highlands, for Gorée and Cape Manuel at Dakar. The Mamelles of Cape Verde are Quaternary.

Important though these exceptions are locally, it remains true that relief is not often a cause of great regional diversity. Nor does relief do much to upset the zonal arrangement of climatic and vegetational belts, except in the Fouta Djallon, the Guinea Highlands, on the Jos Plateau, and the

11

PLATE 1. The Gambaga scarp, northern Ghana

Nigeria–Cameroon borderlands. Indeed, there is even a broad zonal arrangement of relief. In the southwest the ancient shield has been raised, and the south-flowing streams are now regrading themselves across it. North of it is a wide central depression in part, at least, tectonic and extending from Senegal to Lake Chad. Beyond again in the northeast, are the high massifs of Adrar des Iforas and Aïr.

Moreover, near the coast between Cape Palmas and Prampram there is a marine deep some 5 000–6 400 m (16 500–23 000 ft) in depth, and aligned from west to east. This section of the sea bed (particularly near Accra) is steeper than that of any other part of the Atlantic coast of Africa. With such slopes seismic conditions may be expected, and are the probable cause of earthquakes experienced in and around Accra. The Devonian, Carboniferous and Cretaceous rocks of Ghana all slope towards this deep, which may perhaps be correlated with the troughs of the lower Niger and Benue valleys. More certainly it may be associated with coastal submergence, as discussed on page 10.

## Drainage

The drainage characteristics of West Africa[1] may be summarised as follows:

1. Rapid runoff on crystalline rocks, especially on the south or south-western Pre-Cambrian shield, where the rainfall is particularly heavy.
2. Behind the southwestern and Guinea coasts, rivers are cutting down to new base levels, probably because of Miocene and later uplifts, and inward tilting. Thus the Volta river is gaining at the expense of others. The Guinea coast rivers are frequently interrupted by rapids and deposit relatively little alluvium, except close to the shoreline.
3. Greater maturity and indeterminate courses of the rivers of the sandy central lowland zone, compared with the immaturity and vigour of the Guinea Coast rivers. The Senegal, middle Niger and the upper reach of the Volta rivers have cut devious courses from the central zone.
4. Great seasonal variations in river flow. Seasonal rains cause extensive flooding, e.g. along the central Niger. Tributaries frequently become distributaries, e.g. the Sourou (see below). But much water is lost by intense evaporation and percolation in the dry season.

Quaternary eustatic changes of sea level and alternation of wet and dry climates have also been modifying factors. The last of these is shown by the existence of dry river courses on the left bank of the Niger near Gao. Dry courses have likewise resulted from the deposition of dust by the Harmattan wind in the beds of shrunken streams in the dry season. This feature is well seen in the Inland Niger Delta of Mali.

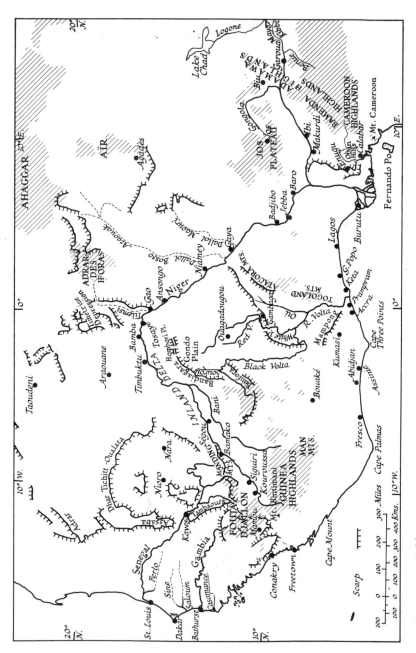

Fig. 2.1. Major relief features

PLATE 2. The River Gambia in annual flood at Basse, Gambia. The buildings are alongside the dry season thalweg of the river and are used as storehouses during the six months dry and trade season. Like other such riverside settlements, houses are farther from the river, on higher ground.

15

Rainfall is heaviest and runoff most consistent in the Fouta Djallon and the Guinea Highlands. Short, rapid streams descend from these direct to the sea. From the inward side of the Fouta Djallon the headwaters of the Senegal, Gambia, Niger and many of their tributaries take their rise.

*The Senegal* began to define its present course in mid to late-Tertiary times, when the maritime gulf retreated from the Senegal area. Recent and rapid accumulation of loose sand has obstructed its central and lower reaches, diverting it southward. Longshore drift and the Marine Trade winds are building a great sandspit, *La Langue de Barbarie*, which ruins the estuary and has prevented St Louis from developing a natural harbour. These various obstructions also cause widespread flooding when the river is full.

The Senegal is navigable (for the navigable reaches of rivers, see Fig. 9.1) from August to mid-October for very small vessels as far as Kayes. After mid-October, navigation is limited to even smaller vessels and ceases at Podor. The flow of the river varies greatly from year to year, and the railway now takes almost all the traffic. The estuary spit and bar are the main impediments to navigation with the sea.

*The Gambia* is a river, whose lower course has become a ria. It is navigable to the limit of the Gambia state, and is by far the best river of western West Africa. Unfortunately, its value has been greatly compromised by the boundary, which has prevented it from serving its natural hinterland.

*The Niger* is some 5 200 km (2 600 miles) long and passes through almost every climatic zone of West Africa. The Upper Niger is a mature river, with a well defined course, and which flowed into the various Secondary and Tertiary inland seas. In mid-Tertiary times, following upon the retreat of the Senegal gulf, the Upper Niger was captured by the Senegal river through the Nara-Nioro sill north-northwest of Ségou. When the climate became drier, sand wastes obstructed that outlet, and the Upper Niger then flowed into the Araouane Lake.

A return to more humid conditions in Quaternary times gave rise to many vigorous streams from Adrar des Iforas and Aïr. Flowing into one great stream around Gao, this broke through the Badjibo sill (above Jebba, Nigeria) to join the headwaters of an existing stream, so forming the southeast flowing Lower Niger. Increasing sand accumulations in the Araouane Lake then caused that lake to subdivide into several lakes, which overspilled at Tosaye to join the Lower Niger.

Sand accumulations are still pushing the river southward at Timbuktu and obstructing its many channels. Yet in and after the rainy season the river floods areas between Ségou and Timbuktu as extensive as England and Wales. This is because of the low-lying country and slight slope of the river. The lakes of this Inland Delta are reminders of former terminal lakes of the Upper Niger (Fig. 15.4).

The Upper Niger is navigable for small ships from Kouroussa to

PLATE 3. The River Niger in the 'double V' between Say and Gaya

17

Bamako between July and October. Below Bamako it is interrupted by rapids, caused by sandstone outcrops from the Manding Mountains. The Middle Niger is navigable from Koulikoro in the full flood, and from Mopti in semiflood. Floodwaters are so delayed that although they are felt at Koulikoro in mid-July, they do not arrive at Timbuktu until about October.

The Inland Delta ends east of Timbuktu, and the Niger passes through the Tosaye quartzite sill, cut in mid-Quaternary times, to link with the Lower Niger. It ceases to be navigable between Ansongo and Tillabéri. Between these places it has often cut down to the ancient basement rocks, whose outcrops cause the Fafa and Labbezenga rapids. Moreover, halfway between Niamey and the Nigerian boundary it cuts through the end of the Atacora ridge by a series of cluses with sharp turns in the shape of a double V (Plate 3). The former Bussa rapids are now submerged in Lake Kainji behind Kainji Dam (pp. 472 and 476–8).

From Jebba, and more easily from Baro, the river is navigable again. There is local high water from early August to mid-November, and high water again from mid-February to mid-April, when the Upper Niger floodwaters, after their long journey and dispersion in the Inland Delta, arrive at last in the Lower Niger. Some of the Maritime Delta mouths are navigable for ocean vessels, and former mouths are often used by local streams.

## The Benue

The Benue is unobstructed by severe rapids, and its course may possibly correspond to a major faultline. The valley has been a routeway for peoples coming from the east and northeast. The river may be navigated up to Makurdi between June and November, between Makurdi and Yola from July to early October, and between Yola and Garoua in Cameroon in August and September.

The Benue has many characteristics of a mature river. It has flat banks which are extensively flooded in the rainy season and offer possibilities for sugar and rice cultivation.

## The Volta

Of the Guinea coast rivers, only the Volta demands special mention. The upper Black Volta flows first in a northeasterly direction, parallel to the Upper Niger and, like it, is a mature stream that must have flowed via the Sourou into Secondary and Tertiary inland seas and an early Quaternary lake. The latter was presumably situated in the Gondo Plain, below the Bandiagara Scarp. In a wet climatic period the lake may have overspilled, sending streams southeastwards to join others farther south. The Sourou is now alternately a tributary and distributary of the upper Black Volta.

The White Volta is also a composite river which (with the Red Volta) has captured, or had directed to it, rivers which once drained northward. Similarly, the uppermost reach of the Oti was probably once a tributary of the Niger. The diversion, to vigorous Guinea Coast rivers, of streams from the great central depression is, indeed, a common phenomenon.

The lower Volta cuts through the Akwapim–Togo range by a gorge, wherein the Akosombo dam and hydroelectric power station have been established (see pp. 390–3).

**Lagoons**

Lagoons are significant means of communication in the Ivory Coast, Togo, Dahomey, and especially in Nigeria.

# 3
# Climate*

## Causation

### Air masses[1]

The fundamental cause of West African climates is the seasonal migration and pulsation of two air masses. The most widespread feature is the mass of Tropical Continental (cT) Air, warm and dusty, which extends from the Sahara, reaching its maximum southward extent in January between 5° and 7°N. Alternating seasonally with it is the mass of Tropical (or Equatorial) Maritime (mT) Air, warm and humid, which moves north in July or August to about 17°N on the coast and to about 21°N inland. Associated with Tropical Continental Air are dry northeasterly winds, and with Tropical Maritime Air wet southwesterly ones.

Because of the differing densities of the air masses, Tropical Maritime Air forms a wedge under the Tropical Continental one. The wedge penetrates northward as Tropical Maritime Air, and becomes predominant in and after May, retreating southwards in August or September. Hence the depth of warm, moist air over any point first increases and then decreases, the rain belt occurring where it is about 900 m (3 000 ft) deep and often at least 1 500 m (5 000 ft). The depth of warm, moist air also varies daily, and rain appears to be associated with such changes, as well as with seasonal advance and retreat.

The discontinuity between these air masses is called the inter-Tropical Front or Inter-Tropical Convergence Zone (ITCZ), and lies north of the Equator all the year. With the penetration inland of Tropical Maritime Air, the Zone pushes northwards, and with the retreat of Maritime Air the Front returns southwards.

As dry air lies over moist, active weather does not occur at the point

*West African climatic statistics should be used with caution. Until 1938 most observations were made from instruments generally located in the grounds of agricultural or medical departments. Untrained observers are prone to errors in reading thermometers. Maximum and minimum thermometers are also liable to develop faults, which may not be noticed or corrected for considerable periods in the hands of inexperienced readers. Instruments were often badly sited and not always read regularly or sufficiently frequently, and their location within a given town has sometimes changed. More recently there has been great improvement, but upper air records are still few. Nor is it unknown for there to be interference with instruments, and rain gauges are sometimes improperly used for the oddest purposes.

of contact of the Zone with the earth's surface. Instead, there is usually a great width of persistent light winds with little or no low cloud, and generally fine weather. The Front is thus a rain screen rather than a rain producer in West Africa.

Above both of these alternating surface air masses and wind systems come first the equatorial easterlies. These are related to the northeasterlies, but are humid, probably originating over the Indian Ocean. They fill the middle layers of the atmosphere over most of West Africa all the year round. These may, perhaps, play some part in line squalls at the change of season (see below); otherwise they are mainly of importance to air navigation. Above again are westerlies, sometimes known as the counter-trades.

## Relief

Once Tropical Maritime air has penetrated northward in sufficient depth, we should expect orographic rain wherever there are highland areas, particularly if they lie across the path of southwesterly rain-bearing winds. Such is the explanation of heavy rainfall in the Fouta Djallon of Guinea, the Guinea Highlands of Sierra Leone and Liberia, the Freetown Peninsula, the Mampong Scarp in Ghana, and on the Nigeria–Cameroon borderlands. In all of these there are often great local differences because of relative exposure. Thus average annual rainfall over ten years at Freetown (Hill Station, 250 m: 820 ft above sea level) was 4 811 mm (189·4 in), whilst at Freetown (Falconbridge, 11·3 m: 37 ft above sea level) it was 1 295 mm (51 in) less. These relief features (as well as others— e.g. the Jos Plateau) also produce rainshadow effects, local and farther afield.

High relief also lowers temperatures and increases the diurnal range. Colonial administrations established hill stations to take advantage of such conditions. Thus Dalaba was established at 1 113 m (3 650 ft) in the Fouta Djallon of Guinea, Hill Station at 250 m (820 ft) above Freetown, and Jos at 1 250 m (4 100 ft) in Nigeria. Several relief climatic zones are distinguished later in this chapter.

## Ocean currents

These play a considerable part in climate. The influence of the cold southward-flowing Canary Current is felt as far south as Cape Verde, where it is deflected oceanwards. It is responsible for occasional fogs, and for low air temperatures which often cause persons travelling to Europe by sea to catch cold. More happily, it cools coastal Senegal. Similarly, cold water which is probably an offshoot of the cold Beneguela Current upwells in the middle of the year off São Tomé, eastern Ghana, Togo

21

and Dahomey. It cools sea and air temperatures and may play a part in causing dry weather, by restricting convectional conditions.[2]

Between the cold Canary and Benguela Currents is the eastward-flowing Guinea Current, which brings warm water to the Guinea Coast for the rest of the year, thereby reinforcing the effects of the already warm and moist southwesterly winds.

## Characteristics and consequences

### Winds

#### THE HARMATTAN

Except on the coast of Senegal, the dry season wind is the Harmattan, which normally prevails to a maximum southerly limit at about 5–7°N in January. It is typically a northeasterly wind, warm and so desiccating that vegetative growth ceases. Clouds are absent, so that temperatures are relatively high during the day but low at night. Visibility is severely restricted by a haze of dust particles carried from the arid north, trapped beneath a strong subsidence inversion.

Cold nights require people to have more blankets—a joy to Europeans and a trial to Africans. Low humidity dries up the mucous membrane of eyes, nose and throat. Lips, fingernails and skin crack. Barefooted Africans may find the skin of their feet so cracked as to make walking very painful. Epidemics of cerebrospinal meningitis are most prevalent at this season. The Harmattan also dries up plants and often coats them with dust particles. Dust penetrates houses, and such things as typewriters and radio equipment.

#### THE SENEGAL MARINE TRADE WINDS

The cold Canary Current cools air above it, so limiting convection and the making of, as much rain as would otherwise occur. Hence the coast is drier than comparable inland stations, although relative humidity is higher. The strength of these northerly or northwesterly winds, especially across the exposed Cape Verde peninsula, is responsible for another contrast, that between the cooler temperatures of coastal Senegal, and the higher ones of the interior.

#### 'LINE SQUALLS'

At the change of season with the northward advance of the Inter-Tropical Convergence Zone east to west or northeast to southwest thunderstorms or 'line squalls' occur, often misnamed tornadoes. It may be that with the change, from May to July and again in October, of the relative depths of the Harmattan and of the southwesterlies, the easterlies of the upper air levels descend to the surface. J. Navarro, however, has shown[3] that these storms are northeasterly rather than easterly, and have several routes towards the Guinea coast, ending in the regions of Mt Cameroon, Cotonou, Abidjan and Tabou. These northeasterly 'line squalls' are the partial cause of almost all rain received on that coast between May and July, and again from September to October. They are created under a long line of instability in upper layers, the humidity being supplied by southwesterlies.

'Line squalls' are preceded by a day or two of high temperatures. Finally, the sky darkens, there is vivid lightning and the noise of wind of high speed. Behind the wind and swirling dust comes torrential rain, the lightning persisting. Winds become southwesterly and then easterly, and temperatures drop 5·5–11°C (10–20°F). Heavy rain, of up to 50 mm (2 in) in under an hour, then gives way to gentler rain without lightning. When the rain ceases, the clouds disappear and temperatures rise again. Such sudden and violent storms and rainfall cause soil erosion and damage to crops, housing and communications. Men and beasts may catch colds or pneumonia. North of about 15°N in the east and 17°N in the west, these line squalls are mainly dry storms or 'dust devils', i.e. in Mauritania, Mali and Niger.

## SOUTHWESTERLIES

Associated with moist Tropical Maritime Air are southwesterly winds. They prevail all the year south of about 6°N, penetrating in July round the coast to about 17°N, and inland to approximately 21°N in August. During their prevalence two or three days' continuous rain may occur on the Guinea Coast, and for much longer on monsoon coasts (see later). Continuous rain is rare inland, where it is generally heavy at first in late afternoon, becoming intermittent and accompanied by thunderstorms in the evening, and ceasing as light rain early next morning. This is especially so at the beginning and end of the rainy season.

Skies are frequently cloudy, and early morning mist is common; otherwise visibility is good, except during actual rainfall. The following figures illustrate some of these points.

*Mean amount of cloud in tenths*

| Time | Jan. | Feb. | Mar. | Apr. | May | June | July | Aug. | Sept. | Oct. | Nov. | Dec. | Year |
|------|------|------|------|------|------|------|------|------|------|------|------|------|------|
| Enugu (6°27′N, 7°29′E)(Average of 5 years) | | | | | | | | | | | | | |
| 0900 | 4·6 | 4·9 | 7·0 | 8·1 | 8·3 | 8·6 | 8·9 | 8·8 | 9·1 | 8·7 | 7·1 | 5·4 | 7·4 |
| 1500 | 4·3 | 4·7 | 5·9 | 7·4 | 7·6 | 7·9 | 8·3 | 8·3 | 8·2 | 7·8 | 6·8 | 4·8 | 6·8 |

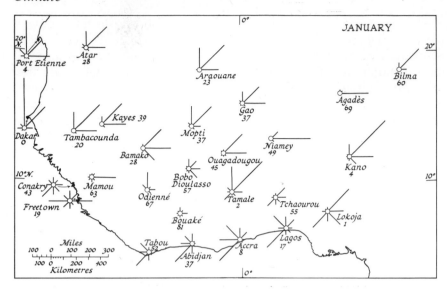

FIG. 3.1. Wind directions in January

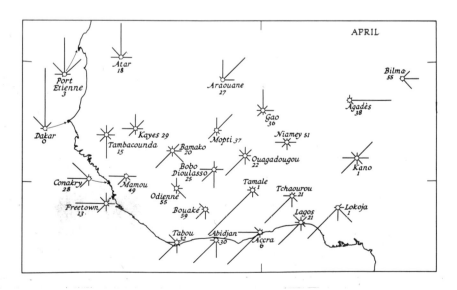

FIG. 3.2. Wind directions in April

24

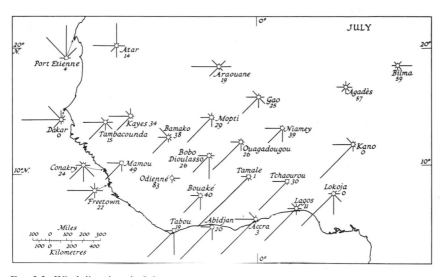

FIG. 3.3. Wind directions in July

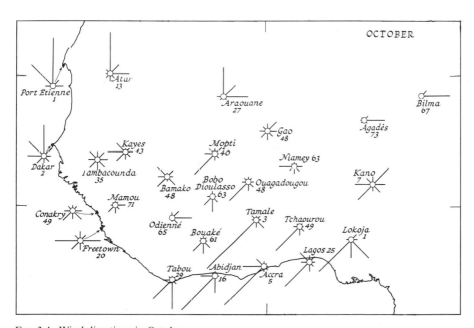

FIG. 3.4. Wind directions in October

The lines are proportional to the percentage of observed winds from each direction. Numbers give the percentage of observed calms. Twenty-eight stations

*Mean number of days with less than 2·5 tenths average*

| Jan. | Feb. | Mar. | Apr. | May | June | July | Aug. | Sept. | Oct. | Nov. | Dec. | Year |
|------|------|------|------|-----|------|------|------|-------|------|------|------|------|
| Freetown (8°30′N, 13°14′W)(Average of 10 years) | | | | | | | | | | | | |
| 12 | 12 | 10 | 3 | 1 | 0·2 | 0·1 | 0 | 0 | 0 | 1 | 7 | 46 |

*Mean number of days with more than 7·5 tenths average*

| Jan. | Feb. | Mar. | Apr. | May | June | July | Aug. | Sept. | Oct. | Nov. | Dec. | Year |
|------|------|------|------|-----|------|------|------|-------|------|------|------|------|
| Freetown (Average of 10 years) | | | | | | | | | | | | |
| 2 | 2 | 3 | 7 | 12 | 16 | 26 | 28 | 23 | 17 | 12 | 7 | 155 |

Cloud cover is intimately associated not only with southwesterly winds, but also with high humidity and low range of temperature. And, although the rainy season may be long or short, fine weather often prevails for several or even many days.

As will be seen later, there are relatively few places with a true equatorial climate. The Gulf of Guinea coastlands mostly have two rainfall maxima, the first and normally greater one being initiated by the line squalls discussed above. These are followed by a relatively dry season from July to August, although cloud cover and relative humidity remain high. This little dry season is often explained as being due to the northward movement of the Inter-Tropical Convergence Zone, but Crowe[4] considers that 'the real key surely lies in the prevalence aloft of the marked inversion normally encountered in the southeast trades at about 900 m (3 000 ft). This is the season when the southeast trades are at their strongest and the waters beneath them are at their coolest. It is, therefore, in no way surprising that their normal inversion is not liquidated at the Equator but roofs over the whole strong southerly air stream. Such a 'roof' may be penetrated in three chief ways—(i) where a gigantic relief features like Mt Cameroon 4070 m (13 350 ft) bodily protrudes through the inversion and stimulates convectional overturnings around its flanks; (ii) where more moderate elevations like the Fouta Djallon plateau are encountered by strong persistent winds; and (iii) by surface heating over a Continental interior'.

ONSHORE AND OFFSHORE BREEZES

Along the entire West African coastline and up to about 16 km (10 miles) inland, sea and land breezes are important. The late afternoon onshore (or sea) breeze results from the relative overheating of the land, compared with the sea. Conversely, there is a offshore (or land) breeze during the night. Except where land descends sharply to the sea, e.g. at Freetown, the sea breeze is usually the stronger. These breezes may partially divert the normal wind, as in Mauritania and Senegal, where by day the north-northwest marine trade winds are common. They may even reverse it, as in Portuguese Guinea and Guinea, where in January a westerly wind frequently replaces the northeast trades during the after-noon. Finally, they may reinforce the usual wind, as along the Guinea coast, where the southwesterlies are particularly strong in the afternoons.

In this section we have discussed the northeasterly Harmattan of the interior, the Senegal marine trade winds, the northeasterly or easterly 'line squalls' of the interior, the wet southwesterlies most prevalent in the mid-year months, and onshore and offshore breezes. Yet this variety is more apparent than real, and the prevailing winds are so over-whelmingly from the northeast or southwest, that a single runway oriented in these directions is sufficient at most West African airports, unlike the runways in various directions found in lands of changeable winds.

Seasonal winds, combined with the trend of the coast and degree of slope of the foreshore, account for the swell and surf of West African coasts. Swell is of relatively minor importance and is almost always from the north along the Mauritanian coast. Along the Senegal coast it is more southerly between June and September. On all other coasts, it is generally from the south and southwest. Surf, by contrast, is severe and hinders the establishment of ports. It helps to build up sandbars, though less from Cape St Mary (Gambia) to Cape St Ann (south of Freetown) where there is great tidal range.

## Temperature

The common belief that West Africa is always exceedingly hot is exaggerated. The very high temperatures, so characteristic of many months in the lowland parts of similar latitudes in East Africa and India, are attained in West Africa only in or near the desert in summer. The writer has vivid recollections of sitting, swathed in a blanket, on a cool August evening, in an open-air Accra cinema, listening to the justified jeers of Ghanaians at the trailer of an American film asserting that the film it advertised brought 'the authentic atmosphere of the steaming hot jungles of Africa'.

West Africa has lower temperatures than world average for similar latitudes during the northern hemisphere winter in the dry far north, during the rains in the south, and almost all the year in highland areas and along the coasts of Senegal, eastern Ghana and Togo. On the other hand, temperatures are higher than world average for similar latitudes in April, July and October in much of the centre and north, especially in lowland areas. Fairly high temperatures are also common in the south at the end of the dry season.

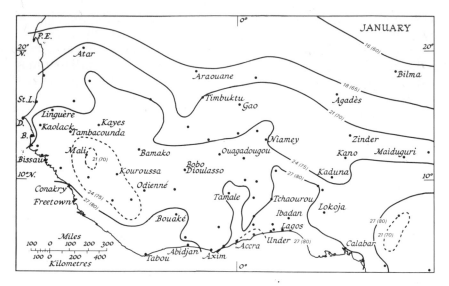

FIG. 3.5. Mean actual daily temperatures in January for 75 stations

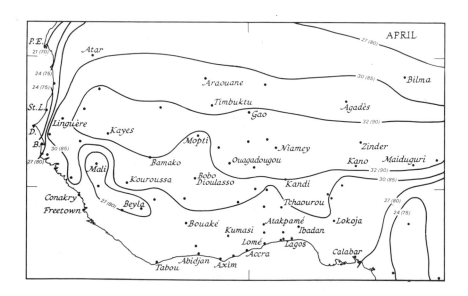

FIG. 3.6. Mean actual daily temperatures in April for 75 stations

28

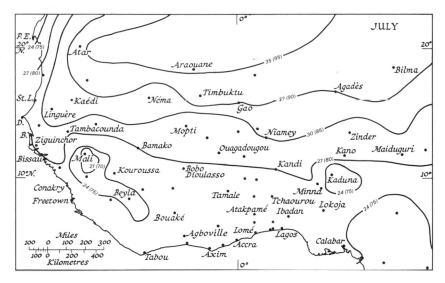

FIG. 3.7. Mean actual daily temperatures in July for 75 stations

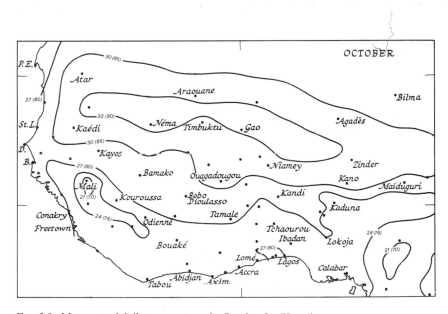

FIG. 3.8. Mean actual daily temperatures in October for 75 stations

Broken lines on some of Figs 3.5.–3.15 indicate conditions below the norm for that latitude

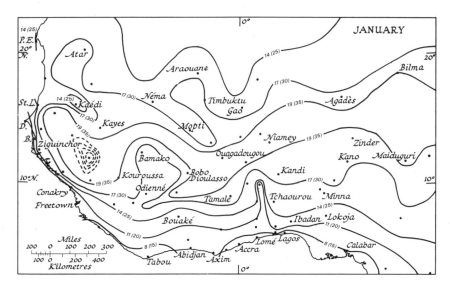

FIG. 3.9. Mean diurnal range of temperature in January for 75 stations

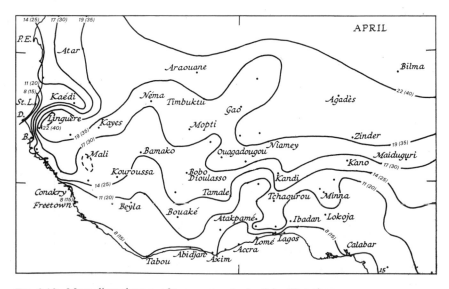

FIG. 3.10. Mean diurnal range of temperature in April for 75 stations

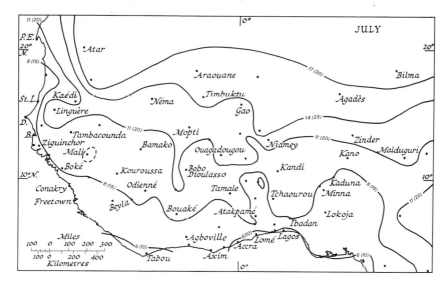

FIG. 3.11. Mean diurnal range of temperature in July for 75 stations

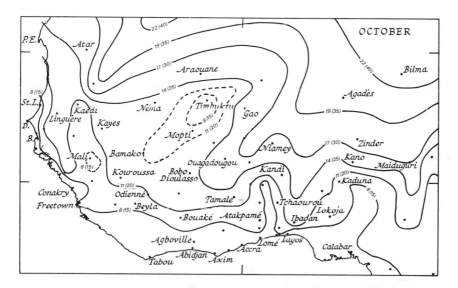

FIG. 3.12. Mean diurnal range of temperature in October for 75 stations

31

High temperatures may cause a skin complaint popularly known as 'prickly heat'. Loose clothing should be worn, and the ample robes of most northern people and their loose caps are very suitable. Thick-walled houses also help to withstand high temperatures.

Yet the high temperatures by day of inland stations are rather-offset by wider diurnal and seasonal range. Figures 3.9–3.12 show the greater range of temperature to be in the centre, northwest, north and northeast. There is a gradually increasing range from the Guinea coast northwards, and a much sharper increase inland from the Senegal coast. The greatest ranges are found at the change of seasons.

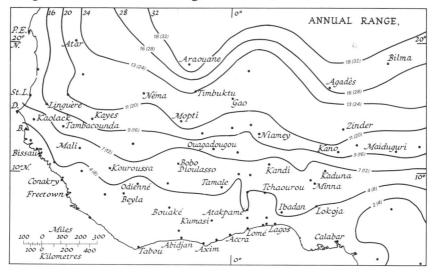

FIG. 3.13. Annual range of temperature for 75 stations

Figure 3.13 summarises the general position for the whole year. Comparison with world averages for similar latitudes reveals that the Guinea coast has a little less than the annual average range for that latitude, an illustration of its somewhat oppressive character. But the interior has more than the average, a well-known characteristic of the Sahara and its fringes.

## Sunshine

Another fallacy concerning West Africa is that a supposedly pitiless sun shines ever fiercely. Such an idea is grossly inaccurate. As night and day are almost equal, hours of sunshine can never exceed about twelve hours, as they may in summer in temperate lands. During the dry season the sun is often obscured by dust haze; during the wet season, clouds as well as early morning mist often hide it. In consequence, the recorded sunshine is often remarkably little. The following figures of mean daily sunshine in hours are representative:

| | Jan. | Feb. | Mar. | Apr. | May | June | July | Aug. | Sept. | Oct. | Nov. | Dec. | Annual mean |
|---|---|---|---|---|---|---|---|---|---|---|---|---|---|
| Freetown (Average of 10 years) | | | | | | | | | | | | | |
| | 8·1 | 8·2 | 7·7 | 7·0 | 6·3 | 5·3 | 2·8 | 2·2 | 4·0 | 6·2 | 6·6 | 7·0 | 5·9 |
| % of maximum possible | | | | | | | | | | | | | |
| | 69 | 69 | 64 | 57 | 50 | 42 | 22 | 18 | 33 | 52 | 56 | 60 | 49 |
| Kumasi (Average of 9 years) | | | | | | | | | | | | | |
| | 3·9 | 4·3 | 4·8 | 5·0 | 3·7 | 2·0 | 1·1 | 0·9 | 2·3 | 3·9 | 4·6 | 3·9 | 3·4 |

Cloudiness (but not necessarily haze) diminishes inland, and is at a minimum near the tropic line.

For protection against the relatively small amount of sunshine a soft, light cloth cap is ideal. Sunglasses are very desirable, although there is a marked deficiency in blue and ultraviolet light, so that the value of the light is less than in temperate lands. It is for this reason that white people rarely get very tanned in West Africa, and that most photographs are underexposed. Total solar radiation is also low, because of high water-vapour content, dust and bush fire haze.

## Rainfall

As elsewhere in the tropics, rainfall is the most vital element in the climate. On its amount (and especially its effectiveness), its degree of certainty, its length and how it falls, largely depend the natural vegetation, agriculture, mode of life and much else in West Africa. The association of rainfall with line squalls and southwesterly winds is discussed above, and the various climatic types (which depend overwhelmingly on rainfall criteria) are outlined below.

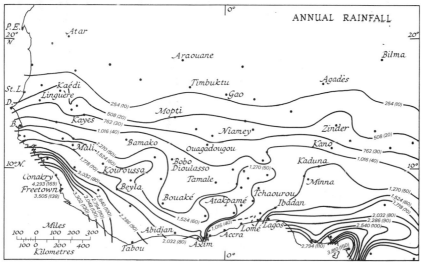

FIG. 3.14. Annual rainfall for 95 stations (minimum period of ten years)

Figures 3.14 and 3.15 show the general picture of annual and monthly rainfall. The heavy monsoonal rainfall (May to October) of the south-western coast is evident, as well as the heavy rain of the Cameroon highlands and Mt Cameroon. The drier central parts of the Ivory Coast, and especially of eastern Ghana and Togo, both annually and especially in August and September, are also clear. Otherwise, annual rainfall diminishes fairly regularly inland from the Gulf of Guinea, both in amount and in duration. The advance and retreat of rainfall from south to north are likewise striking.

Where annual rainfall exceeds about 2 500 mm (*c.* 100 in) per annum, it may be regarded as dangerously excessive, especially if it falls in one sharp season. Such rain causes excessive leaf growth and makes cereals (other than rice) difficult or impossible to grow. Tubers such as cassava and cocoyams, however, can tolerate such rainfall.

Heavy rain leaches out plant nutrients, erodes the soil and interrupts agricultural work and transport. Rainwater may drain away before it can be absorbed, so that increasing study is being made of rainfall effectiveness (residual or available rainfall).

Thornthwaite's formula for computing potential evapotranspiration uses mean monthly temperatures and the latitude of a given station. Although a generally accurate indicator of the latent heat of vaporisation, it underestimates potential evapotranspiration in the West African dry season and overestimates it during the wet one, because insufficient account is taken of moisture vapour in the atmosphere. Garnier has found that if figures for the mean daytime saturation deficit are added to Thornthwaite's mean potential evapotranspiration figures, the values are increased in the dry season and reduced in the wet, especially for interior states. About 2 000 mm may be taken as the maximum mean annual potential evapotranspiration on Saharan fringes. The minimum of under 1 000 mm (39 in) occurs in high parts near the coast. Most of West Africa has between 1 000 and 1 900 mm (39 and 75 in). South of latitude 10°N coastal lowlands and areas above 500 m (1 640 ft) have under 1 300 mm (51 in). Senegalese and Mauritanian coasts have some 400 mm (16 in) less than nearby inland stations. Mean annual water surplus is substantial in the Guineas, Sierra Leone, Liberia, coastal Ivory Coast and southeastern Nigeria. Water deficit corresponds closely with the length of the dry season, but every place has a seasonal water deficit, and the dry Ghana coast an exceptional annual one of 250–500 mm.[5]

About 100 mm (4 in) rainfall per month is often regarded as the minimum for agricultural needs (Fig. 3.16) and three to four months of rainfall is the minimum for growing the quick maturing millets on the outer fringes of the cropping zone. Where rainfall is fairly evenly distributed throughout the year, about 1 270 mm (50 in) annual rainfall seems to be ideal.

Apart from the amount of rain and its effectiveness, the length of

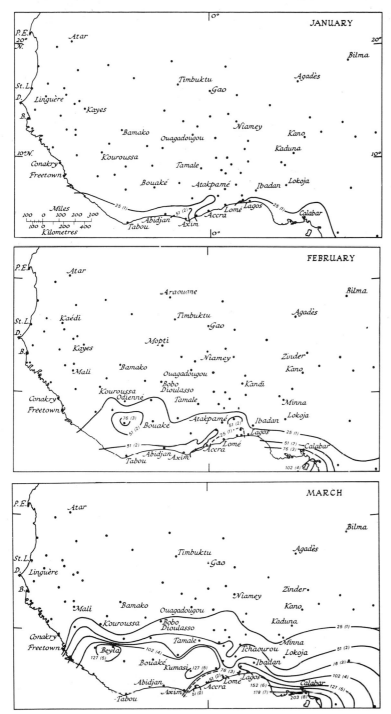

FIG. 3.15. Monthly rainfall for 95 stations. (Minimum period ten years)

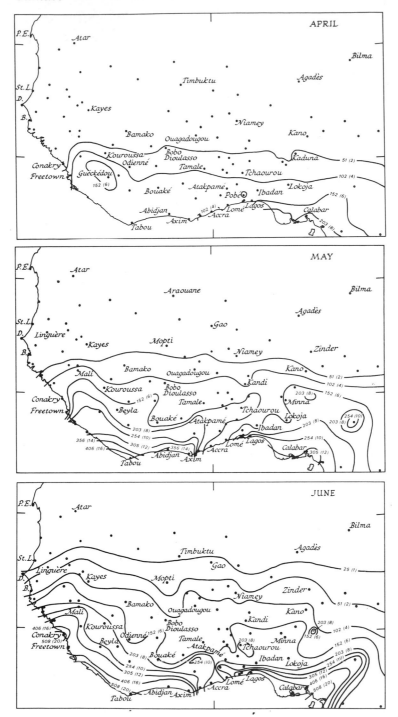

Fig. 3.15—*continued.* Monthly rainfall for 95 stations. (Minimum period ten years)

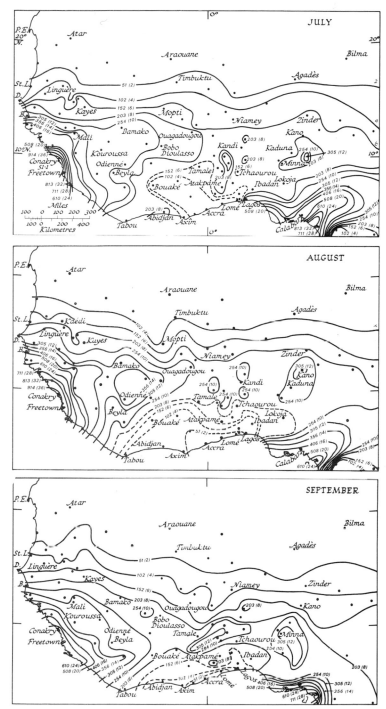

FIG. 3.15—*continued*. Monthly rainfall for 95 stations. (Minimum period ten years)

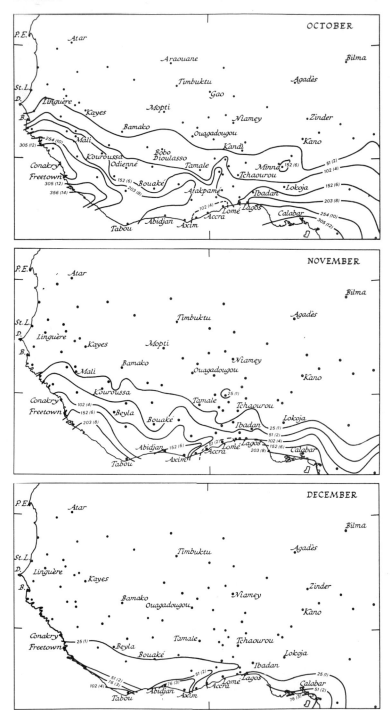

FIG. 3.15—*continued.* Monthly rainfall for 95 stations. (Minimum period ten years)

rainy season is obviously important in influencing which crops may be grown. Kontagora and Abeokuta (Nigeria) have the same average total rainfall, but rainy seasons of about seven and ten months respectively. Where there is a double maximum of rainfall, the short (or middle) dry period, if long enough, provides another harvest time, and so more varied crops may be grown.

Lastly, tropical rainfall is extremely variable in amount, in time of onset and cessation, and in regime. Figure 3.17 shows variability at certain stations in Ghana. Not only is there a high degree of general variability, but also between different districts in the same year.

In the interior and towards the northern limit of adequate rainfall, where water is most precious, variability is greatest. Average figures

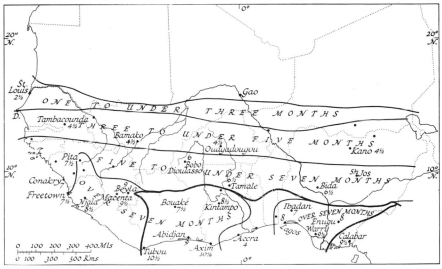

FIG. 3.16. Number of months with at least 100 mm or 4 inches of rain

100 mm of 4 inches monthly rainfall is sufficient for most plant growth. It is also the figure at about which precipitation and evaporation are generally in equilibrium. The heavy line is the northern limit of the double maximum of rainfall. Based on readings from 44 stations

should be used only in the knowledge that in any year the actual rainfall may be about one-half greater or smaller, and that this may happen for several years on end. Thus between 1901 and 1918, rainfall at Banjul (Bathurst) (13°27′N, 16°35′W) was:

|  | mm | in |  | mm | in |  | mm | in |
|---|---|---|---|---|---|---|---|---|
| 1901 | 1 151 | 45·3 | 1907 | 864 | 34·0 | 1913 | 60 | 23·7 |
| 1902 | 747 | 29·4 | 1908 | 1 105 | 43·5 | 1914 | 1 242 | 48·9 |
| 1903 | 1 450 | 57·1 | 1909 | 1 438 | 56·6 | 1915 | 1 209 | 47·6 |
| 1904 | 965 | 38·0 | 1910 | 1 118 | 44·0 | 1916 | 965 | 38·0 |
| 1905 | 1 679 | 66·1 | 1911 | 714 | 28·1 | 1917 | 958 | 37·7 |
| 1906 | 1 636 | 64·4 | 1912 | 864 | 34·0 | 1918 | 1 372 | 54·0 |

39

The average was 1 115 mm (43·9 in). Rainfall in May varied between nil and 48 mm (1·9 in), in June from 56 mm (2·2 in) to 312 mm (12·3 in), and in October from 5 mm (0·2 in) to 231 mm (9·1 in). Whilst it has been objected that such variations are not unknown in the United Kingdom, they are far more critical in the higher temperatures of the tropics, especially near the margins of cultivation, and to wholly rural peoples.

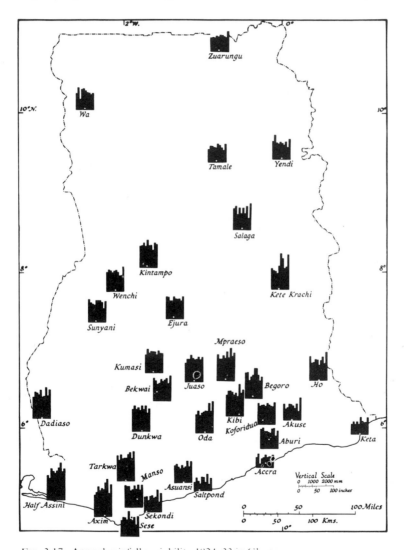

FIG. 3.17. Annual rainfall variability 1924–33 in Ghana

(Based on figures from *Gold Coast Handbook*, 1937; each column represents one year)

Figure 3.18 shows for Zungeru (Nigeria, 9°48′N, 6°09′W) the typical variation over five years in the amount of monthly rain and, particularly, in its distribution. Although average figures show Zungeru with a single rainfall maximum, there was no such neat pattern for any one of the years 1907–11.

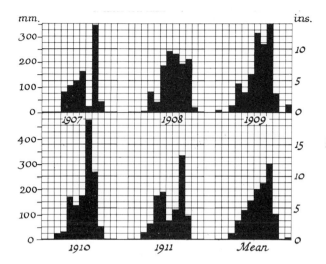

FIG. 3.18. Mean monthly rainfall at Zungeru, Nigeria

(From R. Miller 'The climate of Nigeria', *Geography*, 1952 by kind permission of the author and editor)

## Relative humidity

It is this factor, more than any other, which has given the West African climates a bad name. Yet very high humidity is confined to the rainy areas and rainy seasons, especially in the early morning, whilst during the dry season it is normal to sigh for greater humidity. The following figures are typical:

*Mean percentage of relative humidity*

|  | January | | July | |
|---|---|---|---|---|
|  | a.m. | p.m. | a.m. | p.m. |
| *Monsoon and Guinea coasts* | | | | |
| Conakry (9°31′N, 13°43′W) | 85 | 71 | 92 | 85 |
| Accra (5°31′N, 0°12′W) | 82 | 84 | 85 | 85 |
| Porto-Novo (H°30′N, 2°37′W) | 90 | 77 | 89 | 85 |
| *Interior* | | | | |
| Timbuktu (16°47′N, 3°W) | 39 | 29 | 68 | 46 |
| Bamako (12°39′N, 7°58′W) | 50 | 27 | 89 | 71 |
| Beyla (8°41′N, 8°39′W) | 68 | 31 | 94 | 84 |
| Natitingou (10°16′N, 1°23′E) | 43 | 22 | 81 | 75 |

*Climate*

High relative humidity and heavy rainfall allow dense and rank vegetation to flourish, insects to breed profusely and so spread disease, and the formation of mould and fungi on such things as leather and films. These articles should be kept in airtight tins, clothing in warmed airing cupboards, and machinery should be oiled frequently. Electric cables need far more insulation than in temperate lands. To man, high relative humidity by day generally causes lassitude; by night there may be a sensation of cold, even though temperatures are high. The writer recalls going to bed one night in the rainy season at Bouaflé (Ivory Coast) under three blankets, although the thermometer registered 23·3°C (74°F). In the dry season, when humidity is low, wood dries up and furniture comes apart. Leather and paper become brittle.

## Climates of West Africa*

The climates of West Africa may be classified as follows:

MONSOONAL

Dry Season followed by a long and very wet one:
   *Southwest coast Monsoonal*
   *Liberian*
   *Interior Sierra Leonean*
   *Foutanian*
   *Guinea foothills*
   *Guinea highlands*

EQUATORIAL

Rain in every month, with two maxima.

SEMI-SEASONAL EQUATORIAL

Up to four dry months, or low total rainfall, but with two maxima:
   *Semi-seasonal equatorial*
   *Seasonal equatorial*
   *Accra–Togo dry coastal*

MONSOONAL-EQUATORIAL OR CAMEROON

Rain in every month, variable number of maxima and a very high total rainfall.

---

*Local details of many climates may also be found in the section on climate in certain country chapters. In the following tables, temperatures (T) are means of daily maxima and minima, in degrees Centigrade (Fahrenheit), for each month. Rainfall (R) is in millimetres (inches). After these letters are figures indicating the number of years to which the readings refer. Figures in metres (feet) refer to altitude.

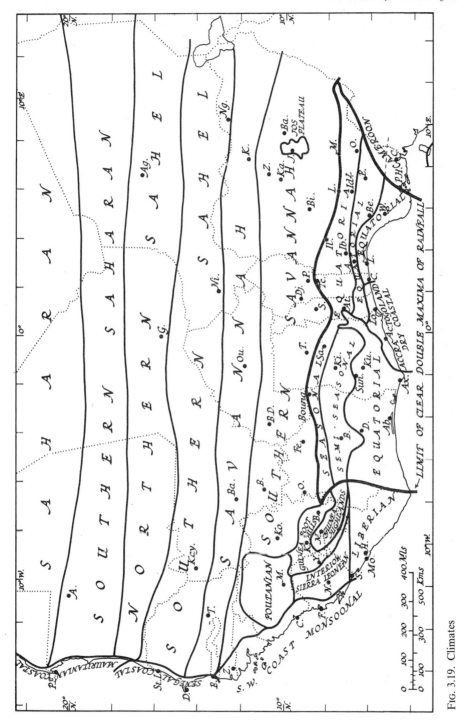

FIG. 3.19. Climates

(For the identification of place names, see cl mate tables)

*Climate*

## TROPICAL (SUDANESE)

One rainfall maximum, becoming shorter inland.
*Southern savanna*
*Jos Plateau*
*Savanna*
*Senegal coastal*
*Southern Sahel*
*Northern Sahel*
*Southern Saharan*


## MAURITANIAN COASTAL

Minute winter rainfall.


## SAHARAN

No regular rain.


## Monsoonal

### SOUTHWEST COAST MONSOONAL

This occurs in the coastal areas of southern Senegal, Portuguese Guinea, Guinea and Sierra Leone.

|  | Jan. | Feb. | Mar. | Apr. | May | June | July | Aug. | Sept. | Oct. | Nov. | Dec. | Year |
|---|---|---|---|---|---|---|---|---|---|---|---|---|---|
| Ziguinchor (Casamance, Senegal) 5·5 m (18 ft) 12°35′N, 16°16′W |||||||||||||
| T5 | 32·6 | 34·5 | 35·3 | 35·4 | 35·0 | 33·1 | 30·9 | 29·5 | 30·7 | 31·4 | 32·0 | 30·7 | 32·7 |
|  | *90·6* | *94·1* | *95·6* | *95·8* | *95·0* | *91·6* | *87·6* | *85·1* | *87·3* | *88·6* | *89·6* | *87·3* | *90·8* |
|  | 16·7 | 17·3 | 19·2 | 19·7 | 22·2 | 24·1 | 23·4 | 23·3 | 23·2 | 23·3 | 21·4 | 18·3 | 21·0 |
|  | *62·1* | *63·2* | *66·6* | *67·5* | *72·0* | *75·4* | *74·2* | *74·0* | *73·8* | *74·0* | *70·6* | *65·0* | *69·8* |
| R10 | 0 | 3 | 0 | 0 | 13 | 142 | 406 | 559 | 338 | 160 | 8 | 0 | 1 626 |
|  | *0·0* | *0·1* | *0·0* | *0·0* | *0·5* | *5·6* | *16·0* | *22·0* | *13·3* | *6·3* | *0·3* | *0·0* | *64·0* |
| Conakry (Guinea) 4·9 m (16 ft) 9°31′N, 13°43′W |||||||||||||
| T5 | 31·3 | 31·7 | 31·9 | 32·1 | 31·7 | 30·4 | 28·6 | 27·8 | 29·1 | 30·1 | 30·7 | 31·3 | 30·6 |
|  | *88·4* | *89·0* | *89·5* | *89·8* | *89·0* | *86·8* | *83·4* | *82·1* | *84·4* | *86·2* | *87·3* | *88·4* | *87·0* |
|  | 22·6 | 23·4 | 24·0 | 24·2 | 24·5 | 23·7 | 23·0 | 23·0 | 23·3 | 23·2 | 24·1 | 23·7 | 23·6 |
|  | *72·6* | *74·2* | *75·2* | *75·6* | *76·1* | *74·6* | *73·4* | *73·4* | *74·0* | *73·8* | *75·4* | *74·6* | *74·4* |
| R10 | 3 | 3 | 10 | 23 | 158 | 559 | 1 298 | 1 054 | 683 | 373 | 122 | 10 | 4 293 |
|  | *0·1* | *0·1* | *0·4* | *0·9* | *6·2* | *22·0* | *51·1* | *41·5* | *26·9* | *14·7* | *4·8* | *0·4* | *169·0* |
| Freetown (Sierra Leone) 11·3 m (37 ft) 8°30′N, 13°14′W |||||||||||||
| T10 | 29·4 | 29·9 | 30·2 | 30·3 | 30·2 | 29·8 | 28·3 | 27·6 | 28·4 | 29·3 | 29·6 | 29·3 | 29·3 |
|  | *84·9* | *85·9* | *86·4* | *86·5* | *86·3* | *85·6* | *82·9* | *81·6* | *83·1* | *84·8* | *85·3* | *84·7* | *84·8* |
|  | 24·1 | 25·1 | 24·8 | 25·3 | 24·8 | 23·8 | 23·2 | 23·1 | 23·3 | 23·2 | 24·1 | 24·4 | 24·1 |
|  | *75·3* | *77·1* | *76·7* | *77·5* | *76·7* | *74·8* | *73·8* | *73·6* | *74·0* | *73·8* | *75·4* | *76·0* | *75·3* |
| R10 | 5 | 3 | 15 | 64 | 150 | 315 | 955 | 912 | 650 | 269 | 137 | 41 | 3 510 |
|  | *0·2* | *0·1* | *0·6* | *2·5* | *5·9* | *12·4* | *37·6* | *35·9* | *25·6* | *10·6* | *5·4* | *1·6* | *138·2* |

There is a hot dry season, somewhat tempered by moist marine winds and quite high relative humidity; and a rather less hot wet one. The monsoon is at a maximum in July and August, has a high persistence of westerly downpours, and is sometimes 3 050 m (10 000 ft) deep. The early and late rains come with line squalls and easterly winds.

During the dry season, vegetative growth may cease for several months. Then the violent and continuous rains impair soil structure and cause severe leaching. All these factors are further deterrents to rich forest development, so that this is the realm of the Casamance Woodland.

The main food crop is rice, the more so as there are many coastal and inland swamps. Tree crops are fairly well suited here. In general however, there is less variety of food crops than elsewhere. Some assert that the heavy rainfall and high relative humidity impair man's efficiency in this zone and have restricted economic development.

## LIBERIAN

Like the Guinea highlands climate, the Liberian type is transitional between the southwest coast monsoonal and the equatorial climates. Compared with the former, there is generally less rain in the Liberian type, though it is much more evenly distributed.

The main characteristic is a drier period from about the last week of July to mid-August, well known in Liberia as 'the middle drys'. Although facilitating transport, these drier days are not sufficient to make harvesting of a cereal possible. The period is often too brief and too irregular in incidence to be recognisable in average monthly rainfall statistics.

| | Jan. | Feb. | Mar. | Apr. | May | June | July | Aug. | Sept. | Oct. | Nov. | Dec. | Year |
|---|---|---|---|---|---|---|---|---|---|---|---|---|---|
| Harbel[1] (Liberia) 30·5 m (100 ft) 6°24′N, 10°25′W | | | | | | | | | | | | | |
| T18 | 31·3 | 31·9 | 32·3 | 32·0 | 30·8 | 29·1 | 27·2 | 26·8 | 27·9 | 29·6 | 30·3 | 30·5 | 29·9 |
| | 88·3 | 89·5 | 90·0 | 89·6 | 87·5 | 84·3 | 81·0 | 80·2 | 82·2 | 85·2 | 86·6 | 86·9 | 85·9 |
| | 20·4 | 21·1 | 21·4 | 21·6 | 21·7 | 21·6 | 21·1 | 21·1 | 21·4 | 21·5 | 21·4 | 20·8 | 21·3 |
| | 68·7 | 70·0 | 70·5 | 70·9 | 71·1 | 70·8 | 69·9 | 70·0 | 70·6 | 70·7 | 70·5 | 69·4 | 70·3 |
| R18 | 25 | 43 | 117 | 158 | 297 | 414 | 467 | 513 | 622 | 371 | 188 | 74 | 3 287 |
| | 1·0 | 1·7 | 4·6 | 6·2 | 11·7 | 16·3 | 18·4 | 20·2 | 24·5 | 14·6 | 7·4 | 2·9 | 129·4 |

## INTERIOR SIERRA LEONEAN

This is a drier variant of the southwest coast monsoonal climate, and occurs not only in Sierra Leone but also in northwestern Liberia. The main rains (July–September) are less, but the early and late ones are usually greater than on the coast.

# Climate

Rainfall regime is akin to the Foutanian type (see below) but temperatures are higher and diurnal variation less, whilst annual rainfall is usually heavier.

| | Jan. | Feb. | Mar. | Apr. | May | June | July | Aug. | Sept. | Oct. | Nov. | Dec. | Year |
|---|---|---|---|---|---|---|---|---|---|---|---|---|---|
| Njala (Sierra Leone) 51 m (167 ft) 8°06′N, 12°06′W | | | | | | | | | | | | | |
| T10 | 31·8 | 33·9 | 34·6 | 33·8 | 32·3 | 30·6 | 28·4 | 27·9 | 29·4 | 30·9 | 31·0 | 30·7 | 31·3 |
| | 89·3 | 93·1 | 94·3 | 92·8 | 90·2 | 87·0 | 83·1 | 82·2 | 84·9 | 87·7 | 87·8 | 87·3 | 88·3 |
| | 19·7 | 20·4 | 21·3 | 21·9 | 22·2 | 21·8 | 21·6 | 21·6 | 21·7 | 21·4 | 21·2 | 20·1 | 21·2 |
| | 67·4 | 68·7 | 70·4 | 71·4 | 71·9 | 71·2 | 70·9 | 70·9 | 71·1 | 70·5 | 70·2 | 68·2 | 70·2 |
| R25 | 8 | 18 | 76 | 130 | 252 | 368 | 406 | 536 | 419 | 325 | 170 | 38 | 2 743 |
| | 0·3 | 0·7 | 3·0 | 5·1 | 9·9 | 14·5 | 16·0 | 21·1 | 16·5 | 12·8 | 6·7 | 1·5 | 108·0 |

## FOUTANIAN

This is a highland variant, within the Fouta Djallon, of the southwest coast monsoonal type and is transitional in character between it and the southern savanna climate.

Rainfall is much less than in the southwest coast monsoonal climate, averaging between 1 525 and 2 030 mm (60 and 80 in), but the rainy season is up to two months longer. There are sharp variations with aspect and altitude, the south and west being wettest. Rain often comes in violent storms which cause severe erosion of the thin soils. Rainfall is less reliable than on the coast, but is steadier at higher elevations. Although mountain mists moderate the aridity of the dry months, relative humidity is lower (annual average 66 per cent) than on the coast, because the Harmattan is the commonest wind.

Temperatures, particularly minima, are markedly low, especially from December to February. Daily variation is far greater, being 16·6–20°C (30–36°F) in the dry season.

| | Jan. | Feb. | Mar. | Apr. | May | June | July | Aug. | Sept. | Oct. | Nov. | Dec. | Year |
|---|---|---|---|---|---|---|---|---|---|---|---|---|---|
| Mamou (Guinea) 744 m (2 440 ft) 10°22′N, 12°05′W | | | | | | | | | | | | | |
| T5 | 32·6 | 33·8 | 34·5 | 33·8 | 30·9 | 28·9 | 26·7 | 26·2 | 27·6 | 28·3 | 29·7 | 31·0 | 30·3 |
| | 90·6 | 92·8 | 94·1 | 92·8 | 87·6 | 84·1 | 80·0 | 79·2 | 81·6 | 83·0 | 85·5 | 87·8 | 86·6 |
| | 12·4 | 14·9 | 17·9 | 18·9 | 19·5 | 18·2 | 18·6 | 18·4 | 18·4 | 17·9 | 16·6 | 13·3 | 17·1 |
| | 54·4 | 58·8 | 64·2 | 66·1 | 67·1 | 64·8 | 65·4 | 65·2 | 65·2 | 64·2 | 61·8 | 56·0 | 62·7 |
| R10 | 8 | 10 | 46 | 127 | 203 | 257 | 335 | 401 | 340 | 203 | 61 | 8 | 2 004 |
| | 0·3 | 0·4 | 1·8 | 5·0 | 8·0 | 10·1 | 13·2 | 15·8 | 13·4 | 8·0 | 2·4 | 0·3 | 78·9 |

## GUINEA FOOTHILLS

This occurs between the Fouta Djallon and the Guinea highlands, in northeastern Sierra Leone (Kabala) and southeastern Guinea.

Total rainfall is about the same as in the Foutanian, but is less than in the Guinea highlands type found at higher altitudes, or in the interior

Sierra Leonean and southwest coast monsoonal types found at lower altitudes. The rainfall regime is transitional between all these climates and the southern savanna. Relative humidity is also intermediate in character between the almost constantly humid Guinea highlands and the more variable conditions of adjacent areas.

Temperatures vary little compared with the Foutanian or southern savanna climates, and are almost as equable as in the Guinea highlands. Lowest means of daily minima are found in December–January, and lowest means of daily maxima in June–August when rainfall lowers afternoon readings.

| | Jan. | Feb. | Mar. | Apr. | May | June | July | Aug. | Sept. | Oct. | Nov. | Dec. | Year |
|---|---|---|---|---|---|---|---|---|---|---|---|---|---|
| Beyla (Guinea) 676 m (2 218 ft) 8°41′N, 8°39′W | | | | | | | | | | | | | |
| T5 | 30·9 | 31·8 | 31·7 | 30·1 | 28·8 | 28·0 | 26·0 | 26·8 | 28·3 | 28·9 | 29·4 | 31·0 | 29·3 |
| | 87·6 | 89·3 | 89·1 | 86·2 | 83·8 | 82·4 | 78·8 | 80·3 | 83·0 | 84·0 | 85·0 | 87·8 | 84·8 |
| | 14·9 | 18·6 | 19·5 | 19·5 | 19·0 | 18·7 | 18·0 | 18·2 | 18·8 | 18·8 | 18·3 | 15·0 | 18·1 |
| | 58 8 | 65·4 | 67·1 | 67·1 | 66·2 | 65·6 | 64·4 | 64·8 | 65·8 | 65·8 | 65·0 | 59·0 | 64·6 |
| R10 | 8 | 41 | 132 | 150 | 175 | 218 | 244 | 264 | 292 | 142 | 89 | 23 | 1 773 |
| | 0·3 | 1·6 | 5·2 | 5·9 | 6·9 | 8·6 | 9·6 | 10·4 | 11·5 | 5·6 | 3·5 | 0·9 | 69·8 |

## GUINEA HIGHLANDS

Like the Foutanian, the Guinea highlands type is a mountain modification of the southwest coast monsoonal type, and is found in the Guinea–Sierra Leone–Liberia borderlands and in the Man Massif of the Ivory Coast.

There is more rain than in the Foutanian, but less than in similar latitudes on the coast. Equatorial influences are evident in that there are only one or two dry months, and two rainfall maxima occur in some years. Relative humidity is high, except in January, and mists are common. At high altitudes the temperatures are remarkably equable for such an inland and mountainous region—a further illustration of equatorial influences.

| | Jan. | Feb. | Mar. | Apr. | May | June | July | Aug. | Sept. | Oct. | Nov. | Dec. | Year |
|---|---|---|---|---|---|---|---|---|---|---|---|---|---|
| Macenta (Guinea) 614 m (2 015 ft) 8°34′N, 9°28′W | | | | | | | | | | | | | |
| R5 | 10 | 48 | 147 | 168 | 196 | 262 | 506 | 587 | 409 | 254 | 203 | 53 | 2 842 |
| | 0·4 | 1·9 | 5·8 | 6·6 | 7·7 | 10·3 | 19·9 | 23·1 | 16·1 | 10·0 | 8·0 | 2·1 | 111·9 |
| Yengema (Sierra Leone) 387 m (1 270 ft) 8°37′N, 11°03′W | | | | | | | | | | | | | |
| T10 | 32·4 | 34·4 | 34·6 | 33·8 | 32·8 | 31·6 | 29·3 | 28·8 | 30·8 | 31·7 | 31·6 | 31·3 | 31·9 |
| | 90·4 | 93·9 | 94·2 | 92·9 | 91·0 | 88·9 | 84·7 | 83·9 | 87·5 | 89·1 | 88·9 | 88·4 | 89·5 |
| | 14·3 | 16·4 | 19·4 | 20·3 | 20·7 | 20·2 | 20·3 | 20·2 | 20·2 | 19·8 | 19·3 | 17·2 | 19·1 |
| | 57·8 | 61·6 | 67·0 | 68·5 | 69·3 | 68·4 | 68·6 | 68·3 | 68·4 | 67·6 | 66·8 | 62·9 | 66·3 |
| R15 | 10 | 20 | 97 | 160 | 229 | 282 | 269 | 412 | 401 | 292 | 145 | 41 | 2 355 |
| | 0·4 | 0·8 | 3·8 | 6·3 | 9·0 | 11·1 | 10·6 | 16·2 | 15·8 | 11·5 | 5·7 | 1·6 | 92·7 |

## Equatorial

The true extent of this type has been frequently exaggerated; it includes only the southern Ivory Coast, southwestern and southcentral Ghana, and western coastal Nigeria.

Temperatures may show diurnal and annual variations of between about 22°C (71°F) and 31°C (88°F). There is constantly high humidity (at least 77 per cent, except around midday), mostly convectional rainfall of at least 25 mm (1 in) in each month, and 1 525 mm (60 in) annually with two maxima. Consequently, plant growth never ceases, and this is the ideal habitat of the lowland rainforest.

| | *Jan.* | *Feb.* | *Mar.* | *Apr.* | *May* | *June* | *July* | *Aug.* | *Sept.* | *Oct.* | *Nov.* | *Dec.* | *Year* |
|---|---|---|---|---|---|---|---|---|---|---|---|---|---|
| **Warri (Nigeria) 6·1 m (20 ft) 5°31′N, 5°44′E** | | | | | | | | | | | | | |
| T5 | 31·3 | 32·7 | 32·8 | 32·7 | 31·4 | 30·1 | 28·1 | 28·4 | 28·8 | 30·0 | 31·6 | 31·4 | 30·8 |
| | *88·4* | *90·8* | *91·1* | *90·8* | *88·6* | *86·1* | *82·6* | *83·1* | *83·9* | *86·0* | *88·8* | *88·6* | *87·4* |
| | 21·9 | 22·3 | 23·2 | 23·3 | 22·8 | 22·4 | 22·2 | 22·9 | 22·2 | 22·2 | 22·4 | 22·2 | 23·6 |
| | *71·4* | *72·1* | *73·7* | *73·9* | *73·1* | *72·4* | *72·0* | *73·2* | *71·9* | *71·9* | *72·4* | *72·0* | *74·4* |
| R46 | 33 | 53 | 135 | 229 | 274 | 379 | 391 | 300 | 434 | 323 | 112 | 36 | 2 698 |
| | *1·3* | *2·1* | *5·3* | *9·0* | *10·8* | *14·9* | *15·4* | *11·8* | *17·1* | *12·7* | *4·4* | *1·4* | *106·2* |
| **Lagos (Nigeria) 3·1 m (10 ft) 6°27′N, 3°24′E** | | | | | | | | | | | | | |
| T5 | 32·5 | 32·8 | 33·1 | 32·5 | 31·1 | 29·0 | 27·9 | 27·6 | 28·8 | 29·8 | 31·8 | 31·8 | 30·7 |
| | *90·5* | *91·0* | *91·5* | *90·5* | *87·9* | *84·2* | *82·2* | *81·7* | *83·9* | *85·7* | *89·3* | *89·3* | *87·3* |
| | 21·0 | 22·6 | 22·8 | 22·1 | 22·3 | 21·8 | 21·1 | 20·9 | 21·4 | 21·7 | 22·1 | 21·6 | 21·8 |
| | *69·8* | *72·6* | *73·1* | *71·7* | *72·1* | *71·2* | *70·0* | *69·7* | *70·5* | *71·0* | *71·7* | *70·9* | *71·2* |
| R55 | 25 | 38 | 99 | 140 | 277 | 439 | 277 | 69 | 142 | 201 | 71 | 25 | 1 803 |
| | *1·0* | *1·5* | *3·9* | *5·5* | *10·9* | *17·3* | *10·9* | *2·7* | *5·6* | *7·9* | *2·8* | *1·0* | *71·0* |
| **Axim (Ghana) 22·9 m (75 ft) 4°51′N, 2°15′W** | | | | | | | | | | | | | |
| T35 | 29·9 | 30·4 | 30·6 | 30·9 | 30·1 | 28·8 | 28·3 | 27·7 | 28·1 | 28·7 | 29·4 | 29·9 | 29·4 |
| | *85·9* | *86·8* | *87·1* | *87·6* | *86·1* | *83·9* | *82·9* | *81·9* | *82·6* | *83·7* | *84·9* | *85·8* | *85·9* |
| | 22·1 | 23·1 | 22·9 | 22·8 | 22·7 | 22·2 | 21·9 | 21·6 | 21·7 | 21·8 | 22·1 | 22·3 | 22·3 |
| | *71·8* | *73·5* | *73·3* | *73·0* | *72·8* | *71·9* | *71·5* | *70·9* | *71·0* | *71·3* | *71·8* | *72·1* | *72·1* |
| R33 | 58 | 61 | 122 | 142 | 404 | 495 | 168 | 58 | 84 | 188 | 196 | 99 | 2 070 |
| | *2·3* | *2·4* | *4·8* | *5·6* | *15·9* | *19·5* | *6·6* | *2·3* | *3·3* | *7·4* | *7·7* | *3·9* | *81·5* |
| **Abidjan (Ivory Coast) 19·8 m (65 ft) 5°19′N, 4°01′W** | | | | | | | | | | | | | |
| T5 | 31·8 | 32·8 | 32·8 | 32·4 | 31·4 | 29·5 | 28·2 | 27·8 | 28·4 | 29·7 | 30·7 | 31·4 | 30·6 |
| | *89·3* | *91·1* | *91·1* | *90·4* | *88·6* | *85·1* | *82·8* | *82·0* | *83·2* | *85·5* | *87·3* | *88·6* | *87·1* |
| | 22·7 | 23·9 | 24·1 | 24·0 | 23·7 | 22·8 | 22·2 | 21·8 | 22·6 | 23·2 | 23·1 | 23·1 | 23·1 |
| | *72·8* | *75·0* | *75·4* | *75·2* | *74·6* | *73·1* | *72·0* | *71·3* | *72·6* | *73·8* | *73·6* | *73·6* | *73·5* |
| R10 | 41 | 53 | 99 | 125 | 361 | 495 | 213 | 56 | 71 | 168 | 201 | 79 | 1 958 |
| | *1·6* | *2·1* | *3·9* | *4·9* | *14·2* | *19·5* | *8·4* | *2·2* | *2·8* | *6·6* | *7·9* | *3·1* | *77·1* |
| **Tabou (Ivory Coast) 4·0 m (13 ft) 4°25′N, 7°22′W** | | | | | | | | | | | | | |
| T5 | 30·3 | 30·7 | 31·1 | 31·4 | 30·2 | 28·7 | 27·8 | 27·3 | 27·8 | 28·8 | 29·7 | 30·1 | 29·5 |
| | *86·6* | *87·3* | *88·0* | *88·6* | *86·4* | *83·6* | *82·0* | *81·2* | *82·1* | *83·8* | *85·5* | *86·2* | *85·1* |
| | 23·0 | 23·2 | 23·3 | 23·4 | 23·3 | 23·2 | 22·9 | 22·1 | 22·4 | 23·0 | 23·4 | 23·1 | 23·0 |
| | *73·4* | *73·8* | *74·0* | *74·2* | *74·0* | *73·8* | *73·2* | *71·8* | *72·4* | *73·4* | *74·2* | *73·6* | *73·4* |
| R10 | 38 | 69 | 99 | 117 | 417 | 579 | 175 | 99 | 198 | 221 | 221 | 117 | 2 350 |
| | *1·5* | *2·7* | *3·9* | *4·6* | *16·4* | *22·8* | *6·9* | *3·9* | *7·8* | *8·7* | *8·7* | *4·6* | *92·5* |

Total rainfall is almost always less, and is more evenly distributed through the year than in monsoonal types. Less erosion and leaching occur, and the drier period between the two rainfall maxima permits the first of two or more harvests. It also facilitates travel and commerce at that time. Winds are gentle and calms frequent.

## Semi-equatorial

### SEMI-SEASONAL EQUATORIAL

This type is found in the southcentral Ivory Coast, northern Ashanti, southern Togo, Dahomey and Nigeria.

Temperatures are similar to those of true equatorial stations, although the diurnal and annual range are greater. A significant difference is the lower rainfall, especially in December and January, when vegetative growth may be halted.

| | Jan. | Feb. | Mar. | Apr. | May | June | July | Aug. | Sept. | Oct. | Nov. | Dec. | Year |
|---|---|---|---|---|---|---|---|---|---|---|---|---|---|
| Bouaké (Ivory Coast) 338 m (1 110 ft) 7°41′N, 5°02′W | | | | | | | | | | | | | |
| T5 | 33·4 | 34·6 | 35·2 | 34·8 | 32·8 | 30·7 | 29·4 | 28·7 | 29·7 | 31·1 | 32·0 | 32·8 | 32·1 |
| | 92·2 | 94·3 | 95·4 | 94·6 | 91·0 | 87·3 | 85·0 | 83·6 | 85·5 | 88·0 | 89·6 | 91·0 | 89·7 |
| | 20·4 | 21·7 | 21·8 | 21·7 | 21·7 | 21·1 | 20·6 | 20·3 | 20·6 | 20·8 | 20·7 | 20·6 | 21·6 |
| | 68·8 | 71·1 | 71·3 | 71·1 | 71·0 | 70·0 | 69·0 | 68·6 | 69·1 | 69·5 | 69·3 | 69·1 | 70·8 |
| R10 | 10 | 38 | 104 | 147 | 135 | 152 | 81 | 117 | 208 | 132 | 38 | 25 | 1 186 |
| | 0·4 | 1·5 | 4·1 | 5·8 | 5·3 | 6·0 | 3·2 | 4·6 | 8·2 | 5·2 | 1·5 | 1·0 | 46·7 |
| Kintampo (Ghana) 369 m (1 211 ft) 8°02′N, 1°52′W | | | | | | | | | | | | | |
| T21 | 32·7 | 34·6 | 34·6 | 33·2 | 32·4 | 30·5 | 29·3 | 28·8 | 29·6 | 31·1 | 32·2 | 32·1 | 31·8 |
| | 90·8 | 94·3 | 94·3 | 91·8 | 90·3 | 86·9 | 84·8 | 83·8 | 85·2 | 88·0 | 89·9 | 89·7 | 89·2 |
| | 19·3 | 21·0 | 21·8 | 21·8 | 21·3 | 21·1 | 20·4 | 20·2 | 20·6 | 20·4 | 20·5 | 19·6 | 20·7 |
| | 66·8 | 69·8 | 71·3 | 71·2 | 70·3 | 69·9 | 68·7 | 68·3 | 69·0 | 68·7 | 68·9 | 67·3 | 69·2 |
| R21 | 10 | 43 | 109 | 158 | 208 | 259 | 175 | 132 | 330 | 229 | 84 | 10 | 1 748 |
| | 0·4 | 1·7 | 4·3 | 6·2 | 8·2 | 10·2 | 6·9 | 5·2 | 13·0 | 9·0 | 3·3 | 0·4 | 68·8 |
| Enugu (Nigeria) 221 m (745 ft) 6°27′N, 7°29′E | | | | | | | | | | | | | |
| T5 | 32·1 | 33·4 | 33·7 | 32·8 | 31·2 | 29·5 | 28·3 | 28·3 | 29·2 | 30·3 | 31·8 | 31·8 | 31·0 |
| | 89·7 | 92·1 | 92·7 | 91·1 | 88·1 | 85·1 | 82·9 | 83·0 | 84·5 | 86·5 | 89·2 | 89·3 | 87·8 |
| | 22·3 | 22·9 | 23·9 | 23·8 | 22·7 | 22·0 | 21·9 | 21·7 | 21·6 | 21·7 | 22·6 | 22·3 | 22·4 |
| | 72·2 | 73·3 | 75·0 | 74·8 | 72·9 | 71·6 | 71·5 | 71·1 | 70·8 | 71·0 | 72·6 | 72·1 | 72·4 |
| R35 | 18 | 25 | 66 | 145 | 264 | 285 | 196 | 175 | 323 | 249 | 53 | 13 | 1 811 |
| | 0·7 | 1·0 | 2·6 | 5·7 | 10·4 | 11·2 | 7·7 | 6·9 | 12·7 | 9·8 | 2·1 | 0·5 | 71·3 |

### SEASONAL EQUATORIAL

This is drier and has a greater range of temperature than the semi-seasonal equatorial type. There are still two rainfall maxima, but there are three or four dry months. Vegetative growth is thoroughly halted, so that the natural forest was frail and is now rare.

|  | Jan. | Feb. | Mar. | Apr. | May | June | July | Aug. | Sept. | Oct. | Nov. | Dec. | Year |
|---|---|---|---|---|---|---|---|---|---|---|---|---|---|
| Salaga (Ghana) 181 m (593 ft) 8°30′N, 0°30′W ||||||||||||||
| T27 | 35·3 | 36·2 | 36·9 | 36·1 | 34·3 | 33·0 | 31·7 | 31·2 | 32·2 | 33·2 | 34·9 | 35·0 | 34·2 |
|  | 95·5 | 97·2 | 98·5 | 96·9 | 93·8 | 91·4 | 89·1 | 88·1 | 90·0 | 91·7 | 94·8 | 95·0 | 93·5 |
|  | 22·7 | 23·1 | 24·7 | 24·3 | 23·5 | 22·8 | 22·5 | 22·3 | 22·5 | 22·6 | 22·7 | 22·2 | 23·0 |
|  | 72·9 | 73·6 | 76·5 | 75·8 | 74·3 | 73·0 | 72·5 | 72·1 | 72·5 | 72·7 | 72·9 | 72·0 | 73·4 |
| R27 | 13 | 20 | 69 | 119 | 145 | 168 | 142 | 183 | 252 | 150 | 36 | 13 | 1 052 |
|  | 0·5 | 0·8 | 2·7 | 4·7 | 5·7 | 6·6 | 5·6 | 7·2 | 9·9 | 5·9 | 1·4 | 0·5 | 41·4 |
| Tchaourou (Dahomey) 326 m (1 071 ft) 8°54′N, 2°36′E ||||||||||||||
| T4 | 34·5 | 36·9 | 36·7 | 35·1 | 33·1 | 31·1 | 29·3 | 28·9 | 29·7 | 31·3 | 33·4 | 34·6 | 32·9 |
|  | 94·1 | 98·5 | 98·1 | 95·2 | 91·6 | 88·0 | 84·8 | 84·1 | 85·5 | 88·4 | 92·2 | 94·3 | 91·2 |
|  | 19·0 | 20·6 | 21·7 | 22·0 | 21·7 | 20·6 | 20·6 | 20·1 | 20·6 | 20·6 | 19·4 | 18·1 | 20·4 |
|  | 66·2 | 69·0 | 71·0 | 71·6 | 71·1 | 69·0 | 69·0 | 68·2 | 69·0 | 69·0 | 67·0 | 64·6 | 68·7 |
| R4 | 0 | 15 | 48 | 89 | 163 | 226 | 109 | 175 | 216 | 79 | 10 | 5 | 1 135 |
|  | 0·0 | 0·6 | 1·9 | 3·5 | 6·4 | 8·9 | 4·3 | 6·9 | 8·5 | 3·1 | 0·4 | 0·2 | 44·7 |
| Ibadan (Nigeria) 227 m (745 ft) 7°26′N, 3°54′E ||||||||||||||
| T5 | 32·9 | 34·2 | 34·4 | 33·6 | 31·6 | 29·8 | 27·9 | 27·8 | 29·3 | 30·4 | 31·9 | 32·4 | 31·4 |
|  | 91·2 | 93·5 | 93·9 | 92·4 | 88·8 | 85·6 | 82·2 | 82·1 | 84·7 | 86·7 | 89·5 | 90·3 | 88·5 |
|  | 20·7 | 21·4 | 22·6 | 22·5 | 22·2 | 21·7 | 21·1 | 21·1 | 21·1 | 20·9 | 21·1 | 20·7 | 21·4 |
|  | 69·2 | 70·5 | 72·7 | 72·5 | 71·9 | 71·0 | 70·0 | 70·0 | 70·0 | 69·7 | 69·9 | 69·2 | 70·5 |
| R48 | 10 | 23 | 89 | 137 | 150 | 188 | 160 | 84 | 178 | 155 | 46 | 10 | 1 229 |
|  | 0·4 | 0·9 | 3·5 | 5·4 | 5·9 | 7·4 | 6·3 | 3·3 | 7·0 | 6·1 | 1·8 | 0·4 | 48·4 |

## ACCRA–TOGO DRY COASTAL

Lands south of a line beginning near Takoradi, and passing through Nsawam, thence near the southern border of the Togo Mountains south of Palimé in Togo, and into Dahomey to the coast west of Cotonou, have less than 1 140 mm (45 in) of annual rain. The coastal fringe between Elmina and Grand Popo has under 890 mm (35 in). The rainfall pattern is equatorial, but the yearly and monthly totals are very low. Days of rain are also few. There are only two or three months with over 100 mm (4 in) of rain, whereas in the seasonal equatorial type there are at least four, and in the semiseasonal and equatorial climates there are at least six months. Relative humidity is a little less than in the equatorial zone, while temperatures are a little higher, except from July to September when they are much lower.

The relative dryness and sparse vegetation were added attractions for the early European traders in gold and slaves. Of forty-five coastal forts, thirty-seven were built within this dry belt and near gold occurrences.

Some have explained the relative aridity of this area by invoking the direction of the coast as being the same as that of the rainbearing winds. This is an insufficient explanation, since not all rainbearing winds are southwesterly. Moreoever, other parts of the Guinea Coast (e.g. around Lagos and Sassandra), though similarly aligned, are not so dry. Furthermore, temperature contrasts over land and sea tend to be more powerful when winds are parallel to the coast, thus making afternoon rain probable.

Land and sea breezes and natural variation in winds also make 'parallelism' ephemeral. Another explanation in terms of the direction of the coast is that its northward curve facilitates the penetration of the dry Harmattan. However, this is not a particularly common wind in the area.

Others have alluded to the proved occurrence of cold water off the Ghana coast from July to September. Cool offshore waters certainly explain the lower temperatures of July and August,[6] which also restrict the conditions favourable to convectional rainfall in those months.

Another explanation is that the southwesterly winds which bring so much rain to the projecting Cape Three Points region, are naturally deviated as westerlies over the land, especially in August. Hence they are drier over the central and eastern Ghana, Togo and Dahomey coastlines, the last two also being somewhat sheltered by the Togo Mountains.

Lastly, it has been suggested that during the northern hemisphere summer the South Atlantic anticyclone moves far enough north (because of the southern ocean—northern landmass contrast) to impinge upon the northern hemisphere in this area. Crowe (see page 26) and others have referred to subsidence and inversion within winds from the southern hemisphere, giving greater stability to southwesterlies, and so less rain.

| | Jan. | Feb. | Mar. | Apr. | May | June | July | Aug. | Sept. | Oct. | Nov. | Dec. | Year |
|---|---|---|---|---|---|---|---|---|---|---|---|---|---|
| Accra (Ghana) 6·1 m (20 ft) 5°31′N, 0°12′W | | | | | | | | | | | | | |
| T39 | 30·8 | 31·1 | 31·3 | 31·1 | 30·4 | 28·9 | 27·6 | 27·1 | 28·0 | 29·4 | 30·6 | 30·8 | 29·8 |
| | 87·5 | 87·9 | 88·3 | 88·0 | 86·7 | 84·1 | 81·7 | 80·8 | 82·4 | 84·9 | 87·1 | 87·5 | 85·6 |
| 29 | 23·1 | 23·7 | 24·2 | 24·2 | 23·7 | 23·1 | 22·5 | 21·9 | 22·4 | 22·9 | 23·4 | 23·4 | 23·2 |
| | 73·6 | 74·6 | 75·6 | 75·5 | 74·6 | 73·5 | 72·5 | 71·4 | 72·3 | 73·3 | 74·2 | 74·2 | 73·8 |
| R47 | 18 | 38 | 56 | 76 | 127 | 191 | 51 | 15 | 38 | 58 | 36 | 25 | 726 |
| | 0·7 | 1·5 | 2·2 | 3·0 | 5·0 | 7·5 | 2·0 | 0·6 | 1·5 | 2·3 | 1·4 | 1·0 | 28·6 |
| Lomé (Togo) 10·4 m (34 ft) 6°08′N, 1°13′E | | | | | | | | | | | | | |
| T5 | 29·5 | 30·4 | 31·1 | 30·1 | 29·7 | 28·2 | 26·5 | 26·0 | 26·8 | 28·5 | 29·7 | 29·6 | 28·8 |
| | 85·1 | 86·7 | 87·9 | 86·2 | 85·5 | 82·8 | 79·7 | 78·8 | 80·2 | 83·3 | 85·5 | 85·3 | 83·8 |
| | 22·3 | 23·3 | 23·5 | 23·3 | 23·3 | 22·6 | 21·9 | 21·6 | 22·0 | 22·3 | 22·5 | 22·1 | 22·5 |
| | 72·2 | 73·9 | 74·3 | 73·9 | 73·9 | 72·7 | 71·4 | 70·9 | 71·6 | 72·1 | 72·5 | 71·8 | 72·5 |
| R15 | 15 | 23 | 46 | 117 | 145 | 224 | 71 | 8 | 36 | 61 | 28 | 10 | 782 |
| | 0·6 | 0·9 | 1·8 | 4·6 | 5·7 | 8·8 | 2·8 | 0·3 | 1·4 | 2·4 | 1·1 | 0·4 | 30·8 |

## Monsoonal equatorial or Cameroon

This type occurs below about 900 m (3 000 ft) in the Cross River basin and its environs of southeastern Nigeria; it is better developed in western Cameroon and Fernando Po. Above the limiting altitude are montane microclimates.

The Cameroon type results from the addition of a monsoonal effect to the equatorial regime. Temperature and humidity conditions of the latter persist, but rainfall totals and high wind velocities in the wet season are akin to monsoonal conditions. The heavy rain may come in several maxima, though, broadly speaking, there is one great upsurge. There are no dry months, as there are in pure monsoonal conditions.

| | Jan. | Feb. | Mar. | Apr. | May | June | July | Aug. | Sept. | Oct. | Nov. | Dec. | Year |
|---|---|---|---|---|---|---|---|---|---|---|---|---|---|
| Calabar (Nigeria) 52 m (170 ft) 4°58′N, 8°20′E | | | | | | | | | | | | | |
| T5 | 30·4 | 31·9 | 31·9 | 31·4 | 30·6 | 30·3 | 27·6 | 28·1 | 28·7 | 29·5 | 30·2 | 30·5 | 30·1 |
| | 86·7 | 89·4 | 89·4 | 88·6 | 87·1 | 86·6 | 81·6 | 82·6 | 83·7 | 85·1 | 86·4 | 86·9 | 86·2 |
| | 22·8 | 23·0 | 23·6 | 23·4 | 23·6 | 22·9 | 22·6 | 22·4 | 22·6 | 22·5 | 22·8 | 22·9 | 22·9 |
| | 73·0 | 73·4 | 74·5 | 74·2 | 74·5 | 73·3 | 72·6 | 72·3 | 72·7 | 72·5 | 73·0 | 73·3 | 73·3 |
| R47 | 43 | 76 | 152 | 213 | 312 | 406 | 450 | 406 | 427 | 310 | 191 | 43 | 3030 |
| | 1·7 | 3·0 | 6·0 | 8·4 | 12·3 | 16·0 | 17·7 | 16·0 | 16·8 | 12·2 | 7·5 | 1·7 | 119·3 |

## Tropical

### SOUTHERN SAVANNA

This type largely coincides with the 'Middle Belt' of West Africa, between about 8° and 11°N in Nigeria, 12°N in the Upper Volta and 13°N farther west. It includes the upper Niger lands of Guinea (but not the Fouta Djallon), the northern Ivory Coast, southern Mali, southwestern Upper Volta, the Ghana Northern and Upper Regions, central and northern Togo, Dahomey and the Middle Belt of Nigeria around the rivers Niger

| | Jan. | Feb. | Mar. | Apr. | May | June | July | Aug. | Sept. | Oct. | Nov. | Dec. | Year |
|---|---|---|---|---|---|---|---|---|---|---|---|---|---|
| Kouroussa (Guinea) 380 m (1 247 ft) 10°39′N, 9°53′W | | | | | | | | | | | | | |
| T5 | 33·6 | 35·8 | 37·2 | 36·9 | 34·6 | 31·7 | 30·1 | 29·5 | 30·4 | 31·9 | 32·9 | 32·7 | 33·1 |
| | 92·4 | 96·5 | 99·0 | 98·5 | 94·3 | 89·1 | 86·2 | 85·1 | 86·8 | 89·5 | 91·2 | 90·8 | 91·6 |
| | 13·8 | 17·1 | 21·7 | 23·0 | 22·8 | 21·6 | 20·9 | 20·9 | 20·8 | 20·6 | 18·9 | 14·4 | 19·6 |
| | 56·8 | 62·8 | 71·0 | 73·4 | 73·1 | 70·8 | 69·6 | 69·6 | 69·5 | 69·1 | 66·0 | 58·0 | 67·3 |
| R10 | 10 | 8 | 23 | 71 | 135 | 246 | 297 | 345 | 340 | 168 | 33 | 10 | 1 684 |
| | 0·4 | 0·3 | 0·9 | 2·8 | 5·3 | 9·7 | 11·7 | 13·6 | 13·4 | 6·6 | 1·3 | 0·4 | 66·3 |
| Bobo Dioulasso (Upper Volta) 433 m (1 421 ft) 11°12′N, 4°17′W | | | | | | | | | | | | | |
| T5 | 34·2 | 36·7 | 38·2 | 38·2 | 35·7 | 32·9 | 30·6 | 29·7 | 31·0 | 33·9 | 35·1 | 34·8 | 34·2 |
| | 93·6 | 98·0 | 100·8 | 100·8 | 96·3 | 91·2 | 87·0 | 85·5 | 87·8 | 93·0 | 95·2 | 94·6 | 93·6 |
| | 15·7 | 16·7 | 20·8 | 22·3 | 21·4 | 21·7 | 20·9 | 20·7 | 20·4 | 20·7 | 19·3 | 16·7 | 19·8 |
| | 60·3 | 62·1 | 69·5 | 72·2 | 70·6 | 71·0 | 69·6 | 69·3 | 68·8 | 69·3 | 66·8 | 62·0 | 67·6 |
| R10 | 3 | 5 | 28 | 53 | 117 | 122 | 249 | 305 | 216 | 64 | 18 | 0 | 1 179 |
| | 0·1 | 0·2 | 1·1 | 2·1 | 4·6 | 4·8 | 9·8 | 12·0 | 8·5 | 2·5 | 0·7 | 0·0 | 46·4 |
| Tamale (Ghana N.R.) 194 m (637 ft) 9°24′N, 0°53′W | | | | | | | | | | | | | |
| T34 | 35·7 | 37·9 | 38·4 | 36·8 | 34·6 | 32·3 | 30·6 | 30·1 | 30·8 | 33·2 | 35·2 | 34·0 | 34·2 |
| | 96·3 | 100·3 | 101·1 | 98·3 | 94·2 | 90·2 | 87·1 | 86·1 | 87·5 | 91·8 | 95·3 | 93·2 | 93·5 |
| | 19·1 | 21·3 | 23·3 | 23·2 | 22·6 | 21·6 | 21·6 | 21·0 | 20·9 | 21·4 | 20·9 | 20·8 | 21·5 |
| | 66·4 | 70·4 | 74·0 | 73·8 | 72·7 | 70·8 | 70·9 | 69·8 | 69·7 | 70·5 | 69·6 | 69·5 | 70·7 |
| R38 | 3 | 8 | 56 | 81 | 119 | 140 | 140 | 206 | 226 | 94 | 18 | 5 | 1 090 |
| | 0·1 | 0·3 | 2·2 | 3·2 | 4·7 | 5·5 | 5·5 | 8·1 | 8·9 | 3·7 | 0·7 | 0·2 | 42·9 |
| Bida (Nigeria) 184 m (605 ft) 9°04′N, 5°59′E | | | | | | | | | | | | | |
| T5 | 34·3 | 36·1 | 36·8 | 36·7 | 34·1 | 31·1 | 29·8 | 29·1 | 30·1 | 32·1 | 34·8 | 34·4 | 33·3 |
| | 93·8 | 97·0 | 98·3 | 98·1 | 93·3 | 88·0 | 85·7 | 84·3 | 86·1 | 89·8 | 94·6 | 94·0 | 92·0 |
| | 21·1 | 23·0 | 24·4 | 25·2 | 23·4 | 22·6 | 22·3 | 22·1 | 22·0 | 21·9 | 21·7 | 20·3 | 22·5 |
| | 70·0 | 73·4 | 76·0 | 77·3 | 74·2 | 72·7 | 72·1 | 71·8 | 71·5 | 71·6 | 71·1 | 68·5 | 72·5 |
| R25 | 3 | 8 | 25 | 76 | 152 | 196 | 193 | 213 | 259 | 97 | 8 | 0 | 1 232 |
| | 0·1 | 0·3 | 1·0 | 3·0 | 6·0 | 7·7 | 7·6 | 8·4 | 10·2 | 3·8 | 0·3 | 0·0 | 48·5 |

and Benue.[7] This climatic zone is roughly coincident with Guinea savanna vegetation.

There is a wide diurnal range of temperature in the dry season. There follows a seven to eight months rainy season, with lower temperatures and less variation. Variability of rainfall is greater than in climates already considered but less than in more northerly ones. Relative humidity varies between about 50 and 80 per cent but in the dry season is under 70 per cent at 9 a.m.

## JOS PLATEAU

This is a highland variant of the southern savanna types and temperatures are much lower. The rainfall regime is similar, but at exposed places on and near the southwestern edge of the plateau annual rainfall may be higher.

Some authorities include this area in the Foutanian type, but temperatures on the Jos Plateau are more equable than in the Fouta Djallon. Moreover, rainfall is hardly monsoonal in character and is certainly less in yearly and in most monthly totals.

| | Jan. | Feb. | Mar. | Apr. | May | June | July | Aug. | Sept. | Oct. | Nov. | Dec. | Year |
|---|---|---|---|---|---|---|---|---|---|---|---|---|---|
| Jos (Nigeria) 1 289 m (4 230 ft) 9°52′N, 8°54′E | | | | | | | | | | | | | |
| T5 | 27·8 | 29·8 | 30·7 | 31·4 | 29·4 | 27·2 | 24·7 | 23·8 | 25·9 | 27·9 | 28·6 | 28·0 | 27·9 |
| | 82·1 | 85·6 | 87·2 | 88·5 | 85·0 | 80·9 | 76·4 | 74·9 | 78·6 | 82·2 | 83·4 | 82·4 | 82·2 |
| | 13·9 | 15·2 | 17·8 | 19·1 | 18·6 | 17·4 | 17·1 | 16·8 | 16·8 | 16·8 | 15·7 | 14·0 | 16·6 |
| | 57·0 | 59·3 | 64·1 | 66·3 | 65·4 | 63·4 | 62·7 | 62·3 | 62·2 | 62·2 | 60·3 | 57·2 | 61·9 |
| R31 | 3 | 3 | 28 | 86 | 203 | 226 | 330 | 292 | 213 | 41 | 3 | 3 | 1 430 |
| | 0·1 | 0·1 | 1·1 | 3·4 | 8·0 | 8·9 | 13·0 | 11·5 | 8·4 | 1·6 | 0·1 | 0·1 | 56·3 |

## SAVANNA

This extends between approximately 11°–13°N on its southern edge and 12°–14°N on the northern one. It includes the southern interior of Senegal, interior Gambia, central Mali, most of the Upper Volta and part of northern Nigeria.

Compared with the southern savanna, rainfall is less and the rainy season is only five to six months in length. The variability of rainfall and the range of temperatures are both greater.

|  | *Jan.* | *Feb.* | *Mar.* | *Apr.* | *May* | *June* | *July* | *Aug.* | *Sept.* | *Oct.* | *Nov.* | *Dec.* | *Year* |
|---|---|---|---|---|---|---|---|---|---|---|---|---|---|
| Tambacounda (Senegal) 57 m (187 ft) 13°46′N, 13°11′W | | | | | | | | | | | | | |
| T5 | 34·9 | 37·2 | 38·9 | 41·0 | 39·6 | 36·1 | 32·2 | 30·7 | 31·6 | 32·2 | 33·4 | 33·9 | 35·4 |
|  | *94·8* | *99·0* | *102·1* | *105·8* | *103·3* | *97·0* | *90·0* | *87·3* | *88·8* | *90·0* | *92·2* | *93·0* | *95·7* |
|  | 14·9 | 16·1 | 19·5 | 21·2 | 24·2 | 23·1 | 21·9 | 21·9 | 22·3 | 21·9 | 17·4 | 15·2 | 19·9 |
|  | *58·8* | *61·0* | *67·1* | *70·2* | *75·6* | *73·6* | *71·5* | *71·5* | *72·2* | *71·5* | *63·4* | *59·4* | *67·9* |
| R10 | 0 | 0 | 0 | 3 | 28 | 175 | 193 | 305 | 216 | 81 | 3 | 0 | 1 006 |
|  | *0·0* | *0·0* | *0·0* | *0·1* | *1·1* | *6·9* | *7·6* | *12·0* | *8·5* | *3·2* | *0·1* | *0·0* | *39·6* |
| Bamako (Mali) 328 m (1 076 ft) 12°39′N, 7°58′W | | | | | | | | | | | | | |
| T5 | 33·3 | 36·0 | 38·6 | 39·6 | 38·2 | 34·6 | 30·9 | 29·8 | 31·2 | 33·3 | 34·4 | 32·8 | 34·4 |
|  | *92·0* | *96·8* | *101·4* | *103·3* | *100·8* | *94·3* | *87·6* | *85·6* | *88·2* | *92·0* | *94·0* | *91·0* | *94·0* |
|  | 17·2 | 19·4 | 23·1 | 24·8 | 25·4 | 23·4 | 22·2 | 21·7 | 21·8 | 22·0 | 19·4 | 17·7 | 21·6 |
|  | *63·0* | *67·0* | *73·6* | *76·6* | *77·8* | *74·2* | *72·0* | *71·1* | *71·3* | *71·6* | *67·0* | *63·8* | *70·8* |
| R10 | 0 | 0 | 3 | 15 | 74 | 135 | 279 | 348 | 206 | 43 | 15 | 0 | 1 118 |
|  | *0·0* | *0·0* | *0·1* | *0·6* | *2·9* | *5·3* | *11·0* | *13·7* | *8·1* | *1·7* | *0·6* | *0·0* | *44·0* |
| Ouagadougou (Upper Volta) 302 m (991 ft) 12°22′N, 1°31′W | | | | | | | | | | | | | |
| T5 | 36·1 | 38·7 | 41·1 | 41·7 | 39·2 | 36·3 | 33·7 | 31·8 | 33·6 | 37·8 | 38·8 | 36·4 | 37·1 |
|  | *97·0* | *101·6* | *106·0* | *107·0* | *102·6* | *97·4* | *92·6* | *89·3* | *92·4* | *100·1* | *101·8* | *97·6* | *98·7* |
|  | 14·2 | 16·1 | 20·9 | 24·3 | 24·9 | 23·1 | 22·1 | 21·3 | 21·1 | 22·0 | 19·0 | 15·3 | 20·4 |
|  | *57·6* | *61·0* | *69·6* | *75·8* | *76·8* | *73·6* | *71·8* | *70·4* | *70·0* | *71·6* | *66·2* | *59·6* | *68·7* |
| R10 | 0 | 3 | 15 | 20 | 74 | 125 | 213 | 264 | 142 | 23 | 0 | 0 | 881 |
|  | *0·0* | *0·1* | *0·6* | *0·8* | *2·9* | *4·9* | *8·4* | *10·4* | *5·6* | *0·9* | *0·0* | *0·0* | *34·7* |
| Kano (Nigeria) 472 m (1 549 ft) 12°02′N, 8°32′E | | | | | | | | | | | | | |
| T5 | 29·8 | 32·2 | 35·4 | 38·2 | 37·4 | 34·7 | 30·7 | 29·5 | 31·1 | 34·2 | 33·6 | 30·6 | 33·1 |
|  | *85·6* | *89·9* | *95·7* | *100·8* | *99·3* | *94·5* | *87·2* | *85·1* | *88·0* | *93·5* | *92·5* | *87·1* | *91·6* |
|  | 13·4 | 15·3 | 18·8 | 22·4 | 23·7 | 23·3 | 21·7 | 20·9 | 20·8 | 20·1 | 16·4 | 13·8 | 19·2 |
|  | *56·1* | *59·5* | *65·9* | *72·4* | *74·6* | *73·9* | *71·1* | *69·6* | *69·4* | *68·1* | *61·6* | *56·9* | *66·6* |
| R48 | 0 | 0 | 3 | 8 | 69 | 114 | 203 | 315 | 130 | 13 | 0 | 0 | 853 |
|  | *0·0* | *0·0* | *0·1* | *0·3* | *2·7* | *4·5* | *8·0* | *12·4* | *5·1* | *0·5* | *0·0* | *0·0* | *33·6* |

## SENEGAL COASTAL

This type is found in a narrow band from north of St Louis southward as far as the Gambia estuary.

Rainfall is lower and comes in a shorter rainy season than in the adjacent Savanna or southern Sahel zones. On the other hand, relative humidity is much higher in the dry season and less variable annually on the coast, because of the prevalence of moist northerly marine trade winds, in contrast to dry northeasterly or easterly winds at interior stations.

Maximum temperatures are not at the end of the dry season, but during the wet one. This is because the marine trade winds have moved away north and the upwelling of cold water also ceases farther north. This more than neutralises the effects of greater cloudiness in the rainy season.

Temperatures are more even and lower than inland, so that the climate is more pleasant, especially as coastal breezes are strong over Cape Verde and Dakar streets are well aligned to catch them.

| | Jan. | Feb. | Mar. | Apr. | May | June | July | Aug. | Sept. | Oct. | Nov. | Dec. | Year |
|---|---|---|---|---|---|---|---|---|---|---|---|---|---|
| | | | | | | | | | | | | | |
| Dakar (Senegal) 32 m (105 ft) 14°39′N, 17°25′W | | | | | | | | | | | | | |
| T5 | 27·8 | 28·2 | 27·8 | 26·7 | 28·0 | 30·8 | 30·9 | 30·4 | 31·0 | 31·1 | 30·6 | 28·6 | 29·3 |
| | *82·0* | *82·8* | *82·0* | *80·0* | *82·4* | *87·5* | *87·6* | *86·8* | *87·8* | *88·0* | *87·1* | *83·4* | *84·8* |
| | 18·2 | 17·9 | 18·2 | 18·3 | 20·0 | 23·6 | 24·7 | 24·4 | 24·7 | 24·6 | 22·8 | 20·0 | 21·4 |
| | *64·8* | *64·2* | *64·8* | *65·0* | *68·0* | *74·4* | *76·5* | *76·0* | *76·5* | *76·3* | *73·0* | *68·0* | *70·6* |
| R10 | 0 | 0 | 0 | 0 | 0 | 31 | 89 | 264 | 145 | 43 | 5 | 0 | 577 |
| | *0·0* | *0·0* | *0·0* | *0·0* | *0·0* | *1·2* | *3·5* | *10·4* | *5·7* | *1·7* | *0·2* | *0·0* | *22·7* |

## SOUTHERN SAHEL

This is found between 12–14°N and 15–17°N, thereby comprising the northern interior of Senegal, southern Mauritania, the southern Niger Bend country of Mali, the southern part of Niger, and the northern fringes of Nigeria.

Rainfall is about 500–750 mm (20–30 in) annually, the rainy season is about three to five months in length but is often erratic, and there is a high range of temperature. This corresponds with the Sahel savanna vegetation zone and is important cattle country. It is the most northerly zone for regular cultivation without irrigation or the use of ground water.

| | Jan. | Feb. | Mar. | Apr. | May | June | July | Aug. | Sept. | Oct. | Nov. | Dec. | Year |
|---|---|---|---|---|---|---|---|---|---|---|---|---|---|
| | | | | | | | | | | | | | |
| Kayes (Mali) 56 m (183 ft) 14°24′N, 11°26′W | | | | | | | | | | | | | |
| T5 | 35·2 | 38·2 | 40·9 | 44·0 | 43·4 | 40·0 | 34·6 | 32·3 | 33·4 | 35·1 | 37·6 | 34·4 | 37·4 |
| | *95·4* | *100·8* | *105·6* | *111·2* | *110·2* | *104·0* | *94·3* | *90·2* | *92·2* | *95·1* | *99·6* | *94·0* | *99·4* |
| | 16·7 | 18·9 | 22·0 | 25·0 | 27·7 | 25·9 | 23·9 | 22·8 | 22·9 | 23·3 | 20·2 | 17·8 | 22·3 |
| | *62·1* | *66·0* | *71·6* | *77·0* | *81·8* | *78·6* | *75·1* | *73·1* | *73·2* | *74·0* | *68·4* | *64·1* | *72·1* |
| R5 | 3 | 0 | 0 | 0 | 25 | 97 | 160 | 241 | 188 | 43 | 0 | 0 | 757 |
| | *0·1* | *0·0* | *0·0* | *0·0* | *1·0* | *3·8* | *6·3* | *9·5* | *7·4* | *1·7* | *0·0* | *0·0* | *29·8* |
| | | | | | | | | | | | | | |
| Niamey (Niger) 216 m (709 ft) 13°31′N, 2°06′E | | | | | | | | | | | | | |
| T5 | 34·3 | 37·2 | 40·6 | 43·1 | 41·7 | 39·1 | 35·3 | 33·0 | 34·5 | 38·7 | 38·7 | 35·7 | 37·2 |
| | *93·8* | *99·0* | *105·1* | *109·6* | *107·1* | *102·4* | *95·6* | *91·4* | *94·1* | *101·6* | *101·6* | *96·3* | *99·0* |
| | 13·8 | 15·6 | 20·1 | 24·1 | 26·8 | 24·8 | 23·4 | 22·3 | 22·8 | 22·6 | 17·8 | 14·8 | 20·7 |
| | *56·8* | *60·0* | *68·2* | *75·4* | *80·3* | *76·6* | *74·2* | *72·2* | *73·1* | *72·6* | *64·1* | *58·6* | *69·3* |
| R10 | 0 | 0 | 5 | 8 | 33 | 71 | 132 | 188 | 94 | 13 | 0 | 0 | 549 |
| | *0·0* | *0·0* | *0·2* | *0·3* | *1·3* | *2·8* | *5·2* | *7·4* | *3·7* | *0·5* | *0·0* | *0·0* | *21·6* |
| | | | | | | | | | | | | | |
| Nguru (Nigeria) 335 m (1 100 ft) 12°51′N, 10°28′E | | | | | | | | | | | | | |
| T5 | 31·0 | 33·2 | 36·7 | 39·8 | 38·7 | 37·9 | 33·5 | 30·7 | 32·8 | 36·1 | 35·4 | 32·3 | 34·8 |
| | *87·8* | *91·8* | *98·0* | *103·6* | *101·7* | *100·2* | *92·3* | *87·3* | *91·0* | *97·0* | *95·8* | *90·2* | *94·7* |
| | 12·1 | 14·3 | 17·6 | 20·7 | 22·6 | 23·5 | 22·8 | 21·9 | 21·6 | 19·2 | 15·1 | 12·6 | 18·7 |
| | *53·8* | *57·8* | *63·6* | *69·3* | *72·6* | *74·3* | *73·1* | *71·4* | *70·9* | *66·5* | *59·1* | *54·7* | *65·6* |
| R11 | 0 | 0 | 0 | 3 | 28 | 38 | 125 | 236 | 109 | 5 | 0 | 0 | 544 |
| | *0·0* | *0·0* | *0·0* | *0·1* | *1·1* | *1·5* | *4·9* | *9·3* | *4·3* | *0·2* | *0·0* | *0·0* | *21·4* |

## NORTHERN SAHEL

This is found between about 15–17°N and 17–18°N in central Mauritania, central Mali Republic and the Niger Republic. Rainfall averages under

400 mm (16 in) per annum and in most cases is under 250 mm (10 in). It comes in about three months, but is highly erratic. Even quick-maturing millets often fail. Thorn scrub is discontinuous but nomadic cattle are numerous.

'Winter' becomes an admissible term in this zone and at some stations in the southern Sahel, as the lowest means of daily maximum temperatures are in the winter months. Rains are insufficient and rainstorms of too short a duration to reduce the very high 'summer' temperatures to the lowest for the year, although there is a lowering of over 10 per cent because of cloud. Yearly and diurnal ranges of temperature are very high. In the Aïr Mountains, daily minimum temperatures are even lower, e.g. at Agadès, and frost may occur.

| | Jan. | Feb. | Mar. | Apr. | May | June | July | Aug. | Sept. | Oct. | Nov. | Dec. | Year |
|---|---|---|---|---|---|---|---|---|---|---|---|---|---|
| Gao (Mali) 267 m (876 ft) 16°18′N, 0°08′W | | | | | | | | | | | | | |
| T5 | 30·7 | 32·9 | 37·3 | 41·4 | 43·3 | 42·3 | 38·8 | 35·7 | 38·1 | 40·1 | 35·6 | 31·7 | 37·3 |
| | 87·3 | 91·2 | 99·2 | 106·6 | 110·0 | 108·2 | 101·8 | 96·3 | 100·6 | 104·2 | 96·0 | 89·0 | 99·2 |
| | 14·7 | 16·1 | 20·7 | 23·1 | 26·6 | 27·7 | 25·6 | 24·3 | 25·3 | 24·8 | 21·8 | 16·6 | 22·3 |
| | 58·5 | 61·0 | 69·3 | 73·6 | 79·8 | 81·8 | 78·1 | 75·8 | 77·6 | 76·6 | 71·3 | 61·8 | 72·1 |
| R9 | 0 | 0 | 3 | 3 | 8 | 31 | 74 | 91 | 25 | 3 | 0 | 0 | 236 |
| | 0·0 | 0·0 | 0·1 | 0·1 | 0·3 | 1·2 | 2·9 | 3·6 | 1·0 | 0·1 | 0·0 | 0·0 | 9·3 |
| Agadès (Niger) 520 m (1 706 ft) 16°59′N, 7°56′E | | | | | | | | | | | | | |
| T5 | 28·0 | 33·1 | 38·1 | 42·0 | 44·4 | 44·0 | 40·9 | 38·7 | 41·0 | 40·6 | 34·6 | 32·3 | 38·1 |
| | 82·4 | 91·6 | 100·6 | 107·6 | 112·0 | 111·2 | 105·6 | 101·6 | 105·8 | 105·0 | 94·3 | 90·2 | 100·6 |
| | 10·1 | 11·7 | 16·2 | 20·4 | 24·8 | 24·7 | 23·2 | 22·7 | 22·6 | 19·8 | 15·1 | 11·8 | 18·6 |
| | 50·2 | 53·0 | 61·2 | 68·8 | 76·6 | 76·5 | 73·8 | 72·8 | 72·6 | 67·6 | 59·2 | 53·3 | 65·5 |
| R10 | 0 | 0 | 0 | 0 | 5 | 8 | 48 | 94 | 18 | 0 | 0 | 0 | 175 |
| | 0·0 | 0·0 | 0·0 | 0·0 | 0·2 | 0·3 | 1·9 | 3·7 | 0·7 | 0·0 | 0·0 | 0·0 | 6·9 |

## SOUTHERN SAHARAN

This is found between 17–18°N and 21°N in northcentral Mauritania, Mali and Niger. Slight rain comes in most years within a six week period mostly from southwesterlies. There are occassional tufts of grass and sage bush, and cattle are still encountered in or near oases. As in the Northern Sahel, the lowest means of daily maximum temperatures are in winter. Lower temperatures occur in Adrar des Iforas and the Aïr massifs.

Araouane (Mali)(285 m: 935 ft, 18°54′N, 3°33′W) and Bilma (Niger) (357 m: 1 171 ft, 18°43′N, 12°56′E) give similar figures to those opposite, except that as one proceeds eastward (as in other west to east climatic zones) rainfall diminishes, the percentage of calm winds doubles and the range of temperature increases by some 10 per cent.

| | Jan. | Feb. | Mar. | Apr. | May | June | July | Aug. | Sept. | Oct. | Nov. | Dec. | Year |
|---|---|---|---|---|---|---|---|---|---|---|---|---|---|
| *Atar (Mauritania) 231 m (758 ft) 20°31'N, 13°04'W* | | | | | | | | | | | | | |
| T5 | 30·4 | 32·8 | 33·9 | 38·7 | 39·7 | 42·3 | 43·2 | 42·1 | 42·0 | 38·3 | 33·1 | 29·5 | 37·2 |
| | *86·8* | *91·0* | *93·0* | *101·6* | *103·5* | *108·2* | *109·8* | *107·8* | *107·6* | *101·0* | *91·6* | *85·1* | *98·9* |
| | 12·1 | 12·9 | 16·8 | 19·5 | 21·8 | 26·7 | 25·1 | 25·9 | 26·0 | 23·1 | 16·9 | 13·3 | 20·0 |
| | *53·8* | *55·2* | *62·3* | *67·1* | *71·3* | *80·1* | *77·2* | *78·6* | *78·8* | *73·6* | *62·5* | *56·0* | *68·0* |
| R10 | 3 | 0 | 0 | 0 | 0 | 3 | 8 | 31 | 28 | 3 | 3 | 0 | 79 |
| | *0·1* | *0·0* | *0·0* | *0·0* | *0·0* | *0·1* | *0·3* | *1·2* | *1·1* | *0·1* | *0·1* | *0·0* | *3·0* |

## Mauritanian coastal

This is restricted to a narrow coastal band in northern Mauritania and Spanish Sahara. The minute rainfall comes mostly in winter months, so that this might be regarded as an extreme southerly extension of the Mediterranean rainfall regime.

Like the Senegal coastal type, relative humidity is consistently high, and north or northwesterly winds predominate. Consequently, temperatures are also exceptionally low and equable for such a high latitude.

| | Jan. | Feb. | Mar. | Apr. | May | June | July | Aug. | Sept. | Oct. | Nov. | Dec. | Year |
|---|---|---|---|---|---|---|---|---|---|---|---|---|---|
| *Nouadhibou (Mauritania) 7 m (23 ft) 20°56'N, 17°03'W* | | | | | | | | | | | | | |
| T5 | 26·3 | 27·9 | 27·4 | 27·3 | 28·2 | 29·9 | 27·1 | 29·6 | 32·7 | 30·3 | 28·7 | 25·4 | 28·4 |
| | *79·4* | *82·2* | *81·4* | *81·2* | *82·8* | *85·8* | *80·8* | *85·3* | *90·8* | *86·6* | *83·6* | *77·8* | *83·2* |
| | 12·2 | 12·7 | 14·0 | 14·4 | 14·9 | 15·9 | 17·7 | 19·9 | 20·7 | 18·6 | 16·4 | 14·5 | 15·9 |
| | *54·0* | *54·8* | *57·2* | *58·0* | *58·8* | *60·6* | *63·8* | *67·8* | *69·3* | *65·4* | *61·6* | *58·1* | *60·7* |
| R10 | 3 | 0 | 0 | 0 | 0 | 0 | 0 | 0 | 8 | 13 | 3 | 10 | 37 |
| | *0·1* | *0·0* | *0·0* | *0·0* | *0·0* | *0·0* | *0·0* | *0·0* | *0·3* | *0·5* | *0·1* | *0·4* | *1·5* |

## Saharan

This is found north of about 21°N, i.e. a smaller extent that often suggested. Rain may fall in some years in any month. Vegetation and livestock are rare and restricted to oases. Temperatures are higher in summer than in the southern Saharan zone but their yearly pattern is similar. L. D. Stamp has noted that: 'The daily range in the heart of the desert is as much as 28–38°C (50–68°F); the highest recorded temperatures on the surface of the earth are claimed by the Sahara. Shade recordings of 58°C (136°F) are said to have been made; the surface of the ground frequently exceeds 77°C (170°F). . . . The annual range is between 17 and 22°C (30–40°F).[8]

## Conclusion

Except towards the Sahara, West Africa does not have excessively high temperatures. The unwarranted bad reputation of its climates is a carry-over from the days when malaria was associated with bad air from swamps, tropical medicine was unborn, and the real cause of diseases unknown. Misapprehensions continue, especially since so many films perpetuate popular misconceptions. Moreover, people working in West Africa tend to emphasise the discomforts, as this arouses sympathy. That the climate is supportable is demonstrated by many missionaries who, although living under spartan conditions, have often stayed in West Africa without leave for some twenty years.

Those who perspire readily, feel fittest in the tropics. Exercise or moderate manual labour is not merely desirable but essential. The idea that manual labour should not be undertaken by non-Africans is false, as shown by many Italians and French. But hard manual labour over long hours in a strict routine is very bad—for Africans as well as for non-Africans. Eating and drinking habits need to be different from those in temperate lands. Less protein and carbohydrate are required, but more vitamins and salts in the form of fruit and vegetables. If the right food is bought, prepared and served thoroughly clean, and fresh water known to be pure is used or else boiled and filtered, insects kept out of houses, the usual prophylactics and daily exercise taken, light cotton clothes worn and strong alcohol avoided or drunk in moderation, then anyone with normal blood-pressure should keep very fit.

Tropical medicine and hygiene, the import and distribution of frozen and canned foods, refrigeration, electrical fans and especially air-conditioning in houses and offices have greatly eased living conditions for those who can enjoy them. Yet the fact that people work and usually sleep better with air-conditioning, and that governments and companies so willingly incur this expense, prove that high temperatures or high relative humidity are disadvantages. Moreover, most Africans enjoy the lower relative humidity of air-conditioning, though much less frequently its lower temperatures. There are other aspects of West African (and other equatorial and tropical climates) which affect daily life. The heat of the midday sun reduces the productivity of agricultural and other labour. The always-dark evenings hinder literacy and education because most people do not have electricity or other good illumination. The influence of climate is still very pervasive.

# 4

# Vegetation

As in other parts of the world, the distribution and character of vegetation result from the interplay of climatic, edaphic (soils and soil water) and biotic influences (animals, especially man, and plants).

In West Africa man has been a ruthless modifier or destroyer of the natural vegetation and fauna. Edaphic factors are often extremely significant or even overriding, especially near climatic margins and where lateritic crusts, saline or waterlogged soils occur.

Of the climatic factors, rainfall and relative humidity normally exert the most powerful influences upon vegetation. Very important factors are the number of months with less than one inch of rain (see Fig. 4.2) and the minimum relative humidity, which is usually that between 1300 and 1500 hours, but is rarely recorded. The duration and frequency of low humidities are very significant. The minimum saturation deficit, which gives a measure of the evaporating power of the air independent of temperature, is even more useful, but is also rarely available.

There are about 7 300 flowering species belonging to over 200 families and some 1 800 genera in West Africa. Although these figures may seem large, they are smaller than for tropical America or Indo-Malaya.

It is not intended to give a systematic account of all the species occurring in each vegetational zone. The aim is to show the outstanding types, characteristics and aspect of the vegetation, where the various types occur, their relationships with other aspects of the environment—physical and human, the value of certain species and some of the problems which arise.

## Strand and sandbank vegetation

This is found on sand, just above high water. It may be showered by seaspray and is always enveloped in moist, saltladen air. Strand and sandbank vegetation is well developed on the sandbar or sandspit coasts of Senegal and the Gulf of Guinea.

Herbs, shrubs and grasses are common but discontinuous. Stunted bushes occur more rarely. On inward margins poor trees are seen.

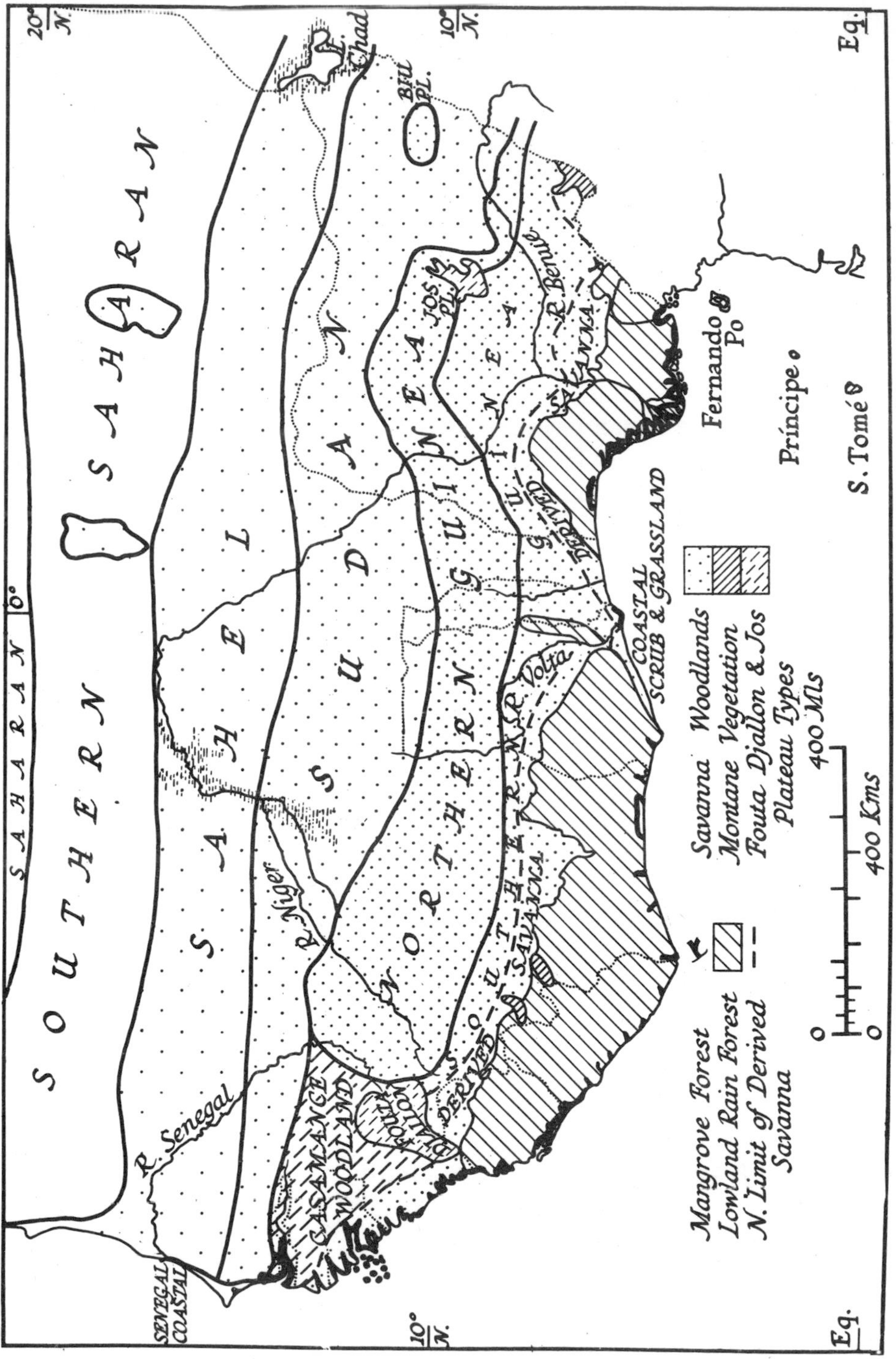

FIG. 4.1. Vegetation zones

(Based on a map by R. W. J. Keay in collaboration with French authorities, with some additions by the present author)

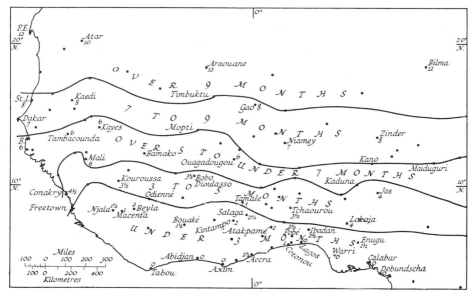

FIG. 4.2. Number of months with less than 25 mm (1 in) of rain

This figure is critical for tree growth. (Based on readings from 103 stations)

## The forest regions (high forest)

### Mangrove forest

This occurs in muddy sheltered creeks, deltas and lagoons, wherever the water is brackish and strongly tidal. Mangrove is best developed in the southwest coast monsoonal, Liberian, equatorial and Cameroon climatic regions, but occurs as far north as the Senegal river. West African mangroves are of the same species as those found along the east coast of America, but differ from those of East Africa and Indo-Malaya. Mangrove rootlets tend to hold loose, soft mud. As alluvium becomes consolidated, young healthy mangrove gives place, on the landward margin, to older mangrove and then to freshwater swamp forest or to rainforest.

*Rhizophora racemosa* (Red mangrove) is overwhelmingly the commonest species. This has the famous 'stilt roots', which do not penetrate the soil, but divide into innumerable rootlets, so making a feltlike underwater raft. Trees commonly reach about 15 m (50 ft) in height. Indeed, they are often far higher in the Niger Delta, where they are only occasionally invaded by very salt water. The trees are evergreen and make a dense canopy, which is the more impressive because of the dark, proplike roots. *R. harrisonii* is dominant in the middle areas, while *R. mangle* is found only on the drier inner limit. Both are smaller than the Red mangrove.

61

Mangrove bark has a high tannin and cutch content. The wood is excellent small constructional timber, and has a high calorific value as fuel, especially as charcoal.

Living mangrove assists land reclamation from the sea. Elimination of mangrove, with protective bunds against the ingress of salt water, often enables rice cultivation, as in the least saline areas of Sierra Leone and Nigeria, where heavy rainfall and river water can be used to flush salt out of the soil. On the Gambia river conditions are less favourable, as salt impregnation is greater and rainfall lower.

### Freshwater swamp forest

This is widespread in the Niger Delta, along freshwater lagoons, rivers and in inland swamps. There is an outer fringe of 'sudd' or 'floating grass', papyrus swamps being a striking feature of Nigerian and some other creeks. Inward are fixed grasses, shrubs or ferns, beyond which are species of Raphia and other palms. This fringing vegetation rarely exceeds 12 m (40 ft) in height.

Inland comes the true freshwater swamp forest, which may attain 30 m (100 ft), many trees having stilt roots. Diameters of the boles are less than those of the biggest trees of the lowland rainforest and most species are different. The canopy is rather open, and in the gaps tangled shrubs and lianes form a denser undergrowth. Climbing palms with hooked spines, related to the rattans of Asia, are characteristic. Useful trees are the Abura or Uwen (*Mitragyna ciliata*), *Pandanus candelabrum* (whose leaves are used for making mats and baskets), and species of Raphia such as *Raphia vinifera* and *Raphia hookeri*, used for roof matting, rafters, piassava for brooms, and for wine. The mahogany *Khaya ivorensis* grows on the drier margin of swamps and is a valuable timber.

### Lowland rainforest

This is the equivalent of Richards's tropical rainforest and of Rübel's *Pluvisilva*, and lies on the northwestern edge of the greater Congo lowland rainforests. Its flora is the richest in West Africa, though poorer than similar forests in South America and Asia.

Separation of the western sector (see Fig. 4.1) of the forest is due mainly to lower rainfall in the gap and to the action of man. The northward limit may once have approximated to a line joining all stations with at least 1 140 mm (45 in) annual rainfall, a minimum mean monthly relative humidity at 1300 hr of at least 40 per cent, and not more than three months with less than 25 mm (1 in) of rain per month (see Fig. 4.2). Although annual rainfall may often be higher north of this line, the dry season is longer and critical afternoon relative humidities are lower.

Lowland rainforest is dense and the highest trees sometimes reach about 60 m (200 ft). Yet they do not rival the taller Californian redwoods or the Australian gums. Trees of the lowland rainforest are highly varied in species, height, girth and age. Girths of over a metre are common, and the trees are typically straight and slender, with few or no branches below the crown. Most barks are thin and smooth. A large proportion of the trees have buttresses extending outwards, sometimes many feet from the base of the trunk. The variety of species is a problem in commercial forestry.

Oddly enough, the lowland rainforest gives an impression of sombre uniformity. This is because many of the different trees have superficially similar trunks, branches and leaves. But there are at least three tiers or layers of this forest with trees up to 18 m (60 ft), between 18 and 37 m (60–120 ft) and between 31 and 61 m (120–200 ft) approximately. The uppermost tier usually has a discontinuous canopy but the lowest a more or less continuous one.

Undergrowth, woody climbers and epiphytes are characteristic, the climbers hanging above in great lengths, loops or festoons. Epiphytes (woody and herbaceous), mosses and lichens are numerous and luxuriant. Ground herbs may also be found.

Sunlight penetrates here and there. There is rarely much accumulation of rotting vegetation because of rapid decomposition. Mature forest on level, well-drained ground is easy to walk through and bare rock outcrops may sometimes be seen.

This forest has been reduced by one-half or more in the last century because it is also the zone of cultivation of many food crops, the oil palm, cocoa, coffee, bananas and rubber. In another century only scattered forest reserves may remain. Yet it is from this zone that so many famous woods are cut in the Ivory Coast, Ghana and Nigeria. Among the best known timbers are certain mahoganies (*Khaya ivorensis* and *K. anthotheca*), Sapele (*Entandrophragma cylindricum*), Guarea (*Guarea cedrata*), Makoré (*Tieghemella heckelii*), African Walnut (*Lovoa trichilioides*) and Dahoma or Ekhimi (*Piptadeniastrum africanum*).

Variations within the lowland rainforest are caused mainly by biotic disturbance (see below) or by differences of relief, soil, slope, drainage, rock outcrops and parent materials.

It seems that the Cross river valley is the western limit of many plants and animals common in Central Africa but which rarely, if ever, extend farther into West Africa. Forests east of the Cross river, growing in an area of very heavy well-distributed rainfall, and on soils derived from volcanic or Pre-Cambrian rocks, are the most completely evergreen and least seasonal forest type in West Africa.

By contrast, the irregular forests of Benin grow mainly on highly porous sands. They contain many mahoganies and a ground flora of wiry creepers. Ondo forests grow on soils from crystalline rocks and have two species entirely absent from Benin, namely, *Nesogordonia papaverifera* and *Mansonia altissima*. The undergrowth is also more shrubby. The Ijebu forests differ again in their poverty of useful trees and in their wide spacing, sparse understorey beneath the emergents, and a poor shrubby and herbaceous undergrowth. This may be ancient freshwater swamp forest developed in turn from mangrove.

A frequent division is made by the separation of *mixed* or *semideciduous* or *dry forest* (once used by Keay but now dropped by him) or *La forêt mesophile* (Aubréville, Mangenot, Schnell, Emberger) or of *Der Subxerophiler Tropenwald* (Milbraed). The present British tendency is to merge this type within the lowland rainforest. In the equatorial semiseasonal or seasonal climatic zones (see Fig. 3.19), where there are up to four months each with less than 25 mm (1 in) of rain (see Fig. 4.2), lower relative humidities and drier soils, the forest may contain rather more deciduous trees, though it is not transitional to woodland or savanna, and is not fire resistant. Although the flora and its physiognomy are similar to the rest of the lowland rainforest, species are fewer and canopies may be more open. Deciduous trees may predominate only in the upper storey, although there are also evergreens. Shrubs and smaller trees, making a strong woody undergrowth, are mainly evergreen. It is for these reasons that botanists dislike the term 'mixed deciduous forest'. There are certainly not enough mature deciduous trees to justify the term 'monsoon forest'. Individual trees are bare of leaves for several weeks annually, but since many trees are evergreen, the forest still presents an evergreen appearance.

Obeche, Wawa or Samba (*Triplochiton scleroxylon*) may represent up to 20 per cent of all dominants. Others of that family are Danta (*Nesogordonian papaverifera*) and *Hildegardia barteri,* which are absent from the wetter forest, *Mansonia altissima* and *Cola gigantea*. Other species are Iroko (*Chlorophora excelsa*), a mahogany *Khaya grandifoliola* (but not *K. ivorensis* or *K. anthotheca* of wetter forests, or *K. senegalensis* of drier regions), Utile, Sipo or Assie (*Entandrophragma utile*), Albizia (*A. ferruginea*) and Afara (*Terminalia superba*). Those with popular names are cut for timber, and many of the trees also occur in secondary and depleted forests. There are often more useful but less valuable trees than in other parts of the lowland rainforest.

Other than the trees, this zone has some tuber geophytes which perennate during dry months, forming underground corms and tubers. Epiphytes are fewer—another indication of seasonal dryness—as is also the fact that herbaceous undergrowth may die down in the dry month or months.

## Biotic modifications of the lowland rainforest

### Depleted forests

Wherever there is or has been selective felling of certain species, the gaps may be colonised by secondary forest species. Often there is a patchwork arrangement of primary and secondary species. Depleted forests are characteristic in Benin and Ondo, and of the timber-producing areas of the Ivory Coast. In Ghana, however, all trees are generally cut, as the land is taken over for food farms.

**Secondary forest**

This results from the cutting and burning of the forest for periodic cultivation. Large trees may be left because they defy primitive methods of clearing, useful ones may be retained for their produce, and others for religious reasons.

The farmed patch is generally abandoned to forest regrowth only when fertility is exhausted. The soils are not only impoverished chemically but also physically, since their humus content and waterholding properties are impaired. The canopy has been broken and the sun's rays may now reach the ground. Consequently, soil temperatures are higher, rainfall more immediate in its action, and relative humidity is lower.

These conditions are unfavourable to complete regeneration for a long time—perhaps for centuries. New plant growth is, however, very rapid, and at first is generally by weeds and seedlings of trees and shrubs. These are quickly succeeded by climbers, such as species of *Combretum*, whose roots generally survive in the ground and which need much light. Lianes and a more or less impenetrable undergrowth are also typical of young secondary growth.

The first new trees are the more tolerant and less valuable, fast growing, softwood, low density species. The Umbrella or Parasol Tree (*Musanga cercropioides*) is often an early dominant, but does not reproduce itself, since it will not tolerate shade. It dies within fifteen to twenty years, thus completing the first stage of regrowth. During this stage, trees are much smaller, thinner and more uniform than in 'primary forest', except for more diverse leaf structure and colour.

Thereafter more variety is seen. Other trees become evident and many are tall, large, light-demanding and useful, such as Samba (*Triplochiton scleroxylon*), Iroko (*Chlorophora excelsa*) and Afara (*Terminalia superba*). The oil palm will often survive from farming days until the forest is high and dense again, when it will be stifled. It is never found in virgin forest.

**Derived savanna**

If secondary forest is frequently cut and burned, or if the original period of cultivation is long and the soil poor, grass progressively invades the cut-over area, and annual fires (intentional or otherwise) gradually kill remaining trees. Fire-tolerant savanna trees may colonise these grasslands, and so there will be derived savanna, typical of the inner fringes

of the lowland rainforest (see Fig. 4.1) and of certain places within it—
e.g. the Sobo plains in southern Benin or of the Ivory Coast near
Jacqueville. Forest patches found in derived savanna are remnants of the
formerly more extensive lowland rainforest.

## Casamance woodland

Coinciding partly with the southwest coast monsoonal climatic zone, this
occurs in the Casamance district of Senegal, Portuguese Guinea and
lowland parts of Guinea.

Though the Casamance woodland might be thought of as akin to
lowland rainforest, it is a woodland with its own very individual
physiognomy and composition. Because of the long dry season it was
originally poorer floristically and has also been heavily cut by man, as
shown by the widespread occurrence of the oil palm.

Originally, and now in a few relicts, it has only two storeys. The upper
storey, 15–21 m (50–70 ft) high, consists overwhelmingly of only four
species: *Parinari excelsa, Erythrophleum guineense, Detarium senegalense*
and *Afzelia africana*. With them are generally many lianes. The trees are
strikingly different from those of the lowland rainforest, because they
are low-branching and spreading. The lower canopy, at 3–6 m (10–20 ft),
of bushes, lianes and herbaceous plants, is likewise deciduous and thick.

On the northern fringes of the Fouta Djallon, where there are poor
lateritic outcrops, the undergrowth is mostly of bamboo and the large
trees are more varied. On sandstone edges and near streams in lowland
Guinea, *Guibourtia copallifera* (gum copal) and *Coffea stenophylla* are
widespread, and on the northern boundary of the zone *Khaya senegalensis*
is common.

## Fouta Djallon

The mean altitude of the Fouta Djallon is about 900 m (2 950 ft), the
highest point near the town of Mali reaching about 1 500 m (4 925 ft).
No clear altitudinal gradations of vegetation occur, nor is there true
Montane vegetation.

Originally, this region may have been the extreme northwestern limit
of the lowland rainforest. If so, it must always have been exceedingly
frail, owing to the marginal position in latitude and altitude of the Fouta
Djallon in relation to the main forests. Moreover, the sandstone weathers
to an exceedingly infertile soil, or even to a lateritic crust, and there
is a four-month dry season, only partly moderated by dew.

It is also possible, perhaps likely, that the Fouta Djallon was originally
covered mainly by Casamance woodland, with some lowland rainforest
additions. The dominant was *Parinari excelsa,* which now survives only in
tiny patches on crests, but is typical of the Casamance woodland.

The original vegetation has been eliminated in the last century and a half, since the immigration of the Fulani. Fire has caused the advent of some species found in secondary forest or in derived savanna, and of a sparse herbaceous and semishrubby flora. The sedge, *Afrotrilepis pilosa*, grows in tufts of fine wirelike leaves on almost bare rock, but itself makes a humus. Nevertheless, the Fouta Djallon is notorious for its *bowé* (sing. *bowal*) or lateritic exposures, almost bare of soil or vegetation.

## Savanna woodland

The present line between lowland rainforest and savanna woodland is one of the world's clearest boundaries, but is rarely, if ever, a natural one. It results from persistent cutting and burning of the vegetation by man.

Savanna is not a climatic climax but a biotic one. But for constant burning, lowland rainforest would change gradually to woodland in areas of lower relative humidity and rainfall. Grass has entered because its roots survive frequent burning; thus grass is a fire climax not a natural climax.

Regular firing (to hunt out animals or to clear land for cultivation) has not only admitted grass and eliminated all trees which will not tolerate fire, but has allowed the advent of those species of trees which are fire resistant. One of these is the common Red Ironwood tree, *Lophira lanceolata* (not to be confused with *L. alata* of the lowland rainforest which is not fire-resistant), popularly known as the Meni oil tree or False Shea butter tree, whose stems are chewed to clean teeth.

Although grass and other species are connected with the occurrence of fire, they may also be encouraged by edaphic factors, such as the occurrence of lateritic crusts with little soil, like the *bowé*, or by the alternation of flood and drought, as in the Afram plains of Ghana.

Savanna woodlands are subdivided on grounds of physiognomy, as well as on botanical differences. Differentiating factors include density of plant cover, height, amount of grass and its character, and whether the plant or tree is deciduous or not in the dry season. Woodlands were less rich floristically than rainforests, and stands are sometimes very uniform.

### Ghana coastal scrub and grassland

Although yearly rainfall is low, the relative humidity is high, so that the original vegetation was probably a mixture of woodland and forest species. The heavy hand of man, over some three centuries or so, has degraded the natural vegetation to dense scrub without grass west of Accra, and to grassland with few trees and patches of scrub east of it. The scrub vegetation is still a mixture of forest and woodland species. East of the Volta is secondary lowland rainforest (oil palm forest) or derived savanna, and north of it is Guinea savanna.

### Guinea savanna

This is found between about 8° and 13°N, and coincides roughly with the southern savanna climatic zone described in Chapter 3, and with the poor 'middle belt'. Rainfall averages 1 020–1 400 mm (40–55 in) annually, there are four to five months each with less than 25 mm of rain (Fig. 4.2), and critical relative humidity may drop to 14 per cent.

#### SOUTHERN GUINEA SUBZONE

On the margins of the rainforest this zone has grass averaging 1·5–3 m (5–10 ft) or more in height. The broadleaved deciduous trees have short boles, are mostly 12–15 m (40–50 ft) high, and occur in clumps. *Anogeissus leiocarpus* and *Lophira lanceolata* are common, as well as *Terminalia glaucescens, Daniellia oliveri, Hymenocardia acida, Vitex doniana, Detarium microcarpum* and *Afzelia africana*. All are fire-resistant, but as they are burned year after year, they usually have twisted gnarled stems and corky bark, and so are useless for timber. The tall, tussocky grasses are mainly species of *Andropogon, Hyparrhenia* and *Pennisetum*.

In swamp areas grass is more dominant and trees are scattered, the Fan Palm (*Borassus aethiopum*) being common. On still moist but better drained slopes, and along rivers, there are outliers of lowland rainforest. On river banks are swamp species.

Leafing and flowering occur commonly at the end of the dry season, well before the first rains. Leafing can be hastened by firing, which is, in consequence, generally done at the end of the dry season. The leaves which soon appear (often with the help of dew and atmospheric moisture) are a wonderful help to starved cattle after the long drought and lack of pastures. But fires at the end of the dry season are naturally fierce and cause much more damage than if started earlier.

#### NORTHERN GUINEA SUBZONE

This is not normally found in contact with lowland rainforest, of which there are only rare outliers. This subzone is also poorer and distinct in its species, although the physiognomy is similar to the southern Guinea one.

The northern Guinea subzone is found in the Niger Valley lands of Guinea, along the borders of the Ivory Coast and Upper Volta, in the southern part of the Mali Republic, central Togo and Dahomey and in northcentral Nigeria.

The original climax vegetation of this subzone probably resembled the great 'Miombo woodlands' of East, Central and South tropical Africa. It is poorer in species than are those areas, the trees are also smaller, fewer and with less development of branches. All this may result from climatic variation in past eras, and from drier winds and more intensive burning in West Africa.

Where there is not too much firing, dominant species are *Isoberlinia doka,* and *I. dalzielii, Monotes kerstingii* and *Uapaca togoensis* (syn. *U. somon*). But *Brachystegia,* so thoroughly typical of this vegetational belt in East and Central Africa, is not found in this zone in West Africa. Moreover, several genera which have many species in Southern and East Africa are represented by very few in West Africa.

This savanna woodland is about 6–12 m (20–40 ft) high and, where the canopy is closed, grass is absent. Where the canopy is open, grass is dominant, though shorter than in the southern Guinea zone. Shrubs are common.

Useful trees such as the shea butter or Karité (*Butyrospermum parodoxum subsp. parkii*), tamarind (*Tamarindus indica*), locust bean tree, *Parkia spp., Vitex doniana, Afzelia africana, Daniellia oliveri* and the rubber climber (*Landolphia heudelotii*) are generally preserved.

## JOS PLATEAU SUBZONE

Keay and others use the old term 'Bauchi plateau', though they do not extend their vegetational type to include Bauchi town. For reasons of relief, morphology and vegetation, the term 'Jos Plateau' is preferable.

The plateau averages 1 220 m (4 000 ft), and rises to just over 1 830 m (6 000 ft) in places. Though at such altitudes montane vegetation might be expected, Keay considers that the vegetation of the plateau is not montane, though there are many plants which show affinities with plants of East and Southern Africa. Others are identical with plants in those areas. Most species of the northern Guinea subzone are found on the plateau, and Keay[1] has concluded that originally northern Guinea vegetation once covered it, with the special additions just mentioned. Monod[2] considers that the original woodland was more montane, and that the present examples of northern Guinea vegetation are not relicts, but advents to the plateau. Ingress to the plateau on the northeastern side is easy because of lower altitudes, gentler slopes and interdigitation of plain and plateau.

Whether the original woodland was montane or northern Guinea in character, it has been so thoroughly destroyed that the most accessible areas are almost treeless and are under grass, which is heavily farmed and grazed. Tin and colombite mining have also greatly impaired the vegetation and drainage. The present plant cover is a highly degraded form of northern Guinea vegetation, with montane additions.

## Sudan savanna

This is found in a belt some 200–400 km (125–250 miles) wide, from Senegal to Nigeria and beyond, north of the Guinea savanna.

In the Sudan savanna annual rainfall averages about 560–1 020 mm

(22–40 in), there are seven almost rainless months, and relative humidity in early afternoons of the dry season may drop to 8 per cent. It may be regarded as the most typical of all savannas and occurs roughly in the climatic belt of that name.

It is one of the clearest climatic, vegetational and human zones, yet one of the most affected by man. It is often densely inhabited—e.g. in northern Nigeria, the Upper Volta and western Senegal—so that there is much secondary vegetation. There has also been some spreading of species from the south, and from the north—particularly of acacias. Consequently, the vegetation of this zone is difficult to define.

Trees, which almost always occur singly, average 8–15 m (26–50 ft) in height and have wide-spreading crowns. The dum palm (*Hyphaene thebaica*), *Sclerocarya birrea, Balanites aegyptiaca* and baobab (*Adansonia digitata*) are common, the latter especially in the west. The last two, as well as the locust bean (*Parkia spp.*), shea butter tree (*Butyrospermum paradoxum subsp. parkii*), *Acacia albida, Tamarindus indica* and kapok (*Ceiba pentandra*), are all protected because of their value. There are also smaller trees, 3–6 m (10–20 ft) high, such as the acacias. Lower again is the bush or shrub of 2–6 m (6–20 ft), in which climbers (e.g. *Combretum micranthum*) are represented, being very common on rocky hills or lateritic outcrops.

Most trees have small leaves, to prevent excessive transpiration, though there are a few broadleaved ones. As one proceeds northward through the zone these disappear, but those with thorns (for example, the acacias) become more common. Most trees lose all their leaves in the dry season, but *Acacia albida* is a most useful exception.

In this zone, grass shoots up only just before the rains. It is also shorter 1–1·5 m (3–5 ft), less tussocky but more feathery than in the zones to the south. Consequently, it is very useful for grazing and is less deliberately burnt, so that fires are not so violent. It is an interesting fact that moderate grazing, by keeping the grass short, can arrest fires and so allow greater tree growth and regeneration.

The original climax (zerothermic) may perhaps still be seen on isolated or inaccessible rocky slopes, or along watercourses. It is thought to be similar to vegetation still seen in southwestern areas of Zambia.

## Senegal coastal vegetation

This coincides with the equally narrow climatic zone fringing the coast in Senegal to a depth never exceeding 50 km (30 miles). Greater atmospheric humidity, together with the higher water table in the *niayes* of Senegal (p. 201) and even in some *aftouts* of Mauritania, permit a naturally more luxuriant vegetation than in the drier interior.

Around the *niayes* and, to a much lesser extent, the *aftouts*, are trees and plants of the Guinea savanna, together with poor looking oil palms and the *Borassus aethiopum* palm. Away from these clay depressions, drier vegetation of the Sudan savanna and Sahel savanna is seen. The baobab is fairly frequent.

**Sahel savanna**

This occurs in southern Mauritania, northcentral Senegal, in much of the Niger bend country of Mali, in the southern Niger, in the extreme northeast of Nigeria, and it has at least eight dry months.

The original climax was probably thorn woodland. This has now become more open, so that it is easy to drive a jeep between the trees. These average 5–10 m (15–30 ft) in height, are deciduous, and finely divided in their leaf structure. They have very spreading and deeply penetrating roots, which fix the loose sand. The trees also have thorns.

The many acacias, with their light foliage and thorns, are always regarded as characteristic. The *Acacia seyal*, 2–4 m (6–13 ft) in height, prefers clay depressions, where there are often dense stands. It is most frequently seen in the Mali Republic and to the west thereof. *A. tortilis subsp. raddiana* is taller, very common and typical of this zone, and prefers light dry sandy soils. *A. senegal, A. laeta, A. ehrenbergiana* and *A. nilotica* are the sources of gum, and grow well on fixed dunes in Mauritania, Mali Republic and the Niger Republic. *A. nilotica* (with several varieties) is found in profusion in the floodplain of the Senegal river and, together with *A. sieberana,* along most streams. These last are up to 12 m (40 ft) in height.

Thorn shrubs, forming tree steppe, are also characteristic. One is *Commiphora africana,* or African myrrh, some 3–5 m (10–16 ft) tall, with a short conical stem and swollen base divided, near the ground, into rigid spreading branches. These branches are straight rigid thorns. Leaves are shed in October, and soon after there are red flowers. It grows in sandy and rocky places, and is particularly common in the Niger. Other shrubs are *Balanites aegyptiaca,* with long spines and small leathery leaves, and *Euphorbia balsamifera,* which is a fleshy spurge found in rocky environments, and used as hedges. Grasses are short, discontinuous, wiry and tussocky, but much used by cattle and sheep. There are no real gallery or fringing forests, only riparian woodland of certain acacias mentioned above.

Fires are far less serious than farther south, because there is neither the density of trees nor height and cover of grass to warrant them, nor such density of population to start them. Soil and water supply exert powerful influence or control on the vegetation.

## Forest outliers, fringing forests and riparian woodland

These extensions of the forest occur along streams, in swamps, ravines, on hillsides and other favourable sites in the savanna woodlands. They depend upon edaphic moisture, rather than upon the low or seasonal rainfall.

Adjacent to rivers in the Guinea savanna are specifically riverine species, such as *Brachystegia eurycoma*, whose brilliant red leaves show up the courses of the rivers. Beyond is a dense understorey of evergreen shrubs and climbers, with widely spaced emergents above, some 12–18 m (40–60 ft) high.

In flatter and poorly drained outer margins of a valley, there may be Raphia Palms with tall dense grass. Even farther out are Borassus Palms and bamboo.

Farther north, in the Sudan savanna, riparian woodland occurs, with dense deciduous climbers and shrubs, alternating with tall grass and isolated trees.

In the Sahel savanna, riparian woodland consists mainly of the more moisture-loving acacias of the same zone and of the Sudan savanna.

## Semi-Saharan and Saharan vegetation

### Southern Saharan

After the small summer rains, grasses and annuals appear. Certain other plants may be sustained by winter dew. Many of the acacias and other trees or shrubs of the Sahel savanna persist. Woody species are mostly tropical but the herbs are mostly Mediterranean. Grasses grow in very isolated tufts. In the less arid and cooler Adras des Iforas and Aïr massifs, there is Sahel savanna vegetation.

### Saharan

In most places there is a very dispersed permanent vegetation of tiny scrubby plants and bushes, with trees in favoured sites. Permanent vegetation here and in the southern Saharan zone depends upon underground water and the nature of the subsoil, rather than upon rain, but seasonal herbs (*acheb*) spring up only after rains and soon mature.

In saline areas there are often chenopods which can provide camel forage; such a fodder plant and fuel provider is Had or *Cornulaca monacantha*. In oases, outliers of the Sahel savanna appear.

## Montane vegetation

### Montane rainforest

Altitude may modify vegetation because of increased and more constant humidity and cloudiness, less sunlight, lower temperatures and less evaporation. Consequently, above about 900 m (3 000 ft) on the Nigeria–Cameroon border and in the Guinea highlands, there is a tall canopied montane rainforest. Lianes are scarce, but bryophytes (mosses), tree ferns

(*Cyathea spp.*), epiphytes (orchids and begonias), and lichens are abundant. Species with temperate affinities also occur.

Above about 1 400–1 500 m (4 600–5 000 ft), trees are smaller and less varied but temperate species are quite common. This zone alone, or this and the previous one, are often termed 'mist forest', since it is usually saturated in mist. At its upper margin, ferns, mosses and epiphytes become less conspicuous than white lichens on trees. The mist zone ceases at about 1 830 m (6 000 ft).

Forest is not usually found above about 1 400 m (4 600 ft) in the Cameroon–Nigeria borderlands, except as tongues. Lesser interference by man has enabled forest in the Guinea highlands to survive fairly well.

## Montane woodland

This occurs on the upper edge of the montane forest and is a drier type with abundant grass. It is easily degraded or destroyed by fire, and is best seen in the Bamenda highlands. Only on the peaks of the Guinea highlands (highest is Mt Nimba 1 837 m: 6 026 ft) does *Parinari excelsa* occur as in the Casamance woodland.

## Montane grassland

This is probably derived from montane woodland as the result of frequent burning, and there are isolated trees. It occurs in the Bamenda highlands and in the Loma mountains of Sierra Leone. Fulani cattle are kept in this zone in the Bamenda highlands.

# Vegetation and the needs of man

The survival of rainforests beyond another century seems doubtful. They are being felled to provide space for food crops to feed the rapidly rising populations, and for profitable cash or export crops such as kola nuts, bananas, coffee, rubber and cocoa. These pressing claims against the rainforests have arisen in the last half-century, though shifting agriculture had, over a far longer period, already converted much virgin forest into secondary bush.

In the past, timber exploitation consisted of the highly selective felling of mahoganies and a few other species. A much wider range of timbers is now exported, and much of the 'useless' timber is used for making fibreboard, etc. Nevertheless, timber is a relatively minor export. Only the Ivory Coast, Ghana and Nigeria export significant amounts of timber and in all of them, at the best, it reaches fourth place in order of value. Rainforests are falling not so much at the demand of the timber merchant, but far more to that of the villager avid for more land.

Another acute problem is the almost entire disappearance or degradation of woodlands, and their replacement by savanna. It is generally agreed that forest and woodland are the only natural climaxes as far as very roughly 15°N.

Bush firing was recorded at the time of Hanno's voyage, nearly 2 500 years ago. It was accentuated by the Ghana, Mali, Songhai and other empires, whose domains lay around the middle Niger up to more than a thousand years ago. A vicious circle of fire leading to grass leading to fiercer fire, has for centuries been shrivelling the life out of the woodlands between about 8° and 15°N. These were originally the most extensive vegetation in West Africa but, because they were frailer and have been the longest attacked, they have largely succumbed to firing by man and to the advent of grass.

North of the 500–700 mm (20–28 in) isohyets, natural vegetation is generally of the Sahel type. This is holding its own and acacias are increasing within it. The short grass does not permit violent fires, the population is slight, and possibilities of cultivation are so restricted that there is no pressure on these lands adjacent to the Sahara.

Far from the Sahara encroaching, as Stebbing[3] once so stoutly maintained, it is now regarded as fairly stable. The relative stability of the Sahel vegetation and of its northern margin seems to confirm this. An Anglo-French Commission, which investigated the matter in 1937, found no instance of live sand dunes along the Nigeria–Niger boundary, no universal lowering of the watertable by natural causes, and no rapid drying out of Lake Chad. They did, however, find deterioration by wind and water through the action of man, and urged protection of head-waters, the reservation of forests and contour farming.

Over geological time, it is certainly true that the Sahara was less extensive; it is equally true that it was, at times, more extensive. We are now in a phase of moderate to major Saharan extension. Whatever the phase, we could do little or nothing to alter it. But as the real trouble is manmade and farther south, we should be concerned.

Contrary to Stebbing's belief, the desperate modern problem concerns not so much the margins of the Sahara, but the realm of the woodlands, which is ever ceding territory to grass. It is all-important to control bush-firing internationally, by preventing it, by limiting its range, or by insisting on firing early in the dry season before vegetation is too dry. However, this last proposal would defeat the whole aim of many pastoralists who fire vegetation to get earlier leafing of trees and herbage for cattle at the end of the long dry season, when cattle desperately need fodder. The over-concentration of cattle and goats, and the cutting of trees for firewood are also matters for concern.

The rainforests must also be defended. In temperate lands, where temperatures and rainfall are lower, removal of large blocks of forest (which is also so much lower and less vigorous in temperate countries) probably has little or no climatic effect. In the tropics, however, temperatures on bare land are obviously higher than in a shaded forest. When the tremendous transpiration from a rainforest and its cooling effect on clouds is eliminated, significant contributions to relative humidity and rainfall disappear.

Aubréville[4] considers that the rainforests of West Africa are responsible for replenishing the southwesterly winds with moisture, without which the savannas would have less rain, lower relative humidity and a shorter rainy season.

Each inroad into frailer parts of the rainforest gives a freer path to the desiccating Harmattan. This has happened in the Fouta Djallon, in the V-shaped bend of the Ivory Coast rainforest south of Bouaké, in the Ghana coastal scrub, on the Jos Plateau and along the Benue, all open to this drying wind.

Removal of forests also greatly affects the drainage pattern. Soils around river sources need tree cover and the binding effect of roots to hold them. Streams often run in forests, even in the dry season, because trees by their cool surfaces induce dew and condensation. Remove the forests and the streams dry up. Cutting of forests often means removal of soil and the clogging of rivers.

Cutting of any woodland frequently leads to soil erosion by wind in the dry season. Cutting of rainforest on steep slopes may assist gully erosion; and cutting on level land may induce sheet erosion and the laying bare of underlying lateritic concretions, like the *bowé* of the Fouta Djallon of Guinea.

Removal of natural vegetation, followed by prolonged over-farming has impoverished many areas. Such is the case between Dakar and St Louis in Senegal (Plate 45), southern Sierra Leone (where the secondary forest is remarkably poor), near Koforidua in Ghana, and in heavily populated parts of Onitsha and Owerri provinces in Nigeria.

Only the restriction of bush-firing and the control of grazing can revive the woodland zone. The rainforest, though less severely degraded, also needs selective protection. Building needs will require wood, and fuel supplies must be assured. But what of the urgent need of land to feed more people and grow more export crops? Better farming on existing land must provide most of the answer. Bush fallowing may suffice and not unduly damage the natural vegetation when the population is small. Increasing land pressure with the same agricultural system must ruin the forest and, in the end, the soils and the people as well. It is not forest reservation but bush fallowing which is so wasteful. Permanent cropping is essential everywhere if the remaining vegetation, the soils and man himself are to survive. Steep slopes and all land not suitable for farming should be retained or replanted as permanent forests. Defence of forest and woodland is one of the outstandingly urgent tasks in West Africa today, for on it depends the very continuance of agriculture—the basis of West African economy.

# 5

# Soils and soil management

During the past twenty years understanding of tropical soils has increased phenomenally; in this expansion West Africa is no exception. Not only has d'Hoore's soil map and monograph correlated and represented knowledge from Africa as a whole, but Ahn's study, among others, epitomises the West African advance, and numerous conference and seminar reports testify to both the importance of interterritorial cooperation and the growing concern with the practical and planning significance of soil studies. In the light of this advance and the applied orientation of much soil research in West Africa it is convenient to consider the soil geography of the area in three parts:

1. A survey of soil characteristics and patterns of variability on different scales.
2. A summary of the essentials of soil–plant relations within the West African ecosystems, with special reference to the implications of traditional and other long-established systems of husbandry.
3. A review of some of the major problems encountered in soil management in West Africa.

## Soil patterns

Regional patterns of soil differences in West Africa may usefully be examined by reference to d'Hoore's map. Figure 5.1 is a simplified version of the West Africa sheet, and sets out the major mapping units distinguished by him in that area.

On the regional scale three main patterns may be distinguished:

1. There is a significant correspondence, though by no means an identity, between the arrangement of the major soil mapping units—the ferrallitic soils, the ferruginous tropical soils, and so on, and the zonation of the major vegetation belts. Furthermore, both the soil units and the vegetation zones show a very approximate latitudinal orientation; thus both soil and vegetation variability, as might be expected, correspond to the equator-tropic climatic gradients. Three observations on this relationship are relevant:

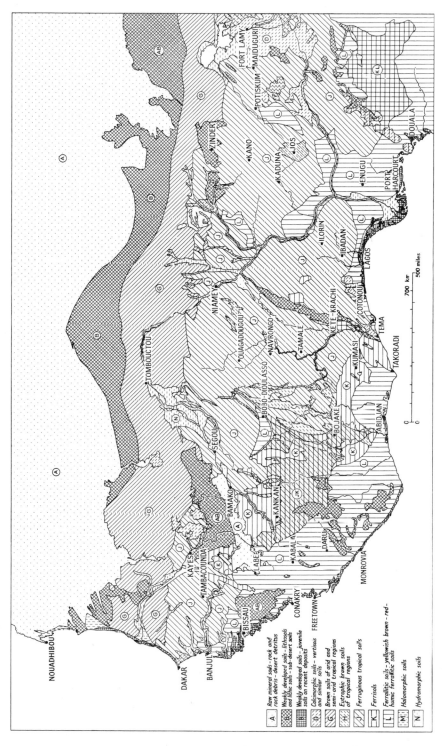

NOUADHIBOU

DAKAR

BANJUL

BISSAU

TAMBACOUNDA

KAYES

CONAKRY

FREETOWN

MONROVIA

DARU

KABALA

LABÉ

KANKAN

BAMAKO

SEGOU

TOMBOUCTOU

NIAMEY

OUAGADOUGOU

BOBO-DIOULASSO

NAVRONGO

TAMALE

KETE-KRACHI

KUMASI

BOUAKÉ

ABIDJAN

TAKORADI

TEMA

COTONOU

LAGOS

IBADAN

ILORIN

PORT-HARCOURT

ENUGU

KADUNA

KANO

JOS

ZINDER

POTISKUM

MAIDUGURI

FORT LAMY

DOUALA

700 km

500 miles

| | Raw mineral soils - rock and rock debris - desert detritus |
| --- | --- |
| | Weakly developed soils - lithosols and lithic soils - sub-desert soils |
| | Weakly developed soils - juvenile soils on recent deposits |
| | Calcimorphic soils - vertisols and similar soils |
| | Brown soils of arid and semi-arid tropical regions |
| | Eutrophic brown soils of tropical regions |
| | Ferruginous tropical soils |
| | Ferrisols |
| | Ferrallitic soils - yellowish brown - red - humic ferrallitic soils |
| | Halomorphic soils |
| | Hydromorphic soils |

FIG. 3.1. Soil map of West Africa (after J. L. D'Hoore)

(*a*) The absence of periods of low temperature in all but the few areas of highest relief in the region, implies that the intensity of soil chemical and biochemical reactions, of processes of chemical weathering, and of biological activity, in the soil and regolith (weathering layer above unaltered bed rock), is little inhibited by temperature factors. Rather is it affected by differences in soil moisture regimes. These in turn are strongly related to the three factors of atmospheric moisture, vegetation structure and composition, and the properties, size and arrangement of minerals in the parent rock in particular locations.

(*b*) The spatial patterns observed result from the interaction of plant character and soil properties in the setting of more general and independent atmospheric and geological patterns. This applies both to patterns of variability in the function of plant–soil systems, and also to the broad patterns of soil and vegetation development. This fact necessitates an examination of soil in the context of the ecosystem in the second part of this chapter.

(*c*) The most marked deviations from latitudinal orientation and from general correspondence with vegetation zones on the part of the major mapping units are associated with parent rock differences. Thus the ferrallitic soils extend inland along the Niger and Benue valleys in association with the outcrop of Cretaceous and Pliocene rocks, largely ferruginous sandstones, thus transgressing both the forest–savanna boundary, and the trend of the isopleths of mean annual rainfall. Even more extensively, the northward swing of the ferruginous tropical soils into the bend of the Niger is associated with the extension of the outcrop of the basement complex rocks, dominantly granitic and quartzitic, into the area underlain by the younger sedimentary rocks of the southern Sahara. There is also a tendency for the subregional distribution of ferruginous crusts in the more northerly savannas to be associated with the outcrops of these Cambrian and Silurian sediments, and even with the recent Pliocene sediments of Senegal.

These broad patterns are associated in terms of soil properties with a general decrease in the intensity of weathering, and the degree of soil development towards the tropic. In the most northerly parts the *subdesert soils* are low in organic matter, show only slightly differentiated horizons, and are biologically very inactive. Some bacteria, such as nitrogen-fixers and nitrifiers, are often completely absent. To the south these soils pass into the *brown and reddish-brown soils* associated with arid and semi-arid moisture conditions. They are darkened by organic matter to some considerable depth, and show some tendency to develop a clear B-horizon, by the vertical differentiation of colour, texture or structure in the profile. Weatherable minerals are a common constituent, and the mineral clay contains a significant proportion of expanding-lattice clays of high chemical activity. Free carbonates often occur, indicating that, because the water additions to the profile by precipitation are rarely sufficient to link up with the groundwater level in the regolith, the soils are not leached through to the regional water table.

The major group (and the most heterogeneous) of soils on d'Hoore's map of West Africa are the *ferruginous tropical soils.* They are typically associated with the extensive areas of savannas of various types, though in some areas, as in the area around and to the west of Ibadan in the Western State of Nigeria, they apparently extend into the forest. They show distinct differentiation into A, B, and C horizons, though the depth to unweathered rock rarely exceeds 3·5 m (11 ft 6 in). The B horizon is distinguished by textural and sometimes structural differentiation, and, though marked separation of free iron oxides frequently occurs, and they may be precipitated as mottles or concretions in the profile, weatherable minerals are often present in significant amounts. The mineral clay is dominatly kaolinitic, though more active clays are usually present also, but free alumina (as the mineral oxide, gibbsite) are generally absent. Thus the chemical activity of the mineral clay is low, but higher than that of the ferrisols or ferrallitic soils.

Between the ferruginous tropical soils and ferrallitic soils in southwestern Ghana, the Ivory Coast and Guinea, there are extensive areas of *ferrisols,* which are intermediate in some properties between these two groups, and chemically more active than either. They occur extensively in association with the former group in Guinea and the Ivory Coast. They are sometimes found also in areas dominated by *ferrallitic soils,* a group which is very extensive in the forest areas of West Africa, being most important in southern Nigeria, the southern Ivory Coast, Liberia and Sierra Leone. They are often deeply weathered with considerable uniformity to several metres below the surface, and contain no reserves of weatherable minerals. The mineral clay is usually dominated by kaolinite, and contains considerable proportions of free iron oxides, as well as hydrated alumina. The mineral clay complex is essentially chemically inactive.

One further group of soils deserves special mention. The *eutrophic* (high in available mineral nutrients) *brown soils* occur in small patches in many parts of West Africa, but more extensively in the northern parts of the Ivory Coast and the southern part of Upper Volta. They are lithomorphic (dominated by parent rock properties) soils derived from very base-rich rocks, volcanic ash or highly basic alluvia. These soils are generally rich in plant nutrients with a large reserve of weatherable minerals, and a mineral clay fraction dominated by chemically very active clays. They are well structured and permeable even with a high clay content. Their chemical activity is maintained even in areas with an annual precipitation in excess of 1 500 mm (nearly 60 in).

Thus on a regional scale there are wide variations in soil character which belie the erroneous suppositions of uniformity which have so often bedevilled geographical consideration of tropical soils.

2. At a smaller scale variability is even more marked in response to differences of parent material. Mention has been made of the general effect of parent rock on the regional distribution of the major groups already described. Within these groups d'Hoore distinguishes subgroups based largely on parent rock differences.

D'Hoore rightly emphasises the essential pedogenetic difference between *parent rock* and *soil parent material*. Individual parent rocks give rise to a wide range of different parent materials by the processes of weathering, erosion, transport and deposition. Furthermore, in many tropical African situations contemporary soil formation is occurring on material which has undergone more than one cycle of weathering. Nevertheless, the mineralogical characteristics of the underlying rock impose a similarity of some significant properties in soils derived from the same parent rock. The properties of the rock important in this respect are: (*a*) the proportion of chemically unweatherable minerals, principally quartz, and their grain size, which considerably affect the texture and sand grain size of the resultant soil; (*b*) the proportion of ferromagnesian minerals, influencing the proportion and character of the mineral clay fraction of the soil; and (*c*) the proportions of iron held in the mineral complex, affecting both soil colour and the form and character of the weathering products. In addition to these effects, the general relationship between forms produced by subaerial erosion and rock character often produces distinct toposequences of soils strongly related to rock type. Examples of these arrangements will be cited later. Thus parent rock often proves a useful tool in generalising soil distributions on a subregional scale.

3. The third regional pattern which requires brief consideration is that of the distribution of hard ferruginous crusts of greater or less areal extent. The origin of these crusts is a matter of controversy which has been exacerbated by the varied use of the term 'laterite'. Some view such crusts as the normal end-product of weathering under humid tropical conditions; others view the hardening as a process subsequent to, and distinct from, the weathering processes which produce the aluminium and iron oxides of which the crusts are dominantly composed. Yet others view the product as the result of alteration of the B-horizon of a tropical forest soil as a consequence of vegetation change from forest to savanna. Most likely the basic decomposition products result from weathering under a fluctuating watertable in areas where slopes are negligible. Subsequently a drop in watertable (possibly also increased surface erosion), perhaps brought about by a change in base level or a vegetation change, results in hardening. Further erosion produces a breakaway, and the hard sheet is broken up, forming detrital ironstone which may then be re-cemented by various processes at a lower level in the land surface. There appears to be considerable morphological variety in the deposits included in these categories, and many mottled clays (which are very extensive in many tropical soils, especially in the forest zone) though

related to the crusts, do not harden when exposed to the atmosphere. Furthermore, there are examples of true *groundwater laterites* quoted from West Africa.

Thus there is considerable confusion surrounding this whole problem; nevertheless, certain facts of distribution are unequivocal. In the first place, in West Africa such crusts, though they are occasionally found under forest vegetation, are principally located in the savanna areas (Fig. 5.1). Though this may perhaps be a genetic effect related to the vegetation, it is relevant to point out that in West Africa the forest is near the sea, and that it is therefore possible to argue that the crusts have been largely removed in the forest areas by normal erosion, whereas in the more distant interior this has not yet taken place. The areas covered by hard crusts form only a small part of the total area, and their importance has been exaggerated by Gourou. D'Hoore's measurements of the areas of the units he maps show that groups which include soils with hard crusts in association with other soils, cover little more than 3·5 per cent of Africa; the total area actually underlain by crusts must be far below the million square kilometres that this percentage represents. Much of what Gourou writes on the soils of the tropics contains an element of misplaced emphasis; large areas of West Africa, at least, must be excepted from his generalisations. Vine's little-known article[1] offers an important and balanced corrective to this viewpoint.

## Local patterns

These regional arrangements contain within them a wide variety of local patterns of soil variability. Hence on smaller-scale maps it is not generally possible to map individual genetic groups, and the mapping units are complexes and associations of various kinds. These local patterns may be of three main types: associations of soils over related parent materials, catenae and toposequences, and undifferentiated complexes (usually in valley and flood plain areas). Each of these is now considered separately.

*Parent material associations* most usefully characterise local patterns where the parent rock or its derivatives possess characteristics which impose special properties on the soils. Thus basic and ultrabasic rocks throughout West Africa give rise to soils of higher base status, a well-developed structure and greater biological stability in most places where they occur. They form distinct soil groups within the more typical soils developed over materials derived from coarser and less ferromagnesian rocks. These geological patterns, which, as was pointed out earlier, are also responsible for regional patterns, override the influence of relief differences which elsewhere are associated with the catenae and toposequences typical of so much of the continent.

While rocks rich in bases give rise to distinctive soils, at the other end of the scale rocks rich in quartz and low in ferromagnesian

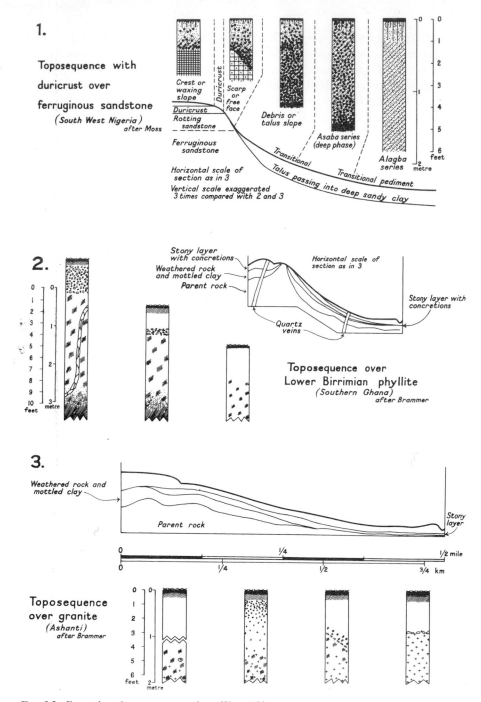

**1.**

Toposequence with
duricrust over
ferruginous sandstone
*(South West Nigeria)*
*after Moss*

Crest or
waxing
slope

Duricrust

Scarp
or
free
face

Duricrust
Rotting
sandstone

Debris or
talus slope

Asaba series
(deep phase)

Alagba
series

Ferruginous
sandstone

Transitional

Talus passing into deep sandy clay

Transitional pediment

*Horizontal scale of*
*section as in 3*

*Vertical scale exaggerated*
*3 times compared with 2 and 3*

**2.**

Stony layer
with concretions

Weathered rock
and mottled clay

Parent rock

Horizontal scale of
section as in 3

Stony layer with
concretions

Quartz
veins

Toposequence over
Lower Birrimian phyllite
*(Southern Ghana)*
*after Brammer*

**3.**

Weathered rock and
mottled clay

Parent rock

Stony
layer

Toposequence
over granite
*(Ashanti)*
*after Brammer*

FIG. 5.2. Examples of toposequences from West Africa

82

minerals also frequently produce distinctive associations. Thus, in Nigeria, quartz-schists and quartzites, consisting almost entirely of quartz and muscovite mica, produce an association of skeletal and rocky soils with soils showing deep, friable, bright red profiles. These bear a strong relationship in terms of properties with some soils derived from Cretaceous and Tertiary ferruginous sandstones. Similar phenomena are implied throughout West Africa by the properties of the categories developed on a subregional scale by d'Hoore.

*Catenae and toposequences* have been used for mapping and classification purposes over wide areas of the continent, the basic concept of the catena having been proposed originally by Milne in East Africa. Though there are essential differences between the two concepts in terms of the processes thought to have produced the relation between soil properties and slope form, they can be conveniently treated together. Examples of both are included in Fig. 5.2. Toposequences may be broadly classified into three main groups:

1. Toposequences with rock outcrops, which are characteristic of much of the region away from the coast. They display great variability in response to rock type, and different sequences occur in response to catenary processes (*sensu stricto*). In these the soil properties in the sequence are genetically related in terms of processes operating within the slope itself, and in relation to the more general processes involved in slope formation, both contemporary and antecedent. These are often related in a complex fashion to the character of the parent rock, and thus particular toposequences may be characteristic of parent material associations. In many situations the toposequential properties of the soils are reflected in the vegetation, so that distinctive plant–soil systems often occur in association with particular facets of the land surface.

2. Toposequences with hard laterite, associated with the areas shown on Fig. 5.1 as having significant areas of duricrusts and cuirasses, are more uniform, and less affected by parent material differences than those with rock outcrops. Characteristically, the hard ferruginous or bauxitic crust occurs at the upper slope or summit position in the sequence, and the soils on the middle and lower slopes are strongly related to the processes of crust disintegration. Frequently, however, secondary deposits forming hard bands are found on lower slopes, either in association with, or independent of, the occurrence of hard crust on the upper slope. Sequences or trains of hard bands at three or more levels in the land surface have been reported, and a number of softer deposits, such as more or less indurated mottled clays, are associated with similar slope forms and soil sequences.

3. Toposequences without rock outcrops or hard duricrusts occur widely, and exhibit considerable variety in association with the differing properties of the underlying rock. Nevertheless, when soil-slope relations in a particular area are understood, slope form can be reliably used as a tool

for predicting the distribution of soil properties. On this basis catenary associations and land systems can be readily mapped.

*Undifferentiated complexes* may be considered a special case of the toposequence, since they are dominantly associated with areas of low undifferentiated relief. They are associated with plains of advanced erosion in the interior of the continent, or with areas of low relief in littoral, lacustrine or alluvial areas. Here soil differences, which may be of considerable agricultural significance and pedological importance, are not related to observable differences in the form of the land surface. Differentiation of soil properties depends principally on relative age, differences of parent material and similar factors at the higher levels, and at the lower levels upon the history of river courses, delta and lagoon development, and drainage history.

The soil patterns of West Africa are thus complex and varied with respect to a wide range of properties, thus belying the myth of uniformity which has for so long hindered the valid appraisal of the role of the soil in the geography of West Africa, indeed of the tropical areas of the continent as a whole. Despite this diversity it is possible to examine the role of the soil in relation to major plant–soil systems in the region, and to pinpoint certain major factors of soil management on a similar scale.

## Soil-plant relations

Soil may be viewed as an element in the ecosystem, and as such it has a particularly significant role in relation to plants, through which nutrients and water are constantly cycled. By this means energy is fixed by photosynthesis and then dissipated through food chains, terminating in the activities of decomposers releasing organic matter and its decomposition products into the soil body.

In tropical Africa the soil has been studied in this way and detailed appraisals are to be found, for example in Nye and Greenland, and Laudelout. As in most plant–soil systems the soil in the tropics performs four important functions with respect to the organisms in the ecosystem:

1. It provides the anchorage for plant roots and the medium in which they develop.
2. It provides a habitat for the macrofauna, such as termites, burrowing mammals, earthworms, etc., and also the environment in which micro-organisms, such as bacteria and fungi perform their essential function.
3. It is the location in which the significant transformations of organic debris to inorganic ions takes place (either chemically, or biochemically through the activities of micro-organisms), thus making them available for absorption by plant roots.

4. It is a store for water and nutrients needed by the plants for metabolism and chemosynthesis.

Clearly, these functions are not independent, and the plants themselves affect the ability of the soil to perform these functions. In particular, the function of the soil macrofauna in pedogenesis needs to be emphasised, especially the significance of termites.

A major contrast in soil–plant relations is provided by the boundary between forest and savanna. The closed forest and the grass-with-trees which compose these two major communities behave very differently with respect to energy, water and nutrients. There is a major contrast in respect of the following properties:

1. The contrast in bulk (that is biomass), which is shown in the figures cited by Nye and Greenland. Developed secondary forest has a dry weight of about 340 000 kg/ha for its aerial parts, compared with much more variable quantities of the order of less than a tenth of this figure for different types of savannas.

2. The difference in structure, with the closed canopy of the forest and its tendency to a layered structure dominating conditions near the ground surface.

3. These contrasts are reflected in the behaviour of the two communities with respect to microclimate, water and nutrients:

(*a*) Exchange between the atmosphere above the upper reaches of the vegetation and that below is considerable in savanna; in forest it is negligible. Thus beneath the forest canopy humidities are high, the air relatively still, and evaporation from the soil surface minimal. Transpiration levels are high. Hence in the regolith below the forest the groundwater level is low, but moisture values are high right to the soil layers adjacent to the surface, even in periods of moisture stress. The amounts of atmospheric precipitation reaching the ground surface by throughfall are negligible, but by stemflow are considerable; run-off also is negligible, even on steep slopes. Hence erosion risks are small, except where extensive areas are cleared.

(*b*) A high turnover of litter and its decomposition also characterises the forest. Furthermore, the extensive root development of the forest plants, together with the root bulk, ensure a continuous supply of organic matter to the soil within itself, by sloughing, death of small roots and exudation. This continues even under cultivation, where, in indigenous practice, roots are commonly left in the soil.

(*c*) In forest there is a considerable cycling of nutrients, substantial storage in the plants, significant storage in the soil, and a 'pumping-up' of nutrients from deep layers in the regolith by the roots of trees, which may well extend 15–20 m (50 or more feet) below the surface. All nutrients except nitrogen seem to be involved.

In contrast to these characteristics, savanna conditions show a more variable, less stable and less vigorous system, more susceptible to meteorological changes in the surrounding atmosphere. Amounts of nutrients depend to a great degree upon the amounts of woody growth present, and this is especially important in respect to calcium, which so greatly affects the behaviour of other nutrient elements in the soil. Furthermore, there is evidence that some savanna grasses, notably the *Andropogoneae,* inhibit the activity of certain soil bacteria, and may cause deficiencies in nitrogen in its availability to plants. Water conditions, which also affect nutrient availability, contrast with those under forest. Owing to lesser water use by the vegetation, and the greater exposure of the soil surface to atmospheric conditions which produces higher evaporation values, the watertable tends to be higher, and soil moisture values lower than under forest in comparable rainfall regimes.

As atmospheric moisture supplies become less in amount and more seasonal in occurrence, the contrast between forest and savanna ceases to be of importance, and is replaced by a contrast, similar in basic character but less striking, between woody savannas with many trees and open steppe grassland.

There is thus a striking contrast in soil behaviour resulting from vegetation differences, particularly but not entirely those relating to structure and layering. Agricultural activity, especially indigenous systems, should be viewed in relation to plant–soil systems, rather than to soil properties alone. Detailed studies have shown that in many areas the interaction between ecological factors of this kind, and social and economic influences, are extremely complex in their effects upon indigenous cultivators.

Four sets of soil properties are of fundamental importance to selfsown plants and to planted crops, and are not, at least on the time scales involved in cultivation and fallow succession, greatly affected by the plants themselves. These sets are:

1. Soil properties which affect the moisture properties of the soil, such as the amounts of silt and clay size particles, and their intrinsic character, together with their arrangement in terms of structural or fabric units.
2. Soil properties which affect the activity of the colloidal system, especially the mineralogical character of the clay and its arrangement in relation to other particles. The character of the colloidal system is fundamentally affected by the amounts and kinds of organic matter present, and this changes with the plants. Nevertheless, the importance of this mineral fraction relative to the behaviour of the complex as a whole clearly depends upon the character and activity of the mineral clay and its proportion. Soils which contain a significant amount of active mineral clay are clearly more stable nutrient systems than those which do not.

3. Characteristics of the regional hydrological system which affect the water properties of the soil, such as regional water table levels and their season of variation.
4. Soil properties, such as the presence of hard layers, of nutrient-rich layers, or profile heterogeneity, which affect the development of the root systems of the vegetation. The rooting volume of the vegetation affects its soil relations as much as, if not more than, the properties of the soil, measured in terms of water and moisture characteristics or chemical and biochemical behaviour in a soil sample.

Thus, in relation to soil use, or soil–plant interactions, it is insufficient to consider only soil properties. A whole gamut of significant factors cannot be understood outside a framework embracing the plants as well, and their ecosystematic role in conjunction with soil. It is within this framework that consideration of soil management problems must take place.

## Soil management problems

### Indigenous agriculture

The African cultivator in particular and the tropical cultivator in general have frequently been portrayed as wasteful, even destructive, exploiters of biological resources, especially in relation to tropical forests. This view, if not completely unjustified, is certainly a gross oversimplification of the actual situation. Indigenous systems based on the cultivation of small areas for short periods, and the subsequent development of a natural fallow, are conservative of biological resources, for the following major reasons:

1. Only small patches are cultivated. This is probably a consequence of the labour involved in clearing forest, but has the effect of introducing only minimal disturbance of the plant–soil system, of reducing the effect of increased run-off by constricting the distance over which movement of material is possible, and of limiting disturbance of microclimatic effects.
2. Cultivation lasts only for a short period, which may be two or three years, or a little longer, after which the plot is allowed to revert to natural fallow. The reason for this reversion has commonly been supposed to be 'loss of fertility', but there is considerable doubt that this is so, at least in itself. Nutrient supply by the soil does not, in many areas at least, decrease as rapidly in successive years as had once been assumed. The measurable amounts of nutrients in the soil, though low by standard in higher latitudes (if the more fertile areas are used for the comparison), may not truly indicate the availability of those nutrients to plants. The activity of the soil water regime characteristic of forest areas for much of the year, and for the wet season in much of the rest of tropical West Africa, probably ensures maximum solution and dissociation of nutrient ions during the growing season of the crop plant. It is likely

that weed problems play a significant role in the decision to abandon a cultivation plot.

3. Many large trees are not cleared, the stools of smaller trees are left in the ground, and the roots are rarely disturbed significantly, particularly in their lower extensions. This means that considerable quantities of organic matter continue to be supplied to the soil while cultivation proceeds, and that as soon as the regeneration of stools and roots ceases to be prevented by the abscission of aerial shoots in the process of weeding, vigorous growth of these plants takes place. Furthermore, under the woody fallow, restoration of the nutrient and organic matter equilibria in the soil is rapidly achieved. Related to this is the fact that seven or eight years is usually a sufficient length of time for the woody fallow to accumulate nutrients in amounts adequate for renewed cultivation.

4. In the process of cultivation the indigenous cultivator leaves a considerable number of adventitious plants growing with his crops. These are rarely weeds, which are by definition useless to the cultivator, but self-sown plants which have a technological, medicinal or food use to the indigenous community. They have the effect of providing a cover of ground plants which conserve moisture, intercept heavy rainfall, and supply some organic matter to the soil.

5. Finally, a significant proportion of forest clearing for food crop cultivation is undertaken with the intention of establishing more permanent managed ecosystems, which include cocoa, oil palm, rubber and other tree crops. These, despite their much greater simplicity compared to developed forest, are analogous to it in respect of a number of basic ecological relationships, and represent an essentially conservative form of land use in the tropical forests.

Thus indigenous cultivation in tropical forests is to a large degree a conservative form of land use, whether it involves the husbandry of food crops or permanent tree crops.

In the savanna areas a similar argument may be developed in respect of indigenous cultivators. However grass-with-trees provides a considerably less efficient method of soil rehabilitation than does a woody fallow, and the labour of clearing is also considerably less. Furthermore, it is significant that even among many of the less numerous and less advanced peoples of West Africa intensive agricultural husbandry attains a high degree of sophistication with developed conservation methods, such as tie-ridging, being used for soil conservation in savanna areas.

### Fertilisers

Having emphasised the conservative character of indigenous agriculture it is necessary to point out that economic increases of yield can be obtained from most crops by applications of fertilisers containing any major nutrient. This has been shown not only in experiments on government farms, but also by extensive trials on farmers' plots. The response to fertilisers is, however, fundamentally conditioned by the soil moisture regime on the one hand, and by the variety of crop grown on the other. Thus, in most situations in West Africa, the effective use of fertiliser depends on parallel development of water control (in the broadest sense), and on the introduction of crop varieties which maximise the effects of the improved husbandry techniques.

With food crops fertiliser application is a fairly straightforward practice, but with tree crops the situation is much more complex. Nevertheless, in major tree crops such as cocoa and oil palm, appropriate fertiliser programmes yield economic results. These must be undertaken in conjunction with programmes of pest control, since pests are most often the principal cause of poor yields in tree crops, especially cocoa, and exist in ecological complexes involving plant diseases as well. Fertilisers should also be combined with more efficient techniques of shading and propagation.

Thus there is considerable scope for the increasing use of manufactured chemical fertilisers in managing tropical soils and crops. Even greater economic returns could be obtained if fertiliser industries could be established in the user countries instead of relying on imported products; one such exists in Senegal.

Farmyard and green manures can also be effectively used, but only where they are produced in quantities large enough to provide adequate and constant applications. This is rarely the case in West Africa. Grass leys and planted fallows have also been used, but these usually need fertilising if they are to produce enough herbage to improve soil conditions significantly and increase crop yields. Thus the use of manufactured fertilisers would seem to offer the best available way of improving crop yields in West Africa.

## Soil erosion and water control

Soil erosion is not a general problem in West Africa under indigenous husbandry systems. It is, however, locally a chronic problem, and in many areas a potential hazard under changing cultivation practices. Soil erosion is intimately associated with problems of water control, and it is thus convenient to consider both together.

Over much of tropical Africa the annual water supply from precipitation is less than the amount of water most crop plants would transpire if adequately supplied with moisture. Furthermore, over much of this area the rainfall is unreliable in amount and occurrence, both seasonally and annually. Also, it is commonly very intense. Thus conservation measures must involve efficient use of the available moisture, and the prevention of the adverse effects of intense rainfall, such as flash floods.

Maintaining a plant cover and mulching, separately or together, constitute one approach to the problem, but the preservation of useless plants simply as a conservation measure involves the waste of moisture which might otherwise go to the crop plant, and is feasible only in areas where the water supply is more or less adequate to the crop being grown. Mulching with dead plant matter is also not usually practicable, since there are other more pressing uses for such materials as straw, plant stems and leaves, which might be used for conservation of this type. Artificial mulches, such as bitumen-in-water, though practicable, are not usually economically or technically possible in the present socio-economic situation in areas where such measures are most needed.

Contour- and tie-ridging effectively achieve conservation of water supplies, and a diminution of runoff velocities. Combinations of the two have proved their worth. These measures offer simple and satisfactory ways of controlling water use and preventing soil erosion, but soil differences still need to be taken into account. The importance of such measures cannot be overemphasised when the problems of stopping and controlling erosion once it has begun are considered. This must almost always involve major schemes of rehabilitation, embracing engineering works, afforestation, considerable modifications of traditional agricultural practices, even of settlement patterns and land apportionment. These imply considerable expense of money and of expertise which could otherwise be used for agricultural improvement, rather than for arresting the effects of past malpractices.

## Conclusion

The soils of Africa vary widely in their characteristics and behaviour in relation to plant growth, and in their response to various agricultural practices. Nevertheless, discernible spatial patterns may be clearly seen on different scales, and thus afford the basis upon which subsequent rational development of the resources may be built. Given adequate local knowledge of soil character, and its satisfactory representation on an understandable map, the technical knowledge is available, by means of which agriculture may develop from the essentially conservative indigenous systems to more ambitious uses. This would effect increased production from already productive areas, and ensure efficient development of areas not yet used. This will involve, as Sir Joseph Hutchinson has pointed out, 'the domestication of the soil as [man] has domesticated plants and animals'. This is already in progress, and much current development represents the beginnings of domesticated, highly fertile soils in the tropics, as they have been developed in Western Europe. To this development, understanding of the basic character and distribution of the soil must make a major contribution.

# Part II

# The resources and their development

*The following chapters relate to the
whole of West Africa. Further details
concerning matters discussed here may
be found in the chapters on the individual countries.*

# 6

# Agriculture

## General considerations

Agricultural pursuits are the basis of almost all West African life. As in any part of the world, important determinants of crop distributions are climate and soils. In the tropics, rainfall (especially its seasonal distribution) is especially significant. Thus the kola nut tree requires a fairly heavy annual rainfall of at least 1 270 mm (50 in). The coconut palm and the groundnut legume must be grown in sandy soils, whereas maize needs at least 760 mm (30 in) annual rainfall and soils of more than average richness.

Biological factors also affect rural economy. Thus, the tsetse fly severely restricts the areas within which large cattle may be kept. Consequently, mixed farming and the renewal of soil fertility are especially difficult where the tsetse fly occurs and only the small resistant *Ndama* cattle survive. In the Sudan and Sahel savannas the tsetse fly is more or less absent, larger humped cattle may be kept, the land is easily cleared and prepared, and mixed farming is possible. Nevertheless, it is not common, because animals are kept mainly by nomads.

In the forest, crops have to be raised from small plots won by periodic cutting and burning. Soils become exhausted and, as there is very little animal manure, and artificials are expensive and difficult to use satisfactorily in the tropics, there is no simple alternative to a long fallow period. Thus the forest farmer generally expends much energy per acre. Yet he is more than compensated by the growth of permanent tree crops such as the oil palm, cocoa, kola and coffee; and by wild or semi-wild forest materials—such as timber and minor forest products. With heavier and more evenly distributed rain, he is also less restricted in his farming calendar.

By contrast, savanna farms are generally larger and less varied in their crops, as the shorter growing period restricts the farmer to one main crop in each season for each field. However, paucity of rain and its unreliability are challenges that may encourage more careful cropping. Population pressure may also induce better farming, e.g. among the Kabrai of Togo, the Hausa around Kano, and others.

The social organisation of some West African peoples, and their conception of the place of women, affect agricultural methods and the crops grown. The area of land farmed may be limited by the amount which a man can cut from the forest, and which the men or women can then cultivate. Yams are generally planted by men; the women in some areas may then plant and cultivate vegetables on the yam mounds. The income from the vegetables may also belong to the women. They often plant and cultivate rice, as in the Gambia.

Inter cropping or double cropping is very common in West Africa. Although this method may seem inefficient and looks a muddle, it saves labour and land, and limits soil erosion by keeping the ground covered. Moreover, some plants may benefit from intercropping. On the other hand, mixed cropping may necessitate the use of crop varieties tolerant of this system. The cotton grown in southern Nigeria is of vigorous robust growth, and will flourish although interplanted among other crops, where a cotton of less robust growth, such as the more valuable Allen type of the north, would fail through competition.

Again, a new process may unduly complicate the farming community by upsetting the relative proportions of men and women's incomes. The income from the cracking of palm nuts belongs to women. Nutcracking machines are more efficient, but are somewhat expensive for Africans, and difficult for women to operate. If they are bought and used by men, social conflict may result. Likewise, cassava processing is women's work and mechanical processing will upset this division of labour and may deny women a source of income.

There is a tradition for or against certain crops. Thus benniseed is especially favoured and grown by the Tiv in Nigeria, and the Fulani cattle-keeping people are averse to fixed agriculture. Miège[1] has shown that the relative spheres of rice and yam cultivation corresponded originally to two great cultural groupings of peoples in West Africa— those of the West Atlantic group (rice growing) and those of the East Atlantic group (yam growing). The boundary between them, in the Ivory Coast, is a major ethnic and crop divide.

Communal or group ownership of land, though now undergoing many changes, is also a restrictive factor in the rational development of crops, especially when farm plots are small and scattered. Cooperative methods may be a solution.

There have been many external factors affecting West African agriculture. Portuguese slave-traders found difficulty in feeding captives on the long voyage to the New World, because most indigenous West African produce from the forest—mainly fruits, insects, rodents, lizards and fish —would not store for long periods. Among introductions from America for this purpose, and later for other reasons including sheer accident, have been cassava, sweet potatoes, groundnuts, maize, lima beans, chillies, tomatoes, papaw, guavas, avocado pears, pineapple, tobacco and American cotton. Early Indo-Malaysian migrants to Madagascar, Muslim pilgrims returning overland from Asia via the Sudan, or the Portuguese bringing them from Asia, are believed to have introduced Indian cottons, certain yams, the cocoyam, aubergines, citrus fruits, mangoes, bananas (later sent on to the New World), certain peas and beans, and sugar cane. More recent introductions are swamp rices from Asia, sisal and cocoa from America. Cocoa was first introduced to São Tomé and Fernando Po, and from the latter to the mainland. Many of these crops are now vital foodstuffs and export crops. Unfortunately, less skilled cultivation than that found in South-east Asia and past lack of selection have sometimes resulted in crops of poor quality.

Governments have sought, in diverse ways, to encourage certain crops. The extreme form of this was in the Ivory Coast after 1912 when, under Governor Angoulvent, there was compulsory cultivation of cocoa and of certain foodstuffs. Export crops were unduly encouraged, e.g. by allocating agricultural research funds almost exclusively to them, rather than to food crops. Former French territories, with small populations, were the first to modify this position.

Overseas export crops are rather more restricted than food crops, both in variety and in distribution. The success of an export crop depends not only on physical factors such as soil and climate, and on economic criteria, but also (and often much more) on such factors as whether a given people is willing to try a crop, and whether it can be fitted into local farming methods. The distribution of export crops is sometimes irrational and incomplete, and West Africa is littered with unsuccessful attempts to introduce all kinds of crops.

More purely economic factors also affect crop distribution. Many African crops can be grown for export only if there is bulk transport. Groundnuts, shelled or unshelled, depend on railways for cheap transport over great distances. Cocoa, being of greater value by weight, can be sent by road. Proximity to transport is a powerful determinant of the extent of cash crop cultivation.

Some produce is still obtained by simple collection, such as piassava and raphia fibre, but most produce comes from mainly subsistence farmers growing small amounts of diverse crops. Some peasant farmers have specialised (e.g. on cocoa or groundnuts), and then crop limits may be more accurately defined by geographical and economic criteria.

Crops grown for a standardised article, or which need processing, such as the oil palm, coffee and fruits, are best grown on plantations. But in British West Africa before independence non-Africans were not normally allowed to establish plantations, and plantation crops were practically absent from British territories, though in Guinea, the Ivory Coast, and the Bight of Biafra islands plantations have for long been important. Africans could establish them, and have done so increasingly, but few possess the capital or technical knowledge. Similarly, rubber is grown for export in Liberia, not only because of suitable climatic and soil conditions, but especially because the Firestone Rubber Company could obtain a large concession. Since just before independence, Nigeria, Ghana and Sierra Leone have shown interest in establishing plantations, usually under the auspices of state or semi-state organisations.

World shortage of certain foods led to trials of mechanised farming. Groundnuts were cultivated mechanically near Kaffrine and Sédhiou in Senegal. In the Inland Niger Delta of the Mali Republic rice and other crops are being partly produced by mechanical methods. Mechanical cultivation may so reduce labour that cultivable areas can be extended.

There are, however, social, agricultural and economic limitations to mechanisation. Mechanical cultivation requires managerial skill and close supervision. Machines need a great deal of careful maintenance because of the rapid deterioration of steel when used on lateritic soils and in conditions of occasional or general high humidity. Spare parts may not always be available because of remoteness from manufacturers, shortage of capital or foreign exchange. Machines cannot normally be used on small farms, certainly not on dispersed plots.

Areas most suitable for mechanical cultivation are moderately or thinly populated savanna areas, where present productivity of the land is limited by the amount of hoe cultivation possible just before and during the short rainy season. Yet is must be remembered that the African hoe, with its blade set acutely to the handle for light soils and nearer to a right angle for heavy soils, though laborious to use and capable of cultivating only a small area, is well adapted to African soils, as it works only the richer top layer. Deep ploughing is dangerous because it brings up poorer soils and greatly loosens the ground. Wind erosion may follow on dry level lands, and after heavy rainfall on steep slopes there may be gully erosion.

Before considering the geographical distribution of collected produce and crops, it is convenient to make a rough classification. First in fame and in daily significance are the oily fruits, especially the oil palm, but also the coconut, sheanut and benniseed. Then there are the cereals— rice, maize, guinea corn, millet and minor cereals. Roots are important in forest areas, especially cassava and yams. Lesser roots are cocoyams, sweet potato, ginger and tiger 'nuts'. Edible fruits are numerous, such as the tree fruits—mango, papaw, orange, lime, grapefruit, banana, plantain and pineapple; in Guinea and especially in the Ivory Coast fruits are grown commercially on a large scale, and on a much smaller but increasing scale in Ghana and Nigeria. The tree fruits of cocoa and coffee have an indirect use and are very important cash crops. Another large group are the legumes, especially the so-called ground-'nut' (used as an oil seed), peas and beans. There are many vegetables, such as onions, shallots, okro, African spinach, peppers, chillies, tomatoes, cucumbers, gourds, pumpkins, melons, aubergines, etc. Other significant products are rubber, sugar cane and tobacco.

# Main crops

Zones may be distinguished within which certain crops are characteristic and common. These reflect climatic differences, whilst edaphic, sociological and economic factors are also significant. This is especially so locally, where the zonal pattern may be modified. Rice is well suited to the monsoonal rains of the southwest coast, and certain other crops such as rubber and bananas do well. Most tubers, maize, and trees such as the oil palm, cocoa, coffee and kola are grown where conditions are most equatorial. By contrast, cereals (except maize) and groundnuts are grown where there is a considerable dry season. Some crops, such as cassava, are tolerant of different conditions and are widely grown, though not everywhere successfully so.

## The southwestern rice and tree crops zone

In Casamance (southern Senegal), Portuguese Guinea, Guinea, Sierra Leone, Liberia and the Ivory Coast west of the Bandama River (except for Tabou District), the dominant food crop is generally rice, as it also is of the floodplains of major rivers in the savannas.

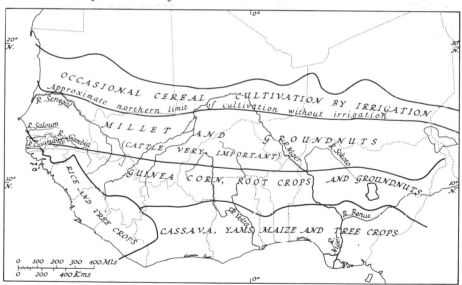

FIG. 6.1. Approximate and generalised crop belts

RICE is much appreciated in West Africa and its cultivation is extending rapidly, in this zone and elsewhere. Rice is a high yielder, the taste is much liked, it keeps well, and may readily be transported for sale far away. It is extremely easy to prepare and cook, compared with most African foods. But cultivation of this crop requires care and skill, so that often it is the more alert peoples who produce it. Thus in Senegal the Serer grow it successfully, but the Wolof generally do not.

Before 1939 large quantities of rice were imported into West Africa from Burma, Malaya and Indo-China. After the war rice could not be imported from those countries, yet demand for it increased because of higher standards of living, increased urbanisation, and because many Africans developed the taste for rice while serving with armies in Asia. Rice cultivation had to be increased in West Africa and, so long as it is grown on flat land, is a good crop to grow. It will tolerate compact and acidic soils, will grow in otherwise useless swamps and, as it needs little or no fallow, it does not upset farming routine, as would the introduction of another tuber crop.

One species, *Oryza glaberrima,* a 'red rice', may have been grown in Africa for some 3 500 years. It probably originated in the Inland Niger Delta or Upper Senegal, whence it was taken to the southwest coasts, via the Gambia and Casamance rivers. This rice as well as *O. sativa* are often grown 'dry' on hillsides, and in light soils wherever the rainfall is at least 900 m (35 in) in the growing season. Dry rice is inter-cropped or grown in rotation with cassava, cotton, guinea corn, millet and maize.

Swamp rices are being increasingly cultivated in former mangrove swamps of the Gambia, Portuguese Guinea, Guinea, and Sierra Leone; swamp rices are also grown in inland swamps, in river flood plains and in the southwest corner of Ghana. In many of these areas, technical aid is provided by Chinese experts. As inland and coastal swamps are being planted for rice, so dry upland rice cultivation should be reduced, to lessen soil erosion. However, some experts think it would also help to distribute improved upland rice seed, so increasing yields and enabling a reduction of areas planted. The greatest problem is that most West African countries must still import large and increasing amounts of this basic cereal.

TABLE 6.1. *West African rice production*

| | Area in thousand hectares | Thousands of metric tons Paddy |
|---|---|---|
| | 1970 | 1970 |
| Gambia | 32 | 35 |
| Guinea | 265 | 350 |
| Ivory Coast | 290 | 395 |
| Mali | 165 | 90 |
| Niger | 15 | 30 |
| Nigeria | 250 | 400 |
| Senegal | 90 | 120 |
| Sierra Leone | 315 | 425 |

Source: *Production Yearbook,* 1971, vol. 25, FAO, Rome, 1971

PLATE 4. Swamp rice in a former mangrove swamp, Jenoi, Gambia. A strip of mangrove has been left along the river on the right for flood control. Rice is growing on the left

A substitute for rice is *Digitaria exilis,* known as 'hungry rice', 'acha grass' (Hausa) or 'fundi' (Temne, Sierra Leone). It is grown in uplands above about 760 m (2 500 ft) and is extremely tolerant of rainfall, as well as of variety and depth of soil. It is much grown on the Jos Plateau, in Bornu and in the Fouta Djallon, as is another variety, *Digitaria iburu*.

CITRUS FRUITS are best grown in upland areas of this zone, where the relative humidity is high, and in areas of high rainfall near the coast in the cassava, yams, maize and tree crops zone.

Sweet orange (*Citrus sinensis*) grows well on the edge of the forest but away from the sea where soils are not sandy. These oranges often remain green when ripe, an impediment to their export, except as juice. The skins have a high oil content, and some is extracted in Guinea near Kindia, Mamou and Labé. A better oil is extracted from the bitter orange (*Citrus aurantium*), which is grown on plantations near Labé.

Limes (*Citrus aurantifolia*) grow in the same conditions as oranges, but at lower altitudes. They are much grown near Cape Coast (Ghana).

Lemons (*Citrus limon*) and grape fruit are grown on plantations in Guinea and especially the Ivory Coast for export.

RUBBER is important in Liberia in this zone and, like citrus fruits, in the adjacent zone to the east. Indeed, more is normally produced in Nigeria than in Liberia, and so this crop is discussed on p. 115.

### The cassava, yams, maize and tree crops zone

This zone includes areas of former or actual rainforest with over 1 150 mm (45 in) of rainfall annually, and occupies the coastlands of the Gulf of Guinea.

Forest is periodically cut and burnt to provide plots for growing

PLATE 5. Cassava (Manioc)

PLATE 6. Cassava tubers

cassava, yams and cocoyams; beans and peas, okro, tomatoes, chillies, fluted pumpkins and other vegetables; fruits such as plantains, bananas and pineapples; sugar cane and tobacco; and cereals such as maize and rice. Useful trees, which are generally planted and safeguarded, are the oil and coconut palms, the kola, papaw, breadfruit, avocado pear, citrus fruits, etc. Some of these are also export crops, cocoa, rubber, coffee and ginger almost exclusively so. Other valuable products are piassava and raphia (see pp. 314–5).

CASSAVA or MANIOC (*Manihot utilissima* or *esculenta*) is a native of South America. It has many varieties, varying in their content of prussic acid; those which tend to have little are sometimes classed as 'sweet', those with more as 'bitter'.

This tuber withstands considerable drought, is unaffected by migratory locusts and, if left in the ground after ripening, is not attacked by insects. Though it does best in well-drained loams, it will grow on almost any soil. For this reason and because it exhausts the soil, it is normally the last crop in a rotation. Extensive cultivation of cassava near towns (e.g. Accra) has exhausted great areas, and it suffers widely from a virus disease known as leaf mosaic.

Cassava prefers a moderate annual rainfall of 760–1 015 mm (30–40 in), so that tubers are produced rather than too many leaves. Thus it is often grown under the shade of trees in areas of heavier rainfall. It thrives especially in southeast Ghana, southern Togo (where there is usually an exportable surplus of flour and tapioca), southern Dahomey and Nigeria, where it is spreading in the north.

Cassava is a perennial which grows to about 1·8 m (6 ft) and produces clusters of long, rather narrow tubers. These are peeled, soaked or boiled to remove the prussic acid, and then pounded and made into a kind of dumpling ('fufu'), which takes the place of bread or potatoes. The tuber can also be boiled or fried (after initial peeling or soaking), or dried and later grated into flour. The moist pulp may be warmed slowly to produce 'gari' meal. Starch is also made, and if this is dropped on to heated plates tapioca is produced.[2]

YAMS. The Yam is a fundamental food in the Guinea Coast countries especially in the 'Middle Belt' or southern Guinea savanna. Of the many edible types, some are indigenous (the white and yellow), but others have been introduced, probably by the Portuguese from Asia. Like cassava, it is a tuber, though larger and with a better flavour. Because of this and its greater weight, the need for rich loamy soils, intolerance of shade and consequently more restricted cultivation, it commands a higher price. Thus it is more of a luxury than cassava, and is the subject of much commerce. Yams are generally the first crop in a rotation, as they require much nitrogen and potash.[3]

Holes up to 0·6 m (2 ft) deep and wide are dug and manured, and

PLATE 7. Yam mounds near Tamale, Ghana. Each mound is protected by a stone to reduce soil erosion. The sides of the mounds are often planted with quick maturing vegetables

PLATE 8. Yam vines around poles in eastern Nigeria

102

separate mounds or continuous ridges are then generally made at least 1 m (3·3 ft) in height. The seed-yams are pushed into the hills at ground level, which are then capped by dried grass and soil or stones. Moisture is thereby retained, temperatures are more even, a mulch is available for the growing vine and erosion is prevented. Maize and upland rice are often sown between the mounds, and women generally raise vegetables on them. Yam vines are trained along a pole, or dried stalks.[4]

The white yam (*Dioscorea rotundata*) and the yellow yam (*D. cayenensis*) produce long tubers and prefer drier areas. The water yam (*D. alata*) is spherical, larger, originates from Southeast Asia, prefers wetter places and will grow on poorer soils. This water yam is softer, exudes water when cut, does not keep well, and is inferior in taste.

The Chinese yam (*D. esculenta*) produces many small tubers and, like the water yam, thrives in wetter areas, where rainfall exceeds about 1 800 mm (70 in) per annum, humidity is constantly high, and dry months few. There are other lesser varieties.

MAIZE or CORN (*Zea mays*), of disputed introduction, is—outside the rice areas—the chief cereal of forest and savanna lands with 750–1 500 mm (30–60 in) annual rainfall. It does best on sandy loam or loamy soils rich in humus; like the yam and sweet potato, it dislikes shade. Two harvests can be secured where there are two rainy seasons, and it is often the first food crop to be harvested.

OIL PALM (*Elaeis guineensis*)[5] is indigenous to the swampy parts of West African forests and occurs as far south as those of the Congo. The densest stands are not necessarily where the climatic and soil conditions are most favourable, but where population is or was considerable, and where there have long been contacts with Europeans. Thus, there are many oil palms in southeastern Sierra Leone but fewer in Liberia; more originally (before cocoa became more profitable) in the Ivory Coast and in Ghana; in Dahomey (planted by prisoners when their disposal as slaves had become impossible); and west and especially east of the Niger and its delta, which, like the Congo, was long visited by slave ships.

The oil palm is not common in high forest but, when the forest is disturbed and habitations are built, the oil palm follows. The connection with man is reinforced, as it is the source of West Africa's best vegetable oil, used in cooking, for illumination, in the making of soap, and in many other ways in everyday African life. Palm kernels and oil are also important exports from Nigeria and Dahomey.

Palm plantations around Abomey in Dahomey were planted at the suggestion of the slave traders looking for new articles of commerce. Later European-owned plantations were few, having been forbidden (except for experimentation) in the British colonies. Being less remunerative than cocoa, coffee or banana cultivation, oil palm plantations were

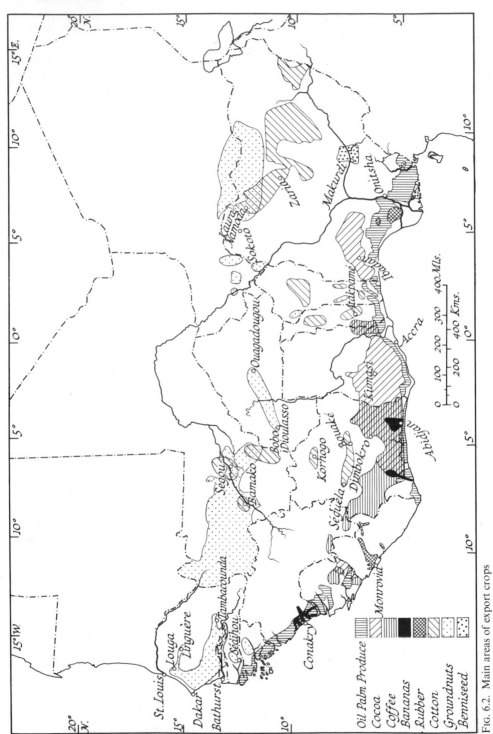

Fig. 6.2. Main areas of export crops

Oil Palm Produce
Cocoa
Coffee
Bananas
Rubber
Cotton
Groundnuts
Benniseed

also few in non-British territories. However, quite a number of plantations have been established since about 1950 as a means of agricultural diversification.

The oil palm ideally requires a minimum rainfall of 2 000 mm (79 in) distributed over at least eight months of the year, but it can survive with as little as 1 300 mm (51 in) if that amount is evenly distributed. Thus it reacts badly to a pronounced dry season. It also needs much sunlight.

In its soil requirements, however, the oil palm is more tolerant; the dense stands in the East-Central and Mid-Western states of Nigeria demonstrate that it will grow on sandy soils where cocoa does not flourish. Nevertheless, it grows much better on moist, deep rich loamy or alluvial soils.

Generally, palms are planted near roads or compounds and are given little or no attention. Tapping for palm wine (the sap) reduces bunch yields. For this and other reasons detailed below, the quality of the semi-wild palm is rather poor.

By contrast, that from plantations in West Africa, Zaïre, Malaya and Sumatra is superior. Yields of fruit per acre are many times higher, the amount of oil in the fruit is also much greater, more of this increased amount of available oil is extracted, and its quality is superior, as it contains less free fatty acid (a noxious ingredient resulting from fermentation of overripe fruit). The superior oil can be used in margarine and tinplate manufacture, and yields more glycerine when used for soap. The poorer oil is used in making soap, paint, candles, and as a lubricant.

In 1900 Nigeria produced almost all the world supply of palm oil, which then represented 88 per cent of her exports. In 1938 it represented 10 per cent of her exports and her plantation rivals exported much more. During and after the Second World War production in Malaya and Indonesia fell away, but Nigerian output increased in quantity and improved in quality. However, Nigeria later fell behind Malaysia and Indonesia, even before the Biafra War.

Exports from the Congo began in 1915, from Sumatra in 1919 and from Malaya in 1926. From Southeast Asia both oil and kernels are available, since less oil is used locally. (Asian kernels are so small, however, that they were but little used until after 1945.) In West Africa only the thinly populated areas are able to export both oil and kernels, the heavily populated areas having only a surplus of kernels.

Because of the spontaneous growth of palms and their struggle for light in West Africa, they grow taller than in Asian plantations, often reaching 18 m (60 ft). The palm bears fruit only after a longer period. The tree has to be climbed, a skilled, distasteful and dangerous task. The fruits are orange-red, tinged with black, and are produced in clusters weighing some 23 kg (50 lb). Two to twelve clusters are produced each year, according to the age of the palm. The weight of each bunch increases up to the eighth year of the tree. Beneath the skin of the fruit

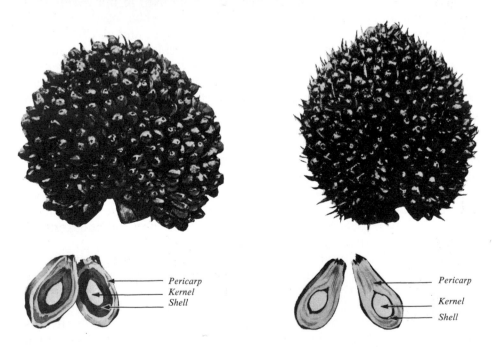

| | | | | | |
|---|---|---|---|---|---|
| | Pericarp | | | Pericarp | |
| | Kernel | | | Kernel | |
| | Shell | | | Shell | |

PLATE 10. Bunches of oil palm fruit. African grown palm fruit (left) usually has a thin mesocarp and thick kernel shell. Plantation fruit (right) has a thicker mesocarp and the kernel is thin shelled

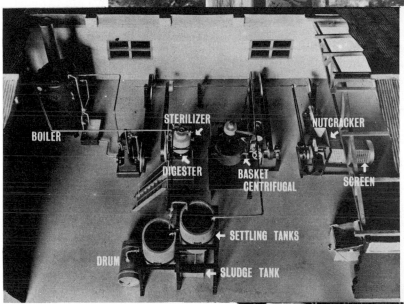

Plate 11. An oil palm hand-press

Plate 12. Model of early small 'Pioneer' palm oil mill

Plate 13. Interior of larger factory-type palm oil mill

is the fibrous mesocarp, which yields palm (mesocarp) oil. Unfortunately, this mesocarp is often thin in West African palms.

Africans extract the oil by boiling, pounding, reheating and skimming in the 'soft oil' process. This is tedious and yields 55 per cent of the total oil, which is of average free fatty acid content. Alternatively, men generally ferment the fruit, trample it, pour boiling water over it, and skim off the oil. This 'hard oil' process (it produces oil which melts at a higher temperature) is quicker, yields 65 per cent of the oil, but this has a high free fatty acid content. It is the more common process where water is available. When the oil is extracted, the nuts are the women's perquisite. They crack them and sell the kernels.

A hand press can extract up to 65 per cent of the oil, which may have less than 2 per cent f.f.a. if the fruit is fresh. A later hydraulic hand press can extract up to 80 per cent of the oil. The machines are expensive for poor farmers but save time and are difficult for women to work.

Another improved method of oil extraction is in small 'Pioneer' mills, which extract up to 85 per cent of good oil from fresh fruit, and which may crack or return the nuts to the women. The much larger factory mills established on plantations, not only extract 90 per cent or more of the oil, but extract the kernel oil as well. Pioneer mills were numerous in Nigeria in the 1950s and early 1960s. There are a few large factory mills, usually associated with plantations, in the Ivory Coast, Togo, Dahomey and Nigeria, but difficulties are experienced by pioneer and even large mills in getting fresh fruit. It is sometimes said that the bulk of the world's palm oil must come from plantations and large factory mills, but small mills and hand presses can give good oil. With improvements in the oil palms, the regularity of fruit supplies, and improvements in oil extraction, the West African peasant should be able to supply a product acceptable to the world market, and at lower prices than the plantation and factory mill product. On the other hand the pre-requisites have often not been fulfilled, while rising populations and improved standards of living have caused greater local demands for oil.

Palm kernels are milled commercially in Europe or America and, until 1939, practically exclusively so. They contain half their weight in oil, which is used in making margarine, cooking oils, soap, toilet creams, glycerine and paints. The pulp residue is combined with sweeter materials to make an excellent cattle-food. In Africa, kernel oil for domestic needs is traditionally obtained either by roasting or soaking the kernels, and then pounding and soaking them in warm water. There are some kernel oil mills in West Africa. The oil is used as skin or hair oil, and as cooking fat.

At the several national and regional oil palm research stations, valuable work is being done in improving cultivation of the oil palm and in selecting and distributing better palms. Use is being made of improved

Asian material as well as of high yielding local palms. But with few plantations in West Africa, it is difficult to diffuse improved varieties rapidly. The cutting out of poor palms and replanting have not been very successful, because of the prejudice of chiefs who dislike the spread of private ownership of the land, which such planting involves.

TABLE 6.2. *Palm oil—exports from principal countries and areas*

| Country | Hundred metric tons | | | | Percentages | | | |
|---|---|---|---|---|---|---|---|---|
| | 1909–13 | 1924–28 | 1934–38 | 1968 | 1909–13 | 1924–28 | 1934–38 | 1968 |
| Nigeria | 819 | 1 281 | 1 370 | 34* | 67·7 | 59·5 | 29·7 | 0·5* |
| Ex-Fr. W. Africa | 192 | 241 | 212 | 105 | 15·9 | 11·2 | 4·6 | 1·4 |
| Zaïre | 21 | 192 | 603 | 1 588 | 1·7 | 8·9 | 13·1 | 21·4 |
| Others | 178 | 173 | 250 | 250 | 14·7 | 8·1 | 5·4 | 3·4 |
| Total Africa | 1 210 | 1 887 | 2 435 | 1 977 | 100·0 | 87·7 | 52·8 | 26·7 |
| Indonesia | — | 253 | 1 709 | 1 419 | — | 11·8 | 37·1 | 19·1 |
| Malaysia | — | 13 | 341 | 2 856 | — | 0·6 | 7·4 | 38·5 |
| Total Asia | — | 266 | 2 050 | 5 192 | — | 12·4 | 44·4 | 70·1 |
| Grand Total | 1 210 | 2 152 | 4 612 | 7 410 | 100 | 100 | 100 | 100 |

TABLE 6.3. *Palm kernels—exports from principal countries and areas*

| Country | Hundred metric tons | | | | Percentages | | | |
|---|---|---|---|---|---|---|---|---|
| | 1909–13 | 1924–28 | 1934–38 | 1968 | 1909–13 | 1924 28 | 1934–38 | 1968 |
| Nigeria | 1 763 | 2 491 | 3 329 | 1 616* | 53·8 | 46·3 | 45·5 | 38·5 |
| Ex-Fr. W. Africa | 523 | 700 | 815 | 318 | 16·0 | 13·0 | 11·1 | 7·6 |
| Sierra Leone | 465 | 654 | 755 | 653 | 14·2 | 12·2 | 10·3 | 15·6 |
| Zaïre | 65 | 677 | 782 | 22 | 2·0 | 12·6 | 10·7 | 0·5 |
| Others | 458 | 824 | 1 019 | 749 | 14·0 | 15·3 | 14·0 | 17·8 |
| Total Africa | 3 274 | 5 346 | 6 700 | 3 358 | 100·0 | 99·5 | 91·5 | 80·0 |
| Indonesia | — | 29 | 363 | 354 | — | 0·5 | 5·0 | 8·4 |
| Malaysia | — | — | 58 | 466 | — | — | 0·8 | 11·1 |
| Total Asia | — | 29 | 421 | 821 | — | 0·5 | 5·7 | 19·5 |
| Grand total | 3 274 | 5 375 | 7 320 | 4 195 | 100 | 100 | 100 | 100 |

Sources for Tables 6.2 and 6.3: Early figures from C. Leubuscher, *The Processing of Copra, Oil Palm Products and Groundnuts*, 1949, H.M.S.O., and for 1968 from *Trade Yearbook*, 1969, Vol. 23, F.A.O., Rome, 1970.

*Abnormally low figures because of the Nigerian Civil War, 1967–70.

COCOA[6] (*Theobroma cacao*) is perhaps the most famous and valuable crop of West Africa, being grown almost entirely for export. Indeed, West Africa produces three-quarters of the world's cocoa. Cocoa accounts

PLATE 14. Ghana cocoa farm

for about two-thirds by value of the exports of Ghana, and for significant percentages of those of the Ivory Coast, Togo and Nigeria.

The tree is indigenous to the Amazon basin, the name being an Aztec one. Cocoa was introduced by the Portuguese to the island of São Tomé in 1822, and unsuccessful attempts were made to grow it in the Gold Coast early in the nineteenth century. But in 1879 it was reintroduced by Tetteh Quashie of Mampong (Akwapim), who, on returning from the Fernando Po plantations, took back six beans to his village. The plant was also taken to Nigeria, and from there the first export from the mainland took place in 1885; the first from the Gold Coast was in 1891.

In Ghana and Nigeria most cocoa is grown on African farms averaging about 0·5 hectare (1·25 acres). This is also the case in he small cocoa area of Sierra Leone (developed since 1938), east-southeast of Kenema, and in Togo. But in the Ivory Coast there are some expatriate plantations in the centre and west. Non-African plantations are also found in north-central Liberia. Since independence some plantations have been developed by government bodies in Nigeria.

Cocoa requires deep soils of heavy loam or light clay, rich in potash, and especially those derived from granites, diorites, schists and gneiss. It will not grow on light sandy soils, so that it fails on such soils in eastern Nigeria, although the rainfall is adequate. Undulating country,

110

like that of southern Ashanti, gives the best drainage.

Cocoa cannot withstand drying winds, so that it must be protected from the desiccating Harmattan. It also requires a gradually developing, long and steady wet season of at least nine months, and an annual rainfall preferably of around 1 500 mm (60 in) per annum. It is grown in shaded clearings of the denser forest, as in Ghana; or in close plantings to make its own shade, as in parts of Nigeria. This keeps the soil moist, provides leaf enrichment, reduces erosion and, above all, protects the shallow roots. The rainfall of Western Nigeria is only just sufficient for cocoa, and the short but pronounced dry season is bad for it, e.g. Ibadan 36 mm (1·4 in) from December to February. In Sierra Leone and Liberia the dry season is also a problem and the rainy season develops too fast and brings rain even into the harvesting months of August and September.

The tree begins bearing economically in the fifth to seventh years and reaches maximum yields when about twenty-five years old. A main crop is secured between October and March, and a minor one from May to August. Large yellow, red or brown pods, each up to about 250 mm (10 in) long, are formed on short stalks hanging mainly from the trunk. These pods are opened, and the 30 to 40 white beans with adhering sticky pulp are then fermented and dried to their chocolate colour, the pulp then being removed.

The United States is the largest market. To eliminate excessive numbers of middlemen, there are marketing boards in most countries, which buy at a rather low fixed price and, with accumulated profits, keep funds to stabilise the income of farmers when prices fall, and to aid cocoa research, education and general development.

Despite the great place of West Africa, and especially of Ghana, in the world cocoa trade, the cultivation of the tree is beset with many problems. Soils are somewhat exhausted in southeastern Ghana and in the former cocoa area south of Abeokuta (Nigeria). Farmers have taken to cocoa cultivation so wholeheartedly that they have often neglected to grow valuable food crops. Food is imported at needlessly high prices and rural indebtedness is often a problem.[7] The attraction of the cocoa areas in Ghana and the Ivory Coast is seen in the yearly movement of the virus disease of Swollen Shoot, the fungus disease of Black Pod, Upper Volta.

Cocoa is a delicate plant and easily degenerates. Severe threats are the virus disease of Swollen Shoot, the fungus disease of Black Pod, and the attacks of capsid insects. It is an unpleasant fact that cocoa has been subject to severe diseases or pests in one producing country after another.

'Swollen Shoot' is a virus disease of which the cocoa tree, the silk cotton tree (*Ceiba pentandra*), and the wild kola (*Cola chlamydantha*) and other trees are hosts. The virus is carried by the mealy bug

TABLE 6.4. Exports of cocoa beans from main producing countries or areas

| Country | Metric tons | | | | | | Percentages of total cocoa exports | | | | | |
|---|---|---|---|---|---|---|---|---|---|---|---|---|
| | 1898 | 1908 | 1918 | 1928 | 1938 | 1968 | 1898 | 1908 | 1918 | 1928 | 1938 | 1968 |
| Ghana | 188 | 12 946 | 67 404 | 223 339 | 261 557 | 335 280 | 0·2 | 6·7 | 24·6 | 43·5 | 37·0 | 31·6 |
| Nigeria | 35 | 1 388 | 10 383 | 49 950 | 97 542 | 208 880 | 0·0 | 0·7 | 3·8 | 9·7 | 13·8 | 19·7 |
| Ivory Coast | — | 3 | 420 | 14 515 | 52 719 | 121 470 | — | 0·0 | 0·2 | 2·8 | 7·5 | 11·4 |
| Togo | — | 84 | 1 576 | 6 317 | 7 628 | 14 340 | — | 0·0 | 0·6 | 1·2 | 1·0 | 1·4 |
| São Tomé and Príncipe | 9 945 | 28 560 | 17 332 | 14 638 | 12 729 | 11 090 | 11·5 | 14·8 | 6·3 | 2·9 | 1·8 | 1·0 |
| Fernando Po and Rio Muni | 800 | 2 267 | 4 220 | 8 664 | 12 212 | 39 670 | 0·9 | 1·2 | 1·6 | 1·7 | 1·7 | 3·7 |
| Cameroon and Rest of Africa | 311 | 3 181 | 3 699 | 8 478 | 24 965 | 83 540 | 0·4 | 1·7 | 1·2 | 1·4 | 3·6 | 7·9 |
| Africa | 11 279 | 48 429 | 105 034 | 325 901 | 469 352 | 814 270 | 13·0 | 25·1 | 38·3 | 63·2 | 66·4 | 76·7 |
| Central and S. America and W. Indies | 72 070 | 138 600 | 162 792 | 181 264 | 229 450 | 54 320 | 83·2 | 72·1 | 59·4 | 35·4 | 32·5 | 5·1 |
| Asia and Pacific | 3 451 | 5 468 | 6 374 | 7 234 | 8 094 | 32 770 | 3·8 | 2·8 | 2·3 | 1·4 | 1·1 | 3·1 |
| Grand total | 86 800 | 192 497 | 274 200 | 514 399 | 706 896 | 1 061 380 | 100 | 100 | 100 | 100 | 100 | 100 |

Sources: Early figures from *Gordian*, April 25, 1939, and for 1968 from *Trade Yearbook 1969*, Vol. 23, F.A.O., Rome 1970.

The diminishing proportion occupied by Central and South American and West Indies supplies is striking, though Brazilian production has maintained its proportion. Within West Africa, the decline of São Tomé is striking, as is the meteoric rise of Ghana.

PLATE 15. Typical swellings produced by Swollen Shoot virus

PLATE 16. Normal pod (left); Swollen Shoot (right), which is also mottled and smaller

(*Pseudococcus spp.*). This is protected by the Crematogaster ant, which feeds on the honeydew secretion of the mealy bug. No cure has been found for this insidious disease, which kills cocoa trees slowly but surely. Each year the harvest is poorer, the pods more rounded and smaller, young shoots become swollen and the leaves mottled. If the disease were left unchecked, cocoa might be exterminated in Ghana. The only checks are the cutting out of infected trees, or the spreading around the roots of a poison, which, when absorbed by the tree, is transmitted to the mealy bug when it sucks the sap. The disadvantages of the first method are its cost, and the natural unwillingness of farmers to see such a method applied to trees which, though diseased and bearing ever smaller harvests, are still alive. The disadvantage of applying poison is that it is impossible to grow food crops nearby, or to keep animals, and it is not certain that the poison may not affect the cocoa bean. What is desperately needed is a simple cure for Swollen Shoot, rather than difficult methods of controlling its spread. Although Swollen Shoot is serious, Black Pod and capsids are more widespread, and are often even greater menaces.

COFFEE is indigenous to Africa and has many varieties, each with different climatic or altitude requirements. Like cocoa, it needs a fertile, well-drained, undulating yet sheltered environment. Compared, however, with cocoa, coffee requires lighter soils and matures more rapidly. It grows in the Rain Forest zone to about 8°N, where these conditions are fulfilled, and where there are roads.

*Arabica,* which originated in Ethiopia, is the best quality. It must be grown at about 600 m (2 000 ft) or over, which limits it to the Cameroon and Guinea Highlands, especially the N'Zérékoré area. *Stenophylla* grows wild, and is also cultivated in Sierra Leone east of Kenema, and in the *arabica* regions just mentioned. *Liberica* is indigenous to Liberia, is hardy and widely grown, but poorer in quality. *Gros indénié* is indigenous

113

to the Ivory Coast, where it is grown especially in the westcentre. *Excelsa* and *Canephora* (with its varieties of *robusta, kouilou* and *petit indénié*), indigenous to Central Africa, are of superior quality to *liberica,* and mature early. *Robusta* is extending rapidly in the Ivory Coast, as *kouilou* and *indénié* are much afflicted with disease.

Coffee requires machinery for proper preparation, so that African farmers may need financial help or cooperatives, if they are to succeed. Alternatively, coffee is well suited to larger plantations.

The Ivory Coast is the third or fourth world producer, and coffee is its greatest export by value, as it was in Guinea in the last years of French rule. Small producers are Sierra Leone, Liberia and Togo. Ex-French lands had a protected market in France until 1964.

KOLA (*Cola acuminata, Cola nitida,* etc.). The second species of kola, indigenous to Ashanti, the Ivory Coast and Sierra Leone, but also cultivated extensively in Nigeria, is the chief kola of trade and is of great traditional or social significance. The first species is native to Nigeria, Gabon and the Congo Basin, but is less cultivated. The trees grow to a height of about 15 m (50 ft) and do not bear a useful crop until they are about ten years old.

Kola has been cultivated in West Africa for a very long time, and trade in its nuts was widespread even before the arrival of Islam. It was almost certainly this trade (as well as that in salt, slaves and gold) which occupied merchants of the Mali Empire in the thirteenth century, and which led to the foundation of colonies of Dioula (Dan) peoples in Guinea, Liberia and the Ivory Coast. Indeed, Beyla in Guinea was founded by Dioula in 1230, as a centre for the slave and kola nut trades.[8]

Within the areas of at least 1 300 mm (50 in) rainfall and of the rain-forest, the main producing districts are the coast lands and southeastern

PLATE 17. Kola nuts

interior of Guinea (Kissi country); southcentral Sierra Leone; the northern fringes of the Ivory Coast between 6°30′ and 7°30′N; southern Ashanti; southern Dahomey, especially around Adjara and Domé; and the Agege–Abeokuta–Benin belt of Nigeria. In several areas (e.g. in the Abeokuta area) it has taken the place of cocoa, because the soil proved insufficiently good to support that crop.

The green, wrinkled pods contain about six to ten nuts, claret, pink or white. The latter colours are rarer but more valued for their sweeter taste, colour and higher caffeine content. Although produced in the forest zone, the nuts are mostly consumed in savanna lands by Muslims. The nuts contain caffeine, kolatine and theobromine, and have a very astringent taste. The effect of chewing them is somewhat similar to that of drinking coffee or tea; namely, a stimulating or sustaining effect. They are often chewed by those doing heavy manual work or on long marches. The white nuts are a symbol of friendship, but the red ones may be emblems of enmity. Kola nuts also have religious (white nuts only) and legal significance. Many Africans consume some 700 nuts per year, or about 10 kg (22 lb). A red dye can be made from the red nuts.

RUBBER exports from indigenous trees such as *Funtumia elastica*, and from vines such as *Landolphia heudelotii* and *L. owariensis,* were important from rainforests up to and during the First World War. The development of plantations of *Hevea brasiliensis* in Southeast Asia practically killed West African wild rubber exports, except during the Second World War. *Heva brasiliensis* was little grown in West Africa until the Firestone Rubber Company began planting in Liberia. Their success has been due to he high rainfall (average 3 300 mm: 130 in), rational methods and high capital investment. In the 'forties rubber accounted for up to 96·6 per cent by value of Liberian exports, but iron ore is now far more important. There are other plantations and also smaller producers in Liberia, as well as in the Ivory Coast, Ghana and the Mid-Western and South-Eastern states of Nigeria. Indeed, Nigeria normally produces more rubber than Liberia.

COCONUT (*Cocus nucifera*) must have sandy or very well drained loamy soils with, preferably, about 1 800 mm (70 in) annual rain, or equivalent irrigation, and high relative humidity. It is a typical sight on coasts, and there are plantations in Togo and Dahomey. Copra is produced and the leaves are used as thatching material but many trees are diseased. Elsewhere, coconuts have only local significance as a food crop, though their cultivation could be extended along the Ivory Coast, Ghana and the southwestern Nigerian coasts.

PLANTAIN (*Musa paradisiaca*) is another important foodstuff brought from Asia at an early date. It is taller than the banana plant, and the fruit is longer, straighter and more outspread.

The green fruit is roasted, boiled or fried in oil. It may also be sliced, dried and then ground into meal or flour. The skins are burned and the ashes mixed with palm oil to make soap. Fibre from the stalk is used for scouring pots, and as a sponge.

BANANAS were more systematically grown in Guinea and the Ivory Coast than in the ex-British countries, because the French permitted non-African plantations and provided a large market at high prices. Yet on climatic grounds Sierra Leone and, to a lesser extent, Ghana and Nigeria offer possibilities for the crop, if plantations could be established and run efficiently. Banana boats would have to be induced to call, and these countries would have to compete with the Caribbean and Canary Islands.

Bananas are often grown in valleys, or round the sides of swamps (thus bananas are often seen near rice), especially where the dry season is pronounced, as in Guinea. There they are grown on small cooperative plantations and smaller private African ones; the most successful are nearest the coast. The first variety grown was akin to the Canary banana. Small, sweet and fragile, it required wrapping for export, but was suited to mediocre soils, and had a fine flavour. The *Gros Michel* variety, introduced from Jamaica to Sierra Leone and Western Cameroon when under United Kingdom Trusteeship and the *Cavendish* or *Poyo* variety used in the Ivory Coast since 1956, require richer soils (or more fertilisers), but produce larger and less fragile fruit, and more of it.

Bananas and plantains require deep, rich, loamy soils and 1 000–2 550 mm (39–100 in) annual rainfall, or irrigation. Because of their fragility, bananas are grown for export near good communications, e.g. on the fairly rich soils of the central Ivory Coast (especially near Abidjan and Agboville on the railway), in valleys near Kindia and Mamou in the Fouta Djallon of Guinea and on its coast near Forécariah and Benty. Outside these areas, bananas are grown for everyday food and to shield coconut, oil palm, cocoa or coffee seedlings.

COCOYAM (*Colocasia esculenta*), indigenous to South Pacific islands, was formerly much grown in the wettest forest areas, e.g. in the Ivory Coast and in eastern Nigeria. An improved cocoyam (*Xanthosoma sagittifolium*), or 'tannia', was introduced to the Gold Coast in 1843 from the West Indies, and is now much commoner there and elsewhere than the other species.

Cocoyams grow easily, and provide shade and conserve dampness for cocoa seedlings. The corm, or underground stem, is round with lesser cormels around it. These are prepared like cassava, and the leaves and stalks are also eaten.

PINEAPPLE (*Ananas comosus*), from Central America, has many varieties and prefers sandy loam soil of low elevation, preferably near the sea and with moderate rainfall. Modest exports are carried on from Guinea and Ivory Coast plantations, where there is some canning of juice and fruit.

SUGAR CANE (*Saccharum officinarum*) is being increasingly grown in riverine soils on estates using irrigation at Bacita near Jebba (Nigeria), Tillabéri (Niger), Komenda and Winneba (Ghana). Sugar has been added for diversification on the otherwise all-rice lands at Richard-Toll (Senegal) and on the mainly rice and cotton lands of the Inland Niger delta in Mali. Like cotton, sugar provides raw materials for local industry, whose finished products also save foreign exchange.

TOBACCO (*Nicotiana tabacum*) is widely grown around compounds. American tobacco is grown in the southcentral Ivory Coast, Ghana and especially in Nigeria for cigarette manufacture in these and other countries.

OKRO or GOMBO (*Hibiscus esculentus*) is indigenous to West Africa and is much grown, the fruit and leaves being used as vegetables. It does well even in sand. Sorrel (*H. sabdariffa*) is grown for its leaves, fibre and oil from the seeds. Kenaf (*H. cannabinus*), indigenous to India, provides rope and material for bags, and the leaves are eaten.

PUMPKINS. Fluted pumpkin (*Telfairia occidentalis*) is often inter-cropped, like Okro, with yams and beans. The shoots, leaves and seeds are edible. The Edible Pumpkin (*Cucurbita pepo*) and small tomatoes are widespread.

BEANS. Lima or butter beans (*Phaseolus lunatus*) are important in humid areas. Haricot beans are extensively grown in the ex-French lands, especially Dahomey. Yam bean (*Sphenostylis stenocarpa*), so called because it has a tuber, is much grown in Ibo country, Benin and southern Ashanti, wherever there is at least 900 mm (35 in) annual rain. Most of the peas and beans listed in the Guinea Corn Zone are also grown.

### The Guinea corn, root crops and groundnut zone

This corresponds roughly with the Guinea savanna. Other important crops are millet,[9] oil seeds and nuts, sweet potatoes and cotton. The main source of vegetable oil is the shea butter tree. Fruits, other than the mango and cucurbits, are few. Almost the same vegetables are grown as in the forest. For millet and groundnuts, see next zone, and for root crops, the previous one.

This is the most southerly zone in which cattle are numerous. They may be the small resistant breeds, the large non-resistant Zebu type, or crosses of these.

GUINEA CORN, GIANT MILLET or SORGHUM[9] has many varieties and its origin is uncertain, but is Ethiopian according to Sauer, and West

African according to Porteres[10]. Some regard it as the most important cereal in West Africa.

The Grass and Sweet Sorghums are used for fodder, but Grain Sorghums are grown for man and animals. The most important of these are 'Durra' (*Sorghum durra*), 'Maskwari' (Fulani name) or 'Mazakwa' (Hausa name) which is *S. cernuum,* and true Guinea Corn (*S. guineense*). All are grown where it is too dry for maize or unirrigated rice, and either where there is an annual rainfall, ideally, of 815–1 015 mm (32–40 in), or where there are annual floods and the crop can be planted as the water drops. It does best where there is only one clear rainy season. It likes the same heavier soils as maize, but *S. cernuum* needs alluvial soils. Guinea corn is grown as an annual or perennial crop for up to three years, interplanted with Bulrush millet.

The plant generally grows up to 3·7 m (12 ft) high and has abundant small grains in loose flowering-heads on the end of a stem. Guinea corn is an excellent human food, and intoxicating drinks are also made from it. The grain is marketed over considerable distances. A red-seeded variety provides a medicine and (from the stems) a red dye for cloth, leather and fibre. Bran and the leaves from mature plants are fed to animals. The stems are also used for fencing, fuel, mats, thatch and as poles for yam vines. *Sorghum dochna, var. technicum,* is grown for broom-making.

SHEA BUTTER TREE (*Butyrospermum parkii*)—French 'Karité—is a major source of domestic oil in the Guinea corn and millet zones. It is widely distributed between 10° and 14°N, but seldom in great density. It requires moderate rainfall of about 900–1 270 mm (35–50 in) per annum, and is tolerant of damp land and sea air. When damaged by annual bush fires it averages about 6 m (20 ft). If not so damaged, it grows much taller—e.g. near compounds.

Because of its dispersion, the problem of collecting fresh fruit and of making an oil (or 'butter') low in free-fatty acid content are greater even than with the oil palm. Moreover, the oil has a distinctly rancid flavour. For this reason, but especially because of the low density of trees, the sparce human population and the remoteness of many producing areas, the product is mostly used locally. Nevertheless, there is a small export from Mali, Upper Volta and Dahomey. It is the kernels which are used, and there is quite an extensive internal commerce in the oil.

BENNISEED, SESAME, TILSEED or GINGELLY (*Sesamum orientale*) is indigenous to West Africa, from where it was introduced to India. It is an annual, and the seeds have a higher oil content than groundnuts, though the yield is much less. Most of the West African exports come from Nigeria, where it is largely grown by the Tiv of Benue-Plateau state. It is also grown by the Dagomba of Ghana, in the Upper Volta, Guinea, Mali and Sierra Leone. The seeds yield more oil if the plant is grown as the last crop on exhausted sandy loam or loamy soils, with plenty of moisture for two months only.

The oil is used outside Africa as a substitute for olive oil, in confectionery, margarine, cooking fats and soap. In Africa, the seeds are used for a kind of porridge and in soup. The leaves are also put in soup. The crop is used as green manure. A poorer variety is *S. radiatum*.

S W E E T  P O T A T O (*Ipomoea batatas*), an introduction from South America, grows where there is 760–1 270 mm (30–50 in) annual rainfall, or in very sandy soils with heavier rainfall. It is important in Guinea, the Mali—Upper Volta—Ivory Coast borderlands, the coastal savanna of the Ivory Coast, the Volta Delta, southern Senegal and northern Nigeria. Like yams, it is grown in mounds or ridges, and is a creeper. The tubers are small and numerous, and the leaves can be eaten by man as a spinach, or raw by animals. It should be noted that in the United States, sweet potatoes are called 'yams'.

C O T T O N (*Gossypium sp.*) is an ancient crop in almost all parts of West Africa, except in the densest forest, but it is most successful wherever the dry and wet seasons are sharply defined. In the south, cotton is generally intercropped with maize or yams; in the north, it is intercropped or rotated with groundnuts or guinea corn. Thus it is a crop which is spread through several climate and crop belts and, though mainly grown for factory and artisan use, some is exported.

American Allen cotton (*Gossypium hirsutum*) is suited to the north, where there are fewer crops to grow and space can be found for single cropping, which this cotton demands. In the Mali Inland Niger Delta, rice cultivation competes with irrigated cotton. When grown dry cotton is more difficult to grow than groundnuts, except on heavier soils.

In the south, where the rainfall is heavier, cotton is grown almost entirely for domestic purposes. There are two varieties of *Gossypium barbadense*: 'Ishan', a tough fibre, and 'Meko', a poorer variety.

In the Middle Belt, neither Allen cotton of the north nor the varieties of the south do well, and there is no good local variety.

TABLE 6.5. *Production of ginned cotton (lint)*

| Country | Thousands of metric tons |
|---|---|
| | 1970 |
| Senegal | 5 |
| Mali | 16 |
| Upper Volta | 12 |
| Niger | 3 |
| Ivory Coast | 14 |
| Dahomey | 10 |
| Togo | 2 |
| Nigeria | 87 |

Source: *Production Yearbook* 1970, vol. 24, FAO, Rome, 1971

INDIGO (*Indigofera arrecta*), indigenous to East and South Africa, is a shrub of about 1·2 m (4 ft), whose leaves are used for the dye. It requires rich soils and about 760 mm (30 in) annual rainfall. In the south, the dye is produced from a wild plant, the Yoruba or West African Indigo (*Lonchocarpus cyanescens*). Indigo dye is used extensively in Nigeria and Sierre Leone. *Henna* is also grown for its dye.

GARDEN EGG (*Solarnum melongena*), known also as Asiatic aubergines, does well with moderate rainfall, as do the peppers (*Capsicum annuum* and *C. frutescens*).

MANGO (*Mangifera indica*) is a native of southern Asia, but is found throughout West Africa, especially in the Middle Belt. The West African unimproved variety has small fruit not always of good flavour. The trees are excellent for shade along roads, provide tanning for leather, and a fairly hard wood.

PEAS. Pigeon or Congo pea (*Cajanus cajan*), introduced from India, requires good soils and dry conditions. Cow pea (*Vigna unguiculata*) should have good soils and at least 635 mm (25 in) annual rain, but will grow in poor sandy soils. Both peas and pods may be eaten. The leaves provide a spinach, and the Cow pea is also a green manure crop.

BEANS. Sword bean (*Canavalia ensiformis*) is much grown on the Jos Plateau. Locust bean (*Parkia biglobosa* and *clappertoniana*) is valued for its seeds, which are boiled, pounded, fermented and then made into balls and sold as *daudawa*, a product rather like cheese. The pulp in the pods is used for soup.

ONIONS are extensively grown in northern Nigeria and in the dry coastal areas of Ghana.

CALABASHES are widely grown for making utensils.

## The millet and groundnut zone

This is the most northerly agricultural zone, and roughly corresponds with the Sudan and Sahel savannas. With millet are found the lesser millets and all the crops of the previous zone, except yams, the shea butter tree and fruits, although cucurbits are grown. This is the ideal region for Zebu cattle, which are often kept even farther north, where permanent cultivation is impossible.

MILLET

Millet (*Pennisetum typhoideum*), known also as Bulrush Millet or Pearl Millet, and in Hausa as 'Gero', is indigenous. It grows about 1·8 m (6 ft) high, and at the head of the spike is a compact, rodlike concentration of grey grains; hence the popular names. One variety matures in two months, another in three months, and a third in four to five months. Their distribution is a reflection of the length of the rainy season.

Millet grows best in light loamy or sandy soils rather lacking in humus, and requires under 700 mm (28 in) annual rainfall. Indeed, it is generally grown with 275–400 mm (11–16 in). It benefits from clear skies, low humidity and considerable diurnal temperature variation.

The plant is used in the same way as guinea corn. It is the main cereal of Niger, central Mali and northern Upper Volta, Senegal and Mauritania and of the driest areas of Guinea, Togo, Dahomey and Nigeria. *Tamba* (*Eleusine coracana*) is a poor type of finger millet, used for food and for beer. *Hungry Rice* and *Iburu* are also much grown. (See p. 99.)

## GROUNDNUTS

Groundnut (*Arachis hypogoea*) is probably native to South America, and is also known as the peanut. It is an important food in most places, but does best between 8° and 14°N (especially between 11° and 13°N), in rich but sandy soils. The latter are essential, as the pod matures in the soil. Rainfall must be at least 355 mm (14 in) per annum in the humid atmosphere of coastal Senegal, or 635–900 mm (25–35 in) in the drier interior lands. If two light rainy seasons occur, two crops can generally be grown.

There are two types of plant—the 'spreading' or 'running', and the 'bunched' or 'erect'. Both are annuals, and the runner is the more common and better yielder. On the other hand, the erect is more suitable for intercropping and for the heavier red clay soils of Zaria (northern Nigeria), where the rainfall is greater. The crop is grown in rotation or intercropped with millet, guinea corn or cotton. Groundnuts, however, really need much lighter soils than cotton.

Until about 1950 the crop was grown exclusively by African peasants, but there is some mechanised production near Kaffrine (Senegal). Other such schemes have failed. In Senegal there are some 450 000 peasant farmers using about 980 000 hectares (2·3 million acres). In addition, some 70 000 casual labourers or 'navétanes' migrate from the poorer districts of Mali, Portuguese Guinea and Guinea into either Senegal or the Gambia (according to which offers the highest prices) as squatters or harvest labourers. In northern Nigeria the average size of farms is 1·2–1·6 ha. (3–4 acres), and the total area under groundnut cultivation in all Nigeria is about 1 million ha. (2·5 million acres).

Export entirely depends upon cheap bulk transport, so that commercial cultivation is intensive in physically suitable areas near means of transport in Senegal, western Mali, southwestern Upper Volta, and

PLATE 18. The groundnut

especially in northern Nigeria north of an east–west line through Zaria and into Niger near its boundary with Nigeria.

The groundnut is not a nut but a member of the pea family. Inside each pod are two seeds which, when crushed, give an oil highly valued for cooking and as a substitute for olive oil, as well as being used in the manufacture of margarine and soap. The outside shell also yields a small amount of oil of poorer quality. The residue of the crushed nuts gives an excellent cattle cake, and that of the shell a fuel.

The first shipment of groundnuts from West Africa was from Rufisque (Senegal) to Rouen in 1840, and annual shipments started in 1845. Intensive cultivation followed the opening of the Dakar to St Louis line in 1885, the Kaolack branch in 1911, the completion of the Thiès–Niger railway in 1923, two branch railways in 1931, and the many roads. Continuous cropping led to soil exhaustion, and cultivated areas are now mainly in southcentral Senegal.

TABLE 6.6. *Groundnut production, 1970*

| Country | Thousands of metric tons |
| --- | --- |
| Senegal | 660* |
| Mali | 100 |
| Upper Volta | 100 |
| Niger | 190 |
| Gambia | 102 |
| Nigeria | 1 175 |

Source: *Production Yearbook 1970*, vol. 24, FAO Rome, 1971
*Exceptionally low. Normally 800–1 000

TABLE 6.7. *Groundnut exports, 1968 (metric tons)*

| Country | Shelled groundnuts | Groundnut oil | Groundnut cake |
| --- | --- | --- | --- |
| Senegal | 243 000 | 198 040 | 24 874 |
| Mali | 11 000 | 5 | 32 |
| Upper Volta | 9 000 | 198 | 57 |
| Niger | 170 000 | 7 500 | 1 100 |
| Gambia | 29 000 | 25 122 | 2 657 |
| Nigeria | 651 000 | 110 946 | 17 345 |

Source: *Trade Yearbook 1969*, vol. 23, FAO, 1970

Senegal is the nearest groundnut producer to Europe. Groundnuts and derivatives (especially oils) are about four-fifths of Senegal's exports. Mali and Niger export much smaller quantities but the crop is vital to them. In the Gambia groundnuts are even more vital. They are almost the only cash crop and constitute almost all of the exports. Nuts pass across the Senegal–Gambia border according to relative prices. In Portuguese Guinea, groundnuts comprise over half the exports by value.

In northern Nigeria the most important areas are around Kano and Katsina, but the crop is significant west to Sokoto, south to Zaria, east to Maiduguri, and north into the Niger. Again it was the opening of the railway to Kano in 1912, the branch from Zaria to Gusau in 1927 and on to Kaura Namoda in 1929, and the extension of the main line from Kano to Nguru also in 1929, that made possible such a vast cash crop. It accounts for about a quarter of the Nigerian railway tonnage and rather less than that proportion of Nigerian exports by value.

An excessive amount of labour is at present used in cultivation. High

123

prices for groundnuts have made worthwhile the use of artificial fertilisers, which are sometimes put in with the seed. The farmer can expect up to a four-fold return for his outlay on fertiliser.

For decades groundnut oil was extracted in Europe, first from unshelled groundnuts and, since the 1950s, mostly from groundnuts decorticated in West Africa. This economises on transport costs but some oil is thereby lost so that the 'nuts' command a lower price. On the other hand, such decortication provides local employment.

Extraction of the oil began in Senegal in the 'thirties, aided by a protected market in the then-French North Africa. But there is only a small market in Senegal for the oil or the crushed nut residue which gives an excellent cattle cake. However, after the fall of France in 1940, groundnut oil came to be extracted on a much larger scale than before. Such a development did not follow in Nigeria until over a decade later, because of its greater remoteness from markets for the oil and residue, and its well-established outlets for decorticated nuts. However, all groundnut-producing countries of West Africa crush increasing quantities of their crop for oil, which is thus of growing relative importance in export compared with the raw groundnut. The cattle cake must also be largely exported, as the nomadic cattle herders of Africa have neither the inclination nor the money to buy it for their animals.

# 7

# Livestock and fisheries

## Livestock

As with crops, there are clearly defined livestock (especially cattle) zones.
These are determined by the tsetse fly, which, so far, has made it impossible
to keep Zebu cattle in the south. Thus this zone has been unable to
develop mixed farming, though its heavily leached soils would benefit so
much from manure enrichment. The north, being freer from the tsetse
fly, is the great cattle zone, from which there is a considerable trade in
cattle to the south. Cattle-rearing could be greatly increased there if
more water were available during the long dry season, and if pastures
and feeding were improved.

Moreover, if the tsetse fly danger of the wet season could be overcome,
cattle movements should no longer be necessary, and the Fulani and
other nomads might be persuaded to become settled and to take up
crop-farming. Sedentary crop-farmers might also take more readily to
cattle-keeping. Such revolutions would enrich both soil and man, and
would extend the cultivated area.

Ethidium bromide and related drugs, together with the Antrycide salts,
have proved highly active against *Trypanosoma congolense* and *T. vivax*.
These are carried by the tsetse fly and are the causes of trypanosomiasis
in cattle. But the prophylaxis seems uncertain after some time, and it is
difficult to carry out periodic treatments on nomadic animals. Their
greatest value is to enable cattle to travel safely through a fly area on
their way to consuming areas for slaughter, as has been shown so
successfully in Nigeria.

### Cattle

South of about latitude 10°N only small, humpless cattle are found
permanently, and they are relatively tolerant of the trypanosome. Their
small stature may possibly be connected with calcium deficiency of soils
and herbage in the forest zone. If so, it is by a mechanism of natural
selection towards the optimum size to suit this poor environment. As
rainfall decreases to the northeast, leaching becomes less severe, so that
calcium content increases and the animals are certainly larger.

PLATE 19. Dwarf Lagoon and Ndama cattle by the sea in Dahomey. Note sizes in relation to the men.

There are three main types of humpless cattle, the most famous being the small *Ndama* found especially in the Fouta Djallon and Guinea Highlands. It has a short, large head, and fawn or brownish-red colouring. It is the main source of meat for Guinea, Sierra Leone and Liberia.

The second or *Dwarf Shorthorn* (*Muturu* in Nigeria), is very small, weighing only about 100 kg (220 lb), stocky and dark or piebald. Subtypes of this are the *Lagoon, Somba,* etc.

On the inner fringes of the forest are types intermediate between the *Ndama* and *Dwarf,* such as the *Baoulé* (Ivory Coast) and most Ghana cattle.

The third type is the large *Chad* (or *Kuri*), found on the shores and islands of Lake Chad, especially in the Niger Republic. This has huge stump horns, a much larger body than the *Ndama*, is whitish-grey in colour and, despite its geographical location far inland, is humpless.

All these types of humpless cattle probably originated from Asia and North-east Africa in the distant past. Before the later arrival of the Fulani people, humpless cattle were found all over West Africa. They yield up to only 55 per cent by weight of meat and very little milk.

Cattle become much more significant between 9–10°N and 12–14°N; they are still humpless and are mainly crosses between the *Ndama* and the larger humped *Zebu*. They have an incomplete resistance to fly. Included in this cross-type are the *Djakoré* of Senegal, the *Bambara*, *Mandé* or *Méré* of Mali, the misnamed *Sanga* of Ghana, and the *Borgu*

126

PLATE 20. A herd of large and varied Zebu cattle, on the north-eastern boundary of Ghana, near Bawku. Note the large humps. Despite the rainy season, these cattle were already in poor condition and had several hundred miles farther to travel

in Dahomey and Nigeria. This intermediate zone may offer opportunities for mixed farming.

North of 12–14°N are found the humped Zebu cattle introduced from Asia perhaps as early as the sixteenth century B.C. With them were introduced to West Africa some of the bare rudiments of cattle-keeping. Most cattle are owned by nomads, are not immune to trypanosomiasis, and before the rains they endure months of starvation. During the rains they are better fed, although necessarily dispersed from rivers and the tsetse fly. Transhumance of these cattle is inevitably extensive. It is difficult to say whether this is the cause of Fulani nomadism, or whether the Fulani and other nomads took to cattle-keeping because it fitted their ways.

Migrations by the Fulani in West Africa since the seventh century, together with yearly transhumance, have led to many types of Zebu cattle. These are taller than the humpless ones (except the Chad), with the longer legs necessary for transhumance. They are generally light in colour—white or grey with black—but they may also be black, fawn, red or piebald. They will support much more work and give more milk than the humpless variety, but only the same percentage of meat to total weight. Moreover, Zebus take up to six years to mature, and often calve only in alternate years.

The main varieties are the shorthorn *Maure, Tuareg, Azaouak, Sokoto*

127

(*Gudale*) and *Shuwa*, all used for transport, milk and meat. They have remained fairly pure because of relative isolation. There are also the medium-horned *Diali* and *Adamawa*. The lyre-horned white or grey *Fulani* cattle occur in Senegal, Mali, Niger and Nigeria, are much affected by movement and crossing with humpless cattle, and are good meat-yielders. Rather similar are the large, red *Bororo*, with long-lyre horns, and known as *Rahaza* in Nigeria.

Table 7.1 shows average weights of certain breeds, according to Joshi, McLaughlin and Phillips. Within each breed the actual weights of animals vary according to sex, age, area, feeding and condition. Some figures are estimates (especially for ex-French West Africa), while some are averages of measured animals. No better comparisons are possible. Nigerian figures for Zebu are higher than those for ex-French West Africa probably because the former are for government·farms and the latter for ordinary stock.

TABLE 7.1. *Weights of mature cows and bulls*

| Type | Cows kg | lb | Bulls kg | lb |
|---|---|---|---|---|
| Kuri | 360–400 | 800–880 | 500–650 | 1 100–1 400 |
| Ndama | 240–350 | 520–780 | 290–420 | 630– 920 |
| Dwarf Shorthorn | 150–160 | 330–350 | 190–200 | 420– 450 |
| Zebu (Nigeria) | 300–340 | 650–750 | 360–540 | 800–1 190 |
| Zebu (ex-French West Africa) | 240–320 | 530–710 | 300–420 | 720– 910 |
| Red Bororo | 360–450 | 790–990 | 350–500 | 770–1 100 |

Nomadic peoples are increasingly ready to learn improved methods, so that veterinary officers have successfully inoculated against rinderpest, pleuro-pneumonia and other diseases. Other difficulties are that most herders will not feed or house their animals, and want an all-purpose beast. But a vast amount needs to be done in the improvement of breeds. Crosses with temperate cattle have been unsatisfactory, except in the Cameroon Highlands, and upgrading can best be achieved by selective breeding of indigenous stock.

The Fulani keeps his animals less for commercial profit, than for subsistence and as a sign of social status. He does little or no selective breeding, keeps as many animals as possible, and sells only when he needs ready cash or finds particular animals useless to him. Thus the whole conception of cattle-rearing and sale is fundamentally different in West Africa from the commercial cattle-rearing countries of the world. This must always be borne in mind, especially when considering cattle areas and trade routes.

The main concentrations of cattle are shown in Fig. 7.1; approximate total numbers in Table 7.2.

TABLE 7.2. *Approximate totals of cattle in West African countries*

| Country | Number of cattle |
|---|---|
| Senegal | 2 600 000 |
| Gambia | 235 000 |
| Mauritania | 2 600 000 |
| Mali | 5 000 000 |
| Upper Volta | 2 800 000 |
| Niger | 4 300 000 |
| Portuguese Guinea | 260 000 |
| Guinea | 1 800 000 |
| Sierra Leone | 240 000 |
| Liberia | 28 000 |
| Ivory Coast | 400 000 |
| Ghana | 630 000 |
| Togo | 180 000 |
| Dahomey | 570 000 |
| Nigeria | 11 550 000 |

Despite the possessive attitude of the Fulani towards his cattle, several hundreds of thousand head of cattle are exported annually from the cattle-keeping republics of the Niger, Mali, Upper Volta and Mauritania to the coastal countries, particularly Ghana.

Cattle provide food for the Fulani and other cattle-keeping peoples, and especially for other better-off Africans living in the more prosperous areas. As wage or salary earning and cash crops develop, and railway, road and droving facilities improve, so the demand for meat increases.

Ghana is easily the greatest *per capita* consumer of meat in West Africa. Annual consumption there is about 200 000 head, coming partly from between Niafunké and Gao in the Mali Republic, and partly from local sources. Thus, 7 million Ghanaians eat over half the amount of meat consumed by ex-French West Africa's 28 million people, who live in more predominantly cattle country.

Kano (northern Nigeria) is the greatest commercial cattle centre in West Africa. Cattle-trains leave daily for the south; the journey takes 1–2 days and the animals arrive in poor condition. Many more are driven south on foot, taking about three months. Some are lost and the survivors likewise arrive in as bad a condition as those sent by railway. Increasing numbers travel most speedily by truck.

If rail charges were lower and more refrigerator vans were provided, cattle could be slaughtered in the north in better condition, and meat sent south, rather than live animals. Meanwhile, several governments have provided pens along the cattle routes, pasturages have been improved, and rest camps established for the drovers. Modern abattoirs exist in some cattle centres but more are needed.

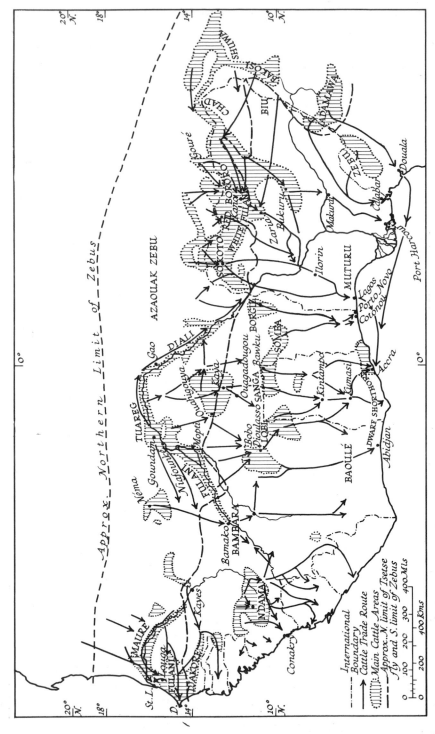

Fig. 7.1. Main cattle areas and trade routes

Kano has also long been a great leather and skin centre. After the opening of the railway to Lagos in 1912, overseas trade in these products was developed by European firms, which have made notable improvements in methods of preparation.

Zebu cattle are relatively poor milk-yielders, dairy produce is made mainly by the Fulani, and little is sold. Most diary produce is imported from temperate countries in tins.

## Sheep

The large sheep are kept by nomads in the Sahel, and are hairy and long-legged; they commonly move in great flocks. Most of them are kept for meat, although the long-haired *Maure* variety of Mauritania and Mali is used more for its skin and fleece. The *Tuareg* type, found generally east of Timbuktu, are good for meat and milk. The *Fulani* type, farther south, are better meat animals but poorer milkers.

*Macina* sheep are found in large flocks, mainly in the Inland Niger Delta of Mali, between 14° and 17°N, and to a much lesser extent in Mauritania and Niger. These sheep are probably of North African origin, medium in build and with an open fleece. This is elastic, light and durable, and is used for blankets and clothing. The meat and milk are poor. These sheep are kept by settled Fulani, whose Negro shepherds (former captives) move with the sheep to the outer dry fringes of the Inland Delta during the rains and floods.

A degenerate variety of the *Macina*, known as the *Goundoum*, is found in small flocks on the banks and islands of the Niger river, between Timbuktu and Niamey. During the floods they are on the higher right bank (Gourma), after which they occupy the islands until the grass is too poor. They are then taken to the low left bank.

Dwarf, short-legged, hairy sheep are found south of 14°N, and are kept in very small flocks by sedentary farmers. They are generally white and black or white and red in colour, and have hair rather than wool.

## Goats

Goats look remarkably like sheep in Africa and they are generally kept together. Goats are easily reared, endure a long dry season without undue ill-effect and also withstand the humidity of the south much better than sheep. Weight for weight, goats give more meat than any other animal in West Africa. Goat meat is consumed in greater quantities than any other.

As with cattle and sheep, there is the same contrast between on the one hand the large type north of 14°N, kept by Fulani, Maure and Tuareg, giving much milk and good meat from the female, but very susceptible to the tsetse, and on the other hand the dwarf goat south of

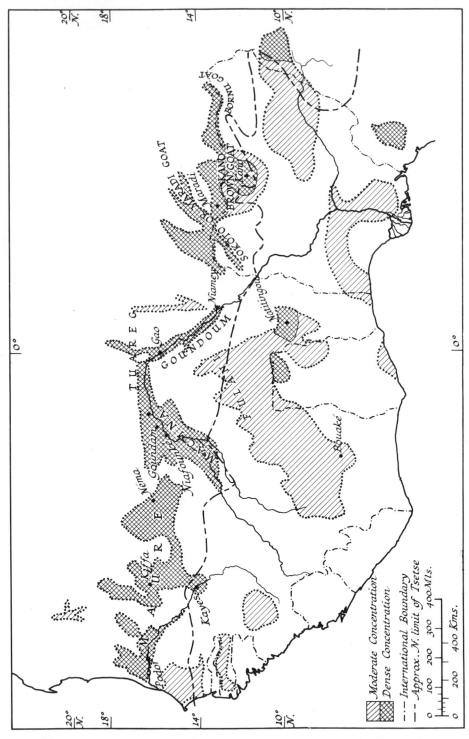

FIG. 7.2. Sheep and goats

14°N, resistant to fly, prolific and giving good meat from the male. Both types originated in Asia, and come here via northeast Africa.

Specially renowned are the intermediate sized *Sokoto Red* or *Maradi*, and the *Kano* or *Zinder Brown*. These are sources of coloured glacé kid leather, a valuable export from Nigeria and the Niger. The goat is small to medium in size, very prolific indeed, and gives good meat and milk. *Bornu* goat-skin is also valuable for suede leather.

Goats and sheep are fundamental to nomadic peoples, as their skins are used for making water-containers, bellows, belts, cords, cushions, saddlery, bags, mats, sandals, etc. Demand is insistent, and made greater by rapid wear resulting from poor preparation.

## Pigs

The African black long-snout pig, probably introduced at an early date by the Portuguese, lives in an even wilder state than the other domestic animals. Pigs are limited to non-Muslim peoples, and are mainly found in the southern parts of Nigeria and Dahomey, southern and central Ivory Coast, the Casamance area of Senegal, and around Dakar and other towns.

Berkshires and Yorkshires have been introduced into most West African countries. Many Lebanese established piggeries to produce bacon and ham. The Middle Belt deserves especial consideration for piggeries, as it is centrally sited for varied fattening foodstuffs, such as groundnut cake, millet, benniseed, sweet potatoes and palm kernel waste.

## Camels

These live in the Sahara and its immediate confines, mainly north of the millet zone. In Mauritania they are especially important in the centre (Trarza and Tagant), east (Hodh), and north (Adrar); in the Mali Republic in the Timetrine and Kidal regions north of Timbuktu, Bamba and Bourem and down the Niger to Gao; and in the Niger around Tahoua, Agadès and the oases.

In the past these animals helped to link West Africa to the Arab world, and so to spread Islam. But the advent of Europeans, the turning of trade southward and the pacification of the Sahara, have greatly reduced their value and the variety of breeds. Camels are now raised which are capable of carrying heavy loads through the desert fringes—e.g. groundnuts from the Niger into Nigeria.

### Horses, donkeys and mules

#### HORSES

No fossil remains or cave drawings of horses have ever been found in

West Africa, and all horses came from North Africa. Most, if not all seem to have been introduced from the seventh to the thirteenth centuries, as a result of the Arab invasions of North Africa. Thus there are the Arab and Barbary types found in the high areas of Mali and the Niger, and progressively poorer varieties of these southward into the basins of the upper Senegal and Niger. Another type, the Dongola, was introduced by Arabs from the Upper Nile towards the end of the thirteenth century. It is now found in Sokoto, Katsina, Kano and Bornu Emirates, with poorer varieties to the north as far as Agadès, Niger, as well as down the Niger river from Say to below Niamey.

Most horses live south of the camels. Horses succumb quickly to the tsetse fly, whose northern outposts are the horse's southern limits, roughly along a line through Kaolack, Tambacounda, Bamako, Bobo Dioulasso, Tenkodogo, Nikki, Bida and Maiduguri. Horses are found mainly in western Senegal near the sea, in Mali (especially in Hodh and around Ségou and Mopti), in the Niger and in northern Nigeria. In West Africa horses are used essentially for ceremonies and sport.

## DONKEYS (ASSES)

These are more acclimatised and tougher than horses, and during the dry season they are used quite far south. Their normal regions are western Senegal; the Trarza and Assaba districts of Mauritania; around Mopti, Timbuktu and Gao in Mali; in the Niger southwards into Nigeria as far south as Bida; and in the Upper Volta around Ouagadougou. There are probably two and a half times as many donkeys as horses, and they are used for cattle-droving, for ceremonies and especially for transport.

MULES. Most African peoples refuse to rear these, except the Hausa, who rear many, especially around Sokoto.

## Poultry

CHICKENS. These are ubiquitous, small, and give only about 60 tiny eggs a year. In most parts they are given no attention, and some peoples refuse, or once refused, to eat eggs—e.g. the Mende of Sierra Leone. But in northern Nigeria the Hausa sell several million surplus eggs each year for despatch southwards, and the Mossi of the Upper Volta also keep many poultry. Early mass production schemes were failures. Day-old chicks are now flown in and inoculated, whilst feed is balanced with imported vitamin-enriched feeding stuffs. In most countries poultry are largely raised by battery and house methods, and eggs are now within the purchasing power of most urban dwellers, though not so poultry.

GUINEA FOWL. These are widespread in the savanna zones, and are much appreciated.

DUCKS. Barbary or Muscovy ducks are numerous along the Senegal, Gambia and Niger rivers, and in the forest zone. They give about double the amount of meat of chickens or guinea-fowl.

TURKEYS. These were first introduced by the Portuguese and are kept mainly in the drier areas of the Guinea Coast.

## Miscellaneous

BEES. These are valued by savanna peoples, and wild honey is sold in markets. Beeswax is collected for export, especially in Senegal and Gambia.

SNAILS. A giant variety is an important source of protein to forest peoples.

# Fisheries

## Sea fishing

Sea fishing by Africans was restricted in the past by the economic state of the countries, by insufficient capital and inability to build anything larger than canoes. Fishing with these means inshore fishing, by daylight, and small returns; however, canoes are now often powered with out-board motors. Dried fish play a considerable part in trade, as meat is generally expensive south of 10°N, where the tsetse fly prevents the keeping of large cattle.

Fishing is most important off Mauritania, Senegal, the Ivory Coast, Ghana and Nigeria, which account for about three-quarters of fish caught in West African waters, but other countries are developing fishing. Mauritanian waters supply much of the Senegal total of about 170 000 tons annually; they are also visited by trawlers from Europe, Japan and the Canary Islands, which return thence with their catch, or land part of it for drying at Nouadhibou (Port Etienne).

Fish processing depots at Nouadhibou (Port Etienne), Dakar, Monrovia, Abidjan, Tema and Lagos freeze tuna and other fish and do a little canning. Total exports of fish from Mauritania and Senegal are about 30 000 tons per annum, mainly refrigerated and dried fish.

In the Gulf of Guinea much of the fishing is done by Fanti, not only from their own Ghana villages, but also far to the west, east and south. Total Ghana landings are about 180 000 tons per annum.

Fishing boats operate from most ports, and Russian and Japanese trawlers come with factory ships, and land the cheaper fish. This and locally caught fish are increasingly distributed in refrigerated containers by lorries.

**Lagoon fishing**

The extensive lagoons of the Guinea Coast are rich in small fish. These are mostly caught by cast nets but some peoples build elaborate mazes of wicker, which extend over considerable areas of the lagoons, especially in Dahomey.

**Freshwater fishing**

The extent and intensity of such fishing varies greatly between peoples and rivers. Some rivers are not fished for religious reasons, e.g. in southern Ghana, whilst others have been overfished like the Senegal. The most intensively fished is the middle Niger in Mali, where certain peoples like the Bozo are essentially fishermen. There is much movement of fishermen upriver from Nigeria and downstream in Mali and Niger to catch fish at particular stages of the flood. Mopti is a centre of trade in dried and smoked fish, which is exported overland to the Ivory Coast and Ghana in very considerable quantities.

The creation of the great Volta and Kainji lakes behind barrages has been followed by some stocking with *tilapia*, sporadic fishing, and hopes of annual catches of 12–20 000 tons.

# 8

# Minerals, fuels and power, and industry

## Minerals

### General

Gold has been mined in West Africa for at least a thousand years. The Empire of Ghana, whose zenith was in A.D. 1000, obtained gold from the Falémé River and the adjacent Bambouk Mountains. The Manding or Mali Empire, which had its zenith in A.D. 1332, probably sent its merchants into what are now the Ivory Coast and modern Ghana to buy gold, ivory, kola nuts and slaves. Gold and some other commodities were traded to the Arabs in North Africa, and from there to Europe. Portuguese, Spanish and Italian coins may have been made from West African gold. Tin was worked on the Jos Plateau long before the advent of Europeans, as was lead at Abakaliki in eastern Nigeria. Salt-digging in the Sahara, and the exchange of salt and cattle for kolas and gold, are ancient trades in West Africa.

Gold brought Europeans to West Africa. The Portuguese landed at Shama, at the mouth of the Pra river, in 1471, and in that year made the first recorded direct export of gold to Europe. Gold was also exported down the Senegal and Gambia rivers from the basin of the Falémé. Gold, gum, spices, ivory and slaves were staple exports for centuries.

Several metals were smelted and worked into objects of everyday use. In Ashanti and the Baoulé countries, brass weights were used to weigh gold. These small weights were delightfully shaped to represent animals, birds, fish, reptiles, insects and allegorical figures. Gold itself was used for ceremonial or ornamental objects such as stools, bowls, staff heads, chains, rings and bracelets. Another famous metal industry was brass and bronze founding at Benin, which may antedate the Portuguese. But if this was so, it is difficult to see how the copper, and especially the zinc, were obtained, though the tin could have come from the Jos Plateau. Tin articles were made in the Naraguta area (Nigeria) at least from the eighteenth century. Iron has long been smelted in small bloomeries almost throughout West Africa, generally for making cooking vessels, hoes, matchets and such articles.

European exploitation of minerals dates from 1878 when gold mining began on the banket reefs of Tarkwa, Ghana. It was hampered by the difficulties of transporting heavy equipment and by poor labour. Gold-mining needs were responsible for opening the Ghana railway from Sekondi to Tarkwa in 1901, its extension to Obuasi in 1902, and for a branch to Prestea in 1912. The need for bauxite caused the opening of the Awaso branch in 1944. In Nigeria the Bauchi light railway was opened in 1914 for the needs of tin-mining, and the Nigerian eastern line to Enugu in 1916 for coal-mining. It was extended to Jos in 1927 to serve the tin-fields directly. Mineral lines were opened in Liberia from Monrovia to the Bomi hills in 1951, to the Mano river 1961, and the Bong mountain in 1965 to permit iron-working, as was that from Buchanan to Mount Nimba in 1963, and from Pepel to Marampa in Sierra Leone in 1933. Many existing railways made possible later mining developments, e.g. of manganese at Nsuta (Ghana). Mining has also stimulated road construction, most notably in the Nigerian oilfields. Special terminals or ports have been built at Nouadhibou, Pepel, Monrovia, Buchanan, Porto-Segouro and Bonny, to cite only the most significant.

Mining plays a major part in West African economy, and has a major share in the total capital invested (and sometimes lost). It pays considerable amounts in wages, whilst mineral traffic is an important element in certain railway revenues. Mining companies often provide housing and free medical attention, not only for their employees but also for dependants. The main minerals worked by government corporations are Nigerian coal and some of Ghana's gold, whilst Sierra Leone's former diamond mining company and Ghana's private enterprise gold and diamond mines have been reorganised with government majority holdings. Mining royalties and taxation are very significant revenues to the governments of Mauritania, Guinea, Sierra Leone, Liberia, Ghana, Togo and Nigeria. Development of oil in Nigeria and of iron in Mauritania and Liberia are revolutionising the fortunes of those countries, whilst potential power and bauxite reserves may industrialise Guinea and Ghana.

Minerals are important too in diversifying economies. They introduce a new item, the price of which is usually rather more stable than that of agricultural produce. Mining requires and teaches new skills, has significant linkage and multiplier effects, e.g. in encouraging the local supply of timber and food, and such industries as explosives and paints. Mining has often activated countries, e.g. Mauritania, Sierra Leone, Liberia or the Rivers State of Nigeria.

In colonial days, French West Africa was less intensively prospected for minerals than the British colonies. French capital also seemed hesitant to invest in mining. All this has changed dramatically, and many important mining developments have taken place in Francophone countries, such as Mauritania (iron and copper), Guinea (bauxite), Senegal and Togo (phosphates).

**Important worked minerals**

It is intended here to give a general survey of each mineral. Fuller details may be found in the regional chapters. Where a mineral is at present worked only or mainly in one country, most information will be found in the appropriate chapter.

## GOLD

Ghana is the only significant producer, although it has but one profitable mine (Obuasi). There are also some four unprofitable ones, abandoned by companies but run by a state corporation (see pp. 386–8).

## DIAMONDS

All production is from alluvial sources. By weight of output, West Africa is far ahead of South Africa, but well behind in value.

Ghana is the largest producer, the diamonds being small and mainly of industrial quality. Merchanised production began in the Birrim valley in 1920. Africans work on their own account in the Bonsa basin.

Larger, and occasionally very large diamonds are found in Sierra Leone, where a state-controlled company works areas at Yengema and Tongo. There are many dispersed and very prolific African 'diggings' particularly along the Sewa valley.

Production near Kissidougou, in southeastern Guinea, began in 1936 and, later, west of Beyla. However, the Guinea government closed all workings in 1966 because of smuggling from the country of so many diamonds. Much of Liberian production is, in fact, the purchase of diamonds smuggled into the country, mainly from Sierra Leone.

TABLE 8.1. *Diamond production in thousand metric carats*

| Country | 1969 |
|---|---|
| Guinea | — |
| Sierra Leone | 1 937 |
| Ivory Coast | 141 |
| Ghana | 2 391 |
| Liberia | 836 |

## IRON ORE

The first exports were of haematite from highly metamorphosed Pre-Cambrian rocks at Marampa-Lunsar, Sierra Leone, which began in 1933. Similar but unworked deposits occur further inland around Tonkolili.

There was no further development in West Africa until the quarrying of itabirite ore began in 1951 in the Bomi Hills, north-northwest of

139

Monrovia. Another deposit, also of itabirite, was opened on the Mano river (the western border) in 1961. More important and much more spectacular is the far greater reserve of haematite on Mount Nimba, on the border of Guinea and the Ivory Coast, opened in 1963, and served by a railway which crosses Liberia to the purpose-built port of Buchanan. Lastly, poorer ore has been produced in the Bong hills, northeast of Monrovia, since 1965. These Liberian mines have transformed the cash economy of that country, and iron ore accounts for some three-quarters of Liberian exports.

Another remarkable development was the beginning in 1963 of export from F'Derik (formerly Ft Gouraud), Mauritania of equally rich but drier haematite. A railway had to be built through utterly desertic country to an ocean terminal at Nouadhibou (formerly Port Etienne). As a result of this new operation Mauritania became a viable country.

TABLE 8.2. *Iron ore production (thousand metric tons)*

| Country | 1969 |
| --- | --- |
| Liberia | 14 786 |
| Mauritania | 5 497 |
| Sierra Leone | 1 800 |

West Africa has become a significant source of rich iron ore, and its importance is likely to grow because other rich Liberian deposits at Wologisi, Kitoma and Mount Putu may also be opened.

Much less rich ore from ferruginous laterite is widespread but rarely of sufficient iron content to be worked. However, such a deposit was exploited near Conakry, Guinea, from 1953 until 1966. Despite its coastal site, the ore proved difficult to sell because of its impurities, competition from richer and better ores such as those from Sierra Leone, Liberia and Mauritania, and because of the shortage of foreign exchange with which to buy mining spare parts.

Somewhat modest content ore (45 per cent *Fe*) exists in substantial quantities at Mount Patti, near Lokoja, Nigeria, close to the navigable Niger. The ore has been considered for use in a proposed iron and steel industry but its mediocre quality and the unsuitability of Nigerian coal for coking present major problems. Electric steel production is conceivable, using power from the Kainji dam, but would be costly for a relatively small non-specialised plant. Furthermore, political wrangling may prevent proper decisions as to the best location.

The Economic Commission for Africa recommended an iron and steel plant should be established at either Monrovia or Buchanan to serve all the West African market in general steel. It could use rich Liberian ore, and the ore carriers would have a return cargo of coke from

American or Europe. However, at least Nigeria, Ghana, Guinea and Mali wish to establish their own plants.

## BAUXITE

Workable deposits of the tropical lateritic type of bauxite, the ore of aluminium, have so far been found only in Ghana, Sierra Leone and especially Guinea, though occurrences have been noted elsewhere.

Quarrying really began in Ghana during the Second World War at Awaso, southwest of Kumasi, and at Mount Ejuanema, near Mpraeso; Awaso alone continued production after the war. Development of other deposits, especially near Kibi, will start after the Volta Aluminium Company decides it can produce alumina from Ghana bauxite instead of importing alumina for its aluminium smelter at Tema.

Guinea probably has one-half of the world's resources of bauxite, and is a major world producer. A small working began on Kassa Island, off Conakry in 1952, and much later another was undertaken on Tamara. Both have now almost ceased due to exhaustion of the ore. Far more important is the Fria mine, north of Conakry, opened in 1960, and associated with a large and modern alumina plant—the first in Africa. Nevertheless, the greatest development is of the huge and rich deposit at Boké. The mine became operational in 1973 and an alumina plant is being added, both served by a 136 km (85 miles) railway to a port at Kamsar.

Other large deposits occur at Kindia (rights held by the USSR), at Tongue (to be developed by a Swiss company), and Dabola (concession granted to a Yugoslav corporation). Working of these depends upon improvement of the existing government railway. Power could be produced on the Konkouré river to smelt alumina to aluminium.

Compared with all these sites the small one in Sierra Leone, opened in 1964, is of very modest significance.

## MANGANESE

Several deposits of manganese occur as surface concentrations from the weathering of manganese-rich rocks in Ghana, the Ivory Coast, the Upper Volta, etc. The only deposit worked is in Ghana at Nsuta, 55 km (34 miles) from Takoradi. Working began in 1916 and for several decades Ghana was a leading world producer. However, the deposit is relatively small and is nearing economic exhaustion. The Ivory Coast quarry at Grand Babou was worked only from 1961 to 1971.

## TIN

The ore is derived from granite and pegmatite. It was washed out from the parent rock by ancient and existing rivers, from whose gravels it is sluiced or dredged on or near the Jos Plateau (pp. 473–5). Some of the ancient river courses and their gravels were later covered by volcanic lava. Tin ore not so covered was first worked by Africans and later by Europeans. All the ore is smelted in the mining areas. A little ore is also produced near Agadès in Niger.

## COLUMBITE

This was formerly a waste product of tin-mining in Nigeria, but the metal it contains is now important in the production of certain classes of stainless steel and other alloys, for jet engines and gas turbines. Nigeria is the main world producer, but production has varied greatly according to needs in the USA.

## URANIUM

Ore is mined at Arlit, in Niger and, with production in Gabon, the Central African Republic and France, provides the latter with her uranium needs.

## COPPER

Working began in 1970 of a small deposit of copper oxide ore at Akjoujt, Mauritania. Development had been delayed mainly by difficulties of ore refining. These were resolved by the 'Torco' process, and concentrates are taken by road for export through Nouakchott pier. Production of 30 000 tons of concentrates is expected for twenty-five years.

## RUTILE AND ILMENITE

The world's largest known deposit of rutile (titanium dioxide) was worked by means of a floating suction dredge north of the estuary of the Sherbro in Sierra Leone for a few years prior to 1971. There were hopes that the country would become the leading world producer, but the company had persistent labour and technical troubles. The deposit may be re-worked by another company, and a second deposit is the subject of interest.

Ilmenite was obtained from Senegal's Petite Côte beaches from 1922 to 1964, and from Gambia's Sanyang beach from 1956 to 1958. Both operations became uneconomic. Unworked deposits occur in Casamance (Senegal); at York and Hastings (near Freetown), Sierra Leone; in the Ivory Coast and Dahomey.

Rutile and ilmenite are sources of the metal titanium, which is increasingly used in rockets, steel alloys (especially as a cutting material), in white paints and glass.

## PHOSPHATES

Calcium phosphate at Lam-Lam and aluminium phosphate at Pallo, both near Thiès, Senegal, were first quarried in 1950 from Lower Eocene strata; however, in 1953 the Lam-Lam quarry proved uneconomic and was closed. Exploitation was then concentrated on a deposit of aluminium phosphate, from which some 160 000 tons are produced, and from which fertiliser is made. A nearby deposit of calcium phosphate has been developed by another company at Taïba, where well over one million tons are produced, all for export as phosphate.

Another large deposit near Anécho, Togo, yields $1\frac{3}{4}$ million tons a year. Unworked deposits exist at Cive (near Matam) on the Senegal River, in the basin of the Lama River in Dahomey, at Abeokuta in Nigeria, and in the dry valley of the Tilemsi north of Gao, Mali.

## LIMESTONE

Limestone, in forms suitable for cement manufacture or for building stone, is relatively rare in West Africa. Yet cement is in great demand and is expensive, especially far from a port. Marly limestone, at the junction of Cretaceous and Eocene series, is worked at Rufisque (Senegal), which has West Africa's earliest cement factory. There are several factories in Nigeria, and some four more in other countries. Imported clinker is also used at port works e.g. in Tema.

## SALT

This has been worked for centuries in the Sahara at Trarza and Idjil in Mauritania, and at Taoudéni in Mali. Saline earths are dug at Kaolack (Senegal) and at Bilma (Niger), and salt is obtained from saline springs at Daboya, Ghana. Sea water is evaporated at Ada, Keta, Accra and other coastal places.

The Saharan deposits were the source of ancient exchange with kola nuts from the south. Movement of salt has been largely changed in direction by imports of cheap European salt through the ports and, to a minor extent, by the output from the factory at Kaolack, Senegal.

## Fuels and power

In early colonial times and before, the only fuel available was wood, which was so much used in early mines and on railways that deforestation resulted in some places.

## Coal

By comparison with other continents, Africa is poorly endowed with coal. The only working of it in West Africa has been near Enugu, Nigeria, (pp. 475–6), where the decision to mine it before the First World War led to the development of that town, of Port Harcourt, and of the railway between them. The coal, unlike most coal, is not Carboniferous but Cretaceous, sub-bituminous, of poor calorific value, and of high ash content. Production never exceeded about one million tons, and is now far less. The coal has been used on Nigerian and other railways, and in electrical generation. Apart from the poor quality of the coal, the mines had many labour disputes, whilst dieselization of the railways and the development of Nigerian oil removed most of the markets. The coal is also non-coking, so that it would not easily be used in the proposed iron and steel industry. It is most suited to chemical byproduct manufacture.

### Lignite

This occurs more widely than coal, both in Nigeria and elsewhere, but with increasing oil production in West Africa lignite is unlikely to be used as a fuel or in a chemical industry.

### Oil

After long and exceedingly costly exploration in the appallingly difficult terrain of the Niger Delta, oil was proved to exist in commercial quantities in 1956 (pp. 469–73). Export began in 1958, and by 1965 oil was Nigeria's leading export. Despite much damage to oil installations and delayed development during the Nigerian War of 1967–70, a record production was soon reached after that, and oil now largely exceeds the total of all other Nigerian exports.

Production is most important in Rivers and Mid-West states, and less so in East-Central and South-Eastern states. Important quantities also come from off-shore. The several companies have their own terminals, the earliest and most important being Bonny. A refinery near Port Harcourt provides most of Nigeria's requirements, so saving much foreign exchange. The oil is of good quality, being low in sulphur content. With Libyan and Algerian oils it shares the advantage of relative proximity to markets.

Although widespread prospection elsewhere in West Africa has failed to find oil in quantities so far warranting commercial production, the indications are that oil may later come to be produced westward along the coast of Ghana and, perhaps, in inland basin formations.

### Natural gas

Gas always occurs with oil, and in Nigeria is sometimes the preponderant product (pp. 472–3). Wherever it leaves the ground it must either be piped away for almost immediate use or burned as waste. A little is used in

144

a few industries and in electrical generation. Greater and more widespread use awaits further industrial needs which, in turn, await markets and a higher standard of living. Gas is piped for short distances in the oil-fields, but a basic national and a possible international gas grid should be developed.

## Hydroelectric power

There are quite a number of possible sites on West African rivers but major developments have taken place only recently and at a handful of sites, which are often remote. African rivers are highly seasonal and so large dams are necessary to control the greatest floods, annual flow, and to create the vital storage and height (head) of water. Insulation of cables is expensive in areas of high humidity, so that transmission is also costly. Breakdowns due to electrical storms accentuate the problem. So the capital cost is heavy, whilst the demand for power is still small. The largest dams of Akosombo (Ghana), Kainji (Nigeria) and Kossou (Ivory Coast) have been built where there is either a great demand from a specific industry (aluminium at Tema, Ghana), from a large population (Nigeria), or a prosperous expatriate community and a thriving general economy (Ivory Coast). Elsewhere, small hydro, oil or gas fed power stations serve still modest local and national needs; only where an industry could use large quantities of power might other dams be built, as on the Konkouré river in Guinea which would provide power for aluminium plants. More-over, as Nigerian oil and gas become available, so the competitiveness of hydroelectric power must be reassessed. Competition is twofold—gas versus electricity, and gas turbines versus water turbines in the generation of electricity. All this may modify the evolution of the Niger Dams Project in Nigeria, in which the present Kainji dam was to be only the first of three (pp. 472 and 476–8).

Akosombo power has been the means of diversifying the Ghana economy by permitting the introduction of a large aluminium plant and by cheapening power costs of all other users. The same should happen in Nigeria and the Ivory Coast. Nevertheless, the greatest prospects are in Nigeria, with its unique variety of fuels (coal, oil, gas) and hydro-electric power, and its relatively large market.

Power from Ghana is taken by a power line to Togo and Dahomey, and a link of only 150 km (90 miles) could be made with the Nigerian grid. The distance between the Ghana and Ivory Coast grids is not much more. If these two links were made, the three most developed countries of West Africa (Nigeria, Ghana and the Ivory Coast) would have inte-grated grids and be able to switch power when needed. The two links would do more to promote international economic development than any project yet achieved or proposed. Such an international grid may be anticipated or succeeded by similar oil or gas pipelines.

## Industry

### The need for industrial development

A major debate between economists concerned with West Africa is whether to concentrate very scarce resources for development in agriculture, or whether to concentrate on industry. The latter tends to be favoured as likely to bring quicker returns, because it operates with fewer institutional and social restraints. Almost all leaders advocate it for this reason, as a symbol of modernisation and advance, and because they often regard agricultural reform as more or less hopeless, certainly in the short run.

Industry will not find an adequate market unless the national population, which obtains most of its income from farming, can increase its income sufficiently to buy industrial goods. So in varying proportions, according to the special circumstances of each country (area, population, resources, infrastructure, etc.), there must be both improvement of agricultural production, processing and marketing, and the development of industry. In some cases, these can be combined, e.g. in the improvement of cotton cultivation and the development of textile and clothing manufacture, or in sugar cultivation, refining and manufacture. Both these provide substitutes for imports, and so should be net savers of foreign exchange, though foreign exchange will be needed to build the factories, provide the machines and pay for foreign technical assistance, unless aid is forthcoming. Even then, the finished product, protected by tariffs from foreign competition, will often be more costly, less varied and of inferior quality to the formerly imported article.

Industries are sought as a means of diversifying economies, and this they have done. However, each industry must be economically justified at its establishment, and remain so during its lifetime. This criterion, rarely if ever sustained with vigour, is the only one for economic health, and was the way the great industrial nations achieved their success. Motives such as providing jobs for school leavers or training new skills are best left to the implementation rather than planning stage.

### Problems of industrial location and development

Most industries are located in ports and, Nigeria apart, in few other towns. Ports attract industries processing exports or imports. Such ports are also usually capitals and often the largest towns, so that they also present other advantages to industrialists, such as nearness to government decision-making, to the best transport facilities and labour supply, and to the largest market.

Industry is overwhelmingly concentrated in a relatively few centres of four countries. The francophone ones are, firstly, Senegal (Dakar) where most industries were founded in the expectation of serving all former French West Africa. The other is the Ivory Coast (Abidjan) where most

146

industries have developed since independence in a *laissez faire* and prosperous economy, where there are far more local raw materials than in Senegal, the market is enlarged by the many Europeans, and by free trade in the four other countries of the Benin–Sahel Entente (Upper Volta, Niger, Dahomey and Togo).

The anglophone countries are Ghana and Nigeria. In the former, Takoradi's deep water harbour, opened 1928, was West Africa's first after Dakar; whilst Tema is West Africa's only completely planned town and industrial city. Like Takoradi it has good access to varied raw materials and markets. Industries in Accra have government departments nearby. All three are well served by public facilities, and Ghana has a relatively advanced educational system and standard of living.

Nigeria has an exceptionally large home market, and sixteen towns have significant industries. Resources, including fuels and power, are also very varied. Nevertheless, one-third of all employees are in Lagos, one-fifth in the northern trio of Kaduna, Zaria and Kano, and one-tenth in Ibadan.

So in West Africa there are only these four countries with really significant industries. Ghana and Nigeria alone have a scatter of industries, with some inland, whilst only Nigeria has really widespread and diverse industry. The outlook for the smaller countries, or ones with low populations is very poor, especially for the inland ones.

The relatively few towns with industries increasingly dominate the economies of their countries. To encourage a more balanced development, the development of, preferably, labour-intensive industries in some other towns is being advocated, as well as the encouragement there and in the larger towns of some smaller industries. Industrial estates, often promoted by national or provincial authorities, may be the means of attaining this, just as they have been important in the existing centres, particularly in Nigeria.

Elsewhere, before an industry (or a mine) can be established much of the environment must be modified. The bush must be cleared and drained, power, water and some housing provided, and often medical and social facilities as well. Raw materials are normally very important to West African industries, despite the declining relative significance of these in older industrialised countries. There are commonly problems of irregular, variable or interrupted supplies of raw materials, e.g. of fruit for canning and of timber for processing. Electric power is often interrupted, causing great problems to industries such as metal refining or soluble coffee manufacture. Perhaps the most fundamental long-term problem is that, whilst most new industries must be the fairly simple processing ones, world markets are increasingly requiring more sophisticated products. Consequently, if world markets are being sought (and they are the only ones that are large), then cocoa-producing countries should produce a cocoa liqueur rather than chocolate, and the timber producers should

147

produce unusual furniture or furniture in unusual woods. Likewise, African soap producers should develop and use local essential oils, such as jasmine. Mali already cans tamarind and guava juices; they deserve an overseas market. Of all raw materials, the oil and natural gas of Nigeria should eventually stimulate a broad range of widely distributed chemical industries.

Industrial skills have improved as countries have developed in general and industrially, but managers and skilled workers are still few. There is a need for better machine maintenance, improvement of technical education, and the quality and relevance of all education. In the francophone countries this is still overwhelmingly French-oriented.

Indigenous capital resources are small, and what is available commonly goes into land, private building, road transport and family celebrations, rather than into industrial enterprises. Consequently, the state must often act as 'capital organiser'; it is the agent through which capital is obtained, and from which it is also in part provided. In varying ways it either wholly runs industrial enterprises (as in socialist Guinea and Mali) or participates in mixed companies (part state and part private enterprise) as in most countries. Almost all have always had certain state enterprises, such as railways, since early colonial times.

As so many West African countries have small total populations, and all its peoples are poor, it is often argued that countries should establish joint industries. Many such proposals have been made, most notably by the United Nations Economic Commission for Africa, which has investigated the prospects *inter alia* in iron and steel, superphosphates, chemicals and textiles. Such proposals have foundered on the economic nationalism of countries which want their own factories, and so have tended to found the same industries, e.g. cement. Prospective partners who are weak and poor would lose revenue from import duties, and probably pay more for the new and probably inferior product from a stronger partner. The poorer partner would lose an employment outlet, a prospect no politician dare let go. Such were the complaints up to 1960 when Dakar had most of the industry of French West Africa. In some cases it might be possible to establish part of the manufacture in one country and part in another, but this is rarely economically possible or geographically realistic. Eventually there need to be joint power lines, oil and gas pipelines.

## The character of industrial development

Industries may be classified in many ways. One is to look at their purpose.

### PROCESSING OF LOCAL RAW MATERIALS BEFORE EXPORT

This was an early and often essential function to make export possible, most notably of gold from Ghana, where even rich gold ore contains only 1 part in 40 000 of gold. Waste must be largely eliminated by local refining. Later on local processing competes with overseas processing of the same materials, and may ultimately supplant it. Thus since before the Second World War in Senegal and after it in other countries, groundnut oil has been increasingly extracted locally, as is palm kernel oil. Bauxite is converted to alumina in Guinea, timber is sawn and further processed or peeled for veneer and plywood, and cocoa beans converted to 'couverture', 'neats', cocoa butter and even chocolate. These represent stages of industrial processing, from the essential removal of waste to carrying out in the production area some of the final processing. More of the 'value added' accrues to West Africa, the industry is not limited by the usually small size of the home market because it is producing for export, and national revenue gains. Yet the scope for such industries is limited, unless they can enter a rising market, compete against established processors, or develop such new products as suggested earlier.

### PROCESSING OF LOCAL RAW MATERIALS, MAINLY FOR THE HOME MARKET

These are import substitution industries, and may be subdivided into those currently using only local materials, e.g. for cotton textiles and clothing, shoes, rubber tyres, and Nigeria's oil refinery; and those which process both local and imported materials, with the hope of eventually finding all the raw material locally, e.g. cigarettes, sack, soft drinks and bulk-beer, and some types of shoes. The products of both categories should improve as purchasing power increases, but at present the goods produced are often more costly, of poorer quality and less varied than the imports which would otherwise come in, and in the second group there are frequent disappointments over local supplies of raw material. Moreover import duties are lost to the state, though precious foreign exchange is partly saved.

### LOCAL PROCESSING OR ASSEMBLY OF IMPORTED GOODS, MAINLY FOR THE HOME MARKET

Such are the flour mills of Dakar, Abidjan or Lagos, the car and truck assembly plants at Abidjan and Lagos. They are the import counterpart to the first group. Again, some of the value added by labour accrues to the African country, but in this case the industry is very limited by the size of the home market, as are all the last three categories. That small market may also prefer the imported article if it or something similar is still imported or can be obtained by smuggling.

The potential for further import or partial import substitution industries is now small in those countries which have most industries, i.e. Senegal, Ivory Coast, Ghana and Nigeria. Nor are prospects good in the

*Minerals, fuels and power, and industry*

other countries with small populations or little industry.

There is manifestly a need to develop specialist products such as Tema aluminium, first made from imported alumina but using local power and exporting most of the output. Yet such industries demand education, managerial skills and enterprise which are very rare in the underdeveloped countries. The best hope lies, perhaps, in the further development of hydroelectric power, oil and natural gas supplies, and their progressive distribution by grid and pipeline. This should make existing industries more competitive, be the basis for the initial production of fertilisers, pesticides and plastics, and the later production of caustic soda and ammonia. With cheaper electrical energy, oil and natural gas, an industrial 'take off' could occur.

# 9

# Transport

With the arrival in North Africa of the Arabs in the eighth century, and their use of the camel, contacts developed across the Sahara with the relatively fly-free interior lands of West Africa. The spread there of Islam is a vivid result of these contacts; in the reverse direction, leather, taken from what are now the northern states of Nigeria, was sold in Europe as 'Moroccan leather'. The fringes of the Sahara were linked by Arab traders and by Islam, but to the south lay the repellent forest. Though trans-Saharan traffic was considerable, it was often interrupted and was very difficult in the dry season. The wells which sustained it were dug and maintained by Negro slaves of the Arabs and other peoples.

After the Turks had barred North Africa, European contact with West Africa was necessarily by sea. But the West African forest repelled Europeans as much as the Arabs. To the difficulties of penetrating the forest were added those of an inhospitable coast, difficult to approach and to land upon. Beyond lay the fly-ridden forest, where animals could not be kept and the wheel was unknown. With other inter-tropical regions easier of access, healthier and more advanced, it was natural that European attention should be mainly concentrated in the Americas, in India and the Indies.

Early European interest in West Africa was in relation to those areas; thus Gorée, off modern Dakar, was a landfall on the way to India. The greatest significance of West Africa was as the source of slaves for the American plantations. By the Treaty of Tordesillas, 1494, the Pope had allotted West Africa as a Portuguese sphere, so that the slave trade was at first mainly in Portuguese hands for predominantly Spanish markets. The only other West African products which were sufficiently valuable to withstand difficult and costly transport were melegueta pepper, ivory and gold. They gave their names to various parts of the coast— the Grain Coast ('the Grains of Paradise'—pepper), Ivory Coast (nineteenth-century name), Gold Coast, Slave Coast—though most parts of the coast traded in several commodities.

From the fifteenth century the various trading nations or companies established forts, particularly along the central and eastern Gold Coast shoreline, where there was a little more protection because of short promontories, the rainfall was low, the forest in consequence less dense, and where all the above-mentioned produce was available. The slaves were brought in on foot and the produce by slave porters. Transport to the coast presented no great problem but one aspect of transport to the new world did do so, namely, how to feed the slaves on their long voyage? The wild fruits then available in West Africa were unsuitable for storage, and so the Portuguese, in particular, introduced new crops (p. 94) to provide food for the long voyage.

The creation of major British interests in India, Dutch and then British occupation of the Cape, the abolition of the slave trade and the independence of Central and South America, all induced decay in the old trades in West Africa. Some competitors had come and gone earlier, and there was a general lack of British interest in West Africa during the second and third quarters of the nineteenth century. Not so among the French, who had been allowed to retain their ancient bases, despite their loss of them in most Anglo-French struggles.

That the French kept their interest in West Africa was a reflection of the fact that inland from St Louis and Gorée lay no forest. After the establishment of St Louis in 1659, the French made regular expeditions up the Senegal, and they were the only power which penetrated inland to any extent in West Africa for nearly two centuries. Their later advance into Algeria, Tunisia and Morocco made them heirs of the old trans-Saharan trade.

In the last quarter of the nineteenth century there was a general revival of European interest in the West African forest lands. Rapid industrialisation and rising populations in Europe needed supplies of vegetable oils and certain minerals which this region could supply, in return for cheap manufactured goods. These new needs led to a scramble inland to control the sources of supply, and at the Berlin Conference of 1884–85 it was decided that title to colonies could be maintained only by effective occupancy. Powers which still retained coastal stations, such as France and Britain, pushed their political influence inland; a newcomer, Germany, secured a foothold. On the other hand, Denmark and the Netherlands had sold their coastal holdings in 1850 and 1872 respectively, at the time of the decay of the old economic regime and before the new large-scale palm oil trade. This added its nomenclature to the coast with the Oil Rivers Protectorate, proclaimed in 1885 over that area in and around the Niger delta which, in 1900, produced 88 per cent of the world's palm produce.

At first, head porterage had to be used for carrying imports; and palm oil was sent to the coast by the curious and expensive method of barrel-rolling. Porterage was a social evil, a political danger and an economic waste. Although railways were frequently constructed under harsh conditions of labour, they were (the few navigable rivers excepted) the first alternative to porterage. Labour was released for agriculture, mining and other activities, which made possible a cash economy.

PLATE 21. The most modern of three passenger-cargo boats plying on the Middle Niger in Mali

PLATE 22. Part of the cargo discharged from a weekly downstream boat at Bourem, (Mali). The goods included Dutch toothpaste, Russian sugar, French sweets, Italian detergent, Mali cigarettes and Chinese goods

## River transport[1]

European penetration was often up rivers, for they seemed to provide a natural routeway. Bulky goods could be carried or timber floated over considerable distances, especially in the rainy or flood seasons, which are precisely the most difficult ones for all other means of transport. However, the Niger and the Gulf of Guinea rivers are obstructed at intervals by rapids, many rivers are wholly or largely unnavigable at low water e.g. the Senegal above Podor, the Niger above Mopti, and all of the Benue. The courses of the Senegal and the middle Niger are also long because of their semicircular detours. Moreover, most areas near rivers are not now of economic importance, except for fairly small areas of Mali, the Gambia, Portuguese Guinea and the lower Niger and its delta. The only naturally excellent river, the Gambia, has been severely underused because the enveloping political boundary shuts it off from the natural hinterland.

River navigation has declined because the leading European companies have withdrawn from most retail trading, and African traders are provisioned by road or rail services. The building of roads and of the Maiduguri branch railway in Nigeria, as well as the almost complete laying up of shipping during the Nigerian war of 1967–70, are other major reasons for the decline. The Benue is probably more important to Cameroon than it is to Nigeria but that use may disappear as the Cameroon railway is extended north. The remaining shallow draught services on the Benue and lower Niger depend upon the uneconomic branch railway to the Niger at Baro for freight and for economic use of shipping in both rivers.

Apart from some use of river water for domestic purposes, for irrigation and for power, use for navigation is likely to increase only for the transport of hydrocarbons, cement and other building materials. The first may later come to be distributed mainly by pipeline.

## Rail transport

Three factors have affected railway construction in Africa:

1. Physical considerations such as the relief and nature of the terrain, the presence or otherwise of navigable rivers, the availability of ballast and, until recently, of water.
2. Political problems, such as the need for effective military control and efficient administration.
3. Economic circumstances, such as the availability of labour and capital, and the prospects of an economic return.

All these have had their weight in varying degrees at different times and places, but it is important to realise that railways—as also roads, ports and airports—have sometimes been built in Africa for political purposes rather than in response to solely economic requirements.

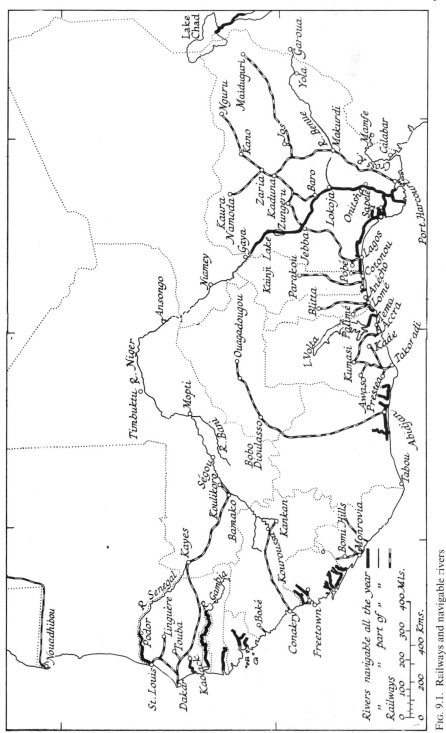

FIG. 9.1.  Railways and navigable rivers
(For greater detail see maps of individual territories)

155

Railway construction in West Africa was undertaken in the face of great difficulties. The Sahara, too great an obstacle for early railway engineers because of the lack of water, is too expensive to cross with a modern railway which, except with heavy mineral traffic, could never pay. Almost all lines have been built from a generally inhospitable coastline. In the early days equipment had often to be offloaded into surf boats. Skilled labour had to be imported at much expense in money and lives, in the infancy of tropical medicine and hygiene. Heavy rainfall necessitates good ballasting, yet ballast material was generally lacking near the coast, precisely where it was most needed. Track maintenance is difficult and expensive in an underdeveloped country, where rainfall can cause many washouts. Bridging has almost everywhere been considerable and expensive—across large rivers, like the Niger at Kouroussa and at Jebba, and the Benue at Makurdi; and across many small ones, lagoons and inland swamps as in Dahomey. River valleys can rarely be followed because of danger from flood and disease-carrying mosquitoes and flies.

Hurried construction of railways through little-known country, difficult to survey, together with the vital need to keep down costs, meant that only minor earthworks were undertaken, gradients were severe, curvature acute, the track devious and often economically ill-placed. In consequence, capacity and speeds are low, and journey times excessively long. Most lines have been realigned at greater cost than that of their original construction.

Long railways pushing north from the Guinea Coast have central sections largely unproductive of traffic and with only thinly peopled country. Thus on the Lagos–Nguru line, there is very little goods and not much passenger traffic from stations between Oshogbo 293 km (182 miles) from Lagos and Zaria 993 km (617 miles), whilst between Enugu 243 km (151 miles) from Port Harcourt and Kafanchan at 739 km (459 miles) there is normally almost no traffic at all. These unproductive sections lie in the poor 'Middle Belt', in which the difficulties of both forest and savanna lands are present, but few of their resources. The paucity of traffic from these long sections is a major economic and operational problem.

Another difficulty was West Africa's deficiency in coal. Until 1915 all coal was imported, but thereafter the mines near Enugu were able to supply railway coal for Nigeria and sometimes to Ghana and Sierra Leone. In French West Africa wood was often used, though it is inefficient as fuel, and timber-cutting caused severe soil erosion, e.g. in Guinea.

After the Second World War diesel locomotives and rail cars were progressively introduced, but they require heavy oils which, except in Nigeria, must be imported at considerable cost in foreign money. Nevertheless, greater efficiency has been achieved.

PLATE 23. One of the first diesel-electric
locomotives in West Africa, introduced about
1948 on the Dakar–Niger line

Railways were, indeed, the means of creating new horizons socially, politically and economically. They introduced many West Africans to wage-earning and mechanical skills. They united peoples and lands which had never before been one, and partly from that union nationalism arose. A wider economy was created, and new towns depending upon the railways developed, such as Kafanchan in northern Nigeria. Housing materials and foodstuffs could be widely distributed. Meat was introduced extensively into the forest zone; dried sea fish, kola nuts and European goods could be distributed in the interior.

Lines in ex-French and ex-British West Africa evolved in different ways as the result of contrasted historical, geographical and political circumstances. The French penetrated eastwards up the Senegal and down the Niger rivers. They were ultimately in possession of continuous territory, in which movement was relatively easy. Their railways were first planned to replace deficient ports, to supplement the navigable sections of the Senegal and Niger rivers, and to link their lands with the Atlantic and Guinea coasts. The systems were officially known as the Dakar–Niger, Conakry–Niger, Abidjan–Niger and Benin–Niger, even though the latter two never reached the Niger. Most of these lines were built for local development but as parts of a general plan for economic integration within the former Federation of French West Africa.

By contrast, British West African railways were all built from the coast, within isolated colonies, as economic or political need arose. Much impetus for railway construction came from the Liverpool, Manchester and London Chambers of Commerce and from that vigorous and far-seeing Colonial Secretary, Joseph Chamberlain. Only with the linkage of the first Nigerian lines from the terminii of Lagos and Baro to a third at Kano was there an aim to integrate with river transport. The common denominator in both French and British colonies was to secure effective political control of the interior, and to attract to, develop and retain within one's own territory as much trade as possible.

Until the 1930s railways were unrivalled as a means of transport. Thereafter, they were increasingly challenged by lorry transport, which has taken away most short distance traffic in valuable produce. Many

157

passengers were lost first to the 'mammy wagon' (Plate 25), and then after the Second World War to private cars and internal air services.

Since the early or mid-1950s, and depending on the line, the country and the economy, railways have taken a poor second place to road transport. Lorry transport now competes for long distance groundnut and similar traffic to and from e.g. northern Nigeria. This competition may not be truly economic, but neither is the Nigerian or other railways, which are all subsidised. Managerial skill is difficult to attract to railways and is especially rare on all but, perhaps, the Ivory Coast line. Deficits have soared and were the lines in private ownership they would have closed long ago, probably with little adverse effects on national economies.

Many lines are in poor repair (especially the Guinea one), and lines have closed in Nigeria, Dahomey and Sierra Leone. Others will do so. Yet more numerous and longer new lines have also been opened—from Bobo Dioulasso to Ouagadougou (Upper Volta) in 1954, from Achiasi to Kotoku (Ghana) in 1956, and from Kuru to Maiduguri (Nigeria) in 1964. New mineral lines are numerous: in Mauritania (1963), Liberia (1951, 1961, 1963 and 1965), and Togo (1960), many short mineral or industrial branches were also added. Railways still seem essential for the transport of heavy mining machinery, minerals, and large amounts of agricultural produce over long distances, and even to distribute petroleum and aviation spirit for road and air competitors. Vigorous management and new enterprise could still bring back other traffic to the railways.

TABLE 9.1. *Provision of railways and railway traffic in West Africa*

| Country | Length of railways (km) | Population per km of track | Area in square km per km of track | Millions of net ton-km 1969 | Millions of passenger-km 1969 |
|---|---|---|---|---|---|
| Senegal | 992 | 3957 | 299 | 183 | 264 |
| Guinea | 662 | 5923 | 371 | n.a. | n.a. |
| Ivory Coast | 625 | 6896 | 516 | 394 | 522 |
| Ghana | 963 | 9373 | 247 | 302 | 474 |
| Togo | 443 | 4192 | 128 | 13 | 88 |
| Dahomey | 579 | 4639 | 199 | 85 | 65 |
| Nigeria | 3475 | 15849 | 254 | 1615 | 728 |

## Roads and road transport

Historically, roads followed railways in West Africa, as in other under-developed countries, and in contrast to European ones. The first important era of road building was the late 1920s and early 1930s, when cheap and reliable lorries or trucks became available. At first roads were built as 'feeders' to the railways. They were usually built at right angles to the

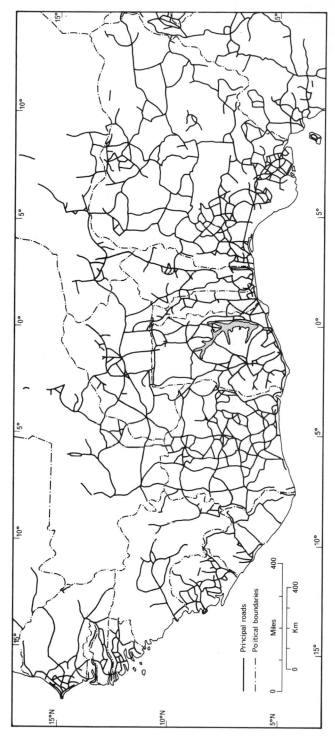

FIG. 9.2. Roads

Principal roads
Political boundaries

Miles

Km

159

PLATE 24. Rivers as impediments. There are few bridges across most rivers, and ferries are of low capacity and take much time. A photo taken at Bamako in 1959, just before the inauguration of the Niger bridge

railway line, so that most early roads in Sierra Leone were north–south, and in the Ivory Coast east–west. In the then Gold Coast some were built north–south, but to open roadsteads such as Cape Coast, instead of to the then sole deepwater port of Takoradi. Apart from these, through road routes were lacking, and so there was no road network. Although a few through roads have since been built in Sierra Leone, and the railway is being closed, the original feeder character of the roads to the railway can still be deduced from Fig. 20.2.

As more roads were built and road transport developed—even on devious routes, so various governments instituted controls of road transport to defend the government railway and its traffic. Such controls, as in the then Gold Coast, took the forms of special licensing and the prohibition of lorry traffic on certain roads or for the transport of specific produce. Some countries still have such controls and many did not encourage long distance buses in the hope of delaying competition to their railway.

Nevertheless, road transport is almost everywhere far more important than rail transport. Roads are increasing fast in length, in quality, and in their national and international links, the latter especially since independence. Figure 9.2 shows main roads and, be they laterite or tarred, the network is far greater, and roads are far more evenly distributed than are navigable waterways and railways (Fig. 9.1). Roads are most numerous in the developed parts of the leading countries i.e. western Senegal, and the southern parts of the Ivory Coast, Ghana and Nigeria. Densely peopled areas such as eastern Nigeria and the Upper Volta also are better provided than the average. Otherwise, the table shows the Ivory Coast to be the best provided. The density of roads in Portuguese Guinea may be partly the result of recent military and

PLATE 25. 'Mammy wagons' in Ghana

PLATE 26. An early long-distance coach on the Gao–Niamey route

PLATE 27. Ore a few months after the opening of the direct Lagos–Benin road

administrative needs. The map shows a paucity of roads in the poor and dry parts of eastern Senegal and western Mali, in Guinea, Liberia and in the 'Middle Belt'—especially of Nigeria.

An important characteristic of roads is their diversity. Somewhat irrespective of their surfacing, they may be all-weather or only seasonally usable. Their surface may be sheer earth, laterite bound, bitumen strips, bitumen or asphalt road, or motorway (Dakar–airport, Accra–Tema only). Some began as private forest or mineral roads, and have been taken into public use. Roads in ex-French countries tend to be wider and better graded than those in ex-British ones.

Good wide roads are costly to build and maintain. Ferries have been progressively eliminated by bridges, especially in the more developed or more productive countries. Ferries can be very time-devouring, and before the Asaba–Onitsha bridge was opened across the Niger in Nigeria in 1965 trucks would often wait about a week for a place on a ferry.

Road transport is subject to interruption or delay in the wet season on poor roads but otherwise it has very few disadvantages. On the other hand, truck transport is capable (given adequate roads) of carrying bulk long-distance traffic, but whether the rates charged are really remunerative is another matter. However, road transport is pre-eminent in hauls of up to very roughly 320 km (200 miles) but is exceedingly flexible as to range, area, passenger and/or goods traffic. Except for long journeys, passengers usually prefer road transport, even in a hot, covered, congested, dual-purpose 'mammy wagon', or on top of a lorry. Long-distance coaches or buses are mainly a phenomenon of the late 1960s, except for the network of services started by the French Cie. Générale Transafricaine (Plate 26). Buses in the large towns appeared mostly in the early 1960s, whilst minibuses and, of course, taxis (often operating like minibuses) are of earlier origin. Cycles are widely used in country areas in the

162

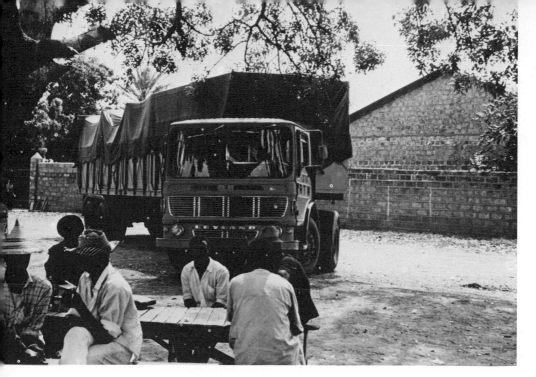

PLATE 28. Long-distance lorry used for Mali–Ivory Coast trade

south, both for carrying goods (one sack between handlebar and saddle, another on the carrier) and for passengers—even first and second class! First-class riders will be taken up all but the steepest hills; second-class travellers must walk up all hills. In savanna lands the donkey is an important means of transport in rural areas.

Road transport has had most important economic and social results. New areas have been brought into the economy. Entirely new settlements have appeared on roads such as Ore near Benin (Plate 27) after the opening of the direct Lagos–Benin road and the link to Ife. Ore is at the junction of these roads. Other new settlements are duplications of older ones away from the road, such as Old and New Idangre, east of Ife. At such settlements there is usually intensive cultivation of vegetables, maize, cassava and yams for sale at the roadside. Road transport has also led to even greater and more frequent mobility than did rail transport.

Road transport is a great African economic activity, especially in the anglophone countries. As such it has been a major means of capital accumulation. Car and truck repairing is both a major enterprise and a supposedly skilled trade. However, many lorries are run uneconomically and most improperly mechanically, so that their life is short.

## Ports

The generally adverse physical characteristics of the West African coast-line have been discussed on pp. 9–10. West African economic development

163

has essentially been one of external contact and trade, so that coastal transfer has throughout been of vital importance, despite the many natural difficulties. Some of the modern ports, such as Dakar, Banjul (Bathurst), Conakry and Freetown have developed where there is natural shelter and deep water. Others enjoy only one of these advantages and needed costly development to overcome the lack of the other one, e.g. Abidjan and Lagos. Together the ports may seem to be quite numerous, but it must be observed that all the first named are on only part of the western coast, and the second group are all on the Gulf of Guinea. Otherwise, this surfbound and sandbar obstructed coast has been countered only at a few other points by the building of long and costly breakwaters to provide an enclosed calm and deep harbour.

River ports are few because of obstructed outlets (e.g. of the Senegal at St Louis), seasonal variation of water level and obstruction by falls, or, in the case of the Gambia, by political restriction of its hinterland. The main river ports are Kaolack (Saloum, Senegal), Pepel (Rokel, Sierra Leone), Sapele, Warri and Burutu (western Niger Delta), and Port Harcourt (Bonny) the last four all in Nigeria.

From the earliest points of contact at the end of the fifteenth century until this mid-century trade passed at first exclusively and then partly through numerous open roadsteads. Ships would lie offshore and be unloaded and reloaded by canoes or lighters. The best roadsteads were those with shelter, with trade goods to offer as well as water and vegetables. The best came to be protected by forts, usually of the merchant companies of the trading powers. These garrisoned forts were also trade depots and residences for the merchants. From the Gold and Slave Coasts hundreds of thousands of slaves were despatched through these forts to the New World.

West Africa's first pier on the Gulf of Guinea was opened at Sekondi, in the then Gold Coast, in 1903, and by the 1930s similar piers had been built at Cotonou, Lome and Port Bouët (Ivory Coast). Goods trains were shunted on to these piers, from which lighters worked to and from ships anchored beyond the surf. This and swell prevented them from tying up at the piers. The last pier to be built is at Nouakchott, Mauritania, opened 1966. Its late construction is suggestive of the semidesertic character and early stage of economic development in which that country finds itself, although it does have an older and naturally sheltered harbour at Nouadhibou farther north. Otherwise, piers came to be vital to the Ivory Coast (and the Upper Volta), Togo and Dahomey (and Niger) until deepwater ports could be built. Meanwhile, the naturally sheltered and deep harbours were also developed and, with greater cost, those already noted as sheltered but requiring deep inlets.

The next economic stage was the progressive substitution of the piers by deepwater harbours, beginning with the replacement of Sekondi pier by Takoradi port in 1928, and continued later with Cotonou in 1965, and

Lome in 1968. To these might be added Monrovia in 1948, despite there having been no preceding pier.

The piers had greatly concentrated traffic through them, although some roadsteads continued e.g. Axim, Dixcove, Cape Coast and Winneba in competition with Sekondi pier. The opening of a deepwater port concentrated trade still further in the then Gold Coast, and absolutely so elsewhere.

The opening of Tema in 1962 and of Buchanan in 1963 illustrate the beginning of the duplication of deepwater ports. Ghana needed another near to the site of the prospective Akosombo Dam, through which the constructor could import heavy constructional equipment. The country also needed a second general port and industrial town. In Liberia the Mount Nimba iron ore mine needed an outlet, and Buchanan was built to provide this. With the opening of Tema, all roadsteads were closed, although by order of the government rather than by economic necessity.

All the deepwater ports built on a surfbound coast have two breakwaters, within which is a substantial area of clam and deep water with quays at which ships can tie up and be unloaded directly. Although Dakar has natural shelter its trading evolution has led to a not dissimilar plan.

The progressive development of new resources has led both to special piers or ports, and to special facilities within ports. Pepel, built for iron ore loading near Freetown, the first special purpose pier, was opened in 1933. Another at Kpémé (Togo) opened in 1961 for the direct loading with phosphate of ships that anchor and tie up a few feet away from the pier. Nouadhibou pier, opened 1963, handles Mauritanian iron ore. Finally, an example of a special facility port is Bonny where ships load oil from pipes.

Among the very numerous examples of special facilities within ports are the phosphate quay in Dakar opened in 1950, an alumina quay at Conakry opened in 1962, three iron ore finger quays in Monrovia for iron ore exports opened in 1951, 1961 and 1965, and many others.

Because of accelerated development and the export of large quantities of minerals, especially iron ore (about 30 million tons annually), port tonnages have increased some fifteen times since the Second World War. Yet no West African port ranks as a very important one by world standards, and collectively their trade is far less than that of Rotterdam. Many of them leave much to be desired in their handling efficiency. Furthermore, trade is usually in diverse articles, so that for exports in particular containerisation is probably not a solution.

Ports are focal points of land, sea and even air transport, and as such they attract a preponderant amount of industry (pp. 146–8). The leading port of a country is usually also the capital. Not only is there congestion at the quays but also in the town, due to its multiplicity of functions and the obvious restriction of space posed by the sea. There is some talk of new sites for capitals, and of encouraging other centres for industries.

PLATE 29. *Air Afrique* plane

## Air transport

Until the Second World War air transport had hardly touched West Africa, but then the loss of the Mediterranean–Suez route, and the campaigns in North Africa, put West Africa on a new and vital supply air route. Airports such as Yundum (Banjul), Lungi (Freetown), Takoradi, Accra, Kano and Maiduguri were vastly improved, or built from nothing, as were many subsidiary airstrips in Ghana and Nigeria. That French West Africa was faithful to Vichy until early 1943 was a further incentive to the air defence of British West Africa. Only after French West Africa joined the Allies did much construction of airports take place there. The fine Dakar airport at Yoff dates from the end of the war, and was built with American aid.

War and peace needs do not necessarily coincide. Dakar, Accra and Kano benefited permanently and are among West Africa's busiest airports. Yundum, the wartime British strategic equivalent to Yoff, cannot rival it in peace. Again, several Freetown airfields were vital to the defence of the naval base and Atlantic convoys, especially when Dakar was unfriendly, but all these airfields are unnecessary in peacetime. Lungi has been retained because it is away from the dangerous mountains behind Freetown, and its runway is the longest and firmest, but it suffers from being on the opposite side of the estuary from Freetown, and has to be reached by ferry from the city, or by light aircraft from Hastings, south-east of Freetown. Monrovia's main intercontinental airport, built by the Americans after 1942, is 90 km (55 miles) from the city.

Traffic development began to be rapid in the early fifties, both on internal and external routes. At first most services were run by European

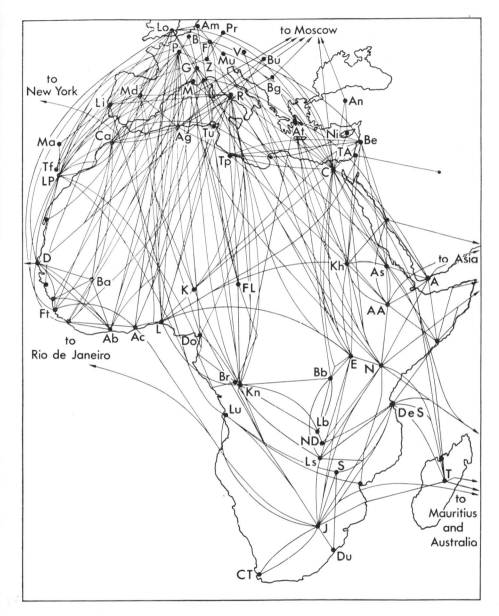

FIG. 9.3. Major intercontinental air links of Africa

Reproduced by courtesy of the *ABC World Airways Guide*, being a simplified version of its map of scheduled air routes to and from Africa

companies. However the British colonies, with British help, formed West African Airways Corporation (WAAC), which provided internal and linking services, while the ex-French colonies in Africa (except Guinea

167

and Mali) later formed *Air Afrique* (Plate 29). Gambia, Sierra Leone and Ghana later withdrew from WAAC, which is now *Nigeria Airways*, and Cameroon and Chad withdrew from *Air Afrique*. All the anglophone and almost all of the francophone countries have their own internal airline, usually very heavily subsidised. The most considerable internal network is in Nigeria but it has suffered from periodic and sudden contractions.

Ghana and Nigerian Airways and Air Afrique run services to outside Africa in pool with a European company. Most external links are with Europe, so services are basically north–south–north. Pure jet aircraft have permitted longer hauls and so there are now fewer calling places; indeed, some Europe to West Africa services are non-stop. Major airlines rarely have more than one intermediate stop, which is commonly on the Mediterranean seaboard or at an inland West African airport such as Bamako, Bobo Dioulasso, Ouagadougou, Niamey or Kano. Air travel has largely replaced sea travel for passengers between Europe and West Africa. Cargo traffic is less important than on many other world routes but is significant to inland airports as well as to those in the more prosperous coastal countries. It is interesting to note the large amount of traffic in French foodstuffs to francophone countries and of British newspapers to anglophone ones.

Even with jet aircraft, climatic factors influence services in several ways. The rainy season makes air navigation more difficult and dangerous, though accidents are very rare. However, this is also the season when fewer air services are required, as commerce is at a minimum. Since prevailing winds are mainly either northeast or southwest one runway in those directions is usually sufficient. Unfortunately, behind the coast low clouds are common in early morning, so that airports should be adjacent to the sea, where this phenomenon is at a minimum. An otherwise much more convenient site at Cotonou (Dahomey) had to be abandoned for this reason, and Ikeja airport, 20 km (12 miles) north of Lagos, is from this point of view, less satisfactory than the earlier one at Apapa. Until the advent of pure jet aircraft in the mid-1960s, the Sahara was always crossed by night, when cold conditions give greater 'lift' and more stable air.

## Conclusion

Railways were pre-eminent as transport media in West Africa until about 1930, when the full challenge of road transport became evident. That from air services became severe about 1955. It is important that wise road, rail, river and air policies be pursued without harmful over-lapping, restriction or excessive subsidy, but with impartial coordination.

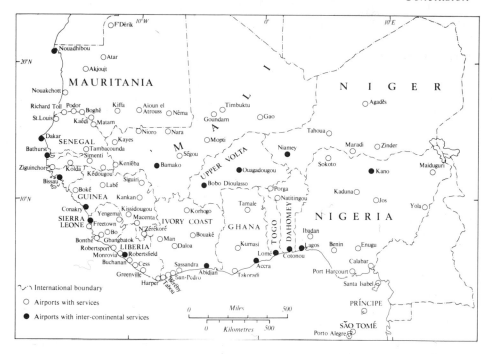

FIG. 9.4. Airports with intercontinental or local West African services

Air routes are not shown, as these change frequently.
Bathurst is now called Banjul

Backward areas of potential value can develop rapidly under the influence of efficient road services. All populated and developed areas obviously need roads. Air services are most helpful for the development of quick cross-country routes for passengers and mail. Nevertheless, railways and rivers (where available) can carry heavy and bulky commodities economically over great distances in all seasons. Bulk transport is the basic requirement for West African trade. These considerations point to the need for a transport plan for each area, worked out in relation to its physical, social and economic geography.

# 10

# Population

West Africa occupies one-fifth of Africa but has nearly one-third of the population, so that this is one of the more peopled parts of a thinly peopled continent. Tropical Africa is less populated than extratropical Africa, but West Africa, whilst comprising one-third the area of Tropical Africa, has nearly one-half of its peoples. Nigeria is Africa's most peopled country; and one in six of all Africans is a Nigerian, and one in two of all West Africans. Compared with Central and West Africa, most of West Africa permits at least subsistence agriculture, and better animal keeping than Central Africa and most of East Africa. In part too, these West African concentrations are reflections of political security and contact with the outer world, first by trans-Saharan trade, and later by maritime contact. In general, West Africa was more readily penetrable than Central or East Africa, and, apart from the minerals of Central Africa, has been the greatest attraction to early traders. Thus it is no surprise that there are major clusters of population in West Africa on certain fringes of the Sahara where political organisation was good and trans-Saharan trade was formerly important, e.g. around Kano, as well as at points of long maritime contact, and in productive forest areas near the coast. There are, however, several real or apparent anomalies, such as the dense cluster of the Mossi in the poor and rather isolated Upper Volta but this is the reflection of cultural circumstance and history.

Like the rest of Africa, West Africa has both high birth and death rates, the annual rate of increase in both cases being 2·4 per cent. West Africa has, alas, Africa's highest fertility and mortality and its lowest life expectancy rates, which explain the somewhat modest rate of increase. As Table 11.1 shows, Niger (2·7) and Ghana (3·0) exceed this figure; while Gambia (1·9), Liberia (1·7), Sierra Leone (1·5) and Portuguese Guinea (0·9) have much lower figures. Thus, the population is generally growing quite fast, the rate is increasing, the proportions of very young and quite old people are rising rapidly, which will add to the social burdens of these poor countries, but there is as yet, no great population explosion. However, there is, as in most of Africa, an 'urban explosion', for the rate of urbanisation in Africa is the highest in the world. West Africa may soon have several lesser-Calcutta's, centres of acute housing problems and health hazards.

In the difficult exercise of interpreting West African population figures, and in drawing conclusions, the deficiencies of almost all censuses should be borne in mind. Dispersion of the rural population, poor transport and communications, and widespread illiteracy make the taking of a census difficult, especially over a short time. Moreover, many fear censuses because they believe they are the prelude to heavier taxation. Counting, especially of human beings, is often regarded as unseemly.

The main purpose of this chapter is to examine the population of West Africa as a whole from the geographical viewpoint, namely distribution, 'man–land' relationships or population pressure, spatial movements and urbanisation. The several chapters of Part III have further information.

## Areal distribution

West Africa has the highest average population density in tropical Africa, yet its population pattern has no simple explanation. Population distribution is not, as in Europe, the result of long trial and error over many centuries by advanced peoples, in each type of environment. Tradition is stronger in West Africa than in most temperate regions; attachment to the soil, even in poor areas, and dislike of nearby fertile but non-traditional areas are important factors. Thus the Ibo of southeastern Nigeria are densely concentrated in a mediocre environment, but to the east are richer and thinly peopled lands. The same is true of fairly heavy concentrations on infertile *bowé* around Labé in Guinea, the Mossi concentration in the Upper Volta, the Kabrai in the Atacora Mountains of northern Togo, and many more.

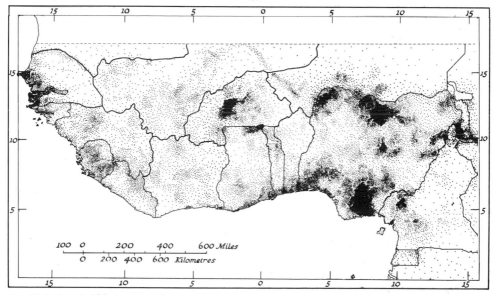

Fig. 10.1.  Rural African population

Compiled by Glenn T. Trewartha and Wilbur Zelinsky, and reproduced with their permission.

Fertile areas were often left unpeopled or only sparsely occupied, either because of slave raiding or the fear of it, e.g. in the Bole region of northwestern Ghana. Tribal conflict also has depopulated many areas; hence the thinly peopled 'no-man's–land' or 'shatter zones' between the well populated old Dahomey state and Yorubaland, the latter and Benin, Kano and Bornu and many more.

Once the population is reduced by these or other factors to about 5 per sq km (12 per sq mile) in country of few streams, or nearer 28 per sq km (70 per sq mile) where there are many streams, tsetse fly infestation often becomes so severe as to make the area uninhabitable. A certain minimum population is required to control fly and make habitation possible.

Most Africans live near the soil, so that the correlation between water supplies and population is close. Thus there are the peopled valleys of the Senegal, Niger and Sokoto, where tsetse are few. Elsewhere, dwelling in such areas means danger from mosquitoes, simulium and tsetse flies. Ibo country again provides a paradox, of a densely peopled area with poor water supplies.

Defence considerations, important in the siting of settlements everywhere in the world at one time or another, have been very significant in West Africa. This was especially true in the days of intertribal warfare, but tradition is so strong that most peoples remain loyal to the ancient nuclei, though the original siting reasons have passed away. Ibadan arose as the Yoruba war camp around Mapo Hill, from which there are excellent views. The Somba live in the poor hill country of the Atacora Mountains in Dahomey, the Dan and the Labe occupy the scarp fastnesses of Bandiagara, and the Birom were pushed on to the agriculturally poor Jos Plateau. The intense peopling of the Fouta Djallon by the Fulani may be partly explicable in terms of easier defence, healthier conditions and the chance to remain cattle-keepers, though settled ones, and with Ndama cattle rather than with their traditional Zebu humped cattle. The Fulani also took Negro slaves to grow crops in the valleys.

In other places the defence factor, though real and fundamental, is less obvious. Many settlements were established close to lookouts, to which retreat could be made if necessary, as at Savalou and Savé in Dahomey. Likewise, the Somono and Sorko first lived near the Niger River, to use it for escape if attacked; and the lagoons of the Ivory Coast, Togo and Dahomey were favoured by some peoples for the same reason. Defence of a culture has also been important; thus non-Muslim peoples left the far north of Nigeria for the Jos Plateau, the Mandara Mountains, Adamawa Highlands and many smaller rugged areas, the better to safeguard their religion.

The varying abilities of peoples to organise their political, social and economic affairs have been important factors.[1] Thus the Kano area is densely peopled because first the Hausa rulers, then the Fulani emirs,

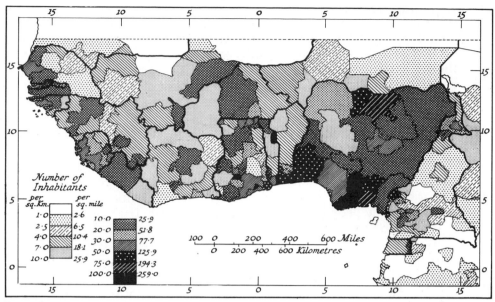

Fig. 10.2. Population density by administrative area

Compiled by Glenn T. Trewartha and Wilbur Zelinsky, and reproduced with their permission

and later the British provided settled government. With this fundamental prerequisite, the alert Hausa farmer has made much of available water and of the light soils. The other emirates of Nigeria generally have more than the average population density of that latitude, for the same reasons of defence and settled government. They have, however, less than for Kano because of poorer water supplies, except for those along the Sokoto River.

Traditional attachment to a state, like that already alluded to for towns, is also strong. Thus New Juaben, formed by Ashanti people outside Ashanti, is a small state around Koforidua. It has the highest rural density of population in Ghana; had the state been larger, the density of population would have been far less.

One of the most arresting features of the West African population map is the existence of the generally thinly peopled Middle Belt, on the outer fringes of the forest, a belt which may be followed from the east through most of the Guinea coastlands, roughly between $7\frac{1}{2}°$N and $10°$N (Fig. 10.1). This belt, which has few natural resources and produces no considerable exports, suffered from slave raiding, has all the diseases and problems of forest and savanna, but no compensating advantages except a general absence of population pressure. Local efforts have been made to re-populate this zone, notably with Mossi in the central Ivory Coast and with Kabrai in central Togo. Peaceful conditions, railways, roads and commerce have also done something to even out or relocate population, but no major alteration has taken place, nor is this likely for a long time.

173

## Population pressure on the land

A matter of increasing urgency in certain areas is pressure of population on the land, which European intervention tended to increase, often as the result of specifically humanitarian work. Tribal wars have virtually ended, tropical diseases cease to take savage toll of life, modern transport brings in relief supplies if famine occurs, and infantile mortality—while still high—has diminished. Consequently, populations are increasing, some rapidly. The land, which formerly produced only subsistence crops, now carries cash crops as well. The fallow period has been drastically shortened, per capita land area is less, and soil erosion has increased. Much the same consequences ensue from overstocking with livestock because of increased demands for meat, and population pressure can well occur in thinly peopled but poor areas of the Sahel.

Population pressure may be evidenced by such misuse of the land as leads to its degradation, to poorer crop yields, and so to a progressive lowering of the standards of living. All this may encourage migration, either short or long term, short or long distance, national or international. Such is the situation of the Mossi of Upper Volta, the Kusasi and the Mamprussi of far northern Ghana. Alternatively, population pressure may lead the same people at a different time or stage of development, or other peoples, to develop more intensive and productive farming. This has been achieved around Kano and other northern Nigerian cities by the Hausa, and in Togo by the Kabrai on their tiny terraces (Plate 94). And, while some Ibo migrate, even to Equatorial Guinea and Gabon, to work, others remain to continue quite intensive farming over much of their crowded homeland.

Population pressure is doubtfully capable of measurement; even if it were, it would, theoretically, change from moment to moment with the total population. The effects are, however, plain for all to see and can be measured. How and when they occur depend on each people over time, their technological, social, economic and political organisation, the efficiencies of these at a given time, the quality of the land, and the vagaries of the climate and weather.[2]

## Migrant labour

People move from areas of poverty and poor prospects ('push' areas), to those of actual or supposed opportunity ('pull' areas). The push areas are commonly regions of population pressure (whether densely or thinly peopled) in the savannas. Migration may be seasonal, for a period of years, longer term—even the rest of a working life, or permanent.

Poverty is not always the sole reason for migration. The migrant is usually young and adventurous, and may wish to break out, if only for a time, from the social constraints of his family, kin and village. Among certain peoples he may be virtually compelled to participate in a migrant labour tradition, a kind of adult male initiation or status symbol, a matter of equal importance to the need for money, which, in turn, is commonly sought for helping relatives and acquiring a wife.

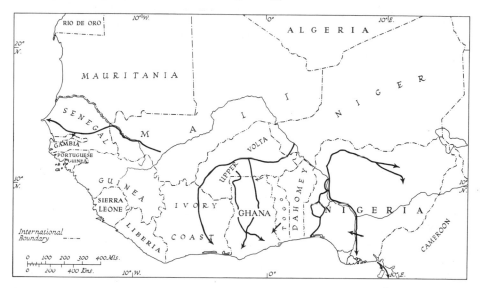

FIG. 10.3. Labour routes

So far as 'pull' areas are concerned, international migration is declining within West Africa, though this is slightly offset by intercontinental movement, e.g. of Maliens to France and some Nigerian Ibo to Britain. There is now little movement into Senegal for groundnut cultivation, because of greater political and currency controls than in colonial days, so that migration is largely confined to the most developed and richer areas of the Guinea coastlands, for work not wanted by the local peoples. Such is work on the coffee and cocoa farms of the Ivory Coast, the mines and cocoa farms of Ghana and Nigeria, and certain jobs in large cities of all West Africa. However, there have been major expulsions, particularly of foreign traders, from the Ivory Coast and Ghana.

The absence of many young and vigorous men may impoverish the agricultural practices and reduce crop yields in the community they leave, a phenomenon well known in South African reserves but acute in West Africa probably only in Upper Volta. Their absence may also upset the demographic balance, loyalties within families, and lead to a dependence by the very young, the women and the old upon remittances from the young migrant men. On their return they may find it difficult to readjust to the poor rural and parochial community, and it to them. More particularly, the skills acquired are rarely useful at home in a different climatic region and socio-economic organisation.

175

While the migrants are away, particularly those in towns, they may sleep twenty or more to a room, eat new and poor food, and that irregularly. Not surprisingly they are often listless, ill—physically and mentally, and so not good employees. For these reasons, but mainly because there are so many seeking so few jobs, there is much un- or under-employment. The latter is often in uneconomic occupations such as shoe-shining, newspaper selling and porterage. Poverty is often acute, and disillusion profound. On the other hand, there is, perhaps, physical and psychological freedom, there are rewards for some of those with intelligence and initiative, and comparison of urban and rural slums may not be wholly to the disadvantage of the former in African eyes.

## The spread of disease

European contact, economic development and independence have each encouraged greater mobility of peoples, but this is greatest in the sector of migrant labour. Mobility of peoples necessarily means dispersion of disease, even though modern medicine has brought other and generally greater advantages. Early European contact brought in such new diseases as influenza, and spread existing ones such as malaria and sleeping sickness. R. Mansell Prothero and John M. Hunter have made many studies of the spread of diseases in West Africa, the former by migrants[3] and the latter more specially of onchocerciasis or river blindness.[4]

## Towns

Precolonial trade routes were few and sharply defined because of inter-tribal wars and the prevalence of deadly flies and disease. West Africa is almost unique in tropical Africa in having had precolonial towns. A considerable number of these owe their origin partly or wholly to being well-defended places on trade routes, e.g. Kano adjacent to its two prominent hills used as lookouts, Zinder, Agadès, and Timbuktu.

Caravan halts were especially important if they were also the place for change of mode of transport, e.g. from camel to donkeys, horses or men—as at Kano—or were adjacent to varied regions, e.g. Bouaké. Some are now much less significant, such as Odienné, because of the decay of a trade route, just as some former Roman towns have decayed in Britain or France.

Religious centres are sometimes significant, especially in Muslim areas; such is the case with Djenné and Mopti. Many towns were state capitals, such as Kano, Gao, Ségou, Ouagadougou, Kumasi, Abomey and Benin.

European conquests led to many new towns, resulting from the new political and economic order. Administrative towns were established, such as Kaduna, Bingerville and, later, Abidjan. New significance was given to smaller centres by the system of 'district' or 'circle' administration.

Early European trading points and forts such as Elmina and Goreé (Plate 37) and gum *escales* like Dagana on the Senegal, are not significant now. They have given place to newer trading centres—both ports and inland centres. River towns arose such as Lokoja, Koulikoro and Kayes. Railways led to the creation of towns such as Baro and Kafanchan in Nigeria, Kindia and Mamou in Guinea. Roads have helped to produce towns such as Ore, west of Benin, on the direct Lagos–Benin road opened in 1963 (Plate 27). Likewise, mining led to such towns as Jos and Bukuru in the Nigerian tin fields, Tarkwa, Prestea and Obuasi by gold mines in Ghana. Currently, the formidable urban explosion is due to the inter-action of many of these influences in certain towns, and especially to those of commerce and industry. These are the attractors of migrants to such rapidly growing centres as Dakar, Abidjan, Tema, Lagos and Port Harcourt.

Many of the port capitals of West Africa suffer from major environ-mental problems. Dakar, Conakry and Freetown lie on peninsulas, the first a dry one, the second narrow, and the last mountainous. Abidjan and Lagos are lagoon-island towns where reclamation and drainage have been costly, and the disposal of sewage and other effluents particularly difficult. The journey to work is often costly, long and tiring, particularly in Lagos. Water supply has often been a severe problem, to be resolved in part in Dakar by bringing in water from the far away Senegal River, and done in Freetown by the construction of the Guma Dam.

Costs of living are high, not only because of the necessarily high costs of transport but because of overcentralisation of governmental services, port functions, commerce, industry and social services in one town—formidably illustrated by Lagos, double capital of Nigeria and of Lagos State. All these services are attractors of migrants, so these towns are social mosaics of their country.

Nor is it surprising that local government is rarely if ever equal to the task. It is commonly both inefficient and corrupt, and most administrations tend to prevent newcomers from seeking membership of their councils, becoming appointed to their staffs, or even from using local services.

Within the urban hierarchy, the major town is almost always a primate city, so that it has far more than twice the population of the next town. Consequently, the rank-size rule, though it may apply to the rest of the hierarchy of the other towns, does not fit for the primate one. Dakar has a population of 474 000, and the next largest town, Kaolack, has 69 500.

Appalling as are all these problems, they are as nothing compared with the basic one—that the urban explosion has occurred ahead of major industrial or agricultural revolutions. Here is the basic contrast with the industrial countries. So there is also population pressure in urban environments, for the population is increasing faster than economic productivity, represented mainly in industry and trade. Thus in Senegal

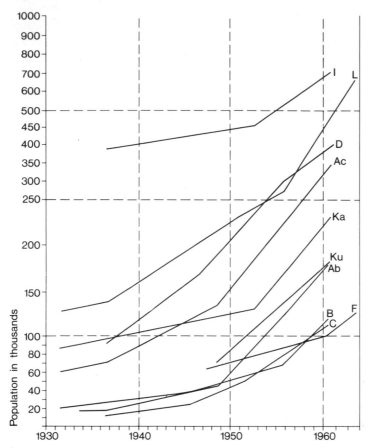

FIG. 10.4. Population growth of selected towns
(From a graph by M. Safier)

the towns have increased by more than 100 per cent in a decade. Enugu, in Nigeria, was an empty site in 1914 and now has a population of more than 80 000; Ibadan, also in Nigeria, has trebled its population in 20 years. And much of this population concentration is packed into the peri-urban fringes, slums and shanty towns.'[5]

Solution of this problem of overgrowth is peculiarly difficult because, on the one hand, there are those who believe the major towns have been and will continue to be vital 'growth poles' for general economic development. Others believe that the smaller (but not small) towns should be developed by some decentralisation of services from the primate city and by the encouragement of industry, so enlarging their currently smaller populations and stemming the flow of people to the congested primate city. This is most practicable in the fairly developed countries which have electric power, such as the Ivory Coast, Ghana and Nigeria, the latter also possessing oil and natural gas. In this connection it is interesting to mention the new town and port of Tema in Ghana, built on garden city lines, and a notable example of a spacious layout, with people living near their work, leisure and shopping facilities.

## Non-African population

African education was widely developed in the ex-British lands, so that there were more Africans in senior posts than in ex-French Africa. European administrators have been replaced by Africans in almost all government departments, except in the Ivory Coast, and non-Africans are now mainly technical advisers, business executives, teachers and missionaries. They are least numerous in the radical states of Guinea and Mali, but very numerous in the conservative Ivory Coast.

Non-Africans could not own land in British West Africa, but were permitted to do so in other countries (except Liberia), where planters sometimes established themselves. They still have some importance in the Ivory Coast, and especially on the islands of the Bight of Biafra. In Senegal and the Ivory Coast Europeans continue to own or manage hotels, cafés, shops, business and industrial enterprises to an extent unknown in former British West Africa even in colonial days.

In most countries the non-African population has become far more varied since independence. It is no longer dominantly from the former colonial power, but usually includes experts from many other European countries, Russia, China or Taiwan, Israel and America. Newly independent countries are keen to use the experience of countries which have themselves faced formidable problems and adopted new methods or techniques in solving them. Advice and help have also been sought from United Nations agencies, so that experts from many countries visit West African states. These and other visitors have stimulated a notable development of hotels in the major towns.

The 'Syrians', as they are almost always called, are, in fact, predominantly Lebanese. They are mainly the smaller traders and shopkeepers of West Africa, particularly up-country, although some have built up large and varied enterprises in the major cities. Indian merchants are also to be found in ex-British states and in Portuguese Guinea.

# Part III
# The political divisions

# 11

# Introduction to the political divisions

The earliest development of statehood in West Africa was in the dry savanna lands of the Senegal and the upper and middle Niger valleys. Tekrur was a state of the Senegal valley in the eleventh century, while in the upper and middle Niger valley Ghana, Mali, and Songhai followed one another between the ninth and sixteenth centuries. Farther east, the Hausa-Bokwoi and Bornu states developed about the fourteenth century, surviving today as the mainly Fulani-ruled emirates of northern Nigeria.[1] These states flourished in a zone that is now much less productive than the forest zone of the coast. Yet the dry zone presented greater geographical advantages in those centuries, for it lay north of the then denser and more extensive forest, much more difficult of penetration then than now because of its greater extent and the simpler techniques available. The states of the dry savannas lay on the southern edge of the Sahara and were often terminals of Arab trans-Saharan trade routes. These were greatly facilitated by the existence of far more wells which were maintained by Negro slave labour. The Senegal and Niger rivers provided water, fish, routeways, seasonal cultivation, and tsetse fly-free pastures to these states, which were also intermediaries in the gold, ivory and slave trades from the smaller, and usually younger, forest-situated states of Ashanti, Dahomey, Yorubaland, and Benin. Gold has been obtained from what is now Ghana for fully a thousand years.

The Turkish occupation of most of North Africa, the penetration of the Portuguese to West Africa by sea, and the trans-Saharan conquest of Songhai by the Moroccans in 1591 contributed to the decay of trans-Saharan trade and of the savanna lands that greatly depended upon it. Instead, the forest lands quickly acquired the advantage of proximity to maritime European traders that the savanna lands had previously enjoyed relative to Arab trans-Saharan merchants. This advantage of proximity has become absolute for the forest lands because of their far greater resources and potential relative to the savannas and to world needs. That the development of the forest zone (like that of the savanna zone) has not been uniform has been due not only to geographical differences, but also to those of political and economic policy.

Most political boundaries in West Africa were hastily drawn between 1885 and 1919 with scant regard for natural and human patterns. Almost

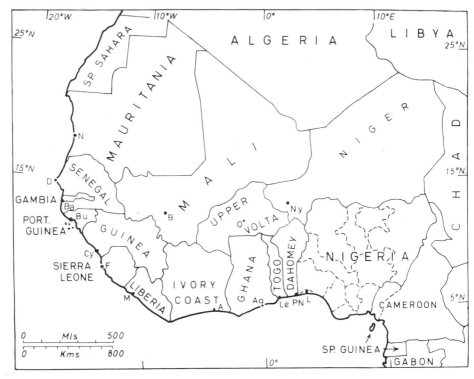

FIG. 11.1. Political divisions and their capitals

all boundaries are geometric lines, or follow rivers, watersheds or other divides which are rarely ethnic.

Boundaries often reflect the limit of colonial military penetration, e.g. the northern boundary of Ghana. Many are the result of compromise, such as the northwestern boundary of Nigeria. Others are the consequence of exchange, such as the British cession of the Los Islands, off Conakry, Guinea, in exchange for an area now in northwestern Sierra Leone.

Rarely have international lines been drawn to respect the unity of African peoples; thus the Niger–Nigeria boundary divides the Hausa people. Even more cynical was the deliberate partition of the Kru people by the Ivory Coast–Liberia boundary, so that French West Africa might secure some of these seafaring people, so useful on West African ships[2]. Less deliberate but more drastic was the partition of the Ewe in Togo under British and French Mandates in 1919, and continued as Trustee-ships from 1946 until 1957 and 1960 respectively (see pp. 396–7).

The already unsatisfactory Niger–Nigeria boundary also bisects natural trade routes. Far more serious in this respect is the Gambian boundary composed of arcs and straight lines, which shuts off the Gambia river from its natural hinterland (see Chapter 13). The lagoon waterway between Porto-Novo, the capital of Dahomey, and Lagos, the Nigerian Federal capital (see p. 399), is crossed by the Dahomey–Nigeria boundary.

From 1904 till 1958 French West Africa was the largest political unit of West Africa, but it broke up in 1958–59 with the independence of Guinea and the later decision of the other seven members to become independent republics. The Ivory Coast, Upper Volta, Niger and Dahomey created the Benin–Sahel Entente, which Togo joined in 1966.

The oldest French settlements were the islets of Gorée (off Dakar) and St Louis (Senegal estuary), founded in 1659. From them the French later penetrated up the Senegal and down the Niger rivers. These provided west–east routes, and the Sahel zone, through which they partly flow, is one which facilitates movement and has fewer hazards from disease than many others.

French ingress from the Guinea coast was subsidiary to their more important line of movement from west to east, and to British lines of advance from that coast. Consequently French West Africa had its main axis and extent in poor Saharan, Sahel and savanna lands, with lesser projections to the richer forested Guinea coast. French West Africa thus had long lines of communication in relatively unproductive country, and was very continental, with a high proportion of land to coastline. Mali, the Upper Volta and Niger are land-locked states.

British West Africa was a mere expression covering four separate colonies, developed from the richer forested lands. The politically and economically diverse and generally richer lands of British West Africa needed shorter lines of communication, and had relatively greater coast-lines, far greater populations and overseas trade.

The former French lands are rather over dependent upon a few cash products. The dry zone countries of Senegal, Mauritania, Mali, Upper Volta and Niger depend overwhelmingly upon groundnuts, cotton and livestock, except for Mauritania's iron ore and Senegal's phosphates. The Ivory Coast and Guinea have the most varied economies, the former with coffee, cocoa, timber, bananas, pineapples and diamonds, the latter with bauxite, alumina, bananas, coffee and diamonds. These two countries have good potentials.

Contrasted political organisation and economic regulation have led to differing economies. Thus, plantations established by non-Africans were permitted and encouraged outside the former British territories. Plantation-produced bananas and other fruits are significant exports from Guinea and the Ivory Coast, but are unimportant ones from the non-plantation lands of ex-British Nigeria, Ghana and Sierra Leone. Cocoa and coffee are also partly produced on non-African plantations in the Ivory Coast, as is rubber (the main agricultural export of Liberia). Since independence, however, most states have been actively encouraging plantations.

Mineral production was slight in French West Africa until 1953, largely because of the unwillingness of private French capital to invest in such enterprise. Even now, iron, bauxite and diamonds are won in the successor republics very largely with foreign capital. Nationalisation and fears of possible nationalisation have caused some hesitancy among private investors towards new developments, particularly in Ghana, Guinea and Mali.

The economic development of Liberia and Portuguese Guinea suffered in the past from shortage of capital, as well as from traditionalist methods or mercantilist conceptions of the means of development. The economies of ex-French West Africa and of Portuguese Guinea were also far more closely integrated with their metropolitan countries than were those of ex-British West Africa with the United Kingdom. Production was often heavily subsidised, prices were frequently far above world levels in the French lands, and exports were commonly directed to protected markets in the metropolitan country or its dependent territories. Such was the case with groundnut oil extracted and refined in Senegal, which enjoyed a protected market in France and the French Community.

British West Africa was not free from restrictions, but those that prevailed resulted more from the decisions of the African peoples themselves, rather than from those of the British Government in London. Economic regulations in British territories proceeded from the bottom upwards; in non-British territories, control proceeded from the top downwards. The non-British colonies had much more restrictive economies, their markets and sources of supply were narrower and, in consequence, imports were less varied, their prices higher and the cost of living greater, characteristics which remain in independence.

British political aims in West Africa contrasted strongly with those pursued by Portugal and France until 1955. These powers sought to attach their territories in a close political and economic union with the mother country, a union that survives in the case of Portuguese Guinea. The culture and outlook of these mother countries were diffused widely, so that as many Africans as possible should become assimilated or at least be closely associated and identified with the former governing power. African customs and institutions were given little encouragement, and African languages were rarely used in education. These policies have tended to produce an African élite often sympathetic to the former or still-governing power but divorced from African life; the majority of the populations had little encouragement of their initiative.

British policy, by contrast, was directed to achieving the political and economic independence of overseas territories. Political and economic links with the United Kingdom were of the loosest kind, diverse and constantly changing. Political, social and economic power rested with African elected legislative councils and with generally wholly African executive councils drawn from the dominant African political party.

TABLE 11.1. *West African states: area and population*

| Country | Capital | Area in sq km and sq miles* | Estimated population 1970 | Annual rate of increase 1963–70 | Density per sq km and per sq mile |
|---------|---------|------------------------------|----------------------------|----------------------------------|------------------------------------|
| Senegal | Dakar | 196 192 *75 750* | 3 925 000 | 2·4 | 20 *52* |
| Gambia | Banjul | 11 295 *4 361* | 364 000 | 1·9 | 32 *83* |
| Mauritania | Nouakchott | 1 030 700 *397 969* | 1 171 000 | 2·2 | 1 *3* |
| Mali | Bamako | 1 240 000 *478 783* | 5 022 000 | 2·1 | 4 *10* |
| Upper Volta | Ouagadougou | 274 200 *105 868* | 5 384 000 | 2·1 | 20 *52* |
| Niger | Niamey | 1 267 000 *489 208* | 4 016 000 | 2·7 | 3 *8* |
| Portuguese Guinea | Bissau | 36 125 *13 948* | 556 000 | 0·9 | 15 *39* |
| Guinea | Conakry | 245 857 *94 930* | 3 921 000 | 2·2 | 16 *41* |
| Sierra Leone | Freetown | 71 740 *27 699* | 2 512 000 | 1·5 (1963–69) | 35 *91* |
| Liberia | Monrovia | 111 369 *43 000* | 1 171 000 | 1·7 | 11 *28* |
| Ivory Coast | Abidjan | 322 463 *124 504* | 4 310 000 | 2·3 | 13 *34* |
| Ghana | Accra | 238 537 *92 100* | 9 026 000 | 3·0 | 38 *98* |
| Togo | Lomé | 56 000 *21 622* | 1 857 000 | 2·5 | 33 *85* |
| Dahomey | Porto-Novo | 112 622 *43 484* | 2 686 000 | 2·5 | 24 *62* |
| Nigeria | Lagos | 923 768 *356 669* | 55 074 000 | 2·5 | 60 *155* |
| Total West Africa | | 6 137 869 *2 369 895* | 100 995 000 | 2·5 | 16 *43* |

*Square miles shown in italic numerals

Needless to say, the aims of such bodies were to develop African culture, institutions and languages, but this was equally British policy. The élite in British territories have sometimes been unsympathetic to Britain, but it is an élite far less divorced, or not divorced, from African life.

Liberia has been an independent state since 1847, whilst Portuguese Guinea is still ruled by Portugal. Otherwise, independence was achieved for the nine ex-French and four ex-British territories between 1957 and 1965, most becoming independent in 1960. The political map is shown on Fig. 11.1 and the statistical details are in Table 11.1.[3]

Colonial West Africa disintegrated into independent states; 'disintegrated' because it was never intended, until 1956 at the earliest, that any of the nine ex-French states should become independent and their boundaries were formerly rather unimportant administrative limits. Nor was full independence expected for the small ex-British colonies of Sierra Leone and Gambia until a few years before that came about. We have, therefore, a mosaic of states nurtured with different policies and methods, and determined to go their own independent, separate and often conflicting ways. The Gambia is but three times the area of Derbyshire, but much is river, freshwater or mangrove swamp, and the population a mere 364 000 (1970). The physically magnificent river, wholly exceptional in Africa, is navigable for ocean vessels all the year far up river, yet is visited by only a few vessels annually because its political boundary and colonial nationalism shut off the economic hinterland. Complete integration with Senegal is so genuinely difficult that it may never occur.

The United Kingdom is a small country, yet Senegal, Gambia, Portuguese Guinea, Sierra Leone, Liberia, Ghana, Togo, and Dahomey are all smaller. Many states have under five million inhabitants, notably all the aforementioned (except Ghana), the Ivory Coast, Guinea and the large-sized Mauritania and Niger. A small population in a large area poses major administrative, social and economic problems. The Upper Volta, a little larger than the United Kingdom, has just over five million people but is grossly overpopulated. The main resource of the Upper Volta is its labour which seeks work mainly in the Ivory Coast and Ghana. Moreover, Mali, Upper Volta and Niger are three of Africa's fourteen landlocked countries, while Mauritania, though not landlocked, has suffered from many of the problems of such countries. Thus most of the independent states of West Africa present immense problems of sheer survival, and give rise to concern as to whether colonialism has been replaced by perpetual dependence on foreign aid. Mali, Upper Volta, Niger, Dahomey and Guinea are in the Unctad list of the world's twenty-five poorest nations, although Guinea has much unrealised potential. Only the Ivory Coast, Ghana and Nigeria, particularly the latter, are economically very viable states, and none can be reckoned free of many major problems.

The division of West Africa into fourteen independent countries is by no means the end of the divisions. There are the new currencies, for where there was previously one British West African pound there are now four currencies; and where there was the CFA franc there are now three more—those of Guinea, Mauritania and Mali. Although the latter may readopt the CFA franc others are proposing to create their own. Association of the ex-French countries with the European Economic Community was a colonial decision, but its divisive effects have been accentuated by Commonwealth West Africa's early isolation from it and Guinea's secession.

Yet attempts at integration are not wanting. The Ghana–Guinea Union of 1958, joined by Mali in 1960 when it was renamed the Union of African States in the hope of more members, was an exciting prospect since it cut across former Anglo-French colonial divisions. It associated three geographically diverse countries with contrasted products and non-competing exports. No substantial results came from this so-called 'union', because the countries are not all contiguous, they have different official languages, constitutions and administrative methods, had three inconvertible currencies, and operate in or through three different financial zones.

Another effort at integration, dating from 1964, is for a free trade area comprising Guinea, Sierra Leone, Liberia and the Ivory Coast. The first two already have trade, payments and other agreements, while the Ivory Coast is a member of the customs free Benin–Sahel Entente and an associated member (unlike the other three) of the European Economic Community. The four countries of the proposed free trade area have two official languages, contrasting histories, constitutions, administrative methods, political aims and economic policies, membership of four trading zones, and four different currencies—one of which is inconvertible. Although these countries have somewhat contrasted environments and products, and are contiguous, their road and trade links are few. However, the nearest port for southern Guinea is Africa's only free port of Monrovia, to which there is access by a fairly good road. Substantial trade moved along it in the 1950s but much less since Guinea lost the main market for its coffee in France and adopted its inconvertible franc. Some trade is now carried on the Buchanan–Mount Nimba mineral line. Otherwise, trade is mainly in small cattle (when available) from Guinea to Sierra Leone and Liberia, and in kola nuts and foreign goods not readily imported directly into Guinea but obtained via Sierra Leone (when Guinea can find the necessary exchange).

A far more successful effort at integration has been the Benin–Sahel Entente formed in 1959 between the Ivory Coast, Upper Volta, Dahomey, and Niger, and joined by Togo in 1966. All were formerly under French rule and so have the same official language. They have similar constitutions and methods, are contiguous, and use the same common currency as before. Moreover, they were already closely integrated

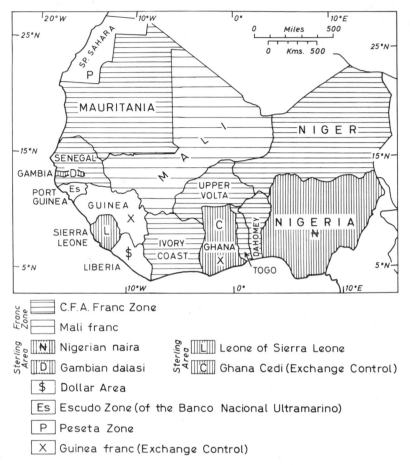

FIG. 11.2. Currencies of West Africa
Mauritania left the CFA franc Zone in 1973

economically in pairs—the Ivory Coast with the Upper Volta by the
Abidjan to Ouagadougou railway, roads and air services, and by Upper
Volta labourers working in the Ivory Coast. Dahomey fulfils a similar
transit function for Niger, although some trade passes through Nigeria.
Again contrasted countries were brought together, but ones well known
to and already needing each other. Yet nothing fundamentally new has
so far come from the agreement—certainly nothing like a much needed
integrated policy for industrial development, which is still overwhelmingly
concentrated in Abidjan in the Ivory Coast.

However, these five countries have freedom of trade, and a unified
system of fiscal schedules and external tariffs. They have common agreements with France, there is a central fund to prepare development projects
and so encourage external aid. There are declared aims of common
administration of public works, road traffic and quarantine, foreign

190

affairs, justice, labour, constitutional and electoral procedures, organisa-tion of the armed forces, public services and a common diplomatic corps.

Another promising association is that of Liptako-Gourma, grouping Mali, Upper Volta and Niger in discussions of the joint development of the Niger Bend lands, especially minerals and livestock. The several basin authorities of the Gambia, Senegal and Niger rivers and of Lake Chad have had their political strains, particularly that of the Senegal, but research has been done which should now be applied.

Purely political associations have achieved little; far more urgently needed are international or regional plans for shared industries, power and better transport links, rather than mere free trade which may harm the weakest countries.

Non-geographers often generalise about countries as if they were homogeneous, yet most states have varied physical and economic environ-ments, and the new tropical ones usually exhibit striking regional in-equalities of many kinds. As Green and Fair have said 'vast differences in the physical environment, in the distribution of natural and human resources, and in the historical sequence of the use of those resources, have resulted in widely contrasting degrees, possibilities and problems of development from place to place'.[4]

Aid and development plans must consider how progress can be achieved regionally and at particular places. It is not just the effect of a policy upon a whole country, but the necessarily differential and unequal effects upon its regions, places, and different peoples that is important. Invest-ments should be made differentially according to the relative advantages of some regions for development compared with less advantageous ones, although social and political considerations often obscure, or are allowed to obscure, regional realities. We can better understand the West African countries, indeed any others, by a knowledge of their very diverse regions, their past and present specialisations, and their potential.

191

# 12

# Senegal: the ancient base

This state, with an area of 196 192 sq km (75 750 sq miles) and a population in 1970 of 3 925 000 is appropriately the first francophone country to be analysed. Although it has fewer people and a lower density of population than some other francophone lands in West Africa, the islands of St Louis in the estuary of the Senegal and of Gorée off Dakar were the first areas in West Africa to be colonised by the French. From the Senegal river the upper Niger was reached and occupied.

Senegal is a leading world commercial producer of groundnuts and has large groundnut oil factories. These products are still the largest export from Senegal, despite the development of phosphates, tuna fishing, and considerable industry especially near Dakar. While the search for oil has so far been unrewarding, small amounts of natural gas have been found which may be used industrially. Dakar is one of the finest ports of Africa and is of importance, too, in world strategy. The federal capital of French West Africa from 1904 until 1959, Dakar is now the capital only of Senegal.

Nevertheless, this country is less rich than the Ivory Coast, which has outstripped Senegal in all but strategic supremacy. Much of central and eastern Senegal is semidesert, where water may be found only at great depths. Even in the settled zones, water is often scarce in the dry season. There has been severe degradation of the soils first tilled for groundnut export between St Louis and Dakar; but for this these lands might more readily have been developed as a source of vegetables and fruit during the European winter, in competition with North African supplies.

## Climate

Senegal has sharply contrasted coastal and interior climates, well shown in the figures for Dakar, Ziguinchor, Tambacounda and Kayes, given in Chapter 4.

The Casamance coast has a southwest coast monsoonal climate; its hinterland has the southern savanna type. The rest of the coast is exceptionally equable, not only for the normal reasons of proximity to water, and the usual afternoon sea breezes and nocturnal land ones, but also because:

(*a*) the north-northeasterly marine trade winds bring a refreshing coolness and greater humidity during the dry season;
(*b*) the land breeze, vigorous in the dry season, offsets the humidity of the marine trade winds by night;
(*c*) the exceptionally cool waters of the Canary current also lower temperatures.

Although rainfall may be low, effective humidity is high. Temperatures are much lower than in the interior, the daily and annual range are less, and there is more movement in the air. Thus the Senegal coastal climate is much more easily tolerated by Europeans than are most West African climates.

By contrast, interior Senegal has the southern savanna, savanna or southern Sahel climates; and is subjected to the usual alternation of intensely desiccating northeasterly Harmattan winds, with a short season of wet southwesterly ones. There is the usual diminution in rainfall, thinning of the vegetation and lowering of the watertable from south to north.

Like all areas near the northern limit of the southwesterlies, Senegal suffers from extremely variable rainfall. St Louis had 127 mm (5 in) of rain in 1903 and 660 mm (26 in) in 1912. Dakar had 381 mm (15 in) in 1937 and 686 mm (27 in) the following year. Furthermore, while rainfall for a year may seem normal in amount, it varies greatly in its onset and termination, especially in central and northern Senegal. Finally, if the rains cease early, the groundnut may fail to secure its necessary 110–25 growing days.

## Geology and relief

Though Senegal is bordered on the east and southeast by Pre-Cambrian and Primary rocks which give higher and bolder relief, most of the country was occupied by Upper Cretaceous and later seas, until their withdrawal at the end of the Eocene period. These and later deposits floor the monotonous plains which rarely rise above 60 m (200 ft). Earth movement and possible faulting caused the higher relief of the Thiès Plateau and its scarp, and the shallow synclines of Cayor, Baol and Sine-Saloum.

Retreat of these seas coincided with Tertiary volcanic activity at Cape Manuel and Gorée. The elegant 'plateau' residential area of Dakar is situated on basalt rocks and these also protect the harbour, constructed on the adjacent flat and soft Quaternary sands.

In Quaternary times, upward movement has been responsible for raised beaches. More volcanic activity took place in the Cape Verde Peninsula, this time at the Mamelles. Their rounded form (the name means breasts),

and the fact that lava from them is found over fossilised laterite, proves their youth.

A former wetter climate was undoubtedly responsible for relic valleys found in the Ferlo, for considerable erosion in the plains of western Senegal, and for the transport and deposition of clay in the Sine-Saloum Delta.

Following that wetter period, there was a vast carpeting of loose wind-borne sands in northeast–southwest trending dunes in western Senegal, which thus has a gently undulating surface. Tertiary and Cretaceous deposits are rarely visible except where they outcrop in cliffs, e.g. at Cape Naze and Cape Rouge southeast of Dakar, in the Thiès scarp, and in the lower valley of the Ferlo.

The only other relief features are the live coastal dunes, extending northeast from Cape Verde. They also trend southwest to northeast, and are often interspersed by clay depressions with generally fresh water lakes or *niayes,* fringed by quite luxuriant vegetation.

## Major regions

### The Fouta

The Fouta is the left bank floodplain of the Senegal river, between Bakel and Dagana, known on the Mauritanian bank as the Chemama.

The Senegal valley (see Fig. 12.1) is 10–19 km (6–12 miles) wide and often contains several streams. The Senegal river also divides, e.g. to enclose the Ile à Morfil (Fig. 12.4), which averages 480 by 13 km (300 by 8 miles).

The Fouta has grey loamy soils, unlike the sand of adjacent regions, and a greater cover of Sahel savanna. With the retreat of the annual floods, the Fouta is fairly intensively cultivated for millet by the sedentary Toucouleur, as well as by sedentary Fulani. At the end of the cropping season, cattle are brought in by nomadic Fulani and Maure until the floods return. This region is very important to nomadic and sedentary peoples, and thus is sharply distinguished from neighbouring regions.

FIG. 12.1. Senegal river floodplain near Podor

Heights in metres. Intermittent streams shown by
dotted lines. (From Podor sheet of 1 :200 000
Institut Géographique National, Paris.)

Towns such as Dagana, Podor and Matam are markets for millet, groundnuts and gum, though gum from the Sudan has reduced this ancient trade.

The Fouta is the scene of several irrigation developments. The earliest which is still in operation is at Guédé, on the Doué branch of the Senegal, southeast of Podor. Work began in 1939 and simple gravity irrigation is used for the most part on nearly 1 000 ha (2 600 acres) divided among some 500 farmers who grow rice and millet. After these are harvested, cattle feed on the stubble, and their droppings are augmented by artificial fertiliser. There is some dry farming on the perimeter. Unfortunately, there have been numerous difficulties. The enclosing dyke is sometimes breached by Senegal floods, violent rain or wind erosion. Water distribution is unequal because of inadequate initial levelling and ill-maintained control gates, distribution and drainage channels. Wild rice is another problem, and there have been fierce quarrels between farmers of different tribes or kinship groups.

195

PLATE 31. Preparing land for flood-retreat cultivation on the River Senegal near Podor

## The Oualo (Senegal delta)

At Richard Toll ('the garden of Richard', Governor 1822–26), the head of the delta, the Senegal divides into several distributaries, especially when in flood. In the Oualo there are also innumerable intermittent or abandoned courses or *marigots,* relic dunes and swamps.

Powerful longshore drift, the northeast marine trades and strong waves, backed by the greatest fetch of open water, combine to turn the mouth of the Senegal southward and to maintain its ever-changing sandspit, the *Langue de Barbarie.* The estuary of the Senegal has always been dangerous because of the variable end of this sandspit, and a bar across the river mouth, yet St Louis has existed since 1659.

*St Louis* lies on an islet, 2 195 m (7 200 ft) by 320 m (1 050 ft), which was easily defended and, though within the difficult Senegal estuary, was

PLATE 32. The Fouta after floods have fully retreated

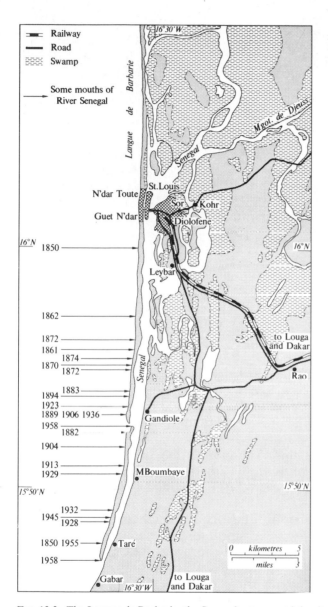

FIG. 12.2. The Langue de Barbarie, the Senegal estuary and the site of St Louis

(Based on the 1:200 000 St Louis sheet of the Institut Géographique National, and maps in
Assane Seek, *Dakar-Métropole Ouest Africaine*, 1970, and A. Bernard, *Afrique
Septentrionale et Occidentale, (Géographie Universelle)*, vol. ii, pt 2, 1939, p. 453

PLATE 33. The old fort of St Louis (left) now housing archives, old balconied buildings, and a hotel

sheltered and adjacent to the trade route round Africa. Up-river were to be found slaves, gum and gold from the Falémé tributary. The Gambia river might have been preferred by the French, but it was mainly in the hands of the British; so the inferior Senegal river became the means of French penetration into West Africa from St Louis.

Nevertheless, the difficulties of St Louis as a port helped the development of Dakar after 1857, and the opening in 1885 of the first railway in West Africa, between these towns. Though supplanted as a port, St Louis remained the capital of Senegal (and of Mauritania) until 1958, when that of Senegal was transferred to Dakar and that of Mauritania began transfer to Nouakchott. The population of St Louis doubled between 1940 and 1951 because of the development of government services. In the latter year it was 62 200, including 1 840 non-Africans but was only 39 800 in 1954.

The island is the administrative and commercial centre, and has an attractive character, reminiscent of small towns of southern France. Its buildings are solid and of stone, in European as well as Creole styles. There is a small trade in groundnuts, millets, gums and imported goods on the river. Quays are mainly on the east side of the island.

The town spread early on to the sandspit, where the northern settlement N'Dar Toute, had Mauritania's administrative offices until 1960. The southern settlement of Guet N'Dar, with mostly Lébou and Wolof, is one of the largest fishing centres in West Africa, fish being prepared by fishermen's wives and by several firms. On the mainland are Sor and Diolofene, the former with the railway station, modern houses and flats.

198

PLATE 34. The barrage at
Richard-Toll on the Taoué

The Richard-Toll irrigation scheme, southwest of that town and near the head of the Senegal delta, was begun in 1947 with the aim of growing rice locally to save expensive and then uncertain imports. Mechanical cultivation with irrigation was adopted and in 1968 some 5 100 ha (12 600 acres) produced 10 200 tons of paddy, a very low yield.

To provide the necessary water, a barrage was built in 1948 across the Taoué, which connects Lake Guier to the Senegal. This was necessary because the Senegal river has so gentle a gradient and so small a discharge in the dry season, that salt water penetrates not only upstream, but even up tributaries. To prevent it entering Lake Guier, local people built a new earth barrage across the Taoué each year; they thus also retained fresh water within the lake for use during each dry season, but the ensuing floods destroyed the earth barrage. Now the sluice gates are opened during floodwater and closed as the floods fall around 15 November.

These developments have disturbed only a few nomads, and the level character, virtual lack of vegetation, the clayey soils, and the possibility of using Lake Guier as a natural reservoir were attractive features. Yet the area is infertile so that heavy applications of artificial fertilisers are

PLATE 35. Quelea birds attacking rice in the Senegal Delta

necessary, while the soils have a high salinity. Irrigation is by the expensive method of pumping, there are problems of preventing sheet erosion by wind during the dry season, and of prodigious losses at harvest time from quelea birds and, to a lesser extent, from ducks and grasshoppers. Wild rice is another nuisance. Although originally about 6 000 ha (15 000 acres) were to be irrigated, no extensions are being made. Capital costs have been written off, and current costs are heavily subsidised. The scheme has made only a modest and very costly contribution to Senegal's rice needs.

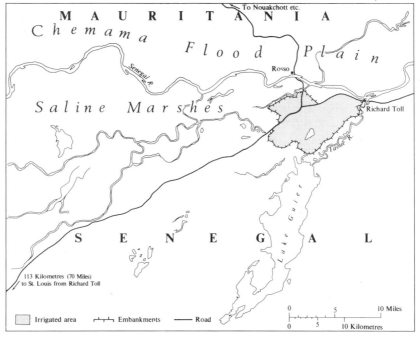

FIG. 12.3. The Senegal delta irrigation scheme

Two modifications have been tried. The first, begun in 1957, was to admit about a hundred peasants, but they too have had poor results. Then, since 1961, the mechanical cultivation of sugar cane has been tried on some 120 ha (400 acres), but it has also suffered from salinity, as well as from attacks by rats and borers. A sugar factory has not been built, and to be viable it would need the whole area to be turned over to sugar.

Downstream, in the delta proper, are other developments. Land and water are readily available, markets are near, transport is easy to them, but salinity and quelea attack are again major hazards. An 80 km (50 miles) protective dyke has been built along the left bank of the Senegal, some 12 000 ha (30 000 acres) have been prepared for cultivation, and villages established for over 3 500 peasant farmers. Land is mechanically prepared for them, there are cooperatives, and an engineering and processing centre at Ross-Bethio on a southern distributary of the Senegal. Initial yields were good, but it remains to be seen if salinity can be countered, and engineering and current costs have been high.

### Diander (Cayor coastlands)

The same factors which are responsible for diverting the Senegal river mouth, and for making an unstable sandspit, have made the smooth coastline of Cayor. Dunes rise to over 40 m (130 ft), often being covered with scrub resulting from the higher humidity and more moderate temperatures of this coast. The dune belt extends up to 24 km (15 miles) inland, and is used by Fulani and Maure herdsmen.

In the north, there are marshy depressions or *niayes* (meaning 'clumps of oil palms') between the dunes, and parallel with the coast. Dew and intermittent streams provide the water, and around their edges is luxuriant vegetation. Vegetables are grown for the St Louis and Dakar markets by men who also fish offshore. Dwarf bananas and coconuts give a Guinea-like atmosphere to these valuable freshwater depressions.

By contrast, in the south and extending into the Cape Verde Peninsula, some lakes are saline and frequently invaded by the sea, e.g. Lake Retba. The sand is also less consolidated and younger.

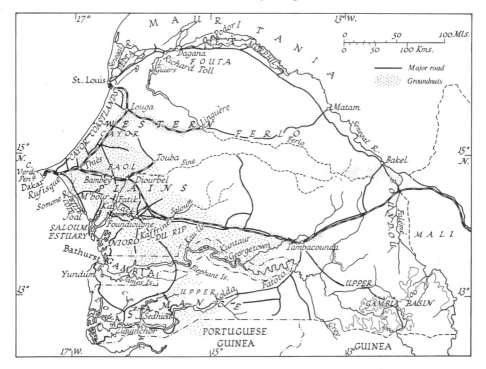

FIG. 12.4. The regions of Senegal and the Gambia

PLATE 36. Cayar fishing village with canoes, and backed by sand dunes on the smooth sandy coast 61 km (38 miles) northeast of Cape Verde

Cayar deep may be a drowned river valley connected with the same postulated fault that may explain the Thiès scarp. The deep is an important fishing ground for fishermen using canoes (most have outboard motors).[2] Along the whole of the Senegal coast there are about 4 000 canoes, 27 000 fishermen, and some 130 000 tons of fish are landed annually by traditional methods, with another 36 000 tons by modern methods.

## Cape Verde peninsula

The eastern limits of this peninsula[3] are often taken to be the Thiès Lower Eocene scarp, yet west of this lies the Cretaceous area around Rufisque. The true peninsula or tombolo was formed west of this latter area, beginning with the volcanism of Cape Manuel.

Immediately south of Dakar are the Miocene basalts of Cape Manuel, Gorée and the Madeleine Islets. Farther west, and constituting Cape Verde, are the two Quaternary volcanoes of the Mamelles (Plate 30). Laterite occurs on top of the Miocene volcanic rocks and underneath lavas from the Mamelles, so dating the laterite as Pliocene. Basalts from the Mamelles form Almadi Point and its reefs—Africa's most westerly point.

Along an otherwise dry, sandy coast, early navigators found the green hills of the Cape Verde Mamelles—green because their projecting rounded

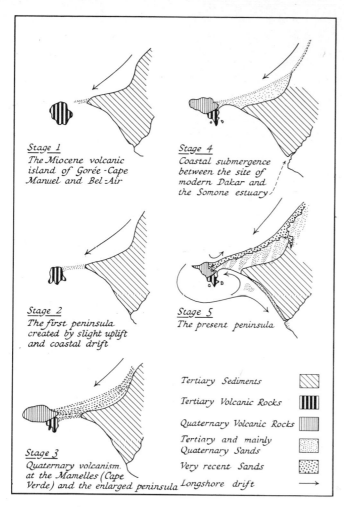

Stage 1
The Miocene volcanic island of Gorée -Cape Manuel and Bel-Air

Stage 2
The first peninsula created by slight uplift and coastal drift

Stage 3
Quaternary volcanism at the Mamelles (Cape Verde) and the enlarged peninsula

Stage 4
Coastal submergence between the site of modern Dakar and the Somone estuary

Stage 5
The present peninsula

Tertiary Sediments

Tertiary Volcanic Rocks

Quaternary Volcanic Rocks

Tertiary and mainly Quaternary Sands

Very recent Sands

Longshore drift

FIG. 12.5. The evolution of the Cape Verde peninsula

(From diagrams by J. Richard-Molard in *La Presqu'île du Cap Vert*, 1949)

forms catch extra humidity. The older basalts of Cape Manuel gave shelter to the equally basaltic islet of Gorée, occupied from the fifteenth century by Europeans (from the seventeenth by the French), the embryo of modern Dakar and—with St Louis—of former French West Africa.

## DAKAR

Dakar[4] was first occupied permanently in 1857—just after the Crimean War had revealed the strategic importance of the site. Work was begun in 1862 on the first pier, which is now incorporated in the southern jetty. A second, longer jetty proved successful in 1866, and the Messageries Impériales (now the Messageries Maritimes) transferred its calling point,

PLATE 37.  Gorée islet, off Dakar

PLATE 38.  Former slave house on
Gorée. Slaves were led out through the
arch to be rowed to vessels anchored
offshore

PLATE 39.  Former house of the French
East India Company on Gorée, a
reminder of Gorée's other early role as a
calling point on the route to India

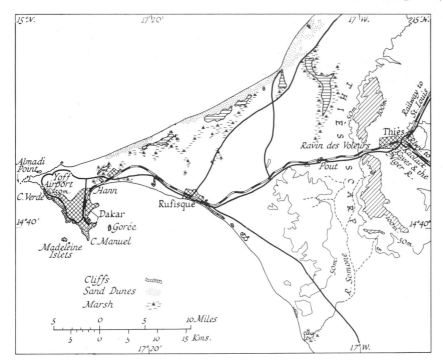

FIG. 12.6. The Cape Verde peninsula

(Heights in metres)

on the route from France to South America, from St Vincent to Dakar. But by 1878 Dakar's population was still only 1 556.

For the next quarter of a century development was steady. In 1885 West Africa's first railway was opened between St Louis and Dakar, to obviate navigation of the difficult Senegal estuary. Thereafter, Dakar attracted most of the traffic to and from the Senegal valley, and St Louis decayed as a port. The new railway achieved even more by stimulating the cultivation of groundnuts along its route. By 1891 the population of Dakar was 8 737. In 1892 the southern jetty was extended and a breakwater built on to it.

The next great impetus came as a result of the decision taken in 1898, at the time of Anglo-French differences and of British troubles in South Africa, to make Dakar into an important naval base. The northern breakwater was built, thus creating a true harbour, and with depths averaging nearly 9 m (30 ft). The southern jetty was again extended and a dry dock built in the western harbour. Shortly after, between 1904 and 1910, great improvements were once more made in the south by the construction of piers (Fr. *moles*) 1 and 2, more dredging, and by the provision of better loading and storing facilities. In 1904 the population had risen to 18 477 and Dakar became the federal capital.

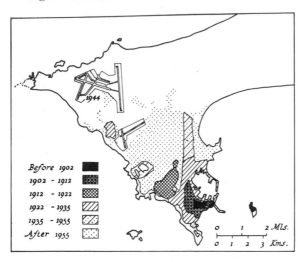

FIG. 12.7. The historical development of Dakar

These naval and civil developments made Dakar into a true port and town, and brought about its planned layout immediately south of the harbour. By 1914 its population was 23 833; 2 772 were non-African civilians and 1 242 non-African army and navy men.

The 1914–18 war brought a great increase of traffic to Dakar, the tonnage of shipping cleared trebling between 1911 and 1918. But a more lasting development was the opening of the through railway from Dakar to Bamako on the Niger in 1923. Thereafter, Dakar was not only the main port for Senegal and Mauritania, but also for the French Sudan (now Mali), and its trade became more diversified. Although Kaolack (linked by railway in 1911) at first excelled Dakar in groundnut exports, the latter benefited much from this trade and the processing of groundnut oil.

Between 1926 and 1933 new port works were again undertaken, this time in the northern sector. Pier 8 was built for the efficient refuelling of ships, the groundnut storage yard was laid out, Piers 5 and 6 built for groundnut export and, later, for shipping groundnut oil by pipeline. These improvements killed Rufique as a groundnut port. Before the works were undertaken, the population of Dakar in 1924 was around 40 000, by 1931 it was 53 982, and in 1936 was 92 634, all figures including Gorée and nearby mainland villages.

Just before the Second World War, the northern jetty was equipped for the discharge of tankers, and Pier 3 was constructed near the end of the southern jetty. Loading and storage facilities and depths of water were greatly improved. Pier 4 has since been built for groundnuts, Pier 1 and the northern jetty have been extended, and a cold store completed to help the fishing industry and the importation of perishable foodstuffs.

Other works include the construction of Pier 7, the improved handling of phosphates, groundnut oil storage and loading, and a new tanker terminal.

Dakar has been fairly prosperous since the war, largely as the result of many new commercial and industrial developments, although since independence these have lost the market of the rest of ex-French West Africa. The presence of over 30 000 non-Africans, much overseas aid, former high prices for groundnuts in France, the rapid increase in air traffic, diversion of ships from the Suez route, the calling of cruise liners, and the beginning of inclusive holidays from Europe have all helped. The population doubled between 1926 and 1936, and again by 1946. In 1955 it was 230 579 including suburban villages and Gorée. By 1961 the figure was 374 700 and by 1972 the built up area had half a million people.

Water and housing have been scarce, and the cost of living very high. The residential development of Dakar has been restricted by several factors. Lébou land rights held up redevelopment in the centre, and the French forces occupied an inordinate amount of land, especially on Cape Manuel. To these specific difficulties have been added those of the high cost of imported materials, and the poor quality of labour. Nevertheless, very many high-rise apartments have been erected in central Dakar, while many fine suburbs in striking styles of architecture, have been built.

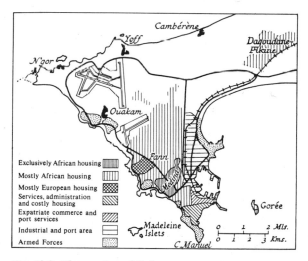

FIG. 12.8. The quarters of Dakar

(Villages in black)

Further water supplies have been obtained by deep borings, there is now an elaborate system of distribution, and great quantities of water are taken on by ships. On the other hand, the watertable shows signs of

PLATE 40. View north over Independence Square (the central business district of Dakar), and its port (with a French naval base, groundnut and groundnut oil wharves on the left, the phosphate wharf in the centre between two buildings, and the fuelling wharf on the right). The peninsula extends northeast in the distance

PLATE 41. View northwest over Dakar, with the dome and square towers of the cathedral in the centre, and the twin volcanic cones of Cape Verde in the right distance

PLATE 42. Northern suburbs of Dakar

being lowered and certainly the vegetation around Dakar has been degraded—perhaps by this, but undoubtedly more by overfarming on the doorsteps of such an attractive market.

Dakar is a very considerable industrial centre. Its industries are mainly located along the railway and road leading out of the peninsula, between Hann (not to be confused with residential Fann to the northwest) and Tiaroye, on former sandy wastes. Groundnut oil refineries, textile mills, soap, sack, shoe and soft drink factories, a brickworks and fish canneries are based essentially on the processing of local raw materials. Mercantile and naval ship repairing, the brewery, match and cigarette factories, the oil refinery, truck assembly, and the flour mill depend mainly upon imported materials. Paper wrapping, metal, furniture and clothing factories make up entirely imported materials.[5] These industries were mostly established when the whole of French West Africa was open to them as a market. This situation ended abruptly in 1959, and many factories barely survived. More recently, tourists have enlarged the Senegal market, whilst textiles, fish products, flour and shoes are significant exports, some of them again going to ex-French West African states.

The port has 216 ha (530 acres) of protected water, 65 ha (158 acres) of which have dredged depths of 10 m (32·5 ft). There are 3 008 m (9 837 ft) of commercial quays with these depths, and in all there are 7·8 km (5 miles) of quays, at which some forty-six ships can be accommodated, and from which over 5 000 ships are cleared annually. This demonstrates the major role of Dakar—that of a calling port, especially for ships on

209

South American, West and South African routes, and for many others since the closure of the Suez Canal.

Dakar has supplanted St Vincent in the Cape Verde Islands but is usually second to Las Palmas which, incidentally, is usually visited by passenger boats and most British ships of all kinds. Petroleum companies furnish oil at cheaper rates there than at Dakar, the shipping lines find useful freight in fruit and vegetables from the Canary Islands, and the stop is popular for its tourist attraction. But if Dakar could compete with Las Palmas in price of fuel oil, it might attract ships outward bound from Europe.

By its strategic position adjacent to the most westerly point of Africa and at the nearest point to South America, Dakar has been able to attract increasing air traffic on the Europe–South America and North America–South Africa routes. It is also the centre of some West African services and is touched by other African systems. The superb airport is served by almost all European air corporations and by several others. About 160 000 passengers pass through Yoff airport annually and 6 000 tons of freight are handled.

Given the strategic position of the general site, the development of the town has been greatly favoured by the Miocene basalts of Cape Manuel, and the Eocene limestone plateau with superficial laterite. This fairly level plateau, with an average height of about 30 m (100 ft), is excellent for residences and for government buildings. North and northeast of it are

210

loose Quaternary sands, easy to excavate for port works. Dakar harbour is always easy to enter, since there is no current or drift, the tidal range averages only 406 mm (16 in), it is naturally sheltered from the north-northeasterly and westerly winds, and harbour works have provided shelter from the southwesterly ones.

For its residents, especially for its non-Africans, Dakar has the advantage of a far more pleasant climate than almost any other part of West Africa except, perhaps, Accra. Temperatures are very moderate. Daily maxima are 31°C (88°F) from June to October and daily minima are 18·3°C (65°F) from January to April. Daily range varies from 5° to 9·4°C (9° to 11°F) during the year. Its rainfall of nearly 585 mm (23 in) comes mostly in four months. Not only does it have the usual onshore and offshore breezes of all coastal stations but the narrowness, digitated nature, and planned road alignment of the peninsula ensure that these breezes have their maximum effect. Furthermore, it enjoys for nearly nine months the north-northeast marine trade winds, not the dry and dusty Harmattan of interior Senegal.

French people live in Dakar (and in Abidjan) exactly as they do in France, with cafés, restaurants, and many-storied offices and apartment blocks. Because of Dakar's situation as a calling place on world trade routes, and the considerable European market, it can command an import of temperate fruits and vegetables (often from Morocco) far cheaper and in greater quantities than can most West African towns. Again, because of its large European population and its more fixed character, general imports are much more varied than through most West African ports.

Dakar is unique in West Africa. It forms a vivid contrast to Lagos and Accra where no Europeans live permanently. Many children have their secondary and university education in Dakar. The plateau is thoroughly European in aspect and more beautiful than many cities in Europe of equivalent size.

### The Rufisque Cretaceous region

This region lies east of the Cape Verde peninsula and the Dakar area, with which it is frequently considered. Geologically it antedates the formation of the peninsula, and the limestone (Cretaceous-Eocene) of Rufisque contrasts with the loose sand, basalt and laterite of the peninsula. Limestone rocks also outcrop south of the Somone estuary and extend inland to Diourbel and Gaouane.

*Rufisque*, antedates Dakar by several centuries and was first named Rio Fresco by the Portuguese, who stopped here regularly for fresh water, which they obtained from seepages in the dunes. Rufisque was for long the main exporter of groundnuts until Dakar and, for a time, Kaolack replaced it. Between the two wars it was quite moribund, but has revived as an industrial town with groundnut oil refineries, a cretonne cotton

PLATE 44. West Africa's first cement factory at Bargny, near Dakar. Cretaceous limestone is used

factory, a tannery and shoe factory, pharmaceutical works, engineering assembly shops and, nearby at Bargny, West Africas's first cement factory.

On the edge of this region lies the clay marshland of Pout, which belongs to the Cayor coastlands or to the Cape Verde peninsula. Pout is significant for its brickworks.

### The southern or 'petite côte'

Beyond Rufisque are cliffs formed of Eocene deposits and laterite, followed by cliffs of Cretaceous rocks beyond the Somone (see Fig. 12.4). It is therefore unlike any other part of the Senegal coast. Popenguin, Portudal and Joal were early European points of contact, probably because the area had more fresh water seepages, a denser vegetation, is more sheltered, and has less swell and surf than the northern coast. But these roadsteads were supplanted first by Rufisque and later by Dakar.

The modern significance of this coast has also declined because of the cessation in 1964 of the extraction of titanium and zircon ores from its beaches and those of the Sangomar peninsula. First worked in 1922 these ores were for long the only significant Senegalese minerals. Concentration of the first ore by electromagnets and of zircon by mechanical means was effected at Djifère, on the Saloum. These operations became uneconomic in competition with large Australian and Malaysian producers, and

212

because of the difficulties of navigating the Saloum estuary.

Fishing is still important here. Main catches are of white fish, which is sent dried or fresh to Dakar, Rufisque, Thiès and Kaolack. Joal has firms drying and canning fish. The pastures of la Petite Côte are visited in the dry season by Fulani herdsman.

## Saloum estuary

South of Joal the long sandspit of Sangomar begins. The spit is an analogue of the *Langue de Barbarie,* and diverts the Saloum southward, though like the Senegal, it occasionally flows across the spit.

A ria coast commences here and continues southward into Sierra Leone. The Saloum estuary or ria was probably formed from the drowning of a very shallow relic valley. The land has since gained, and the estuary is clogged by much silt. Around the many channels are salt flats or *tannes*, which, if only they could be desalted, would be valuable ricelands. Dykes with flap valves have been built, especially near Fatick, to keep out salt water and to retain fresh floodwaters until a certain height is reached. Then the valves let out the fresh water, without admitting salt water. Behind the *tannes* are areas cultivated for rice, millet and groundnuts.

Despite a bar at its entrance, and a meandering course, the Saloum is navigable to Kaolack for small ocean vessels. After the decline of Rufisque, this was Senegal's leading groundnut port until, in turn, displaced by Dakar and even by downstream Lyndiane, which has a groundnut oil mill. Kaolack's main activity is salt production and export (usually 40–50 000 tons annually) to other francophone countries.

## The western plains

These extend from just west of the St Louis–Dakar railway eastward and also southward into the Gambia, where they are known as the Sandhills. On the southwest they terminate in the Thiès scarp (Fig. 12.4), which is about 60 m (200 ft) high, and a vivid feature of the landscape. Its altitude, like that of the Mamelles of Cape Verde, is sufficient to cause heavier rainfall (about 75 mm (3 in) more at Thiès than at Dakar) and the so-called 'Forest' of Thiès.

Most of this slightly undulating plain is under 40 m (130 ft), and consists of lacustrine and continental Mio-Pliocene argillaceous sandstones which cover Eocene and earlier formations. In many places there are relic dunes, aligned from northeast to southwest, which again give a pronounced 'grain' to the country. Superficial sand is absent only in parts of the Ferlo valley and along the coast around M'Bour. This deep blanket of sand has so choked most valleys that, for example, the Sine above Diourbel is scarcely evident, except for a band of denser vegetation.

PLATE 45. Degraded former groundnut lands north of Thiès

## THE CAYOR

The northern part (north of 15°N) of this large region, known as the Cayor, has deficient rainfall—255–400 mm (10–16 in)—so that it has Sahel savanna, and crop lands are not continuous. The naturally sparse vegetation has been much devastated by fire, overpasturing, and felling of acacias by the Wolof whose farming practices are destructive.

*Louga* is a small town lying on the northern edge of this region, in contact with the coastal dune region, and where pastoral Fulani nomads meet sedentary Wolof groundnut farmers. Louga is the leading cattle market in Senegal, being admirably situated between the main cattle rearing regions to the north and the meat consuming towns of St Louis, Kaolack, Thiès and Dakar. Louga has been served by a railway since 1885, and in 1931 became a junction with the opening of the Linguère branch. Though many of the surrounding groundnut lands are largely exhausted, Louga is a groundnut and millet marketing centre, and has a groundnut oil refinery and associated soap works.

Thiès[6] is the main centre of the Western Plains. It has been connected by rail with Dakar since 1885, and from 1923 has been a junction for the St Louis and Niger lines. A double track exists to Dakar, and Thiès is a notable road centre.

Communications have helped to encourage its groundnut market. Industry started with the large railway workshops. Nearby are the Pout brickworks, and a phosphate refinery using aluminium phosphate from the Pallo quarries. Larger deposits of calcium phosphate are worked at Taïba, near Tivaouane, northwest of Pallo. The phosphates are of great significance in that they are near farming areas in desperate need of fertiliser. There is also some export of the latter, and of all the unrefined calcium phosphate.

214

PLATE 46. Phosphate quarry and fertiliser works

## THE BAOL

The Baol, which lies south of Cayor and north of the Saloum River, has Sudan savanna vegetation. Between Fatik and Bambey the country is inhabited by the Serer people, who conserve the useful trees by putting thorn branches round them in the dry season to ward off livestock. The Serer are also most unusual in that, as well as growing crops, they keep cattle and fertilise their farms with manure. Fields are hedged with thorn bush to restrict the movement of cattle. Such conservation practices and mixed farming are very exceptional among African peoples. They are certainly in very marked contrast to those of their neighbours, the Wolof of Cayor and Nioro du Rip.

Wherever the Serer live, the Baol has the appearance of a well-kept park, with many baobab, acacia and mango trees. Groundnuts and millet are the main crops, with beans and cotton as lesser ones. The Serer country of Baol is the most peopled and socially knit part of Senegal.[7]

## THE NIORO DU RIP

This country lies south of the Saloum and is peopled by Wolof. Lying in a zone of heavier rainfall it is naturally more wooded, and this characteristic has been retained as it has a smaller population and is less farmed.

PLATE 47. Brushwood protection of the useful mango tree and of a village. A typical scene in the better wooded Serer country between the Dakar–Niger Railway and the Saloum River

PLATE 48. Groundnut lands being prepared after the first rains near Bambey

**The Ferlo Plateau**

Central Senegal is a little higher and far drier than the western plains, but is otherwise similar, except that its sandstone is more ferruginous. It extends into the Gambia, where it is termed 'Sandstone Plateau'.

In the Ferlo, villages are practically confined to relic river valleys, where water may be found near the surface. Elsewhere, water is so deep that vegetation is Sahel savanna and the area is almost uninhabited, except for Fulani nomads[8] who, until recently, have tried to retain the Ferlo for their exclusive use. Water from deep borings 50–80 m (160–260 ft) has begun to change the vegetation, and Wolof have been entering to grow groundnuts.

On the eastern fringes is a subregion where the argillaceous sandstones thin out in contact with the metamorphic rim. Again there is an almost complete mask of sands, clays and laterites, but the rivers are incised and bordered by borassus palms. On the southern margins, near to and south of the railway, are important groundnut lands and some fixed Fulani herdsmen.

**The Boundou**

This is the rim of Pre-Cambrian schists, quartzites and sandstones. Hills rise abruptly to nearly 180 m (590 ft) and there is evidence of erosion surfaces.

The region is crossed by the Dakar–Niger railway, but is only poor seasonal pasture land, though in past centuries alluvial gold was of great importance from the Falémé Basin.

**Niokolo (Upper Gambia)**

This is an undulating plain, averaging about 90 m (300 ft), with occasional higher plateaux and hills, e.g. around Mako, which attain nearly 400 m (1 300 ft). These are fragments of the Pre-Cambrian eastern rim, of the Palæozic sandstones and the Pre-Cambrian quartzites of the Fouta Djallon in the southeast, or formed from eruptive rocks. Apart from these, there is a general cover of superficial deposits, either of sand, clays or laterite in the area which largely account for the very poor vegetation and bare uninhabited countryside. Only the hills and river courses are slightly more fertile.

**Casamance**

This territory lies south of the Gambia, so that it was somewhat isolated from the rest of Senegal, especially until the Trans-Gambian road was built by the French across the Gambia in 1958.

Because of its southerly position, Casamance has monsoonal conditions and more vegetation than other parts of Senegal. Ziguinchor has nearly three times as much rain as Dakar, and twice as many rain-days. Rice is the dominant food crop.

The river and its tributaries are bordered in tidal areas (as far as 120 km (75 miles) up river) by fairly thick mangroves, behind which marshes have often been reclaimed for rice cultivation. Raphia and oil palms, bamboos, teak and silk-cotton trees are all found. Argillaceous sandstones cover the whole area, with much alluvium along the rivers and in the estuaries.

Three subregions are distinguishable:

(*a*) Lower Casamance[9] from the ocean to Ziguinchor. Here there is a succession of low marshy areas deeply penetrated by tidal arms. As in Portuguese Guinea, mangrove or rice fields are backed by valuable stands of oil palms. Ziguinchor the headquarters of Casamance, stands on the left bank of the river, 68 km (42 miles) upstream, on the first considerable piece of firm ground. It can be reached by boats of about 800 tons, and there are river jetties. It is also served by air.

(*b*) Central Casamance lies beyond Ziguinchor, and produces more groundnuts than the previous region. Even more might be grown but for tsetse fly infestation of great areas believed to be suitable for cultivation. In 1949 an experimental mass-production groundnut scheme, using mechanical cultivation, was begun near Sédhiou, but it failed.

(*c*) Upper Casamance is higher and drier. There are abrupt edges to the river valleys, succeeded by considerable expanses of bare *bowal* (laterite surfaced country), suitable only for intermittent pastures. In the better areas, groundnuts are grown. Kolda is the main regional centre. This country merges into the Niokolo (Upper Gambia) region.

## Economic resources

### Agriculture

#### MILLET

Millet is overwhelmingly the main foodstuff and is grown in rotation with groundnuts, the virtually exclusive cash but also a food crop, and with beans a lesser food crop. Other significant food crops are rice and maize, grown mainly in river valleys, especially of Casamance; cassava produced mainly in exhausted soils formerly used for groundnuts in Louga, Thiès and Kaolack districts; and sweet potatoes grown in Casamance and the Thiès district.

## GROUNDNUTS

Groundnuts are the very lifeblood of Senegal, which is the fourth or fifth largest world grower, the second cash producer, and the nearest one to Europe. Groundnuts and groundnut products (mainly groundnut oil and cake) account for most of the exports of Senegal. Until after the Second World War, outside Dakar and St Louis, there was almost no other economic activity. Senegal and the Gambia are outstanding examples of cash monocultures, which are the more dangerous because rainfall variability causes vast differences in annual production, especially in Senegal.

The texture of Senegal soils is ideal for groundnuts. Most soils average 3·4 per cent only of clay, the ideal percentage being between 2 and 5 per cent. Nevertheless, because of overcultivation, the chemical and humus contents of soils in the older areas of cultivation between St Louis and Dakar have greatly deteriorated from even their natural mediocrity. The Wolof have impoverished their central and northern region by overcutting and firing the natural vegetation. On the other hand, the Serer, who live mainly in the naturally wooded Sine-Saloum area, have protected the vegetation and manured the soils. In view of the poverty of Senegalese soils and their increasing exhaustion by man, locally produced phosphates from the groundnut region itself are of great significance.

Groundnuts have been a peasant subsistence and export crop for a very long time. Exports date back to 1840; they were encouraged, as in the Gambia, by the needs of French soap manufacturers and by the lack of a French import duty on groundnuts. The earliest cropped areas were around Podor, Matam and Bakel in or near the Senegal valley, near St Louis, and in and near the Cape Verde peninsula. The soils of all these areas are now largely exhausted.

A great impetus to production and switch in producing areas came with the opening of the St Louis to Dakar railway in 1885, along which lands were soon given over—all too exclusively and intensively— to groundnut cultivation. The second impulse and change came with the building of the railway eastward from Thiès. It reached Diourbel in 1908, Guinguinéo in 1910, Kaolack (by a branch) in 1911, Koussanar in 1913, Tambacounda in 1914, and the through route was opened to the Niger in 1923. Groundnut cultivation spread in the Baol, especially as far east as Koussanar, where the climate is more suitable and the soils richer than between St Louis and Dakar. In 1931 branch railways were also opened, from Diourbel to Touba, and from Louga (on the St Louis to Dakar line) to Linguère.

More significant than these branches was the construction of roads, mainly after 1923, and especially in the later thirties. Roads have extended cultivation far beyond the railways. Yet rail transport still canalises much of the export trade.

The Sine-Saloum normally accounts for over two-fifths the area planted to groundnuts and for that part of the production, followed by Diourbel (nearly one-quarter), Thiès nearly 15 per cent, and Casamance about 12 per cent in each respect.

Mechanical cultivation of groundnuts is being tried at Boulel, north of Kaffrine. The soils are suitable but the area was uninhabited. Water is now available and the Department of Agriculture is in charge. Some 3 240 ha (8 000 acres) have been cleared. There, and near Touba, near Taïf, and southeast of Kael, agriculture has been encouraged by marabouts of the Mouridism Islamic movement. At these other places smaller but still large-scale clearing has gone on, partly for community cultivation of groundnuts. Modern economic and technical methods have been interwoven with an Islamic community and sect of feudal character.[10]

Towards the end of the First World War, some local shelling of groundnuts was undertaken to save cargo space. This led later to the establishment of small oil-extraction works at Kaolack, Diourbel, Ziguinchor and Louga. The first one at Dakar was opened in 1924, and groundnut oil was first exported from Senegal in 1927. Until 1937–38 exports were limited to 5 500 tons of groundnut oil per annum, because extractors in France had become alarmed at this competition. During the war the limit was raised to 12 000 tons and later to 45 000 tons annually.

The Second World War gave an enormous impetus to Senegal oil extraction. After the fall of France, Senegal could neither export groundnuts, nor import fuel oil. So in 1941 a large-scale extraction plant was opened in Dakar (by a Dunkirk firm whose factory was overrun by the Germans), with a capacity of 20 000 tons of crude oil per annum, which was first used in North and West Africa as a substitute for diesel fuel oil. This and other factories in Dakar now carry out complete refining of groundnut and other vegetable oils.

Outside Dakar, complete refineries are located at Lyndiane (near Kaolack) and Louga, whilst crude oil refineries are located at Rufisque, Kaolack, Diourbel and Ziguinchor, whose oil is finally refined at Dakar.

Senegal refineries have the capacity to deal annually with almost the entire annual cash crop. So far, however, about one-half of the groundnuts in shell are crushed locally. Three-quarters of the oil is crude and the rest refined oil. Crude oil is exported for final refining.

The early use of so much of the Senegal crop for local oil extraction contrasts with the situation in the Gambia, where little local oil was produced until the late fifties. Likewise, in Nigeria oil was first extracted locally in a small Kano factory only in 1949, twenty-eight years after the first mill began in Senegal, and in the face of governmental indifference in Nigeria.

Local processing reduces transport costs, and the acid content of the oil. It provides a valuable fuel from shell waste, local employment and revenue. On the other hand, oil tankers have to return to Dakar in ballast, and the now large-scale oil industry in Nigeria has never enjoyed a large protected market, as did the Senegal crushers until 1965.

## Livestock

Senegal has only moderate numbers of livestock, most of its needs in meat being met by cattle driven southwestward from Mauritania. The fact that the Serer people are cattle keepers as well as crop farmers accounts for the greatest concentration of local cattle southwest of Diourbel and around Kaolack. Sheep and goats are likewise important southwest of Diourbel, but also near M'Pal (east of St Louis) and Mekhé. By relating the density of the livestock population to the human population, however, northern Senegal is shown to have many herds, kept mostly by nomadic or seminomadic Fulani.

Deep sea fishing by European, Russian and Japanese trawlers for tuna has long been important, and has more recently been undertaken from Dakar, where freezing and canning is undertaken (see also Chapter 7). Annual landings are about 170 000 tons mainly by canoes.[11]

## Minerals

Mineral working is restricted in range and recent in its development. The oldest worked mineral is salt from marine salt evaporation works on the Saloum opposite Kaolack (p. 213). Phosphates near Thiès (p. 214), some manufactured into fertiliser, and limestone for cement manufacture near Rufisque (p. 212) are more recent. Basalt and laterite are quarried for road making.

## Industry

Industry in Senegal arose from the processing of the main crop and export  groundnuts. Industrial development progressed because of the highly protected market in all French West Africa, and from the con-tinuing substantial market of Dakar. This is considerable because of its size—about half a million people, some 30 000 of whom are usually well-off expatriates. The Dakar market is further nourished by the many calling ships and aircraft, passengers in transit, and the growing cruise liner and package holiday traffic. Thus Dakar as almost the only export port of groundnut derivatives, and as far and away the main general port and market, is an exceedingly strong locating point for industries, the more so as the former capital of highly centralised French West Africa, and as the present one of equally centralised Senegal. Reference should be made to the texts on Dakar and groundnuts in this chapter, and to Chapter 8.

## Transport

### RIVERS

The Senegal was the earliest means of French ingress into the interior. Its place has now been taken by the railway, but a little local traffic remains on the river. Small ships can reach Podor (285 km: 177 miles—from St Louis) all the year; between July and January boats can reach Matam (644 km: 400 miles from St Louis); and in August and September Kayes (Mali) is the limit (970 km: 603 miles) from St Louis. For the Saloum river see p. 213, and for the Casamance p. 218.

### RAILWAYS

The St Louis–Dakar line was the first in West Africa. Though built to overcome the insufficiency of St Louis as a port, the line was even more successful in developing groundnut cultivation along its route. There is considerable passenger traffic, about eighteen diesel-electric trains running weekly in each direction.

The through route from Dakar to Bamako and Koulikoro, on separate navigable reaches of the Niger River, was opened in 1923. The link between the Senegal and Niger Rivers had been finished in 1904 and projections into the gap from Thiès and from Kayes were started in 1907. The important branch to Kaolack was completed in 1911, and the lesser ones from Diourbel to Touba in 1931, as was the branch from the St Louis–Dakar line from Louga to Linguère. The through railway provided an efficient lifeline for the French Sudan (now Mali), and replaced through transport on the poor and seasonal Senegal river. It also serves the main groundnut areas of western and south-central Senegal, and halted the diversion of trade to the then British Gambia. Normally there are three through passenger trains weekly in each direction between Dakar and Bamako 1 238 km (769 miles). There are diesel rail cars three times a week in each direction between Dakar and Kaolack.

### ROADS

These were somewhat neglected until after the Second World War in defence of the railways. However, there are tarred or other good roads from Dakar to most of western Senegal, to St Louis, Rosso and into Mauritania, up the Senegal to Podor, across the Ferlo to Matam, across the Gambia to Casamance, and southeastward to Kédougou, but the road to Mali is poor (see Fig. 12.4).

### AIR[13]

Apart from the international services passing through Dakar, there are local services between major towns.

## Conclusion

Despite its northerly latitude, Senegal has a relatively cool and humid coastline, compared with the interior. Dakar may be said to enjoy an almost semitropical climate of remarkable freshness, whilst in the centre of Senegal are barren, dry wastes.

Senegal is largely summed up in two words—Dakar and groundnuts. Dakar is one of the most developed of all West African towns, and is a sea and air calling point of major significance. Groundnuts are the only important cash crop, and there seems to be no foreseeable alternative to this presently soil-exhausting crop. Groundnut produce provides over 80 per cent of Senegalese exports.

# 13

# The Gambia: a riverine enclave

The Gambia has an area of 11 295 sq km (4 361 sq miles) and a population of 364 000 in 1970. By far the smallest state in Africa, and with much water and swamp, it is entirely surrounded by Senegal, except for the short coastline. Some common policies and shared services are being developed between the two countries, but complete integration is unlikely in view of their very different systems.

## Historical outline[1]

The first European to describe the Gambia was Alvise da Ca'da Mosto, a Venetian, who sailed up the river in 1455. Soon afterwards, by the Treaty of Tordesillas of 1494, the Portuguese secured exclusive rights of trade on the West Coast.

In 1588 a claimant to the throne of Portugal granted the right to trade along the Gambia river to certain London and Exeter merchants. These grants were later transferred to other merchants, after being confirmed by Queen Elizabeth I.

About 1651 James, Duke of Courland, erected a fort on an islet 26 km (16 miles) up-river. It was captured by an English fleet in 1661, renamed James Fort, and thereafter used by successive English trading companies.

In 1765 James Fort and other settlements were taken over by the Crown and administered as part of Senegambia, with its capital at the captured French town of St Louis on the Senegal river. But in 1783 Senegambia ceased to exist, as Senegal was returned to the French, and the Gambia reverted to the Africa Company until 1821, when Crown rule was established.

In 1857 in exchange for the renunciation by the British of their gum rights at Portendik (Mauritania), the French ceded their remaining rights at Albreda, on the north bank of the Gambia.

The present state averages only some 24 km (15 miles) in width (48 km: 30 miles near the coast) and extends along either bank for 470 km (292 miles) to the tidal limit of the finest navigable river in Africa, but its usefulness has been greatly reduced by the political boundary.

If the French had possessed this fine waterway, it is likely that they would have used it rather than the Senegal river as their main way into the interior. 'Dakar' might have developed on the Gambia river, and a shorter and more direct railway could have been built from it to the Niger. Money thus saved might have been put to better use in developing western Senegal, although this alternative site for Dakar would have been less good and less healthy than present day Dakar. Again, though groundnut cultivation might have been less developed without the existing Senegalese railway, a shorter one from the present Mali to Kuntaur, at the limit of ocean navigation on the Gambia, would have hastened development of that poor inland country.

A fine waterway has been divorced from its natural hinterland and rational economic development of 'Senegambia' gravely compromised. Political ruination of a natural waterway, and the division of Senegal into two limbs, could be ended by closer association with Senegal.

## The river

In the dry season, the Gambia river is navigable only in the Gambia, but in the wet season launches may reach the Grey river. Ocean vessels of up to 5·8 m (19 ft) draught can always reach Kuntaur, 241 km (150 miles) from Banjul, and even Georgetown, 283 km (176 miles), if of lesser draught. Vessels not exceeding 2 m (6·5 ft) in draught can go on to Fatoto, 464 km (288 miles) from Banjul the last wharf for steamers. Launches and canoes can reach Koina, 470 km (292 miles), the last village in the Gambia, where the tidal range is still 0·6 m (2 ft). There are thirty-three wharf towns at which government steamers call.

Kuntaur is the most important groundnut centre on the river and is a rice-growing centre.[1] Above Kuntaur floods are more significant than tides to navigators and riverside dwellers, especially if they are rice farmers. Floods can cause rises of up to 9 m (30 ft) on certain parts of the river.

The estuary is generally considered to commence at Elephant Island, 150 km (93 miles) upstream, where the river is 1·6 km (1 mile) wide. This is the wet season limit of salt water, and of fringing mangroves, but in the dry season salt water penetrates to about 221 km (137 miles) upstream. There are depths of 9 m (30 ft) at the estuary mouth. The mile wide navigable channel to Banjul has two sharp turns, and there is a bar which ships of over 21 000 tons cannot cross.

## Climate

The rains arrive first in the interior, which they reach in April, and they end there in September. On the coast they begin only in June or July, but last until October. August is normally the rainiest month everywhere. During the wet season, 762–1 143 mm (30–45 in) of rain may be expected.

On and near the estuary, as in coastal Senegal, the intensity of the dry season is lessened by heavy dew, by high relative humidity, lower temperatures, and by sea breezes—though these are less strong than at Dakar. Marine trade winds account for 43 per cent of the average readings at Banjul, the Harmattan for 17 per cent, and the rain-bearing westerlies or northwesterlies for 18 per cent, the rest being calms. The fact that even the rain comes predominantly from the northwest is interesting. Upriver, where the Savanna climate prevails, the Harmattan accounts for some 60 per cent or more of the readings.

## Major regions

### The coastal region

This is a flat and monotonous area of unconsolidated marine and aeolian sands, low dunes being typical, as in Senegal. Some 2·8 m (10 ft) below the level surface is Tertiary ferruginous sandstone, which occasionally forms cliffs up to 6 m (20 ft) high, e.g. at Cape St Mary.

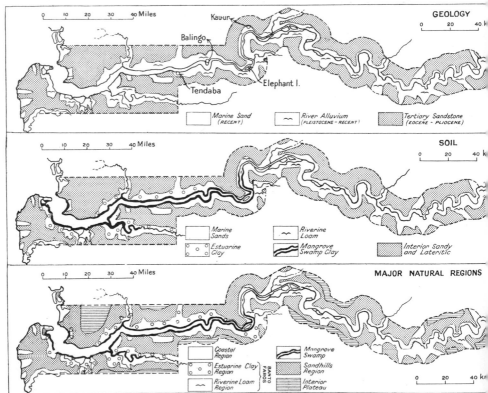

FIG. 13.1. Geology, soils and major regions of the Gambia

Source: H. R. Jarrett, 'Major natural regions of the Gambia', *Scottish Geogral Mag.*, **65**, no. 3, (1949), pp. 140–44 by kind permission of the author and editor. See also Fig. 13.4

226

As in western Senegal, the soil is light in colour and texture, originally low in chemical nutrients and very infertile. However, the *niayes,* or wet hollows, so typical and useful there, are not found here. The oil palm provides the only significant resource.

St Mary's Island, 5·6 × 2·0 km (3·5 × 1·25 miles), separated from the mainland by Oyster Creek, is really a sandbank. It ends eastward and southward in a sandspit, occupied by a once insalubrious part of Banjul, known ominously and—until recently— correctly as Half Die.

## BANJUL

After Gorée Islet (off Dakar) was returned to the French in 1816, another base was required to suppress the slave trade on the Gambia river. So a fort was established on Banjul Island, which was soon re-named St Mary's Island. The town developed as merchants and missionaries settled round the fort, and was named Bathurst, after Earl Bathurst, then Secretary of State for the Colonies. Bathurst was renamed Banjul in 1973. Part of Banjul is known as Portuguese Town, after slaves set free from Portuguese slave ships in the nineteenth century.

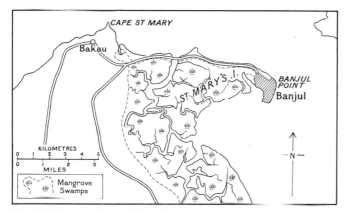

FIG. 13.2. The position of Banjul

Source: H. R. Jarrett, *A Geography of Sierra Leone and Gambia,* 1954, by kind permission of the author

The fort was undoubtedly fixed for strategic reasons at the constriction point on the river, where it is only 3·2 km (2 miles) wide; otherwise, the site is bad. Banjul is situated on two sand dunes about 1·8 and 2·4 m (6–8 ft) high, separated by a depression at water level, and adjacent to a river subject to yearly floods. Until 1949 annual floods caused the town to be likened by a distinguished surgeon to 'a water-logged sponge, floating in a sea of its own excreta';[3] especially was this so in Half Die and other reclaimed parts. Despite the town's broad streets, regular plan and at least one large open space, Banjul was until then aptly described by President Roosevelt to Mr Churchill as 'that hell-hole of yours'.[4] Malaria and yellow fever were formerly severe, and the infantile mortality rate from dysentery and allied diseases exceeded 250 per thousand until 1938. President Roosevelt caught fever here in 1943, hence his remark.

The problem of redeveloping Banjul was made more acute by shortage of space and overcrowding. In 1942, 10 per cent of the population regularly slept in the streets. One typical compound of three two-roomed houses and five one-roomed huts housed sixty people. The population has grown as follows:

| | |
|---|---|
| 1911 | 7 700 |
| 1921 | 9 305 |
| 1931 | 14 370 |
| 1944 | 21 152 |
| 1951 | 19 602 |
| 1967 | 31 800 |

Fig. 13.3. Plan of Banjul (after Town Plan)

PLATE 49. A street in Banjul with a central drain, part of a town system that stopped the erstwhile seasonal flooding of the town. The three-storied houses are in typical Creole style, erected in the nineteenth century by ex-slaves and typical of early Banjul, Freetown, Liberian coastal towns and of Lagos. The right hand building is a commercial house, with shop and warehouse below, and living accommodation above, likewise typical of early commercial houses

Following a report of 1943, flood and storm drains were put in along many roads, low-lying areas were cleared, and a new road and bund built in 1949 northwest from Half Die at the southern tip. Flooding has ceased and the town is now quite healthy, and congestion has been virtually eliminated.

Banjul has many small wharves owned by commercial houses (Fig. 13.3), and a deepwater one of 9 m (30 ft). Ships can also be offloaded to lighters while anchored. The main functions of the town are administrative and commercial, it being the organising centre for groundnut exports. Inclusive holidays, first organised by a Swedish firm, have led to the construction of several hotels and are a most useful stimulus to a small town.

### Mangrove swamps

The soils of the estuary are of clayey alluvium, heavily impregnated with salt. They are difficult to reclaim but there has been a good deal of clearance for swamp rice cultivation behind a 'curtain' of mangrove, which is left along the river to restrain flood waters (Plate 4 and Fig. 13.5).

### Banto Faros

These are Manding words meaning 'beyond swamp'. They are grasslands which are submerged in the flood season but are above water in the dry season, when their coarse grasses wither. The Raphia palm provides piassava for local use, and might be more exploited.

229

PLATE 50. Banto Faro; up river in the Gambia. The sunny areas are on a slight slope and under rice. Raphia palms are in the left-centre

Soils in this riverine ribbon are of lighter alluvium, and more fertile than those of the previous region. But below Kau-ur, where the Gambia river commences its great southward turn, the soils are saline and of little use. Above Kau-ur, salt does not occur, and the 'banto faros' of the Gambia river and its tributaries are fairly intensively used for rice cultivation by the women. The men are mainly engaged in growing groundnuts for sale, millet and guinea corn.

### The sandhills region

This is underlain by light Tertiary sands and sandstone, and is well—even too well—drained. Low hills alternate with shallow valleys. Much laterite or ferruginous crust is encountered, and the area is infertile. Above Niankwi Tenda this zone is very narrow; below that point it averages 5 km (3 miles) on either side. Tall grass alternates with baobab, locust bean and kapok trees.

### The sandstone (interior) plateau

This level area, which has an average altitude of 30 m (100 ft) in the west, 37 m (120 ft) in the middle river, and 46–49 m (150–160 ft) in the upper river, is an extension of the Eocene–Pliocene Ferlo Plateau of Senegal. Except in its flatness and slightly higher altitude, it resembles the sandhills region. Ferruginous or lateritic outcrops are frequent and the Gambia river has cut a gorge in these between Niankwi Tenda and Fatoto. At the latter point the cliffs are 46 m (150 ft) high.

These last two regions are well populated because they are beyond danger of flood, are healthier and more useful. Though infertile, the sandy soil is light and suited to the groundnut, the produce of which has long

230

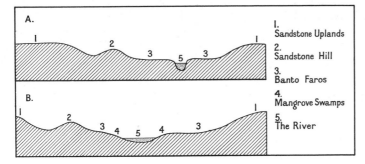

FIG. 13.4. Profile of major natural regions of the Gambia

Source: H. R. Jarrett, *A Geography of Sierra Leone and Gambia*, 1954, by permission of the author

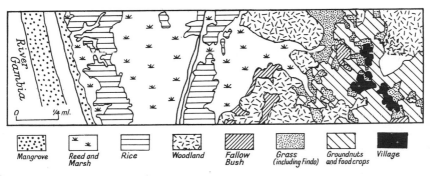

FIG. 13.5. Land use transect

From the Dunkunku sheet 1:25 000 Land Use, Directorate of Overseas Surveys map DOS 3001 sheet 6/IV,
Crown Copyright Reserved, by permission of the Controller of HM Stationery Office

accounted for some 95 per cent by value of Gambia's exports.

Most Gambian villages stand on the dry, quickly drained, sandy soils adjacent to groundnut patches and to 'banto faros' suitable for rice (Plate 50 and Figs 13.1 and 13.4–5). As the latter cannot be so easily grown in the lower river because of mangrove and saline soils, truly rural population tends to be greater up-river.[5]

# Economic resources

## Agriculture

### GROUNDNUTS

These are the only major cash crop, and occupy two-thirds of the cultivated 'uplands'. The crop is grown entirely by small farmers on some 85 000 ha (210 000 acres). Average yields are low, and a unit of the Medical Research Council found the soils to be extremely deficient in magnesium, copper and boron. Improved varieties of groundnuts and better farming methods are also required.

231

Groundnuts were first exported from the Gambia in 1830 and have been the leading export since 1845. That the Gambia is excessively dependent on groundnuts is all too evident, yet it is not easy to find alternative exports. The most promising development is increased rice cultivation, since imported rice often costs three times as much per ton as exported groundnuts.

### RICE

Rice, the favourite though not the main foodstuff, is of ever-increasing importance. There has been some remarkable clearance of mangrove swamp in the lower river and of fresh-water swamp in the upper river by farmers for rice cultivation.

### MILLET

Millet is the basic food and is grown in rotation, or intercropped with groundnuts. It is said that by intercropping, the extensive roots of millet dry out the soil and hasten the maturing of the groundnuts.

### LESSER PRODUCTS

Lesser crops are maize, guinea corn, cassava, hungry rice (findo), sweet potatoes and other vegetables, the oil palm and the coconut—the last two mainly in the coastlands.

Apart from groundnuts, the only agricultural products exported are palm kernels, hides, skins and beeswax; the first of these accounts for some 1–2 per cent of exports only. Limes have been tried at Yundum since 1967 for the possible export of lime oil and juice. Cotton is grown for local cloth.

## Conclusion

The Gambia river has been prevented from serving its proper hinterland, and the tiny Gambia has suffered severely from the disadvantages of a one-crop economy. Increased rice cultivation and tourism may do something to alter this.

Although the country is an enclave, no advantage has been taken of this fact, e.g. the Gambia might have developed many oil factories to attract Senegal groundnuts. Trade from across the frontier in hides and skins might also have been encouraged. Banjul could have been developed as a free port, like Monrovia, Liberia. The future should lie in closer association with Senegal. The Gambia river would then be available to cheapen the transport costs of groundnuts and other goods from an enlarged hinterland, and the river towns and Banjul should prosper.

# 14

# Mauritania: the link with North Africa

## Introduction

Although Mali and Niger also adjoin North African lands in the Sahara, Mauritania is the truest link with North Africa, particularly Morocco. Contacts between peoples are of long standing, and the predominant inhabitants of Mauritania are known in French literature as *Maures*. These people call themselves *Bidanes* ('whites') and have Berber and Arab blood, with some Negro admixture. They are often light in colour and dress in blue robes in order, it is said, to accentuate their pale colouring. They are of medium height, spare in build, with wavy black hair, and are predominantly nomadic keepers of livestock. The few agriculturalists are generally their semi-slaves or descendants of slaves. The Moors are well known for their hospitality and are great drinkers of sweet green tea, said to have been introduced about a century ago from Morocco. Their way of life derives from their nomadic existence and Islamic faith.

## Historical outline

Despite its name, modern Mauritania does not coincide with the former Roman Province of *Mauretania Tingitana*, whose limits did not extend beyond the Draa river, far to the north. Indeed, it was in the period after the decay of the Roman Empire and at the height of the Arab conquests, that contacts between the areas now occupied by Mauritania and Morocco were closest.

As with most other parts of West Africa, the first European contacts were in the fifteenth century by Portuguese who, after seeking a route round Africa to Asia, revisited this coast to trade first in gold and then in slaves. They established a fort on Arguin Island, which was later captured by the Dutch and English. Probably because of the sparse population, the slave trade soon gave way to that in gum arabic, over which there was intense rivalry between the Dutch and French, until the Dutch finally withdrew from the coast in 1727. Thereafter, the rivalry was between the French and British, until the British withdrew in 1857, against French cession of Albreda on the Gambia river. However, the trade in gum declined in the twentieth century, in face of competition from the Sudan.

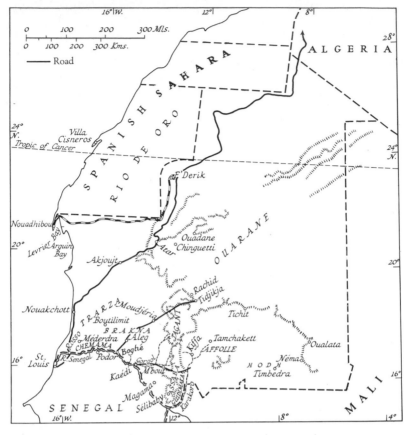

FIG. 14.1. Mauritania

Most of modern Mauritania, as distinct from points on the coast, was occupied between 1902 and 1914. It became a colony in 1920 and independent in 1960.

The country extends northeastward from the Senegal, ultimately into pure desert. Mauritania's area of 1 030 700 sq km (397 969 sq miles) makes it the third largest state of West Africa, and the size of France and Spain combined. Mauritania is larger than Nigeria, yet the measure of the aridity of the former is its population of only 1 171 000 in 1970. Over 90 per cent of the mainly nomadic population live in the southern two-fifths of the country, whilst another two-fifths are virtually uninhabited. Although the capital of Nouakchott, built since 1958, has over 10 000 inhabitants, and the newer iron ore railway terminal towns of Cansado (part of Nouadhibou) and F'Derik (Fort Gouraud) have about the same populations, there are only a handful of other towns of over 3 000 inhabitants. With by far the lowest density of population in West Africa, and one that is very dispersed in a harsh environment, Mauritania is indeed a country with immense problems—but also one with promising resources in minerals, livestock and fish.

# Climate

The outstanding features of the climate of this territory are the persistence in the interior of the Harmattan winds, the consequent aridity, and the great variation between day and night temperatures.

Cool marine trade winds are felt along the coast, but they bring little rain, and that mostly in 'winter'. The wet southwesterlies reach as far as the centre or north between August and October, but to a very variable extent and intensity. In the extreme southeast of the territory, where the southern Sahel climate prevails, the annual rainfall is about 460 mm (18 in) at Kaédi and 650 mm (26 in) at Sélibaby. At Rosso it averages nearly 305 mm (12 in). North of Rosso the northern Sahel climate is found.

In the north-centre about 75 mm (3 in) annual rain occurs in the Southern Saharan climate, e.g. at Atar. Although the rainfall is so small, the cooling effect may be significant and very welcome. Heavy dew at night throughout the territory provides vital moisture. North of 20–21°N rain is rare and Saharan conditions prevail.

So far as temperature is concerned, the diurnal variations exceed the annual ones. As a rough average, the diurnal range is 11–17°C (20–31°F) on the coast and 17–19·5°C (31–35°F) inland.

## Water resources

It is obvious from the above that water is a fundamental factor in Mauritanian life and development. It is generally found at great depths in the north and often so even in the south.

Water is most readily available in the Chemama or Senegal valley, in clay depressions in the south where it can generally be found not deeper than 18 m (60 ft), and at the base of large dunes where it may be as much as 90 m (300 ft) down.

In the region limited by Aleg, Podor and Kaédi, there is much water available at 40–59 m (130–195 ft) in depth, but it can be tapped extensively only with costly equipment. To the west, in Trarza, the water table is nearer the surface and was reached by the local people, but its exploitation has been greatly improved by the French. Originally, there were only a few earth barrages in Mauritania, which often lasted no longer than a year. There are modern ones at Aneikat-Gaoua (Brakna), a similar one at Mokta Sfera, near Kiffa, and some ten others. So far some 18 000 ha (45 000 acres) have been brought under cultivation with water from dams. More are needed, however, especially along regular cattle routes.

## Geology and natural regions

Pre-Cambrian rocks are present in northwestern Mauritania, but elsewhere they are often covered by other series. In western Mauritania they are much obscured by great accumulations of Quaternary sands, which occur in northeast to southwest trending dunes, some being live and some fixed. Central Mauritania sees the thinning of these sands. Cretaceous and Post-Eocene rocks occur in Trarza and Brakna; to the north and east Pre-Cambrian rocks outcrop or are near the surface. In eastern Mauritania Ordovician, Silurian and—to a lesser extent—Devonian sandstones give rise to magnificent scarps which can be traced through the country from near Sélibaby to far beyond Atar (see Fig. 14.1).

## The coastal zone

The same smooth shore backed by mobile dunes occurs as in Senegal, but with significant differences. First, a few capes and islands break the coastline, as at Arguin, and these were used as slave depots and, for much longer, as gum-trading points. Secondly, instead of the freshwater *niayes* of Senegal, with their luxuriant vegetation, there is, in the north, a succession of salt encrusted mudflats (*sebkhas*), marshy only after rare rains, which are remnants of former lagoons. South of Nouakchott, is the Aftout-es-Saheli clay depression, which is almost always marshy in character. In the far south is a former Senegal outlet, and beyond this marsh is a long spit upon which, within Senegal, at St Louis, were the government offices of Mauritania from 1920 to 1960.

The coast has shifting sandbanks, e.g. at Portendik and Arguin, and the action of the dry winds on loose sands often causes sandstorms; whilst the waters of the cold Canary Current, in contact with warm air, produce fog and mist. These and the smooth shoreline add to its dangerous character. Yet there is a considerable continental shelf with much plankton, so that ships from Europe, the Canaries, and even from Japan visit these waters, catching some 270 000 tons annually.

*Nouadhibou*[1] lies on the east side of the Cape Blanco peninsula (the western half of which is Spanish), and so on the west side of the sheltered Lévrier Bay. Founded in 1907 as a fish drying base it has six drying, freezing or canning factories, which also produce fish oil and meal and other fish products. A modern quay and fish hall was opened in 1968. Dried fish are exported to Congo and Zaïre.

Far more important now is the iron ore export pier farther south, where there were natural depths of 13·4 m (44 ft) and where 150 000 ton ore carriers can tie up. Associated with it is the township of Cansado (Plate 54). Water is brought in by railway and also distilled from sea water, as it also is at Nouakchott.

*Nouakchott*, the capital, has a wharf built for general cargo but increasingly used for the export of copper concentrates from Akjoujt.

PLATE 51. Nouakchott, capital of Mauritania, built since 1958

## The Chemama

The Mauritanian half of the Senegal floodplain is the country's only large area of arable land, cultivated mostly by Toucouleur as the annual river flood retreats. From this area comes much of the millet consumed in Mauritania. *Kaédi, Boghé*, and *Rosso* arc important river trading towns.

## Plains of southern Trarza and Brakna

South of the Méderdra–Aleg–Moudjéria line, the country is composed in part of northeast to southwest trending fixed dunes (*sbar*), which are infertile but covered by fairly dense Sahel savanna. Otherwise, between the dunes are clay plains (*aftout*), fertile and cultivable, especially after the rainy and flood season. These are important cattle areas, and gum arabic is collected.

## Central plains of northern Trarza, northern Brakna and Akjoujt

These lie north of about 17°N and are also known locally as the Sahel. Dunes are progressively barer and more mobile, and north of about $18\frac{1}{2}$°N Sahel savanna gives way to southern Saharan vegetation. Hills have spurges, while acacias and useful grasses occur only in damp depressions.

Southwest of Akjoujt, there is an *aftout*, some 48 km (30 miles) wide, which reaches the coast. Copper is mined near the same settlement (see below).

237

**The granite mass of Zemmour**

Situated in the northwest, astride the Rio de Oro boundary, greater height and impervious rocks enable acacias and other dwarf trees, shrubs and grasses to survive to a surprising extent. Camels are extensively raised here.

**Guidimakha**

This region extends around Sélibaby, in the extreme southeast of Mauritania, and is similar to the Bondou region of Senegal, except that Guidimakha also has steepedged mesas, which are outliers of the Primary sandstone scarp of Assaba. The seasonal Gorgol streams provide opportunities for millet cropping and intermittent pasturing; tamarisks, acacias and small palms are common.

**The sandstone plateaux**

These occupy almost all eastern Mauritania. South of the scarp running northeastwards from Atar, the plateaux are of Ordovician and Silurian sandstones and shales, probably similar to the Voltaian system of Ghana, and equally infertile. In Mauritania their barren character is heightened by aridity and masks of loose sand. In the far north the sandstones are of Devonian to Lower Carboniferous age, dip north and have northeast–southwest scarps (Fig. 14.1).

As in Ghana, the edges of the sandstone are impressive scarps. Continuing from the Mali Republic, they run east to west at Tichit, north to south near Kiffa and towards Sélibaby and Rachid, northwestward to near Akjoujt, and then mostly northeastward in several series. The scarps average 60 m (200 ft) in height, are sometimes broken into several mesas and etched by ravines (Plate 52). Indeed, south of Atar the scarp is eroded into a rather chaotic collection of valleys and flat-topped masses. Springs are fairly frequent at the base of the scarps and have helped such settlements as Ouadane, Atar, Rachid, Tidjikja and Tichit. Some seasonal torrents have been dammed to make possible the greater production of millet.

*F'Derik* lies on the Moroccan road, and eastward lies the Kédia d'Idjil hills whose north-eastern peaks have rich haematite iron ore, Mauritania's most important resource (p. 240). To the northwest lies the Sebkha of Idjil, once much exploited for salt, but now worked mainly for local sale to the nearest settlements.

*Atar* is an important centre with a trade in dates. *Moudjéria* also trades in dates.

On the plateau the only settlements of note are the oases *Chinguetti, Ouadane* and *Tidjikja*; they too produce dates.

PLATE 52. Cambrian and later limestones and sandstones are associated with flat-topped massifs (here of Adrar), deep valleys and springs. The latter are vital for man, camels and dates. A view of Atar

## Economic resources

### Agriculture

Both because of the nature of the country and the attitude of the people, agriculture is of minor importance. Real cropping is found only in the Chemama, in oases, along seasonal rivers such as the Gorgols and Karakoro (respectively west and east of Assaba), and adjacent to barrages. It is done mostly by descendants of former slaves—by Wolof below Dagana, Toucouleur from Dagana to Magama, and by Sarakollé above Magama. Millet is the main crop, with much smaller amounts of maize, rice and water melons. Rice is almost only grown towards M'Bout and in Guidimakha by the Sarakollé. Irrigation of rice being tried at several points on the Senegal river, especially west of Rosso.

DATES are important near centres mentioned above. Unfortunately, they are not produced in sufficient quantity or of such quality as to be exported. However, improved palms have been planted in substantial numbers.

GUM ARABIC is produced from the *Acacia senegal* and *A. arabica*, the first giving the harder and better gum. The gum is employed in pharmacy, cooking, textile industries and in the manufacture of dyestuffs. It first came to medieval Europe from the ports of Asia Minor, whose merchants had obtained it from Arabs in Red Sea ports, who in turn had bought it from the areas in the Sudan. Because of the trade being in the hands of Arabs, the gum came to be known as 'gum arabic'.

When Europeans went to the Mauritanian coast, the gum trade soon predominated, and was the source of rivalry between the Dutch, French and British from the seventeenth century to the nineteenth. The Sudan again controls the market by exporting gum of higher quality.

Gum is obtained by tearing strips of bark from the trees, which bear from the fourth or fifth year until the twentieth to twenty-fifth year. The tree also provides fibre for rope and nets. Most of the Mauritanian production comes from areas situated between 15° and 17°N. In Trarza the trees grow on the northeast to southwest trending sand dunes, especially east of the road from Rosso to north of Méderdra. The dampness of sea breezes and dew by night are important factors in their growth. In Brakna rainfall is greater and more certain, but the sandy-clay soils are less suitable than the dune soils of Trarza.

## Livestock

Cattle, which must move in search of seasonal pastures, are the traditional resource of this poor country[2] and are overwhelmingly the *Maure* type of Zebu. Maure cattle are very hardy and weigh some 360 kg (800 lb) on average. Extensively used as beasts of burden, they will carry up to about 90 kg (200 lb) each. Most cattle are found in the Hodh and near the seasonal Gorgol rivers. There is an abattoir and freezing plant at Kaédi, as well as a tannery, but they operate far below capacity in default of outlets. Most livestock are exported on the hoof to Senegal and the Gambia.

Sheep and goats are mainly concentrated in the coastlands, in Tidjikja, and especially around Tamchakett. Lesser concentrations are in Brakna and Trarza. Mutton is a very important item in the diet of the Moors. Sheep and goat skins are used in making saddlery, cushions and much else. Only in the south are there sufficient skins for export.

Donkeys are important as beasts of burden in the better-watered areas, especially near the coast and in the southeast. Camels are important everywhere as beasts of burden and are extensively hired to Senegal merchants during the groundnut trading season. The main area for camels is around Akjoujt.

## Minerals

IRON. Mauritania has been transformed politically, economically and socially by the opening of rich haematite iron ore deposits in 1963.

PLATE 53. Tazadit iron ore mine east of F'Derik, Mauritania

These occur as thick cappings on the northern peaks of the Kédia d'Idjil hills, east of F'Derik. There are at least 200–250 million tons of 64 per cent iron content, half of which can be mined open cast (Plate 53), the ore has few impurities, and is very dry. A company with French, British, German, Italian and Mauritanian government capital is mining the deposit, and a 635 km (397 miles) railway takes the ore to Nouadhibou. A direct route across Spanish Sahara was ruled out in the face of onerous Spanish terms; nevertheless a 2 km (1¼ miles) tunnel had to be built at a cost of £3 million to keep the track within Mauritania at the southeastern corner of Spanish Sahara. Nearby fixed sand dunes required spraying with heavy oil to secure a stable base for the track, while nearer Nouadhibou mobile dunes may require periodic realignment of the track. Townships were built at each terminal in utter desert (Plate 54) and water is conveyed to each by the railway. Annual export of iron ore is 9–12 million tons, and from 1963 to 1971 this constituted 95 per cent or more of Mauritanian exports.

COPPER ORE (1·9–2·9 per cent copper) has been mined at Akjoujt since 1971, a development made possible by the use of the Torco process in refining the oxide ore. There is also sulphide ore below. Four units concentrate the ore to 65 per cent Cu, which is then taken by road to

241

PLATE 54. Cansado township, south of Nouadhibou, built for employees at the Miferma railway terminal and shipping quay. A similar township was built in equally desertic conditions near the mine

PLATE 55. Miferma terminal and shipping quay, at Cansado, south of Nouadhibou

PLATE 56. Akjoujt copper mine. A 'Torco' smelter

PLATE 57. Copper concentrate being loaded into a lighter at Nouakchott pier for transfer to an off-shore vessel for export

Nouakchott for export via the pier. An ultimate annual export of 34 000 tons is intended but low prices for copper occurred as this rather costly production began.

SALT is mined near Akjoujt to serve the copper refinery. A little salt is dug near F'Derik and Nouakchott by traditional methods for domestic use.

OIL is still being prospected and there are possibilities of other mineral developments.

## Conclusion

The metamorphosis of Mauritania from the direst poverty to modest viability is akin in style, if not in degree, to that of some Arab sheikdoms. As in them, the traditional economy remains outside the nevertheless increasingly numerous nodes of the modern one. The country is also socially and politically a mixture of traditionalism and radicalism.

For some eight years after independence Mauritania was claimed by Morocco but relations are now more normal. Meanwhile, Mauritania, like Algeria and Morocco, lays claim to Spanish Sahara.

## 15

# Mali: Marxian socialism in an inland state

Mali is some five times the size of Great Britain and has an area of 1 240 000 sq km (478 783 sq miles). The population in 1970 was estimated at 5 022 000 so that it has an average density of no more than 4 per sq km (10 per sq mile). The country is landlocked and arid or dry, except along its southwestern fringe. Elsewhere, cultivation depends almost entirely upon flood water control or irrigation from the Niger river and its tributaries, mainly for rice cultivation or pasture. The greatest (but nevertheless underdeveloped) resource is livestock. An indication of the poverty of Mali is that men migrate to work in Dakar (Senegal), the Ivory Coast and Ghana, and also to France.

Since 1960 Mali has pursued an intensely state-directed form of socialism, akin to that in far richer Guinea and Ghana (under Nkrumah). Although there were modifications after the fall of Modibo Keita in 1968, state companies run most enterprises but rarely efficiently so. The rupture with Senegal in 1960, Mali's closure of the through railway to Dakar until 1963, and the creation of the Mali franc in 1962 all reduced foreign trade, and discouraged farmers and traders. Activity was more directed to self-sufficiency, and there was much smuggling across the many borders. On the other hand, the infrastructure, notably roads, was much improved.

Following devaluation in 1967 there was considerable agricultural revival, notably in the dry farming of cotton and groundnuts, and an increase in floodwater control for rice cultivation. Industries are being made more efficient, some private enterprise has been restored in commerce, and more varied imports permitted. The Mali franc is again within the franc zone.

## Historical outline

It was in the lands that at present constitute Mali that the most famous ancient empires of West Africa were centred. The first of these was that of Ghana, which may have been established in the fourth century AD, and is mentioned in Arab writings from the ninth century onwards. In the eleventh century it was probably at its zenith, but after 1076 was conquered by peoples from North Africa, and its rulers became converted to Islam. It finally declined after a second conquest in 1240. Ruins of its capital exist at Koumbi Saleh, about 322 km (200 miles) north-northeast of Bamako.

Ghana was succeeded by the Mali (or Manding) Empire. This originated in the seventh century, was at its climax in the thirteenth or fourteenth centuries, and had its capital at Mali on the left bank of the Niger. In the fifteenth century this empire declined at the hands of the Gao or Songhaï Empire, which likewise traced its origin to the seventh century.

The Songhaï Empire split up after 1591 and, until the arrival of the French at the end of the nineteenth century, there were a number of minor states under the Fulani and Bambara.

The three empires of Ghana, Mali and Gao were quite highly organised and received considerable revenues from trans-Saharan trade. The later period of the Ghana and the whole era of the Gao Empire were strongly influenced by peoples from North Africa, and there can be little doubt that even the Mali Empire, although indigenous, ultimately depended upon North Africa for its economic survival.

The most famous explorers of this area were the Arab Ibn Batuta in the fifteenth century; Mungo Park who travelled down the Niger between 1795 and 1797 and again on his fatal journey in 1805; Réné Caillé, who visited the area in 1827; and Barth in 1850–55.

The route up the Senegal and down the Niger was an obvious one for European penetration, since it offered great stretches of river navigation with no major physical obstacles. The French established their first permanent fort on the upper Senegal as early as 1712. Expeditions were sent to Bambouk (Falémé valley) in search of gold in 1730–31, 1756 and 1824, though by the latter date gum was of greater general importance.

Advance beyond the Senegal river was initiated by Faidherbe, and by 1866 Ségou on the Niger had been reached. Forts between the Senegal and Niger rivers were built from 1879 to 1881. The railway was begun in the latter year, being opened to Koulikoro in 1904; it linked the upper limit of navigation on the Senegal river with two navigable reaches of the Niger. The through line to Dakar was opened in 1923.

The territory became a separate French colony from 1892–99, and again from 1904. It has had its present name since independence in 1960, a reminder of the earlier empire.

## Climate and vegetation

Typical average rainfall figures are Araouane 51 mm (2 in), Gao 229 mm (9 in), Mopti 508 mm (20 in), Kayes 762 mm (30 in), Bamako 1 118 mm (44 in) and Sikasso 1 397 mm (55 in). Most of Mali is dry; north of 19°N there is virtually no rain and Saharan conditions prevail. Even in the mountainous Adrar des Iforas, there is less rainfall than in the Aïr Massif of Niger.

245

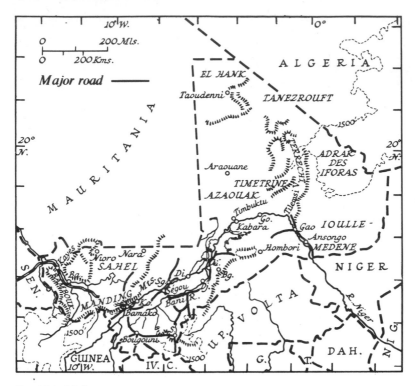

FIG. 15.1.  Mali

M = Mopti, Bg = Bandiagara, Dj = Djenné, Di = Diafarabé, Sg = Sansanding, Ko = Koulikoro,
S = Sikasso, Ba = Bafoulabé, Go = Gourma Rharous

South of about 19°N, extending nearly to Timbuktu, and farther south in the east and west, are semi-Saharan conditions.

From about 17° to 15°N in the Northern Sahel and Southern Sahel climatic zones rainfall is light, variable and of short duration. Diurnal temperature ranges remain high, because of almost unimpeded insolation and the high degree of refraction. Evaporation is also intense, so that the human body can feel cold even when the temperatures are 16–21°C (61–70°F). In building reservoirs for watering the large numbers of livestock, account must be taken of this high evaporation. The Niger and its tributaries may modify conditions by their flood or irrigation waters. Near the rivers are extensive swamps; otherwise the vegetation is Sahel Savanna.

Between 15° and 12°N the Savanna climate prevails and the vegetation is Sudan Savanna except, again, near rivers.

South of about 12°N, in the extreme southwest, the Southern Savanna climate occurs and the wet season is longer. Because of the many ferruginous crusts, the rainfall is less effective even here than might be supposed and the vegetation is poor Northern Guinea Savanna.
(See also Chapters 3 and 4.)

# Geology and relief

Most of Mali is very flat. Yet it is well known for its sandstone mountains and plateaux which are limited by steep scarps. The sandstones are probably Ordovician and Silurian in age, are flatbedded, and lie unconformably on Pre-Cambrian schists and gneisses. In the sandstones are sheet intrusions of dolerite and gabbro. The most famous sandstone scarps are Tambaoura south of Kayes, that of the Manding Mountains, and the long and almost continuous scarp which extends from Banfora in the Upper Volta northwards to Bandiagara, south of the Niger Bend. The other major relief feature is Adrar des Iforas, which consists of Pre-Cambrian schists and granitic intrusions.

The Niger and its tributaries flow through the depression which is so much a feature of West Africa between the ancient rocks of much of the Guinea Coast and the massifs of the Saharan interior. In this depression was a late Tertiary—Quaternary lake, which was drained by overspilling into the lower Niger, whose sources were then in Adrar des Iforas.

The western part of Mali benefits from the Senegal river, with which the upper Niger river communicated via the Nara–Nioro sill until the Tertiary inland lake was formed.

# Major regions

## Bambouk and the Manding Mountains

These mountains of Palaeozoic sandstone are northern spurs of the Fouta Djallon of Guinea. The Bambouk Mountains terminate westward in the impressive Tambaoura scarp, overlooking the Falémé river. A rocky sill in the Senegal river, just above Kayes, is an outlying remnant, and makes that town the limit of seasonal navigation on the Senegal.

### KAYES

Before the completion of the Dakar–Niger railway, Kayes was a transhipment point between the Senegal river and the railway to the Niger. The town is a cattle and sheep market, dependent upon the export trade in livestock to Senegal by rail and road. It also trades in groundnuts, gum, hides and skins; there is a tannery, and a cement works at Diamou.

The Manding Mountains lie east of the Bafing and end east of Bamako, where their southern edge dominates the Niger left bank and is occupied by Koulouba, the administrative quarter of Bamako. These mountains are flat-topped and often covered by laterite. As in the case of the Senegal at Kayes, there are outliers in the Niger below Bamako, so making that city the lower limit of navigation of the upper Niger.

247

## BAMAKO

The capital of the Mali Republic was a mere village when occupied by the French in 1883. It developed rapidly, not so much as a result of the separation of the territory from Senegal, but rather from the opening of the railway in 1904. In consequence of this, it became the capital in 1908, which had previously been at Kayes. The greatest impetus, however, came after 1923, when the through railway to Dakar was opened, and transhipment at Kayes to the Senegal river ended. The Niger bridge, opened 1960, has helped develop the south bank.

The political departments are at Koulouba; the technical ones, the railway, the commercial and most other quarters are on the plain between the scarp and the river. The town has been very well planned and varied trees line the roads. Some of the buildings are in an interesting neo-Sudan style.

Bamako is an important administrative and military centre, as well as one for railway, road, local and international air communications. It is also a very important market, especially for cattle and kola nuts. Industries have developed almost entirely since independence. Those using local materials include an abattoir and cold store, with some export of meat by air to the coastal countries, a cotton ginnery, textile mill and a

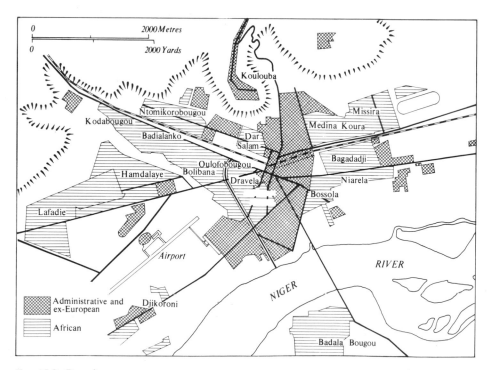

FIG. 15.2. Bamako

brickworks. Guava, tamarind and other rather unusual fruit juices are canned at Baguineda near Bamako, and should be developed for export. A cigarette, tobacco and match complex built by the Chinese partly uses imports and, increasingly, local produce. Factories using imports comprise agricultural equipment, cycle and transistor assembly, a milk reconstitution plant, the making of metal furniture and enamelware. An industrial quarter has grown up between the Sotuba and Koulikoro roads, and a new airport has been built 12 km (7·5 miles) south of Bamako. Bamako has grown rapidly in population—1946, nearly 37 000 people; 1954, 65 000; 1960, 131 900; 1966, 182 000, and 1971, over 200 000.[1]

KOULIKORO

Just as Bamako owes some of its importance from being at the lower end of the navigable upper Niger, so Koulikoro is significant as being at the commencement of the much longer navigable middle Niger. The railway joins the towns and the two navigable reaches of the river. Koulikoro is a collecting centre for goods railed westwards to the coast, and for the despatch of imported goods down the river. Apart from its significance as a river port, Koulikoro has a groundnut oil and soap factory.

**Sahel**

This is an area of sandy lowlands lying northwest and north of the Niger river, as far as Ségou and extending into Mauritania. It was through the Nara–Nioro sill that the upper Niger once drained to the Senegal river, and present intermittent drainage is still in that direction.

In this region the Ghana Empire had its capital, but today the area is very poor; nevertheless, it supports great numbers of livestock, especially sheep. The regional centres are Nioro and Nara.

**Azaouak, Tanezrouft and El Hank**

Azaouak is the vast sandy plain and cattle country north of Timbuktu, drier than the Sahel but otherwise similar. Tanezrouft is flat stony desert, while El Hank in the far north is broken desert country.

**Timetrine, Terrecht and Adjouz**

In these regions Tertiary limestones and arid erosion forms give broken country, with occasional scarps. Ouadis from Adrar des Iforas sometimes have water but, as their courses are often blocked by dunes, marshes tend to form. The eastern edge of Terrecht is known as the Kreb de Terrecht and adjoins the dry Tilemsi valley. All these lands are very dry.

249

## Tilemsi valley

A sandy trough, this averages 48 km (30 miles) in width and some 270 km (170 miles) in length. It is a magnificent example of a valley etched in a wetter period, when the Tilemsi was the upper part of the presentday lower middle Niger.

## Adrar des Iforas

This great highland somewhat resembles the larger Aïr Massif and is an extension of the Ahaggar Massif. Adrar des Iforas averages 610 m (2 000 ft) above sea level and is drained westward to the Tilemsi. Archaean schists comprise most of the north, east and south; granite intrusions make up the western heights towards the Tilemsi. Quaternary rejuvenation has made the ouadis narrow and deep. Broken and trenched, Adrar des Iforas is also barren. It is almost uninhabited, unlike Aïr, home of some Tuareg.

## Ioullemedene

Lying between Adrar des Iforas and the Niger river, and extending into the Niger Republic (see Djerma Ganda) and the Sokoto region of Nigeria, this area is very dry and eroded. The annual rainfall at Menaka is about 200 mm (8 in). Many mesas occur, and north of Menaka is a rather large group of hills which rise 91 m (300 ft) above the plain.

## The Niger valley

The Niger and its tributaries are the lifegivers of Mali. Water is used for rice cultivation, the rivers for navigation and for fishing, and it would appear that, in the inland delta region at least, rainfall is increased by the amount of water in the many channels of the river. Downstream, as far as the annually flooded areas (between Diafarabé and Timbuktu), the river plains are generally well peopled and sometimes cultivated with the plough in a system of simple mixed farming.

Although the annual floods of the Niger have long been utilised to grow millet, it is only since about 1940 that great efforts have been made to harness them to grow rice and cotton. There are two main methods of using floodwaters:

(*a*) By canal irrigation fed from the Sansanding Barrage. For this the Office du Niger has had to undertake great engineering works on the Niger, build canals, level vast areas accurately and completely, and attract its labour force and colonists. In return, water control is complete.

(*b*) By simple works undertaken by the Génie Rural, to modify flooding, especially at the beginning and end of seasonal floods. Little expense is

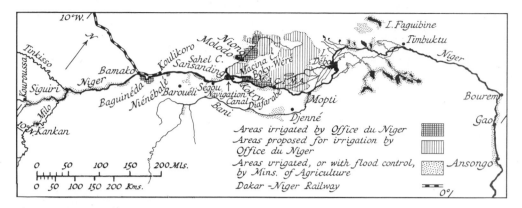

FIG. 15.3. Irrigated areas in part of Guinea and Mali

incurred and, as the riverine lands are generally already used, the aims are to make better use of the water and to increase the cultivable area.

Yields from the latter method are often inferior but costs are less, and the areas improved are much greater. The Office du Niger has effectively irrigated about 42 000 ha (approx, 104 000 acres) and the Génie Rural 64 000 ha (158 000 acres), both having been in full operation for comparable periods. Moreover, areas effectively irrigated by the Office du Niger are declining, whilst the Génie Rural provides water control to new areas each year.

The Niger valley comprises several distinct sectors:

## UPPER VALLEY

In both Guinea and Mali tributary rivulets are being harnessed by simple barrages near confluence points with the Niger. Canals direct water to farmers who thereby get their water earlier and in a gentler and more systematic way. The main stream is often paralleled by a tributary, and this may be used as a drainage canal, or as a reservoir. Apart from earlier encouragement of rice, cotton and tobacco have been developed since 1967, the latter for the factory at Bamako.

The upper Niger is navigable from Kouroussa downstream to Bamako and the Milo can be used from Kankan, but traffic on these is much less than on the middle Niger.

## THE DJOLIBA SECTOR FROM KOULIKORO TO SANSANDING

The river plains are intensively cultivated, but the river flows in a slightly confined valley, so that annual flooding is restricted. Simple water management schemes are numerous in this sector, particularly above and below

251

PLATE 58. Sansanding Barrage. Note one of three travelling arms for adjustment of sluices

Ségou, at Ké-Macina, above and below San, at and below Mopti.

*Ségou,* the Bambara capital from 1660 to 1861, is the headquarters of the Office du Niger. Goods come to its market from the Niger, and by lorry from the Bani river at Douna. There is trade in fish, cattle, hides, salt and cotton, and there is a large textile works in the town.

### THE INLAND NIGER DELTA

This area corresponds to a former lake of late-Tertiary times, with a series of deltas, and which was drained when it overspilled to connect with the lower Niger. In this former lacustrine area, between Sansanding and Timbuktu, the Niger has an almost insignificant gradient and is easily diverted into a more southerly course, whenever a valley becomes obstructed by Harmattan windborne sand. The inland delta area may be subdivided into the dead delta from Sansanding to Diafarabé, and the live one from Diafarabé to Timbuktu.

It is in the dead part that the main works of the Office du Niger are located. Above Sansanding is a barrage nearly a kilometre (half a mile) long, extended northward by an embankment to prevent lateral percolation. The barrage has 488 small sluice-gates, each adjustable like deckchairs by means of three travelling lifting arms. There is a navigation canal, and over the barrage and the embankment is a bridge, one of only eight across the Niger. The Sansanding barrage was begun in 1934 and

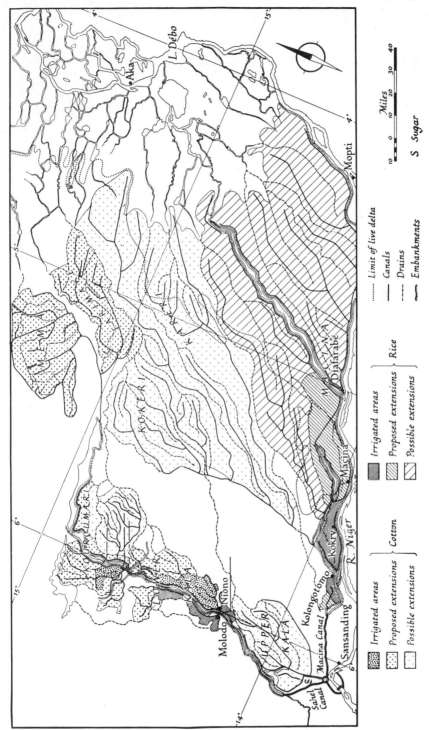

FIG. 15.4. The inland Niger delta

253

PLATE 59. Combine harvesting of rice

completed in 1941, except that temporary wooden sluices were in position until 1947.

The immediate effect of the barrage was to raise the level of the Niger by some 4 m (14 ft). A feeder canal leads water into the Sahel and Macina canals, which have been cut through sand to unobstructed parts of former Niger thalwegs, now once again filled with water. Hence, the essential aim has been to revive the dead delta by sending water down abandoned valleys.

From the main canal, lesser ones send water to the mechanically levelled and prepared fields, excess water being led off by drains. The scheme has been in full operation since 1947, but by 1971 only 42 000 ha (approx. 104 000 acres) had been or remained irrigated to support 3 200 families or 30 400 people in all.

These peasants had come from eastern and southern Mali and in the past from the Upper Volta.[2] They had no resources and no knowledge of irrigated farming. They were provided with huts, gardens, animals and simple cultivation equipment, food and training. Although the land is prepared mechanically, each family has its own leased holding.

Originally the aim was to create a second Nile valley, where vast quantities of cotton could be produced to free France from American supplies. However, inexperienced farmers allowed the cotton to degenerate, and the soils are seldom rich enough because the Niger has not deposited silt to anything like the depth found along the Nile.

From 1941 to about 1960 the emphasis was changed to rice, which has come to occupy most of the irrigated area. The southeastern areas of Bcky-Wéré and Kokry, fed by the Macina canal, have always been mainly concerned with rice cultivation because of the damper and more impermeable soils. Some of the crop is mechanically cultivated at Molodo and Sokolo in the north on the Sahel canal. There are some 12 000 ha (29 650 acres) so cultivated, out of a total of 28 000 ha (approx. 69 200 acres) devoted to the crop.

The Sahel canal feeds the formerly mainly cotton areas of Niono, Molodo and Kouroumari in the north. Mechanical cultivation of this crop was encouraged after 1960 under Russian guidance, as a means of supporting local industry. However, the cost and difficulties of doing so were progressively realised, particularly as far more cotton is now produced more cheaply by dry farming here and especially elsewhere in Mali. Consequently, irrigated cotton is no longer officially sponsored by the Office du Niger.

The latest modifications have been under Chinese technicians, who have encouraged sugar cane on some 1 300 ha (approx. 3 212 acres) north of Markala, and 4 000 ha (9 885 acres) may be planted ultimately. The crop is crushed in a nearby experimental mill, soon to be replaced by a large and permanent one, which should supply a substantial part of Mali's needs in sugar. Pigs have also been introduced at Molodo, to feed mainly on rice waste.

The Office du Niger was conceived on a grandiose scale in terms of engineering, but has been too autonomous and too costly, and has achieved only very mediocre results agriculturally. These are understandable in view of the poor environment and lack of irrigation background among the peasants.

Below Diafarabé is the live sector of the inland delta, as the Niger here subdivides into the Diaka branch, which rejoins the main stream in Lake Débo. The Diaka and Niger have natural levées which are occasionally breached, and water control consists in modifying the gaps and strengthening the banks. This and the next sector are the most important for fishing.

## THE LACUSTRINE SECTOR

This comprises numerous channels and lakes, beginning with Lake Débo, and extending to Kabara—the 'port' of Timbuktu. Lake Débo is an interior lake which, in the flood season, extends considerably in size and depth. It acts as a secondary regulator of floods to the Sansanding barrage. Beyond Lake Débo the Niger flows in a vast network of streams, which has a slackening effect upon the current. These streams have also built their banks above the general level of the countryside, so that when lakes are eventually filled by floods, they do not empty into the river.

Millet and rice are grown around these lakes. Rice is first sown on the highest fringes, and then, as lake level declines by evaporation, the rice is transplanted two or three times to lower levels. Thus water control schemes seek to equalise, for as long as possible during the year, the

PLATE 60. A large herd of Zebu cattle crossing the Niger in the Diaka region at Diafarabé

water entering the lakes, so that more land can be sown as the floods decline.

In both the inland delta and the lacustrine reaches of the river there are nutritious pastures, visited seasonally by large herds of cattle, which find here their richest sustenance. There is thus some conflict of interest between pastoralists and farmers, though in many cases it is people associated with the pastoralists who grow rice and millet, while they are near the river with the cattle.

A more acute problem is raised by irrigation schemes either on former pasturelands (as along the Diaka) or cutting across transhumance routes (as with the Office du Niger works in the Macina). Traditional pastures should be respected, as also cattle routeways, for which canal bridges are necessary.

There is also the effect upon the Niger river of abstracting water for irrigation. Some fear that this will so impair its flow, that annual floods will no longer be strong enough to remove obstructing sand, deposited in the shrunken dry season river by the northeastern Harmattan wind. It has also been said that the lakes are no longer completely filled each year. This may or may not be due to removal upstream of irrigation water. If it is due to this, then it may be said that more land has been revived than has been destroyed. Another barrage near the downstream end of the lacustrine region would enable full water control to be provided for all the lakes.

Wherever floods are to be expected, permanent settlements are on higher ground. Such is the case with Macina, Niafunké (famed for its camel and goat hair blankets) and Goundam, where there are hills 60–90 m

(200–300 ft) high.

*Timbuktu* has for centuries been an admirable example of a market at the meeting place of desert and water. Here, at the end of a trans-Saharan caravan route, produce from Europe and North Africa, desert salt, dates and tobacco, were bartered for slaves, kola nuts, gold, ivory, millet and rice.

The town originated under the Tuareg in the twelfth century. It was put by them in the charge of Buktu, a female slave: hence the name, meaning 'the place of Buktu'. It became part of the Mali empire in 1325 but was reoccupied by the Tuareg in 1434. Prosperous and fairly well known, Timbuktu declined after capture by the Songhaï empire in 1468. Later a ruler enabled it to attain great prosperity in the sixteenth century, but in 1591 the town was overwhelmed by an expedition from Morocco. It was governed by local pashas, again by Tuareg, Fulani, and others until the French captured it in 1894. From a population of 45 000 in the sixteenth century, it lost its importance because of the decline of the desert caravans. Tourists have brought some revival.[3]

In the course of some eight centuries the Niger has moved south from the town, which is now served by Kabara or Korioume on the river.

POST-DELTAIC SECTOR

Below Kabara, the Niger is again one stream, and flows in a valley 10 or 11 km (6 or 7 miles) wide. This is a semi-desert zone, and for irrigation it is necessary to construct dykes to retain water.

*Gao* was the Songhaï capital whose zenith passed with Moorish occupation in 1591. It is a trade centre on the left bank of the Niger, and is served by road, river and air transport.

**The Bani plains**

The plains lying around this great Niger tributary often have expanses of bare laterite or ferruginous crust, giving rise to *bowal* wastes. To these bare, hot and secluded plains, the Bani brings a ribbon of fertile watered lands locally improved by water management, and a means of transport.

*Djenné*, a Songhaï town probably founded in the eighth century, was a centre for Koranic studies. A market (especially for fish) and a centre for artisans making leather articles, cloth and blankets, it has nevertheless lost ground to Mopti and Ségou, better served by communications. Djenné has a large mosque rebuilt by the French in 1907 in neo-Sudan style.

*Mopti* lies on the right bank of the Bani, just above its confluence with the Niger, and is a considerable fish and cattle market, much trade being with the Ivory Coast and Ghana. Petroleum products and other

PLATE 61. Djinguereber mosque, Timbuktu

PLATE 62. Timbuktu

imports are also imported via Abidjan and despatched down the Niger.

### The Minianka, Sikasso, Bandiagara and Hombori plateaux and scarplands

East of the Bani river, the land rises almost imperceptibly to the great east-facing scarp of Palaeozoic sandstone, which extends into the Upper Volta as the Banfora scarp. In Mali, the highest points are at 760 m (2 600 ft).

The most impressive and famous scarp is that of Bandiagara, which has an almost sheer drop of 244 m (800 ft) (Plate 63). Inhabited by the Dogon people,[4] the settlements lie on the scree and spring line of the lower slopes, and terraces have been built to make fields often as small as a few square feet. A notable speciality is the cultivation of onions. In the Hombori Mountains, practically deserted by man, are some sheer drops of 610 m (2 000 ft).

In all this sandstone country water is scarce, and the annual rainfall is only 585 mm (23 in) at Bandiagara, 483 mm (19 in) at Mopti and rather less at Douetza. The main markets of this large region are Bougouni, Sikasso, and Koutiala.

### The Niger bend lands

South of the great loop of the Niger is a monotonous low and dry plateau. Pre-Cambrian gneisses and schists form low hills northeast of Hombori, through which the Niger cuts a gorge above Bourem, the point of overspill of the middle Niger. There are occasional tors and some laterite. As the rocks are impermeable, the region is marshy in the wet season (when water collects in hollows), but exceedingly dry for most of the year. There is extensive transhumance between these lands and the Niger river and lakes. Immediately south of the Niger are the Takamadasset Hills, which are fixed dunes.

## Economic resources

### Agriculture

#### Millet

Most of Mali lies within the millet zone, so that this crop is usually the main food, except near the river floodlands or irrigated areas.

#### Rice

As elsewhere in West Africa, this cereal is in increasing demand as a food and imports have sometimes been necessary. The bulk of the harvest comes from riverine areas often with simple floodwater management,

259

from the Office du Niger which is again encouraging the crop, and especially from the areas under development near the Niger and Bani rivers above Mopti.

## COTTON

While irrigated production of cotton by the Office du Niger, its original aim, has been abandoned, dry farming of the crop has been remarkably successful in the Sikasso, Koutiala, Ségou and Bamako regions. Production increased nearly four times between 1961 and 1971 and yields have much improved. Cotton is a major export, as well as supplying textile factories in Ségou and Bamako.

## GROUNDNUTS

This crop is grown where there are light soils and enough rain near the railway in the west, or close to roads not far from the railway. About half the crop is sold, some to the oil extraction factory at Koulikoro. The haul of 1 207 km (750 miles) to the coast is a severe deterrent to extending cultivation for other than local needs. Production fell between 1964 and 1969 but then rose with better prices and French technical aid. The main production areas are Kita, Kolokani, Bamako and Koulikoro. The crop is rotated or intercropped with millet and cotton.

## Livestock

Livestock are more important than in any other country in West Africa, except Nigeria. There are reckoned to be some 5 million cattle and ten million sheep and goats.

Because of the Niger river, its tributaries and the occurrence near them of the tsetse, only Ndama cattle occur in the Bamako area, and south and east of it; Zebu cattle are found north of 15°–16°N. The increase of livestock is entirely dependent on the provision of more wells or barrages. On the other hand, irrigated lands often conflict with transhumance routes. There is extensive transhumance between the floodland pastures along the Niger and its tributaries (with the fine 'bourgou' grass), and the poor and dry pasture lands of the north and northwest.

There is considerable export of cattle towards the Ivory Coast, Ghana and, to a much lesser extent, to Dakar, Liberia and Nigeria. The total export is estimated at 160 000 head annually.

## FISH

Fish are of great importance to riverine peoples, especially along the Niger. The greatest market is Mopti. Some 10 000 tons of smoked and

PLATE 63. The Bandiagara scarp, with several Dogon villages at the base

dried fish are exported, especially to the Ivory Coast and also to Ghana, but there is increasingly severe competition with sea fish in these countries.

## Minerals

There has been fairly intensive mineral prospection, especially for oil, but without promising indications.

PHOSPHATES of rather poor quality occur in the dead valley of the Tilemsi, 130 km (80 miles) north of Gao, which might be worked in collaboration with the development of manganese at Ansongo (Mali) and Tambao (northeastern Upper Volta), all of which could use a common means of transport.

IRON occurs as magnetite near Kayes, and as non-phosphoric haematite near the railway between Kayes and Bamako. Were the Senegal developed for power, it might be possible to establish an electric steel works using these deposits and run by the Senegal riverine states.

SALT mining at Terhazza was described by El Bekri in the eleventh century. Salt rock is still mined at Taoudeni, and transported in slabs by camels to Timbuktu, Gao and other riverine points. Most salt is, however, imported from Senegal (Kaolack) or Europe.

## Industries

No other sector has seen such development since independence as industry. As a basis electrical production doubled between 1961–71, with some help from the small Sotuba hydroelectric power station opened 1966. Industries have been established mainly with Russian and Chinese aid, and as state concerns. They are located mainly in or near Kayes, Bamako and Ségou (see pp. 247–9 and 252).

## Transport

There has also been a great effort since independence to improve the means of transport, particularly the roads. The main ones from Bamako to Bougouni, Sikasso and the Ivory Coast border, and from Bamako to Ségou, San and Mopti are tarred, whilst about 7 500 km (*c.* 4 700 miles) of other roads are motorable all the year.

The middle Niger is a slow but useful means of transport from mid-July or August to mid-December between Koulikoro and Gao, and from the end of December to March between Mopti and Gao. Downstream traffic is mainly in imports via Koulikoro and Mopti, whilst upstream traffic is mainly rice from the Office du Niger. The upper Niger is navigable from Bamako to Kouroussa from July to December, but the

Milo tributary is more used as far as Kankan. The Senegal is navigable for about eight to ten weeks from August to mid-October, and groundnuts and cotton are in part exported by this means.

## Conclusion

The basic problems of the geographical situation of the country remain— vast areas are semidesert, and lines of transport are very long. However, there are considerable possibilities for more rice, cotton and groundnut production, and for a wider spread of industry. Better livestock management, and improved fish processing are longer-term aims.

# 16

# Upper Volta: land of the Mossi

Upper Volta is far smaller than the other dry lands of West Africa. It is also considerably farther south, lying within both the millet and Guinea corn zones, so that most of its lands are, theoretically, capable of cultivation. There is no desert, though there are many unproductive and unpeopled areas.

Although the Upper Volta had a population of 5 384 000 in 1970 within its relatively small area of 274 200 sq km (105 868 sq miles) most of the country is relatively infertile. Over one-third is uninhabited, including up to 20 km (12 miles) either side of the three Volta rivers where there is danger from floods, sleeping sickness and river blindness. The latter is also widespread in the swampy area north of Pama (Fada N'Gourma district). River blindness is caused by the Simulium fly, which lives near fast flowing water and whose bite may cause blindness (Onchocerciasis) by the larvae entering the eye. Southeast of Banfora is another uninhabited area, in this case empty because of a deep water table and for historical reasons, yet having fertile soils.

Consequently, a great problem of the Upper Volta is pressure of population in the centre of the country. The republic has many times more people per square mile than any other dry country in francophone West Africa, and this in a land whose soils are often thin and eroded.

In the western sandstone country, water is usually deep because of rapid percolation, and in the rest of the republic it is difficult to find in wells in the Pre-Cambrian rocks because of rapid runoff. In general, rainfall may be collected only by constructing barrages in hollows, or from the intermittent rivers.

Unfortunately, there seems to be no easy means of diversifying or increasing production in the Upper Volta. As in the overpeopled parts of Ibo country in Nigeria, men must migrate temporarily for work. Some 200 000–250 000 go annually to the towns, farms or mines of Ghana, or the Ivory Coast. A few settled in the irrigated areas of the inland Niger delta. Economic reasons are not alone in causing this migration; the love of adventure, freedom and the prestige of such a trip also play their part.[1]

Another problem of the Upper Volta is that, like Mali and Niger, it is landlocked, and so is very remote from markets and sources of

264

supply, though the railway from Ouagadougou gives direct access to the deepwater port of Abidjan. While this railway is of great value in lessening the cost of imports, it is difficult to develop much export traffic, since the Upper Volta has so little of value to offer. The rail journey from Ouagadougou to Abidjan is 1 144 km (711 miles), a great distance to carry any but valuable goods at a profitable rate.

## Historical outline

Most of the country formed part of the main Mossi empire, the present dynasty of which dates back to the early eleventh century. It has had its capital at Ouagadougou since the fifteenth century. The present population of this part of the country is over 2 million. The dynasty of the Mossi kingdom of Yatenga (capital Ouahigouya) dates back to the twelfth century.

Apart from the Mossi peoples, other more or less original inhabitants are the Bobo, Somo, Lobi, Gourounsi, Gourmantche and Dagari. These people are also non-Muslim and are almost entirely settled farmers.

Muslims number about 800 000 and are mostly pastoralists or in commerce. The pastoral groups are the Fulani and the Tuareg; the commercial peoples are the Dioula.

French conquest dated from 1896 to 1901, and the country became a separate colony from 1919 to 1932, and again from 1947. Upper Volta became an independent republic in 1960 and is closely associated with the Ivory Coast, Niger, Dahomey and Togo in the Benin–Sahel Entente.

## Climate

Owing to its more southerly latitude than the other dry lands of Mauritania, Mali and Niger, the Upper Volta has more rain. In the southern savanna climatic zone, for example at Bobo Dioulasso, rains begin in May, extend to October, and average 1 170 mm (46 in). At Fada N'Gourma, which has the savanna climate, they begin in May and extend to September, averaging 840 mm (33 in). For the same period they average 740 mm (29 in) at Ouahigouya. The northern limit of the country has the southern Sahel climate.

Temperatures tend to be high at the end of the dry season—the mean of daily maxima in March and April at Ouagadougou is 41°C (106°F)—but temperatures are considerably lower in the southwest. At Ouagadougou, from January to March, relative humidity is exceptionally low, being 12–16 per cent at 13 00 hrs.

Owing to the general thinness of the soils and the widespread occurrence of laterite, the countryside and its vegetation look even drier and poorer than the above rainfall figures suggest. The southwestern part of the country consists of northern Guinea savanna, with scattered trees or

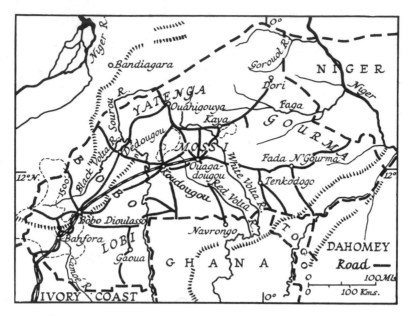

Fɪɢ. 16.1. Upper Volta

clumps; the rest of the country is Sudan savanna, with infrequent trees. In the north, the paucity of trees is due to climate; in the heavily populated Mossi lands it is due to the intense population, since only the large and useful trees (especially the shea butter) are kept.

## Geology and relief

Most of the Upper Volta is composed of Pre-Cambrian rocks and with the Birrimian in the west-centre (Fig. 1.1) are associated hills, and very fertile and much farmed soils. The country is mostly monotonously flat, with only a slight southward slope and occasional steps or edges. Laterite is frequent and the watertable is very deep. Because of the impermeable nature of many of the rocks and rapid runoff, rivers are alternately dry or in sudden flood. Water shortage is made more acute by the high density of population.

The southwestern borderlands, however, are composed of overlying Silurian sandstones, which give infertile flat country, comparable with that found in the Voltaian Basin of Ghana. The sandstone region of the Upper Volta is likewise limited by an impressive scarp, that of Banfora, some 150 m (500 ft) high, which has its steep edge facing southeast. The upper part of the Black Volta River drains the sandstone region and once flowed north along the course of its tributary, the Sourou, to the great central depression of West Africa; however, the stream has been

PLATE 64. Yatenga–Mossi country, Upper Volta. Soils are thin and poor but villages are numerous

captured by the rejuvenated and, therefore, more vigorous Black Volta. The upper waters of the Camoé drain the scarp in impressive falls. The other Volta streams follow the general trend of the ancient rocks of the rest of the country. (See also Chapter 3.)

## Major regions

### Yatenga–Mossi country

This lies in the northwest of the country and is rather dry. Sand and lateritic or ferruginous crust ridges overlie the Archaean base. Both soil and vegetation are thin and poor, in part the result of the actions of the peoples of the ancient Yatenga Mossi kingdom. There has been infil-tration by Fulani pastoralists, as this area is practically free of tsetse.

### Gourma and the eastern fringes

Voltaian sandstone and more recent sands overlie part of the Archaean base, and the surface is heavily laterised. Seasonal rivers flow eastward to the Niger river in wide, shallow valleys. Broken country encloses the Gôrouol valley.

The settled Gourmantche population is poor, as are the Fulani nomads, though there are many livestock. The population rapidly becomes less dense towards the southeast.

*Fada N'Gourma* lies on the Niger–Volta watershed, and is largely a French creation.

## Mossi lands of the south-centre

These are geologically akin to Yatenga. Despite the thin soils and rather low rainfall (890 mm; 35 in) they are the densely settled lands of the main Mossi kingdom of Ouagadougou. Vegetation is thin, the grass short and the trees bushlike, except for the locust bean and shea butter trees which are safeguarded.

*Ouagadougou*, the capital, has been the Mossi capital for centuries and the French retained the Morho Naba in some semblance of his spiritual, though not political, authority. In 1970 the population was 90 000.

*Koudougou* is an important market, and has textile and shea butter mills, and a cotton ginnery.

## Lobi and Gaoua country

This has the same Pre-Cambrian base and there are many tors. The Lobi and Bobo can produce groundnuts, cotton, shea butter kernels and benniseed for export, as population pressure is less. The population of this area may once have been greater, and then reduced by sleeping sickness. It has increased again with the progressive elimination of that and other diseases, and the Mossi have been penetrating Bobo country as far as Bobo Dioulasso and down the Black Volta.

## Eastern extension of the Sikasso plateau

This is the Silurian sandstone plateau, which terminates in the eastward facing Banfora scarp. Geologically, this region is in contrast to the rest of the Upper Volta. To some extent the porosity of its rocks is offset by the greater rainfall, and because of this and the better farming methods of the Bobo, the soils are less eroded. The region produces the same surplus commodities as the previous one.

*Bobo Dioulasso*, 'the town of the Bobo and Dioula', with a population in 1966 of 60 000, is one of the main entrepôts of Dioula trade, and lies where the north–south route from Mali to the Ivory Coast meets the east–west one from Guinea to northern Nigeria. The town is just west of the scarp and is the second town of the Upper Volta. From 1934 to 1954 it was the railway terminus and then completely over-shadowed Ouagadougou in economic importance. This has partly changed but Bobo Dioulasso is a collecting centre for cotton, ground-nuts, shea butter and cattle. Small industries include oil seed crushing, brewing, soap, corrugated iron, plastic shoe, tyre inner tube, cigarette and sweet manufacture, cycle and scooter assembly. Bobo Dioulasso is also served by road and air transport.[1]

# Economic resources

### Agriculture

The Upper Volta is within the Guinea corn and millet zones, the former corresponding roughly with Bobo country and the latter with Mossi country. Beans are often intercropped with guinea corn, millet, cotton or groundnuts.

The Mossi are so numerous and their soil so poor, that the maximum effort must be made to cultivate as intensively and continuously as possible. Because of land hunger and the distance to ports, little can be produced for export. For the same reason, the Mossi attempt self-sufficiency and, consequently, they cultivate varied crops. The Bobo seem to be better cultivators, but this may be because they have less eroded soils, and more certain rainfall. Population pressure is also less severe among them.

COTTON is the most valuable crop and production has increased remarkably in recent years. After livestock, cotton and cotton seeds together comprise about 20 per cent of exports, and also provide some local industrial employment.

GROUNDNUTS are normally the next most important export and are decorticated. Part of the crop is used for food and, like cotton, crushing for the oil provides employment.

BENNISEED, another significant crop, is grown almost entirely for export.

SHEA BUTTER nuts (which are collected), are an important oil food as well as export. Again there is some processing.

### LIVESTOCK

The northern limit of the tsetse is roughly along a line from Ouahigouya to Kaya and Fada N'Gourma. Consequently, only the northern part of the country is free from this fly and has Zebu cattle. In the south the small Ndama and Lobi resistant cattle are found, the latter around the northwest corner of Ghana.

Sheep are of two kinds, the *Fulani* which has horns, and the *Tuareg* of the Dori country in the east which has no horns.

About 50 000 cattle are exported annually from the Upper Volta (by far the country's most valuable export), as well as many more in transit from Mali. Most go to Ghana and about a third to the Ivory Coast. A modern abattoir has been established at Ouagadougou.

**Minerals**

About 10 million tons of manganese occur in the northeast of the country, at Tambao, 120 km (76 miles) from the Niger river. The deposit is too small as well as too remote to work on its own, so investigations are being made into its development jointly with another manganese deposit at Ansongo and phosphates north of Gao, both in Mali. Other minerals are known to exist, but remoteness has so far made development impossible, except for a small gold deposit. There are indigenous workings of iron near Banfora and Ouahigouya, where there are small and simple iron bloomeries. The smelted iron is used to make household and farming implements, and souvenirs.

## Conclusion

The Upper Volta is afflicted with remoteness, a dense population which is often undernourished, with thin and often poor soils, and water scarcity. Minerals seem few and would be costly to export. There are only small surpluses of cash or other crops, so that transit trade between Mali, Ghana and the Ivory Coast, and remittances of Upper Volta labourers mainly in Ghana and the Ivory Coast are important sources of revenue. The Upper Volta is often considered to be the poorest state in the world.

# 17

# Niger: a finger into the desert

Niger has an area of 1 267 000 sq km (489 208 sq miles), and is West Africa's largest state. Such is the measure of its aridity, however, that its population as estimated in 1970 was only 4 016 000. Nearly all its peoples live in the south, near the Niger river and the Niger–Nigeria border.

Niger has an extreme width of nearly 1 600 km (1 000 miles) and averages 1 050 km (650 miles) from north to south. The only cultivable area lies within the millet zone, and like the Upper Volta and Mali (which is not much smaller than Niger), Niger is landlocked.

## Historical outline

The Tuareg (singular Targui), the most famous inhabitants, are Berbers and came to the Aïr Massif from Egypt, via the Fezzan. They obviously had considerable contact with the Romans, because they use Roman names for the months and for many other things. Although not Christian, they use many ornaments of cruciform pattern and, whilst professing Islam of a non-dogmatic kind, the men are veiled (for protection against the sand), but not the women.[1]

The Tuareg probably established themselves in the Aïr Massif in the eleventh century and their Sultanate of Agadès dates back at least to the fifteenth century. Political and economic power was largely derived from its place on trans-Saharan caravan routes. In 1515 Agadès was captured by the Songhaï. Trans-Saharan trade declined, though the trade with the south remained important and Agadès was supreme as a political centre until 1870. Meanwhile, Bornu had become significant as a semitributary state on the south, was at its zenith from 1571 to 1603, but was conquered by the Fulani in 1808.

French occupation was effected between 1897 and 1900. The boundary with Nigeria, although according Niger a well-watered road between the Niger river and Lake Chad, divides the Hausa people and cuts across north to south trade routes. Whenever the controlled prices for ground-nuts in Niger and Nigeria are different, there is some movement of groundnuts across the boundary, particularly from farmers living near it but remote from buying and control posts on the roads. Many imported goods are smuggled, especially from Nigeria.

Niger was established as a colony in 1922, and the capital was moved from Zinder to Niamey in 1926. The present boundary with Chad was fixed in 1929 and that with Libya in 1935. Niger became independent in 1960.

The Hausa, who number about 2 million, are the largest group and are the sedentary people of the southern border, with close contacts with their kin in Nigeria. The Djerma and Songhaï (about 800 000) are the next largest group and are also sedentary people, but live in the south-west around the Niger river. They emigrate in considerable numbers to Ghana, where they engage in commerce. The almost wholly nomadic Fulani number about 450 000 and are mostly in the south; the Tuareg and Arabs (about 350 000) are mainly in Aïr and its western and southern environs. The Kanuri and Manga of the southeast number 300 000.

## Climate

The climate of Niger is similar to that of other hot, dry lands of West Africa. North of 20°N there is normally no rain, except on high ground. Storms may appear but, because of the intense evaporation, rain rarely reaches the ground. Along the southern border, in the southern Sahel climatic zone, about 560 mm (22 in) annual rainfall occurs. Tahoua, on the northern border of this zone, has 350 mm (15 in). Agadès (alt. 524 m:

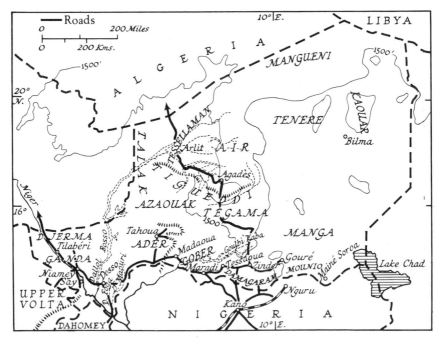

FIG. 17.1. The Niger

272

1 719 ft), in the northern Sahel climatic zone, has about 150 mm (6 in). At Bilma in the southern Saharan zone, 25 mm (1 in) of rain may occur annually. As in all such lands, rainfall is highly variable from year to year. The diurnal and seasonal range of temperature is exceptionally high. (See also Chapter 3.)

## Geology and relief

Pre-Cambrian rocks appear significantly only round Zinder and in the Aïr Massif. Elsewhere, there are mainly Secondary and Tertiary rocks in the western and central borderlands adjacent to Nigeria. Secondary rocks are rarely found in extensive areas in West Africa, except here and in adjacent parts of Nigeria. In Niger they are mostly sandstones, much affected by semi-arid erosion and by varying degrees of laterisation. Quaternary sands cover vast areas in the south-centre, east, northeast and northwest, thereby accentuating the great aridity.

## Major regions

### Djerma Ganda

Because of the distance of this part of the Niger river from its sources and the slackening of its flow in the inland delta, floods come in mid-January, in the dry season. This phenomenon is a very great help to the local farmers near the river. A sugar estate and factory is being developed at Tilabéri.

The lands on the left bank are composed of Miocene and Pliocene continental soft sandstones and clays, with some laterite. These level plains (as well as southern Azaouak) are crossed by wide, shallow, yet sharply defined relic river valleys, known as *dallols*. In Quaternary times these were vigorous tributaries of the Niger and they are evidence of former wetter conditions in this part of the Sahara. Along these old river beds water may still be found below the surface, and acacias and borassus palms line their banks.

Beyond the valleys these plains have acacias and African myrrh. Water is generally to be found only at depths of 30–76 m (100–250 ft), except near the river where the watertable is higher and the vegetation denser. This whole region ends northwards in the Adrar Aouelaouel and eastwards in the Tahoua scarp.

*Niamey*, population 80 000, capital of the Niger, lies above the left bank of the Niger river, is a river, road and air centre, and has a textile mill. Nodality caused it to be preferred to Zinder as a capital, despite the fact that Niamey is in the far west of the country, and that Zinder is more central.

PLATE 65. Flood control for irrigated cotton and guinea corn in the Ader Maggia valley at Koré, near Tahoua, Niger

## Ader

This is a plateau of Eocene series, often capped with laterite. Rainfall averages 380 mm (15 in), but percolation is rapid, and Ader is drier than might be expected, being covered by thin and small Thorn Bush.

*Tahoua* is a market for the produce of nomads and sedentary peoples.

## Gober

Sandy plains occur east of Madaoua as far as the road north from Tassaoua. They are practically uninhabited, except near the intermittent Goulbi Kaba stream. Vegetation is again poor Thorn Bush.

*Maradi* was situated by a stream of the same name but disastrous floods in 1947 and 1950 caused it to be resited on higher ground. It is a prosperous town, being a collecting point for groundnuts, cotton grown along the stream, Maradi Red Goat skins, hides and cattle. Groundnut oil is extracted in a local mill, and Maradi is also an important administrative centre. There are ties of kinship and trade with Katsina and Kano in northern Nigeria.

## Damagaram and Mounio

These are largely a clay plain, where the watertable is much shallower. Moreover the rainfall is greater, being 560 mm (22 in) at Zinder, and seasonal lakes and semipermanent rivers occur. This is the most important groundnut area, despite the fact that the soils are not so suitable as the sandy ones of Maradi. It also has the greatest density of gum trees, particularly in the Gouré and Mainé Soroa districts. If the price of gum became more favourable, more could be exported from this region.

*Zinder*, was the Niger capital from 1911 to 1926, and is still a major commercial centre. The town lies on a plateau between two ouadis and is really composed of three nuclei. Zinder is a great groundnut, hide and skin market, has craftsmen making articles in skin and leather, and blankets from camel, goathair and wool. The town is a lesser Kano, with which it has close trading relations. There are several groundnut oil mills between Zinder and the border.

## Manga

This is a sandy semiwasteland around Lake Chad. Although the rainfall may reach 460 mm (18 in) or more a year, percolation is so rapid that the area is very dry. Pastures are found only near the lake.

## Tenere and Kaouar

This vast area along the eastern boundary is a continuation of Manga. There are sand-dunes with occasional tors.

*Bilma* is an oasis on the edge of the desert. It has some trade and salt is produced nearby.

## Mangueni plateau

This is a broken desert country of Archean schists and gneisses and Palaeozoic sandstones, with superficial sand and gravel. Former rivers have caused great erosion, so that there are frequent outlying mesas.

## Aïr

This vast and vivid relief feature of Pre-Cambrian gneisses and granites, together with some black volcanic lavas, tuffs and ashes of Quaternary age, rises abruptly from the surrounding lands. It extends for about 400 km (250 miles) from north to south and 240 km (150 miles) from east to west. Many subsidiary massifs may be distinguished, and all lie between 1 070 and 1 525 m (3 500–5 000 ft) above sea level. The southern limit of Aïr is taken to be at the Tigueddi Scarp. There is a Tuareg saying that 'wherever there is stone it is Aïr; wherever there is sand it is Tenéré'.

Rainfall is some 255 mm (10 in) or more on the exposed parts, despite the fact that much of Aïr lies north of 18°N. This rainfall is highly erratic and almost all of it comes in thunderstorms which cause severe erosion. Because of its dryness, and the altitude which modifies the otherwise great heat and also causes greater daily range of temperature, Aïr is exceptionally healthy. Drainage is westward to the Tessellaman depression by short rivers, whose deep valleys were cut by streams in a wetter climate than now; their grasslands are of great value to nomadic herdsmen. Rich uranium deposits occur in the massif, and their development is bringing new life to Aïr (p. 278).

*Agadès*, some 520 m (1 700 ft) up, is the centre of Aïr. It lies on a foothill, at the side of a ouadi in a Lower Cretaceous clay plain like that of Tessellaman. It had its most opulent period in the sixteenth and seventeenth centuries. After subsequent decline it survived as a cattle market centre for herdsmen, and for craftsmen making saddles and sheaths.

## Talak

These plains lie west and southwest of Aïr, and are composed of loose Quaternary sand over Cretaceous limestones. Talak is almost pure desert and practically devoid of population.

## Tessellaman and northern Azaouak

This is an island of rich pasture within the desert of Talak, extending west and southwest of Aïr, and is composed of Lower Cretaceous clays. Pastures are nourished by streams draining the western side of Aïr and collecting within this semi-swamp, which is of great significance to nomadic cattle keepers, especially those from Aïr. There is an extensive range of vegetation, particularly of grasses and acacias, especially *Acacia seyal*.

## Tegama plateau

This vast plateau extends between Aïr in the north and Damagaram in the south. It has infertile soils derived from flat Cretaceous or possibly Triassic sandstone, and the area is semi- or complete desert. The sandstone has been considerably eroded by the Goulbi Kaba to expose underlying clays in wide valleys; only in these is water available.

# Economic resources

## Agriculture

### CROPS

Permanent cropping is almost confined to the lands near the Niger river, and eastward and northward from it to about 130 km (80 miles) north of the Nigerian boundary. Northward for about another 160 km (100 miles) there are rare and isolated patches of cultivation where water is available. Thus the distribution of crop land is similar to that in Mauritania, where the only important zone is along or near the Senegal river or its tributaries on the southern border.

Again, the predominant cereals are various kinds of millet and—to a lesser extent—guinea corn in clay or other moist soils. Some hungry rice (iburu or fonio) is grown in dry areas. As in Guinea and Mali, rice cultivation has been improved in the Niger valley, with water control from the river. Cotton, indigo, temperate cereals and vegetables (especially beans and onions) are grown in gardens for local needs. Dates are grown in the northern oases.

The only considerable cash crop is the groundnut, grown between Maradi, Tessaoua, Zinder and the Nigerian boundary, and, to a much lesser extent, in the southwest, and which accounts for about one-half of the agricultural exports by value.

### LIVESTOCK

The effective northern limit of livestock rearing is generally 15°N, except for Aïr and its confines. Thus the areas suitable for livestock are far less extensive than in Mali. Moreover, the cattle keepers—even the true nomads—are very much concentrated in the western and southern regions. Extension of livestock rearing depends upon the provision of more water. Apart from that which may be found in the valleys of Aïr at depths of only 4·6–6·1 m (15–20 ft), most underground water is between 30–76 m (100–250 ft) down, as in the post-Eocene continental beds east of the Niger.

The curious large-horned humpless Chad cattle live near that lake; otherwise all cattle are Zebu. *Arab Zebu* are found east of Gouré and in the north, the *Azaouak Zebu* is short-horned, small and strong, whilst the *Bororo Zebu* has large lyre-shaped horns. Most of the cattle trade is with Sokoto, Katsina and Kano for sale to other parts of Nigeria.

Types of sheep tend to vary with each tribe. The *Tuareg* is good for meat and milk; the *Goundoum* kept by the Songhaï and valued for its skin and wool, is a poor variety of the *Macina*, and is found along the banks of the Niger.

Goats are very numerous and the *Maradi* is especially valued as a source of coloured glacé kid leather, being almost as valuable as the *Sokoto Red*.

Camels are important for trade between Aïr and Kano in the trading season. For the peoples along the borderlands, donkeys are the main beasts of burden.

PLATE 66. Uranium quarry, Arlit, Niger

## Minerals

After intensive prospecting, the quarrying of uranium ore was begun commercially in 1971 at Arlit, Aïr, by a company in which there is West German, Italian, Niger and French participation, the latter by government and two companies. Up to 750 tons of concentrate are to be produced from nearly 500 times that amount of ore. Together with deposits developed in France, Gabon and the Central African Republic, France now controls 10 per cent of the uranium resources of the West, and is a seller of uranium alongside the USA, Canada and South Africa. Another mining and refining complex may be developed near Arlit in 1974, with Japanese participation.

Very small amounts of tin and wolfram have been mined near Agadès for some time. Oil is being prospected.

## Transport

The shortest links of Niger with the outside world are by road from Maradi to Katsina, or from Zinder to Kano. From Kano traffic passes along the 1 127 km (700 miles) railway to the deep-water Nigerian port of Lagos, and most of the groundnut export travels this way. Alternatively, traffic passes through the port of Cotonou in Dahomey, by rail to Parakou and on by road. This route was much developed for reasons of economic

278

nationalism, and most imports come this way. Return freight is mostly groundnuts. Both routes are expensive because of the distances involved and breaks of bulk.

Trunk roads along the Niger and eastward towards Lake Chad have been improved, and there are bridges across the Niger at Niamey and Gaya (the latter preventing navigation, except by canoe). Air services link Niamey (the international airport) with Tahousa, Agadès, Maradi and Zinder.

## Conclusion

Within the vast Niger there is a great variety of relief and of population, yet over the whole country lies the uniform problem of water supplies. The only relatively well-developed parts of the country are the south-centre, between Maradi and Zinder, and the Niger valley. Aïr, healthy and beautiful, is too far north and too remote to be capable of much development for stock-rearing or agriculture, even if more water could be obtained. On the other hand the uranium ores of Aïr may be the means of making Niger more self-supporting.

Niger is likely to remain poor, not only because of its poverty of resources and its aridity, but also because it is secluded north of Nigeria, far from overseas markets and sources of supplies.

# 18

# The Portuguese province of Guinea:
# land of estuaries and rivers

The Portuguese province of Guinea or, more popularly, Portuguese Guinea, is about one-half the size of Sierra Leone, or one-third that of Portugal. Like the islands of São Tomé and Príncipe, Portuguese Guinea is a reminder of the very early contacts of Portugal with West Africa.

## Historical outline

After its discovery by Nuno Tristão in 1446, fortified posts were established for the trade in slaves, gold, ivory and European goods. But penetration of the interior was impossible, as the Mali and Wolof islamised kingdoms, which had cavalry troops, were hostile.

As usual, slaves were obtained through African intermediaries. Some were sent to Bahia, one of the earliest points of colonisation in Brazil, where there is much evidence of cultural transfer from Portuguese Guinea. Slaves were also despatched to the Cape Verde Islands for work on plantations; their descendants form the Creole population of that archipelago. Trading posts and castles at various places on the Gulf of Guinea were first administered from the Cape Verde Islands; from the latter many Creoles have come to Portuguese Guinea to engage in agriculture and have brought with them their Portuguese Creole *lingua franca*.

In 1879 Portuguese Guinea was separated from the Cape Verde Islands administration. By then the French had occupied Ziguinchor (Casamance Senegal), which still retains some Portuguese features, and the British were at Bolama. So the first capital was established at Geba, at the limit of navigation on the Geba river. Although unusually central for an early capital, it was in a swampy area where there was much malaria; consequently, it was later abandoned in favour of Bolama, after that island was ceded by the British in 1890.

In 1941 the capital was retransferred to Bissau, in the Geba estuary, on a well populated island joined to the mainland by a causeway, in the economic centre of the country, and with depths of 11 m (36 ft) at low water for anchorage and of 6 m (20 ft) at quay.

The interior was only finally pacified in 1912. At that time Bissau was a fort surrounded by ramparts and palisades, with a few houses

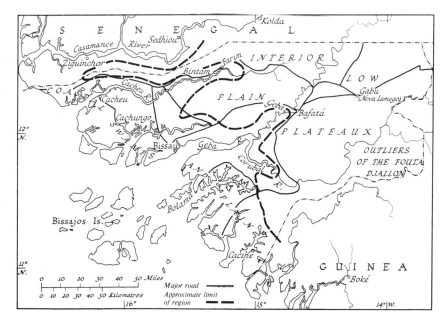

FIG. 18.1. The Portuguese province of Guinea

The broken line shows the tidal and mangrove limit. It is also a great climatic, vegetational and human divide

belonging to Cape Verde people. It is now a well planned, flourishing town and port.

## Population

In an area of 36 125 sq km (13 948 sq miles), Portuguese Guinea had a population of 556 000 in 1970, so that the average density per square kilometre was 15 (39 per sq mile). It is highest in the coastal regions, and in the north, lower on the islands, in the south and the interior.

Of the 1950 total of 510 777, 502 400 were African, 4 568 were of mixed blood (many being Cape Verdians), 2 263 were White, 10 Indian and 203 Lebanese. The 'civilised' population, which, until 1961, alone had full citizenship, numbered only 8 320. It comprised all whites, Indians and those of mixed blood, but only 1 478 Christian Africans 'assimilated' to Portuguese culture. In and around the old towns of Farim, Cacheu, Geba, Bissau, Bolama, etc., Portuguese Creole is spoken and Portuguese rather than African names are common.

The towns of Farim, Cacheu and Cacine are in decline as the result of political and economic changes in recent decades; and the first capital of Geba is in ruins and invaded by bush. Bafata and Canchungo, on the contrary, are developing rapidly. Bissau, the young capital, and Bolama have most of the 'civilised' population and enjoy municipal status.

281

PLATE 67. Bissau, capital of Portuguese Guinea, and founded 1941. The mud flats show the great tidal range along this southwestern coast. At Bissau it is over 5 m (about 17 ft)

Human differences reinforce physical contrasts within Portuguese Guinea. As in other matters, the line of demarcation is approximately along the limit of tides and fringing mangroves (see Fig. 18.1). Inland live the Manding and Fulani. Both are Islamic and basically pastoral. Even where the Fulani have become semifixed, their huts resemble tents, in that the roofs reach almost to the ground. Moreover, settlements are small and abandoned frequently. Agriculture is rudimentary and shifting, being concerned mainly with millet and groundnut production. The Manding are more fixed, have larger villages, and are often craftsmen, Islamic missionaries, smugglers, traders and, in the past, warriors. Although they cultivate groundnuts, cotton, vegetables and fruit gardens, they really disdain agriculture.

By contrast, in the estuarine swamps and coastal plains live the animist, vigorous, expansionist but settled Balante. These people, and the less numerous Floup of the extreme northwest, have been the great reclaimers of mangrove for swamp rice cultivation, using bunds for water control and applying manure. Their buildings are large and permanent and house families, animals, grain and all belongings. Settlement is in hamlets. Animals are kept mainly for manure and, in the wet season, are kept indoors, away from crops.

Most other peoples of the coast are culturally similar, but they also undertake fishing, navigation and coconut collection. Such are the Papel of Bissau Island and the Mandjac, who live west of Bissau. All the coastal peoples keep pigs and small cattle (although the Papel and Mandjac do not use manure). They collect and prepare the usual products from the coconut, oil and raphia palms. These were the conditions of traditional life before the political troubles of 1963 and after.

282

PLATE 68. Protective and dividing bunds or embankments in a swamp rice field

## Climate and vegetation

The coastal area has the southwest coast monsoonal climate. There are five very wet months, in which the relative humidity often reaches saturation point, and violent storms are common. During the longer dry season, the maritime trades are far more common than the Harmattan, which appears only towards the close of the season. The interior, by contrast, has the southern Savanna climate.

The vegetation shows the same marked division. Along the coast and up the many wide and deeply penetrating estuaries mangroves grow luxuriantly, but have often been cleared for rice cultivation. Behind the mangroves comes much freshwater swamp forest and then Casamance woodland. In the drier interior there is Guinea savanna, with an exceptional amount of grass in the hills.

## Geology, relief and major regions

Portuguese Guinea is sharply divided on grounds of climate, vegetation, relief, human types and economy, between the flat coastal swamps and plain on the one hand, and the interior plain, low plateaux and Fouta Djallon outliers on the other hand.

Recent marine transgression drowned the lowest reaches of the rivers, so creating ria estuaries, which are good waterways and are indentations of the coast. Off the coast are some sixty islands; some of these adjoin the mainland, and are connected at low tide (tidal range is about 3·7 m: 12 ft) by recently developed lateritic rock. The Bissajos Islands are farther out, but were doubtless separated in the same way. Drowning of rivers with such gentle gradients has contributed to the slackening of flow and silting of their lower courses.

The coastal and interior plains both belong to the southern extremity of the great Senegal basin, whose deposits are post-Eocene. Flat and monotonous, these plains are nearing the end of a cycle of erosion, the rivers making vast and numerous meanders and flooding severely in the wet season, or at high tides. Minor relief features result only from the outcrop of lateritic rocks, or occasional cliffs of up to 50 m (160 ft) in height.

Behind the coastal and interior plains are the low plateaux of Pre-Cambrian rocks. One such plateau is that of Gabu-Bafata, with a clear western edge at the latter town and following, approximately, the line of the Geba river. The rivers are incised, and lateritic crusts are widespread.

In the extreme southeast, approximately south of the Corubal river, are outliers of the Fouta Djallon. Valleys are separated by flat-topped interfluves, averaging 107–213 m (350–700 ft) in height. These have widespread and bleak exposures of older lateritic crusts, practically bare of soil, and supporting only poor grass used by nomadic Fulani cattle keepers. These are the *bowé* of French writers.

## Economic resources

### Agriculture

Unlike the Portuguese islands of São Tomé and Príncipe, Portuguese Guinea is a low-lying country. Plantations are almost unknown, and the economy is based on traditional farming and the collection of wild produce by Africans.

RICE is the basic food and the main crop in coastal, riverine and inland swamps. The Balante people are renowned in West Africa for the reclamation of mangrove for rice cultivation.

OIL PALM PRODUCE is produced mainly in the same areas as swamp rice, especially along the coast and on the islands. Most of the oil is consumed locally, though a little is exported. Palm kernels are, however, the second export by value.

GROUNDNUTS are the main export of Portuguese Guinea and leading cash crop of the plateaux, being especially important around Farim, Bafata and Gabu (Nova Lamego). As in Senegal and Nigeria, they are grown mainly by Muslim peoples. An increasing amount is being processed locally. There are three mills (two also process rice), and the oil cake is sent to Europe.

Oil seeds (groundnuts, cake and oil, palm kernels and oil, copra) account for about 90 per cent of Portuguese Guinea exports. They are sent mainly to Portugal and there handled by a large company whose extensive works constitute the largest industrial concentration of the Portuguese capital.

**Transport**

The three main rivers (Cacheu, Geba and Corubal) are each navigable for about 160 km (100 miles). They and coastal channels are cheap and important means of transport and make the construction of a railway unnecessary.

The rivers have been well supplemented by over 3 200 km (2 000 miles) of earth roads, comprising an excellent network for this small country.

Bissau airport is served by a service from Lisbon. Bissau is also the main port but is supplemented by Bolama.

## Conclusion

Portuguese Guinea has developed rapidly since the 1930s, particularly in the cultivation of rice. It would seem that much more can still be done to develop that crop and its internal and external markets. There is a less favourable prospect for the groundnuts. Economic development, except for roads, has been affected by disturbances since 1963.

## 19

## Guinea: Marxian socialism
## in a highland watershed

Guinea has an area of 245 857 sq km (94 930 sq miles) and a population estimated at 3 921 000 in 1970. The density of 16 per sq km (41 per sq mile) is higher than of most francophone Africa, although low compared with that of Sierra Leone or of the rest of anglophone West Africa.

The country is one of exceptional interest, alike on political and geographical grounds. Alone in French Africa, Guinea voted for independence in 1958, a decision that was met by the French government with the withdrawal of most equipment, personnel and aid. Guinea might have succumbed had not Ghana provided immediate financial aid, followed quickly by Russia and other communist countries. Guinea left the franc zone, created her own inconvertible franc, and refused to associate with the European Economic Community, or with the airline *Air Afrique* founded by most francophone states in 1961. With Ghana and Mali, Guinea became a proponent of rapid political integration in Africa and of nationalisation at home. All overseas and most internal commerce was nationalised, as were the banks, insurance companies, diamond mines, and most industries. Rather strangely, the Fria bauxite and alumina plant and the iron mining company were allowed to remain under private foreign enterprise, the former quickly becoming responsible for most of Guinea's exports but the latter collapsing (not entirely or even mainly because of political decisions) in 1966. The Bauxites du Midi concessions on the Los Islands and at Boké were cancelled, the former then being given to a Hungarian concern until the deposit was exhausted, and the latter later being regranted to an American company.

Economic decline ensued, except in the Fria operation. Decline was especially notable in coffee (the leading export in pre-independence Guinea), in banana and pineapple cultivation (though this was largely due to the loss of quotas and of tariff preferences in France), and in diamond production or official sales. Public services and parts of the infrastructure deteriorated, most notably the government railway, although foreign aid has maintained or improved most roads and air services. Food supplies especially of rice and meat, have often been short in towns, especially Conakry, and there has been a sharp reduction in the range of goods and in their quality. Life has become more complicated and circumscribed by comparison with other West African countries, even with formerly likeminded Ghana and still more or less likeminded Mali.

Yet Guinea has very considerable potential. There are very great reserves of bauxite and of hydroelectric power which have been developed much less rapidly than have similar resources elsewhere since independence. Diamond production has actually ceased for politico-economic reasons, whilst coffee and other agricultural exports are far less than from the neighbouring Ivory Coast. Almost the only encouraging feature is the Boké bauxite and future alumina plant.

## Historical outline

French interests in the coast date back to the seventeenth century at least, but were in competition with the Portuguese and the British. The establishment of 'factories', however, dates back no earlier than the nineteenth century, when there were also German ones. At the beginning of that century this coast was also a hideout for slave boats, still operating at the end of the slave trade in defiance of British and other antislavery patrols. British political interests in the coast were mainly centred in the Los Islands, which remained British until 1904.

The first assumption of French sovereignty was in the Boké region in 1849. There was considerable advance after 1854, when France was anxious to occupy the area before the British could link the Gambia with Sierra Leone. In 1868 there were negotiations between Britain and France with the object of exchanging the Gambia for a part of what is now Guinea, but these parleys had no result, and the boundaries with Sierra Leone were defined in 1882 and 1889. German interests were eliminated in 1885. The boundary with Portuguese Guinea was agreed in 1886 and that with Liberia in 1911. In 1891 this territory, until then governed from Senegal, became a separate colony and in 1893 was named French Guinea. It became the Republic of Guinea in 1958.

## Climate

Owing to the high relief and the southeast trending coast, there is considerable climatic variety. Climatic regions are here determined by relief rather than by latitude.

As one would expect, rainfall is highest on the coast and on the western slopes of the Fouta Djallon. The rains start in March in the south and reach Conakry in early May. They end in the north in November and in the south by December. July and August are everywhere the wettest months, and until October movement may be difficult, owing more to the floods than to heavy rain.

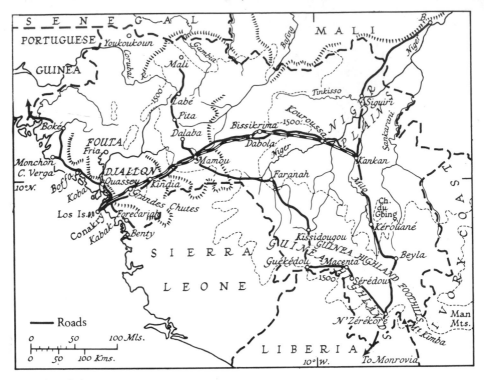

Fig. 19.1. Guinea

## Southwest coast monsoonal zone

Here the rainfall is heavy, 4 300 mm (169 in) at Conakry and 2 800 mm (111 in) at Boké. Rain is regular from the end of June to early October, and much comes at night. In July and August, and sometimes even in September, there may be rain for several days on end. Annual relative humidity averages 70–80 per cent.

Days are hottest in April, reaching about 32°C (90°F). In August they are cooler because of rain, but nights tend to be oppressive.

Because of the high rainfall and humidity and small range of temperature, this climate is unhealthy. This, together with the treacherous estuaries and fly infestation, may explain why this coast was relatively little visited between the fifteenth and nineteenth centuries and, until the mid-nineteenth century, less affected by the slave trade.

For the Foutanian, Guinea foothills and Guinea Highland climates, see Chapter 3.

## Southern savanna

This is found in the Niger and tributary valley lands of the northeast, and in lowland areas on the northern and northwestern border. Kouroussa,

Kankan, Siguiri and Youkounkoun are typical stations. Local conditions conform with those of the rest of this climatic zone (see p. 52), but rainfall is particularly variable. It tends to come in the afternoons as sharp storms, though rarely at night.

## Geology, relief and major regions

In Guinea differences of relief and geology powerfully determine the various regions.

### Coastal swamps

As in Portuguese Guinea, the coast is a recently submerged one, the inlets being drowned valleys and the islands remnants of old hills. As there is no constant longshore drift, and the tidal range is high, sandbars or lagoons do not readily form.

The estuaries are muddy and bordered by mangrove. There are two theories concerning this mud accumulation. The first is that mud-laden river water coming into contact with salt water drops mud particles. The second explanation is that near the shoreline there is a compensatory upward movement to balance coastal submergence, thus assisting mud accumulation.

The coast was so unhealthy in the past that slave traders hardly visited it until the nineteenth century. Then its tricky channels and dense

PLATE 69. Swamp rice cultivation near Dubréka, Guinea

289

vegetation provided concealment from British antislavery naval patrols operating from Freetown and from the Los Islands.

The Baga have long been renowned for rice cultivation in reclaimed mangrove swamps, protected by bunds, and efforts are being made to reclaim mangrove for rice cultivation. (See also under Agriculture, p. 296).

The muddy mangrove coastline and the coastal plain are broken at two points by rocky spurs—at Cape Verga and behind Conakry. The former consists of schists and quartzite and the latter of granite and ultra-basic intrusive rocks, found also in the Los Islands and in the Kakoulima area, northeast of Conakry.

*Conakry,* the capital of Guinea, lies on Tombo Island. This is a little over 3 km (2 miles) long and 1·6 km (1 mile) in width, and is

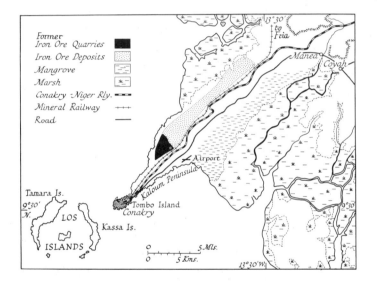

FIG. 19.2. Conakry, its environs and mineral deposits.

connected by a causeway to the mainland. Conakry has deep water and no surf, though approach has to be from the south. The port is somewhat sheltered by the Los Islands and by breakwaters. Despite natural advantages, Conakry remained a minor port until 1953 (when iron ore began to be exported), largely because of the relative poverty of the then colony. Concrete wharves or piers are on the northwest side of the island and are equipped for handling passengers, iron ore (although export ceased in 1966), alumina and bananas. Other exports are palm produce, coffee, and pineapples.

The population of Conakry grew from 13 600 in 1936 to 26 000 in 1946 and 184 000 in 1967. About 55 000 of these live on the island. Roughly speaking, the northwest sides of both Tombo Island and the peninsula have the administrative and good residential quarters, whilst the southeastern side of the island is much overcrowded. Newer quarters have been built on the mainland.

As more hydroelectric power becomes available, so new industries are being established under state control. Since independence a furniture works, a textile mill, and a large cigarette, tobacco and match factory and other plants have been built near Conakry. Older concerns are soft drinks and soap factories, fruit canneries, a paint and plastics works, and a mining explosives factory.

*Benty* is, 16 km (10 miles) from the sea, on the south bank of the Mellacorée river, where it widens out into a drowned estuary or arm of the sea. Economically, it is a supplement to Conakry, as it is easily accessible and has no bar.

**The coastal plain**

Between the wide mangrove belt and the Fouta Djallon foothills is a coastal plain of sandstone gravels, washed down from the highlands, and overlying laterite and a substratum of granite and gneiss. This gravel plain, 48–80 km (30–50 miles) wide, narrowest in the northwest but wider and flatter in the southeast, is sheltered from coastal breezes by the broad mangrove but has a heavy rainfall, high humidity and temperatures. It also suffers from waterlogging after heavy rain.

Nevertheless, villages are more numerous here than on the foothills or outlying mesas. The villagers grow rice, hungry rice, maize, kola nuts and the oil palm, the latter being the main resource. Many of these villages have also reclaimed mangrove swamp for rice. There are banana plantations around the inland end of the Conakry (Kaloum) peninsula (Plate 70), and near Forécariah and Benty. Pineapples are also grown at Benty and Ouassou (northwest of Dubréka).

**The Fouta Djallon**

This great highland mass is mainly within Guinea. It rises on the west and north by a series of fault steps, but the eastern slopes are gentler and their valleys shallower. Some 13 000 sq km (approx. 5 000 sq miles) are higher than 915 m (3 000 ft), figures which might suggest unimpressive mountains, yet such is their dissection that they are indeed majestic. The Fouta Djallon consists mainly of level, westward sloping, siliccous Cambrian to Ordovician sandstones, which cover Birrimian rocks to a depth of some 760 m (2 500 ft). Here are possibly the largest bauxite resources in the world, with especially important deposits at Boké and Fria (both worked), and as yet unworked ones at Friguiagbé, Tougué, Dabola, etc.

PLATE 70. Western edge of Fouta Djallon near Dubréka and Conakry, with irrigated bananas and dry rice on hillside. See northern limit of Fig. 19.2

On the remarkably level plateaux there are expanses of bare and hard impervious and ferruginous crust or *bowal* (plural *bowé* = 'no trees'). These bowé are especially bare in the extreme north, and are most extensive in the west. Oddly enough, the highest areas are the most densely peopled, mainly by the Fulani, who comprise two-fifths of Guinea's population, and who were attracted by the healthy conditions and pastures. Nevertheless, the tsetse fly forced them to keep the small Ndama cattle and to become semifixed pastoralists. They retained prisoners of war as slaves to grow crops for them in the valleys, where the Negro settlements are still found. The worse the bowal, the more captives were required to provide food; hence the coincidence of denser population in poor high parts used for wet season pastures, and in valleys used for crops and dry season pasturing.

Basic eruptive gabbros and dolerite often occur in the sandstone as sills or dykes, so causing some of the vivid rock edges, over which there are often waterfalls, e.g. near Pita. Soils on these rocks tend to be richer; near Labé are plantations of bitter oranges grown for their oil, of jasmin for perfume, and of arabica coffee. On the western edge of the Fouta Djallon, gabbros often form the peaks, e.g. Mont Gangan, 1 106 m (3 627 ft) near Kindia, or the Kakoulima Massif 998 m (3 273 ft) northeast of Conakry.

The sandstone has been intensely and curiously dissected, by Caledonian or Hercynian warpings, by fractures in the underlying Pre-Cambrian rocks, or as the result of tension during the Alpine earth movements. It may be along these lines of weakness that the rivers have worked. Evidence of rejuvenation (probably Miocene) is widespread. Uplift may still be continuing as the rivers, like many others in West Africa, show signs of youth in an otherwise mature landscape.

292

Valleys are almost always narrow and deeply trenched, often in a north–south direction. Rivers frequently take rightangled turns through gorges to another valley, suggestive of fault guidance or capture. Thus the highland is cut into a chequerboard pattern of blocks isolated by vast chasms. The most obvious north–south trench is that east of Kindia, which almost separates the Fouta Djallon into two parts. There is also a west–east trench partly followed by the railway and by the Tinkisso tributary of the Niger.

On this dissected and divided highland there falls heavy seasonal rainfall, so that mighty rivers take their rise here. Among them are the Bakoy and Bafing headwaters of the Senegal, the Gambia, and some northwesterly headwaters of the Niger. The flora is special, because of the heavy rain and flooding followed by months of dryness, the frequence of ferruginous crusts or laterite, high relief and relative inaccessibility. Yet owing to the depredations of man, especially late bush firing to provide green shoots for cattle at the end of the dry season, the original forest rarely remains on the plateaux (see Chapter 4).

Soil conservation is vitally important in the Fouta Djallon, as so much soil has already been washed down the rivers. Moreover, the relatively dense population uses such thin soils that they are constantly loosened by heavy rain, as well as being thoroughly leached of their chemical nutrients.

Apart from subsistence crops, the keeping of livestock, and the above-mentioned plantations, bananas are cultivated in damp valleys as far east as Mamou, though most plantations are nearer Kindia, e.g. in the Kolenté–Kakrima depression. Valley cultivation of bananas is essential to permit growth during the dry season, many estates having made their own reservoirs along the rivers. By contrast, pineapples and citrus fruits are grown on higher drier ground.

The main towns of the Fouta Djallon are first the old ones of Mali, Pita and Labé, although Timbo, the former capital of the Almamis of the Fouta Djallon state, is now no more than a village. Secondly, there are the colonial creations of Kindia, Mamou and Dabola, on the railway, which are route and trading centres.

## Guinea Highlands

Along the north-northeastern part of the Sierra Leone–Guinea boundary, the mountains narrow and the mighty Niger takes its rise. Had it not been for the political boundary, this could have been an ideal crossing of the highland mass for a railway from the coast to the upper Niger. It is also here that the flat sandstone cover and lateritic surfaces disappear south of about 9°N and the Guinea Highlands begin.

The Guinea Highlands are very different from the Fouta Djallon. They are composed of granite, gneisses, schists and quartzites. The summits are generally rounded and forested, but Mounts Nimba and Simandou are quartzite ridges. Although the Guinea Highlands trend northwest–southeast, dissection has cut them into several northeast–southwest segments.

Heavy and well-distributed rainfall, steep slopes and relative inaccessibility have allowed the survival of rainforest. Fairly rich gneiss-derived soils encourage cultivation of the oil palm, kola, maize, rice, cassava and cocoyam. There are coffee plantations, of tea at Macenta and of cinchona at Sérédou. Haematite iron ore is mined on the Liberian flank of Mount Nimba and will later be on the Guinean side, as well as on Mount Simandou, as soon as the evacuation route can be decided to the satisfaction of the Guinea government (p. 300).

*N'Zérékoré* is a trading centre, with roads north to Kankan, southeast to the Ivory Coast, and to the nearest deepwater port at Monrovia. Some palm kernels and coffee are exported by this route. *Macenta* and *Guékédou* are other market centres. The latter trades with Sierra Leone.

### Guinea Highland foothills

Although geologically similar, and sometimes as high, these are more dissected than the Guinea Highlands. Impressive foothills are the steep edge near Boola, the Pic du Tio north of Beyla, the Chaine du Gbing east of Kérouané, and the Dongoroma mountains to its west.

There are good Ndama cattle on these grassland foothills, which are more fertile than the Guinea Highlands because of lesser leaching and deeper soils. Rice and tobacco are grown in excess of local needs.

The rainforest formerly extended here, but there are now few trees, except along streams. Diamonds have been mined in this region (see under Minerals).

*Beyla* was probably founded by the Dioula around 1230, as a centre for the slave and kola nut trades. It markets surpluses of rice, tobacco (burley) and cattle. *Kissidougou* and *Faranah* are other markets.

### Niger plains

The eastern limit of the Fouta Djallon is clear orographically and geologically, the horizontal sandstones ending in a steep edge north and south of Bissikrima. This overlooks the Niger plains which are composed of the same rocks as the Guinea Highlands and foothills, except that granite intrusions are commoner and laterite is widespread—a grave disadvantage.

The average elevation of these plains is about 300 m (1 000 ft), but there are several upstanding relief features. These are either steep sandstone outliers of the Fouta Djallon, or rounded granite domes. Both are to be seen west of Siguiri, and the Pre-Cambrian rocks are responsible for the rocky river sill at Kouroussa which stops navigation up the Niger.

Along the rivers, rice cultivation has been increased by flood control works.[2] Elsewhere, Ndama cattle are kept, and crops of cassava, sweet potatoes, millet and groundnuts are grown. The shea butter tree is very evident. In general, crops are poor because of the laterite covering.

*Kankan*, the eastern terminus of the railway, is on the Milo tributary, easier to navigate than the Niger. It is served by road, railway, river and air, is a market for local produce (especially rice), and for produce from or going to the Guinea Highlands. *Kouroussa*, at the limit of Niger navigation and on the railway, is subsidiary to Kankan.


## Soil conservation

Soil conservation is of vital importance in Guinea. If a land with similar soils existed in Europe, two-thirds of it would be regarded as unsuitable for agriculture or stockrearing, and would be left as open space or forest. But in Guinea many of these poor sandy soils are quite intensively used because of pressure on the land. Rice and hungry rice are often sown in areas where there is less than 100 mm (4 in) of soil, but where rainfall of up to 4 070 mm (160 in) per year can come to wash it away.

It has been estimated that about 60 per cent of the country ought not to be cultivated, but should be used for intermittent pasturage. About 30 per cent could be used if proper cultivation and anti-erosion methods were employed. Only about 10 per cent, mostly situated on the coast and in river valleys, is capable of being cultivated without particular precautions.

Guinea suffers not only from thin soils and devastatingly heavy rainfall, but also from severe bush firing by the pastoral Fulani at the end of the long dry season. As the source of so many great rivers, it is also more than usually subject to severe erosion.


## Economic resources

### Agriculture

As with all matters in Guinea, agricultural production is much determined by the sharply contrasted regions, though cassava is grown everywhere. In general, the oil palm, rice, bananas, hungry rice, maize and kola nuts are the subsistence crops of the coastal plain and of the Guinea Highlands. In the former, rice and bananas are also grown as cash crops. In the Guinea Highlands the main cash crop is coffee.

In the Fouta Djallon the subsistence crops are upland rice, some swamp rice, hungry rice, maize, millet and bananas. The export crops are bananas grown in the valleys, citrus fruits and pineapples grown on sloping ground, all mainly on plantations.

In the Niger plains the subsistence crops are rice near the rivers, hungry rice, maize and millet elsewhere. There is no important cash crop.

## RICE

Rice has developed to such an extent in Guinea, that it is the main food in most areas. In the past, relatively little rice was grown and all of it was upland, but the country now produces much rice from swamps.

Along the coast there has been the same effort to reclaim mangrove swamps for rice as in Portuguese Guinea and Sierra Leone. In the northern part of the coastal plain the Baga are skilled in reclaiming mangrove swamp and in building polders. It is not certain whether they learned this skill from the Mali kingdom of the middle Niger, from the early Portuguese, from the Portuguese via Africans, or developed the skill themselves. They have reclaimed considerable areas in the north, where water control, climate and soils are good.

Large reclamation schemes have also been undertaken to permit mechanical cultivation of new areas. Thus the French tried to develop about 2 025 ha (5 000 acres) at Monchon near Boffa, and 760 ha (1 875 acres) at Koba. Africans, with European help, have reclaimed 1 517 ha (3 750 acres) on Kabak island (Forécariah District), at Dukréka near Conakry, and at Bintimodia south of Conakry.

When mangrove is cleared for rice cultivation, salt must be eliminated from the soils by flushing with fresh river water, and sea water must be excluded. At Monchon it was difficult to sustain the supply of fresh water to the lands, as the river is silting up. In Portuguese Guinea, Guinea and Sierra Leone it has also been found that lands which appear to be free of salt often have toxic alkalis appearing in the soil, once rice cultivation has been started.

Also of significance has been the reclamation of inland and riverine swamps, most of them along the Niger and its tributaries. Water control is similar to that undertaken along the same rivers in Mali. The greatest project is that for the reclamation of 13 150 ha (32 500 acres) in the Siguiri area.

## BANANAS

Once a leading export, this crop has declined greatly since independence, partly because of changed politico-economic circumstances and partly because of disease.

As in the Ivory Coast their cultivation depended upon a preferential tariff in France. Exports rose from 188 tons in 1918 to 4 326 tons in 1928, 54 765 tons in 1938, 32 515 tons in 1948 and 64 900 tons (the record) in 1958. Then Guinea's bananas were shut out of the French market, so that other outlets had to be sought, mainly in Eastern Europe, where imports are controlled and not considerable. With the interruption of regular exports in 1958–60, many European and Lebanese planters left, and plantations were often abandoned or converted to tomato, pineapple or food crop cultivation. Some plantations were, however, divided into small and much less efficient banana farms, but a long-present problem of the fungus *Cercosposiose* became devastating. Banana cultivation has ceased east of Kindia, remaining only in the Ouassou–Benty–Kindia triangle, where water is plentiful and transport to port is easier and quicker, but where soils are poor, much fertiliser is needed, and banana diseases and pests are widespread.

## PINEAPPLES

Cultivation of pineapples for export began in 1934, also aided by French tariff preference. The fruit is grown on well drained slopes, mostly near Kindia and Mamou, but some is produced on the coastal plain, near Forécariah, Benty and Ouassou in growing competition with bananas. Unfortunately, like bananas, pineapples have their main harvest at a time when they are in competition in Europe with temperate fruits. Ways of overcoming this difficulty are by canning, which deals with most of the harvest, and by trying to force the fruit to mature earlier. Production has increased greatly since independence, for new markets have been easier to find than for bananas.

## KOLA NUTS

Kola trees are fairly widespread in the coastal plain and in the Guinea Highlands. There is extensive trade in kola nuts, especially from the latter towards Kankan and Mali. Indeed, the roads which now lead northward from the Guinea Highlands have been made from the old trails followed by merchants taking kola nuts one way, and salt and cattle in the other direction.

## COFFEE

This developed remarkably in the Guinea Highlands and accounted for about one-third of Guinea's exports at independence. Since then it has fallen to a low figure because of the loss of the French market, smuggling into Liberia or the Ivory Coast, and through disease.

## LIVESTOCK

There are nearly 2 million cattle in Guinea, almost all of them in the Fouta Djallon or in the Niger plains. They are of the small, humpless

Ndama type kept by the Fulani—this being the only country where the Fulani keep such cattle.

The most important cattle area is around Labé, and from there live-stock are sent to the rest of Guinea, to Sierra Leone and to Liberia. Although the cattle are small, the proportion of meat available per carcass is normally about 45 per cent and in the richer pasture lands around Beyla may reach about 53 per cent. The meat is also of higher quality than that normally obtained from average Zebu cattle.

## Minerals

### BAUXITE

The huge and high quality (55 per cent alumina) bauxite deposits of Ghana are typical of those in tropical countries in that they are tri-hydrates. The most important sources so far prospected are those at Boké, Fria, Kindia, Friguiagbé, Dabola and Tougué, whilst others on the Los Islands have been almost worked out. Export of bauxite took place from Kassa Island between 1952 and 1966, and from Tamara Island (Fig. 19.2) after 1968. Until 1962 the concession was held by Bauxites du Midi, then by a Hungarian state concern, and finally by Harvey Aluminium Company of America, which also secured the immensely more important Boké concession of Bauxites du Midi.

An international company with American, French, British, Swiss and German participation has been mining bauxite (33 per cent alumina) since 1960 at Fria, 145 km (90 miles) north-northeast of Conakry, and con-verting it to alumina in a very modern plant (Plate 71).[3] Since inde-pendence this has been Guinea's leading and most vital export, upon which her survival has largely depended. Much of the French company's share of the alumina is taken to Cameroon for smelting to aluminium

PLATE 71. The Fria bauxite and alumina works at Sabende

at Edea. The question is sometimes posed as to why the American share is not taken to Tema (Ghana) for smelting in the American plant there; the answer is that different and competing companies are involved. Near Fria are the Souapiti falls on the Konkouré river, which could be harnessed for power to enable aluminium smelting. Russia at one time agreed to develop the power, but nothing has so far come of it, perhaps because Guinea prefered to see development concentrated at Boké.

The Sangaredi (Boké) deposit is the largest and richest bauxite deposit so far known. Development was stopped in 1961–62 by disputes with the first concessionaire, and then delayed by the relatively small firm of Harvey needing to bring in other participating companies. Moreover, the Guinea government had to arrange loans to build the mining and port townships, the 136 km (85 miles) railway from the mine to the new port of Kamsar, and to build the latter. Harvey, its American, Canadian, French (the same firm as originally held the concession), West German and Italian associates, as well as the Guinea government, have capital in the mine, which was to open in 1973 with an initial production capacity of 4·7 million tons of bauxite annually, to rise later to 6·6 million. Later on, part may be converted to alumina at Boké. Hydroelectric power could also be developed, and then an aluminium smelter might be installed.

Other concessions have been granted—to Russia to exploit the Debele (Kindia) deposit, to a Swiss company to develop those at Tougué, and to the Yugoslavs to exploit that at Dabola, in each case with a 65 per cent Guinean share of the profits, as is to be the case at Boké. However, these other concessions cannot be worked until the main railway is converted to standard gauge and greatly strengthened. This was to be done by Russia but has since been accepted, in principle, by China.

## DIAMONDS

Commercial production of diamonds began in 1935. They occur in alluvial gravels of tributaries of the Makona river in the same way as in Sierra Leone, and the company which worked the Guinea occurrences until 1961 was connected with companies in Sierra Leone and Ghana. The workings lay southwest of Kerouané, whilst other workings were east of Kissidougou and west of Beyla.

As in Sierra Leone most of the diamonds were small, but a good number were gem stones. Again, as in Sierra Leone, there was always a problem of illicit diggings, and until 1958 there was much smuggling of diamonds into Sierra Leone or Liberia. Then control and production increased in Ghana until 1961, after which losses again became severe because of the inconvertibility of the new Guinea franc. Part and then all of the two concessions were nationalised, and the illicit diggers were organised and licenced in cooperatives. Poor management and smuggling led to the cessation of all production after 1966, so these valuable deposits are lying undeveloped.

IRON ORE

Ferruginous magnetite of 51 per cent iron content, low in phosphorus but with many other impurities, was mined only 8 km (5 miles) east of Conakry (Fig. 19.2) from 1953–66. Production then ceased, mainly because of competition from the richer haematite ores of Mauritania, Liberia and elsewhere, and because of import restrictions on mining equipment affecting operational efficiency.

Of immensely greater potential importance are the 300–600 million ton reserves of haematite on the Guinea side of Mount Nimba, and of 500 million tons on Mount Simandou just west of Beyla. British, Belgian, Italian, Spanish, Dutch, Swedish, Yugoslav, Romanian, American, Australian and Japanese concerns have expressed great interest in one or both of these deposits. That on Mount Nimba could have been developed in the mid-1960s if Guinea had been willing to see the ore exported to Buchanan (Liberia), with the Liberian ore from Mount Nimba. One proposal for the evacuation of Simandou ore is for a 710 km (444 miles) Guinean branch railway via Kissidougou to the main railway, and then by another branch to a new port south of Conakry. Another 50 km (31 miles) of line could be added from Mount Simandou to Mount Nimba, or the latter might after all be served separately via Buchanan. Guinea favours a branch from both sources to the existing railway near Kankan and using the present railway, duly widened and strengthened. This would then also carry bauxite from Dabola, Tougué and Kindia. An agreement signed in 1973 provides for mixed corporations to mine these deposits, financed by Guinea, Liberia, Algeria, Nigeria and Zaïre, and by Japanese, Yugoslav and Spanish companies.

## Hydroelectric power

Because of the heavy rainfall, the many deep gorges in the Fouta Djallon and the level plateaux, there is a high potential for hydroelectric power. On the other hand, evaporation is high during the long dry season, the thin vegetation on the plateaux is unhelpful to water and soil conservation, and lakes are rare.

A great impetus to the development of hydroelectric power has been given by the development of iron and bauxite deposits. If vast quantities of cheap electricity can be produced on the Konkouré river at least, it should be possible to establish aluminium plants at both Fria and Boké. Power could help existing factories and might encourage the development of other industries, including iron and steel. Meanwhile, there are small plants near Conakry and Pita, and the consumption of electricity (mainly thermal produced) has increased about twelve times since independence.

## Industry

Guinea has a considerable endowment of raw materials and of potential power for industrial development, so that she has the possibility of developing the extended processing of exports. On the other hand, the home market is small and poor, and is unsupported by numerous better-off expatriates as in Dakar and Abidjan. Hence the prospects for import substitution and consumer good industries are much less good than they have been so far in Senegal, the Ivory Coast, Ghana or, above all, in Nigeria. Furthermore, political principles, whilst encouraging fairly widely distributed state industries, have discouraged expatriate and private enterprise. Reference should be made to the texts on Conakry and bauxite in the present chapter, to Chapter 8, and especially to K. Swindell, 'Industrialization in Guinea', *Geography*, 1969, pp. 456–58.

## Transport

In a territory with so much high country of a particularly dissected character, it is obvious that means of transport are of more than usual importance. Moreover, the highland mass obstructs communications between the coast and the upper Niger and its various tributaries, which are modest means of communication in the northeast.

At the end of the nineteenth century, when France and Britain were rivals in the area now occupied by Guinea and Sierra Leone, the interior could be held only by means of railways. Thus, the Guinea and Sierra Leone railways were rival routes into the interior, and that in Guinea was built to prevent the British from reaching the lands of the upper Niger. It also had the object of creating a hinterland for Conakry, at that time subsidiary commercially to Freetown.

Unfortunately, the narrowest part of the highland mass, the waist line between the Fouta Djallon and the Guinea Highlands, lies on the boundary with the northeastern part of Sierra Leone. Had this not been so, such a route would have been the easiest one for a railway or road. The French railway was built in the face of appalling engineering difficulties, through precipitous country and at great cost in lives, material and money. As the boundary kept the British from the Upper Niger, the Sierra Leone Railway was built for the strictly local purpose of serving oil palm areas, and was too near the southern coast. Because of an unfortunate political boundary, both railways had unsatisfactory routes, were built at considerable cost, and secured only moderate traffic to offset high capital burdens.

The Guinea railway was begun in 1900, reached the Niger at Kouroussa in 1910, and the more easily navigated Milo tributary in 1914. It rises to 715 m (2 346 ft), but this figure gives little idea of the steep gradients and sharp curves on the railway, the lines of which are frequently on the narrow ledges of precipices. The scenery of this railway is magnificent and quite exceptional in West Africa. As already mentioned it may be rebuilt, mainly for new bauxite and iron ore traffic.

There are some good trunk roads. An accord with Liberia and the Lamco company permits Guinea to send or receive up to 40 000 tons of merchandise through Buchanan and the Liberian mineral railway to Mount Nimba.

Conakry, Boké, Labé, Kissidougou, N'Zérékoré, Kankan and, in the dry season, Siguiri and Macenta are served by air.

## Conclusion

Guinea has, for West Africa, an exceptionally varied environment and economic resources. The low and rainy coastal plain is well suited to the production of oil palm produce and rice, for all of which there is keen demand. The Fouta Djallon is suited to the growth of pineapples on its slopes and to banana cultivation in its valleys. Coffee in the Guinea Highlands developed very rapidly initially, and could be resuscitated. Rice cultivation in the Niger plains can also be extended.

In addition to varied cash and food crops, mineral production is important, though less varied than in the last two decades of colonial rule. Mineral developments since independence have been much affected by state control. Development of bauxite at Boké and of iron at Mount Nimba have been seriously delayed, as have hydroelectric power development and the possibility of aluminium production. Banana and coffee cultivation have greatly declined, largely but not wholly because of the loss of the French market. Although pineapple and tomato have partly taken the place of bananas in the Mamou area, agriculture is not prosperous.

On the other hand, there has been a determined effort to establish industries, particularly in and near Conakry. These mainly process local or partly local supplies in the textile, cigarette, tobacco and match, shoe and tanning, and brick-making plants. Outside Conakry the main works are food canning at Mamou, a groundnut oil mill at Dabola, a wood and furniture complex at N'Zérékoré, tea packing at Macenta, sugar refining at Medina Oula, and a cement works at Mali.

Trade is fairly evenly divided between France, the communist and capitalist countries (the rest of the Six, the UK and the USA).

# 20

# Sierra Leone: Britain's contribution to the settlement of freed slaves

## Historical outline

There is a legend that Hanno the Carthaginian watered his ship in the Freetown Estuary about 500 BC. The first written reference appears in an account, written in 1462 by Pedro da Cintra, of a Portuguese voyage to the coast. To the rugged and high peninsula on which Freetown now stands he gave the name Sierra Leone or 'Lion Mountains', because, compared with low-lying coast north and south of Freetown, the shape of the mountains as seen from the sea reminded him of a lion. The name was later extended to the whole country.

From the sixteenth to the eighteenth centuries the Rokel Estuary was constantly visited by European slave traders. But at the end of the eighteenth century the mountainous peninsula became the scene of Britain's partial reparation for her part in the trade. With the support of the British Government and a few philanthropists, Granville Sharp assembled a pioneer party, mainly of destitute ex-slaves, which arrived in 1787. Other parties came later.

These groups were joined by former American slaves who had fought with the British in the War of American Independence. They had been assembled in Nova Scotia, whence they were taken for settlement at Freetown in 1792. Among many other early immigrants were Maroons from Jamaica, who arrived in 1800, though most of them and their descendants later migrated to the Gold Coast or returned to Jamaica.

This town of freed slaves and others, most of whom had not been born in Africa, endured hostility from the peoples of the interior, and attack from the sea by the French during the Revolutionary and Napoleonic Wars. In 1808 Britain took control of the new settlements, proclaiming the Sierra Leone Peninsula a Crown Colony and the slave trade illegal. From 1817 to 1819 several hundred discharged African soldiers were settled in Freetown, and in the appropriately named villages of Waterloo and Wellington.

The British Navy played the major rôle in suppressing the slave trade by sea from West Africa. Freetown was the main naval base and, whenever between 1808 and 1854 slave ships were captured, freed slaves were resettled in and around Freetown, if their homeland could not be determined or reached. Up to 1833, 34 000 slaves had been liberated at sea and sent here, e.g. to such aptly villages as Wilberforce, founded in 1811.[1]

Descendants of ex-slaves are generally known as Creoles. They are characterised by their mixed blood, part African but partly non-African culture, and higher standards of education and literacy than most Africans of the interior. This was especially so in the past.

After the initial hostility of the local Africans, there was little advance beyond the peninsula. But, with the general 'Scramble for Africa' in the last quarter of the nineteenth century, it became necessary to define the boundaries with Liberia and French Guinea, the latter having expanded around the north and eastern sides of Sierra Leone and hemmed it in. By 1898 the Protectorate had come into existence and all boundaries were defined, except for one sector with Liberia, finally agreed in 1911. Thus organisation of the Protectorate started a century after that of the Colony; the Protectorate was, in consequence, in contact with European ideas and methods for a much shorter time.

As Freetown was the main naval base and the senior British settlement, it was responsible, during much or the nineteenth century, for the government of other territories down the coast. Many Creoles were engaged in this service; others were in business and in education, but as the other countries developed their educational systems and become economically and politically more powerful than Sierra Leone, the Creoles no longer found their position so privileged. Moreover, the Protectorate peoples improved their social, political and educational status. Rivalry between these peoples has been an important obstacle to unity in Sierra Leone.

Although Sierra Leone has a longer history of education and social services than has any other territory, it has been overtaken in recent years by the larger lands of West Africa, where greater and more varied resources have brought larger revenues. Unlike Nigeria or Ghana, Sierra Leone began mineral workings only in 1929, but she is now an important producer of diamonds and iron.

Before the Colonial Development and Welfare Acts and later aid, Sierra Leone was one of those poor countries which became relatively poorer because of her inability to afford necessary expenditure upon such things as bridges and roads. She has also been retarded by the colony–protectorate division, but upon independence in 1961 this administrative division was eliminated.

## Population

The 1970 population of Sierra Leone was estimated to be 2 512 000, giving a density of 35 per sq km (91 per sq mile), a fairly high figure by West African standards, especially in view of the character of its agriculture and possibly rapidly wasting mineral economy.

## Climate

As in Guinea and Liberia, there is the same rapid onset of an exceedingly rainy and almost uninterrupted wet season which generally lasts from May to October or November.[2]

Along the Sierra Leonean coast, as far as Bonthe Island, the southwest coast monsoonal climate prevails. But at Sulima there is generally a short but clear break in the rains, so that town is the approximate western limit of the Liberian climate.

Unlike neighbouring lands, Sierra Leone has a range of mountains reaching the sea in a northwest to southeast trending peninsula. This lies across the path of rain-bearing winds and has a particularly heavy rainfall, amounting to 6 366 mm (250·63 in) at Guma valley and 3 360 mm (144 in) at Freetown. However, as in most tropical lands, there is wide annual variation.

Unexpectedly, perhaps, the interior Sierra Leonean climate has more rain than the Foutanian of central Guinea, despite the lowland character of much of western Sierra Leone compared with the Fouta Djallon. The northeastern mountainous border of Sierra Leone has the Guinea Foothills climate, and the eastern upland border that of the Guinea Highlands.

Unfortunately, the heavy rainfall of Sierra Leone and its neighbours causes runoff, soilwash and severely leached soils. Heavy rain and high temperatures may have helped to produce lateritic soils. There are great areas of lateritic sand or gravel and sandy loam, upon which only poor grass will grow. The long dry season halts vegetative growth for several months annually, and this fact and the leached soils account for the naturally poorer forest, itself heavily degraded by man—especially in the north.

## Vegetation

The small size of trees and poor nature of the vegetation in this country of high rainfall require explanation. In Guinea the vegetation is likewise poor in the mountains, but that can be attributed to infertile sandstone and lateritic coverings. In the lower areas of Sierra Leone, where the rainfall is everywhere over about 2 300 mm (90 in) a year, the vegetation should be richer.

'As it is, the vegetation has been so affected by farmers, that the once extensive areas of rain forest have disappeared and there remain only islands of forest. . . . There are extensive swamp areas in the coastal zone . . . tidal mangrove forest near the sea coast, and flooded sedge and grass swamps behind. Sometimes scattered trees are present in the latter giving a park-like effect. These swamp types of vegetation have grown up on the more recent geological deposits and are not thought to be derived in any way from the degeneration of rain forests.

There are many evidences that in the past the greater part of Sierra Leone was covered by Rain Forest but that, unhappily, is now far from being the case. The forests have gone down before agricultural demands and shifting cultivation. As these became progressively more intensive, owing to increasing population, forest was converted to high bush, high bush to low bush, and low bush to orchard bush with grass; while in isolated cases, where other conditions, such as drainage have not been propitious, the ultimate degradation to grass flats has been reached'.[3]

The proportions of the country under the various types of vegetation are roughly as follows:

Forest (excluding Mangrove) 3–5 per cent—stable through forest reservation; mainly on eastern ridges and in southeast.
High bush (secondary forest) 20–25 per cent—rapidly decreasing, found in southeast.
Low bush (poorer secondary forest) 20–25 per cent—stable in area but decreasing in value, found in south-centre.
Savanna and grasslands 35–45 per cent—especially in north, increasing in area and declining in value.
Swamps—all kinds 10–20 per cent—see below.

Inland seasonally flooded grasslands ('bolilands')[4] and coastal mangrove swamps are a feature of Sierra Leone. These are often suitable for wet season cultivation of swamp rice, to replace upland rice which tends to assist soil erosion. Upland soils are severely leached and lateritic in nature, and increasing population has led to their over-intensive use. It is by better farming and swamp cultivation that degradation of soils can be halted, forests improved, and the livelihood of man made more secure.

## Geology and physiographic regions

### The Freetown peninsula

This northeast trending peninsula, at the northern end of which stands Freetown, is about 40 km (25 miles) long from northwest to southeast, and averages 16 km (10 miles) across from northeast to southwest. Mountains rise steeply from the sea to nearly 900 m (3 000 ft) and are very different from the rest of Sierra Leone, being composed of a varied complex of basic intrusive igneous rocks (gabbros, norites, etc.).

At the base of the hills are flat expanses of lateritic pan, and raised beaches.[5] At the lowest levels mangrove occurs. The hills are now a forest reserve, constituted to restore soil cover and, by restraining run-off, to protect water supplies both for present domestic needs and hydroelectric power.[6]

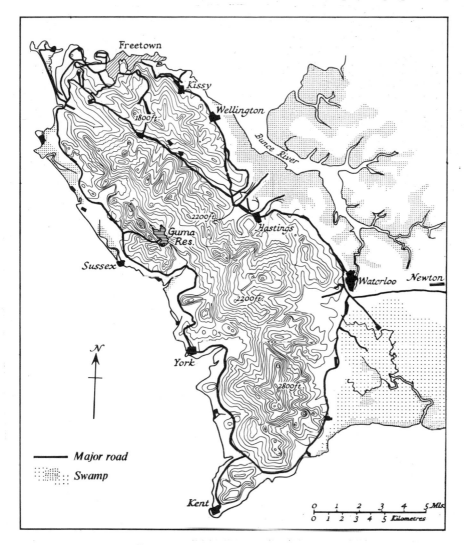

FIG. 20.1. The Freetown Peninsula

The stippled areas indicate swamps.
Based on a map from H. R. Jarrett, *The Port and Town of Freetown, Geography,* April 1955, by permission of the author and editor

On this peninsula are settled the Creoles who comprise part of the population. Villages are mostly 30 m (100 ft) up, along the main road around the peninsula, and especially on the eastern side near the road. Many of these Creole settlements, which have characteristic street plans and house types distinguishing them from other villages, have decayed. Creoles no longer have a privileged position in village commerce, and have moved to Freetown and its dormitory suburbs. Moreover, the

307

fertility of the soil has seriously declined in this area of long settlement, overintensive farming of cassava, leaching and eroding rainfall.[7] Erosion has been halted by the forest reserve mentioned above, but the farming area is necessarily restricted and what remains tends to be overworked. Only in the small valley swamps is there systematic manuring of land, in this case for the production of vegetables. Farms and the marketing of produce are badly organised and villages now depend more upon fishing.

One logical redevelopment could be the encouragement of tree crops. These hold the soil, provide humus from their leaves, and the crops would be near the Freetown market and the port. Another activity, sponsored by the agricultural station at Newton (just east of the peninsula), is the improved rearing of pigs and chickens. This activity is limited by the availability of sufficient feeding stuffs from groundnut cake and palm kernel residue of oil extraction.

The first mineral won in Sierra Leone was alluvial platinum from York, 1935–41 and 1945–49. The alluvial nuggets were derived from lodes or bands of basic igneous rock, through which the streams have cut. Unfortunately, the parent rock has not been found. Ilmenite is also abundant in the rocks and streams near York, Hastings and Middle Town. It assays 47 to 53 per cent titanium dioxide and contains appreciable quantities of platinum. Other minerals known to occur in the peninsula are felspar, hypersthere, diallage, olivine and titanomagnetite.

## FREETOWN

Freetown, capital of Sierra Leone, was founded in 1792 as an atonement for the evils and miseries of the slave trade. It was chosen as a well-known site, superior to most places on the Sierra Leone coastline. It stands on raised beaches at the northern end of the hilly peninsula, adjacent to which is a deep channel of the easily entered, sheltered and large estuary. Pure water was also available. It was therefore ideal also as a naval base for suppressing the slave trade and, in times of war, has been important to the defence of the Atlantic and the protection of convoys.

Oddly enough, by comparison with the rest of the West African coastline, nature was here so lavish in her natural shelter, that a deepwater quay was opened only in 1953, and extended in 1970. Upstream at Pepel is a deepwater loading installation belonging to the Sierra Leone Development

PLATE 72. Freetown from Fourah Bay College (University of Sierra Leone) on Mount Aureol. Central and historic Freetown lies near the right waterfront. Inland and upward from this is the next ridge of Tower Hill with State House (below in trees) and the Parliament Buildings on the left edge. Next comes King Tom Pensinsula with King Tom Point, Murray Town Peninsula with Murray Town Point, and, finally, Aberdeen Hill over 8 km (5 miles) away

Company and used for shipping iron ore.

Freetown has been the subject of much unfavourable (if incidental) comment,[8] but like Monrovia it has much more character than most West African cities, especially other ports. The older three storied frame houses, with first floor balcony and upper floor dormer windows, are copied from the American colonial style. As at Monrovia, it was the only style ex-slaves from America had known.

In 1799 a Royal Charter empowered the appointment of a mayor and corporation. Freetown has been a bishopric since 1852 and was British West Africa's first diocese. Here also were the first hospital and railway in British West Africa. Fourah Bay College, founded in 1827, has provided some university education for over a century, far longer than any other institution in West Africa.

Like other West African cities it has distinctive quarters. There are the usual ones such as Kru Town, but also some more unusual sections. Thus (as also at Banjul, Ouidah and Lagos) there is a Portuguese Town, southeast of Kru Bay, where lived Portuguese recaptives, and Maroon Town, on the east side of Kru Bay, where the Jamaican Maroons established themselves in the nineteenth century.

Behind the old lighter wharf the land rises steeply to Tower Hill. Fort Thornton, on the gentle lower slopes of Tower Hill, was the first government office, and the hill the early military headquarters. Between Fort Thornton (Government House) and the old wharf is the oldest part of the town containing the Law Courts, Secretariat, Post Office, Cathedral and commercial quarter. Residential quarters lie to the west and east. Farther east, the deepwater quay,[9] rice and groundnut mills in Cline Town form a second harbour zone. There is, as yet, little industry as the national market is so modest. However, there is an industrial estate farther out of Freetown, at Wellington.

Freetown had an early Hill Station, at first exclusively reserved for European officials. It lies southwest of and about 245 m (800 ft) above Freetown, and was reached from 1904 to 1929 by a railway, which had its only distinction in being the steepest non-funicular railway in the world. Mount Aureol, on the southeast side of Freetown, is now occupied by Fourah Bay College (part of the University of Sierra Leone).

In 1948 the Freetown population of 64 576, comprised 17 331 African non-natives (largely Creole), 46 081 African natives, 372 Europeans and 792 Asians (Lebanese and Indian). In 1971 the population was estimated to be 187 000.

Freetown has the usual problem of replanning an old site, made more difficult by the hilly environment. This has also affected the location of the airport. At the end of the Second World War there were airfields at several places along the east coast of the peninsula, and at Lungi across the estuary. Only the latter can take large and fast planes, because of the dangers of the nearby mountains on the Freetown side.

Consequently, a road and ferry journey or extra flight is necessary between Freetown and Lungi.

## Coastal swamps

The coastal swamps, which average some 32 km (20 miles) in width, are well defined because of their liability to wet season flooding. They are mostly composed of Tertiary and Quaternary sediments (Bullom Series), have special types of vegetation and land use, and are threaded by navigable, tidal waterways. Flooding occurs because of the heavy rainfall (over 3 175 mm—125 in), which falls on a flat and low lying area, where much of the sub-soil is clay or sand.

The coastal swamps have alternating bands of gravels, grits, sands and clays. Along the south coast are large areas of coarse marine sand ridges, relics of former beaches. Lacustrine, lagoon, estuarine, deltaic and marine conditions have occurred widely here in recent geological times.

On the west coast, although there are some fine silts, most of the swamps consist of different kinds of clay, including pottery and brick clays. Lignite occurs near Newton, east of Freetown. When this lignite is dried, cleaned, ground to powder and briquetted, it might be used as fuel, but its calorific value is only one-quarter that of coal, and it has other disadvantages. Salt occurs north and south of the Scarcies estuary; rutile, monazite and zircon are widely distributed and are concentrated in the gravels of many rivers near tidal limits.

Martin[10], distinguished four types of coastal swamp vegetation:

1. *Mangrove swamps*, found at the mouths of most rivers. Mangrove has been cut to make swamp rice farms. The clay soils are very suitable for holding water in rice fields but salinity is a problem.
2. *Sedge swamps*, found behind the mangrove swamps of many rivers. These are badly drained and are frequently flooded to over 1·5 m (5 ft) throughout the rainy season; by the end of the dry season all but the deepest parts are dry again. Soils are alluvial, deep and rich, though generally slightly saline near mangrove swamps.
3. *Flooded grasslands* are found on the larger rivers above the tidal zone. Soils are much lighter and flooded only when the rivers are in spate.
4. *Coastal parkland, farm bush and scrub* are found in Pujehun and Bonthe districts, wherever coarse marine sands occur. These are water-logged in the wet season and very dry in the dry season. Consequently, trees are stunted and widely spaced.

It is only in inland and coastal swamps, and fertile tidal areas, that permanent cropping has so far succeeded. In cleared mangroves the elimination of salt in the soil, the prevention of toxic (ferrous sulphide) accumulations on empoldered lands, and defence works against tidal scour have sometimes proved problems. With Portuguese Guinea and

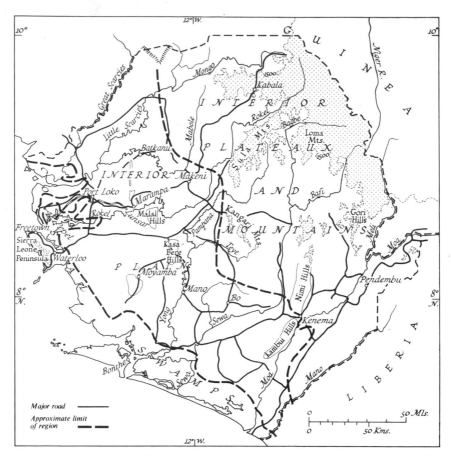

FIG. 20.2. Relief and regions of Sierra Leone

Guinea, Sierra Leone is famed for its mangrove clearance for rice cultivation. As swamp rice replaces upland rice production, so forest and soil
degradation and erosion should diminish.

About 1880 some Temne found that the less saline mangrove swamps
could be utilised for rice, and development accelerated after both wars.
In eighty years 35 500 ha (90 000 acres) have been planted. By far the
most important of the reclaimed mangrove areas are in the lower Great
and Little Scarcies rivers and around Port Loko, where over 26 325 ha
(65 000 acres) are used for rice farming (see Fig. 20.4).

The average rice farm has three acres. Initial clearing and preparation
is exceedingly arduous (getting labour is the basic problem), but once
cultivation can be started, annual work is easy. Fertility is maintained
by the continual deposit of silt from river water, and weeds are checked
by saltwater floods. Near the sea, fields must be bunded to prevent
deep flooding by saline water. High up, bunding is not essential and

312

PLATE 73. Rice cultivation along the Great Scarcies river, north of Bumpe. Rokupr town is in the extreme right centre, the site of a rice research station. Most of the farms have mature rice

quick-growing (four-month) varieties are used. The main rice growing area starts about 10 km (6 miles) from the sea and extends upstream for 24 km (15 miles). Wherever natural drainage is adequate, and the river water at high tide is fresh for at least five months, the salt deposited during the dry season will be cleared sufficiently by rain and fresh water floods.

In the south, clearing of mangrove has been done mainly since 1938. The south has been developed later for two main reasons. Although there are more extensive areas available than in the northwest, they are dispersed, being interrupted by unsuitable areas of coarse sand. Secondly, the area is more remote from the chief market of Freetown. There is only about one-third the acreage found in the Scarcies, and about two-thirds is mechanically ploughed. On both the south and west coasts there are still some undeveloped mangrove swamps, although those easiest to develop have been cleared.

Behind the mangrove swamps are riverine grasslands on the southern littoral, and swamp grasslands and sedge swamps in the Scarcies areas, some of which may be suitable for tractor cultivation.

Where flooding is deep, tall erect rices must be used. In still deeper water the so-called 'floating' rices of Indo-China, such as are used in Mali, are suitable. The strong root system of sedges and grass is a

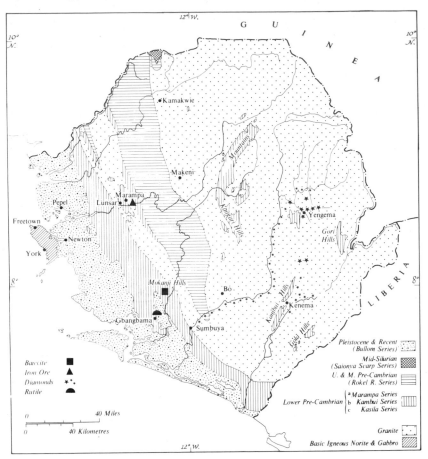

FIG. 20.3. Geology and minerals of Sierra Leone

problem in these areas, entailing much preparation in the early years. Thereafter work is easier, and the soils have such a high content of organic material that they can be cropped with little or no fertiliser. In the drier parts, sweet potatoes and early cassava are grown in the dry season.

Piassava, the other product of the coastal swamps, derives its name from a Brazilian word for the prepared fibres from the base of the leaf-stalks of the Raphia palms (*R. vinifera* and *R. gaertneri*), which grow in South American and West African swamps. The best quality (Prime Sherbro) is mainly limited to the Bonthe district riverine areas, including Gbap, Taigbe and the Lake Kwarko area (see Fig. 20.4). The poorer standard Sulima quality comes from the Lakes Mabesi and Mape, and the Pujehun, Zimi and Sulima areas. The differences of quality result from better methods of preparation, rather than from the fact that *R. vinifera* predominates in Bonthe and *R. gaertneri* in Sulima areas. A large swamp

314

on the northwest of Lake Kwarko produces Prime Sherbro piassava, because retting is done by the local people in sunny stagnant water which, except for a brownish tinge, appears to be clear. In the Sulima area, however, retting is done in small pools in high forest. The water is cool and does not cover all the bundles. But some piassava produced around Lakes Mabesi and Mape, and at Zimi, is excellent when fully retted.

The first export was from Sulima in 1892. From this area, which produces the bulk of Sierra Leone's piassava, production spread to the riverine areas of Sherbro. Piassava exports go mainly to the United Kingdom, the USA and Western Europe. Piassava is used in the manufacture of brooms and scrubbing brushes but there is severe competition with nylon fibre; it can also be used in removing air bubbles in the manufacture of steel castings, but chemical silicones have supplanted it. Piassava exports are now a very minor item.

Bananas are grown widely but haphazardly in the coastal swamps in the areas just east of the Freetown Peninsula and across the estuary in Lungi, near the airport. If there were plantations and more uniform fruit could be produced, a considerable export would be possible, provided that banana ships called regularly. A plantation near Songo has bananas with interplanted beans which, with unwanted bananas, are fed to bacon pigs.

The coastal swamps of Sierra Leone have an attractive future, so long as they can be continuously developed for rice, and piassava can be sold and is improved in quality and quantity. Considerable income could also come from systematic banana exports, and from the rearing of pigs for the Freetown market. Soil fertility in the mangrove and riverine swamps, initially greater than anywhere else in Sierra Leone, is being sustained. The agricultural potential of Sierra Leone lies in the coastal swamps.[11]

**The interior plains**

This region extends inland from the coastal swamps to about 160 km (100 miles) from the coast, rising in gentle undulations to about 120 m (400 ft) at the foot of the scarp marking the edge of the interior plateaux and mountains. From the plains rise residual hills showing accordances at 137, 160 and 213 m (450, 525 and 700 ft), indicative of former levels of planation.

Underlying the lowland are northwest to southeast belts of metamorphic and other rocks of Pre-Cambrian (Birrimian) age. Immediately east of the Pleistocene deposits of the coastal swamps are the metamorphic Kasila series, consisting of gneisses and granulites, which occur in a belt averaging twenty miles from west to east. The Moyamba hills belong to this series. The area around Port Loko is singularly infertile, with only thin soil over a lateritic pan.

East of the Kasila series are the scattered occurrences of metamorphic Marampa schists, as well as granites. Marampa schists, which occur around Marampa and northward across the boundary, consist of altered argillaceous and arenaceous Birrimian sediments, in which there is high grade but occasionally phosphoric haematite iron ore, containing 52–69 per cent iron. The largest deposits and those of better physical condition and iron content are in the Sula mountains, and may be worked later.[12]

The more accessible iron occurrences at Lunsar were first worked in 1933, and occur in thick deposits caused by overfolding in two abrupt hills. The ore is simply scraped off the hills, one having been lowered 30 m (100 ft) in thirty years of working. Most of the richer red haematite ore has been removed; washeries or concentrators deal more with grey, soft, schistose powder ore of 45 per cent iron, which they upgrade to 63 per cent iron.

The ore is taken by a private mineral railway to the loading pier at Pepel, 90 km (55 miles) away on the northeastern side of the Rokel estuary. The pier can accommodate 100 000 ton ore carriers. The concession is owned by the Sierra Leone Development Company, which the Sierra Leone Government once wished to nationalise. If this occurs, there is a possibility that the present company might not wish to continue. Meanwhile, some 2 000 workers are employed and annual exports are over 2 million tons of ore, or about one-eighth of Sierra Leone exports by value. The deposits are among the most accessible to Europe and America but the company also has contracts to supply Japanese mills until 1979.

The Rokel series extend from near Sumbuya in the south, to beyond Saionya on the north-central boundary, and average 32 km (20 miles) in width. The series comprise sandstones, shales, conglomerates and some intrusive rocks. As the Rokel series are less resistant than granite or the Marampa schists, the resulting landscape is lowland, with savanna and rare forest patches, e.g. near Tabe and Bumpe in the south, Kumrabai Mamila in the centre, Batkanu and Samaia in the north. It is likely that this belt of sediments has never been thickly forested. In the rainy season the Bolilands are usually flooded, and swamp rice cultivation is being encouraged, but in the middle of the dry season all but the larger streams become intermittent. Villages are rare and there is a vivid contrast between the low population on the Rokel series and the denser population on the granitic rocks found to the east, e.g. towards Makeni and Kamalu. Yet the sandstones of the Rokel series hold water, which could be secured from wells and bore holes, so that more people could be sustained. No significant minerals have been found in the series.

It is generally the ancient volcanic rocks, associated with the Rokel series, that form numerous abrupt and isolated hills, such as the Kasabere hills near Yonibana, the Malal hills east of Marampa, and ridges southwest of Batkanu. However, the steep Saionya scarp, rising to 767 m (2 515 ft) on the northwestern boundary, is formed of flat bedded Silurian sandstones and shales, with intercalated sills of diorite, and is part of the Fouta Djallon.

Over the rocks of the interior plain, laterite and lateritic gravel are widespread, with sandy patches in valleys. Another characteristic is the low, poor secondary forest, resulting from infertile soils and man's depredations. The crops, which resemble those in the next region, are considered in the section on Agriculture.

## The interior plateaux and mountains

East of approximately the 120 m (400 ft) contour is a plateau region belonging to the Guinea Highlands and mainly 300–600 m (1 000–2 000 ft) above sea-level. Most of it is floored by granite with dolerite sills, but there are important occurrences of Kambui schists, a highly metamorphosed and mineral bearing formation of the Birrimian series.

The most important relief features are shown on Fig. 20.2. Many of them are series of scarps and plateaux; some have residual domes, notably tooth-like Bintimani in the Loma mountains. It rises to 1 948 m (6 390 ft) and is capped with Palaeozoic dolerite. The Sula mountains, extensively surfaced by laterite, contain great unexploited reserves of rich haematite iron ore. The Kangari mountains are severely dissected and thickly wooded.

There are many smaller hill masses, and bare granite domes and pinnacles are common. Otherwise, the surfaces of the plateaux are flat over considerable expanses, though trenched by deep V-shaped valleys to depths of about 60–90 m (200 300 ft).

The Kambui schists are important sources of minerals, especially of diamonds. These are alluvial and occur in gravel beds 20–50 mm (8–20 in) deep, lying beneath an overburden of about 0·9 m (3 ft). The parent rock is almost certainly Kimberlite, as in South Africa, though some believe the diamonds originated in Palaeozoic dolerites. The stones are larger than in Ghana; indeed, the largest gem stone ever found in an alluvial deposit in Africa was recovered in 1972.

A company with a majority of its shares held by the government operates near Yenegema, west of Sefadu, and at Tongo, south of Sefadu. In highly mechanised mining the overburden is removed and the diamond-bearing gravels are washed, sorted and concentrated. The concentrate is passed over greased shaking tables, to which the diamonds adhere, while the heavier minerals pass on. The operation is simple and inexpensive (except for costs of security), and yields are very high.

After widespread illicit diamond digging and smuggling in the late 1950s the monopoly was ended, the company compensated, and restricted to their most profitable areas. Diggers were then licensed, and there are over 4 000 licensees, each of which employs gangs of about eleven men. Although some system is being brought into their work, much ground is

PLATE 74. One of the many diamondiferous gravel treatment plants of DIMINCO, near Yengema

left unworked, and small diamonds fall through their sieves. While their production is currently very important, it could decline rapidly. All this output should pass through government buying offices, but there is much illicit dealing and smuggling. Diamonds account for about two-thirds of Sierra Leone exports.[13]

In the southern part of the interior plateaux and mountains, where the rainfall exceeds 2 540 mm (100 in), the vegetation is secondary forest. In the north where the rainfall is less, the vegetation is Guinea savanna. Almost anywhere else in West Africa the rainfall would permit rainforest, but the soils have been heavily leached by the torrential rainfall and impoverished by overfarming.

In the south and in the better areas of the north, farms are usually cultivated for one or two years only. But in the poorest areas of the north, where level farmland is scarce, it is usual to farm for two or

318

PLATE 75. Diamond diggers at work on a terrace of the Sewa river, Sierra Leone

even three years before reverting to the seven- to nine-year fallow. Consequently, poor lands become poorer.

In the north and west, where land must be farmed for more than one year, rice is always the first crop after fallow. The following year is used for pure or mixed crops of cotton, hungry rice, groundnuts, guinea corn, millet, cucurbits, benniseed and, to a lesser extent, sweet potatoes, cassava and peas. In the south and east, where land is used only for about one year, subsidiary crops such as maize, cassava, sweet potatoes, yams and beans are always intercropped with the rice. If the rice is grown in a swamp, other food crops are grown in the dry season and regular annual cultivation is generally possible.

Ginger, grown in Moyamba and Bo districts, is the only crop grown purely for cash. A special farm is cut from bush for it, and it takes the place of rice in rotation. Other crops may be partly sold for cash, but are grown primarily for subsistence. The oil palm, cocoa, coffee and kola nuts are also cash crops, but are not grown in the system of fallow farming. It is interesting that the Temne cultivate their soils much more deeply than do other peoples.

## Economic resources

### Agriculture

RICE

Sierra Leone's rainfall of 2 280–4 320 mm (90–170 in) annually is the main factor in causing rice to be the greatest food crop. It is the chief object of farming, except in a few areas of Temne country (northwest centre), near towns where cassava may be more important, and in the northeast where millet is somewhat more significant. With the oil palm and minerals, rice is a major element in the country's economy. Although all rice grown is for home consumption, and there are heavy imports, the drift away from rice cultivation to diamond mining could be reversed if diamonds become more elusive.

For centuries rice was grown almost entirely on upland farms by the system of shifting farm patches, but since 1923 there has been a rapid increase in swamp cultivation, resulting largely from the enthusiasm of agricultural officers.

Upland or dry rice production is considered deleterious, not only because it accelerates erosion and prevents soil conservation and afforestation, but also because the increases in population and in the percentage of non-farmers require greater production and new areas of cultivation. It is doubtful whether primitive upland rice farming can support a population of more than 23 per sq km (60 per sq mile), which is below the average for Sierra Leone.

Fig. 20.4. Sierra Leone: economic

Many times that number may be supported by using inland, riverine and coastal swamps for rice production. Cultivation of inland swamps, e.g. the Bolilands, cannot cause erosion, but they are usually infertile and require fertiliser; mangrove swamp soils are generally quite rich and fallowing is not usually needed. Yields are therefore better, though inter-cropping is impossible; the work in swamps is unpleasant and may be unhealthy. There is also considerable prejudice against the taste of swamp rice among those accustomed to upland rice.

Of the swamp rice areas, the inland swamps (mainly in Bo, Makeni, Kenema and Kailahun districts) are more extensive than the coastal ones. Inland swamps are easier to clear than mangroves, and are also more compact. Clearing of coastal swamps is a major operation, requiring

321

hard work and skill. Their successful cultivation requires care and capital for drainage, and there has been considerable trouble with toxic accumulations in bunded fields. Meanwhile, Sierra Leone has been very successful in the reclamation of mangroves, though behind Portuguese Guinea in this respect.

## OIL PALM

Palm produce, a vital food, and once Sierra Leone's leading export, accounts for about one-tenth of the exports. The oil palm is widely distributed, but the densest areas are around the Scarcies rivers, in the west-centre and in the southeast.

There are a number of old and new plantations, but most palms are scattered on farms or in the bush, so that the fruit is often allowed to drop from the trees, so impairing the quality of the oil.

A major problem with Sierra Leone palm fruit is that it has a very narrow mesocarp and a large nut. Consequently there is little available palm oil, and this is badly extracted. Communities have been helped to plant improved *Deli* and *Angola* palms, which have thicker mesocarps containing more oil. Nut-cracking machinery has been distributed and some ten small oil mills have been established. These extract more oil and secure a better quality, but operating costs have been high and they have not increased total output. The oil is consumed locally, but better extraction methods ought to bring larger quantities and better qualities for home and export use. About 50 000 tons of kernels were exported annually until 1965, when a kernel crushing factory was opened at Wellington, capable of crushing this amount.

PIASSAVA. See under coastal swamps.

## COCOA

Cultivation dates mainly from 1925, since when planting has been concentrated in the forest areas of Kenema, Segbwema and Kailahun. The long, intensely dry season can be tolerated by cocoa only where there are at least 2 540 mm (100 in) of annual rain. To the northwest the vegetation is too open, and towards the coast the soils are too poor for cocoa, or swamps forbid its cultivation. Little is grown towards the Gola forest because of insufficient labour and poor communications. Present exports are about 3 000 tons annually, or 3–5 per cent of exports by value.

## KOLA NUTS

Being a tree crop, these are, like the oil palm, cocoa, coffee and other trees, admirably suited to soil conservation practices. Kola trees are most numerous in southern Kono, Moyamba and the Freetown peninsula. Nuts are produced for local consumption and for export to the Gambia, whence some pass to Mali. The quality of the nuts is high and the varieties differ from those found in Ghana and Nigeria.

## GINGER

This is grown on small plots outside the usual rotation as a very minor export, the principal area of production being around Moyamba, where it is the main product. Some areas are exclusively under ginger but the annual production is quite small. Sierra Leone ginger is used medicinally, and this restricted sale accounts for the low demand and output. This may be fortunate, because its cultivation on sloping farms induces soil erosion.

## COFFEE

Coffee is grown mainly in the cocoa areas, but it also extends westward and especially northward, as it can withstand some drought. *Robusta* and *liberica* are grown. Exports are developing and, like cocoa, it accounts for about 3–5 per cent of Sierra Leone exports.

## GROUNDNUTS AND BENNISEED

Both of these are important northern food crops. A groundnut mill at Bo produces oil locally, so reducing imports. The principal groundnut areas are Kambia, Bombali and Koinadugu districts in Northern Province, and Kailahun in Eastern Province. As groundnuts are best grown in Sierra Leone on sandy sloping surfaces, their cultivation is not being encouraged because of the risk of soil erosion.

BANANAS, SUGAR, RUBBER and TOBACCO could all be grown successfully if their cultivation were efficiently organised. Markets for the first are, however, restricted, the main potential being in Eastern Europe. The other crops could also nourish local import substitution industries, whilst tobacco could bring more cash into the poor northern districts.

## LIVESTOCK

Ndama cattle can alone be kept safely in Sierra Leone. They are fairly common only in the northeast, where they are kept mainly by nomadic Fulani. Cattle number about 240 000 but others come in from Mali and Guinea, across the northern and eastern boundaries.

Through the energy of the Agricultural Department, the breeding of European pigs has developed at Newton, Njala and Kenema, and by private enterprise near Freetown, at Hangha, and elsewhere. Groundnut and rice mills provide some feeding stuffs.

## Minerals and power

See Fig. 20.3. For diamonds see pp. 317–18, iron p. 316, lignite p. 311 and platinum p. 308.

### BAUXITE

In 1964 a Swiss company began mining a capping deposit averaging nearly 10 m (30 ft) in depth over some 30 km (18 miles) of the Mokanji hills. Production is some 600 000 tons per annum, and washing and concentration are done before despatch by road about 32 km (20 miles) to Bagru Creek, from where lighters take the ore to ocean vessels which anchor near Bonthe.

### RUTILE

Near the bauxite deposit is a large one of rutile, said to be the largest by content in the world. Rutile is a source of titanium, used in aircraft engines and in missiles because of its heat resistance. Rutile is also a source of titanium dioxide used in paint and other materials for whiteness and opacity. An Anglo-American company worked the deposit but had management and technical problems which led to closure in 1971. Dry opencast mining may need to be substituted for dredging by another company taking up the operation in 1973. Other deposits are being prospected in beach sands of the Freetown peninsula and in the Little Scarcies river.

Minerals represent about three-quarters of Sierra Leone's exports, although none were mined before 1929. Many other minerals are known to exist and might become economic to work, given power and better transport.

### HYDROELECTRIC POWER

A Canadian concern is building a dam and power station at the Bumbuna Falls, east of Magburaka. There is considerable other potential.

## Transport

In the nineteenth century, when only the Freetown peninsula was under British rule, head porterage and canoe transport sufficed. The south and southwest-flowing rivers of the interior also came to be used and still have local importance, especially near coastal areas. Some 800 km (500 miles) of launch routes are still used.

The 500 km (310 miles) government railway was opened in stages between 1899 and 1908, and a branch between 1908 and 1916. The main line was built mainly to serve the oil palm districts, but it cut across navigable waterways and for many years could not compete with water transport, or even with head porterage in some areas. The railway was built economically with the narrow gauge of 0·76 m (2 ft 6 in), sharp curvature and steep gradients, all of which reduced its capacity and speed.

Once suitable vehicles were available, roads became vital to hasten development, yet for many years they were few, and were disconnected 'feeders' to the poor and unremunerative railway. By 1930 lorry competition had become severe for the railway, as road haulage was taking goods to and from the rivers. The government restricted this competition by imposing tolls on certain roads.

Only during and since the Second World War were the elements of a road network constructed. Freetown was connected with the interior by road only in 1941. Road transport, now unrestrained by tolls, is still handicapped by ferries. As late as 1950 there were no organised ferries to make a connection with Guinea, and it cost £5 to £6 to persuade local people to ferry cars across the Great Scarcies river at Kambia or the Moa river at Sanibalu. The road between Kabala and Faranah (Guinea) was opened only in 1950. In 1951 American aid made possible the replacement of ten ferries by bridges.

After the Second World War the future of the low capacity and under-equipped railway was doubtful, but in 1949 and again in 1964 it was decided to retain and improve it. The track was improved, and diesel locomotives introduced, but the branch line has been closed and the railway is being phased out.

Sierra Leone is served through Lungi by European and African air services. Internal services began in 1958.

## Conclusion

Sierra Leone is a small country; much of it is mountainous and two-fifths is very poor. Indeed, the coastal and inland swamps are the only fertile areas; elsewhere the soils are very leached and soil erosion is acute on steep slopes.

Not only is the rain very heavy but the rainy season is followed by a sharp, dry one. Apart from the usual problems which any dry season poses to the farmer, intense drought after severe rain gives a less vigorous vegetative cover to the soil, and inhibits the good growth of crops like cocoa. Nor is such violent seasonal alternation kind to man, and some have seen in this a partial explanation of slow economic progress in Sierra Leone and adjacent lands.

The fact that Sierra Leone was to some extent the 'Mother of British West Africa' for long caused it to rest on its laurels. Self-satisfaction, provincialism and colony-protectorate rivalry were evident, at least until independence in 1961. Since then there has been some political instability, and the country is much affected by the dominance of diamonds in the economy. Farming is neglected or abandoned in favour of 'trying one's luck' at diamond digging. There is much illicit digging, selling and smuggling of diamonds, and public morals have often declined sharply in the diamond areas. There is potential in other minerals and in rice cultivation, but inflation is severe and labour is attracted most of all to diamond digging. The small size of the country and of its population hinders diversification, and especially industrial development. An interesting development is the establishment of a small diamond cutting and polishing industry.

# 21

# Liberia: 'The love of liberty brought us here'

## Historical outline

Liberia resulted from the efforts of the American Colonisation Society (founded in 1817 and still in existence) and other societies, to settle American ex-slaves in West Africa. Americans, with varied motives, had been impressed by British efforts at the resettlement of former slaves in and around Freetown in Sierra Leone.

The first but abortive effort by the American Colonisation Society was at Sherbro Island in Sierra Leone in 1820; the first permanent settlement was in 1822 on Providence Island at Monrovia. Many more parties arrived, there and elsewhere in subsequent years, including slaves freed by the American Navy. The American Colonisation Society had some responsibility for the government of their settlements until 1847, but in that year Liberia became an independent state and took as its motto the words quoted above. In 1857 the colony of 'Maryland in Liberia', with its capital at Harper, was admitted as a county of Liberia.

From the beginning Liberia had tremendous problems. The ex-slaves, who had come mainly from America, were generally several generations away from tribal life, and were more American than African. They also lacked techniques, experience and capital. It is true that the American Colonisation Society gave subsidies from year to year, but these did not enable them to acquire specific skills or to set up trades in their new home. Even if the former slaves had possessed technical training, they would have had little chance to make use of it, and they were anxious to forget their past and to live comfortably in the future. They turned to politics and trading, instead of to agriculture.

It must also be remembered that these poor ex-slaves, with their sorrowful background, were landed on what is probably the worst part of West Africa. It has the heaviest rainfall, a very difficult shoreline and leached soils. From the first they encountered the hostility of the Africans; and European powers, especially the French and British, were unhelpful and, on several occasions, aggressive to the new state.

In recent years the Republic of Liberia has undergone rapid economic growth and profound changes. Until 1926 it was chronically in debt and exported only small quantities of palm oil and kernels, piassava and

327

coffee. But in 1924–26 the Firestone Rubber Company of America secured a concession to plant rubber, in return for which the Liberian Government was granted a large new loan and yearly revenue from the concession's activities.

The greatest impetus to advance has been since 1942 when America secured the right to land troops in Liberia at a time when this area was of strategic importance in the Second World War. From 1944 to 1971 Liberia had in President Tubman a most devoted and energetic head of state. The combination of his drive, American money, Firestone revenues and iron ore royalties all helped immensely. Liberia has two deepwater ports, an international airport and roads which, although insufficient, do include one through to Guinea bringing some transit trade and links with Sierra Leone and the Ivory Coast. There have also been political reforms, whereby the Africans of the interior are associated with the government of the country, so that after 1945 officials of tribal origin have been appointed to nearly all important administrative or political positions in the hinterland.

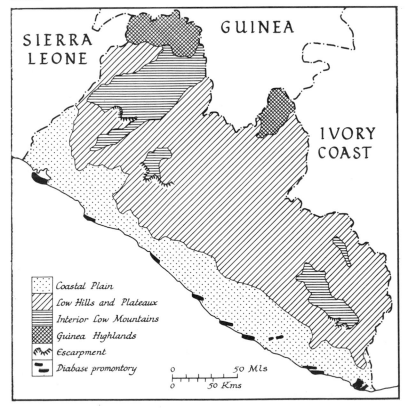

Fig. 21.1. Physiographic regions of Liberia

(Based on a map by P. W. Porter in 'Liberia', *Focus*, American Geographical Society, September 1961)

# Population

The area of Liberia is conventionally quoted as 111 369 sq km (43 000 sq miles), and the population was estimated to be only 1 171 000 in 1970, giving a low density of 11 per sq km or (28 per sq mile). The descendants of the settlers, formerly called 'Americo-Liberians', number 15–20 000 and live almost exclusively in coastal towns on promontories (Fig. 21.1), or in townships along the St Paul, St John, the Sinoe and Cavalla rivers, near their mouths.

Densities of 20–60 people per sq km (50–150 per sq mile) are found in the above areas, on the Firestone and iron ore concessions, and near the main roads. On the other hand, one-quarter of the country has densities of 2–6 per sq km (5–15 per sq mile), and a further one-third has under 1·5 per sq km (4 per sq mile). Large tracts are uninhabited. The lowest densities are in the extreme west-centre and in the eastern third of the country, where there are large forests. Shortage of labour is a major problem in development.

## Climate

The coastal areas of Liberia have over 4 000 mm (about 160 in) of rain annually in the northwest, and some 2 550 mm (100 in) in the southeast, although high points like Cape Mount have up to 5 100 mm (200 in) on average. The wet season lasts from late April or early May until October or November, with a secondary 'middle-dry season' in July or August. This minor dry season is variable and erratic in its occurrence and extent, but it is this which distinguishes the Liberian climate from the southwest coast monsoonal type. Relative humidity is generally about 95 per cent in the wet season and 82 per cent in the dry season.

Mean daily temperatures are 26°C (79°F) and rarely exceed 32°C (90°F) or drop to under 17°C (63°F). The average diurnal range is about 10°C (18°F).

In the interior conditions are considerably better because the rainfall is about one-half or less than that on the coast and it falls in a shorter season, generally from June to October. Range of temperature is greater and relative humidity less.

## Geology and physiographic regions

Most of Liberia is composed of Pre-Cambrian gneisses, granites, and schists. It lies mainly on the lower southwestern slopes of the Guinea Highlands, whose outliers are in general accord with Huronian trend lines. Rivers flow rapidly over the bedrocks and have many rapids and falls, which give Liberia a great potential of hydroelectric power, so far tapped only at the Mount Coffee station (34 mw) on the St Paul and by Firestone on the Farmington river (4·2 mw).

Intrusive rocks, such as granitic bodies, pegmatites, diabase and gabbro dykes (mostly inland) and diabase bodies on the coast are also found. The latter give the relief features of Cape Mesurado 71 m (233 ft) on which lies the old centre of Monrovia, Baffu Point, and Cape Palmas on which stands Harper. The highest coastal point is an elliptical norite plug at Cape Mount 326 m (1 068 ft) near Robertsport. These promontories are broadly similar to the Conakry (or Kaloum) peninsula in Guinea, and the Sierra Leone peninsula behind Freetown.

Frequently associated with the relief features of the Liberian coast, or with river estuaries, are northwest trending sandbars, which are being built by wave action. Behind the sandbars are lagoons, the largest being Fisherman's Lake at Robertsport. Mangrove is not extensive, extending inland only up creeks or the main rivers.

**Coastal plain**

This is about 15–55 km (10–35 miles) wide and has a forest-savanna mosaic of patches of forest and low bush, with gallery forests along the rivers, mangrove swamps, clusters of thorny shrub, and grasslands with some oil palms and dwarf trees.

MONROVIA

Monrovia, th capital of Liberia, was founded by ex-slaves from America in 1822. The Afro-American settlers ultimately established themselves on the upper part of the diabase body of Cape Mesurado and built a town, the style of which is very reminiscent of the Southern States of America. The foot of the hill and settlements on Bushrod Island are, by contrast, rather squalid, though no more so than similar quarters in other West African ports.

The deepwater harbour on Bushrod Island[1], just north of Cape Mesurado, built as an American Lend-Lease project between 1944 and 1948, and operated by a company, consists of long breakwaters which approach each other to give an entrance of 245 m (850 ft) and a dredged channel of 12·2 m (40 ft). The commercial quay can accommodate three ships of up to 10·7 m (35 ft) draught. Three finger piers for shipping iron ore extend into the harbour and can accommodate 90 000 ton carriers. There is also an oil jetty and a fishing quay.

Monrovia is a free port, and foreign goods may be unloaded, stored,

PLATE 76. Monrovia looking east from a hotel roof on the top of Cape Mesurado.
On the left, in the lagoon, is Providence islet where the first ex-slaves from America settled. The left hand street is Ashmun Street, named after one of the pioneers, and the next is Broad Street (the main business street), with the Executive Mansion. On the far right overlooking the sea is the presidential palace.

mixed, repacked or manufactured, and then forwarded by land or sea without payment of duty. Liberian products may even be taken into the free trade area and brought back into customs territory without the payment of duty, although they may have been combined with or made a part of other articles in the free area.

Despite these advantageous provisions, there is little industry in Monrovia because of the small total and low purchasing power of the country's population. However, the industrial estate has an explosives factory which serves the mines and exports e.g. to Mauritania, a brewery and soft drinks works, a fish processing plant, and a small oil refinery.

Rubber latex for export is brought by boat down the Farmington river and a short distance westward along the coast. Iron ore, from the Bomi hills, Mano river and Bong mountains, comes by mineral lines, while goods in transit to and from Guinea travel via the Monrovia–N'Zérékoré road opened in 1947. There is also a shipping service between Monrovia and the other coastal settlements. Buchanan exports Mount Nimba iron ore and handles some Guinean trades. Greenville takes ships of up to 6 000 tons, whilst Harper is a roadstead.

The intercontinental airport at Robertsfield, constructed in 1942, adjoins the Firestone Harbel Estate, 89 km (55 miles) from Monrovia. The airport at Monrovia has West African services.

### Low hills and plateaux

These hills, considered as part of the interior plain in Sierra Leone, are about 122–366 m (400–1 200 ft) high. They are mainly under rainforest.

### Interior low mountains

These are mainly in the Western Province, where several ranges trend northeast to southwest. They are again under rainforest and have a very low population. Much of this country is virtually unexplored.

### Steep scarps

The southern edge of the mountains is limited by some vivid scarps, e.g. at Reputa on the Monrovia–Ganta road.

### Guinea Highlands

These are found along the northern border, and crests of up to 1 372 m (4 500 ft) occur in Liberia, especially Mount Nimba, rich in iron ore.

Except for the coastal plain, Liberia has a rather complex relief. In the lower parts there are often separate hilly masses, which may rise to 914 m (3 000 ft). The higher points are mostly in the northwest.

# Economic resources

## Agriculture

Liberian coastal soils are extremely leached, so that the most suitable crops are tree products. This may account for the success of the Firestone plantations, especially as rubber trees take little from the soil.

About one-half of Liberia is considered suitable for cultivation, and most farmers use the customary slash and burn system for subsistence agriculture. Land is farmed for one or two years and then rested for between seven and fifteen years. Rice and tree crops are ideally suited to the climate, the former in swamps, the latter on slopes. Unlike Portuguese Guinea, Guinea and Sierra Leone, there has been little development of swamp rice cultivation except in northwestern Lofa County. Taiwan specialists have helped develop the Gbedin swamp north of Ganta. Cassava is another important food crop.

### RUBBER

Rubber is overwhelmingly the most important cash crop. The earliest production of rubber in Liberia was from wild rubber on behalf of a British company in the early years of this century. But as early as 1907 some 800 ha (2 000 acres) were planted on Mount Barclay by Sir Harry Johnston's Liberian Rubber Company. This plantation was abandoned in 1920 because of poor prices. When these led to the Stevenson Plan to increase world prices by controlling exports, particularly from the Far East, an agent of the Firestone Rubber Company became interested in the abandoned British plantations and rented them in 1924. Although they were in a semiderelict condition a small export of rubber was made to the USA in 1925.

After long and involved negotiations, the Firestone Rubber Company[2] secured a concession in 1926 of up to one million acres (about 405 000 ha). The company has one large estate on the Farmington river around Harbel, and a small one up the Cavalla river on the eastern border. So far the company has leased only about 65 000 ha (160 000 acres) and has cleared and planted some 36 400 ha (90 000 acres). There are some 10–11 million rubber trees ranging in age up to nearly thirty years. About 31 161 ha (77 000 acres) are in production. Production is approximately 40 000 tons annually.

Despite these impressive figures, the achievement is much less than the Firestone Company originally intended. It has only one-sixth of the planned area under lease and less than one-twelfth planted. Instead of employing the intended 350 000 workers, they employ about 16 000. The original production estimate was 200 000 tons of rubber, and it was proposed to invest about seven times as much money as has been put in so far, which is about £6 million. Nevertheless, it is by far the largest

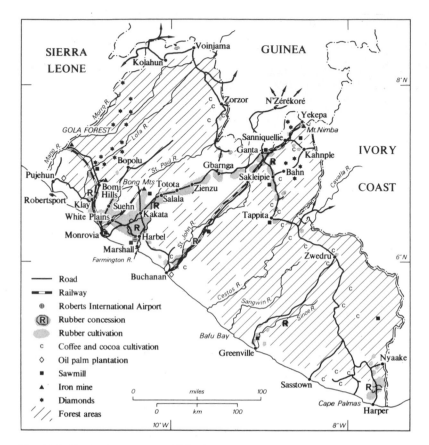

FIG. 21.2. Economic resources of Liberia

rubber operation in the world, with the greatest concentration of high-yielding rubber trees. Yet rubber from Liberia covers only about one-third of the natural rubber requirements of the Firestone Rubber Company, and less than one-sixth of its total natural and synthetic rubber needs. During the Second World War these plantations and others in Ceylon were the only sources of natural rubber latex available to the Allies.

High-yielding rubber strains, known as 'proven clones', have been introduced into Liberian buddings. The buddings have been multiplied thousands of times and then bud-grafted to the original planted seedlings; 80 per cent of the present productive acreage is of budded rubber. It is hoped that eventually yields of about 2 018 kg/ha (1 800 lb/acre) will be achieved, in contrast to the 159–227 kg (350–500 lb) which were average yields of ordinary seedling rubber trees in the past. Present average yields are about 1 457 kg/ha (1 300 lb/acre) at Harbel and 1 171 kg/ha (1 050 lb/acre) on the Cavalla plantation.

The Harbel plantation has all the services of a city. There is a small hydroelectric power station, two powerful wireless stations, 21 schools, 4 churches, 2 hospitals, a brickworks and, needless to say, a Coca-Cola bottling plant.

The Firestone plantations have had a very great influence on the economic development of Liberia, upon its exports and its national revenues, and upon the availability of natural rubber to the dollar area. Moreover, there are many other rubber plantations—foreign and Liberian. There are six more expatriate plantations occupying some 20 240 ha (50 000 acres). Two of these originally planted other crops such as bananas (at Greenville) or cocoa and coffee (between Ganta and Sakleipie), but they changed to rubber when those crops failed. Some 4 500 Liberians have rubber farms occupying about 56 660 ha (145 000 acres) (one-half more than Firestone), one-half of which is mature but yielding poorly because of inefficient methods, despite the gift of over $10\frac{1}{2}$ million seedlings and advice from Firestone, which will also buy their rubber.

There are 113 720 ha (281 000 acres) under rubber in Liberia. In 1945 this crop accounted for 96·6 per cent of Liberian exports; the percentage has now dropped to around one-fifth because of the rapid development of iron mining. Until this occurred Liberia was dangerously dependent upon the crop, essentially upon one plantation. Even now, it is almost the only cash crop, and is not without some pressing problems. The mines, with their higher wages, are attracting labour, while Firestone must replant large areas of old trees.

COFFEE was the main export until 1880, when Brazil began to dominate the market. Coffee again has some significance, especially in the well populated areas between Voinjama and Kolahun, around Zorzor, along the trunk road between Gbanga and Ganta, and in Nimba County. The principal variety of coffee produced in northern Liberia is *robusta*, whilst in the coastal townships the indigenous *liberica* is grown.

COCOA was probably introduced about 1920 by labourers returning to Liberia from the plantations of Fernando Po. So far, however, cocoa is of little importance. It may be that the dry season and its low relative humidity are disadvantageous to it, as in neighbouring Sierra Leone. There are a few plantations, and farms in northern and south-central Liberia, particularly in Webbo district.

KOLA NUTS are mostly grown in the north-centre; they are, in part, traded to Guinea.

PALM OIL is widely produced and palm kernels have been exported since 1850, when Liberia is said to have started this export in West Africa. Large palm oil plantations are being developed near Buchanan and Robertsport.

PLATE 77. Mount Nimba iron ore mine. The precipitous ridge continues into Guinea and descends on the right into the Ivory Coast. On the left a transfer point on the 3 km long conveyor belt may be seen

SUGAR is grown rather more in Liberia than in adjacent countries. Most of it is grown in the better populated areas where it is used for making rum.

GROUNDNUTS and COTTON have local significance in some parts of the interior and, as is common elsewhere, country cloth is made from the cotton.

## Forestry

In the nineteenth century there was some export from Liberia of camwood, then in demand as a dyestuff. After the cessation of that export, because of the competition of synthetic dyes, not much timber was cut, though various companies or agencies made surveys and small exports through Monrovia, Harper and Greenville. Exports developed rapidly only after 1967.

About one-third of Liberia has timber capable of commercial exploitation. The largest forest area is in the east, where Sikon (*Tetraberlinia tubmaniana*) occurs in single dominant stands and in great numbers. A large concession, mainly for timber, but also for palm produce and minerals, is held by a British company in the southeast. The other large

336

forest area is in the west, particularly in the Gola forest, astride the Sierra Leone boundary, where there are fine woods. In both areas extraction is difficult because of competition with mines and rubber plantations for labour, the paucity of roads, and the lack of a deepwater port until Greenville[3] was opened in 1964.

## Minerals

### IRON ORE

Quarrying began in 1951 in the Bomi hills, northwest of Monrovia, to which they are linked by the first of Liberia's four mineral railways. The concession is held by an American company, and much of the ore goes to the USA. Originally there were 20 million tons of magnetite and haematite containing about 65 per cent iron but these have been worked out and 100 million tons of itabirite containing 35–50 per cent iron lying in a basin formation are now being worked. This ore is upgraded at the mine.

A second mine was opened, also by an American company, in 1961 on the Mano river, and linked by another railway worked as an extension to the Bomi hills line. Here there are another 100 million tons of itabirite, this of 55 per cent iron content. It too is concentrated at the mine.

The third mine, high on precipitous Mount Nimba and belonging to several interests but mainly American and Swedish, began operations in

PLATE 78. Iron ore washing and pelletising plant at Buchanan

1963 on its first ore body containing at least 300 million tons of 60–70 per cent iron. There are similar reserves over the boundary in Guinea, whilst adjacent mountains (e.g. Mount Tokadeh where mining started in 1973) have comparable ore reserves of up to 60 per cent iron content. The Nimba haematite deposit has almost no overburden, impurities are insignificant, and the ore could be used untreated. The mineral is carried by Liberia's third and longest railway to the country's second deepwater harbour of Buchanan.[4] There the ore is washed and some is pelletised to further enhance its high quality before being loaded into ore ships of up to 90 000 tons.

The fourth mine, belonging to German firms, opened in 1965 and is in the Bong hills, northeast of Monrovia, to which it is joined by yet another line. Here there are 200–250 million tons of poorer itabirite ore averaging 38 per cent iron but beneficiated to 65 per cent. In 1970 a pelletising plant was added at the mine.

Within fourteen years Liberia became Africa's largest iron ore exporter, and the third world exporter after Canada and Sweden. Many other deposits are known in Liberia, e.g. at Wologisi in northwest Liberia, which is to be developed by another mineral railway to Robertsport and a new ore loading pier. An iron and steel plant is also planned ultimately at Robertsport.

The Nimba mineral railway is also used for timber and rubber traffic to and from adjacent Liberian areas, as well as for some Guinean imports and exports. Iron ore prospectors in Guinea would like it to be used to develop deposits there, but the Guinea government has so far insisted upon an all-Guinea outlet if its ore is to be worked.

DIAMONDS

Diamonds were first recorded in 1910 from alluvial flats along several rivers. There have for long been intermittent workings on the Lofa river in its central and lower reaches, and diggings near Mount Nimba. Exploration is active in these and other areas. Figures of exports are inflated by diamonds smuggled in from Sierra Leone.

**Transport**

Poor means of transport have been limitations upon the development of Liberia. Until the early days of the Firestone Concession, Liberia had no real roads, except in the immediate environs of Monrovia. Elsewhere the country was served by narrow trails—still the means of communication over much of the country. Goods are often carried by porterage.

Most rivers are obstructed by rapids. The St Paul is navigable from its mouth at Monrovia to White Plains, a distance of only 28 km (15 miles).

Much of the recent renaissance in Liberia stems from the development of communications. The deepwater harbour at Monrovia has the added merit of being a free port, and coastal steamers link it with the main coastal settlements. A deepwater port was opened in 1963 at Buchanan for the export of iron ore from Mount Nimba and it also has some general trade. Another deepwater port opened in 1964 at Greenville for timber export, and Harper has been improved.

Roads have been built by the rubber, iron ore and timber concessionaires, Firestone having built about 1 000 km (680 miles). The Liberian government, too, has been able to build more roads now that its revenues have increased so spectacularly. The most important road is that through the country from Monrovia to Ganta and on to N'Zérékoré in Guinea. From it there are branches to Harper via Tappita, to Lola via Sanniquellie–YeKepa, and to Kailahun via Zorzor, Voinjama and Kolahun. Connections exist from Greenville to the Zwedru–Harper road, and from Kle to Pujehun north of Robertsport. There is quite a network of roads round Monrovia, and in the main Firestone plantation.

As already noted, international air flights mostly pass through Robertsfield, but there are services to some West African and Liberian towns from Monrovia.

## Conclusion

Until recently Liberia was undeveloped, partly because of chronic indebtedness and lack of capital for productive purposes. The price of self-government has been isolation, exposure to pressure and intermittent bullying from the great powers, and the lack of true economic assistance.

Since the 1930s and particularly since 1942 there has been a great quickening of the economy of the country, almost exclusively as the result of the drive of various companies and official agencies, and of the late President Tubman. Economic development is restricted in two main ways. The first is that this rice growing country must still import large quantities of that food. The second problem is that the population is very much less than was supposed, and thus the numerous firms which have been granted concessions in recent years are competing for manpower. It will be impossible for all of these to develop fully without the importation of labour.

Exports arise very largely from the operations of foreign concessionaires, rather than from African farmers and entrepreneurs as in most West African countries. Apart from the 4 500 independent rubber farmers, the ordinary Liberian contributes little to either export or internal trade.

# The Ivory Coast: high capitalism in a land of great potential

The Ivory Coast, with an area of 322 463 sq km (124 504 sq miles), is, after Nigeria, the largest country in the forest zone of West Africa and has, by reason of its varied economies and resources, a great potential. The opening of the Vridi Canal in 1950 was a vital step towards realising this potential.

The population in 1970 was 4 310 000, and there were about 50 000 non-Africans. Although one-third larger than neighbouring Ghana, the Ivory Coast has only one-half the population. To overcome the effects of this low population, great efforts have been made to encourage immigration from the overpopulated Upper Volta; indeed, from 1933 to 1947 the largest part of that territory was attached to the Ivory Coast essentially for this reason and for economy.

Among many other contrasts, the Ivory Coast also differs from Ghana in having non-African planters who produce most of the bananas, many of the pineapples, and some of the coffee and cocoa exported. The Ivory Coast has also comparatively few mineral workings. Any student of West Africa will find stimulating contrasts and comparisons between these neighbouring lands.

## Historical outline

Within the confines of the present Ivory Coast the once famous city of Kong was founded by the Senoufo people in the eleventh century. After considerably extending their domain, they were interpenetrated in the sixteenth century by the Dioula, who came southward from Ségou when the Mande Empire broke up, and ultimately became the overlords. By predilection they were and are itinerant traders. Kong became famous as a caravan centre, where kola nuts from the south were bartered against cattle and salt from the north. When Binger, the French explorer, visited Kong in 1888 there were some 15 000 inhabitants, but it was destroyed in 1895.

In the eighteenth century the Ashanti extended their control to the Bondoukou area, which they held until 1874. Moreover, the Agni of the southeast Ivory Coast and, to a lesser extent, the Baoulé of the south-centre, resemble the Ashanti in their social and political organisation.

340

These groups comprise a quarter of the present Ivory Coast population.

By contrast, west of the Bandama river, in the western Ivory Coast, the tribes have always been highly fragmented in their geographical distribution, social and political organisation. So bad was their reputation, that in the past the western coast was marked on maps as *La Côte des Mal Gens*, in contrast to that of *La Côte des Bonnes Gens* in the east.

Along all the coast there was heavy surf, a lack of harbours, dense forest, a sparse population and little or no gold. Thus the attention of mariners seeking gold and slaves was directed earlier and more intensively to the favoured Gold Coast.

French contacts were in three phases. The first was from 1637 until 1704, when there were rare visits by ships of several companies and by missionaries to Assinie, a town near the Ghana boundary destroyed by the sea in 1942.

From 1843 until the Franco-Prussian War, forts were established at Assinie, Grand Bassam and Dabou, whilst French rights were fairly vigorously proclaimed along all the coast. Northward from Assinie, the town of Aboisso became an important trading post, at the head of water navigation and on the caravan route to Ashanti. Both caravan route and market have ceased with the erection of the boundary with the ex-Gold Coast. As in other parts of the world, the French withdrew at the time of the Franco-Prussian War; nevertheless, her interests were looked after by Verdier and Treich-Laplène, just as British ones had earlier been kept alive on the Gold Coast by Maclean.

The next phase opens with the enunciation of the principle that title to territory could be legally sustained only by effective occupancy. Treich-Laplène spent two energetic years from 1887 to 1889 making treaties with chiefs in the interior, and in the latter year the name 'Ivory Coast' was given to all the French part of the coast. The colony was proclaimed in 1893, with its capital at Grand Bassam. After terrible epidemics of yellow fever, the capital was moved to Bingerville from 1900 to 1934, since when it has been at Abidjan. The deep water port, opened in 1950, heralded an economic upsurge of great magnitude.

## Climate

There is the usual system, common to all Gulf of Guinea countries, of two clear rainfall maxima on the coast, merging into one maximum at approximately 8°N. However, in the Ivory Coast there are two special features. First, the mountainous area of the west around Man is wetter than other places in the Ivory Coast in the same latitude. Its rather heavy rainfall of some 2030 mm (80 in) comes in one season, which builds up evenly to a maximum in September and diminishes again in the same way. This area has a monsoonal climate of the Guinea highland type. Secondly, although all the southern part of the Ivory Coast has an equatorial regime, there are marked variations in rainfall along the sea-board, which brings to mind much sharper contrasts along the Ghana one. In the Ivory Coast, the southwestern and southeastern extremities are wettest; the central part of the coast between Sassandra and Lahou is less wet. Tabou, at the extreme southwestern end of the coast, averages over 2 340 mm (92 in) of rainfall, falling in 130 days; Sassandra has under 1 525 mm (60 in) falling in seventy-five days. Abidjan to its east, is wetter with 1 960 mm (77 in) in 150 days.

Although the central coastline, the centre, north-centre and northeast of the Ivory Coast all have less than 1 525 mm (60 in) rainfall, there is no area so dry as around Accra, on the Ghana coast, where the rainfall is only some 635–760 mm (25–30 in).

Consequently, despite the considerable rainfall variations, the equatorial belt is exceptionally well developed in the Ivory Coast. The rainforest was so difficult to penetrate in the early days that the railway was built to force a way into the more open interior; it was built across the narrowest part of the forest, where the rainfall is least. The forest is now the realm of production of the Ivory Coast's greatest cash crops and likewise valuable export of timber.

Beyond the equatorial zone, the semi-seasonal equatorial type is very well developed, and typified by such places as Séguéla, Bouaké and Bondoukou. Although the forest was originally semi-evergreen, man has converted much or it to poor grass woodland, with gallery forests.

To the west lies the Guinea highland climatic zone, mentioned at the beginning, while to the north is a narrow seasonal equatorial zone, typified by Bouna. Lastly, on the northern fringes is the southern savanna zone, with its single rainfall maximum. Relative humidity varies between about 45 and 80 per cent. Yet rainfall is often as high as or even higher than in the seasonal and even semi-seasonal equatorial zones, according to whether one is considering the wetter west or drier centre of any zone. Thus Odienné averages 1 550 mm (61 in) of annual rainfall on about ninety-two days and Ferkessédougou 1 300 mm (51 in) on 100 days, although there are great variations from the average.

## Geology, relief and major regions

### The coastal plain

As far east as Fresco, the coast is characterised by low cliffs, averaging about 60 m (200 ft) in height, with rocky points and intervening sandy bays, similar to much of the Ghana coast but, as already noted, little visited in the past.

*San Pedro* is being developed as the country's second deepwater port, particularly to open up the hinterland, especially to timber cutting. Later will come the opening of the Bongolo iron ore field near Man, and manganese deposits at Odienné. Agriculture is to be encouraged, especially the cultivation of rice, oil and coconut palms, bananas and cocoa. By 1980 the population of San Pedro is expected to be 50 000; meanwhile, ships drawing up to 9·7 m (31·5 ft) can use the port and there is an airport.[1]

*Sassandra* lies in a semicircular bay with deep and sheltered water. The town lies on a rocky promontory and a wharf, opened in 1951, handles 250 000 tons of goods annually. With the help of roads to Gagnoa, Soubré and Tabou, and from San Pedro to Soubré, the production and export of bananas and wood has increased greatly. However, the wharf may come to be supplanted by the harbour of San Pedro.

East of Fresco, the coast becomes smooth and sandy, with a long and ever-increasing sandbar; this is broken by the Bandama river at Grand-Lahou, by the Comoé at Grand Bassam, and by the Bia river and Aby lagoon at Assinie. The sandbar is everywhere bordered by lagoons on the landward side; on the north shore of the lagoon are Tertiary marine and estuarine deposits. These are the presumed Tertiary shoreline and former estuaries (or rias), e.g. the Aguien and Potou lagoons, near Bingerville. By contrast, the Aby lagoon is probably partly of tectonic origin. Near the Vridi canal at Abidjan is the *trou sans fond*, a submarine trench which some consider to be the former valley of the Comoé. Others consider it to be a structural feature.

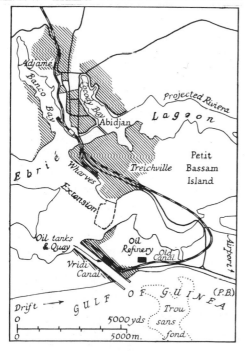

Fig. 22.1. Abidjan and the Vridi canal

*The Ivory Coast: high capitalism in a land of great potential*

The possible causes of this remarkable lagoon and sandbar coast, which is repeated east of the Volta Delta, have been discussed in Chapter 1. Whatever they may be, it was a great impediment to the development of the country. After the failure to keep open a canal cut across the sandbar near Abidjan between 1904 and 1907, the Ivory Coast had to be content until 1950 with wharfs at Grand Bassam and at Port Bouët.

The Vridi canal, begun in 1936, halted during the Second World War, and completed in 1950, made Abidjan into a fine, sheltered, spacious and deepwater port,[2] and rendered obsolete the pier at Port Bouët. Not only did traffic increase rapidly but the whole economy of the Ivory Coast was greatly stimulated.

Other important stimuli have been the opening of the railway to Ouagadougou (Upper Volta) in 1954. Then there was the transfer of French settlers and their capital from Guinea in 1958 onwards, and the removal of Guinea's competition in the French market for coffee, bananas and pineapples. Moreover, France continued the guaranteed purchase of large amounts of Ivory Coast crops (especially coffee) at higher than world prices until 1965. The break-up of French West Africa freed the richer Ivory Coast from subsidising the poorer members, whilst the diversion from Senegal of Mali's overseas trade from 1960–63 (some still retained), and of Niger overseas trade from Dahomey between 1963–65 also helped. The European Economic Community, and the Benin–Sahel Entente formed at the suggestion of the Ivory Coast and composed of the Ivory Coast, Upper Volta, Niger, Dahomey and Togo, have greatly benefited Abidjan's port and industries.

On the east side of the canal are the petroleum wharves and depots. Here is a newer industrial area, with an oil refinery, chemical, truck and car assembly works, and many other industries. Still further east is the large airport.

Petit Bassam Island is being joined to the sandbar by new fishing (80 000 tons of fish are landed annually) and general cargo wharves. The main wharves are on the western and northwestern ends of Petit Bassam Island, which is connected by two wide bridges with Abidjan proper. Beyond these wharves is the oldest industrial quarter. Here are the expected processing plants of coffee (Plate 80), cocoa, timber, rubber and fruit, the usual consumer industries of flour, textiles, soap, beer, soft drinks and furniture, but also some quite elaborate electrical and engineering factories, radio and transistor assembly. Farther east is the dominantly Ivoirien quarter of Treichville.

Abidjan proper is spaciously laid out on the mainland between Banco and Cocody bays. The town has some elegant public buildings, notably the town hall and several hotels—one even with an ice rink! Whilst Banco Bay is used for timber floating (Plate 81) and shipping, Cocody Bay is mainly overlooked by hotels, embassies and the very pleasant Cocody suburb. Near here the Club Méditerranée has a base and there

PLATE 79. A view over Abidjan looking south. At the top of the photograph is the sea and the Vridi canal with its oil terminals, and nearby oil refinery. On the western and northwestern sides of Petit Bassam Island are wharves, railway lines, and then Treichville. The road and rail bridge links with the mainland commercial quarter on the left (east), from where there is now a second bridge to Treichville. The rest of the mainland is mainly administrative and residential

PLATE 80. Soluble coffee plant at Treichville, Abidjan

PLATE 81. Timber awaiting shipment at Abidjan

is a project for a 'riviera' residential and tourist complex. As at Dakar, but increasingly so here, there is a large and high-income European community of some 40 000. The population increase of Abidjan since it became the capital in 1934, and since the opening of the Vridi canal in 1950, is witness to its own and the Ivory Coast's prosperity. In 1937 the population was 17 143; in 1946, 46 000; 1955, 125 153; 1959, 185 000; 1966, 360 000, and the built-up area certainly has half a million. The port is West Africa's leading general one in terms of general cargo imported and exported, having overtaken Dakar and Lagos.

*Grand Bassam*, southeast of Abidjan, dates from the earliest days of French contact in 1700, and was the capital from 1893 to 1900. The first wharf operated from 1901–22 and the second from 1922–50; between 1908 and 1931 it was the sole wharf of the Ivory Coast. Grand Bassam has been supplanted by Abidjan's deepwater harbour, but was for long the major shipper of wood, brought along the lagoons. Although Grand Bassam is an old commercial centre, its site is unsatisfactory, and the town has decayed, particularly as it no longer has a wharf.

East of Grand Bassam the smooth sandbar coast has been built up in front of the estuary of the Bia river, now represented by the Aby lagoon, which penetrates farther inland than any other. It was in this region that the earliest French contacts were made.

The fact that Miocene and Pliocene rocks fringe the north side of lagoons east of Fresco, but not west of that point, may be allied with the existence of an offshore hinge line. In any case, 16–19 km (10–12 miles) offshore the continental shelf ends abruptly.

346

Dense forest extends to the lagoons, except from Fresco to the Ghana boundary, where patches of derived scrub savanna occur. These result from early timber cutting on sandy soils and overintensive farming. These poor areas, reminiscent of sandy heaths in temperate lands, are being gradually re-colonised by trees.

## The interior plains and plateaux

These comprise most of the Ivory Coast and are underlain almost entirely by Pre-Cambrian rocks. The most extensive, especially in the west, is granite. Domes are frequent, especially in the northwest, and around them the soil is often more fertile and water occurs readily. Pronounced northeast to southwest warpings are responsible for the gentle undulations.

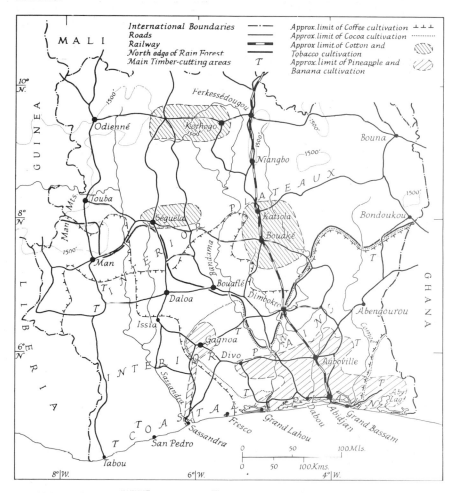

FIG. 22.2. Regions and production areas of the main exports of the Ivory Coast

There are also a number of low hills, composed of the Birrimian series, e.g. the Grabo chain crossed by the Cavally river north-northwest of Tabou, the Baoulé and Korhogo hills. These are usually 200–430 m (650–1 400 ft) high and do not upset the generally low plain and plateau character of most of the country. Birrimian metamorphic schists are found in many places, especially in the east.

It might appear from the foregoing that there is some physical variety in the Ivory Coast, but this is not so. The landscape is remarkably monotonous, the more so through severe laterisation north of 9°N. Some of the laterite has itself undergone surface decomposition to a red clay and is covered by acid (i.e. leached) soil.

The greatest distinguishing factor within the interior plain is the occurrence of rainforest in the south. There, are produced the most significant cash crops—coffee and cocoa (which together account for one-half of the exports by value), bananas, other fruits and oil palm produce. With timber, these account for almost all exports.

Beyond the rainforest are generally lateritic or sandy soils with Guinea derived savanna, broken only by occasional gallery forest or granite domes. Large cattle cannot be kept because of the tsetse fly, there are few cash crops, and the people are poor. This is part of the Middle Belt of West Africa and covers fully one-half of the Ivory Coast.

Significant towns of the forest are Daloa, Gagnoa, Divo, Agboville and Abengourou (the Agni capital). Man, at the foot of the great Man mountains (see below), Dimbokro and Bondoukou are on the fringes of the forest. In the derived savanna are Séguéla and Bouaké.

*Bouaké*, population 102 000 is the second largest town of the Ivory Coast, a great market and route centre, and is served by air, roads and the railway. Northwest of it is a cotton spinning and weaving factory employing over 1 800 people and using local cotton. In Bouaké itself are cigarette and sisal product factories.

*Korhogo* is an ancient focus at the edge of several food crop belts. It is a cotton and food crop market, and an older centre than *Ferkessédougou*, on the railway, which has rather supplanted Korhogo, an administrative centre.

### The Man mountains

These which rise to about 1 220 m (4 000 ft), lie between Man and Odienné, in the northwest, and arc the eastern extremity of the Guinea highlands. Upland rice, maize, guinea corn and cassava are the staple food crops grown in a four to seven year rotation, followed by four to ten years fallow.

# Economic resources

## Agriculture

There are the usual subsistence and export crops, and also non-African (mainly French) plantations of bananas and other crops. They are most numerous around Gagnoa, Divo, Agboville, Abidjan, Lahou, Daloa, Man, Aboisso and Sassandra.

Not only are there these varied techniques of production, but also a greater crop variety than usual. The Ivory Coast includes in the west the rice zone of West Africa, i.e. in western Séguéla, Touba, Daloa, Gagnoa, Man, Grand Lahou and Sassandra districts. Eastward yams become more significant, e.g. around Bouaké. Cassava and plantains are also grown there, together with maize and guinea corn in the centre and north.

### COFFEE

Coffee is a forest crop, particularly in the east and centre, and its cultivation has expanded westwards. The *liberica* variety was first grown by Verdier in 1891 at Elima, by the Aby lagoon. Soon after 1900 the *robusta* and *kouilou* varieties of *C. canephora* were tried, especially near Agboville and Gagnoa. After trouble with a parasite in 1925 the *gros indénié* was widely distributed to African farmers, as being more easily grown. There has been much root disease in coffee trees, particularly those of the *indénié* and *kouilou* varieties, so that *robusta* is now most favoured, a variety very suitable for soluble coffees.

Most coffee is produced in the Dimbokro, Daloa, Abidjan, Gagnoa, Agboville, Abengourou, and Man areas. There are some 650 000 ha (1 606 185 acres) under coffee, of which all but 2 530 ha (6 250 acres) are African owned.

Extension of cultivation and an increase of exports were rapid after 1930, and again in the 1950s when a guaranteed market at high prices was available for large quantities of coffee in France. In consequence, coffee was planted far beyond its ideal areas, and the Ivory Coast became the main African producer and the world's third supplier. An international quota limited sales in the 1960s, and in 1965 the Ivory Coast also lost the high prices for large fixed amounts of coffee in France; on the other hand, she gained preferential entry to the markets of the other five countries of the European Economic Community. Also nearly one-third of the crop is sold to the USA and other countries. Coffee has fallen from occupying a peak of one-half of Ivory Coast exports in 1960 to about one-third, and some coffee farms are being diversified.

### COCOA

Cocoa comprises about one-quarter of all exports by value, though before the Second World War it was the leading export. The country is the only important cocoa producer in francophone West Africa.

Cocoa was introduced from the Gold Coast in 1895, sixteen years after it had arrived there. Cropping was begun in the east by Europeans, but the Forced Agriculture Policy (1912 onwards) of Governor Angoulvant, whereby Africans were compelled to plant specified amounts of cocoa (and other crops) did much more to extend it. Exports mounted rapidly from 1 023 tons in 1920, to 14 515 in 1928, 55 185 in 1939, and 146 000 tons in 1970.

The southeastern districts together produce about half the crop, and lie west of the Ghana cocoa belt. African production accounts for almost all of the total, the very small non-African production being from some 1 825 ha (4 500 acres) on the western and southern fringes of the African areas, which occupy about 330 000 ha (815 450 acres). Compared with coffee, more cocoa is grown on African farms and in the east, where there are good soils derived from schists and basic rocks. Production is about one-fifth that of Ghana. Sales are about equal to the franc zone, the other countries of the European Economic Community, and the USA and other countries.

## BANANAS

First grown for export in 1931, bananas are produced mainly by French planters or companies on concessions totalling about 130 000 ha (321 237 acres), of which about two-thirds are regularly cultivated. Because of the fragile and perishable nature of the product, concessions are mostly near the railway, roads or lagoons in the Aboisso and Abidjan areas and the Agboville district, from which the distance to the port of Abidjan is small. However, there are developing areas around Sassandra, served by the wharf at the latter.

Production has increased remarkably since the opening of Abidjan as a deepwater port in 1950, the introduction in 1956 of the Giant Cavendish or Poyo variety to replace the small Chinese or Canary type (so eliminating costly packing), and the cessation since 1959 of competition from Guinea in the French market. Although, compared with Guinea, the Ivory Coast has a longer sea haul to Europe, its advantages are richer soils, more uniform temperatures and relative humidity, less violent rainfall, more flat damp land, better opportunities for supplementary overhead irrigation, fewer pests, and a more even monthly production. The use of mulching, overhead irrigation, fungicides and fertilisers is widespread, and there is an excellent cooperative organisation for advice, buying supplies in bulk, and marketing. Banana exports comprise some 3 per cent of exports.

## PINEAPPLES

Production trebled in the decade 1961–70, reaching 90 000 tons in the

PLATE 82.  Banana plantation on the Abidjan–Dabou road

PLATE 83.  Pineapple plantation west of Abidjan

later years. Most of the fruit is canned as fruit or juice. About one-tenth of the crop is exported fresh, mainly from the European estates. The main areas are near Divo, Abidjan, Tiassalé, and Grand Bassam. There are cooperatives and canning factories at the latter three towns, the last two having plantations (Plate 83).

## OIL PALM

It has been estimated that there are some 35 million oil palm trees in the Ivory Coast, mainly semi-wild, though there are over 67 000 ha (165 500 acres) of systematic plantations. Production has suffered by competition from the more remunerative and more easily cultivated crops discussed above. In the past the remoter areas had most oil palms because they could not compete in the production of the more remunerative crops. The need to reduce the area of coffee and to plant other crops has led to much planting of oil palms in the coastal sedimentary areas. Old estates and stands are also being revived and replanted. Large palm oil mills operate, e.g. at Dabou and Abidjan, the latter with associated soap production.

## OTHER CROPS

The need for diversification has also led to the encouragement of the pineapple and other fruits (mainly citrus), and of coconuts on the coast. Rubber plantations were started in 1953, and, although exports began in 1961, the policy is now to use the latex locally in tyre manufacture. Kola is significant in some forest areas and the nuts are traded to Mali, and Upper Volta.

Cotton is important in the drier areas of the centre and north, and is grown for hand weaving and for mills near Bouaké, Korhogo and Boundiali. Groundnuts are often intercropped with cotton, and as imports of these crops are also necessary, both are being increasingly grown. Like most West African countries, the Ivory Coast imports substantial quantities of rice and sugar, and the local cultivation of these and tobacco is likewise encouraged. A large sugar factory is scheduled for 1974.

## Forestry

There were probably greater stands of useful timber in the Ivory Coast than in any other West African country, and they are the nearest to Europe. The Ivory Coast is Africa's leading timber exporter, surpassing Ghana and Nigeria combined in weight and value of timber, which comprises about a fifth of Ivory Coast exports. The forest is a high and dense evergreen one on the seaward side, and is best developed in the rainy southeast and southwest. It is more deciduous in character on the drier inward margins, including the drier centre, where the forest narrows south of Dimbokro. The best stands are in thinly populated and rainy country between Man and Sassandra.

In the early years of this century the forced labour policy brought some 15 000 men to timber cutting along the lowest navigable reaches of the rivers and along the lagoons. Logs were floated to Assinie, Grand Lahou and to Grand Bassam, which remained the chief exporters until the Vridi canal was opened in 1950, when much of the timber came to be floated to Abidjan by rivers and the lagoon. This facility, the deepwater port there, the wharf at Sassandra, and roadsteads have helped to achieve a massive increase in exports, especially from western areas around Daloa, Gagnoa, Issia, Sassandra, Béréby and Tabou.

The most important timber, both for logs and sawn wood, is Sipo or Utile (*Entandrophragma utile*), which comprises nearly half the sawn timber by value and weight, and it and Samba or Obeche (*Triplochiton scleroxylon*) account for half the logs by weight and nearly that proportionate value. There are some thirty-five sawmills, of which ten are large, and several plywood, veneer, furniture, box and match factories. On the other hand, a factory using wood from the Umbrella and Silk Cotton trees to make packing paper soon proved uneconomic. About 13 000 men are employed in the timber and wood industries.

The area of rainforests has been more than halved since 1900. Replantings amount to only a tiny fraction of areas cut, so that the forest will disappear if present trends continue.

## Minerals and power

There are alluvial diamond exploitations on the Bou tributary of the Bandama at Tortiya 97 km (60 miles) south of Korhogo, and near Séguéla. Manganese was quarried on a modest scale near Grand Lahou from 1961–71. There is very active prospecting for iron ore, copper, molybdenum and oil. Iron ore may be developed near Man.

Hydroelectric power was first developed on the Bia river in the southeast of the country by two stations at Ayamé, with a total capacity of 50 mw.

A large dam and power station have been partially inaugurated at Kossou on the Bandama, with a capacity of 171 mw. The dam is creating a lake about 140 km (88 miles) long which will extend to Tiassalé and necessitate the resettlement of nearly 80 000 people. The number is identical to those resettled in Ghana following the filling of Lake Volta; the Ivoiriens will mostly be resettled around nearby Yamousoukro. Cultivation of rice, sugar, food crops, fruit and vegetables will be encouraged by irrigation. The price of electricity will be greatly reduced, so further boosting industry in the country.

## Transport

Lagoons were the only natural means of communication, and in 1923 the Asagny canal was opened to link the Ebrié and Lahou lagoons. Barge traffic is quite considerable, the object being to bring logs and other produce toward Abidjan and to distribute bulky imports, such as constructional material.

All other means of communication have been built in the face of great difficulties. The rivers are practically unnavigable, and the great struggles and final triumph in building a deepwater port at Abidjan have been described. The rainforest, another great obstacle, was overcome only by the opening of the railway as far as Dimbokro in 1909, and Bouaké in 1912. Bobo Dioulasso became the terminus in 1934, so making a line of 813 km (505 miles). In 1954 a further extension to Ouagadougou was opened, making a grand total of 1 144 km (711 miles) of rail artery from Abidjan through the Ivory Coast and Upper Volta. Fast diesel rail cars operate between Abidjan and Bouaké, and most of the passenger and goods traffic originates between these towns.

Roads were built during the First World War, and the country is now well provided with them. Those serving the timber concessions, others from Man and Séguéla to the railway, and the international roads have also been much improved in recent years, especially into the Upper Volta, Mali and Guinea.

Abidjan has air services to Europe, and local ones along the coast and inland to five centres. Few, if any, countries in West Africa were so isolated by hostile coast, useless rivers and dense forest. Even the lagoons could not be used to reach the interior. Yet no land has been so much changed by man's communications; the Vridi canal and Abidjan's first road and rail bridge rank among the engineering marvels of Africa.

## Conclusion

The Ivory Coast should have a great economic future. Already its resources are varied, and the range can be increased by extending the number of raw products (especially if more minerals could be developed) and through even more industries. Though Dakar has a strategic site, Abidjan has much the richer hinterland, and is the political and economic heart of the Benin–Sahel Entente grouping Togo, Dahomey, Niger and the Upper Volta with the Ivory Coast.

The Ivory Coast is a major world producer of coffee, and the leading one in Africa. It is the third world producer of pineapples, the fourth of cocoa, the sixth of bananas, and a leading African producer of timber. For its size of population and area, and in terms of foreign trade, the Ivory Coast is the most productive country in West Africa. Unfortunately, much of its wealth leaves the country, and prosperity is highly localised in the south (especially in Abidjan) and amongst the élite.

# 23

# Ghana: land of cocoa and minerals

Ghana is one of the most developed countries of tropical Africa. Gold has been won for many centuries, it is the world's largest producer of cocoa and the third world producer of diamonds by weight, all of which help to explain its relatively high standard of living, national revenue and expenditure.

These material advantages, combined with an older and more developed educational system than that of any other similar country in Africa, quickened Ghana's path to independence. This is a fine achievement for a relatively small country of only 238 537 sq km (92 100 sq miles), approximately the equivalent of Great Britain, and with only some 9 million people. Within this relatively small area almost all the wealth and revenue derives from only about one-quarter the total area.

## Historical outline

The original inhabitants may have been pygmies who used stone implements, made pottery and lived on elevated sites in the forests. The ancestors of the present Akan peoples probably arrived in the thirteenth to seventeenth centuries, after the successive decline of the Ghana, Mali and Songhaï Empires. It is likely that they came in periodic invasions from the northwest, as well as by a much smaller movement along the coast from the east. Some or all of them came with knowledge of metal smelting, since traces of old iron smelting ovens are widespread, brass was in common use, and gold dust served as currency until the introduction of coins by Europeans.

The first completely authenticated landing by Europeans upon the coast was in 1470–71 by a Portuguese. By the papal award under the Treaty of Tordesillas, 1494, the Portuguese were granted a monopoly of trade in Africa. Other nations and traders disregarded this monopoly and the first known English voyage was in 1553. The Dutch came by 1595, the Swedes about 1640 (just before the Dutch expelled the Portuguese in 1642), the Danes soon after and the Brandenburgers in 1683.

Castles were built as quarters, the first being that constructed at Elmina in 1481–82 by the Portuguese. This magnificent structure is excellently preserved and is now used as a police training depot. Most castles were, however, built in the seventeenth century at the height of the slave trade. Slaves were kept in the castle dungeons, later to be led out on to the beaches to start their tragic journeys to the New World. In the castles were also stored other articles of trade—exports of gold, ivory and spices and imports of guns, cloths and ornaments. Merchants lived on upper floors.

Until about the mid-nineteenth century Europeans scarcely penetrated the interior, contenting themselves with trading through their forts. The English companies traded from 1618 to 1820 under Charter or Act of Parliament, sometimes with financial grants from the British Government. Founded in 1750 with a government subsidy of £13 000, the African Company of Merchants, open to all British traders, was the governing body until 1820, and had its headquarters at Cape Coast Castle.

By 1820 the trading position of the company had weakened through the suppression of the slave trade and by attacks from the Ashanti. It was, therefore, dissolved and all assets and administration passed to the Crown, exercised by the Governor of Sierra Leone. This distant arrangement continued until 1874, with two breaks. From 1828 to 1843 an arrangement rather similar to the earlier one prevailed, whereby the Committee of African Merchants was responsible, through their celebrated Governor George Maclean. After another period of Crown rule from Sierra Leone for seven years, the Gold Coast became a distinct dependency between 1850 and 1866. Thereafter Sierra Leone was again the headquarters for eight years, the Gold Coast finally becoming a separate colony in 1874.

There were seven Ashanti attacks on coastal peoples and their British allies in the nineteenth century and ultimately Ashanti was annexed in 1901. In the same year the Northern Territories became a Protectorate, having come under British influence in 1897.

Only the English, Danes and Dutch survived into the eighteenth and nineteenth centuries. During the nineteenth century, especially in the first three-quarters, the trading outlook was bleak. The African Company of Merchants was wound up in 1820, the Danes withdrew in 1850 and the Dutch in 1872; British withdrawal nearly occurred. The cruel but lucrative slave trade had gone, but palm oil did not become important until the last quarter, when modern methods of gold mining also encouraged new hopes. Cocoa, introduced in 1879, did not become the leading export until 1924.

Although cocoa so largely sustains the modern economy, gold, diamonds, manganese, bauxite, timber and aluminium are significant items. There is thus a more diversified economy than is often the case in Africa, though the production of other products is being encouraged.

In 1922 a landlocked portion of former German Togoland was put under British Mandate, which became a Trusteeship in 1946. In consequence of a plebiscite in 1956 it became an integral part of Ghana when the latter became independent in 1957.

Ghana owes much to Sir Gordon Guggisberg, Governor from 1919 to 1927. It was he who had the eastern railway completed, the central line begun, the magnificent Achimota School established, and the first port of Takoradi constructed.

Since independence there have been successes and failures. Independence brought a spurt of initiative which led to a great expansion in industry, road building, schools and hospitals. However, many state farm and industrial enterprises were started which were not efficient, cocoa prices fell in general, the population has grown rapidly, and food imports—even of non-essentials like tinned sardines—were heavy. Dr Nkrumah was responsible for most of these successes and the many failures. The Volta dam, which he inaugurated just before he was deposed, can be regarded as due to his insistence. When aluminium is made from Ghana's bauxite, and not just from imported alumina, Volta power may do more to increase development and diversify the economy. Meanwhile, Ghana has fallen behind the Ivory Coast in many aspects of development.

# Population

Distribution of Ghana's population[1] is shown in Table 23.1:

TABLE 23.1. *Population distribution in Ghana*

| Region | Per cent of Ghana area | Population 1970 | Per cent of Ghana population | Population per sq km | Population per sq mile |
|---|---|---|---|---|---|
| Western | 10·3 | 768 312 | 9·0 | 32 | 83 |
| Central | 4·0 | 892 593 | 10·4 | 90 | 234 |
| Greater Accra | 1·1 | 848 825 | 9·9 | 330 | 853 |
| Eastern | 8·4 | 1 262 882 | 14·8 | 63 | 164 |
| Volta | 8·7 | 947 012 | 11·1 | 46 | 119 |
| Ashanti | 10·5 | 1 477 397 | 17·3 | 61 | 157 |
| Brong-Ahafo | 16·2 | 762 673 | 8·9 | 19 | 50 |
| Northern | 29·4 | 728 572 | 8·5 | 10 | 27 |
| Upper | 11·4 | 857 295 | 10·0 | 31 | 81 |
| Total Ghana | 100·0 | 8 545 561 | 100·0 | 36 | 93 |

The Eastern and Western regions were created before independence, and the Central region afterwards. Small areas on the eastern side of the Eastern region and west of the Volta river have been incorporated in the Volta region. The Ashanti region comprises the southern half of the Ashanti of the Gold Coast, and is the historic core of Ashanti. Brong-Ahafo region, created in 1959, incorporates lands conquered in the past by the Ashanti in the Wenchi, Sunyani and Goaso districts, together with the Yeji and Prang areas of the former Northern Territories. The

Northern and Upper regions are otherwise the successors of these. The Volta region includes all the areas of the former United Kingdom Trusteeship of Togoland from the Krachi district southwards, plus certain areas inhabited by Ewe people around the Volta delta formerly in the Eastern region.

Over two-fifths of the population of Ghana live in the southern quarter of the country in the Western, Central and Eastern regions, and Greater Accra. If these be added to well-populated Ashanti, then over three-fifths the population of Ghana lives in one-third its area. By contrast, in the

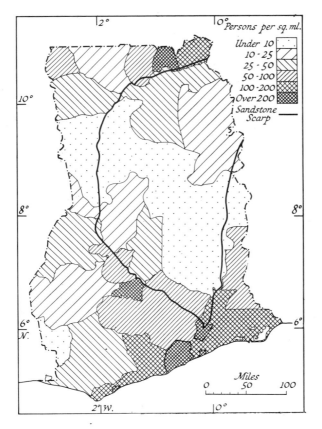

FIG. 23.1. Density of population in Ghana (1960)

Northern and Upper regions, two-fifths of the country, live only a fifth of Ghana's peoples, despite the existence of dense clusters of poor people in the extreme northeast. The Volta region has both the characteristics of the well populated south in its southern districts, and those of thinly populated central Ghana in its north, whilst Brong-Ahafo is thinly populated especially in the centre and east.

The greater concentration of population in the south may be explained as follows:

(*a*) Many areas are suitable for cocoa cultivation and it was here that cocoa cultivation commenced.
(*b*) Most mining is carried on here.
(*c*) This area has been longest in contact with the outside world.
(*d*) It contains Accra (the capital and by far the largest town), Tema, Takoradi-Sekondi, and the densest network of communications.

By contrast, the low density of population in central and eastern Brong-Ahafo and in the Northern region is largely caused by the occurrence of the infertile Voltaian Sandstone. Water is scarce in the dry season, floods abound in the wet one, tsetse is rife, few minerals occur and none are exploited, cocoa can rarely be grown except on the southern fringes, and the area is rather isolated.

Yet remoteness does not necessarily exclude high population densities. The extreme north of the Upper region lies beyond the infertile Voltaian Sandstone and has better soils derived from crystalline rocks. Water is more easily found, though there are only 1 015–1 270 mm (40–50 in) of rainfall annually in one season. Population pressure is acute in most of Zuarungu, and many Fra-Fra males must seek work in the south. These areas of high population density and poverty are extensions into Ghana of similar areas in the Upper Volta, where these problems are even more acute.

Although the soils of the far north of the Upper region are fairly fertile, they are thin and much eroded where there are great population densities, as in Mamprusi. The Tumu subdistrict of the Upper region and the Bole subdistrict of the Northern are less densely peopled. Bole district was depopulated by Ashanti warfare and slave raiding, and then emptied by the tsetse fly; given control of tsetse it is an area of potential resettlement.

Areas for potential settlement lie mainly in the west of the Brong-Ahafo and Western regions, towards which cocoa cultivation and settlement are extending. On the other hand, the rapid development of Tema and especially its industries may arrest or reverse that tendency, by bringing people into the sparsely populated Lower Volta plains. Lake Volta behind the Akosombo dam has required the resettlement of some 78 000 people from poor areas of the Voltaian basin to rather better districts on the lake margins. The west of the Northern and Upper regions are areas of modest potential for resettlement.

Cocoa-farming, mining, power development, a developing aluminium industry and the second port all continue to increase the attraction of population from the overpopulated districts of the Upper and Northern regions, the Upper Volta and beyond. Tema has attracted far more people than expected, and is growing very rapidly indeed.

## Climate

There is greater variety of climate in Ghana than in most West African countries.[2] Rainfall diminishes from the very wet southwest, where there are two rainfall maxima, towards the northeast, where there is only one. But there is also an extremely dry area in the southeast which, nevertheless, has two rainfall maxima.

Four climatic regions are commonly distinguished.

### Southwestern equatorial

Annual rainfall varies from over 2 030 mm (80 in) in the extreme southwest to 1 460–1 525 mm (55–60 in) on the other margins. Rainfall is least variable behind Axim, and wherever there is over 1 780 mm (70 in) rainforest predominates. This is an important timber producing area, which is also well suited to rice cultivation.

In the rest of the area, where annual rainfall is approximately 1 400–1 780 mm (55–70 in), it is the ideal habitat not only for valuable forest trees but also for cocoa, especially where the rainfall is over sixty inches.

### Semiseasonal equatorial

Although rainfall may be greater than at many places in the previous zone, there are normally two relatively dry months when vegetative growth may be halted. The forest was, therefore, less vigorous and dense, especially as the northeastern part is on poor Voltaian Sandstone soils.

### Seasonal equatorial

Rainfall is under 1 270 mm (50 in) north of a line roughly through Techiman and Yeji. Bole and Salaga both have just over 1 040 mm (41 in) of rain, with two maxima and four relatively dry months.

### Southern savanna

All stations, north of approximately the latitude of Tamale, have a single rainfall maximum and a drought of four to six months. Yet, as in the Ivory Coast, rainfall totals may be rather higher than a little farther south. As one would expect from the direction of the rain-bearing winds and the higher relief, stations along much of the northwestern border are a little wetter.

Nevertheless, the vital point is that the effective rainfall is far less and the variability much greater than in the equatorial zone and, wherever sandstone occurs, percolation is usually rapid. Water is almost everywhere a problem and relative humidity may drop to under 10 per cent in dry season afternoons at Tamale. It is understandable, therefore, that population densities tend to be greater on the more impermeable 'granite soils' of northern Mamprusi and Lawra. (See also Chapter 3.)

## Geology, relief and natural regions

Ghana is divisible geologically and geographically into contrasted regions. The northern and western fringes, together with the southwestern third of the country, consist of Pre-Cambrian rocks with granite and other intrusive formations. Their trend lines are predominantly northeast to southwest, except in the far northwest, where they are north–south. In all cases the relief is in close accord with these trends.

Along the northern and northwestern borders, and as far south as beyond Bole, the country is floored mainly by granite, with Birrimian series occurring along the boundary with the Voltaian basin and in the Bolgatanga–Zuarungu district. West and northwest of Wa and through Lawra to the northern boundary, the Upper Birrimian occurs.

South of Bole, in Ashanti and in the Western, Central and Eastern regions, Upper and Lower Birrimian, the Tarkwaian, granite and other intrusives occur frequently. In the southeast and on the east-centre boundary are found the Akwapimian and Buem series of the Akwapim hills and Togo mountains.

Northwest of these is the largest feature of all—the Voltaian basin, filled with Primary sandstones. It occupies northern Ashanti and the southern and central Northern region. Except on the southern edge, it is infertile, has no important minerals and yields little water. It is also rather featureless, except where its upturned edges form the magnificent Mampong, Wenchi, Konkori and Gambaga scarps (Plate 1).

There are small outcrops of marine-Devonian rocks at Accra, of Carboniferous or Devonian ones east of Axim, while Upper Cretaceous rocks occur westward from Axim.

Southeast of the Akwapim and Togo mountains are Archaean and granite rocks, deeply covered southeastwards by Tertiary and Quaternary sands in the Volta delta.

The explosive caldera or meteoric scar of Lake Bosumtwi probably dates from early Pleistocene times.

### Lower Volta plains

Southeast of the Akwapim–Togo mountains are plains floored by Archaean gneisses and schists, with granite intrusions. This area was partially drowned by Tertiary and Quaternary seas. Thus crystalline rocks which floor the plains are masked seaward by up to 18 m (60 ft) of marine and fluviatile sands, gravels, silts and clays. Raised beaches are further evidence of the progressive retreat of the sea and the Volta delta is a good example of deltaic formations.

Accra may be taken as nearly the western limit of these plains which, as the *Terre de Barre*, extend eastward into Togo and Dahomey. The Lower Volta plains are gently undulating, by no means uniform, and there is evidence of several peneplanations in numerous inselbergs and ridges. Wide and rather ill-defined valleys of seasonal rivers cross the plains. Soils are poor, except for the *Terre de Barre* clays, the alluvial soils along the Volta river, and loamy soils around freshwater lagoons.

The Lower Volta plains may be subdivided as follows.[3]

## (*a*) THE COASTAL AND LAGOON LOWLANDS

These lowlands have loose Quaternary sands and are devoid of inselbergs. Bluffs end eastward at Old Nugo, east of which former exits of the Volta river may be deduced. Lagoons are numerous, the Avu and Ke almost alone having freshwater.

Rainfall averages only 635–760 mm (25–30 in) on about forty to fifty days. Along the sea shore sedges, herbs, creepers and grasses occur with planted coconuts. Nutritious grasses grow best around the freshwater lagoons and provide fairly good pasture. Around the saline lagoons, and for a mile up the Volta river, are stunted mangroves.

Fishing here and on adjacent coasts is the most important occupation. Herrings, horse mackerel and other fish are smoked by women, who find a good market for them in Accra and inland. There is also some lagoon and river fishing. Salt is obtained by evaporation in the lagoons, for local use and for sale.

Other than fishing, cattle rearing is most important. Again there is a ready market in Accra, the country is predominantly grassland, and the tsetse fly is almost absent. Nevertheless, small West African Shorthorns are kept because they are very resistant to disease and because of tradition. They are most numerous northwest and northeast of the Keta lagoon and around the small freshwater lagoons. Sheep are found mainly east of the Volta. Goats, pigs and poultry are common near the lagoons, where they are kept under coconut trees.

These lowlands are fairly productive, especially round the Keta lagoon, and their economy is more varied than that of most of the Lower Volta plains. Other than fishing and stock-keeping, there is intensive cropping of vegetables, cassava and maize, the latter despite the sandy soils and dry climate. The chief producing areas are between the sea and the Keta lagoon, where porous sandy marine soils meet the heavier ones of the lagoon, and the grasslands north of the lagoons, again with loamy soils and with over 890 mm (35 in) of rain annually.

When cassava is grown in light sandy soils, the product is tough and reddish in colour, starchy and sticky when boiled. Hence it is fed to

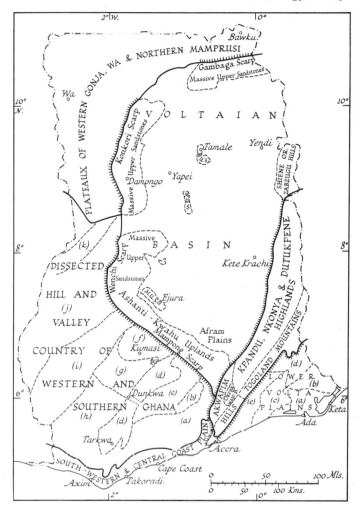

FIG. 23.2. Natural regions of Ghana

The italic letters of subregions refer to names in the text

animals, used as fish bait, or converted into garri, starch and tapioca. The best cooking cassava and sweet potatoes are grown in deeper loamy soils around the freshwater lagoons.

Vegetables are grown for sale in Accra and Lomé. Onions and shallots are intensively grown in great numbers on the edge of the lagoon between Anloga and Keta. Maize, tomatoes and okro are also planted here, and groundnuts and lima beans in drier sandy areas.

*Keta,* is an important market, especially for cotton cloth woven around Keta lagoon, for fish, salt and onions. There normally is much traffic to and from Lomé and Accra. The town has suffered severely in the past from wars and from sea erosion. Much of it is now built on land

363

reclaimed from the lagoon.

*Ada,* or *Ada Fua*, lies west of the Volta mouth and was established by Europeans as a commercial centre near the Chief's town of *Big Ada,* now much smaller in size. When trade up and down the Volta was important, Ada Fua was far more significant.

### (b) THE TERRE DE BARRE

Northeast of the Keta lagoon, the Terre de Barre has red clays derived from Eocene formations, extending towards the Volta river from Togo and Dahomey (*q.v.*). As in those countries, they are well planted with oil palm and maize, and are more densely settled than other parts of the Lower Volta plains.

### (c) THE BLACK CLAY BELTS

This belt results from the weathering of gneiss. Extending northeast from Prampram to beyond the Volta, this area has very poor vegetation and is virtually empty. 'Shortage of water prevents settlement or stock raising and the cultivators, with their present equipment, are unable to till the intractable clays. . . . Communications are unusually bad, as only a slight shower will render the motor tracks impassable.'[4]

### (d) THE SOUTHERN VOLTA AND TRANS-VOLTA PLAINS

These are geologically akin to the Accra plains, but have about 1 270 mm (50 in) annual rainfall on 100 rain days. Rainfall is more reliable, grass is taller, Borassus and oil palms and even forest trees occur in valleys and along the edge of the Togo hills. Yet the soils are thin and cultivation is confined to broad basins with deeper soils. Yams and cotton (formerly much more important for the weaving of 'Kente' or 'Keta Cloth') are

PLATE 84. Weeding shallot beds, Anloga

still significant in a belt of country 8–16 km (5–10 miles) wide, extending 81 km (50 miles) from west to east in the centre. Forest crops are grown on the northern fringes. The tsetse occurs and few animals are kept.

## (e) THE ACCRA PLAIN

The Accra plain[5] lies west and southeast of the Black Clay Belt. The plain is low and has long spurs and outliers of the Akwapim hills.

Rainfall is only about 760–1 140 mm (30–45 in) annually, on some seventy rain days. With such low and often erratic rainfall, and with mainly porous sandy soils, the vegetation is Scrub and Grassland. Low deciduous trees and bushes occur along intermittent streams. *Elaeophorbia drupifera, Antiaris africana* and Baobabs (*Adansonia digitata*), are common. Grazing is poor, except near Achimota, and yields of cassava, maize and vegetables are low.

*Dodowa,* an old halfway halt on the overland route from Akuse to Accra, is a market between the forested Akwapim hills and the dry plains.

*Tema*, is Ghana's most modern port,[6] specially equipped for the rapid handling of cocoa, but also important for general import cargo, and it has a developing fishing fleet. There are numerous and diverse industries, especially an aluminium smelter, oil refinery, a cement works and a small steel works, cocoa processing and many consumer goods industries. The town is planned on garden city lines, and has notable public buildings and social facilities.[7]

Almost everywhere in the Lower Volta plains water is scarce and restricts settlement, stock-keeping and crop-farming. Water is generally 12–37 m (40–120 ft) down, but nearer the surface near the Akwapim–Togo mountains, and around outliers and inselbergs. Settlements tend to concentrate in these places, around freshwater lagoons, along the Volta and other (mainly intermittent) rivers, along the Accra water pipelines, roads and the sea. In the latter case the villages may be only temporary. Permanent villages rarely have over 500 inhabitants.

The Lower Volta plains are a fascinating field for the historical geographer and economic historian. The Danes took Christiansborg from the Swedes in 1659 and built subsidiary forts at Ningo, Ada and Keta in 1784, and in Teshi in 1787. Slaves were brought down the Volta river from the collecting centres of Yapei (Tamale Port), Kete Krachi and Yendi.

But the Danes were the first nation to abolish the slave trade, doing so in 1792. This undermined Danish trade, as other nations continued the traffic. Moreover, Danish trade in palm oil from the forests, ivory from Kete Krachi, hides and skins from Yapei down the Volta to the forts was less than that of other merchants farther west. The Danes sold

PLATE 85. Africa's most extensive harbour at Tema, Ghana, opened in 1962. On the extreme top right (west) are two large cocoa sheds which can deliver 1 000 tons of bagged cocoa per hour direct to holds of ships at Quay 1 to their left. Beyond is the general and passenger quay. At the land end of the eastern breakwater (centre) are slipways, a dry dock and a fitting-out quay (which projects west), and at the sea end of the breakwater is the oil berth. Fishing and naval harbours are east again at the left base of the photo

PLATE 86. Aluminium ingots from Tema smelter

PLATE 87. Bus and coach assembly at Tema

their forts to the British in 1850 and their economic significance continued to diminish.

Trade down the Volta and through this coast declined even more sharply when cocoa cultivation further activated areas to the west. The opening of the Accra–Kumasi railway in stages between 1910 and 1924 channelled cocoa export by rail first through Accra and later through Takoradi.

A revival is now at hand. The new port of Tema has created a new market for meat, fish and vegetables. With Accra, there is an almost continuous conurbation of 800 000. If irrigation is brought to these plains agriculture may be more productive, but the Accra plains are exceedingly poor and not worth costly or extensive irrigation, which might be more advantageously directed to the coastal and lagoon lowlands.

*Accra,* capital of Ghana, lies in a very small basin of the Akwapimian series which has been infilled with sandstone, grits, mudstones and shales of mid-Devonian age.

Fairly frequent earthquakes make this site unfortunate for a capital. Major shocks since 1858 have occurred in 1862, 1906 and 1939; and lesser ones in 1863, 1883, 1907, 1911, 1918–19, 1923, 1925, 1930, 1933–35 and 1953. The tremor of 1862 almost completely destroyed Accra and was severe east of the town, a fact of significance to Tema harbour. Every stone building in Accra was razed to he ground and Christiansborg castle and the Accra forts were rendered uninhabitable. Some quarters of the town were almost completely ruined. In 1906 many government buildings were cracked and the castles and forts again damaged. In 1911 Lomé wharf was destroyed by a tidal wave occasioned by a sea earthquake. In 1939 sixteen people were killed, 133 injured and hundreds of thousands of pounds worth of damage was done to buildings. These earthquake shocks probably come from the base of long steep slopes of an offshore deep. There is also an unstable zone along the Akwapim–Togo range as far as Atakpamé, which could affect the Akosombo dam.

The Ga people came to the Accra area by canoe or along the beach from Nigeria in the sixteenth century, making their first capital at Ayawaso, on an outlier of the Akwapim hills, northwest of Accra.[8] In the first part of the seventeenth century a settlement was started east of Korle lagoon and towards the sea, where there were better possibilities for trade with the Portuguese. The Dutch later became supreme, and in 1650 built Fort Crévecœur (now Ussher Fort) to replace an earlier lodge. In 1673 the English built Fort James, by the present breakwater. Both forts are now prisons.

The seventeenth century town was between these forts (only 457 m 1 500 ft) from each other) and the lagoon. Sites of the slave markets may still be seen, and Ussher Town and James Town are the modern names of these oldest and most overcrowded parts of Accra. Three miles to the east was Christiansborg (Osu), the Danish headquarters from 1659. Walls of its slave market still remain and the castle is now the offices of the head of state.

Although Accra was (and still is) the capital of the Ga people, the economic significance of its three forts—Dutch, English and Danish— was not so great as of forts to the west, where gold and slaves were more readily obtained, or of Ada farther east. Nevertheless, in the latter half of the eighteenth century the Fanti introduced the art of sea fishing and this increased local trade.

When the slave trade as abolished, 'legitimate' trade through Accra was maintained, as forest products were brought there more easily than to the Volta mouth. In 1850 the Danes sold Christiansborg and their other castles to the British. The Dutch sold Crévecœur in 1867 and remaining castles in 1872. In 1876 the capital was transferred here from Cape Coast Castle, which had, until then, been the chief British fort. With the Danes and Dutch eliminated at both towns, Accra was felt to be more suitable as a capital, because animals could be used here for transport.

Victoriaborg, between Ussher Town and Christiansborg and behind cliffs where there is always a breeze, was begun as a European residential quarter. Until the era of cars it retained this character, which it has now lost to that of government and to being part of the central business district. The Ridge and the Cantonments, northeast of Victoriaborg, are now better residential areas.

The railway from Accra was begun in 1909 and opened to Pakro in 1911, Koforidua in 1912, Tafo and Kumasi in 1923. Until Takoradi was opened in 1928, Accra was the chief exporter of cocoa, and this more than anything else led to rapid growth. In 1891 the population was 16 267; in 1901, 26 622; in 1911, 29 602; and in 1921, 42 803, a figure raised by the inclusion of Labadi and twenty-six villages. These villages were included in and after 1921 because they were served by piped water, first provided in Accra in 1915, and another powerful attractor of popula- tion to Accra.

The governorship of Sir Frederick Gordon Guggisberg saw the opening of Korle Bu Hospital and the bridging of Korle Bu lagoon in 1923, so enabling suburbs to be built west of it. In 1925 Achimota school, north of Accra, was opened. Construction of hospital and school brought in workers, and Korle Gono was planned and settled southwest of the bridged lagoon. Houses also spread northward along the road to Achimota, taking in Adabraka, formerly a separate Muslim village. In 1931 the population was 60 726 and in 1948 135 926, of whom only 54 per cent were born there. The 1970 figure was 633 880.

Development since 1931 has been more the consequence of the general development of Ghana, as Takoradi and Tema now ship all the cocoa. Yet Accra is the greatest administrative, and commercial centre, as well as having considerable industry. It has an excellent airport, served by many airlines. Although ocean vessels had to anchor half a mile out, it was Ghana's second port until 1962, handling some 400 000 tons annually through its jetty (protected to the west by a breakwater) and surfboats. There is still a submarine pipeline, which enables tankers anchored off-shore to discharge oil into tanks in Accra. Many men are engaged in fishing.

The overwhelming importance of Accra is somewhat remarkable, as Takoradi might have been expected to rival it in size; such is the case in Dahomey, with Cotonou the port and Porto-Novo the capital. Kumasi might also have been more of a competitor with Accra had Tema not been built.

Tema has supplanted Accra as a port. Industrial and commercial functions may also be restricted in Accra, but the administrative and cultural rôles will remain. Accra forms part of an urban area of some 800 000 people, so rivalling Dakar and Ibadan. Like the latter, and so many other West African cities, it lacks cohesion and has suffered from uncoordinated though impressive development.

### The Akwapim–Togo mountains

These mountains begin as prominent hills west and northwest of Accra; a fault near Senya Beraku on the coast is believed to have caused their termination there. They trend northeastward across Togo and northern Dahomey, where they straddle the Niger river. In northern Togo and Dahomey they are known as the Atacora mountains.

Overfolding and thrusting from the southeast, with consequential thrustfaulting and shearing, have caused the very abrupt edges to these ranges which average only about 300–460 m (1 000–1 500 ft) in height. Synclines and anticlines correspond closely with downfolds and upfolds, the regional dip of the rocks being southeastward. Earthquake shocks were recorded in 1906, 1930, 1933 and 1939 and, as the Volta dam and hydroelectric power station are in the Volta gorge, it is obvious that earthtremors from faultslipping are a menace. The gorge separates the Akwapim hills to the southwest from the Togo mountains to the northeast.

These ranges are composed of the Akwapimian (or Togo–Atacora) series on the east and the Buem series on the west, both of younger Pre-Cambrian age. In the Akwapimian series, schists are very common, metamorphism has converted some sandstones into quartzites and silicified limestone occurs. Yet unaltered sandstone is widespread. There are also intrusive rocks, although granite is only locally important in the southeast. The quartzite series occur in long, narrow, tightly folded ranges adjacent to the Archaean shield rocks to the southeast. On the west, the Buem group consist of calcareous, argillaceous, sandy and ferruginous shales much more easily weathered.

369

AKWAPIM HILLS. These hills or low mountains, begin southwest of Accra, as two simple masses, separated by the Densu gap, which shows evidence of drainage diversion. North of another gap, Kokoasi, used by the Accra–Kumasi railway, are two parallel ranges. On the east is a continuous, narrow, steep-edged range, preserved because it is composed of resistant white quartzite and of a band of granite on its eastern edge. This eastern range is also sheltered from the full force of the rain-bearing winds and has narrow valleys. By contrast, to the west is a lower, more dissected but wider belt of rounded hills of the Buem shales. Many hills have been isolated in the west but few in the east.

Northeast of Adawso, on the Akropong–Mangoase road, erosion has proceeded so far in the western range and between it and the eastern one, as to produce the Okrakwajo basin. In all probability, the many headwaters of the Pawmpawm have worked on faults and flexures in this zone, near to the Voltaian series on the northwest.

THE TOGO MOUNTAINS. These are higher than the Akwapim hills and have wider valleys; indeed, the Tsawe and its tributaries have cut down to the underlying Archaean rocks. To the west of the Togo mountains are the north–south trending Kpandu, Nkonya and Dutukpene highlands.

Annual rainfall averages 1 400 mm (55 in) on the western range of the Akwapim hills and 1 140 mm (45 in) on the eastern one, but reaches 1 400–1 800 mm (55–70 in) in the Togo mountains and the several highlands to their west and north. Valleys have some 255 mm (10 in) less rain. The western ranges are forested and cocoa is grown, as well as the usual forest food crops, as well as yams and upland rice.

The Krobo, whose original home was in the dry Accra plains and have tended to migrate northeastwards into the forest lands of Akwapim, are well-known growers of food crops for cash in the Akwapim hills and the Okrakwajo basin. Their peculiar method of land purchase has given rise to a strip system of farming known as *huza*.

It was in the Akwapim hills that cocoa was first planted in 1879, and came to replace the oil palm as a cash crop. However, the soils are thin, and there has been much soil deterioration as well as severe swollen shoot in the cocoa. New Juaben has the highest population density of any rural area in Ghana, and in an extremely small area. The very small farms now perforce produce food crops rather than the far more remunerative cocoa.

The Togo mountains lie mainly within the Ho district of the Volta region. *Ho* lies at the foot of the Togo mountains where they adjoin the southern Volta plains of the Lower Volta. It is a notable route centre and collecting point for cocoa. *Hohoe* and *Kpandu* are other centres. The fact that there are significantly more males than females tends to substantiate the westward movement of Ewe from Togo, at least in the past.

## The Voltaian basin

This great syncline, infilled with Ordovician, Silurian or Devonian flat bedded sandstone series is mostly 90–180 m (300–600 ft) in elevation. However, it has upturned edges which produce vivid scarps, notably the Mampong scarp in the south averaging 610–670 m (2 000–2 200 ft) between Koforidua and Mampong, with flat topped residuals rising higher. Between Mampong and Techiman the scarp is lower but reaches about 550 m (1 800 ft) near Wenchi. The highest point on the Gambaga scarp (Plate 1) is 518 m (1 700 ft).[9]

These scarp edges are composed of massive Upper Sandstones of mudstone, shale and arkose, with beds of conglomerate and sandstone. These wear down to better soils than those in the centre of the basin, and water supplies are also superior. These margins are the most cultivated and populated parts of the basin.

The Ashanti and Kwahu uplands east of the Mampong scarp are the most favoured, cocoa can be grown near the scarp, and in every way the uplands are more akin, except geologically and pedalogically, with the regions to the south. There are also modest bauxite deposits near Mpraeso.

The basin occupies some 103 600 sq km (40 000 sq miles) and is drained by parts of the Volta rivers and their tributaries, partly submerged by the artificial Lake Volta which occupies nearly one-tenth of the basin. The basin also extends into northern Togo, then along the Dahomey–Upper Volta boundary, and just enters Niger. In Ghana the basin occupies nearly one-half of the country, yet it has no more than one-sixth the population. Moreover, most of its peoples live on the better southwestern, western and northern fringes, so that the remaining four-tenths of Ghana has only one-tenth the population.

Not only are soils both poor and not easily improved, and water scarce, major problems to those resettled from lands flooded by Lake Volta, but the desiccating Harmattan penetrates strongly and the vegetation is poor Guinea savanna. Flyborne and other diseases are widespread. Minerals are also few and unexploited.

However, all is not negative. Ghana must grow more of its food and the basin is being more cultivated, mainly for food crops such as yams, pulses and rice. The latter is a suitable crop in certain areas of alluvial soil adjacent to Lake Volta, and where irrigation may be developed. Tobacco is encouraged by a manufacturing company and the crop is tolerant of poor sandy soil.

Some 78 000 people from 15 000 homes and 740 villages have been resettled from the areas covered by Lake Volta. Most are regrouped in over fifty new settlements, varying in size from a few hundred to several thousand inhabitants. The only town to be much affected was Kete Krachi, which has been rebuilt on a new site and is a waterway port.

Each new settlement has a planned location and layout, sewage disposal

371

and piped water, although water supplies have been understandably difficult. Care was taken to ensure that people were grouped with those with whom they had some affinity. There are new main and access roads and, for some of the settlements, the prospect of better farming, fishing and trade on the waterway. For all there are new homes, with the chance to enlarge those provided free by the government, land, advice on methods of cultivation and the crops to be grown. Although many mistakes were made, partly because of the short time available for resettlement, the long-term prospects are better for some than they were in this hitherto poor and secluded region.

*Tamale* is by far the largest town of the Voltaian basin and lies in a peopled but poor area. Around the town there are signs of soil exhaustion and population pressure, not found elsewhere in the basin. Tamale is the headquarters of the Northern region and a significant commercial and transport centre.

### The mainly granite plateaux of western Gonja, Wa and northern Mamprusi

This area corresponds to the interior plateaux of the Ivory Coast. Apart from predominant granite, these areas have Birrimian rocks in central Mamprusi along the fringes of the Voltaian basin and the western border in Wa. The country averages 183–366 m (600–1 200 ft) in elevation, is gently rolling with north–south trending hills in the west through Wa to Bole and south from Tumu. Residual granite domes and bare rock are frequent, as they are across the border in the Upper Volta.

Granite and the other rocks wear down to better (though still thin) soils than do the Voltaian sandstones. Rainfall is rather higher than farther south and this, combined with the greater impermeability of the rocks and more fertile soils, makes for better conditions for farming.

Population is, in fact, generally far greater on the 'granite soils' than on the sandstone ones, though slave raiding, warfare and tsetse have de-populated some relatively fertile areas, such as Bole in western Gonja.

There is population pressure in Zuarungu, where there is much poverty and over 230 people per sq km (600 per sq mile). But with tsetse and simulium fly control,[10] less erosion of populated watersheds and more all-season roads, there should be good prospects of settlement in eastern Wa and Bole. Population is mainly in the east; potential areas for resettlement are in the west. However, there is great resistance to permanent migration.

Meanwhile there is a regular exodus of males from the more populated districts for temporary work in mines and on cocoa farms in southern Ghana. Absence of many males has led, as in Central and South Africa, to poorer farming methods and, together with general pressure of population and consequent overcropping to soil erosion in Zuarungu and other areas. These problems are being partially met by some contour

372

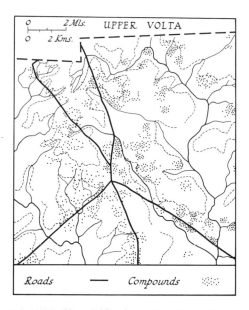

FIG. 23.3. Dispersed compound settlement in Kusasi country of Navrongo district

Streams are generally avoided because of the danger from
tsetse and simulium flies. Watersheds are often eroded,
so that the middle slopes of interfluves are most favoured.
Roads converge on Navrongo
(From the 1:125 000 Navrongo sheet, Ghana Survey)

cropping, and mixed farming, afforestation of river sources, watersheds and steep slopes, and by the provision of weirs and dams.[11]

Northern Mamprusi exhibits an unusual settlement pattern. Very numerous farm compounds are found scattered over the countryside but, because of fly, tend to avoid the rivers. *Bawku,* an important point of transit for cattle coming from the Upper Volta and Niger, and, to a lesser degree, *Bolgatanga* are the only true towns. Zuarungu and Navrongo districts have only administrative nuclei. To the west, however, towns reappear, e.g. Wa and Lawra.

Although inherently richer than the Voltaian sandstone areas, over-population of some granite areas has lowered their productivity and caused erosion. Population redistribution within the granite areas is highly desirable, although difficult to achieve. Both granite and sandstone areas of the Northern and Upper regions have suffered from very low incomes, poor and costly communications, so that there is little variety of foodstuffs or of other necessities. Diets are poor and disease rampant. The Northern and Upper regions, although divided into two contrasted regions of granite and sandstone, are throughout the poor relations of Ghana, neglected in the past because they could neither produce exports nor offer a market.

**Dissected hill and valley country of western and southern Ghana**

Corresponding to the interior plains of the Ivory Coast, this region consists of dissected residuals and ranges of hills, separated by wide flat-bottomed valleys. The country has a steady fall to the south; the general level is below 300 m (1 000 ft), but the higher hills and ranges rise to 460–760 m (1 500–2 500 ft) above sea level. It has northeast to southwest bands of the Lower and Upper Birrimian and Tarkwaian series, with granite and small occurrences of basic intrusives. The Birrimian, predominant in the Western region and western Brong, is by far the most important mineral-bearing series in Ghana, yielding gold, manganese and other minerals. The Tarkwaian series, practically confined to Ghana, has been an important source of gold from south of Tarkwa to Konongo. Other occurrences of the Tarkwaian, not important for minerals, are southwest to northeast of Bamboi on the Black Volta and in the Kibi hills. Granite and gneiss predominate south of 6°N, the granite as usual forming rounded hills and isolated domes.

These areas of varying relief have at least 1 270 mm (50 in) annual rainfall, which is more reliable than farther north. Even more important, the Wenchi and Mampong scarps shield most of western and southern Ghana from the Harmattan, so that the forest survives. Here is grown the cocoa, which is the country's chief export; subsidiary crops are kola, oil palm, citrus fruits and many food crops. Valuable timber is cut, and almost all the minerals are won here, so that this region has most of the revenue-earning resources of Ghana. Two-thirds of the people of Ghana also live in this region, which covers only one-third of the area. Yet, despite this higher density of population, there are still lands in the southwest, west and northwest, where land is available for cropping and settlement, though these will be at the expense of the forest and of the timber industry.

This large region may be subdivided into the following smaller ones:

(*a*) THE DENSU AND PRA BASINS. The basins are floored by granite of which their scenery is typical. Cocoa has been important here from the earliest days but has suffered severely from swollen shoot and from soil deterioration. Some cocoa has been replaced by kola, citrus fruits and food crops, the latter much grown by Krobo immigrants. Population density is over 260 per sq km (100 per sq mile).

*New Tafo*, headquarters of the Cocoa Research Institute, *Koforidua* in New Juaben and *Nsawam* are cocoa collecting centres.

(*b*) THE KIBI HILLS are composed of Birrimian and Tarkwaian rocks, have good reserves of bauxite, and are well forested. They are abrupt, rise quickly to a maximum height of 764 m (2 505 ft), and extend southwestward some 53 km (33 miles). Between them and the Mampong scarp of the Voltaian series is the Osino gap, barely 3 km (2 miles) wide,

PLATE 88. Drying cocoa in a hamlet near Tafo

used by the Accra–Kumasi railway and road. At the southwestern end of the hills is *Asamankese*, where there are diamond mines.

(*c*) THE BIRRIM PLAINS, west of the Kibi hills, are higher than the Densu basin and are floored by Lower Birrimian rocks. The typical wide, flat-bottomed valleys have an annual rainfall of over 1 650 mm (65 in). This is another important but younger cocoa-producing region, where cocoa developed after the opening of the Accra–Kumasi railway in 1923 and of roads to Winneba, Saltpond and Cape Coast. Fully one-third of the men are engaged in growing cocoa and about one-fifth of the women, but land is still available for cultivation and settlement.

Most of Ghana's diamonds are produced in this basin and the largest workings are at Akwatia. The Central Railway, opened in 1927, stimulated diamond and timber production. Population density is about 35 per sq km (90 per sq mile) and is increasing.

*Oda,* is a flourishing route centre near diamond mining, timber cutting and rice growing areas, the latter lying along the marshy Birim river.

(*d*) THE TARKWAIAN HILL COUNTRY consists of narrow elongated and parallel strike ridges and valleys, showing a fold and fault structure. Faults have given rise to many transverse valleys and gaps. The region begins midway between Tarkwa and the sea and extends northeastward to Konongo, where Tarkwaian rocks disappear under the Voltaian sandstones. The Tarkwaian sediments form part of a long and narrow northeast trending geosyncline. The total thickness of the rocks is roughly

375

2 440 m (8 000 ft). Near Tarkwa the folding is open, but elsewhere closely packed folds are the rule. In general, metamorphism is much less than in the Birrimian, although there are some basic intrusives.

These mountains are wooded, and through their narrow valleys the Takoradi–Kumasi railway winds its way from south of Nsuta to Obuasi. Roads rather skirt the region, except at Tarkwa, Dunkwa (Ofin gap), Obuasi and Konongo.

If the Birrimian rocks along the margins are included, this area accounts for almost all the gold and manganese mining in Ghana. The gold-bearing banket conglomerates of the Tarkwaian are akin to the banket reefs of the South African Witwatersrand. They are auriferous between Eduapriem and Damang but have been mined on the eastern edge from Tamsu through Tarkwa and Abosso to Cinnamon Bippo. The other past or present gold-mining areas within the 'gold channel' but in the adjacent Birrimian are Prestea, Obuasi, Bibiani and Konongo. The Nsuta manganese deposits are also in the Birrimian.

The principal towns are Obuasi, Tarkwa, Konongo and Prestea. The five former or still active mining towns of Abontiakoon, Aboso, Nsuta, Tamsu and Tarkwa form an almost contiguous but depressed urban area.

In the south, mining is the dominant economic activity and cocoa is relatively little grown, food crops for the miners and timber for fuel being more significant. In the north, however, cocoa is more important, Konongo also being a cocoa collecting point.

The average density of population is low because of rugged terrain and poor, thin soils, but urbanisation is high.

(*e*) LAKE BOSUMTWI, southeast of Kumasi, is either a meteoric scar or an explosive caldera. A lake 10 km (6 miles) wide lies within a possible crater 104 sq km (40 sq miles) in area. If it is a crater it was probably formed in early Pleistocene times by explosions followed by subsidence, and it has an unbroken rim rising 442 m (1 450 ft) above the lake, which is 80 m (260 ft) deep.

Much lore and superstition are connected with this remarkable natural phenomenon. Lake fishermen are forbidden to use boats, so they go fishing astride planks. The 'name for the country round the lake is Amanse, "the beginning of nations" . . . Most of the important divisions of Ashanti say that they "came out of a hole in the ground"[12], which might refer to this lake.

(*f*) THE KUMASI PLATEAU, dissected, and averaging 245–275 m (800–900 ft) in elevation, is the heart of Ashanti. The plateau is closely settled, and there is a remarkable radial network of roads, as well as the railways to Takoradi and Accra.

Composed mainly of granite rocks, the plateau is probably more intensively planted with cocoa than any other area in Ghana, about one-half of the male population over fifteen years of age and one-fifth of the women being cocoa farmers. Near Kumasi, however, the villages are also concerned with growing food crops (especially maize and cassava) for sale in the city. In the upper Ofin country on the west, kola is also much grown for sale to the north; this crop may spread east of Kumasi, where there has been some soil exhaustion, especially near the city.

*Kumasi* is the Ashanti capital and a great political, cultural and commercial centre. When described by Bowdich,[13] it lay on the side of a hill 'insulated by a marsh close to the town northwards and by a narrow stream'. He put the population at 12–15000. The 1901 census revealed it as reduced to about 3000 by the Ashanti Wars.

In 1903, two years after the end of the last of those wars, the railway from Sekondi reached Kumasi, where the station was then along the West Subin river. By 1911 the population was 18853, and in 1921 it was 23694.

In 1923 the railway from Accra was completed and a new central station was built by draining the marsh of the East Subin river. Henceforth served by two railways, Kumasi was further assisted in 1928 by the opening of the deepwater harbour at Takoradi. Radial roads were also built and these confirmed its commercial supremacy as a cocoa collector, a market for cattle, yams and maize from the north, and as an imports distributor for Ashanti and the north.

By 1931 the population was 35829; in 1948, 53626; in 1960, 180600 and by 1970 it had reached 342986. The city is now fairly clearly separated into separate functional areas, each on a ridge separated by a valley. In the northeast is Manhyia, with the Asantehene's palace and other notables' houses. In several outer areas there are quite impressive housing estates. Mainly across the valley occupied by the Accra railway is the Zongo or northerners' town, as well as many schools. West of both these sectors was the swamp now occupied by the lorry park, station and a park. On a hill immediately to the west is old commercial Kumasi, beyond which is the original European military and official quarter around the fort. Offices of technical departments are located here, west of which are barracks, fine hospitals and the old Ashanti Royal Mausoleum at Bantama. Across the West Subin valley to the southwest is the formerly exclusively European and newer 'political Kumasi'. On the southeast side are many industries, notably timber mills.

The city has grown fast, partly as the result of the advent in 1953 of the college of technology, now a university, and of industries. Replanning is needed, and the railway goods station is to be removed to the northeast part of the city.

(g) THE LOWER ODA and OFIN BASINS (DENYIASI) roughly correspond with Bekwai district. Lower Birrimian rocks underlie this region of gentler relief and lesser population density than the Kumasi plateau. Cocoa growing is again important, especially in the north and east, where communications are good, and more than a fifth of the male population is employed in cocoa cultivation.

*Bekwai* is an old Ashanti political centre, and a cocoa and foodstuffs market made possible by numerous roads and the railway.

(*h*) THE WASAW LOWLANDS may be defined as the country south of the Ofin river, southeast of the greenstone ridges and behind the coastal plain. Like the Lower Oda and Ofin basins, they have mainly Lower Birrimian rocks, but also some granite west of the lower Ankobra river. Moreover, they have at least 1 500–1 800 mm (60–70 in) annual rainfall and a low population density. They constitute the main forested area of Ghana. As the timber is cut, so land is being put under oil palm or cocoa, and population will increase in this 'pioneer fringe' of the Western region.

(*i*) THE BIRRIMIAN GREENSTONE RIDGES OF THE UPPER TANO. These hills, formed mainly of volcanic and pyroclastic rocks with igneous intrusions, extend from the Ivory Coast, through Enchi, Nyinahin and Wiawso. Their narrow, densely forested ridges tend to hamper communications between the east (e.g. Kumasi) and west.

Gold was mined at Bibiani, and there are bauxite quarries near Awaso and Kanayerebo, but the vast reserves at Nyinahin await the second stage of the Tema aluminium works. Meanwhile, the Dunkwa–Awaso railway, opened in 1944, has not only made possible the export of bauxite from Awaso, but has greatly increased timber exploitation.

(*j*) WESTERN BRONG-AHAFO comprises Birrimian and granite country of those parts of Wenchi and Sunyani districts west of the Voltaian sandstones. Within northwestern Brong-Ahafo the sharp Banda hills (*k* on Fig. 23.2), extending northeastward across the Black Volta into the Northern region, form a marked subregion. A second Volta dam has been suggested at Bui.

The whole area is developing rapidly and cocoa cultivation has spread widely. About one-fifth of the men and many women are engaged in it, yet kola, yam and subsistence farming, as well as timber cutting, are probably more important.

## Southwestern and central coast plain

With an elevation of under 60 m (200 ft), this extends inland irregularly, up to 32 km (20 miles) northwest of Accra. The Lower Volta plains, east of the Akwapim–Togo mountains, have been considered separately, because of their younger deposits and greater aridity.

Continuing from the Ivory Coast and as far as Axim, the coast remains smooth. At first there is a sandbar backed by the Ehy and Tendo lagoons, into which the Tano river empties and along which lies

378

the boundary. Cretaceous–Eocene marine sands, with thin pebble beds and some limestone, lie behind the lagoons up to 16 km (10 miles) inland. As in the Ivory Coast, oil and gas seepages are known and the limestone is used for cement making. There is a chance that oil might be found, as it was in similar series in Nigeria.

Coconuts are grown along the strand; inland, food crops and the oil palm are most important. As the southwestern coast has over 2 030 mm (80 in) annual rainfall and swamps are frequent, rice is also a very important food crop. Timber cutting is significant. Oil palm and rubber plantations have been established, the latter sustaining a tyre industry, and the former one or two palm oil mills. On the much drier central coast dwarf cattle are quite numerous.

There is a denser human population on this central coast because of longer development, better transport and trading possibilities. Pre-Cambrian and Primary rocks outcrop in small promontories upon which slaving and trading castles were erected. These sites were good for defence from land attack, and forts could afford protection for ships anchored in a sheltered bay to the leeward. Most points also offered freshwater and were near a river estuary.

*Sekondi*, was the first railway terminus in Ghana and until 1923 most trade passed through its piers. The town is still an important residential and commercial centre having close connections with Takoradi.

*Takoradi*, just west of Sekondi, was Ghana's first deepwater harbour, and took five years to build, in the face of great difficulties. Takoradi was from the first recognised as a superior site to Sekondi, where the first wharf was built and the railway was based for economy.

Takoradi harbour consists of a long southern breakwater, which turns north seaward to give a narrow entrance between it and the shorter direct northern breakwater quay. The narrow entrance at the northeast is thus kept clear of silt brought by west to east drift. Takoradi greatly cheapened and simplified the export of cocoa and even more so that of manganese and timber.

In 1953 new quays and docks for timber, a larger main wharf with three new berths, and better loading facilities for bauxite were completed. Cox's Fort Hill was removed, so levelling 10 ha (24 acres) clearing 1·75 million tons of rock and reclaiming 20 ha (49 acres) from the sea for marshalling yards. The port is now fully mechanised and is dealing with about two million tons of cargo annually, primarily exports, particularly timber, minerals and some cocoa.[14]

Takoradi has cocoa-processing factories; the most modern makes cocoa butter and powder, while another makes 'neats' (a halfway stage between cocoa and chocolate) and 'couverture' (biscuit and cake chcolate). There are also timber, plywood and veneer mills, a factory making paper goods from imported tissues, cigarette, hardware, cement, aluminium sheeting and furniture works, and a boatyard.

*Cape Coast,* has long been an important centre, and three of its four forts survive. The castle, which was the British capital before Accra, is now used as government offices. Another castle is the lighthouse. Cape Coast is a famous educational centre, and has a university. Lime juice and sugar are produced from plantations in the neighbourhood. Around both Cape Coast and Saltpond are quite intensive citrus growing and food cropping areas. *Winneba*, like Cape Coast, has many fishermen. For Accra and the coast plain to its east, see pp. 366–9.

## Economic resources

### Agriculture

COCOA

Cocoa more than any other resource dominates Ghana's economy. Whilst mining, forestry and commerce are partly in the hands of external companies, all cocoa is grown by Africans, mainly on small farms.

The tree was planted unsuccessfully early in the nineteenth century but was properly established by Tetteh Quarshie of Mampong, Akwapim, who in 1879 returned from a Fernando Po plantation with some beans. Some germinated and the young trees grew so well that the governor visited them. In 1887 there was an official distribution of seedlings raised from seed imported from São Tomé.

Export began in 1891, and thereafter plantings were made with immense rapidity, rubber-tapping and palm fruit collecting being forsaken. The almost empty countryside was repeopled with small villages and the Accra–Kumasi railway was built in stages between 1908 and 1923 to facilitate exports. So also were many roads. Ghana became the leading world producer in 1913 and has remained so. Cocoa became the largest export of the country in 1924 and continued so thereafter. Record exports of over 500 000 tons have occurred in some years, a remarkable achievement, especially after a long and hard struggle against swollen shoot and other diseases. This has involved cutting down many millions of trees, replanting as many, spraying, and careful extension work with farmers.

Cocoa still accounts for about two-thirds of Ghana exports by value. The value of cocoa exports rose twenty-five fold between 1938 and 1970 to £129 million. Ghana produces one-third of the world's cocoa, but competition is increasing from, e.g. the Ivory Coast and Cameroon, which have had preferential entry to the European Economic Community, and from other countries, notably Nigeria.

The price obtained for cocoa determines more than anything else the prosperity of Ghana. The non-cocoa areas (except the coastal towns) are almost always poorer than the flourishing cocoa districts. From profits and taxes on cocoa have come many impressive developments.

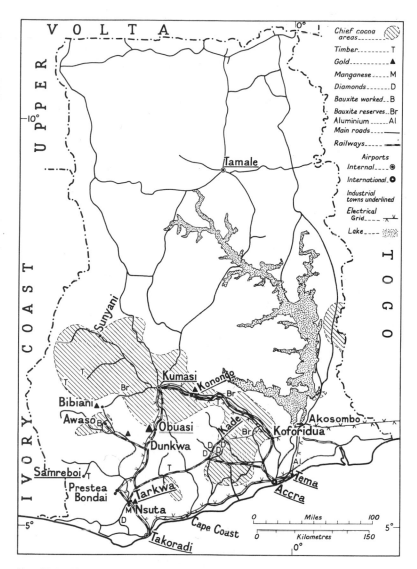

FIG. 23.4. Ghana: economic

In Brong-Ahafo over two-fifths, in Ashanti nearly two-fifths, and in the Eastern region one-quarter of all males fifteen years of age and over are growing cocoa. The crop is responsible for making the Kumasi plateau one of the most thickly populated parts of Ghana.

The physical conditions required for cocoa and the relative place of Ghana production are discussed in Chapter 6. Cocoa has spread west[15] and northwest from the Akwapim hills, so that it is now found in Ashanti, in western Brong-Ahafo, and in Western, Central and Eastern regions,

381

except near the coast. The first area of maximum production was in the Densu and Birim basins between Koforidua, Begoro, Kibi, Kade, Oda, Swedru and Nsawam; this area declined to insignificance as the result of endemic swollen shoot. Newer and less heavily infected areas are: southwest and northeast of Nkawkaw; within a circle around Kumasi limited by Obuasi, Konongo and Mampong; west and northwest of Kumasi to beyond Sunyani; and northeast of Kpandu. There are probably 1·3 million hectares (3·5 million acres) under cocoa.

Although swollen shoot has not been cured, it has been countered, and cocoa remains dominant in the Ghana economy. It is, however, too dominant, for when prices fall the whole economy of the country is imperilled and thousands of people are impoverished. Nor can power from the Volta river scheme provide equivalent industrial employment.

## Minor crops

Kola trees are grown with cocoa in the upper Densu-Birim valleys, where they are largely replacing cocoa, as well as northwest of Kumasi towards Sunyani. The nuts are sent to northern Ghana, the Upper Volta, Mali and Niger. The official figure for annual exports is about £1 million, but the real one is higher. Coffee is developing in the Volta region. Coconut, oil palm, rubber and banana plantations and sugar estates have been established in the south-central and southwestern coastal areas with some success. There is an older lime plantation near Cape Coast. Cotton is being encouraged in northern Ghana. These crops provide only a tiny fraction of exports but some serve local needs and significant industries.

The usual food crops are grown, plaintain and cocoyam occupying unusually large areas. Food crops are being encouraged to save food imports and to diminish excessive reliance upon cocoa. There are, however, problems of incentive and of land availability.[16]

## Livestock

About two-thirds of Ghana's relatively high consumption of meat is imported from Mali and Niger. The vast majority of cattle pass through Mogonori and Pusiga but substantial and increasing numbers enter near Navrongo. There is an unsuccessful meat-packing plant nearby at Zuarungu, but many animals are driven south along well-marked but badly equipped routes to converge on Prang for Kumasi and Accra. The condition of the cattle is much impaired, and better provision is required for pastures, kraals and water, especially as there is increasing competing demand in the Ivory Coast for cattle.

Ghana herds could be increased if the measures suggested were taken. Although most are in the Northern region, some are kept around Cape Coast, Winneba, and in the Lower Volta plains.

## Fishing

Fanti fishermen are especially well known in West and West-central Africa, and some 50 000 men at least are engaged in fishing in Ghana. In most coastal towns it is the main occupation.[17] Many women are also fish processors and sellers, fish is an important item of internal commerce, and a major source of protein. Locally based trawlers have not been really successful; instead larger catches have come from power driven canoes. Annual lands of sea fish are about 190 000 tons, and of freshwater fish (mainly from Lake Volta) some 20 000 tons.

## Forestry

As in the neighbouring Ivory Coast and in Nigeria, forestry is an important part of the economy. Reserves are barely sufficient to protect water supplies, control erosion and to provide a permanent supply of timber, with a surplus for export. With an expanding population, however, further reservation is desirable, if Ghana wishes to continue as a large exporter.

Some timber comes from unreserved forest, which is fast being cut by farmers. As the timber will, in any case, be removed by them, the aim is to cut and market it in a systematic way before it is ruined. Most felling is done where farming needs will require the forested area within the next ten years.

Rainforest is largely confined to Ashanti, southwestern Brong-Ahafo, the Western, Central and Eastern regions. It is found on the western boundary as far north as 7°30'N and extends over the Ashanti–Kwahu uplands and into the Togo mountains, wherever the rainfall is at least 1 270 mm (50 in). Timber exploitation is mainly in the thinly peopled parts of Ashanti, Brong-Ahafo and the Western region, and there is also a large area to the west of the Cape Coast–Fosu road.

Woods from the wetter forests include various mahoganies (*Khaya ivorensis* and *anthotheca*), Makore (*Tieghemella heckelii*), Scented Guarea (*G. cedrata*), African Walnut (*Lovoa trichilioides*) and Sapelç (*Entandophragma cyclindricum*). Attractive veneers are obtained from these. A very heavy evergreen tree is Dahoma (*Piptadeniastrum africanum*). Among semideciduous trees from the drier forest are Odum—better known by its Nigerian name of Iroko (*Chlorophora excelsa*), a superb wood of many uses. As it is the traditional building timber of Ghana, its export is prohibited. Wawa (*Triplochiton scleroxylon*) is soft and relatively light; it is used in West Africa for canoes and is exported for commercial plywood and corestock for cheap furniture, shuttering and box-making. Kokorodua (*Afrormosia elata*), Utile (*Entandrophragma utile*), Mansonia (*M. altissima*), Albizzia (*A. ferruginea*) and Danta (*Nesogordonia papaverifera*) are others, the latter being an excellent wood for axe and tool handles.

PLATE 89. Part of Samreboi timber, plywood and veneer works

Unlike Nigeria, most Ghana logs must be moved at high cost on roads (often specially constructed) and by rail. Timber is shipped exclusively at Takoradi.

The expansion in volume and value, variety of timber marketed, and in its processing is one of the most remarkable features of Ghana, as illustrated in Table 23.2.

TABLE 23.2. *Ghana: timber exports*

| Exports | 1938 | 1966 |
|---|---|---|
| Logs in cubic feet | 667 000 | 16 883 000 |
| Sawn timber (cu ft) | 39 000 | 7 233 000 |
| Veneers (cu. ft) | Nil | 95 000 |

Substantial quantities are also sold in Ghana.

In early years 95–99 per cent of timber exports were of mahogany; that wood now represents a very small part of exports. Other popular woods are wawa, makore, sapele and utile; much more may yet be achieved in diversifying demand and so using forests more fully.

Lastly, there is the vast increase in local processing. Previously, almost all exports were in log form and until 1945 there were only six small saw

384

mills. There are now some fifty saw mills whose capacity is vastly greater. Sawn timber output (as distinct from export) has exceeded log export since 1952, and over half the sawn timber is exported. Manufacture of veneers started in Ghana in 1950.

Timber shipments fell by well over one-half after 1960 because of Ivory Coast competition, and political and economic difficulties in Ghana. Total annual timber exports are now valued at about £15 million, or rather under 10 per cent of Ghana exports. Most go to the USA and Europe; much capital is invested in the industry, which provides much employment, as well as requiring many contractors and subcontractors.

## Mining

Although cocoa is by far the greatest present resource of Ghana, it was gold which gave the first name to the country and lured Europeans there. Yet at the beginning of the present century the average annual value of minerals won was only £38 000. In 1914 it was £1 744 500 but in 1928–29 only £710 000. In 1970 it reached £11 million.

As with cocoa cultivation, all major mineral workings occur in the Western and Central regions and Ashanti. Indeed, almost all minerals are obtained from within a radius of 100 km (60 miles) from Dunkwa, on the Takoradi–Kumasi railway. This was one of the world's richest concentrations of minerals, and around the Obuasi mine is probably the richest square mile in the world.

Factors which have helped this remarkable concentration are:

1. The wide and deep geosyncline of slightly metamorphosed Birrimian and Tarkwaian rocks in the Western region and Ashanti.
2. Deepseated faults and shear zones formed during the folding of the Birrimian rocks, and during their intrusion by granitic rocks.
3. The intense pre-Tarkwaian and Tertiary to Recent erosions of the Birrimian. The first erosion probably concentrated gold in the Tarkwaian banket reef and diamonds in the Tarkwaian basal conglomerates, while it enriched the manganese oxide concentrations. The latter erosions also enriched bauxite and oxidised auriferous ores.

The Obuasi mine of the Ashanti Goldfields Corporation (Lonrho) has the best grade ore of any large gold mine in the world. There is a concentration of alluvial diamonds near Akwatia and Atiankama (Birim valley), which has yielded more than 25 million carats, over 5 million carats of which have come from an area of less than 0·6 sq km (0·5 sq mile) at Esuboni. Substantial amounts of high-grade manganese ore have been mined since 1916 at Nsuta, alongside the pre-existing railway line. The opencase mine there was earlier the largest individual producer of high-grade manganese ore in the world and probably the largest producer of crystalline manganese dioxide (for batteries). Lastly, the vast and concentrated bauxite deposits at Kibi and Nyinahin will be used in the second phase of the Volta river project.

Mining employs many men and is an attractor of labour from northern Ghana, Upper Volta, Mali and Niger. Previously thousands also panned for diamonds; they now work for the State Diamond Mining Corporation.

GOLD

As explained at the beginning of Chapter 8 (p. 137), gold was planned or dug for hundreds of years before modern deep mining began. Previously, gold reached Europe via the Sahara and Arab traders, and from 1471 onwards via the coast (Gold Coast) and European traders. The slave trade later became more profitable than that in gold, yet in the early part of the eighteenth century annual shipments of gold to Europe in peace years were worth about £250 000.

British soldiers returning home after the Ashanti War of 1873 made known the occurrence of gold and its use by the Ashanti. Due largely to Pierre Bonnat, a French trader and explorer, large scale methods were begun in 1878. Exclusive concessions soon caused the decline of the very narrow shaft or pit mining by Africans.

The railway from Sekondi reached Tarkwa in 1901 and Obuasi in 1902. Publicised comparisons with the Johannesburg Rand caused a bubble of speculation, some 400 companies being formed in 1901; none survives. There is now only one company and a few state mines. Gold exports average £10 million annually, three-quarters coming from the company mine at Obuasi.

Gold occurrences and workings may be classified as follows:

(*a*) *Ores in Birrimian rocks.* Most of the gold worked since the advent of European companies has come from quartz reef lodes and sheared rocks at Obuasi, Prestea, Bibiani, Bondaye and Konogo. The lodes are found mainly in metre wide veins of quartz, deposited in fissures on the flanks of synclinal depressions. These depressions commonly occur near the boundary between the Upper and Lower Birrimian, and between the Upper Birrimian and Tarkwaian on the western edge of the Tarkwaian geosyncline. Occurrences are also close to intrusions of younger granite and porphyry. The largest ore bodies are in deepseated shear zones, faults or fractures.

Birrimian gold was extensively worked along outcrops by Africans, e.g. at Bibiani, where, in 1891, there were some 915 m (3 000 ft) of workings with some pits up to 30 m (100 ft) deep. Much the same was true at Obuasi in 1895 when it was visited by E. A. Cade and he obtained his rich 259 sq km (100 sq miles) concession which later led to the establishment of the Ashanti Goldfields Corporation.

(*b*) *Ores in Tarkwaian rocks.* Banket or conglomerate reef lodes, akin to

PLATE 90. Obuasi, the sole centre of profitable gold mining in Ghana

those of the Witwatersrand, have been mined near Tarkwa and southeast of Kumasi. Nearly 30 per cent of gold obtained since the advent of European companies has come from the Tarkwaian series. They were also previously worked by Africans, especially the surface oxidised ores.

(*c*) *Placer deposits.* These have been formed by past or present rivers draining gold-bearing areas, but workings have been confined to present-day rivers. Previously there was extensive exploitation of gravels and sands on valley flats and low terraces of the Ofin, Jimi, Pra, Ankobra, Tano, Fura and Birim rivers by Africans and, after 1897, by European companies. Only one dredger is now working, at Bremang.

(*d*) *Ores in acid igneous rocks intrusive to the Birrimian.* These were extensively worked by Africans, but have never been worked by Europeans.

Most mining is now done from shafts of up to 1 130 m (3 700 ft) in depth, but low-grade, weathered (oxidised) Birrimian and Tarkwaian ores, occurring near the surface, have been worked in the past by large draglines. Placer, or alluvial deposits, were worked by dredges. Africans now do only insignificant panning, because diamond panning is more profitable.

Formerly gold was a major export but it declined relatively during the

387

PLATE 91. A compressed air drill making a hole for an explosive charge to loosen hard gold-bearing rock. The deep gold mines of Ghana are West Africa's only important underground mines

First and Second World Wars. There was a recovery from 1931 to 1941, and again during the 1950s, but there has been a general decline since then because of labour difficulties, high costs, and the low official price of gold. Many mines have closed, and there has been much concentration in capital and mining. Gold now accounts for about 5–8 per cent of Ghana's exports.

### MANGANESE

Occurrences of manganese ore are widespread, but those of economic importance are the deposits in the Upper Birrimian at Nsuta, 63 km (39 miles) by railway from Takoradi, smaller unworked ones at Hotopo on the Sekondi–Axim road, and at Yakau near Dixcove.

The Nsuta ores form five hills on two parallel ridges 4 km (2·5 miles) long, running in a north or north-northeast direction. The ores were discovered in 1914, and mining began two years later. The ore is cut away in terraces by power shovels and loaded into railway trucks. The mine, formerly the largest in the world and a leading producer, is near to economic exhaustion. The ore is used in steel making and some in paint, varnish and dry battery manufacture. Manganese exports are much below those of gold in value.

### DIAMONDS

Ghana diamonds are probably derived from Upper Birrimian rocks, are alluvial in occurrence, and mostly of the smallest industrial type. They

PLATE 92. Manganese mine, Nsuta

were discovered in the Birim and Bonsa valleys in, respectively, 1919 and 1922. In the former they are worked by a British company in which the Ghana Government has a majority holding. The diamonds, which occur profusely in terraces and in very shallow stream beds, are concealed by 0·6–6 m (2–20 ft) of silt overburden. The company excavates, washes and screens mechanically, and the diamonds are then collected on greased tables.

The Bonsa deposits worked by Ghanaian licensees, are much more restricted in area and thickness, and were unworked until 1933. The diggers work singly or in family groups, washing the gravel in calabashes. About a quarter of the diamonds in the gravel are lost and 20–30 per cent of the gravel is never treated because of haphazard digging. The proportion of diamonds won by diggers is small, and the conditions of work are exceedingly bad.

Ghana is the fourth world producer by quantity but produces only 5–10 per cent of world output by value. Diamonds represent about 8 per cent of Ghana exports.


BAUXITE

Whilst present production is minor, prospective quarrying near Kibi for conversion of bauxite to alumina for the Volta Aluminium Company's (VALCO) works at Tema makes this mineral of great potential importance.

The largest deposits are at Nyinahin west of Kumasi, at Asiakwa near Kibi, between Awaso and Bibiani northwest of Dunkwa, and at Mount Ejuanema above Nkawkaw on the Mampong escarpment. There are some 200 million tons at Nyinahin on flat-topped hills about 32 km (20 miles) long, the bauxite being 6–15 m (20–50 ft) thick. The deposit near Kibi has at least 88 million tons of ore and is to be developed by Valco with a link to the eastern railway by 1975, it being more accessible to Tema and so cheaper to develop than Nyinahin. The last two areas have much smaller reserves but were opened in 1942, the Awaso deposit by a branch railway from Dunkwa and a continuing road, Mount Eyuanema exclusively by road from Nkawkaw. The latter soon ceased operations, and the Awaso deposit was exhausted in the 1960s, being replaced by another quarry at Inchiniso, nearer Bibiani. Until the Kibi deposit is opened for Valco, only the Inchiniso deposit is being quarried for the shipment of relatively small quantities of bauxite through Takoradi.

OIL

Oil seepages have long been known in the southwest coastal region, whilst the geology of the Lower Volta basin, especially around Keta is favourable. Moreover, oil was prospected in 1896, in 1909–13, 1923–25, 1956–57, 1966 and since 1970, but by 1972 no commercial quantities had been found, despite intensive onshore and offshore searches.

**Volta power**

The Akosombo dam in the Volta gorge of the Akwapim–Togo mountains was inaugurated in 1966. Behind it is a 400 km (250 miles) long lake, perhaps the longest artificial one in the world. Lake Volta has flooded some 3·5 per cent of Ghana, fortunately areas of low fertility and thinly peopled. With such an area of water it may marginally induce heavier rainfall in the drier north, by increasing atmospheric humidity.

Between inauguration and 1972 power generation was below capacity while the Valco aluminium smelter at Tema was building up production, and while other uses for the power were being encouraged. In 1972 the sixth and final turbine was installed, bringing generating capacity to 882 mw. Valco takes 300 mw of this and was the main reason for the dam and power scheme. Valco's capacity is 145 000 long tons of aluminium per year, but may rise later to 210 000 tons, at which point Ghana would be a major refiner of aluminium.

Until 1974 at least alumina is being imported but Valco appears likely to develop the Kibi bauxite deposit and to build an alumina plant there or nearby, so using another local asset, providing further employment (the smelter already employs about 1 700 people), teaching new skills, and further diversifying and strengthening Ghana's economy. Lake Volta, Akosombo dam, the very modern aluminium smelter, and the prospective bauxite quarry with alumina plant, together comprise West

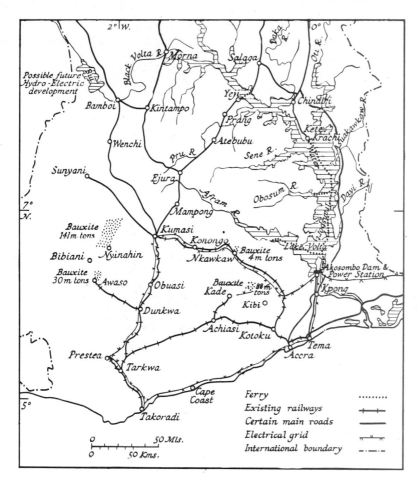

FIG. 23.5. Volta power development

Africa's greatest development. Indeed, the smelter is the largest in the world outside North America.

The subsidiary uses of both the power and the lake are important, or potentially so. The power is distributed by grid (Fig. 23.5) to the major towns, industries and mines of Ghana, to Lomé (Togo) and, prospectively, to Dahomey, Upper Volta and, perhaps, Mali. This power is cheaper than that produced by using imported oil in diesel generators, is more reliable, and has strengthened the efficiency of the consumers it serves.

The lake provides a new and potentially cheaper routeway to and from northern Ghana, when barge transport can be organised. There was a dramatic rise in the fish population soon after the creation of the lake because of the increase in plankton, in turn due to the submergence of vegetation. These early phenomena may not continue, so that the fish

391

PLATE 93. Akosombo dam, Ghana

population may need restocking, but there is always likely to be an annual harvest of at least 20 000 tons. Meanwhile, the protein deficiency disease of kwashiorkor has virtually disappeared among the fish eaters of the lakeside villages and towns. Water supplies are guaranteed to Tema and Accra. There is some irrigation in a pilot scheme producing vegetables at Kpong (Fig. 23.5), and at the not very successful Asutsuare sugar estate in the Lower Volta plain. More may be attempted on selected fringes of the lake, but it should be remembered that the areas near the lake belong mainly to the infertile or intractable Voltaian basin and Lower Volta plains. There is also some tourist interest in the dam and lake, and more might, perhaps, be developed.

However, there are also some disadvantages. Bilharzia has spread rapidly and widely in the settled areas round Lake Volta, through the advent of infected Ewe fishermen to fish in the new lake. Furthermore, river blindness (Onchocerciasis) has spread to the Volta river below the dam, where there is now faster flowing water. Nor are the resettled 78 000 entirely content with their tiny one-room houses, ill-conceived for polygamous families, and often aligned in serried rows in each town. Stabilised, cooperative agriculture has been difficult to learn, particularly in poor environments where soils and water supplies are mediocre. Agricultural services have not been adequate, and some new settlements are isolated. Fishing is increasing at the expense of farming. Finally, the dam lies in an earthquake-prone zone, and the weight of water in the lake increases the earthquake danger.[17]

## Industry

Ghana has a very notable range and distribution of industries. This has come about as the result of the use of available raw materials such as timber, minerals and of power, the fairly considerable and compact local market, and one with a higher than average per capita income. Thus there are also varied import-substitution industries, especially those making consumer goods. There has been a great drive to industrialise, notably under Dr Nkrumah (1951–66), especially after independence in 1957, but many factories have proved uneconomic. Ghana is one of the few African countries where industrial location has been mainly planned and is broadly based, though particularly in Takoradi, Accra, Tema and Kumasi, especially the first three. In Tema, where there is the greatest variety of industry, there are, inter alia, cocoa bean processing, fish freezing, truck assembly, an oil refinery, a scrap steel smelter, a clinker cement plant, a printing and stationery works, radio and television assembly, and factories making insecticides, shoes, textiles, aluminium sheets and utensils, paints, storage tanks and pipes, sandcrete blocks, etc. Tema's new town layout and industries are comparable with a British new town. Further reference should be made to the texts in this chapter on Volta power, mining, forestry, the major towns, and also to Chapter 8.

## Transport

The original impetus to railway construction came from the gold mining companies at Tarkwa, to which the railway from Sekondi was opened in 1901. By offering a financial guarantee the Ashanti Goldfields Corporation secured the extension of the railway to Obuasi in 1902, and it was completed to Kumasi in 1903 for political reasons. Gold mining companies were also the cause of the construction of the Tarkwa–Prestea branch opened in 1912, and urgent needs of bauxite for aluminium caused that from Dunkwa to Awaso to be built in 1943–44.

If gold was the main reason for building railways in the west, it was cocoa in the east, where the line from Accra was built in stages from 1909 and completed to Kumasi in 1923, after wartime delays.

The central line, opened in 1928 from Huni valley to Kade, was a liability, as it runs into an area well served by more direct roads. A branch from Achiasi to Kotoku (on the Accra–Kumasi line), opened in

1956, provides a direct line from Takoradi to Accra. A shorter rail route than the devious one through Kumasi was long needed, but the newer line competes with an even shorter road. Now that Tema serves the eastern Ghana coast, it is difficult to envisage much rail traffic passing between Accra and Takoradi. A branch—the first from the Accra–Kumasi line—was opened in 1954 from Achimota to Tema. Another branch may be built in the 1970s to open bauxite deposits for Phase Two of the Volta power development.

Kumasi, the inland terminus, is only 270 km (168 miles) from the coast and beyond lies most of Ghana. A rail extension beyond Kumasi has been much discussed, but it is difficult to see how it could develop traffic that could not be more economically developed by road transport. Moreover Lake Volta could provide an excellent waterway as far as Yeji for cheap all-season bulk transport for non-perishable goods. Finally, the Abidjan (Ivory Coast) to Ouagadougou (Upper Volta) line, completed in 1954, is a competitor for traffic to and from the Upper Volta.

Without the existing railways mining could never have been developed to its present scale, nor could cocoa cultivation until about the mid-1920s when lorry competition appeared. On the whole, the relatively short railway lines have been confined to the most productive areas of the country.

The railway has long been used to capacity for goods traffic, especially timber haulage. Consequently, the track was doubled from Takoradi to Tarkwa in 1953. There is intense lorry competition for cocoa and passenger traffic, and from air services for passengers between Takoradi, Accra and Kumasi.

Road competition became acute in the 1930s, and until the Second World War it was legally restricted in certain areas. There is a good network of roads in the well populated areas of southern Ghana; and one of the outstanding characteristics of the country has been the very extensive Ghanaian and Lebanese ownership and operation of lorries. One Ghanaian company operates services to Khartoum (5 470 km: 3 400 miles) en route for Mecca, and to Lagos.

Air services between Accra, Takoradi, Kumasi and Tamale provide many flights a week. The country is also served by Nigerian and other West African services and by intercontinental services through Accra.

## Conclusion

The periods preparatory to and after independence saw many new economic and social developments, mainly as the results of the dynamism of Dr Nkrumah, the devotion and zest of Sir Charles Arden-Clarke, and the very considerable financial reserves available at independence. Tema and the Akosombo dam were built, and the aluminium smelter became Ghana's most impressive industry. Many factories were established in the larger towns, and especially in Tema, but quite a number proved uneconomic.

Cocoa farming still provides by far the major employment in Ghana, and should long continue to do so. Agricultural diversification into food crops and into plantation cultivation of the oil palm, rubber and other import substitution or industrial raw material crops is proceeding, but is far behind the Ivory Coast. Truly economic agricultural diversification and really viable industrial development are both necessary, because over reliance upon a fragile crop like cocoa and its semiluxury product chocolate is dangerous, whilst the future of gold, manganese and even diamond mining is uncertain.

Because of political controls, mismanagement, and differences in economic organisation, Ghana has fallen behind the Ivory Coast in many respects but development in Ghana is far more indigenous than in its western neighbour.

# 24

# Togo: diversity in miniature

With an area of only 56 000 sq km (21 622 sq miles) and a population (1970) of 1 857 000, Togo is the larger and eastern part of former German Togo, and includes all the coastline, the capital and railways of that colony.

The boundary between the British Gold Coast and former German Togo, agreed in 1904, divided the Mamprusi, Dagomba and Gonja people of the north between the British and the Germans. The Dagomba capital at Yendi became German, and to govern his divided people, the paramount chief delegated authority in the Gold Coast to a subchief at Savelugu. On the other hand, in the south, the same boundary put four-fifths of the Ewe people under German administration, and one-fifth of them in the Gold Coast, east of the Volta river.

After the First World War, the effect of the present boundary was to reunite the Mamprusi, Dagomba and Gonja but to further divide the Ewe, so that some three-fifths were under British administration and two-fifths under French. The Ewe protested, but only under the trusteeships were they able to make oral representations; thus their division received most publicity after 1946.

The problem arose not merely from division by a boundary but also from the contrasting principles and practice of British and French rule. Thus, the British encouraged the use of the Ewe language; the French favoured French. The British developed elected local government in villages and districts, but the French very little. Togoland under United Kingdom Trusteeship had representatives in the Gold Coast Legislative Assembly and a minister in the all-African Executive Council, with an African Prime Minister. Togo under French Trusteeship had an assembly only from 1946, and its powers, compared with that of the then Gold Coast, were small.

In 1956 universal suffrage was introduced in the French Trusteeship, the assembly was given legislative powers on all internal matters, and a ministerial system was established. A referendum taken in October showed wide support for these changes, for the termination of the trusteeship, and for its replacement by an autonomous republic, which was proclaimed shortly after. It became independent in 1960; but the Ewe will not be reunited unless Togo ever decides to join or federate with Ghana.[1]

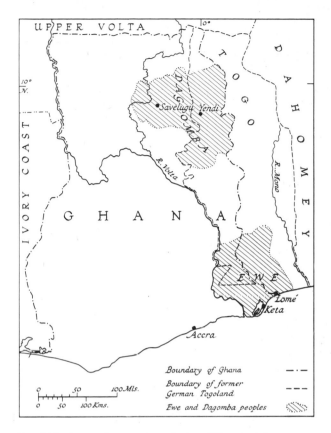

FIG. 24.1. Past and present boundaries of Togo and the distribution of the Ewe and Dagomba peoples

## Historical outline

Little is known of the origins of the people of the centre and north, but the Ewe came to their present home in the south from the Niger valley, under pressure from the east, five or six hundred years ago.

The Portuguese visited this coast in the fifteenth and sixteenth centuries, from their headquarters at Elmina, and from its successor at Ouidah. They probably shipped slaves locally from Grand Popo, Petit Popo (Anécho) and Porto-Ségouro, whose names are somewhat Portuguese. They introduced coconuts, cassava, maize and other crops to provision the slave ships, and the intensive cultivation of these along this coast and in Dahomey is partly their legacy.

The French established a trading post at Anécho in 1626 and in 1787, but on both occasions it was short lived. German contacts probably originated with the arrival of traders at Grand Popo in 1856, but from 1865 to 1883 the French were again active politically and commercially at Anécho and at Porto-Ségouro. In 1880 more German traders arrived

397

and acute rivalry ensued. Finally, in 1884 a German protectorate was declared along the coast, so creating the first German territory in Africa. Dr Nachtigal had made a treaty with the chief of Togo village, on the north side of a lagoon behind Porto-Ségouro, east of Lomé. The village name, an Ewe word meaning 'behind the sea', was taken for that of the whole territory. The Germans had their first capital at Baguida, then at Zébé, and from 1897 at Lomé.

German Togo was conquered in August 1914 by French and British units from neighbouring colonies. The country was divided, so that the British held all the coast and railways, and the French the interior. In 1919 the situation was reversed. The Mandates were made definitive in 1922 and became Trusteeships in 1946, the British one being terminated in 1957 when Ghana achieved independence, and the French one in 1960 when the Republic of Togo was proclaimed.

## Climate

The coastal belt of Togo has the exceptionally dry Accra–Togo dry coastal climate (see Fig. 3.19). Lomé averages 893 mm (35 in) annual rainfall, with an average of eighty-six rain days. Although relative humidity is high, Lomé and Anécho have by far the lowest rainfall and fewest days of rain in all Togo. Baobab trees are common up to about 10 km (6 miles) inland.

Between Tsévié and Nuatja, on the central railway, and to the west and east, the semiseasonal equatorial climate prevails, in which there is rather more rain than on the coast. Thus Tsévié has 1 011 mm (39·8 in) on seventy-three days and Nuatja 1 077 mm (42·4 in) on eighty-one days. Only in and near the Togo mountains are conditions typically equatorial. Palimé has 1 504 mm (59·2 in) on 100 rain days. Klouto, nearby, with 1 765 mm (69·5 in) on 199 days, is probably the wettest settlement in Togo. Atakpamé lies in the seasonal equatorial climatic zone, near to where the equatorial climate makes its most northeasterly projection inland.

All Togo north of a line near Blitta has the southern savanna climate. At first there is rather heavier rainfall than for comparable stations in Ghana. Thus Blitta has 1 313 mm (51·7 in) on eighty-four days, Sokodé 1 356 mm (53·4 in) on ninety-eight days, and Bassari 1 288 mm (50·7 in) on 102 days. In the far north, however, Sansanné Mango with 1 044 mm (41·1 in) on seventy-three days and Dapango with 1 085 mm (42·7 in) on sixty-nine days are rather drier than similar places to the west.

## Geology, relief and major regions
### Sandbar coast and lagoons

As in Dahomey, the smooth sandbar is backed by lagoons, which in Togo extend deeply inland as Lakes Togo and Ouo. These lakes are the

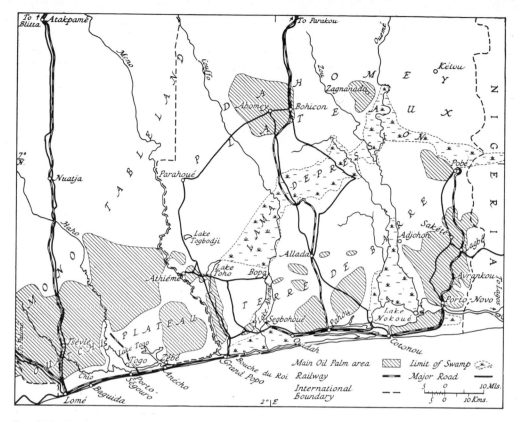

FIG. 24.2. Southern Togo and southern Dahomey

former estuaries of the Chio, Joto and other rivers.

Beginning in 1886, the sandbar has been closely planted with coconut palms, now heavily diseased. Under the palms small lagoon cattle are grazed. Lagoon and sandbar villages are mainly engaged in fishing, the collection of coconuts, and in the preparation and marketing of these products which are important in internal trade.

*Lomé*, the capital, with a population of some 95 000, adjoins the Ghana boundary. Served by railways terminating at Palimé, Blitta and Anécho, by roads, intercontinental and West African air services, and by a port, Lomé is also the commercial headquarters. There is normally a great deal of traffic across the boundary to Keta and Accra (Ghana), mostly in cassava flour and tapioca, and in dried sea and lagoon fish.

The western part of Lomé is largely the administrative quarter. It was well laid out by the Germans, is shaded and attractive. The centre is the commercial quarter; the east is an industrial zone. Living quarters are on the inland side of the town.

Until 1968 all Togolese overseas trade had to pass through a wharf, which severely limited national economic growth. The present deepwater harbour, with four berths at a finger quay, is 6 km (4 miles) east of Lomé,

399

and has permitted a substantial increase in trade, although capacity is only one-third greater than that of the wharf. Handling is easier, faster, safer and cheaper. The harbour is capable of much enlargement, and the next priority is for better roads to up-country Togo and into the eastern Upper Volta. Lomé so far lacks international traffic such as Dakar. Abidjan and Lagos all handle.

*Anécho* (*Petit Popo*), near the Dahomey boundary, lies more on the southern shore of the lagoon than on the coast. It is much older than Lomé and, as well as being on the Ghana–Togo–Dahomey–Nigeria road, is the terminus of the coastal railway from Lomé. It is an important cassava and dried fish market.

## La Terre de Barre or Ouatchi plateau

This corresponds to similar country behind the lagoons in Dahomey. As there, 'la Terre de Barre' is limited by a clear northern edge and divided by rivers. Where there is adequate water, it is well cultivated and settled, with up to 60 per sq km (150 per sq mile). Compared with the Dahomey sector, the oil palm is less densely planted but maize, yams and cassava are more important and are traded to Ghana, especially Accra.

## Mono tableland

Beyond the northern edge of the Terre de Barre, some 48–64 km (30–40 miles) inland, comes the usual monotonous and silicious clay-covered tableland. Because of the low rainfall, baobabs occur widely along the southern edge, and poor southern Guinea savanna is dominant up to the northwestern limit along the Togo–Atacora mountains near Palimé, Atakpamé, Sokodé and Lama-Kara.

Villages are rare, except along the railway and north road, and cultivation is restricted to areas round them. Yams and maize are dominant, the oil palm is important around Atakpamé, the shea butter tree towards Blitta and Sokodé, with groundnuts also around the latter. Some cotton is grown for sale. Nuatja is the most important local market for all crops.

In the Atakpamé district a three year rotation is common, with crops grown on yam mounds to prevent erosion. In the first year yams and cotton are grown, in the second, maize and cotton or guinea corn and, in the third year, cassava with groundnuts, beans, etc. Rice is grown dry with yams, or wet in the Mono valley. Fallow periods are from eight to fifteen years.

In the extreme northeast of this area, in the Kabrai massif, southeast of the Atacora mountains, there is a very dense population in the Lama–Kara division and across the border in Dahomey. The average population, over more than 2 590 sq km (1 000 sq miles), and embracing between 200 000 and 235 000 people with a yearly increase of 5 000–6 000,

PLATE 94. Kabrai country, Togo

is 72 per sq km (180 per sq mile). Yet the environment is so rugged that only one-third of the land is cultivable. Thus the effective average population density is about 200 per sq km (500 per sq mile), but reaches 600 per sq km (1 500 per sq mile) in some mountainous cantons. This is possible only because of the relative fertility of soils derived from granites, gneiss and basic green diorite, and because of intensive cultivation. Tiny terraces are laboriously built by the Kabrai and, to a lesser extent, by the Naoudemba and Lamba, and are manured and irrigated.

Resettlement has been going on since 1926 between Atakpamé and Sokodé, where some 40 000 people now live. People moved from over-populated areas are allotted new villages, farming equipment, seeds (especially cotton), animals, some money until the first harvest and freedom from taxation for two years.[2] Individual emigrants also go to the Bassari district, and to southern Togo and Dahomey. Unfortunately, the farming methods of the Kabrai sometimes deteriorate in a lowland environment.

*Palimé* lies in a hollow near Mount Agou. It collects local cocoa, and railway and road link it with Lomé. *Atakpamé*, in a narrow valley and on adjacent hills, is likewise a regional market, collecting palm oil, kernels and cotton, there being ginneries in the town.

*Sokodé* is the northern administrative centre and market. *Lama-Kara*, the Kabrai administrative centre, is situated at the outlet from the only point where the Kara river may be crossed easily in all seasons.

401

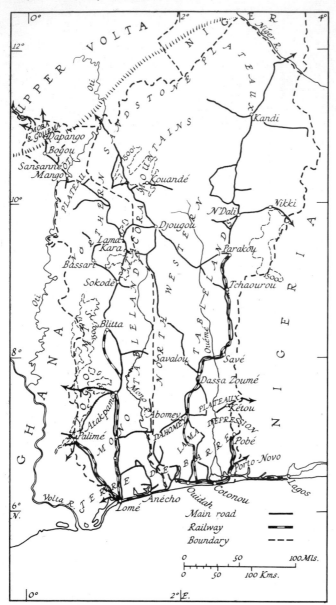

Fig. 24.3. Togo and Dahomey

## Togo–Atacora mountains

These denuded thrustfold ranges are highest and widest in Togo. This massive and rugged double range, with deep valleys and abrupt-edged plateaux, begins near Accra as the Akwapim hills, and is aligned north-eastwards across Togo into Dahomey, where it obstructs the Niger river in the famous double **V**.

The southeastern range is composed of the Akwapimian–Togo–Atacora series (probably Middle Pre-Cambrian), and the northwestern wider one of the higher folded, consorted and faulted Buem series (Upper Pre-Cambrian). The double range is usually called the Atacora mountains in the northeast. Around Sokodé is a low saddle, which divides these from the Togo mountains in the southwest. Before the arrival of Europeans the whole range kept apart Islamic and animist peoples in this area.

By reason of their more northeasterly position, the Atacora mountains are drier and poorer, with thinner soils and poorer vegetation. Millet is the dominant food crop; groundnuts, tobacco and kapok are almost the only cash ones.

In the Togo mountains rainfall is heavier (1 200–1 500 mm : 47–59 in) than elsewhere in Togo, and this is the only mainly forested area. Temperatures are lower than on the coast, and it was here, around Klouto and Akposso, that German plantations were early established for cocoa, coffee and rubber. Cocoa is still grown on some plantations with Kabrai labourers, as well as on Togolese-owned farms. Coffee is now entirely grown by Togolese, and is Togo's second or third most important export. Upland dry rice, maize and millet are the main food crops.

### Oti sandstone plateau

This is the eastern part of the Voltaian sandstone basin, continued from Ghana and extending into northern Dahomey. As in the other areas, this plateau is infertile, and subject to alternation of flooded and baked-out soils. Consequently, population is slight and the crops of groundnuts and millet are, like the people, poor. The Bombouaka scarp is the lower eastern continuation of the more impressive Gambaga scarp of Ghana's Upper region. *Sansanné Mango* is the main market.

### Moba and Gourma granite lands

North of the Bombouaka scarp granite occurs. There is here, as in the extreme dry north of the Ghana Upper region, a denser but poor and isolated population. The Moba and Gourma cultivate groundnuts, cotton, irrigated rice, and millet, and take to keeping livestock fairly well. *Dapango* is the local market.

## Economic resources

### Agriculture

Until 1960 Togo found its resources exclusively in agriculture, and about 40 per cent of the country is cultivated.

In the south the main food crops are maize, cassava, the oil palm and yams, the first three being grown in surplus. Cassava is normally sold to Ghana traders, mainly from Keta; palm oil and kernels go overseas. There is a palm oil factory at Alokoègbé and one at Ganavé for cassava starch.

In the centre, cassava, yams and maize remain basic food crops, but cotton (intercropped with yams) becomes the main cash crop southeast of Atakpamé. A modern spinning and weaving mill at Dadja is using much of the cotton crop.

The southeastern lower slopes of the Togo mountains produce cocoa and coffee, with rice for local food. A little coffee is also grown nearer the coast in la Terre de Barre.

In the centre and north, guinea corn, millet and beans are the basic foods. Yams and rice are locally important, e.g. north of Bassari and Sokodé. Groundnuts and cotton are grown both for subsistence and export. Shea butter nuts are collected in most areas and kapok north of Bassari.

The main exports by value are, approximately, phosphates (35 per cent and increasing), cocoa (20–40 per cent), and coffee (16 per cent). Although it is generally the major crop export, the amount of cocoa varies greatly according to relative prices on either side of the boundary with Ghana. Cassava flour is sent over land boundaries in quantities difficult to determine.

## Minerals and power

Calcium phosphate deposits northeast of Lake Togo have been worked since 1960. They occur mixed with clay in a layer 5·5–8·5 m (18–28 ft) thick, covered by 6–24 m (20–80 ft) of soft overburden (Plate 95). A 23 km (14 miles) railway takes the phosphate to a concentrator and

PLATE 95. Phosphate quarry near Lake Togo. The large excavator is cutting away the overburden, and the smaller one is taking out the phosphatic earth and putting it on a conveyor belt

wharf east of Porto–Segouro. Annual exports are about 1·75 million tons of 80 per cent phosphate. A cement works, which also serves the Ivory Coast market, uses limestone from Tokpli on the eastern border.

Copper-bearing sulphide deposits have been found near Palimé, which are believed to be economically viable. Chromite occurs in several places, and other minerals are known.

A little hydroelectric power is produced at Kpimé, near Palimé, whilst much more power is brought by grid from Akosombo dam, Ghana (Fig. 23.5).

## Conclusion

The resources of this small but regionally varied country are modest, although they do include a mineral—calcium phosphate—and they are greater than those of neighbouring and larger Dahomey. Togo also benefits a great deal from illicit trade to and from Ghana.

# Dahomey: ancestral home of many Brazilians

Dahomey, one-fifth the size of France, has an area of only 112 622 sq km (43 484 sq miles), and a population in 1970 of 2 686 000 giving an average density of 24 per sq km (62 per sq mile).

This higher-than-average population is explained by concentrations in the south, continuing from the days of the famous Dahomey kingdom. Like Ashanti, Yorubaland and Benin, this was a powerful state, famous for the women's battalions of its army, which were first raised in 1729. It was notorious for its 'customs' or human sacrifices and for its vast part in the slave trade up to their eventual suppression after the mid-nineteenth century.

## Historical outline

Ouidah (Ajuda in Portuguese and sometimes Whydah in English) was for long the greatest slave exporter of the Gulf of Guinea. Vivid accounts have been left by Bosman, Dalzel, Burton and others. The Portuguese established themselves in 1580 at this town, which later became their headquarters after the Dutch evicted them from the Gold Coast between 1637 and 1642. Some 5 ha (11 acres) of Portuguese territory survived until 1961 at Ouidah, with military and civil governors but no population! A French fort was founded in 1671, and the English and Danish also established forts, the buildings of which are still in use. These forts did not originally have political rights, as did such establishments elsewhere in West Africa; instead, they were subject to the Dahomeans (who occupied the town in 1741) through a local representative, the Yevogan or 'Resident Minister for White Affairs'.

At the end of the seventeenth century 20 000 slaves were exported annually, but in the early nineteenth century the number had fallen to 10–12 000 per annum, because of excessive human sacrifices of potential slaves. So in 1810 a famous Brazilian mulatto, Francisco de Souza, himself the descendant of ex-slaves, stepped in to depose the Dahomey Regent, reduce the sacrifices, and so revive the slave trade. In this he and his descendants succeeded until 1885, despite the desperate efforts of the British Navy. In that year the last Portuguese slave ship left Ouidah.

In 1847 the Governor of the Gold Coast visited Guezo, the Dahomey

King, but, as the latter had already limited the annual sacrifices, he could not easily also stop the supply of at least 8 000 prisoners, then exported annually as slaves. Fearing British intervention, Guezo made a treaty with France in 1851. By Franco-British efforts the slave trade through Ouidah, Lagos and Badagri mainly ended about 1863. France finally took political control of Cotonou in 1878 and of Porto-Novo in 1883. Portugal declared a protectorate over all the coast in 1885, but withdrew it in 1887.

Behanzin, the last real monarch, who began his reign in 1889, soon attacked the French. His state was conquered in 1892, and he was deported in 1894. Thereafter, the lands north of African Dahomey were also occupied, and the present boundaries were achieved by treaties with German Togo in 1897 and with Nigeria in 1898.

The former state of Dahomey and the late survival of the slave trade have left their mark. In the former capital at Abomey are the old royal residences (one with the tomb of Behanzin), where many descendants of the royal families live. Around Abomey are the extensive oil palm plantations, established by prisoners when these could no longer be exported as slaves. Former slave merchants advised the establishment of these plantations as an alternative income. Today they provide Dahomey's chief export and are among the few extensive African-owned plantations in West Africa.

The capital is at Porto-Novo, in the extreme southeast, once a rival and later a vassal state to Dahomey. It was the first to ask for French protection and has remained the capital, despite the rise of Cotonou as the commercial centre. Ouidah, the former slave roadstead, is the headquarters both of Catholic missions and of the local Fetish, whose buildings face each other.

## Climate

Along the Dahomey coast, between Ouidah and Cotonou, the extremely dry Accra–Togo dry coastal climatic zone comes to an end. On the Togo border, Grand Popo has only 823 mm (32·4 in). Occasional baobabs may still be seen and, were it not for swamps in the neighbourhood, they would be even more numerous and scrub more general. Eastward, Ouidah has 1 095 mm (41·7 in), Cotonou—where the equatorial climate recurs—1 265 mm (49·8 in) and Porto-Novo 1 285 mm (50·6 in); the rain days also increase from only fifty at Grand Popo to 100 at Porto-Novo.

Rainfall inland from the coast in the semiseasonal and seasonal equatorial climatic zones remains low, as in Togo, being 965–1 270 mm (38–50 in) per annum on about seventy rain days. The amount of rain is thus much the same as on the coast, though it is progressively less effective. Were it not for the fertile soils of the Terre de Barre and the high humidity, oil palms could not survive as they do with as little as 940 mm (37 in) of rain.

North of the Savalou–Tchaourou line the southern savanna climate occurs. The heaviest rainfall in Dahomey is at Djougou in the Atacora mountains, which averages 1 346 mm (53 in) annually. Kouandé, Natitingou, Nikki and Bemberéké, in about latitude 10°N and on high ground, get about 1 270 mm (50 in) annually and this area was originally covered with rainforest.

North of the Atacora mountains rainfall diminishes sharply to about 965 mm (38 in) annually, and is highly variable. This low average, combined with the widespread occurrence of lateritic crusts, accounts for exceptionally poor Sudan savanna vegetation.

## Geology, relief and major regions

### Sandbar coast and lagoons

In Dahomey this type of coastline is well developed, lagoons being continuous from Togo into Nigeria. In the west they are narrow, the first being very near the sea; in the east they are broader and deeper. The Porto-Novo lagoon provides a waterway to Lagos, but is impaired economically by the international boundary which crosses it.

As in Togo, the coastline was built offshore from river estuaries. Relics of these are represented by Lake Ahémé, fed by the Cuffo whose old estuary is now the lake, and Lake Nokoué, formerly part of the estuary of the Ouémé river. In this latter case, however, there has been great siltation, and above the former estuary or present lake the river has divided into two parts, the Zou and the Ouémé proper. Between them is the well-populated delta, which may be improved for palm cultivation on the northern fringes, and on the southern side for rice in the wet and maize in the dry season.

There are two outlets to the sea. One is the *Bouche du Roi,* east of Grand Popo, where erosion is going on, and the other from Lake Nokoué at Cotonou, where deposition formerly occurred. Fish were caught in great numbers in this and other lagoons, and prepared by families living in villages built on stilts in Lake Nokoué. However, after the construction of the deepwater harbour of Cotonou, west of the outlet of Lake Nokoué, a backwash of seawater surged into the lake. The consequences were that the stilt supports of lake houses perished, and fish died out. Lake fishermen have had to take up sea fishing or migrate to the towns.

On the seaward half of the sandbar are considerable coconut plantations, mostly owned by non-Dahomeons, in contrast to the predominantly African-owned ones of Togo. The railway from Segbohoué via Ouidah, Pahou and Cotonou to Porto-Novo runs along this sandbar. Beyond the railway, on the lagoon side, the sand is less consolidated and is heavily laden with freshwater. Here oil palms flourish, in contrast to the seaward side, and there is an oil mill at Ahozon, near Ouidah.

Many former lagoons have become partly silted, especially west of Cotonou. In these marshes, and on those along obstructed rivers, patches are cleared for cocoyams, maize, cassava and vegetables. As mentioned above, rice could be added if the technique were mastered.

· *Porto-Novo*, population 81 000 (1968), is the capital and an old African centre. It lies on a slight eminence on the north side of the Ouémé lagoon, which communicates eastward with the sea at Lagos and, with difficulty, westward with Lake Nokoué and Cotonou. Originally, much external trade passed via Lagos until the deepwater port at Cotonou was opened in 1965. The railway north to Pobé serves the palm belt, but Porto-Novo lacks direct roads to central and northern Dahomey. Most trade, almost all embassies, and the technical departments of the government have moved to Cotonou.[1]

*Cotonou*, population 128 000 (1968), is the commercial headquarters of Dahomey and a European creation. It has Dahomey's deepwater port[2] and lies immediately west of the outlet of Lake Nokoué. There is an industrial suburb to the east of the outlet, with textile and palm kernel oil mills, clinker cement, car assembly, soap and perfume works, nail and furniture factories, a brewery, and soft drink manufacture. Cotonou is served by railways to Porto-Novo and Pobé, to Parakou, to Ouidah and Segbohoué, and by many roads. There are air services in each direction along the coast, and to other countries.

*Ouidah,* is on the north bluff of a reed-obstructed lagoon. On the coast there remain only ruined buildings to remind one that from here hundreds of thousands of slaves were shipped to the New World in the course of several centuries. In the town the old Danish and English forts are used as commercial houses, and the Portuguese retained symbolic territorial rights until 1961. Ouidah is the military and religious head-quarters of Dahomey.

## La Terre de Barre

*Barre* is a French corruption of the Portuguese *barro*, meaning clay. This region, subdivided by the Cuffo and Ouémé rivers, lies north of the lagoons, and averages about 90 m (300 ft) in elevation. Its loams and clayey sands are formed from Miocene and Pliocene rocks, and there are occasional outcrops of ferruginous sandstones or lateritic sands and clays. The soil is light red in colour. Fertility has been increased by the use of waste, and the land is continually cropped, but there are signs locally of exhaustion.

This region is densely planted with the oil palm[3] for cash; maize, cassava, sweet potatoes and beans are grown for food, maize being by far the most important annual crop. Cultivation is most intensive near

PLATE 96. An oil palm grove, with food crops of maize and vegetables

the towns, near which small lagoon cattle are tethered in the fields and sold for meat.

Population is less dense in the Grand Hinwi (Allada) sector, mainly because it was on the slave route between the Dahomean capital at Abomey and the sea at Ouidah, and also because water is usually found only at about 50 m (over 160 ft).

## The Lama depression

This arc-shaped clay swamp is less than 30 m (100 ft) above sea level, is limited by clear bluffs, and has fertile peaty soils and patches of rainforest. Because of annual flooding it is little used, though it could support rice. The Lama was the southern boundary of the Dahomey State and was a major obstacle in the construction of the central railway.

## The Dahomey plateaux

There are four plateaux, around Parahoué, Abomey, Zagnanado and Kétou. These are akin to the three plateaux of the Terre de Barre, but water is even deeper. All are planted with the oil palm. Oranges are also an important cash crop near Abomey, some being sent by lorries to the coast and to the north. Of all these plateaux, population is densest on the first two. *Abomey*, the old Dahomey capital, is now mainly of historical interest, but remains an important market and crafts

410

centre. *Zagnanado* was the Dahomey war base against the Egba and other Yoruba peoples. *Kétou* is mostly inhabited by Yoruba, of whom there are 220 000 in Dahomey.

### Northwestern tablelands

Bare domes and lateritic cappings are frequent, and soils are poor and thin. A few forests survive e.g. at Banté, beyond the limits of the old Dahomey state. To the north, however, vegetation generally becomes poorer, though around N'Dali there are fine forests.

As far as Savé the railway is mainly within fertile country; thereafter its local traffic is slight, since much of the upper Ouémé basin is thinly peopled. The main crop is cotton. Parakou is the rail terminus and transfer point for Niger transit trade and northern Dahomey groundnuts.

### Atacora mountains

As in Togo, these mountains are well peopled. They also have the heaviest rainfall in Dahomey—over 1 270 mm (50 in). With the removal of the original forest cover, there has been severe erosion around the headwaters of the Ouémé.

*Djougou* has cotton ginneries, is an important route centre and has a much greater population than any other town in central or northern Dahomey.

### Northern sandstone plateaux

These slope in gentle undulations to the Niger river. In the northeast, Pre-Cambrian rocks are covered by Pliocene clayey sandstones, which are themselves capped by ferruginous lateritic crusts. In the extreme northwest, primary Voltaian sandstones lie along the border and are also infertile.

Everywhere the vegetation is very poor Sudan savanna. Many areas are unpeopled, except by Fulani nomads. Where cultivation is possible and there are people to do it, millet, guinea corn and cotton are grown, and shea butter and kapok trees are protected.

## Economic resources

### Agriculture

The peoples of the south are alert and vigorous, and have long been in contact with Europeans. Their elaborate political organisation encouraged early specialisation, so that many people did not grow their own food. Furthermore, large quantities of food had to be grown for provisioning slave ships on their long voyages, as well as for slave merchants and their employees. Thus there was, early on, much specialised agriculture, especially in growing cassava, yams, sweet potatoes, maize, peas, chillies, beans and groundnuts, which would keep well on slave ships. These crops (especially maize and vegetables) are still overwhelmingly the most important in the south, and are mainly grown under oil palms. Comé, near Grand Popo, has a factory for making cassava flour and tapioca. Crops of the north are yams, rice, millet, beans, peas and vegetables. Cassava and groundnuts are grown almost everywhere.

Nature has also been kind to intensive food cropping in southern Dahomey. The rainfall of some 1 000 mm (about 40 in) is admirable in amount and distribution, and the country has more alluvial soils than many. The Terre de Barre is easily worked and retentive of moisture, though the actual watertable is deep and the soils mediocre. On the other hand, rainfall and vegetation conditions do not favour cultivation of the more lucrative cocoa or kola crops.

## OIL PALM

Oil palms were planted by prisoners of the Dahomey and Porto-Novo kings after 1839, and especially after 1848 (when France abolished the slave trade), as they could no longer all be sold as slaves. The plantations were well laid out, the seeds selected and the trees tended, probably under the guidance of ex-slave merchants. There are some 30 million trees, occupying nearly 4 145 sq km (1 600 sq miles) as far as $7\frac{1}{2}°$N. Oil palm produce is Dahomey's main export. The oil is notable for its high carotene content—1·7–2 per cent.

Pobé research station has distributed several million seedlings of improved varieties, whilst in 1962 SONADER, a state company began to plant selected palms in large blocks for cooperative farming, and occupying some 16 000 ha (40 000 acres). All this is the more necessary, since the annual rainfall averages less than 1 015 mm (40 in) in the palm areas, and the low water table is a further demerit. Against these problems may be set the constantly high humidity and clay soils.

There are seven palm oil mills, capable of extracting 90 per cent of the oil, and with annual capacities of 2–4 000 tons. That of Gbada is near Porto-Novo, Avrankou is north of that town, whilst others are at Ahozon near Ouidah, at Houin Agame on the Mono river, at Bohicon, Grand Hinvi and Agonvi. As in other countries they suffer from irregular and insufficient supplies of fruit. This is often kept back for primitive methods of treatment to secure oil for domestic use by the rapidly increasing population. Some factory-expressed oil is used in the Porto-Novo and Cotonou soapworks.

PLATE 97. Avrankou palm oil mill, Dahomey

COCONUTS are grown on mainly non-African plantations along the sandbar; and by Dahomeans there, near lagoons, and between Grand Popo and Athiémé. It is usually more profitable and far less trouble to sell the fresh nuts as fruit or for local soap production, than to undertake the expensive preparation of copra for export.

COTTON has been much encouraged by the French Textiles Company (CFDT) and, as elsewhere, cotton is produced for local use and for export. Allen varieties are most important in the north, and Ishan in the south. There are some six ginneries, Parakou having the largest and most modern one (capacity 18 000 tons).

GROUNDNUTS are important in the Abomey, Savalou and Natitingou districts. The first crop is kept as food and the second one in the north is exported. In all, some three-quarters of the crop are retained within Dahomey and about 5 000 tons of shelled nuts are normally exported annually, mainly from the drier and less peopled northern districts. A groundnut mill has been built at Bohicon.

SHEA BUTTER TREES are widespread in the centre and north, but particularly localised in Natitingou, Abomey, Kandi, Nikki and Parakou districts. Internal trade in shea butter nearly equals that in cotton, and kernels are exported.

### Minerals

A little gold has been washed from the river Perma near Natitingou, whilst fairly rich iron ore and chrome exist, as well as rutile and phosphates. Oil has been under prospection offshore since 1967.

## Conclusion

Old Dahomey was famed as an African state but notorious for its human sacrifices and as the last great exporter of slaves to the Brazilian and European slave merchants. Its oil palm plantations, established by prisoners for legitimate trade, survive and are unique in Africa. Also exceptional is the intensive cultivation of food crops from the oil palm plantations, and from the unusually extensive alluvial areas. However, Dahomey is overdependent upon vegetable oil and oilseed exports, and needs to diversify its economy. Great hopes are pinned on the discovery of commercial quantities of petroleum, and on the cultivation of cashew.

Like Togo, Dahomey has suffered from its small size, the poverty of the north, and from the lack of a deepwater port until 1965. This port is a main inlet and outlet for Niger's overseas trade, though in competition with Apapa (Lagos).

# 26

# The Federation of Nigeria:
# the giant of West Africa

With an area of 923 768 sq km (356 669 sq miles) and an estimated population in 1970 of 55 074 000, Nigeria is the most populated country in all Africa. Its area is four times that of the United Kingdom, or three times that of Ghana and Sierra Leone together. Although it occupies only about one-seventh of the settled and productive area of West Africa, it has over half of the population. Indeed, Nigeria has at least three areas of high population density.

Because of its latitudinal extent from approximately 4° to 14°N, Nigeria has exceptionally varied physical conditions, human types and economy. Rainfall varies from some 3 050 mm (120 in) at Calabar, to not much more than one-fifth of those figures in the Chad basin. In the southeast there is an excess of rain all the year; in the north there is adequate rain only in two or three months. There is a corresponding vegetational range, though a characteristic of Nigeria is the unusual width of the Guinea savanna.

Relief is likewise varied, and there is higher land here than anywhere else in West Africa. The southeastern boundary extends along the fringes of the Cameroon and Bamenda highlands, most of which average 1 220–1 525 m (4 000–5 000 ft). Most of the Jos plateau lies at 1 220–1 830 m (4 000–6 000 ft). The geology is also unusually diverse because, apart from Pre-Cambrian rocks, Cretaceous to Recent sedimentary series and volcanic rocks are fairly widespread.

Ethnic variety is likewise great. Between the four main groups—Hausa and Fulani in the north, Yoruba in the southwest, and Ibo in the southeast—there are great differences of outlook and organisation.

The size and variety of Nigeria are likewise reflected in its economy, though this is perhaps less varied than one expects. There are only a few outstanding exports—cocoa from the southwest, mineral oil, palm oil and kernels from the south, groundnuts, cotton, hides and skins, and tin from the north. Moreover, these exports come from relatively restricted areas. On the other hand, food crops are well represented (as one would expect in such a densely populated country), and there is a large internal commerce in them, as well as in kola nuts and livestock. Nigeria is, indeed, the only West African country producing forest crops in the south, as well as possessing great numbers of the humped livestock in

415

the north. She is also one of the few large timber exporting countries of West Africa, and has other unusual resources such as oil, gas, coal and tin.

There is more of a network of communications in Nigeria than elsewhere in West Africa. The Niger, Benue and Cross rivers, the various streams of the Niger delta, and the many lagoons are useful waterways. There are 3 505 km (2 178 miles) of railway and 90 120 km (55 000 miles) of road, with marked concentration in the main cash crop areas. There is also a network of air services.

Lastly, human variety and differing outlooks are reflected in the federal constitution with varying constitutional arrangements in the twelve states.

## Historical outline

The establishment of the Hausa in the north goes back at least to the tenth century. Their political and social organisation were much influenced by the penetration of Islam in the thirteenth century, when the Fulani were also spreading eastward. For centuries the crop-growing Hausa and the pastoral or aristocratic Fulani lived in peace, but in 1802 Othman dan Fodio quarrelled with the King of Gobir and rallied Muslims in a religious war, and Fulani rule was extended over most of the Hausa kingdoms.

Some consider that the Yoruba originated in northeastern Africa and, having come early into West Africa, acquired Negro characteristics by intermarriage. Yorubaland once extended farther westward, and Yoruba peoples also live in Dahomey. Southward penetration by the Fulani to Ilorin, later to Oshogbo and perhaps to Abeokuta much affected the Yoruba, as did slave raiding from north and south. These towns were the extreme southern limits of the Fulani. Tsetse made advance very dangerous to their cavalry, and further penetration was impossible. Benin was independent but was influenced by barbaric fetish priest domination and by the slave trade. Less is known of the early history of the Ibo and other peoples of the east.

The earliest documented European contact was by the Portuguese in 1472. As the overseas slave trade developed they were followed by other nations. Geographically, the Nigerian coast was well suited to the trade, and to its late survival, by reason of the many creeks of the Niger delta. The Yoruba civil and other wars provided slaves, who were also easily captured by African intermediaries from the socially fragmented Ibo, and from as far north as Nupe country around the middle Benue. Slave-raiding was a feature of the north for much-longer, though the slaves were generally used locally.

After the British abolition of the slave trade in 1807, the penetration of the interior of Nigeria was due to Buxton's thesis that legitimate

416

trade rather than armed force was the best way to stop slave-holding. Penetration was made easier by the discovery in 1830 of the true course of the Niger; though there were fearful losses from disease by expeditions until 1854, when Baikie showed that many of these could be avoided by doses of quinine. During much of the century, especially during Gladstone's administrations, there was either indifference or even hostility to British political expansion in Africa.

Lagos was taken in 1861 in order to suppress its slave trade. In 1879 the United African Company (later the National African Company and, finally, in 1886 the Royal Niger Company) finally opened up the Niger river and undertook the government of the interior. Meanwhile, in 1885 the Oil Rivers Protectorate was proclaimed over most coastal territory from Lagos towards Cameroon, but no administration was provided until 1891. In 1893 the protectorate was enlarged over the hinterland, and the name changed to the Niger Coast Protectorate. Benin was occupied in 1897, and appalling human sacrifices there were stopped.

By 1897, therefore, Lagos was under the Colonial Office, the interior under a private company, and the coast under the Foreign Office. But in April 1899 the Colonial Office took over the Niger Coast Protectorate from the Foreign Office, and in January 1900 the Charter of the Royal Niger Company was revoked. In their places, respectively, the Protectorates of Southern and of Northern Nigeria were proclaimed. The Fulani and other emirates of Northern Nigeria were brought under British control by 1903. Lugard introduced indirect rule through the emirs, on condition that they prohibited slave raiding and trading. Islam was to be respected and the entry of Christian missions subject to permission from the emirs—a fact which caused the educational retardation of the north.

In 1906 Southern Nigeria and Lagos were merged. In 1912 the through railway from Lagos to Kano was opened and also the then main line from Kano to Baro on the navigable Niger. With such improved communications it was possible to proclaim a unified Nigeria in 1914. Sir Frederick (later Lord) Lugard, who served the Royal Niger Company in the 1890s, was later High Commissioner for the Protectorate of Northern Nigeria, then Governor of both the Southern and Northern Protectorates in 1912, and first Governor of Nigeria in 1914.

In 1939 the Southern Provinces were divided into Western and Eastern Provinces, and in 1946 Regional Houses of Assembly were created in Ibadan for the Western Region, at Enugu for the Eastern, and at Kaduna for the Northern Region.

Under the 1951 Constitution, far greater powers were given to these regions. In 1953–54, at the wish of Nigerians, regionalisation and home rule were increased. Western and Eastern Nigeria became self-governing in 1957, Northern Nigeria in 1959, and the whole Federation achieved independence in 1960. A fourth region—the Mid-West—was created in 1963.

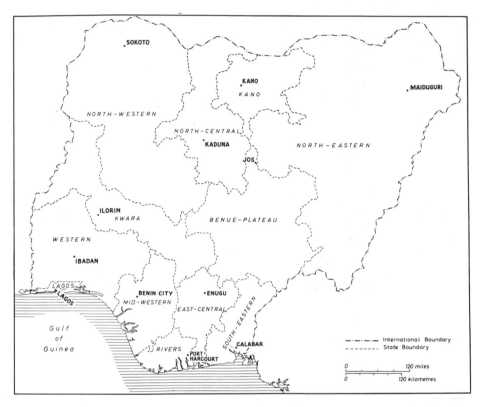

F<small>IG</small>. 26.1. Nigerian states

The Cameroons and Bamenda provinces of the Cameroons under United Kingdom Trusteeship, dissatisfied with representation in the Eastern Regional Assembly, secured a legislative and executive council and became the Southern Cameroons in 1954. Responsible government came in 1958, and detachment from Nigeria in 1960 to remain awhile under trusteeship. In 1961 it joined then federal Cameroon as Western Cameroon, but in 1972 became an integral part of unitary Cameroon.

The Northern Region dominated the rest of Nigeria by its size, population and voting strength. It became clear that to save the federation more nearly equal component areas were essential. So in 1967 twelve states were substituted for the four regions. Northern Nigeria was subdivided into six states, Eastern Nigeria into three, the already small Mid-West Region was merely renamed, Lagos Federal Territory was enlarged by additions from Western Nigeria, the rest of which became the Western State (Fig. 26.1). Between 1967–70 the Eastern Region attempted to secede as 'Biafra'.

418

TABLE 26.1. *Nigeria: size and population of states (1963)*

| State | Capital | Area sq km | sq miles | Population 1963 | Population sq km | sq miles |
|---|---|---|---|---|---|---|
| 1. Lagos | Lagos | 3 577 | 1 381 | 1 443 568 | 97 | 251 |
| 2. Western | Ibadan | 75 369 | 29 100 | 9 487 526 | 111 | 289 |
| 3. Mid-Western | Benin | 38 648 | 14 922 | 2 535 839 | 65 | 168 |
| 4. Rivers | Port Harcourt | 18 151 | 7 008 | 1 544 313 | 90 | 233 |
| 5. East-Central | Enugu | 22 652 | 8 746 | 7 227 559 | 274 | 711 |
| 6. South-Eastern | Calabar | 35 561 | 13 730 | 3 622 599 | 101 | 263 |
| 7. Kwara | Ilorin | 74 260 | 28 672 | 2 399 365 | 32 | 82 |
| 8. Benue Plateau | Jos | 101 538 | 39 204 | 4 009 408 | 37 | 95 |
| 9. North-Eastern | Maiduguri | 272 014 | 105 025 | 7 893 343 | 30 | 78 |
| 10. Kano | Kano | 43 071 | 16 630 | 5 774 842 | 131 | 339 |
| 11. North-Central | Kaduna | 70 209 | 27 108 | 4 098 305 | 61 | 158 |
| 12. North-Western | Sokoto | 168 720 | 65 143 | 5 733 296 | 34 | 88 |
| Federation | Lagos | 923 769 | 356 669 | 55 670 052 | 60 | 156 |

## Population

Figure 10.1 shows that there is an exceptional range of population density in Nigeria, from many almost uninhabited areas to those with about 540 per sq km (1 400 per sq mile) in areas near Owerri and Onitsha. Because of the varied physical character of the country and the diverse antecedents and character of its peoples, there is no simple explanation of this wide variation; nevertheless, the factors discussed in Chapter 10 are well exemplified in Nigeria.

### Ibo lands

Densely peopled Ibo lands extend southeastward from Onitsha towards Calabar. Although there is a very dense population, there were almost no true towns until the Europeans came, and the Ibo live mostly in frequent clusters of mud houses. They maintained themselves because the tsetse fly isolated them from Fulani attack, and the forest shielded them from severe attacks by slave raiders from the coast or the interior.

The very numerous Ibo have survived in their restricted and poor homeland by intensive and careful cultivation of mediocre soils, and with a basically vegetarian diet. Although conditions are not ideal for the oil palm, it will tolerate light soils (as cocoa will not), and oil palm produce, cassava, yams and cocoyams are the basic crops.

There is almost certainly overpopulation in and around Owerri and Onitsha, with severe underemployment and unemployment. Because of this and the high literacy rate, Ibo are normally found in clerical, technical and executive occupations elsewhere in Nigeria, as well as in plantations on Fernando Po and in forestry in Gabon.[1]

419

**Yorubaland**

The Yoruba concentration, between Lagos and Ilorin, contrasts in most ways with conditions in Ibo country. Most soils are derived from Pre-Cambrian rocks, rainfall is lower and less continuous, and fallow periods are longer. Water is generally freely available in central Yorubaland.

The low population density in northern Oyo results from Fulani attacks, from this area being a no-man's-land between Yorubaland and Dahomey, and from the lower rainfall, poorer soils and restricted cropping possibilities. Elsewhere, political organisation and military power enabled most of the Yoruba concentration to survive.

Large towns are an outstanding characteristic of Yorubaland,[2] many old cities having over 50 000 people. Ibadan, the second city of tropical Africa, had 627 379 inhabitants in 1963. One half at least of the urban population of Nigeria is Yoruba and, whereas over half of the population of Western Nigeria is urban, only 14 per cent is so in the eastern states, and 9 per cent in the northern ones. This urbanisation came about by the concentration of farmers in protected towns by night, while still farming some distance away by day.

The railway runs through the heart of Yorubaland, serving its main centres but roads have done more to extend urban concentration and have made more profitable the cultivation of cocoa for export, and of kola nuts, cassava and yams for internal sale, all on a large scale.

**Ondo, Benin and Warri**

Ondo, Benin and Warri lie between the Yoruba and Ibo concentrations. In northern Ondo and Benin the population survived Fulani raids because of the rugged terrain of the Niger–Bight of Benin watershed. Southern Ondo and Benin are thinly populated or even unpopulated because of Yoruba civil wars, slave raiding and Benin human sacrifices in the late nineteenth century, the depth of the water table, thin, poor and dry soils and, in part, because of dense forest. Yet in Ibo country similar physical factors were no impediment to dense population.

**The Middle Belt**

The generally thinly peopled Middle Belt (see also pp. 447–51) comprises two-fifths the area of Nigeria but has only one-fifth the population. This low density results in part from slave raiding from south and north, and from infestation by tsetse and other pests. It is also a 'shatter zone' or 'no-man's-land' between the contrasting northern and southern peoples, and has few large ethnic groups. Furthermore, many of its soils are poorer, water is scarce and rainfall variable. Indeed, it seems to have the disadvantages of the south and north, with none of

420

their advantages. There are no large towns of Middle Belt peoples. Such towns as exist are either mainly Yoruba, such as Ilorin; rare capitals such as Bida and Yola; or European in origin, such as Kaduna, Minna and Jos. Except round the latter town, communications are also rather poor in the Middle Belt.

A few 'islands' of greater than average density in the Middle Belt should, however, be noted. Broken country around Abuja, the Jos plateau and on the eastern boundary north of the Benue saved so called 'pagan' (non-Muslim) peoples from extinction. European influence tended to spread them out on to new lands. Tin mining on the Jos plateau has, however, brought in far more people. Where the Fulani settled, they often added notably to the population density, e.g. in Nupeland (Bida Emirate), and around Yola.

Notable Middle Belt peoples are the Nupe and the Tiv, who live in the Niger–Benue plains. The Tiv went there in the eighteenth century, settling at first in the southern districts on the margin of the Benue plains, rather as emigrants to the United States tended at first to congregate in New York. Thus Tiv country southeast of Makurdi has locally severe overpopulation; but across the Benue river, in the northwest of Tiv country, there are much lower densities.

## Northern clusters

The northern clusters attain their highest densities in the Sokoto valley, around Katsina, Kano and Zaria and, to a lesser extent, in the heart of all emirates. Settlement was facilitated by light soils and relative freedom from the tsetse fly, but limited by water, e.g. northwest and southeast of Sokoto and east of a line through Nguru and Potiskum.

Wherever there was water, other favourable factors encouraged particular concentrations. Sokoto is a religious centre of the north. Sokoto, Katsina, Kano and Zaria were on trans-Saharan caravan routes, but their survival was due to superior political and military organisation. Soils are easily tilled, but no more so than those of many thinly peopled areas in Nigeria. Much of the explanation lies in the intensive cropping methods of the Hausa, their use of night soil and of animal manure. First the railway and then roads have provided an outlet to markets for their groundnuts, cotton and surplus foodcrops, as well as for Fulani cattle.

## Overpopulated areas

Calculations of overpopulation rarely allow for differences in soil fertility, farming method and social custom, which much affect productivity. Nor do all people live exclusively from farm crops; there is also much wild produce, such as fruits, firewood and game. Many are supported by part

421

or whole-time non-agricultural work, such as commerce, transport and crafts. Nevertheless, there is overpopulation in parts of Ibo[3] and Tiv countries.

Conversely, about one-half of Nigeria, mainly in the Middle Belt, might take more people, even with present farming techniques, so long as tsetse flies are controlled and pure water supplies assured. The Anchau scheme, by which people were resettled in an area cleared of tsetse lying between Zaria and Jos, showed that at least 27 people per sq km (70 per sq mile) are needed to keep the tsetse at bay, and so keep the area peopled at all. In practically tsetse-free Bornu, resettlement depends upon the provision of wells, as the rainfall is too little for farming development without expensive irrigation.

The government has undertaken other resettlement schemes,[4] such as that at Shendam on the southern edge of the Jos plateau, to receive people from the plateau whose soils are ruined by overfarming or by tin mining. More elaborate but unsuccessful schemes were undertaken at Mokwa, and by the Eastern Nigeria Development Corporation in the Cross river–Calabar project. The solution of social problems and economic pressures has proved difficult.

## Climate

Nigeria has a greater variety of climate than any other West African country; the Cameroon, equatorial, semiseasonal equatorial, seasonal equatorial, southern savanna, Jos plateau, savanna and Sahel types of climate being found. Apart from latitudinal extent, the wide range of relief increases the variety.[5]

There seems to be a rainshadow effect in the lower Niger–Benue valleys and, possibly, towards Lake Chad. In general, however, rainfall diminishes from the southeast and south, towards the north and northeast.

An outstanding contrast exists between western and eastern Nigeria. In the former, rainfall averages 1 016–1 525 mm (40–60 in) and there is a 'little dry season' from about mid-July to the middle of September. This enables a greater variety of crops to be grown and two harvests to be secured. In eastern Nigeria, where the equatorial and Cameroon climates are extensive, and which lies generally farther south than western Nigeria, there is heavier rainfall, in a longer season and, normally, no 'little dry season'. Consequently, soils are more leached, crops are perforce less varied than in the west, harvesting is more difficult, and dry storage of crops is a problem. The oil palm, tolerant of poor soils and preferring the greater rainfall, is the main cash crop and the moisture-loving cocoyam is often found.

In the Middle Belt, although rainfall may be as high as in the southwest, it is far more variable from year to year in amount, times of onset and cessation, and distribution. Thus the Middle Belt is climatically hazardous to farmers. The north has less rain than the Middle Belt, but the fall is often more regular and reliable.

## Vegetation

As one would expect from the climatic and altitude range, there is great vegetational variety in Nigeria. Mangrove vegetation is well represented around Lagos, west of Warri, south of Port Harcourt, and around Calabar. Inland lies much freshwater swamp, continuous from the eastern boundary to Port Harcourt, and extending up the Niger to north of Aboh.

Inland again is rainforest to an approximate northern limit through Ilaro, Abeokuta, Offa, Owo, Onitsha, Okigwi, Obubra, Ogoja and Obudu. Thus forest is poorly represented in much of Yoruba country but is still well seen in Ondo, Benin and eastern Calabar. In the Owerri area it is mostly secondary forest with planted oil palms, and in southeastern Oyo and Ibadan districts secondary forest with cocoa.

Northward of the rainforest is an ever widening belt of derived savanna, the northern limit of which runs approximately through Iseyin, Ilorin, Kabba, Oturkpo, near Obudu, and then northeastward. This line approximately represents the former limit of rainforest.

Beyond lies a broad wedge of Guinea savanna, with its northern edge near Bussa, Gusau, Ningi, thence south to east of Shendam, north of Jalingo, and south of Yola. This zone was formerly occupied by open woodland which has suffered severely from cutting and burning by man and has been replaced by savanna. This vegetation is especially typical of much of Nigeria, because the belt is wide and occupies quite half the country, coinciding roughly with the Middle Belt. Within it lies the Jos plateau, which has exceedingly poor short grass.

Most of the rest of northern Nigeria is occupied by Sudan savanna, except that Sahel savanna occurs north of a line through Geidam to the southern edge of Lake Chad.

## Geology

Pre-Cambrian igneous and metamorphic rocks occupy four large areas. The largest of these—the High Plains of Hausaland—lies north of the Benue and Niger rivers. This area is connected by a narrow neck to the second large area, which extends over most of Ilorin, Kabba, Oyo and Ondo. The third area mainly occupies Ogoja, Benue and Adamawa. The fourth area lies north of the Benue. These areas occupy nearly two-thirds of the country. The older of the granites give rise to numerous smooth-domed inselbergs. Younger granites, which are more resistant, form rugged hills, e.g. near Jos. The weathering of these younger granites has given tinstone, columbite, wolfram and pyrochlore, and these have been concentrated in ancient stream beds mainly on or near the Jos plateau.

Severance of South America and Africa is thought to have taken place in Cretaceous times, first along a rift now occupied by the Benue west of Yola, and extending off the Guinea Coast to beyond Cape Palmas, and later along a downwarped trough now followed by the Niger south of Bourem (Mali) and extending seaward towards Angola.

The Benue valley and central Sokoto have early Cretaceous marine rocks and late Cretaceous terrestrial formations. The Niger valley has only the later Cretaceous formations, which also occur around the Gongola tributary of the Benue. In eastern Nigeria Cretaceous deposits are up to 4 570 m (15 000 ft) thick.

At Nkalagu, younger Cretaceous limestones are used for cement manufacture. In late Cretaceous times the sea became shallower and the vegetation of its fringing swamps and lagoons decayed to form the coals now found in Onitsha, Kabba, Benue and eastern Bauchi. That worked at Udi is the only coal exploited in West Africa and is poorer than most coals worked in the world. As well as the limestone and coal seams, the Cretaceous series consists of shales, sandstones, sands and clays. Oil is being worked at many places in southern Nigeria from this series.

The early Cretaceous rocks of eastern Nigeria and the Benue were strongly folded before the accumulation of later series, which are unconformable and only slightly folded.

At the end of Cretaceous times, the land sank and the sea advanced again, so that Tertiary (Eocene) marine clays, shales and sandstones overlie Cretaceous rocks across the southern edge of the country, as well as in northwestern Nigeria where there was another Eocene sea.

Above these deposits are deep beds of sand and clay, with lignite seams. The latter occur near Benin, Owerri and Onitsha. Lignite indicates that the Tertiary sea was withdrawing, leaving lagoons and swamps on the coastlines. In the south, Cretaceous and Tertiary sediments break down into the acidic and easily eroded formations often loosely and erroneously called the Benin sands.

Erosion surfaces have been used to suggest that the fluvio-volcanic series, found widely on the Jos plateau, is of early Tertiary age. The fluvial sands on the Jos plateau include tin bearing sands and gravels, above which are thin beds of clays and sometimes more sands or partly decomposed basalts, which are also usually weathered to clays.

Younger unweathered basalts overlie some tin bearing gravels and have also overflowed the edge of the plateau. Volcanic cones may still be seen.

In Pleistocene times, downwarping in northeastern Nigeria formed the Chad basin, in which were deposited terrestrial and lacustrine sands and clays of Pliocene to Pleistocene age.

Pronounced outward monoclinal tilting of the coastline is shown by the linear outcrop of the Eocene rocks, upon which rests the base of the Pleistocene–Recent delta. Later outward tilting is indicated by the drowned lower courses of all the rivers, although these are masked seaward by sandbars and spits. Easy excavation of the soft sediments of the Benue and Niger valleys has supplied abundant material to the Niger delta.

# MAJOR REGIONS[6]

## Lagos State

### Sandspit coast

This stretch of coast[7] lies south of the Porto-Novo creek or Victoria lagoon, from east of Lagos to Porto-Novo, which is an excellent waterway. Were there no political boundary to restrict traffic, it could be much more used.

South of the lagoon are recurved spit ends, shaped by eastward-moving material. South of the recurves are subparallel sand ridges, separated by strips of former swamp mud. Vegetation is always greater on the sand ridges. In the west these are relatively few, close together and clear; eastward they diverge, and breaks in continuity are more frequent. Between these subparallel sand ridges and the sea is a broad belt of sand, terminating in the surf beach. The sandbelt has fishing villages and coconut plantations, as in Dahomey.

Just west of Badagri the subparallel sand ridges end abruptly marking a former breakthrough between creek and coast. Consequently in the Badagri area the outer sand belt is backed immediately by recurved spit ends.

*Badagri*,[8] on the mainland, is an old European point of contact and missionary headquarters, now reviving somewhat. Behind it lies a system of east–west trending belts of sand and mud, indicating former open creeks between islands and mainland. Three miles east of Badagri the recurved spit ends cease, and, consequently, as far as Lagos there is only a comparatively narrow and geologically recent sandbelt.

*Lagos*,[9] with a population in 1963 in the then federal district of 665 246, is the capital of Nigeria, its most important and best equipped port, and the largest town.

The broad and calm Lagos lagoon, with several islands, a permanently open outlet to the sea fed by the Ogun river and fringing mangroves afforded unusual possibilities for defence and trade. Lagos Island was first settled by Yoruba who began by establishing themselves at Isheri, north of Lagos, moved later to Ebute Metta, and subsequently to Iddo Island. From the latter they began to cultivate on Lagos Island, though they made few settlements. However, peaceful penetration of Benin people became intense, and by the end of the fifteenth century they predominated, Lagos falling under their overlordship.

About the time this happened, the Portuguese appeared and applied the name Lago de Curamo. Later they called it Onin and, finally, Lagos, after one of their home towns. The site was unhealthy because of its low elevation and bad drainage, encouraging bubonic and other plagues, and because of malarial mosquitoes in the occasionally flooded areas. Nevertheless, it was an excellent lair for slave-traders, near the sea, yet easily protected from sea attack. To it slaves could be sent by inland waterways from the Dahomey, Yoruba and Benin kingdoms, which were willing to sell their military and political captives.

Because of these physical advantages, and the exceptionally heavy supply of slaves from the Yoruba civil wars of the nineteenth century, Lagos remained one of the last great centres of the illegal slave trade. To stop it, the British occupied Lagos in 1851 and installed a new king and a vice-consul. Portuguese merchants restarted the trade, so in 1861 Lagos was taken to suppress it, restrict the sources of supply, and develop legal commerce.

The island of Lagos became a colony in 1862, was added to in 1863, and between 1883 and 1895. In 1866 it was included (rather as a necessary encumbrance) in the 'West African Settlements' under the governor resident in Freetown, Sierra Leone. In 1874 Lagos came under the governor of the Gold Coast, but in 1886 it regained independent administration as the 'Colony and Protectorate of Lagos'.

The oldest and most densely peopled part of Lagos Island is the north-northwestern part (Fig. 26.2). After 1861 the southwestern corner became the commercial quarter and many firms established wharves. The south-eastern part came to be occupied by government, missions, schools, hospitals and major European residences. Behind it, in the centre of the island, ex-slaves from Brazil had settled earlier in the area then called the Brazilian quarter. Beyond this, on the northeast, were late nineteenth and early twentieth century African houses. The eastern extremity of the island was at first the European quarter.

The governorship of Sir William MacGregor (1899–1904) saw much development and improvement. The MacGregor canal was dug along the then eastern limit of the town, so creating Ikoyi Island. This was used for the cemetery and farther east for the later European (now Senior Service) residential quarters. The railway was opened to Ibadan in 1901 and, at the same time, the Denton railway bridge between Iddo Island and the mainland, and the Carter road bridge from Iddo Island to Lagos. The latter was rebuilt in 1931, when the former was transformed into a causeway.

The fusion in 1906 of the Colony of Lagos and the Protectorate of Southern Nigeria eliminated the danger of a railway being built from a rival port west of the Niger; it also concentrated the trade of a larger

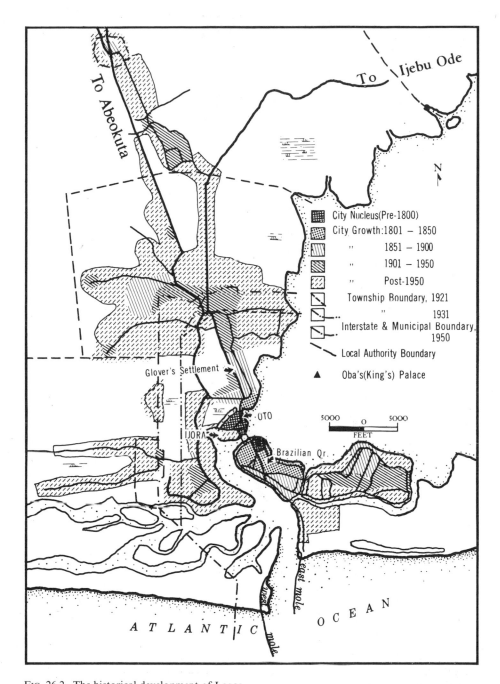

FIG. 26.2. The historical development of Lagos

This and the following two maps are by Dr P. Sada, University of Lagos, who kindly permitted their use here

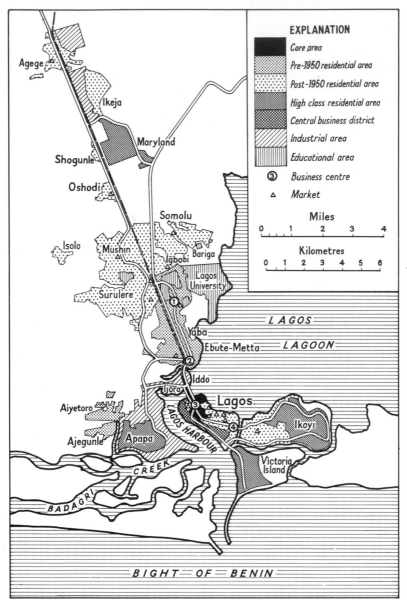

FIG. 26.3. Lagos areas

political unit at Lagos.

Ocean steamers were still unable to enter Lagos. Passengers were transferred by 'mammy chair' to surf boats or tenders offshore, while cargo was transhipped at Forcados to 'branch boats' of 900–1 200 tons which could enter Lagos.

With rapidly increasing trade this became intolerable, so that dredging

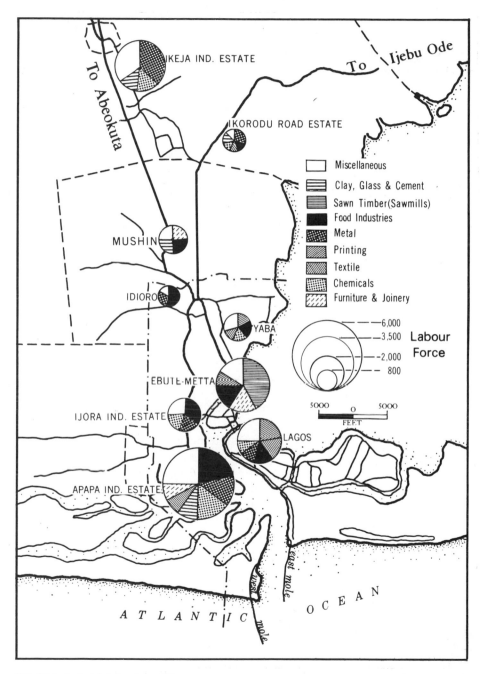

Fig. 26.4. Industrial structure of Lagos

and the construction of moles and training banks on either side of the entrance were begun in 1906. Ocean vessels first entered in 1914, just as the opening of the Lagos–Kano railway in 1912 and the unification of Nigeria in 1914 (with its capital at Lagos) were concentrating ever more trade on it.

The inauguration in 1926 of the Apapa wharves on the mainland west of Lagos greatly increased port capacity, though lighterage was sometimes necessary to Lagos wharves. A few ocean vessels still use Lagos berths, whilst others anchor in the intervening channel to wait for berths or for unloading into lighters. Apapa was further extended southeastward in 1955 and again in 1965. A lighter wharf was also provided.

Northwest of the Apapa wharves is the largest industrial estate of Lagos (Fig. 26.4). The exceptionally varied factories include a flour mill, a brewery (which started by using empty bottles from competing imported beers), a truck assembly and repair plant, metal container manufacturing, soap and margarine works, a bulk palm oil installation, mineral oil depot, and an oxygen works.

To the west of Apapa are housing estates of the Lagos Executive Development Board. This body encouraged industry to move to sites adjacent to the Apapa wharves, and the movement of Lagos Island dwellers to new houses at Apapa. Congestion on Lagos Island was reduced, but unfortunately many people must still commute between Lagos and Apapa by road or ferry. Moreover, high rise development took place in the late 1950s and '60s on Lagos Island, especially along and near the Marina, so that there is also much movement into Lagos Island, and severe traffic congestion.

North of Apapa and of Lagos Island is Iddo Island, now linked by a second bridge to Lagos. Iddo has the railway terminus, West Africa's largest thermal power station, and Ijora industrial estate. West of it, on the mainland, is the northern end of Apapa industries which are continued by those of Iganmu (Plate 99).

Northwards on the mainland is Ebute Metta, the earliest indigenous suburb, first established for railway workers, some of whom work in the adjacent railway workshops and railway headquarters. Here is another industrial estate.

Northwest again is Yaba, with hospitals, a college of technology, and another industrial estate. The University of Lagos lies northeastward towards the lagoon. On the northern edge of former federal territory is Sure Lere, and the generally poorer settlements of Mushin (with more industries), Igbobi and Shomolu beyond the former boundary but all now in Lagos State. Still farther on are the Ikorodu road industrial estate, and at Ikeja the airport and an impressive industrial estate with many factories making a variety of consumer goods such as textiles, shoes, drugs, beer and hardware, as well as paints and asbestos cement, etc. The area benefits from proximity to the port of Lagos, yet it avoids

PLATE 98. Corrugating machine in a packaging material factory, Apapa, Lagos

PLATE 99. Beer storage tanks at Iganmu brewery, Lagos

PLATE 100. Textile mill, Ikeja, Lagos State

its disadvantages, such as congestion.

Lagos is in danger of becoming another Calcutta, with severe concentration and congestion of people, activities and functions. Thus over two-fifths of all industrial enterprises are in Lagos State, and one-third of industrial employees.

# Western State

### Southern Abeokuta and western Ijebu[10]

These have the same Eocene clays, sand and sandstones as the Togo and Dahomey 'Terre de Barre' and Dahomey plateaux (see p. 409). Similar food crops are grown, vegetables being especially important west of Ilaro and rice in swampy valleys. Lagos and Ibadan offer excellent markets.

Previously this area was extensively planted with cocoa, but the soils are too light, poor and quick draining. There has been considerable replanting with kolas, rubber, citrus, bananas and pineapples. Citrus fruits and pineapples are canned at Agege, Abeokuta and Ibadan.

### Central Yorubaland

This lies on the southern side of the Niger river–Gulf of Guinea watershed, the relief of which is higher and more broken in the east, e.g. around Ilesha and Akure. Central Yorubaland is the fortunate possessor of fertile loamy soils, derived mainly from Pre-Cambrian hornblende–biotite gneiss.

The Yoruba has generally been a careful and fairly intensive farmer. Yams, cassava, maize, plantains and palm produce are important food

PLATE 101. Lagos–Ibadan road, with electric power line from Ijora. Underneath are oil palms, cocoyams, maize and bananas. On the right are kola trees and palms

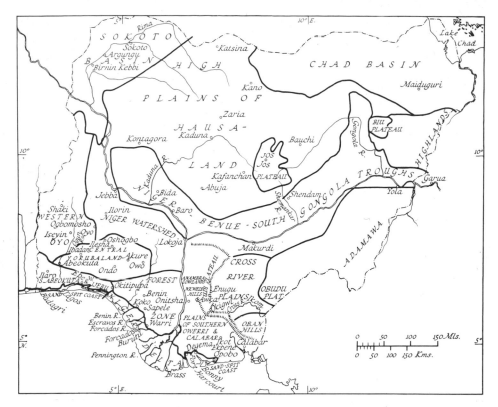

FIG. 26.5. Geographical regions of Nigeria

crops,[11] but there is not much surplus for sale because of the dense population. The Yoruba farmer still tends to live partly in towns, so that large cities such as Ibadan and Abeokuta are an outstanding feature of Yorubaland. Population density is everywhere over 77 per sq km (200 per sq mile), and often over 116 per sq km (300 per sq mile). The area is well served by roads.

This is probably the most productive area in Nigeria, deriving its wealth from cocoa farming and commerce.[12] Cocoa production is limited by insufficient humidity on the northwest and north and by leached sandy soils on the south and east. There are about 445 000 ha (1·1 m acres) under cocoa, cultivated by some 350 000 farmers, so that most Yoruba are directly dependent upon the crop as their major source of income. Farms are commonly 0·4–0·8 ha (1–2 acres). Cocoa is affected by swollen shoot, especially east of Ibadan, but less so than in Ghana. The main cocoa belt extends east-northeast from Abeokuta for some 320 km (200 miles) and is about 64 km (40 miles) from north to south. In area about 25 900 sq km (10 000 sq miles), it includes Abeokuta, Ibadan, Oshogbo, Ondo, Akure, Owo and Ikare. The last two lie near its eastern boundary,

433

beyond which there is some expansion on poor soils. In the centre of the cocoa belt over half the farm lands have been planted with cocoa, often now old. Cultivation is less intensive but more recent in Ondo.

Commerce is largely in cocoa, yams from northern Oyo and northern Ondo, cassava from Ijebu (as central Yorubaland no longer produces sufficient food crops), kola nuts from southern Abeokuta and Ijebu going north, fruit for canning or for despatch to the north, and in local craft goods and imports for the massive urban populations.

*Abeokuta,*[13] centre of the Egba people, like Ibadan owed its foundation about 1830 to the disintegration of the Oyo–Yoruba kingdom. Abeokuta is near contrasting soils and cash crops—mainly cocoa and yams to the north; kola, citrus, pineapple and cassava to the south. There is a brewery, as well as fruit canning and juice production in the town, which is also an important market and collector of these crops. Ewekoro cement works is nearby.

*Ibadan,*[14] population 627 379 (1963) is the largest truly indigenous city in tropical Africa. Ibadan is also the capital of Western State, the site of a university, a major collecting point for farm produce, and a great centre of commerce, crafts and of some industries. Despite all this and its size, about one-fifth of its population is engaged in farming, so that Ibadan is often described as a gigantic village. Farmers may reside partly in a village and partly in Ibadan. Within 32 km (20 miles) there is a rural population of 300 000.

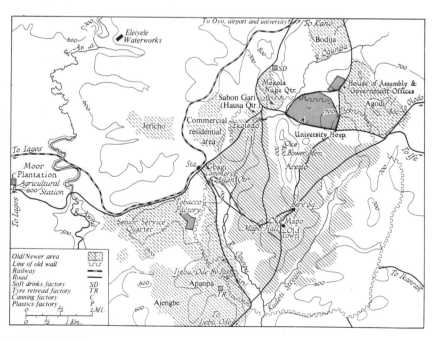

FIG. 26.6. Ibadan

PLATE 102. Air view of Ibadan looking east-northeast over the Jericho estate, the
railway station, the central business district and densely peopled quarters of the old town. In
the left distance are the wooded slopes of Oke Aremo and on the right Oke Mapo with Mapo hall

435

PLATE 103. Cigarette making in the Ibadan tobacco factory, opened 1937, and one of the first true factories in Nigeria

Ibadan was founded near the end of the eighteenth century as a camp of outlaws. The modern settlement dates from about 1829, when it became a rallying point and Yoruba military headquarters after the Owu Wars (1821–25), which had disrupted Yorubaland. It also sheltered refugees from the Fulani conquest of northern Oyo.

By 1851 the town had 18 km (11 miles) of walls, which, in time of conflict, provided protection by night for farmers who by day cultivated land up to 10 km (6 miles) away. Successful protection for a population of about 60 000 accounted for the survival and growth of Ibadan. When it came under British rule in 1893 the population had risen to about 120 000. Commercial and European quarters were soon built and the railway came in 1901.

In the centre of the town are narrow north–south quartzite hills, the highest and most northerly one being Oke Aremo, so commanding an excellent view of possible attackers and aiding defence. The southern hill is Oke Mapo, on whose eastern and southern slopes the original war camp was established. It has Ibadan's oldest houses, largely inhabited by descendants of the original settlers.

On either side of these hills run streams, but disease had the effect of keeping early settlement on the hill slopes and adjacent pediments. Draining of the marshes brought settlement nearer the streams, along which vegetables and sugar cane are still grown. On the northeastern Agodi hill are government offices.

436

Within the 22 sq km (8·5 sq miles) inside the old walls, the population density is about 20 800 per sq km (54 000 per sq mile), averaging 24 per house and up to 100 per compound.

There are three exceptionally large markets. The major traditional crafts are weaving, indigo dyeing and metal work, mostly found in compounds in the oldest quarters. Tailoring (the most common undertaking), cycle and car repairing, and woodworking are more modern and scattered, and are more important than the traditional crafts. Industry is, for example, represented by a tobacco factory, a cannery dealing with grapefruit and pineapple, and by a tyre-retreading works.

Other major towns of central Yorubaland are Ife (the spiritual centre of the nation and with a university), Ilesha, Iwo and Oshogbo. Most of those developed, like Abeokuta and Ibadan, to house farmers whose fields might lie well away from the town. They had double wall systems, with farmlands between inner and outer walls to withstand siege. Protected town dwelling by night was the Yoruba answer to war and civil war. It was not urbanisation as found in Europe.

## Western Oyo

This is distinguished from the former area by shallow and sandy soils which are far less fertile, lesser rain of the seasonal equatorial type, poorer vegetation and eccentric position. For these reasons, those of history and of forest reservation, population density drops sharply. There are few towns, Ogbomosho, a marginal town, being the largest. Low population density and few towns result from this having been a no-man's-land between the Yoruba and Dahomey peoples, and from Fulani attacks. Cocoa and the oil palm cannot be grown economically, and although crops are more varied there are no very valuable ones grown over extensive areas.

As the annual rainfall is under 1 145 mm (45 in) and the population sparser, there is a surplus of yams and cassava for sale, and guinea corn and millets are grown for local subsistence. Another cash crop is tobacco[15] (grown for the Ibadan factory). Cotton, indigo (much used in dyeing at Oyo and Iseyin) and chillies are also grown for sale. Zebu cattle are even kept in the north of Oyo. There is an interesting goat- and sheep-skin leather craft industry at Oyo, as well as cloth weaving and dyeing.

This area, undoubtedly impoverished in the past, is capable of development, although it may never be as productive as central Yorubaland.

## Conclusion: Western State

The State has considerable physical and human variety. Cocoa is an important export; kola nuts, food crops, palm oil and kernels are major cash crops for internal marketing.

Mostly richer soils and lower rainfall than are usual in southern Nigeria have enabled the careful Yoruba farmer to find in cocoa an outstandingly valuable crop, though it is one of possible danger in view of diseases, pests, new competitors, and fluctuating prices.

## Mid Western State

### The Niger delta

This magnificent example of a delta may be taken to begin 100 km (62 miles) east of Lagos. Surf, sand, palms and undergrowth give way to smooth water running over a wide mudflat with mangrove and swamp. This great change coincides with a southeastward turn in the direction of the coast.

Instead of an easterly longshore drift there is a northwesterly one on the west side of the delta. The rivers Benin, Escravos and Forcados, unobstructed by sandspits, are nevertheless increasingly impaired by large submerged bars, that in the Forcados mouth being 5 km (2 miles) wide, seven times wider than in 1899. The depth of the navigable channel over that bar decreased from 6·4–4·0 m (21–13 ft) between 1899 and 1947. Until 1914 goods for Lagos were transhipped at Forcados but then, partly because of the state of this bar, Forcados decayed. Instead, the narrow Escravos entrance was opened in 1940 (minimum depth now of 6·7 m: 22 ft), and soon became to be preferred to the Forcados entrance, as giving deeper water and being easier to navigate. Yet the Escravos entrance requires a longer journey for ships using Burutu and Warri, though a shorter one for those using Koko and Sapele. It has been dredged, and maintained by a breakwater to the south (Fig. 26.7). Forcados has been redeveloped as an oil terminal.

Warri and Burutu export some groundnuts, cotton, cotton seed and cake brought down the Benue river from Cameroon and Chad; groundnuts from regions along the Benue, and from northern Nigeria brought by rail to Baro and thence down the Niger; and cocoa, palm oil, kernels, rubber and timber from those parts of southern Nigeria near the Niger river. Imports are distributed to the same areas.

*Burutu* was a nineteenth century creation of the Niger River Transport Company, and has two ocean berths. Here goods are transhipped to and from river vessels, which include petroleum barges. The port is a base for offshore petroleum exploration and production.

*Warri* performs similar functions. It is an old settlement, which in the fifteenth and later centuries saw Portuguese missionaries and Portuguese and Dutch slave traders. It is heavily oriented to the import of oil-mining equipment, and will have Nigeria's second oil refinery.

*Sapele,* 113 km (70 miles) up the Benin river, is the site of a timber mill, plywood and veneer factory (see p. 468), as well as of rubber plantations, oil palm estates and mills.

*Koko* has bulk palm oil plants, and rather abortive attempts have been made to develop it as a general port.

The delta mouths offered shelter to the early slave traders and easy concealment in the last days of the illegal trade. In addition to the many mouths, there is a continuous line of creeks and lagoons from the Pennington river northwestward via Forcados, Epe and Lagos to Porto-Novo in Dahomey. This provides a calm inland waterway for small

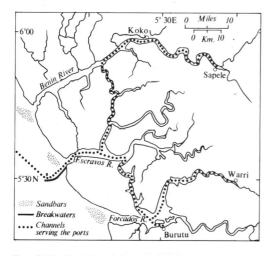

FIG. 26.7. The West delta ports

vessels. On the landward or inner side of this waterway, freshwater swamp vegetation is found from which Raphia is obtained, and obstruction by water vegetation occurs in some parts of the creek-lagoon waterway. On the seaward side, mangrove is cut for tanning material, constructional timber and fuel. Swamp rice cultivation is developing where salt content of the soil is low.

## The forest zone

Soils of this zone are derived from post-Middle Eocene sands which drain rapidly. As the rainfall is 2 285–3 050 mm (90–120 in) in an equatorial regime, and the soils were originally poor, they are now severely leached and acidic. Water is generally found at great depth, so that settlement was probably always sparse in southern Ondo and western Benin. As this area was also a frontier zone between the Yoruba and Edo (Bini) peoples, and was raided for slaves, its sparse population was reduced still further. Nigeria's best and most accessible timber reserves are being developed here, mainly in the Mid-Western State.

In the south and southeast, where the rainfall is highest, the oil palm, rubber and rice are significant crops. Rubber comes mainly from the Warri–Sapele–Kwale–Benin areas, and rice from along the many rivers. In southern Benin, the Sobo grasslands were probably caused by over-farming and forest regeneration is prevented by annual burning.

In eastern Benin, westward from the Niger river, where the annual rainfall is still over 2 285 mm (90 in), is an extension of the main palm belt from eastern Nigeria. There is the same oil palm bush, with associated cocoyam, cassava and maize as food crops. Moreover, this has scattered houses of the Ibo, unlike the usually linear villages of the Bini, or the compact large villages or once-walled towns of the Yoruba.

Population density exceeds 70 per sq km (180 per sq mile) in Asaba division. Consequently, although palm oil production is high, so much is consumed locally that the amount available for export is smaller than farther south or west, where the population is less. Export of kernels is much higher than that of oil.

Northeastern Benin, being drier and less populated, produces less palm oil and kernels, but is a significant producer of rice, yams and of cotton. As it is rather remote from communications and markets, the economy is essentially a subsistence one.

*Benin*, population 100 694 (1963) is the capital of the Mid-Western State, the centre of the Bini people, and a commercial, artisanal and educational centre. Benin was visited by the Portuguese in 1485, when it was a powerful independent kingdom. It soon engaged fully in the pepper, ivory and slave trades, and later fell under a tyranny of fetish priests who made huge annual human sacrifices. The famous brass figures, and the less well known wood and ivory articles are still made.

### Conclusion: Mid-Western State

At first sight the Mid-Western State—less developed and with only one-quarter the population of the Western State, would seem to have poor prospects. However, it has very important resources of mineral oil and gas, timber, rubber and palm oil. Some natural gas is being used in industry and electrical generation. The delta ports have improved access, and are of increasing importance for local commerce as well as serving as inlets and outlets for modest transit traffic to and from northern Nigeria and beyond, in competition with congested Lagos and Port Harcourt. Given good government and sensible policies the Mid-West could be very prosperous.

# Rivers, East-Central, and South-Eastern States[16]

## The Niger delta

The western part of this occurs in the Mid-Western State. Rainfall often exceeds 3 560 mm (140 in) per annum, mangrove vegetation is luxuriant and swamps widespread. The latter are being developed for rice; otherwise fish are the main resource.

As permanently-dry points are rare, roads are few. The infrequent, and essentially fishing villages are on or near waterways, which alone provide constant access. With such difficulties and the unhealthy character of the country, the population density is no more than 15 per sq km (40 per sq mile) in Brass division. Population may also have been lowered by slave raiding, for here were the slave and oil trade ports of the Oil Rivers, such as Akassa, Brass, Degema and Bonny. Most of these have declined, though Opobo and Abonnema have palm oil bulking plants, and Bonny is a major mineral oil export terminal.

*Port Harcourt,*[16] population 95 768 (1963), capital of Rivers State, lies 66 km (41 miles) up the Bonny river, at the limit of mangrove, where there are depths in the river of 13·4 m (24 ft) at high water, and firm dry land. These advantages were noticed by Sir Frederick (later Lord) Lugard in 1913, when he was seeking a terminus for a railway to serve the coalfield at Enugu. The railway between the two was opened in 1916, and Port Harcourt became a distributor of coal by sea to other ports, the rest of Nigeria and, on occasion, other countries in and even outside West Africa. It also immediately became an exporter of palm oil and kernels from the nearby oil palm belt and now has a large bulk palm oil plant.

The railway was extended to Kaduna and Jos in 1927. After this, and especially after 1932, when the Benue bridge was completed, Port Harcourt became the port for the Jos tinfields and for some of the produce of northern Nigeria, especially groundnuts.

The town is built above and east of the Bonny river, between it and Amadi creek on the east and another creek on the south. It is Nigeria's second port, the main one of eastern Nigeria and has road, rail, river and air connections.

Port Harcourt is the centre for the eastern part of the oilfields, and has a refinery. Natural gas is piped to the Trans-Amadi estate where tyres, aluminium sheets, bottles and other goods are made. Port Harcourt could become a major Nigerian town and industrial centre of the federation.

## Sandspit coast

This occurs east of the delta, but lagoons are ill-developed and creeks take their place.

*Calabar,* once known as Old Calabar, lies 77 km (48 miles) up the

Calabar river, a tributary of the Cross river. It was a notorious slave port, the last illegal ship leaving only in 1839. Calabar was also the centre of the subsequent palm oil trade and of the famous 'ruffians', or masters of trading hulks moored in the rivers. Trading houses were not built ashore until the 1870s.

The Oil Rivers Protectorate was proclaimed in 1885, and Calabar became its headquarters until, in 1906, the Protectorate (by then called Southern Nigeria) was amalgamated with Lagos Colony.

A Presbyterian mission was founded in 1846, and Calabar remained the headquarters of that church. The palm oil trade and the mission are still dominant in the town, but Calabar has suffered relative economic decline compared with Port Harcourt. Calabar is, however, served by air, by a few roads, and by the Cross river. This is navigable in the wet season to Mamfe in Cameroon, for which Calabar acts as a trade centre. A road also connects these towns, and Calabar may become an outlet for more of eastern and northeastern Nigeria.

After declining in competition with Enugu and Port Harcourt, Calabar may have a new lease of life as the capital of the South-Eastern State. Industries are also developing, such as plywood and veneer, and clinker cement. Calabar people are important in fishing and commerce in all the Bight of Biafra.

### Plains of southern Owerri and Calabar[17]

These lie inland from the previous region and south of the north-facing Eocene sandstone scarp. This begins west of Akwa (near Onitsha, see Figs 26.8–9) and extends southeastward as the edge of the Akwa–Orlu uplands to just north of Calabar, and so into Cameroon. In the northwest this scarp is some 122 m (400 ft) high and severely gullied, but it is lower in the southeast. Other than the fringing scarp, the deposits are clays, sandstones and lignites of post-Middle Eocene age.

Acid sandy soils are again found, similar to those dominant in the forest zone of the Mid-Western State. They are even more leached in the east, partly by very heavy rainfall of at least 1 780 mm (70 in). Severe leaching is not only a function of the heavier rainfall, but also of the generally uninterrupted rainy season of the Cameroon type. In southern Owerri and Calabar, heavy lateritic soils occur in lower-lying and ill-drained areas, which are also less peopled and unhealthy.

In place of the original rainforest, oil palms now predominate. The climate for the oil palm is ideal and, although the soils are poor, it tolerates them. There has been much replanting under the Palm Grove Rehabilitation Scheme.[18] This is the heart of the oil palm belt and from here comes the bulk of the production. Pioneer mills and hand presses have increased the extraction of oil and its quality. Cassava is the main food crop, followed by yams, cocoyams, plantains, maize and vegetables.

PLATE 104. Government sponsored oil palm
replanting near Uyo

Production of palm oil for the large local population and kernel export
dominates the rural economy. There are also some oil palm and rubber
estates east and north of Calabar.

The density of oil palms is closely allied with that of human population
—this despite the most unfavourable conditions of sandy soils and elusive
water supplies. Settlements are compounds, rather than villages or towns.
Though the area is intensively farmed, the pattern of settlement contrasts
strongly with the urban clusters of Yorubaland.

Population densities here are the highest in Nigeria, and average
about 345 per sq km (nearly 900 per sq mile). Even higher densities
of up to 615 per sq km (over 1 600 per sq mile) occur in Orlu in the
north of Iboland, and of 460 per sq km (nearly 1 200 per sq mile) in
Uyo division of Ibibioland near Calabar. Moreover, such densities are
truly rural ones. These densely peopled core areas are separated by the
former shatter belt between the Ibo and Ibibio in Bende and Aba
divisions, where figures are nevertheless about 210 per sq km (550 per
sq mile). There is severe pressure of population in Orlu and Uyo divisions
at least, the visible consequences of which are the renting of farmland
outside the areas, petty trading and minor service activities and, normally,
the migration of labourers to other parts of Nigeria, to Fernando Po
and Gabon. The dense road network is a reflection of the dense population
and intense economic activity.

*Onitsha* lies on the higher east bank of the Niger, and has for long
been a market for goods first brought by canoe and now mainly by road
transport, facilitated by the Niger bridge opened in 1965. Onitsha was
severely damaged in the 1967–70 war.

443

## The Cretaceous country of the Anambra lowlands, Udi plateau and Cross river plains[19]

The constituent regions are:

(a) THE CROSS RIVER PLAINS in the southeast and east, which are drained by the Cross river and its tributaries, and vary in altitude from 213 m (700 ft) in the northwest to less than 61 m (200 ft) in the south. Beneath them are intensely folded Middle Cretaceous shales, sandstones and limestones.

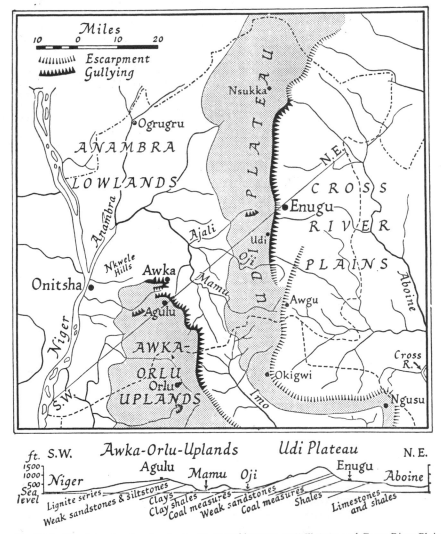

Fig. 26.8. The Anambra Lowlands, Awka–Orlu Uplands, Udi Plateau and Cross River Plains

(From A. T. Grove, 'Soil erosion and population problems in South-East Nigeria', *Geographical Journal*, **117**, no. 3, 1951, 295, by permission of the author and editor)

(*b*) THE UDI PLATEAU, running north–south, is bounded on the east and north by a bold escarpment.

The plateau rises in places to over 457 m (1 500 ft) above sea level and slopes southwestward into the syncline of the Anambra lowlands. These several features result from the sub-aerial denudation of an anticline, whose eastern limb has been eroded.

The cuesta is composed of Upper Cretaceous Coal Measures, hard sandstones and shales; the dipslope has false-bedded sandstones. These are also exposed in the northern sector of the scarp (north of the Oji river and south of Udi), and it is these sandstones which have been easily eroded in gigantic gullies. South of the river another scarp, formed of far more resistant Awgu sandstone, overlaps the northern sector and gullying is absent.

The Udi cuesta runs southward to near Okigwi, where it swings eastward as a hog's back to near the Cross river, and then turns south and southeast[20] to Cameroon. Some 15–30 km (10–20 miles) separate it from the Eocene scarp of the plains of southern Owerri and Calabar.

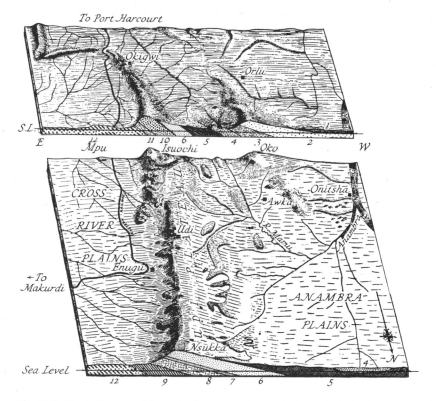

Fig. 26.9. Block diagram of Anambra Plains (lowlands), Awka–Orlu Uplands, Udi Plateau and Cross River Plains

(From A. T. Grove, *Land Use and Soil Conservation*, Bulletin no. 21 of Geological Survey of Nigeria, 1951, p. 2, by permission of the author and director)

(*c*) THE ANAMBRA LOWLANDS (or plains), in the northwest, between the Niger river and the Udi plateau, are floored by sandstones and shales of the Upper Cretaceous Coal Measures. On the southern edge is the Eocene scarp of the Awka–Orlu uplands and the post-Middle Eocene Nkwele hills very near Onitsha.

Rainfall varies between 1 525 mm (60 in) in the north to 2 045 mm (85 in) in the south, and the Udi plateau has a generally higher rainfall than the Anambra lowlands or Cross river plains. Rainfall is of the seasonal or semiseasonal equatorial type, and the original vegetation was probably rainforest. On the uplands, economically useful trees survive only on steep slopes and around villages—'cool green islands set in poor grassland where fire resistant species . . become more numerous as the distance from the nearest village increases. The barren appearance of this outside farmland is surprising in a region with such a high annual rainfall'.[21] Grassland also covers wide areas below the Udi escarpment and in the Anambra lowlands.

The Udi plateau has poor and acidic soils, and those of the Anambra lowlands and Cross river plains are often lateritic. In the Anambra lowlands water is found only at about 75 m (nearly 250 ft) or more, and is insufficient or remote for most people on the Udi plateau. Only on the scarp are there numerous springs.

On the plateau population density averages 135 per sq km (350 per sq mile), and because of the poor environment population pressure exists. People rent farms elsewhere and migrate for work.

The main income is from the oil palm, supplemented by food crop sales in the cases of the less populated lowlands, and by employment in the coal mines and the cement works at Nkalagu east of Enugu. Further employment might be provided by the exploitation of clays for brick-making.

*Enugu*, population 138 457 (1963), lies at the foot of the Udi scarp, where coal-mining began in 1915. Enugu owes its origin and development to mining, to being a capital, and to asbestos cement and scrap steel factories.

### The Oban hills

Lying northeast of Calabar, these are a northwesterly projection of the Cameroon highlands and consist of Pre-Cambrian basement rocks. Rainfall is 2 540–3,555 mm (100–140 in) annually, population is sparse, and the hills are thickly covered with rainforest. On the southern edge are rubber estates.

### The Obudu plateau and Sonkwala hills

Also Pre-Cambrian, these are northwestern projections of the Bamenda highlands, drained by the Katsina Ala tributary of the Benue. The higher parts of the Obudu plateau are covered by tsetse-free grassland where an 8 000 ha (20 000 acres) ranch has been established, as well as a holiday centre. However, access is tortuous.

### Conclusion: Rivers, East-Central and South-Eastern States

These states are the successors of the Eastern Region, the poorest region until 1962. Then the mounting development of mineral oil and gas transformed it into the richest one, revenue-wise, only to be contraried by the civil war of 1967–70.

Agriculturally, there are severe problems. There is excessive dependence upon the oil palm and the poor food crops of cassava and cocoyams, although there are other better ones. Most soils are inherently poor and severely leached as well, with locally acute gullying on escarpments.

The East-Central State, the Ibo homeland, is by far the most densely peopled state with, in 1963, 274 persons per sq km (711 per sq mile). The figures must now be far greater as the result of Ibo refugees from the rest of Nigeria. Their resettlement in an already heavily peopled countryside posed immense problems, vastly aggravated by dislocation and destruction during the civil war. Reconstruction has been costly, difficult and rather slow. Given the energy and enterprise of the Ibo, the long term prospects are better, but depend upon cooperation between all three states.

## The Northern States: 1. The Middle Belt[22]

One of the most distinctive divisions of Nigeria, as indeed of all West Africa, is the Middle Belt which lies between about 8° and $10\frac{1}{2}°$N. It is

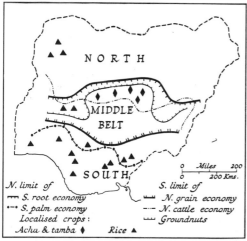

FIG. 26.10. The Middle Belt

(From K. M. Buchanan, 'Nigeria', *Economic Geography*, 1952, p. 308, by permission of the author and editor)

PLATE 105. Pig farm at Minna in the Middle Belt

particularly clear in Nigeria, because of the size of that country, and because the belt separates the 'Nigerian Sudan' from the forest lands.

Geologically and physiographically the belt has no unity, but climatically it roughly corresponds to the realm of the southern savanna climate. There is also close correspondence with the southern and northern Guinea vegetational zones.

Although the Middle Belt produces both the grains of the north and the root crops of the south, tsetse fly usually prevents the keeping of humped cattle, except where forest has been cleared (e.g. around Shendam) or in high areas notably the Jos plateau and the Adamawa highlands). Cocoa cannot be grown (except for a little in Kwara State), and only poor oil palms survive along some water courses. Thus the advantage of the Middle Belt in combining some northern and southern food crops is offset by the paucity of other crops, except the rather unimportant benniseed.

Thus, although the Middle Belt covers at least one-quarter of Nigeria, it contributes little to export and not much to internal trade. Development requires reduction or elimination of the tsetse fly to permit the widespread keeping of Zebu cattle, and to reduce sleeping sickness in man. A greater population could then grow more food crops for the rest of Nigeria. Pig rearing might be further developed by these non-Muslim peoples, using local root and grain crops. Hydroelectric power from the Kainji dam might be used for the development of more industries. Meanwhile, the main significance of the Middle Belt is in the rather modest production of food crops for deficit areas.

The Middle Belt may be divided into the following regions.

## The Niger watershed

This is the divide through which runs the boundary between the Kwara and Western states, following the main limit of Fulani conquest, rather than the precise water-parting. The boundary leaves within Kwara a Yoruba majority in the Ilorin Emirate.

The watershed is composed of Pre-Cambrian rocks, its soils are thin, and the vegetation Guinea savanna. Tobacco is increasingly grown for manufacture at Ilorin, whilst yams, beans, onions and rice are the main food crops, sold mostly to the cocoa growing areas with a food crop deficit.

Ilorin, the seat of a Fulani but Yoruba-speaking Emir, is the capital of Kwara State. There are tobacco and match factories, and pots are made in traditional fashion.

## The Niger–Benue–South Gongola troughs

These are probably of tectonic origin, and have Cretaceous deposits, which weather into fairly productive soils, used for benniseed cultivation north and south of Makurdi, and for some cotton in Kwara. Alluvial soils along the rivers are being increasingly used for rice, and at Bacita for irrigated sugar cane.

The Benue is navigable to *Garoua* (Cameroon) for about two and a half months annually but *Makurdi* is the flood season headquarters for Benue push-tow barge 'trains'. Baro is another minor transhipment point for river traffic, in this case 'fed' by a branch railway originally built as a trunk route. Waterborne traffic has generally declined, first to the railways, then to road traffic and, lastly, through interruption by the civil war. However, the navigational locks at and below the Kainji dam (pp. 472 and 477) should encourage navigation as far as the low bridge at Gaya (Niger Republic). The construction of *New Bussa* and of parts of Yelwa result from the flooding of lands behind the dam (Plate 118). *Lokoja,* on the right bank of the Niger and opposite the Benue confluence was formerly an important centre of river traffic, but has declined greatly. However, it may revive with a new road to be built to link Jos with Warri, crossing the Niger upstream at Koton Karifi, and even more so if iron ore on nearby Mount Patti is exploited and smelted locally. *Bida,* the Nupe centre, is famous for brass, silver, glass and raphia craftsmen.

## The southern high plains of Hausaland

These plains consist of Pre-Cambrian schists and quartzites, and their elevation varies between a little over 300 m (1 000 ft) in Kontagora to over 900 m (3 000 ft) southeast of Kaduna.

Kontagora is thinly peopled because of past slave raiding and consequential tsetse infestation and human avoidance. By contrast, broken country around Abuja may have helped to keep its people independent from the Fulani (who, nevertheless, attacked them), and there is a pocket of denser population. Various efforts have been made to resettle more or less empty areas; thus in Kontagora the local authority tried land settlement with mixed farms, but this and the Mokwa scheme both failed. The only considerable cash crops are cotton, tobacco and sugar.

*Kaduna,* with a population estimated at 255 000 in 1970, was made headquarters of the Northern Provinces in 1917, later became the capital of Northern Nigeria, and in 1967 that of North-Central State. Kaduna is a major administrative, military and industrial centre with five textile mills and other works. It will have Nigeria's third oil refinery.[23]

## The Jos plateau

This is often misnamed the Bauchi plateau, but Bauchi town is beyond the plateau. The highland extends some 105 km (65 miles) from south to north and 81 km (50 miles) from east to west, with an average height of about 1 310 m (4 300 ft). Granite masses, some reaching about 1 830 m (6 000 ft), have formed a resistant core throughout many erosion cycles, compared with less resistant surrounding gneisses. The plateau surface has very gently undulating grassy plains, with occasional granite tors, some flat-topped hills of the Fluvio-Volcanic series, and clusters of small recently extinct volcanic cones with basalt flows.

The edges of the plateau are much indented, the granites causing bold or rocky scarps and buttresses. Between these are embayments, with gently sloping floors, eroded on less resistant gneiss. With larger outcrops, the embayment floors continue to rise inward toward the plateau centre, thus somewhat facilitating rail and road access, e.g. the Kaduna–Jos road and the Kafanchan–Jos railway past the Assob basalts.

West and east, the plateau scarps are frequently 457–610 m (1 500–2 000 ft) high; on the south, they are 915 m (3 000 ft) or more. The structure is complex and the relief rugged. In places two or three bevels, with sharp scarps, intervene between plateau surface and the plains; falls, developed for hydroelectric power, are caused by these intervening scarps.

Whereas the Fulani penetrated and settled in the Fouta Djallon in Guinea, despite its abrupt edges and many deep gorges, they did not do so until recently on the Jos plateau. This is higher, but it has the advantage over the Fouta Djallon of being free of tsetse fly and of being less divided by gorges.

The Jos plateau was the refuge for peoples who had been attacked by the Fulani. The economy of the plateau has been retarded by isolation, the poverty of the soils, and the limited cropping possibilities offered by these in conjunction with the cooler rainy climate. The main cereals have been the poor Acha (*Digitaria exilis*) and Tamba (*Eleusine coracana*). Temperate vegetables are also produced for sale.

Tin mining (see pp. 473–5) has been the greatest economic activity on the Jos plateau since about 1903. Although this mining has benefited Nigeria as a whole, it has ruined some of the plateau farm land and discouraged its peoples from agriculture. On the other hand, tin mining is the major employment.

There is local land pressure, which the Shendam Agricultural Development and Resettlement Scheme has sought to alleviate. Many farmers and their families have been resettled in the formerly thinly populated Shendam district, where rice can be grown.[24]

Mining has had other more beneficial results; it has led to the development of hydroelectric power on the plateau edges and to the construction of many roads. But if the several minerals become unprofitable to work, the Jos plateau might become a problem area.

*Jos* is a European creation. It is the headquarters of Benue–Plateau State, is the organising centre for the tinfields and has some industry. By reason of its Hill Station, museum, climate and pleasant surroundings, Jos has some tourist trade, which might be fostered. Jos is served by road, air and rail.

## The Adamawa highlands

These lie on the border of Nigeria and Cameroon, mainly in the latter. The Adamawa highlands, unlike the Bamenda highlands farther south, are almost devoid of volcanic outcrops and so the soils are poorer. The highlands average 762 m (2 500 ft) in elevation, but in places reach about 2 042 m (6 700 ft). Divided by the Benue trough, they rise steeply but their summits are mostly smooth. Vegetation is Sudan savanna, the original woodland having been degraded.

South of the Benue river, the population is exceedingly sparse, communications poor and the country underdeveloped. The farmers terrace their lands, use manure, rotate crops, plant trees and keep animals. Some have moved to the plains on the west, but they often farm wastefully there. Their crops are guinea corn, millet, peppers, okro, yams, potatoes and cotton, and they collect wild produce. Small cattle are kept in the highlands, and Shuwa, Red Longhorn and White Fulani Zebu in the plains.

Those parts of the former United Kingdom Trusteeship of the Cameroons which opted to join Northern Nigeria in 1961 were far more closely identified with Nigeria than with Cameroon. This is because of kinship ties, closer economic relations and means of transport. Distances from the outside world are the main problem, and roads are especially necessary in the southern districts.

## The Northern States: 2. The 'Nigerian Sudan'

Like the Middle Belt, the Nigerian Sudan has no geological or physiographic unity, but climatically it belongs mainly to the savanna type and its vegetation is that of the Sudan savanna.

The Nigerian Sudan stands in sharp contrast to the Middle Belt, not only in its climate and vegetation, but also·in its cereal and groundnut cash crops, rarity of tsetse fly and the importance of livestock. It provides most of the revenue of the northern states; here also are great and sometimes extensive clusters of population. Restrictions upon development are the availability of water and roads. The Nigerian Sudan may be divided into the following regions:

### Northern high plains of Hausaland

These are the continuation of the southern high plains of Hausaland, which they resemble geologically, except that some Cretaceous deposits occur on the boundary between Katsina and Daura. Altitudes vary from about 305 to 762 m (1 000–2 500 ft). In the south there are more granite domes and rock masses than in the north, where the surface is very flat because of masking by sand. The Niger–Chad watershed is tilted towards the north and east. The rivers, dry for up to seven to eight months, flow seasonally in broad and shallow trenches.

Soils are light, sandy but water-holding in the Kano and Katsina areas, where they are ideal for groundnuts. In northern Zaria, eastern Sokoto and southern Katsina they are heavier, and more suitable for cotton. Nevertheless, these crops are often either intercropped or rotated. Tobacco is the subsidiary cash crop to cotton in Zaria, and follows groundnuts and cotton in importance in Gusau district. The main food crops are guinea corn, bulrush millet, beans, cow peas and a rapidly increasing amount of cassava. In town gardens and in the *fadamas* (flood plains) of all provinces, where darker alluvial soils occur, maize, rice, sweet potatoes, sugar cane, onions, tomatoes, indigo, tobacco, wheat and henna are grown, often in tiny irrigated fields. The protected shea butter tree provides oil, and the locust bean fruit a kind of edible cake and a hardening material. Baobab leaves are used in soup and as spinach, the fruit is edible and used in dyeing, and the bark is used for ropes. These are also made from the fibre of the dum palm.

Around large towns there is extremely 'close farming', sustaining dense populations by permanent and intensive cropping, fertility being maintained with town waste and manure brought from the towns on donkeys, who return with firewood. The population of the Kano close-settled zone[25] was about $2\frac{1}{2}$ million in 1962, living at densities above 135 per sq km (350 per sq mile). Farms average about 1·3 h (3·3 acres), and some 85 per cent of the land is cultivated every year. Almost every

PLATE 106. Farm near Kano. Despite the thin soils and the lateritic layer evident near the surface (right), there is intensive cultivation of guinea corn, groundnuts, chillies and other food crops. This is made possible by the use of town refuse and manure. The baobab trees also provide varied produce, and the lateritic layer provides building stone

PLATE 107. Donkeys which take out town refuse and droppings in the mornings are returning here in the afternoon with firewood. Guinea corn stocks are evident in the fields. A view near Kano but typical of all northern Nigerian town-country trade

PLATE 108. Kano from Dalla hill, looking southeast across the centre of Kano to the large mosque. In front is a 'burrow' pit from which earth has been taken for house building. Better-off people often have their houses whitewashed

piece of ground is or has been used, and the intensity of cultivation recalls Flanders. During the dry season, when food may be insufficient, some farmers engage in handcrafts, small-scale trading and seasonal employment.

These are among the few areas in Africa where indigenous farmers have, to use a French term, 'humanised' the countryside. In the wet season the impression is that man is dominant, rather than nature.

*Zaria*,[26] population 110 000 (1963) lies near the southern edge of this region on a defensive site, and was the capital of the Hausa kingdom of Zazzau. The walled town has tanning, weaving, dyeing and basket-making crafts. Outside, on the north, across the Kubanni stream and around the railway station (junction for a branch to Kaura Namoda), are agricultural and railway workshops, a cotton ginnery, textile works, a cigarette factory and a printing press. Near Zaria is Ahmadu Bello University, the largest employer in the town.

*Kano*,[27] population approximately 300 000, is one of the most interesting towns of West Africa, and the principal commercial centre of northern Nigeria. Neolithic stone implements suggest early occupation, and these and local legend point to the probable importance of Dalla hill as a source of ironstone, sought after by blacksmith settlers. Certainly, there was an influx in the tenth century. Dalla and Goron Dutsi hills served as watchtowers, like those in Ibadan. Kano was at the height of its

454

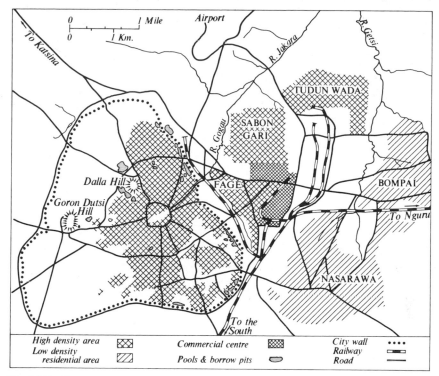

Fig. 26.11. Kano

glory and prosperity from 1463 to 1499, when trans-Saharan trade was considerable.

Within the walls are the two hills, the Jakara stream and grazing and agricultural land, perhaps to help withstand siege. There are also many 'borrow pits' from which earth has been taken to build the flat-roofed and interestingly patterned houses. The central market, astride the Jakara rivulet, is a particularly busy one. Also in the walled city are many brass and silversmiths, leather tanning and ornamental leather workers, makers of mats and rope, indigo blue and purple dyers, weavers, blacksmiths and potters. Tailors are now, however, the most numerous workers. Fulani dominate the southern quarters and Hausa the northern ones.

The British occupied Kano in 1903. At first Europeans lived in Nasarawa, in and around the Emir's suburban house. In 1905 government headquarters were developed at Bompai, where more water was available, but between 1909 and 1926 all but the Police, Judicial and Military departments moved back to Nasarawa. In 1912, on the arrival of the railway, the commercial township (where the Asian community lives) was begun. Between it and the east wall of Kano is Fage, the settlement for Hausa-speaking strangers. Northeast of Fage is Sabon Gari, for people from the south. Away to the north, is the intercontinental airport, with direct services to Europe, some towns in Africa and in Nigeria.

455

Modern industries are also situated outside the walled city. They include soft drink, cosmetic, confectionery, tile, furniture and soap factories, groundnut oil (Plate 110) and flour mills, cotton weaving, the making of hollow ware and rubber shoes, tyre retreading, tanneries, a cannery, and a bone-crushing plant. There is also a huge piggery, managed by non-Muslims.

Kano lives a great deal by commerce. Its largest market has been mentioned. Camels and lorries also bring in produce from Niger, especially groundnuts, hides, skins, gum, salt and natron. Kano is the largest centre of the groundnut, cattle, hides and skin (especially goat) trades in Nigeria.

*Katsina* was founded about 1100, is smaller than Kano, but was a successful commercial rival to it until the Fulani Jihad in the early nineteenth century. Building, metal and leather working, pottery, embroidery, calabash carving and tailoring are the main crafts.

Katsina lies where Cretaceous rocks extend into a hollow of the impervious Pre-Cambrian series, forming a semi-artesian basin. Water is rarely more than 9 m (30 ft) down, though three-quarters of the 711 mm (28 in) of average annual rainfall are concentrated between July and September.

## The Sokoto basin

Lands to the south-east of Sokoto belong to the northern high plains of Hausaland just described. By contrast, Pre-Cambrian rocks are covered in the centre by Cretaceous series, and in the west by Tertiary ones. This part of the Sokoto basin, 'is characterised by gently undulating plains broken at intervals on the northwest by ranges and isolated groups of steep-sided, flat-topped hills capped with ironstone and scored by numberless gullies. The natural vegetation consists mainly of thorn scrub.'[28]

The gentle undulating plains have light, dry, coarse soils, the cultivation of which depends largely upon the availability of water. Where this is sufficient, groundnuts, millet, cotton and tobacco are important crops. Areas of low density are those where water is scarce, or were formerly areas of strife between the emirates of Katsina and Sokoto.

The most intensively cultivated and usually the most peopled areas are the Sokoto and Rima dallols or fadamas (seasonally flooded wide valleys). As the floodwater retreats so rice, onions, tomatoes, and sugar are cultivated. Mechanical cultivation, mainly for rice, has not been very successful. The only surplus commodities from these areas are hides, skins, onions and fish.

*Sokoto,* the spiritual headquarters and first centre of the Fulani, is capital of North-Western State, and has a cement works. *Gusau,* east of the basin and on the branch railway from Zaria, has a textile mill.

### The Biu plateau

This small but highly distinctive region, lies east of the Gongola tributary of the Benue, and averages 700 m (2 300 ft) in altitude. The plateau has Tertiary and younger volcanic rocks overlying the Pre-Cambrian series. Volcanic activity was probably associated with faults in the Gongola valley. Soils are thin and the region is poor but is being activated by road transport.

### The Chad basin

There has been a gentle downwarping of the Chad basin, and Tertiary and Quaternary rocks mask the Pre-Cambrian rocks.

The basin is under 487 m (1 600 ft) in elevation and has light sandy soils with patches of black cotton or 'firki' soils, especially in the north-east. Southern Sahel conditions prevail over the north of the basin, except for marshes near Lake Chad, but otherwise the basin has Sudan characteristics. Aridity alternating with floods and poor communications hindered settlement, which was also obstructed when the centre of the basin was the shatter zone between the Fulani and Bornu empires.

However, artesian boreholes have countered the natural aridity, whilst roads and to some extent the railway have enabled the cultivation of groundnuts and cereals and more grazing. Tarred roads extend to Baga on Lake Chad and to Fort Lamy (Chad). The former has encouraged fish, salt and natron traffic, and the latter transit trade through Nigeria for Chad. Irrigation is being developed along the Yobe (Nigeria–Niger boundary), as is more intensive fadama (flood retreat) cultivation near Maiduguri.

*Maiduguri* is a state capital, and has an oil mill.

### Conclusion: Northern States

The creation of the six states in 1967 ended the long dominance of the north in Nigeria. There is great diversity of physical and human conditions; outstanding are the contrasts between the Middle Belt and the Nigerian Sudan. Within each of these are such physical contrasts as that between the Niger–Benue–Gongola troughs and the Jos plateau in the Middle Belt; and such human contrasts as that between the craftsmen and dealers of the cities, with their intensive suburban farmers, and the nomadic Cow Fulani.

Development is, like the population distribution, very uneven. Probably the greatest contribution to agricultural advance will be by irrigation, especially in view of the proposals for perennial cropping on very large areas of upland Kano, using water from the Tiga dam, under construction on the Kano river. Irrigation should also make a great impact in the northeast, and it should be remembered that many northern peoples are well versed in the use of water in agriculture.

Improved livestock management depends on enhanced grazing and tsetse control, more economic attitudes among the cattle keepers, and better transport and marketing arrangements. The future of tin mining on the Jos plateau is uncertain in view of rising labour and transport costs. The latter are a major problem in all aspects of development in the north.

# ECONOMIC RESOURCES

## Agriculture

### General considerations

Of all West African lands, Nigeria is alone able to produce the complete range of foodstuffs described in Chapter 6.[29] Range of latitude, the varied relief, climate, vegetation and soils, differing peoples with their contrasted methods and crops, and the existence of plantations, make this possible.

As elsewhere in West Africa, subsistence farming is common, especially in the Middle Belt and in other more remote areas. However, as in Senegal and Ghana, ordinary African farmers produce massive quantities of surplus crops. These are especially cassava (gari), yams, cotton and kola nuts for the internal market and palm produce, cocoa, rubber and groundnuts for export. Plantations produce a relatively small part of the palm produce exported, but much more of the rubber.

Despite the spectacular rise of petroleum production and of manufacturing, fully three-quarters of the population depend upon agriculture, which accounts for two-fifths of national income. Agriculture is also labour intensive and nourishes many developing processing industries, e.g. textiles. Moreover, the rapidly rising market for foodstuffs is not being supplied adequately, so that food imports are rising fast. The improvement of agricultural productivity is thus urgently necessary.

### Agricultural zones

The following zones are based upon those used in the latest agricultural census, with later information.[30]

1. Low-lying oil palm belt. Cassava, yams and maize grown for subsistence and sale.
2. Cocoa zone, with kola in the southwest.
3. Food crops, with subsidiary cocoa, oil palm and citrus. Yams are the main crop, followed by cassava, maize and cow peas.
3a. Udi plateau and environs. Subsistence farming, mainly for yams.

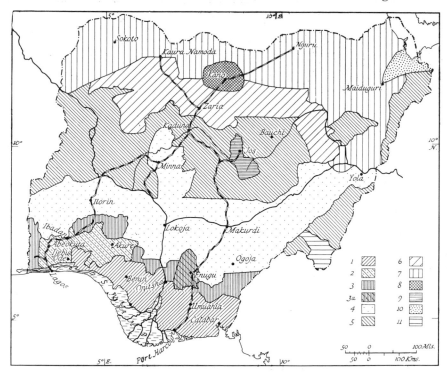

Fig. 26.12. Agricultural zones of Nigeria

(After map in *Sample Census of Agriculture* 1950–51, Department of Statistics, Lagos. See also W. B. Morgan, 'Agriculture in Southern Nigeria', *Economic Geography*, 1959)

4. Yam zone, with maize in the south, and guinea corn and millet in the north. Food crops are sold mainly to southern towns. Rice is important on the Niger flood plain and in Ogoja, and benniseed in Tiv country.

5. Subsistence grain zone (millet and guinea corn). Rice is important in swamp areas of Bida division, and groundnuts elsewhere.

6. Cotton zone, with subsidiary groundnuts and tobacco. Guinea corn, millet and cow peas are the principal food crops. Fadamas are cultivated for vegetables and sugar cane.

7. Groundnut zone, with greatest production in northern part of Kano State. Food crops as in Zone 6.

8. Permanent cropping of Kano country districts, with market gardening by irrigation adjacent to the city. Otherwise, crops as in 7, except that millet is the leading food crop.

9. Jos plateau. Acha the main food crop, with durra, tamba, millet and yams. Temperate vegetables are grown for cash.

10. Dry-season guinea corn zone of Lake Chad black cotton soils (Firki). The crop is planted at the end of the rains, when most of the land is flooded. It ripens as the floods recede during the dry season. Irrigated cultivation of rice and wheat is planned.

11. High grassland zone. Some Fulani herdsmen have settled, with a high density of cattle throughout the year. Varied crops, especially cocoyams, cassava, maize, sweet potatoes, bambarra groundnuts, African and European vegetables, and some arabica coffee.

## Crops

CASSAVA is certainly the most widely grown crop. It is increasing rapidly in northern and eastern Nigeria, in the latter at the expense of yams. Cassava is a very tolerant crop, easy to grow, but impoverishes soils.

YAMS are a much appreciated food but rarely one which farmers will grow in competition with more paying cash crops like cocoa. Hence cash cropping of yams tends to be restricted to the Middle Belt, where there are few competing cash crops, and to land near the railway or roads leading to the best markets in the prosperous cocoa country of the Western State.

GUINEA CORN, MILLET, SUGAR CANE and COW PEAS, all grown mainly in the north, give rise only to commerce for home consumption. Plantation sugar cane is grown with irrigation at Bacita, just east of Jebba, on the Niger alluvial plain. Further development is in hand there, and is proposed at Numan on the Benue. Sugar cane is also grown on small plots in most northern alluvial valleys.

PLATE 109. Irrigated sugar cane at Bacita, near Jebba, a plantation that produces a significant percentage of Nigeria's sugar. A 'rainer' and its feeder-pipe may be seen in the centre

RICE cultivation has vastly increased in recent years in area, as have yields. In the northern states it is grown in fadamas. Areas are being developed along the Sokoto, Rima, Niger, Benue, Gbako (near Bida) and other rivers. Inland and coastal swamps are also being brought into cultivation for swamp rice, including those around and near Lake Chad, to take the place of upland rice. Nevertheless, coastal swamps are less suitable in Nigeria than in Sierra Leone.

## OIL PALMS[31]

The oil palm not only provides a considerable range of produce for local needs, such as building material, fibre for mats, wine, oil for cooking, cleaning and illumination, but also important exports. Most of the oil is consumed in Nigeria, but almost all kernels are exported, either as kernels or crushed for the export of kernel oil. The export of palm oil goes back to the earliest days of trade with Europe, and Nigeria is still a leading world exporter, though exports fell very heavily as the result of the civil war of 1967–70.

In the southwest or Yoruba country, the oil palm reacts badly to the marked dry season, the mesocarp is thin, and cocoa cropping is far more profitable. The small amount of oil produced is mainly used locally, but there is an appreciable export of kernels.

In the Mid-Western, East-Central and South-Eastern States the rural economy is based on the oil palm. Stands are densest here because rainfall is generally over 1 525 mm (60 in) annually, the density of population is high, and the palm will tolerate mediocre soils. There is normally an appreciable surplus of oil from the Mid-Western and of kernels from the other states for export, the oil being of average quality.

There is an increasing number of plantations, notably near Sapele, Ahoada and the Cross river, and they contribute good quality oil and kernels. The quality of oil from Nigerian-owned palms improves eastward, and is especially good around Port Harcourt.

One of the most notable economic changes in Nigeria in the early 1950s was a remarkable improvement in the quality of ordinary palm oil, lifting most of it from the non-edible grades into the higher priced edible category. This was done by bonuses for the best qualities, and by encouraging the use of hand presses and small 'pioneer' oil mills. These extract much more oil and, normally, oil of better quality. Most of these mills were found near Aba, Opobo, and Abonnema, and as far north as Oguta. However, many have closed because of irregular supplies of fruit, poor maintenance, damage or disruption in the 1967–70 civil war, and opposition from hand pressers.

The next necessity is more widespread planting of new and better palms, greater care in their cultivation and in gathering and bringing in fresh fruit. The oil also needs quick bulkcarrying facilities. Bulking plants remove dirt and water, thus slowing down the formation of free-fatty-acid (f.f.a.), store the oil in clean and safe conditions prior to shipment, and pump it into coastal or ocean vessels.

## RUBBER

Rubber is produced in much the same areas as the oil palm but most of the output comes from the Warri–Sapele (Fig. 26.13)–Kwale–Benin areas, and from near Calabar. *Hevea brasiliensis* is alone important. Nigeria normally produces more rubber than Liberia, though most of the Nigerian output is inferior in quality to that from Liberia.

Like the oil palm, rubber tolerates the poor soils of much of the Mid-West and South-Eastern States. Most of the farmers' output leaves much to be desired. The trees are rarely well spaced, are tapped with insufficient care, and not according to a proper rhythm, while the rubber is badly processed and is often dirty, so that it fetches a low price. Farms are not properly tended, are often overgrown, and only semi-productive. Most rubber has been of $B_2$ quality, used for tyres.

There are also large plantations, partly belonging to foreign companies and government boards, Nigerian companies or individuals, at Ilushin east of Ijebu Ode, near Sapele, Ahoada, Calabar and Oban. These have their own processing plants and produce the highest grade rubber, but there was substantial damage to those near Calabar during the Civil War.

No crop has been more subject to price fluctuations than rubber, so that exports have varied enormously; and rubber has rarely been a profitable crop for ordinary farmers. However, farmers' rubber, properly processed and graded, can command high prices, and crepe and sheet-rubber factories have been built for farmer-produced rubber, especially near Benin and Warri. Moreover, rubber is used in tyre manufacture at Ikeja and at Port Harcourt, and in small amounts in other local manufactures.

## COCOA

Cocoa was probably introduced from Fernando Po by Squiss Bamego in 1874, thus antedating by five years its final establishment in the then Gold Coast. Nigeria also began exporting before that country. Yet Nigeria has never come near to achieving the Ghana export figures. Favourable conditions are much more restricted in Nigeria, where cocoa must be grown in areas with the rather low annual rainfall of 1 145–1 525 mm (45–60 in), and with a distinct dry season from December to March. Cultivation is made possible, however, by moisture-holding soils. It is limited on the west and north by insufficient rain, and on the east and south by unsuitable light sandy soils. Early plantings near Bonny and

Calabar failed for this reason and, more recently, cocoa has given way to kola, the oil palm, citrus and food crops in southern Abeokuta. Cocoa growers have also been troubled by exceptionally low rainfall in the Ibadan area, especially during the critical drier months.

Cocoa is the leading cash crop in Ibadan, and adjacent parts of Oyo, Ondo and Abeokuta. The western area has an unduly high percentage of old trees, and much replanting is required. Swollen shoot is also most severe there. Capsid infestation is general throughout the cocoa area. Blackpod is worst in the wetter areas of Ondo and Ijebu but much less so around Ibadan. Much use is made of pesticides to combat diseases.

Cocoa accounts for most of the Western State's exports. Cocoa cultivation, trade and transport (by road and by lagoon) support quite one-half the people of that state, and cocoa exports are tending to increase.

KOLA cultivation has developed greatly north of Lagos, in southern Ijebu and Abeokuta on soils unsuitable for cocoa, but also in Ibadan and Oyo, whenever there is ready access to roads or the railway. Agege, Ifo and Shagamu are important markets for the nuts which are sent to the north.

BENNISEED is an oilseed and almost a Tiv monopoly, although poor prices have caused some shift to rice cultivation. Benniseed is the only significant export crop of the Middle Belt, whose poor soils it tolerates. India is the main producer, compared with whose production that of Nigeria is insignificant. Nevertheless, India exports little and Nigeria is often the main exporter.

TOBACCO[32] is grown in almost all parts of Nigeria, but types used in the cigarette factories are grown mainly in the west and north. Farmers produce tobacco on small plots, in addition to other crops.

Most tobacco is of the air-cured variety, which does well in Zaria, Sokoto, Katsina and Kano areas. Much of the production is from fadamas. The great advantage of this tobacco is that it does not require expensive flue curing.

In the Western State cigarette tobacco cultivation is important north of the cocoa belt. Of its somewhat smaller production, four-fifths are air-cured and one-fifth is flue-cured.

## COTTON

Cotton[33] cultivation is widespread in Nigeria because it is needed for the very considerable local artisan and factory spinning and weaving of cloth, and because several varieties have been selected to suit differing climatic and other conditions.

*Ishan* is one variety grown in the forested south, especially from a little south of Abeokuta to about Oshogbo, in losing competition with cocoa.

463

Ishan was developed by selection from cotton found in the Ishan division of Benin, derived from the *Vitifolium* subvariety of *Gossypium barbadense*, probably originally introduced by the Spanish. The product is coarse and used in western Nigeria.

Another subvariety, *Peruvianum*, which grows best in the drier south, was the source of the cotton first developed and exported from the Abeokuta region, and was probably introduced by the Portuguese. Selection and breeding of a plant of this variety, taken from a field at Meko, have given rise to the *Meko* variety, widespread in southern Nigeria. The product is short, rough and dark.

Cotton grown in the Lokoja district of the Middle Belt developed from a mixture of various American and *G. barbadense* varieties. They are now being replaced by an Allen variety.

The north produces 90 per cent of Nigeria's cotton, and *North American Allen* is grown, first imported in 1909. It thrives in the clay loams or deep loams of the black soil regions of southern Katsina, southeastern Sokoto and northern Zaria, which are, in that order, the main producers of cotton. Minor areas are Gombe division of Bauchi, Kontagora division of Niger, and Benue. Ideal rainfall is 890–1 270 mm (35–50 in) annually but 510–1 400 mm (20–55 in) may be tolerated. The ideal altitude seems to be between 365–915 m (1 200–3 000 ft).

The cultivation of *Allen* cotton in northern Nigeria results from the initial efforts of an industrial missionary of the Church Missionary Society, the British Cotton Growing Association, and the first Director of Agriculture in Nigeria. It was also much encouraged by the arrival of the railway in Kano in 1912, and after 1949 by the Northern Nigeria Development Corporation. Strict control of the crop is effected by the distribution of selected seed. Ginning out-turn is at least 34 per cent and the colour very white. The grade is 'good middling' or 'strict good middling' and so commands a higher price than 'American middling'. Most of the best quality cotton is taken by mills at Kaduna, Zaria, Kano, Ikeja, Mushin (Lagos), and elsewhere.

GROUNDNUTS

Groundnuts are the major crop of the northernmost states of Nigeria. Although Senegal is the leading West African processor, Nigeria is the greatest exporter of groundnuts in the world. They normally represent about two-fifths of the world trade in this commodity.

The massive production of northern Nigeria is a consequence partly of the use of groundnut oil in margarine manufacture since 1903, and partly of the arrival of the railway at Kano in 1912. Up to 1911 export had never exceeded 1 936 tons (1907); in 1913 it was 19 288 tons. About 40 per cent of the crop is crushed locally, and is an increasing source of local edible oil and food.

The crop is well suited to the sandy 'drift' soils of northern Nigeria, though they benefit from dressings of lime, phosphorus and magnesium. About nine-tenths of the export crop comes from an area enclosed by a line from west of Kaura Namoda south to Zaria and northeast to beyond Nguru. In the southern part of this area the soils are heavier and cotton is more profitable, but groundnuts are useful as the last crop in the rotation. The 'upright' variety is grown, which is better suited to heavier soils, but its yield is only two-thirds that of the 'spreading' variety used farther north. There, e.g. around Kano, the soils are lighter and the rainfall of 760–1 015 mm (30–40 in) is ideal. Farther north still, e.g. around Katsina (and in Niger), the soils are even lighter and poorer, and the rainfall only 510–760 mm (20–30 in). Yields are lower, but the crop is the most profitable export one. Over one-half of the groundnuts come from Kano State and most of the rest from Katsina, Sokoto and Bornu. The crop is generally produced for export near the railway or roads. Kano is the most important railing point.

The area under groundnuts is about 1 m ha (2·5 m acres), and almost all of it has come about since 1911. The average farmer devotes about one-third of his land to the crop, grown alone or intercropped with millet. Some three-fifths of the people of Sokoto, Katsina, Kano and Bornu depend upon the crop for cash.

Groundnut oil mills were established in Nigeria only in the later 1950s. Unlike Senegal, which had a protected market for the oil in North Africa, Nigeria had no such market and only small amounts of oil and cake can be sold in Nigeria. Moderate sized mills in Kano and elsewhere had their groundnut purchases restricted by the former Northern Nigeria Government, anxious to retain its place in world nut markets.[34]

Better roads to ports and quicker rail handling are required to enable the crop area to be extended, e.g. in Adamawa, Bornu and Sokoto. More research on the crop, cheaper fertilisers, and better storage are other needs.

PLATE 110. Kano groundnut oil mill, with bags of groundnuts stacked either side of the factory

## Livestock

Trans-Saharan trade in Nigerian red goat skins goes back many centuries. They were carried by camel to Morocco and on to Europe, where their high quality made them world famous as 'Morocco' leather.

Livestock are today of outstanding significance in Nigeria. They are important for the internal trade in meat and dairy produce, and for the home and export trade in hides and skins. Animals in the north are an important source of fertiliser. Despite all this, however, most livestock are kept as a sign of wealth and often slaughtered for non-economic purposes.

About nine-tenths of the cattle are in northern Nigeria, mainly in Sokoto, Katsina, Kano and Bornu. Nomadic Fulani keep the humped non-resistant Zebu cattle in tsetse-free areas; the main breeds are the

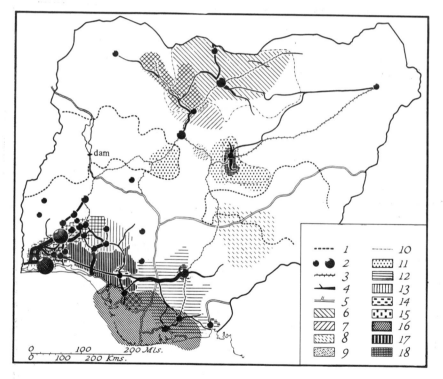

FIG. 26.13. The economic geography of Nigeria

Numbers refer as follows: 1, areas of very low population density; 2, major towns; 3, railways; 4, traffic flow on major roads; 5, navigable waterways (wet season); 6, major groundnut producing area; 7, major cotton region; 8. benniseed (sesame) area; 9. commercial ginger production; 10. major cattle areas; 11. dairying regions of Middle Belt; 12, major oil palm regions; 13, cacao belt; 14, plantation rubber production; 15, commercial kola production; 16, mineral oilfields; 17, major commercial lumber region; 18, major mining areas.

(From K. M. Buchanan, 'Nigeria', *Economic Geography*, **28**, no. 4, October 1952, 320, by permission of the author and editor. Subsequent changes have been added) widespread *White Fulani,* the less common *Gudale* or *Sokoto,* and the red *Rahaja* (or *Bororo*). There is also the humpless *Kuri* or *Chad*, kept by the Kanuri, and found near the lake.

In the Middle Belt are humpless crosses of Zebu and other humpless cattle, but they are not resistant to the tsetse, which infests the belt. Hence cattle keeping is unimportant there, except on the Jos plateau and the eastern borderlands, though if the tsetse could be eradicated, cattle should increase, as the belt has good pasture and fodder crops.

In the south the small humpless *Muturu* is tolerant of trypanosomes. In aspect like the European *Shorthorn*, they are so small as to be of little value and are usually less well cared for than the Zebu of the north.

To supply meat to the southern peoples, cattle are sent south mainly from Sokoto and Bornu, and from Niger. Kano is the most important railing point of cattle, but meat is also carried in refrigerated vans. However, most cattle go south 'on the hoof' by well-recognised cattle routes (see Fig. 26.13). There is a heavy loss in weight and quality on treks of between twenty and sixty days, and many animals die or become diseased.

Improvements in Nigerian cattle keeping depend upon eradicating the tsetse fly, growing and making available more feeding stuffs (especially guinea corn), getting more crop farmers to become mixed farmers, and settling the nomadic Fulani. These show a readiness to abandon the nomadic life when unchallenged rights to land and adequate water and fodder for their cattle can be assured to them. Ranches have been established at Mokwa and Obudu, and one is proposed at Badagri.

Sheep are kept widely in the north and goats everywhere in Nigeria, but the *Sokoto Red* and *Kano Brown* goats are kept essentially for their skins. Apart from those, hides and skins are a minor export item but are of much greater importance in internal trade. To this must be added the great value of the meat trade inside Nigeria.

Dairy produce is made haphazardly by the Fulani. More significant is butter production on modern lines at Vom, Jos, Kano and a little elsewhere, with milk mostly purchased from the Fulani.

The Jos plateau has fly-free and well-watered pastures, numerous cattle, cooler conditions, and a network of roads. This combination of favourable factors is found nowhere else in West Africa, though with roads the eastern borderlands might be so developed.

Yorkshire and Berkshire pigs are kept increasingly to satisfy the domestic demand for bacon and ham. The battery keeping of poultry is widespread, and has greatly reduced the price of eggs and poultry.

## Forestry

Nigerian timber production is more than double that of all the other West African countries put together, although its exports are less dominant, both internationally and nationally. Furthermore, Nigerian reserves are far greater than those of her West African competitors, she is making more attempts to replant, and is more aware of the dangers of illegal and overfelling.

The country is pursuing a cyclical felling policy, whereby part of a reserve or estate is felled and then allowed to regenerate. Thereby, forest reserves should be at least maintained, as well as providing sustained annual yields of timber. Intensive rather than selective felling is also the rule, so that full natural regeneration can be effected. This contrasts with much 'salvage felling' of timber in Ghana, most of whose forests are destined for agriculture in the future. Commercial trends are, however, similar in both countries, with increasing variety of species cut, more local processing and rising local timber demands.

About one-tenth of Nigeria is covered by official forest reserves, but in the Mid-West State the proportion is much higher. There is also nearly twice as much unreserved forest in that state, where about half the area is occupied by highforest. The Mid-West produces most of Nigeria's sawn timber and logs, 80 per cent of the total output by value, and almost all the exported timber.

The main producing areas are Ijebu, southern Ondo and southwestern Benin (three-fifths of all trees felled and four-fifths of exports), all in former no-man's-lands between towns. Minor producing areas are in the South-Eastern State east of the Cross river and in eastern Ogoja. Here access is difficult, but in the Mid-West State the many streams make floating easy, especially to Sapele. Thus Nigeria (and the Ivory Coast) are

PLATE 111. Sapele (*Entandophragma cyclindricum*) log at Sapele

PLATE 112. Veneer peeling in a Sapele mill

at a great advantage compared with Ghana, where much timber has to be carried by rail, and where rivers can rarely be used.

Despite the pronounced tendency to the exploitation of more species, Obeche (*Triplochiton scleroxylon*) still accounts for over one-half the volume and value of logs exported, and about one-third the volume and value of sawn timber. Timber and wood products account for only a tiny percentage of Nigerian exports, even excluding mineral oil.

## Mining

Although Nigeria is about four times the size of Ghana, Nigerian mineral production was much less important until the opening of the oilfields in 1958. The output of oil developed so fast that it almost immediately overtook tin in value, and by 1965 was Nigeria's leading export. Since 1970 oil has been far more important than all other Nigerian exports put together. Consequently, Nigeria's mineral output (almost all oil) is not only the most valuable in West Africa, but probably exceeds the total of all other minerals in the region. Mining in Nigeria provides many millions of pounds of revenue to the federal and state governments, and the companies spend large amounts of money in the country, activating many other trades and industries.

### Mineral oil and natural gas[35]

The search for oil lasted from 1937–41 and from 1946–56, when commercial quantities were proved west of Port Harcourt. By then some £15 million had been spent on exploration, mostly in mangrove or

PLATE 113. Prospection for oil by seismic recordings in a mangrove swamp. Shooting equipment is mounted on a makeshift platform just above the water level. Smoke from the fire deters insects

PLATE 114. A drilling rig barge on the left and a production well on the right

PLATE 115. Pipe-laying barge at work in a swamp in Rivers State

PLATE 116. Port Harcourt oil refinery at sunset. In the left centre is a petroleum gas liquiefaction plant

freshwater swamps of the Niger delta. This is probably the most arduous prospecting area in the world, and is further complicated by seasonal rains and flooding. Furthermore, the transport of oil is possible only by costly laid and maintained pipelines.

Oil is produced from several hundred wells by nearly ten companies on and offshore. Other companies are prospecting. The producing areas, main pipelines and oil terminals are shown on Fig. 26.14. Bonny was the first terminal, and is still the leading one. Some Mid-West terminals are offshore. A refinery near Port Harcourt refines for the Nigerian market, and other refineries are to be built at Warri and Kaduna.

Somewhat offsetting the formidable difficulties of exploration, production and transport, Nigerian oil, though medium heavy in gravity, has a

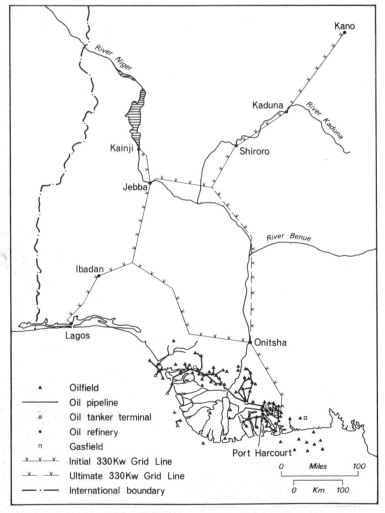

FIG. 26.14. Fuel and power in Nigeria

very low sulphur content, and is relatively near Europe. On the other hand, Japan is an increasingly significant customer.

Gas has been found in far greater quantities than can be used at present. Minor quantities are employed in electrical generation near Port Harcourt and at Ughelli, and in industry in these places and at Aba. Gas may later be exported in liquid form, and could be taken by pipeline to other places in Nigeria, though the Nigerian government currently favours the use of hydroelectric power. Alternatively, if gas were distributed and sold cheaply in small containers, it could displace costly wood for domestic cooking in Nigeria and elsewhere, so reducing the destruction of trees for firewood. Oil and gas could be the bases for fertiliser, polyethylene and other petrochemical production. For gas, as for oil, the prospects are bright, and Nigeria is in the top ten oil producing countries of the world. Fortunately for Nigeria, oil will never entirely dominate the economy as it does in Libya or the Arabian producers.

## Tin

In 1884, when the Benue valley was being opened for trade by the Royal Niger Company, Sir William Wallace found that the tin used locally was produced by Nigerians at Naraguta on the Jos plateau. It was smelted nearby at Liruein Delma, from where it was distributed in the form of thin rods or 'straws'. Previously it had been thought that the tin was obtained from across the Sahara.

In 1902 Wallace took back to England a sample of tin concentrate from the Delimi stream. As a result, a prospecting party went out in the same year, and in 1903 systematic mining was begun. Development was necessarily slow, because transport had to be by porterage to and from the Benue river at Loko and then by canoe on that river.

Public attention was drawn to the deposits in 1909, and from 1911 transport was by porterage to Rigachikun (north of Kaduna) on the Lagos Kano railway. This and the increased number of operating companies greatly stimulated exports. In 1914 the Bauchi light railway from Zaria to Bukuru was opened, just as there was a prodigious demand for tin during the First World War and consequent expansion of production. After that war there was a slump from 1921 to 1923, but the building of a branch of the eastern railway to Bukuru and Jos in 1927 reduced costs of transport in Nigeria by one-third.

Under the Tin Production and Export Restriction Scheme of 1931 Nigeria agreed to limit production, and prices went up. In the Second World War, after the loss of Malaya in 1942, Nigeria and Bolivia were the main producers of tin for the Allies.

Pegmatite, associated with some of the Older Granites, contains workable tinstone and, in certain places, columbite-tantalite. But the principal

PLATE 117. A Walking Dragline excavating tin bearing gravels. Mixed with water these are then sent down the four sluice boxes in the foreground. The boxes are arranged in steps, and the heavy tin gravels collect on the lower steps

deposits of Nigerian tinstone and columbite have been formed from the weathering of tin veins and lodes in the Younger Granites emplaced into a region of Pre-Cambrian rocks. The minerals have been concentrated in former and present stream beds and, in many places, covered not only with soft overburden but by Tertiary or Quaternary volcanic basalt as well.

So far it is alluvial tin which has been obtained almost exclusively in Nigeria. Nigerian and early European workings were in the existing rivers. Since approximately 1936 more and more attention has been directed to former stream beds obscured by considerable soft overburden. There was once concern whether the tin (but not the columbite-tantalite) of these thick alluvial deposits may be exhausted. Consequently, the larger companies envisaged underground exploitation of tin gravels in old stream beds covered by basalt, an expensive operation and possible only if tin prices were sufficiently high.

Meanwhile, four-fifths of the present output is from south of Jos. Most of the rest is from the Bauchi area. Production was again restricted by international quota from 1957–60 but is now around 9 000 tons, or 5 per cent of the world total. Nearly half the output comes from one company, and much of the rest from many small ones.

In the past most mining was by very simple methods. Water was and still is used to loosen the overburden, which is often dug out by men and carried away by women, here the traditional porters. The tin-bearing gravels below are then washed in calabashes, until the heavier black tin oxide remains. This method is still used by the numerous small companies, private operators (Nigerian, European and Lebanese) and by individual African 'tributors', of whom there are some 1 500, and who work for the companies or operators.

About one-half of Nigerian tin is produced by mechanical means, operated by large companies. The simplest method is to direct a powerful waterjet (rather like a firehose) to wash out the tin-bearing gravels. These are then pumped up for concentration at the lower end of a range of sluice boxes, down and through which the water and gravels pass. Quicker excavation is by a dragline which cuts large blocks of earth at each 'dig' and can move by mechanical 'legs' to new ground. The material it excavates is washed as described above. Mechanical shovels and dredges are also used.

As so much water is used, reservoirs have been built to store it; nevertheless, water shortage through variable rainfall sometimes restricts output. The industry also has need of much motive power and, when the Enugu coal deposits were opened in 1915, it looked forward to a railway between the Jos plateau and Enugu to bring in coal supplies. But as the railway did not reach Jos until 1927, the companies had meanwhile developed hydroelectric power sites at the Kurra, Kwall, Jekko and Ankwill falls on the plateau's southern edge. Tin smelting began near Jos in 1961.

Early tin-mining caused much of the present severe deforestation on the plateau. Excavation and spoil dumps have degraded the soils, destroyed farm land (though compensation was paid), and silted the rivers. Some farmers have become discouraged in the face of increased quarrying and creation of spoil dumps, though mining leases now contain a restoration clause.[36]

## Columbite

Columbite, the main ore of the metal niobium, has come into prominence because of its use as an alloy in making heat-resisting steels for gas turbines, jet engines and rockets. Almost all the world's supply comes from Nigeria, where the mineral occurs in association with tin, tantalite and uranium in the radioactive granites of the Liruein–Kano hills, and as a primary constituent of the Younger Granites, all on the Jos plateau.

Production of columbite is more dispersed than tin mining, largely because it was for long rejected as a waste product and is now being recovered from dumps of abandoned, as well as from active tin workings. Small amounts of tantalite are also mined on the around the Jos plateau.

## Coal

Coal was first found in the Ofam river at Udi in 1909, and production began in 1915 when the railway was built from Port Harcourt to Enugu to make this possible. Coal occurs in places as far apart as Ankpa and Gombe in the northeast, and near Benin in the southwest, but is mined only in one adit mine near Enugu. The coal yields much gas and tar oils on distillation, and would best be used for gas or chemical byproduct manufacture. However, this would bring it into competition with plentiful natural gas. Consequently, it is mainly used in electric power generation. The combustile character of the coal, resulting from high gas content, makes it dangerous to transport, and its poor coking character renders its use in an iron and steel industry unlikely, although iron ore of 45 per cent content occurs nearby.

**Limestone**

Limestone is used for cement manufacture at Nkalagu, 40 km (25 miles) east of Enugu's coal mine, Ukpilla (near Auchi) in Mid-West State, Ewekoro (near Abeokuta) and Sokoto. A branch railway has been built from Ogbaho to Nkalagu, and a power station for the factory at Oji river. Some of the other works are less well-sited and less efficient. Imported clinker is used in works at Lagos, Port Harcourt and Calabar. Three more inland works are planned, to use local limestone.

## Hydroelectric power: the Kainji dam

Kainji dam[37], the first of three projected dams, was inaugurated early in 1969. Kainji is 103 km (64 miles) above Jebba. Present capacity is 320 mw, and additional generators will raise this to 960 mw. Power is distributed to Kaduna, Lagos, Benin and the Onitsha areas, thereby encouraging industrial and general development. By about 1982 another dam and power house may be constructed at Jebba, with an ultimate capacity of 500 mw, and by 1986 a third may be needed in the Shiroro gorge of the Kaduna tributary with a capacity of 480 mw.

Jebba will be the base-load station, as it will have the most even flow, being backed by its own lake and by that of Kainji, as well as by the middle and upper Niger. Jebba and Kainji will be further helped by high water from local rains from June to September, and by another peak from December to March from the same rains in the upper Niger basin, the effects of which are brought to Nigeria months later through the tortuous channels of the Niger's middle reaches. The local flood of the Kaduna will immediately generate power, because of limited storage capacity. Meanwhile, the Jebba and Kainji lakes will be filling again to be ready for operation when the Kaduna is low. When both are at a minimum in March or April, the Kainji and Jebba reservoirs will be lowered until the first flood occurs—that of the Kaduna. The scheme is an example of using different river regimes, as well as being part of a national scheme also incorporating electric generation with oil, natural gas and coal.

The relative merits of hydroelectric power versus gas or oil-generated electricity were investigated in 1960–61. The first is an inexhaustible means of electrical generation, whilst at that time, when a decision was taken, the extent of the oil and natural gas reserves was not known. Had they been, Kainji might not have been built, or built so soon, and local use of oil and natural gas might have been more encouraged. The other two prospective dams will need reappraisal in the light of oil and gas reserves and prices.

Finally, there are interesting comparisons with the Akosombo dam on the Volta in Ghana. Kainji does not lie in a gorge, and so is much longer. Kainji power is for general use, rather than mainly for an aluminium smelter as in Ghana. Nevertheless, the inauguration of Kainji nearly doubled the capacity of electrical production in Nigeria, although only one-third of the generators were installed at Kainji. As with Akosombo, some power is to be exported by grid to a neighbour, the Niger in the case of Kainji. Resettlement at the latter was most effective in the partially new town of Yelwa and wholly new one of New Bussa, whose architecture is essentially traditional yet also modern (Plate 118). Subsidiary benefits of navigation and fishing occur in both cases. At Kainji, when locks work efficiently, navigation should be possible for barges as far as the low bridge at Gaya (Niger–Dahomey border). Fishing is likely to be less important on Lake Kainji because it is only one-seventh the area of Lake Volta. Kainji has been the cause of adding to the Nigerian road system, whilst Lake Volta obstructed many Ghanaian

PLATE 118. New Bussa, built to replace Bussa, now under Lake Kainji. People have been rehoused in modernised dwellings built in very traditional style, unlike the houses built for Lake Volta evacuees

roads as well as inducing others. The Kainji dam crossing adds another Niger bridge, and one especially useful for cattle, since it is in a less tsetse infested area than Jebba.

## Crafts and industries

Most countries still have certain traditional crafts, and at least some modern industrial units. Nigeria is unique in the survival of so many varied and vigorous crafts, alongside the emergence of numerous and diverse modern industries.

Among its many traditional crafts, the weaving and dyeing trades are well represented in the north and west of Nigeria. In the latter, women produce fine patterns either by sewing stones and pieces of wood in the material before dyeing, or by making a pattern with starch on the undyed cloth, the starch hardening before immersion in the dye vat. In the former process, the pattern is revealed after dyeing by undoing the stones and sticks; in the latter method, the pattern is seen after scraping off the hardened starch, so revealing undyed spaces. Indigo and other vegetable or local dyes are used, as well as imported synthetic ones. Indigo is most used in the Western State. At Akwete, in East-Central State, vivid coloured embroidery in parallel geometric patterns is worked on black cloth.

Raffia and fibre mats, baskets, etc., are made at Ikot Ekpene (South-Eastern State), Kano, Bida and elsewhere. At Benin woodworking in ebony has a long history. Wooden goods with Ibo patterns are made at Akwa, near Enugu. Calabashes are carved in Oyo and Kano.

Leather working is a major craft in the north, and dyed goat and sheep skins are used for cushions, bags and saddlery. Kano is the main centre. Oyo (Western State) produces black-and-white cushions.

Gold and silversmiths work in most towns, but they are renowned at Bida and Kano. Benin brass figures have been famous for centuries. The making of domestic and agricultural iron goods is widespread. Pottery is important at Ikot Ekpene, Abuja and Ilorin. Glass articles of personal adornment from Bida are well known.

Kano, Bida, Benin and Ikot Ekpene are centres of several crafts. From Kano, Bida and other towns, Hausa traders peddle goods through many Guinea lands.

To these traditional crafts have been added such modern and more important ones as tailoring, plumbing and carpentry, house building, car and lorry repairing.

Capitalist enterprise, as elsewhere, was first directed to the processing of Nigeria's numerous and diverse raw materials, such as palm oil, timber, mineral oil, rubber, groundnuts and cotton.

Factories making consumer and other goods for the large diverse and developed domestic market have been established, mostly since 1950.

Nigeria is normally virtually self-sufficient in almost all refined petroleum products, cotton cloth and simple garments, asbestos cement, tyres, plastic goods (including sandals), furniture, cigarettes, soap, paints and steel rods; whilst she produces substantial proportions of cement, canned or bottled drinks, and hardware. Radio sets, transistors, cycles, scooters, trucks and some cars are also assembled.

Most factories have been concentrated on industrial estates in Lagos and its environs (Fig. 26.4), Ibadan, Ilorin, Sapele, Port Harcourt, Aba, Umuahia, Enugu, Jos, Kaduna, Zaria and Kano. The relatively numerous Nigerian towns have aided industrial development by reason of the services, labour and markets they offer.

Regional and state rivalry has played a part in industrial evolution, sometimes leading to wasteful duplication and consequent narrowing of the market for each factory. This is especially noticeable in the establishment of textile mills, cigarette factories and cement works, as well as in the negotiations for an iron and steel industry. The latter may be established with blast furnaces in one state and the steel furnaces in another![38]

## Transport

Nigeria is unique in West Africa in the diversity and extent of its means of transport. In view of the size and variety of the country, communications have probably done more than anything else either to encourage or, where lacking, to restrict economic development.

### Waterways

In its provision of natural waterways, nature was kinder to Nigeria than to most West African lands. There are some 6 400 km (4 000 miles) of waterways permitting cheap transport at high water.

The Niger river was the first means of export from northern Nigeria and, in conjunction with the Minna–Baro branch railway, still carries some seasonal traffic to and from the north. Likewise, the Benue river is useful to parts of eastern Nigeria and, via Garoua, to the northern part of Cameroon. The Cross river permits seasonal traffic between Calabar and Mamfe, in Cameroon.

Parallel with the coast is a lagoon waterway, from west of Lagos to the many streams of the Niger delta. There is also much coastal sea traffic, especially in the transhipment of oil and other produce between Port Harcourt, the West delta ports and Lagos.

Port facilities at Lagos and Port Harcourt have been severely overloaded, but extensions at both have done something to meet the situation. Calabar is likely to be developed and entry has been much improved to the delta ports by breakwaters at the Escravos mouth, and by dredging.[39]

**Railways**

The line from Lagos to Ibadan was opened in 1901, to develop trade and improve living conditions in Lagos. As Lagos was not then a deepwater port, it was far from clear whether the railway should be extended, or a new one built from some other port; moreover, Lugard favoured a railway from the highest point of navigation on the Niger river. In 1907 it was decided to build a railway from Baro on the Niger to Kano, and to extend the Lagos railway to meet it; both were opened in 1912. The through line to Lagos soon became the main line, and the export of groundnuts, cotton, hides and skins increased enormously. However, the Minna–Baro branch is vital to the maintenance of the Niger–Benue river fleet. The main line was extended from Kano to Nguru in 1927, and the branch from Zaria to Kaura Namoda was built in 1929.

The line from Port Harcourt was opened to Enugu in 1916, primarily to distribute coal. Extensions were made to Kaduna and Jos in 1927, and to Maiduguri in 1964.

Although the railway serves the main cash crop areas and population clusters, its western and eastern lines have long traverses of the unprofitable Middle Belt, and there is no direct west–east line.

**Roads**

The first road, from Oyo to Ibadan, was built as early as 1906. There are now about 90 120 km (55 000 miles) of roads, of which 16 100 km (10 000 miles) are tarred. Often the main form of transport is by road and it is estimated that road traffic exceeds a thousand million ton-miles. The densest road networks are in the palm and cocoa belts, the tinfields, and around Kano, Katsina and Lagos. Better roads are required from Lagos to northern Nigeria; more roads are needed almost everywhere, but especially in northern Nigeria.[40]

**Air services**

Some twelve towns are served by scheduled air services at least once a week, often several times weekly. Lagos (Ikeja) is a major West African airport, and Kano also has international traffic. Air transport has done a very great deal for Nigeria, especially in facilitating movements between west and east.[41]

# Conclusion

With Nigeria's great physical, social and economic diversity it is appropriate that it should be a federation. Size and diversity have encouraged a more varied internal economy and a wider range of exports than is usual in West Africa. No one commodity is supremely important. Local food-stuffs are diverse and are the basis of an important internal trade. State exports (cocoa from the West; mineral and palm oil, rubber and timber from the Mid-West; palm produce, rubber and mineral oil from Eastern States; groundnuts, cotton, hides, skins, tin and columbite from Northern States) are exceptionally varied.

Only about nine countries in the world (including four in the Common-wealth) normally export more to the United Kingdom than Nigeria. It produces about one-third of the United Kingdom's imports of vegetable oil and oil seeds, and of cocoa; one-quarter of the imports of tin and of hides, and a tenth of the hardwoods.

Yet Nigerian diversity presents difficulties; in particular, its peoples seem less united than those of some other countries. The Middle Belt is a vast poor area in the centre of the country, impeding exchange between north and south, and contributing little. Many other areas await develop-ment, such as the thinly peopled lands between Kaura Namoda and Sokoto, between Maiduguri and Kano, the southern Adamawa highlands, eastern Calabar, eastern Ogoja, and much of Benin, Ondo and Oyo.

If the tsetse fly could be eradicated, water made available cheaply and widely, and social resistance to resettlement overcome, then there are many areas in Nigeria capable of development.

Industrial development has far better prospects in Nigeria than else-where in West Africa, mainly because of the potentially large market. Over one of every two West Africans is a Nigerian, as is one in five of all Africans. Factories such as the very modern Kaduna textile mills, the other numerous textile and cement works, and the oil refinery are very much oriented to this large market. Industries are also being encouraged by varied resources, such as natural gas. This gas, with coal, lignite and oil, could activate a whole complex of industries. Nevertheless it is oil which is the economic saviour of Nigeria.

# 27

# Conclusion

*L'Afrique—Terre qui Meurt* (Title of J. P. Harroy's book, published 1944).
'Africa to-day remains a continent of uncertainties' (*The Times*, 5 March 1955).
'Africa is the new continent; she is a focus of twentieth century development' (*The Times*, 1 December 1949).

West Africa is a mosaic of many countries in which, except for Liberia, European powers pursued their divergent and often contradictory aims. The nine ex-French and four ex-British countries all became independent between 1957 and 1965. Only Portuguese Guinea, still in close association with Portugal, has no democratic institutions. Liberia, for long politically independent, lives largely by concessions, which, in the past, kept it in closer relationship with the United States of America than most ex-colonies ever were to their metropolitan country. Although there is no other area of Africa with such a mosaic of political units and contrasting policies, West Africa has, for the most part, been saved the added social stresses of multi-racial communities.

Three outstanding problems result from the many and varied political units. As the territories became independent there has been an unfortunate tendency to break up into smaller entities. Nigeria has accentuated its internal divisions from three regions and the Lagos Federal Territory at independence, to four regions in 1963, and then to twelve states in 1967. There are Nigerians who wish to create more states, although they acknowledge the importance of the federation. The Federation of French West Africa has given place to eight individual countries whose policies are often at variance, and whose boundaries have become major divides, e.g. between Guinea and Senegal. Although new groupings such as the Benin–Sahel Entente of the Ivory Coast, the Upper Volta, Niger, Dahomey and Togo have been formed, West Africa is as divided politically as ever, and more so economically.

Secondly, many problems result from the lack of information on what is going on across the artificial boundaries. Despite the work of the Organisation for African Unity, the United Nations Economic Commission for Africa, and many West African bodies, much research is pursued in ignorance of similar work across the boundary.

Lastly, the unrealistic boundaries created by the colonial powers, have been inherited, but each country seems determined to hold what it has. The new nations have contrasted legacies of language, administrative method, tax and tariff structure, currency zone allegiance, educational system, and so forth. All these are major impediments to political or economic integration, and even simple collaboration.

Almost all means of transport have been constructed from nothing in little more than a half-century. It is not surprising, therefore, that economic development has been patchy and largely coastal. Development of the interior is not only impeded by its greater dryness, water shortage and length of communications, but also by the existence of the intervening Middle Belt. Lying between approximately 8°N and $10\frac{1}{2}$°N, it contributes little to West Africa or the World.

Crucial to the development of the Middle Belt is the elimination of the tsetse; a pioneer fringe would then become available for settlement. Cattle raising could also develop. Elimination of the tsetse is no less vital elsewhere, to man and beast. But so long as this fly is widespread, more attention might profitably be given to improving the small resistant cattle. The south is also in need of cheap suppressives of malaria. Poor physique starts the vicious circle of low initiative and productivity, leading to low income and poor nutrition.

Fundamental to all life in West Africa is agriculture. While it is possibly the case that for the cultivation of food crops the optimum areas and conditions have been found by African farmers, this is not always true of export crops. These must generally be grown near lines of transport. Nor is the best use always made of the optimum areas where they are known.

There is potential danger in static or even declining food crop production. Farmers' sons prefer more remunerative and less arduous occupations, and the remaining farmers, especially near the coasts, turn more and more to export crops. Moreover, certain food crops are in rapid decline, such as yams—which are tedious to cultivate—in favour of cassava, which is easily grown. On the credit side, however, is the increasing cultivation of swamp rice, although rice imports are still unduly large.

Export crops were exceedingly prosperous after the Second World War, but there has been some recession. With increasing competition from other tropical producers, especially from plantations, more is likely. The threat is grave because so much revenue depends on so few export crops. Furthermore, prosperity has resulted not only from increased production but from the good fortune of high prices for certain periods, and from heavy demand. On the other hand, due credit must be given for the notable improvement in the quality of Nigerian palm oil and cotton, and the great output of Ghana's cocoa.

It remains doubtful whether there will be any great increase in agricultural output, except by the development of new areas, by a technical revolution, or both. Some alternative to the land-wasting system of bush fallowing will force itself upon West Africa as the population increases. It has already done so in certain areas of high population density, such as in the Kabrai country of northern Togo where there are tiny terraced fields and permanent rotational farming using vegetable and animal waste.

Some have seen an answer in mechanisation. Outside Africa it has not been applied to small farms, so that it is unlikely to be useful in the difficult physical conditions of West Africa, further complicated as it is by unhelpful forms of land tenure. Mechanisation is limited by the high cost of clearance, the difficulty of maintaining fertility when shifting cultivation is abandoned, low crop yields compared with more intensive cultivation, scattered and tiny cultivated patches, and the cost and difficulty of mechanical maintenance and repair. Mechanical cultivation may be valuable for rice cultivation in treeless valley bottoms, and on level dry land in thinly populated areas. It is not certain to pay even in these environments; it is almost certainly no solution elsewhere.

Publicity has been given to the dangers of soil erosion. They are real, but the extent of the disaster has been grossly exaggerated. Far more important, in area and in degree, is the loss of soil fertility. Man needs quicker, easier and cheaper means of restoring fertility than by bush fallowing. Especially is this so in cash crop areas, where plant nutrients are exported overseas, e.g. in the form of the massive crops of groundnuts from Nigeria or Senegal.

Great progress has been made in industrialisation, especially in Nigeria, Ghana, the Ivory Coast and Senegal. Socialist methods of control and development have been tried in Ghana, Guinea and Mali. However, countries such as Mauritania, Mali, Upper Volta, Niger, Gambia, Portuguese Guinea, Liberia, Togo and Dahomey have such small, poor or dispersed populations that they cannot at the moment support most types of industries. Furthermore, each country excludes most industrial products from other African states. Industrial development also depends not only upon the possession of the requisite raw materials but upon the existence of sufficient engineering, managerial and other technical skills, the availability of capital, and of an adequate market. The most immediately hopeful lines for industrialisation are in the further processing and grading of local materials, already grown or produced cheaply in West Africa and in world demand, such as cocoa, palm oil and other vegetable oils. There are also good prospects for most consumer-good industries and assembly plants. The future for heavy industry is mainly linked with the massive generation of cheap hydroelectric power in Ghana and Nigeria, and with the more varied use of Nigeria's oil, gas, coal and other resources.

West Africa has been in contact with North Africa for a millennium, with Europe for half that time, but with world economy for barely a century. Intensive and generalised economic development dates only from the Second World War. West Africa already has far more than its proportionate share of Africa's population and external trade; it has also been the scene of some of the most interesting political and economic developments.

# Notes and references*

## Introduction
1. See R. J. Harrison Church, 'The history of projects for a Trans-Saharan railway', in L. D. Stamp and S. W. Wooldridge, eds, *London Essays in Geography*, Longmans, 1951, pp. 135–50.

## Chapter 1   Geology, coasts and shores
Dr N. R. Junner, OBE, MC, DIC, MInst MM, Director of the Gold Coast Geological Survey 1930–46, has given me most helpful criticism of this chapter. Professor C. A. Cotton and Professor J. C. Pugh have done likewise for the section on coasts and shores.
1. For the effect of Miocene uplift on rivers see Chapter 2.
2. Y. Urvoy, *Les Bassins du Niger*, Paris, 1942, p. 56.
3. J. C. Pugh, 'A classification of the Nigerian coastline', *J. W. Afr. Sci. Ass.*, **1**, no. 1, 3–12 at p. 4.
4. E. F. Gautier, 'Les côtes de l'Afrique Occidentale au sud de Dakar', *Annls Géogr.*, 1931, 163–74.

### Supplementary references and maps
FURON, R. *Geology of Africa*, Edinburgh, Oliver & Boyd, 1963.
*International Atlas of West Africa*, Organisation of African Unity, Sheet 1, Seas and coasts of West Africa.
1 : 5 Million International Geological Map of Africa and *Notice Explicative* by R. FURON and G. DAUMAIN, 1963.
1 : 5 Million International Tectonic Map of Africa, 1968.
(Both sets of maps are published in Paris by Unesco and the Association of African Geological Surveys.)

## Chapter 2   Relief and drainage
Dr N. R. Junner also gave most helpful criticism of this chapter.
1. See D. C. Ledger, 'The dry season flow characteristics of West African rivers', in M. F. Thomas and G. W. Whittington, *Environment and Land Use in Africa*, Methuen, 1972.

*Abbreviations used in the references are detailed on p. 517.

## Chapter 3   Climate

Statistics used in this chapter are reproduced from information in the British Meteorological Office; from the *Mémento du Service Météorologique* (Dakar) for ex-French West Africa; from the Meteorological Departments of Ghana and Nigeria by courtesy of the Directors, and various official publications.

I am also deeply indebted to Professors Gregory and Crowe for many helpful suggestions concerning this chapter.

1. I have profited from P. R. Crowe, 'The seasonal variation in the strength of the trades', *Trans Inst. Br. Geogr.,* 1950, 25–47; 'The trade wind circulation of the world' and 'Wind and weather in the equatorial zone', *ibid.,* 1949 and 1951.
2. Crowe, *op. cit.,* 1951, p. 33, quotes the following temperatures at the end of Lomé wharf (6°08′N, 1°13′E):

|  | Jan. | Feb. | Mar. | Apr. | May | June | July | Aug. | Sept. | Oct. | Nov. | Dec. |
|---|---|---|---|---|---|---|---|---|---|---|---|---|
| °C | 26·7 | 27·2 | 27·2 | 27·8 | 27·8 | 26·1 | 23·9 | 22·2 | 23·3 | 25·3 | 26·7 | 26·7 |
| °F | 80 | 81 | 81 | 82 | 82 | 79 | 75 | 72 | 74 | 78 | 80 | 80 |

3. J. Navarro, 'Les grains du Nord Est et le régime des pluies sur la côte du Golfe de Guinée' (typescript), 1950.
4. Crowe, *op. cit.,* 1951, p. 33.
5. B. J. Garnier, 'A method of computing potential evapotranspiration in West Africa', *Bull. IFAN,* **18**, A, 1956, 665–76, and 'Maps of the water balance in West Africa', *ibid.,* **22**, A, 1960, 709–22.
6. J. H. Hubbard, 'Note on the rainfall of Accra, Gold Coast', *Geographical Studies* **1,** no. 1, 1954, 69–75, and 'Daily weather at Achimota, near Accra, Gold Coast', *ibid.,* **3**, no. 1, 1956, 56–63.
7. See R. A. Pullan, 'The concept of the Middle Belt in Nigeria: an attempt at a climatic definition', *Nigerian Geogrl J.,* 1962, 39–52.
8. L. D. Stamp, *Africa: a study in tropical development,* 3rd edn, Wiley, 1972, p. 74.

### Supplementary references
*General*

BATES, J. R. 'Tropical disturbances and the general circulation', *Q. Jl roy. met. Soc.* **98**, 1972, 1–16.
GARBELL, M. A. *Tropical and Equatorial Meteorology,* Pitman, 1947.
HAURWITZ, B. and AUSTIN, J. M. *Climatology,* New York, 1944.
KENDREW, W. G. *The Climates of the Continents,* OUP, 1961.
MALONE, T. F. *Compendium of Meteorology,* Boston, Mass., American Meterological Society, 1951.
PALMER, C. 'Tropical meteorology', *Q. Jl roy. met. Soc.,* 1952, 126–64.
RIEHL, H. *Tropical Meteorology,* New York, McGraw-Hill, 1954.

*West African*

AUBRÉVILLE, A. *Climats, forêts et desertification de l'Afrique tropicale,* Paris, 1959.

BARGMAN, D. J., ed. *Tropical Meteorology in Africa,* Nairobi, Munitalp Foundation, 1960.

CARTER, D. B. 'Climates of Africa and India according to Thornthwaite's 1948 classification', Johns Hopkins University Laboratory of Climatology, *Publications in Climatology* 7, no. 4, 1954.

DAVIES, J. A. and ROBINSON, P. J. 'A simple energy balance approach to the moisture balance climatology of Africa', in M. F. Thomas and G. W. Whittington, eds, *Environment and Land Use in Africa,*

ELDRIDGE, R. H. 'A synoptic study of West African disturbance lines', *Q. Jl roy. met. Soc.* **83,** 1957, 303–14 and **84,** 1958, 468–69.

GERMAIN, H. 'Synoptic analysis for West Africa and the southern part of the Atlantic Ocean', *Final Report of the Caribbean Hurricane Seminar,* Ciudad Trujillo, 1956, pp. 173–86.

GREGORY, S. *Rainfall over Sierra Leone,* Research Paper no. 2, Geography Dept, University of Liverpool, 1965, and 'Rainfall reliability', in Thomas and Whittington, *op. cit.*

HAMILTON, R. A. and ARCHIBOLD, J. W. 'Meteorology of Nigeria and adjacent territory', *Q. Jl roy. met. Soc.* **71,** 1945, 231–64.

*International Atlas of West Africa,* Organisation of African Unity, Sheets 10–13.

MORAL, P. 'Essai sur les régions pluviométriques de l'Afrique de l'Ouest', *Annls Géogr.,* Nov.–Dec. 1964, 660–86.

*A Pilot's Primer of West African Weather,* Meteorological Office, 1944.

TREWARTHA, G. T. 'The Sahara, Sudan and Guinea Coast', in *The Earth's Problem Climates,* University of Wisconsin Press, 1961.

WALKER, H. W. *The Monsoon in West Africa,* Ghana Meteorological Dept, Accra, 1958.

*Weather on the West Coast of Tropical Africa from latitude 20°N to 20°S, including the Atlantic Ocean to 25°W,* Meteorological Office, 1954, 492.

## Chapter 4    Vegetation

I am most grateful to Professor Richards, Dr Keay and Mr Hepper for giving me criticism and much valuable help with this chapter. Botanical names are as far as possible in accord with R. W. J. Keay, and F. M. Hepper's revised edition of J. Hutchinson and J. M. Dalziel, *Flora of West Tropical Africa,* 1954–72.

1. R. W. J. Keay, *An Outline of Nigerian Vegetation,* 2nd edn, 1953, pp. 29–30.
2. Th. Monod, 'Notes sur la flore du Plateau Bauchi', *Melanges Botaniques,* Dakar, IFAN, 1952, pp. 11–37.

3. E. P. Stebbing, *The Forests of West Africa and the Sahara,* Chambers, 1937, and 'The threat of the Sahara', *J. roy. Afr. Soc.* **36**, supplement. For a summary and reply see L. D. Stamp, 'The southern margin of the Sahara: comments on some recent studies on the question of desiccation', *Geogrl Rev.* 1940, 297–300, and Aubréville, *Climats, forêts et desertification de l'Afrique tropicale,* pp. 309–44; also A. T. Grove, 'The ancient erg of Hausaland, and similar formations on the south side of the Sahara', *Geogrl J.* 1958, 528–33.
4. Aubréville, *op. cit.,* pp. 333–38. Richards, *The Tropical Rain Forest* (see reference below), p. 405, lists authorities on this controversial matter.

**Supplementary references**

I have drawn in particular on the works asterisked, all of which contain maps and extensive bibliographies.

\*AUBRÉVILLE, A. *Climats, forêts et désertification de l'Afrique tropical,* 1949.

*Commonwealth Forestry Handbook* (for nomenclature of timbers).

GUEST, S. HADEN, WRIGHT, J. K. and TECLAFF, E.M., eds. *A World Geography of Forest Resources,* New York, Ronald Press, 1956, Ch. 16.

HEDBERG, I. and HEDBERG, O., eds. 'Conservation of vegetation in Africa south of the Sahara', *Acta Phytogeographica Succica,* **54**, Uppsala, 1968.

HOPKINS, B. *Forest and Savanna,* Heinemann Educational, 1965.

\*KEAY, R. W. J. *An Outline of Nigerian Vegetation,* 2nd edn, Lagos, 1953. (Also unpublished material by the same author.)

LAWSON, G. W. *Plant Life in West Africa,* OUP, 1966.

\*RICHARDS, P. W. *The Tropical Rain Forest,* CUP, 1966.

\*ROSEVEAR, D. R. 'Vegetation', *The Nigerian Handbook,* 1953, 139–73.

\*SCHNELL, R. *Contribution à une étude phyto-sociologique et phyto-géographique de l'Afrique Occidentale: les groupements et les unités géobotaniques de la région guinéenne,* Dakar, IFAN, 1952.

*Timbers of West Africa,* London, Timber Development Association Ltd.

\*TROCHAIN, J. *La Végétation du Sénégal,* Dakar, IFAN, 1940.

*Vegetation Map of Africa.* OUP, 1959.

**Chapter 5    Soils and soil management**

This chapter was contributed in 1972 by Dr R. P. Moss, Professor of Biogeography in the University of Birmingham.

1. H. Vine, 'Is the lack of fertility of tropical African soils exaggerated?', *Proc. 2nd Inter-African Soils Conf.,* 1954, vol. 1, doc. 26, 389–412.

**Supplementary references**

BURINGH, P. *Introduction to the Study of Soils in Tropical and Subtropical Regions,* Wageningen, 1968.

D'HOORE, J. *Soils Map of Africa: Monograph to accompany the Soils Map,* Lagos, CCTA, Inter-African Pedological Service, 1964.

LAUDELOT, M. *Dynamics of Tropical Soils in Relation to their Fallowing Techniques,* FAO, 1961.

MOSS, R. P., ed. *The Soil Resources of Tropical Africa,* CUP, 1968.

NYE, P. M. and GREENLAND, D. J. *The Soil under Shifting Cultivation,* Commonwealth Agricultural Bureaux, Farnham, Bucks., 1960.

WALTER, H. *The Ecology of Tropical and Subtropical Vegetation,* Edinburgh. Oliver & Boyd. 1972.


## Chapter 6  Agriculture

I am greatly indebted to Dr S. A. Agboola, University of Ife, for his help with the present version of this chapter.

1. J. Miège, 'Les cultures vivrières en Afrique Occidentale', *Cah. Outremer,* 1954, 24–50.
2. On cassava, see W. O. Jones, *Manioc in Africa,* Stanford Univ. Press, 1959; and 'A map of manioc in Africa', *Geogrl Rev.* 1953, 112–14.
3. On yams, see D. G. Coursey, *Yams,* Longmans, 1967.
4. M. D. W. Jeffreys, 'How ancient is West African maize?', *Africa,* 1963, pp. 115–31; and M. Miracle, *Maize in Tropical Africa,* Wisconsin Univ. Press, 1965.
5. An important text is C. W. S. Hartley, *The Oil Palm,* Longman, 1969.
6. For worldwide studies of cocoa see D. H. Urquhart, *Cocoa,* 2nd edn, Longman, 1961; and G. Viers, 'Le Cacao dans le monde', *Cah. Outre-mer,* 1953, 297–351.
7. Reference should be made to the many studies by Polly Hill.
8. See M. H. Le Long, 'La route du kola', *Revue de Géographie Humaine et d'Ethnologie,* no. 4, 1949, 35–40.
9. On sorghum, see H. Doggett, *Sorghum,* Longman, 1970.
10. Discussed by J. D. Fage, 'Anthropology, botany and history', *J. Afr. Hist.,* 1961, 299–309.


**Supplementary references**

ALLAN, W. *The African Husbandman,* Oliver & Boyd, 1965.

ARE, L. 'An assessment of some plantation problems in West Africa', *J. Trop. Ag.* 1964.

BENNEH, G. 'Systems of Agriculture in Tropical Africa', *Econ. Geog.,* 1972, 244–57.

CLARK, C. and HASWELL, M. *The Economics of Subsistence Agriculture,* 3rd edn, Macmillan, 1968.

DUMONT, R. *Types of Rural Economy,* Methuen, 1970, Ch. 3.

FOOD AND AGRICULTURE ORGANISATION, *Africa Survey. Report on the possibilities of African rural development in relation to economic and social growth,* FAO, 1962.

GOULD, P. R. 'Man against his environment: a game theoretic framework', *Ann. Ass. Am. Geogr.,* 1963, 290–97.

GOUROU, P. *The Tropical World,* 4th edn, Longmans, 1966.

GOUROU, P. 'The quality of land use of tropical cultivators', in W. L. Thomas, ed., *Man's Role in Changing the Face of the Earth,* Univ. of Chicago Press, 1956, pp. 336–49.

HAVINDEN, M. A. 'The history of crop cultivation in West Africa: a bibliographical guide', *Econ. Hist. Rev.,* 1970, 532–55.

HUNTER, J. M. 'Ascertaining population carrying capacity under traditional systems of agriculture in developing countries', *Professional Geographer,* 1966, 151–54.

IRVINE, F. R. *West African Agriculture,* vol. 2: *West African Crops,* OUP, 1970.

ISNARD, H. 'Agriculture et développement en Afrique Occidentale', *Cah. Outre-mer,* 1963, 253–62.

JOHNSTON, B. F. *The Staple Food Economies of Western Tropical Africa,* Stanford Univ. Press, 1958.

MAY, J. M. *The Ecology of Malnutrition in Middle Africa,* New York, Hafner, 1965.

MORGAN, W. B. 'The forest and agriculture in West Africa', *J. Afr. Hist.,* 1962, 235–39; 'Food imports of West Africa', *Econ. Geog.,* 1963, 357–62.

MORGAN, W. B. and PUGH, J. C. *West Africa,* Methuen, 1969, Chs 2 and 10.

PAPADAKIS, J. *Crop Ecologic Survey in West Africa,* 2 vols, FAO, 1965.

PHILLIPS, J. *Agriculture and Ecology in Africa,* Faber, 1959.

SCHNELL, R. *Plantes alimentaires et vie agricole de l'Afrique Noire,* Paris, 1958.

SCHULTZ, T. W. *Transforming Traditional Agriculture,* Yale University Press, 1964.

SPILSBURY, C. *West Africa's Fats and Oils Industry,* 1959.

STEEL, R. W. 'Population increase and food production in tropical Africa', *African Affairs,* special issue 1965, pp. 55–68.

THOMAS, M. F. and WHITTINGTON, G. W. *Environment and Land Use in Africa,* Methuen, 1970, 1972.

WILDE, J. C. *et al., Agricultural Development in Tropical Africa,* 2 vols, Johns Hopkins Press, 1967.

WRIGLEY, G. *Tropical Agriculture,* Faber, 1960.

Further references on the respective countries may be found under chapters 12–26.

## Chapter 7   Livestock and fisheries

I am indebted to Mr I. L. Mason of the Institute of Animal Genetics, Edinburgh, for most valuable comments on several occasions on the livestock section.

**References**
*Livestock*
DESHLER, W. 'Cattle in Africa: distribution, types, and problems' (with map), *Geogl Rev.* 1963, 52–58.
DOUTRESSOULLE, G. *L'Elévage en Afrique Occidentale Française,* Paris, 1947.
JOSHI, N. R., MCLAUGHLIN, E. A. and PHILLIPS, R. W. *Types and breeds of African cattle,* FAO Agricultural studies no. 37, 1957.
MASON, I. L. *The Classification of West African Livestock,* Farnham, Bucks., Commonwealth Agricultural Bureaux, 1951.
VEYRET, P. 'L'élévage dans la zone tropical', *Cah. Outre-mer,* 1952, 70–83.

*Fisheries*
*Yearbook of Fishery Statistics,* FAO.

## Chapter 8   Minerals, fuels and power, and industry

**Supplementary references**
*Minerals*
LERAT, S. 'Les gisements de minerai de fer d'Afrique Noire Occidentale, *Cah. Outre-mer,* 1969, 75–87.
*Mining Annual Review,* published by *Mining Journal.*
SWINDELL, K. 'Iron ore mining in West Africa', *Econ. Geog.* 1967, 333–46.
WHITE, H. P. and GLEAVE, M. B. *An Economic Geography of West Africa,* G. Bell, 1971, Ch. 6.

*Fuels and power*
SMITH, N. *A History of Dams,* Peter Davies, 1971.
WARREN, W. M. and RUBIN, N. *Dams in Africa,* Cass, 1968.

*Industry*
EWING, A. F. *Industry in Africa,* OUP, 1968.
MABOGUNJE, A. L. 'Manufacturing and the Geography of Development in Tropical Africa', *Econ. Geog.,* 1973, 1–20.

*Notes and references*

PLESSZ, N. G. *Problems and prospects of Economic Integration in West Africa,* McGill, 1968.

VILJOEN, D. J. 'Problems of large scale industry in Africa', in E. A. G. Robinson, ed., *Economic Development for Africa South of the Sahara,* Macmillan, 1964.

WHITE, H. P. and GLEAVE, M. B. *op. cit.,* Ch. 7.

*Statistical and Economic Review,* United Africa Company, Sept. 1959.

Reference to national resources will be found in appropriate chapters.

## Chapter 9   Transport

1. See also Chapter 2.

**Supplementary references**
*General*

CHURCH, R. J. HARRISON. 'The pattern of transport in British West Africa', in R. W. Steel and C. A. Fisher, eds, *Geographical Essays on British Tropical Lands,* Philip, 1956.

CHURCH, R. J. HARRISON. 'Geographical factors in the development of transport in Africa', *United Nations Transport and Communications Review,* **2**, no. 3, 1949, 3–11.

HILLING, D. 'Politics and transportation—the problems of West Africa's land-locked states', in C. A. Fisher, ed., *Essays in Political Geography,* Methuen, 1968.

TAAFFE, E. J., MORRILL, R. L. and GOULD, P. R. 'Transport expansion in underdeveloped countries: a comparative analysis', *Geogrl Rev.* 1963, 503–29.

THOMAS, B. E. *Transport and Physical Geography in West Africa,* Washington, National Academy of Sciences, 1960.

*Statistical and Economic Review,* United Africa Company, Sept. 1954, March 1955, March 1957, March 1961.

WALKER, G. *Traffic and Transport in Nigeria: the example of an underdeveloped tropical territory,* UK, Colonial Office, 1959. (See remarks on Gould book below.)

WHITE and GLEAVE. *op. cit.* Ch. 9.

*River transport*
Netherlands Engineering Consultants (NEDECO), *River Studies and Recommendation on Improvements of the Niger and Benue,* Amsterdam, 1959.

*Rail transport*
CHURCH, R. J. HARRISON. 'The evolution of railways in French and British West Africa', *C. R. 16e Cong. Internationale de Géogr.,* Lisbon, 1949, vol. 4, pp. 95–114.

492

CHURCH, R. J. HARRISON. 'Trans-Saharan railway projects' in L. D. Stamp and S. W. Wooldridge, eds, *London Essays in Geography,* Longmans, 1951.

GOULD, P. R. *The Development of the Transportation Patterns in Ghana,* Department of Geography, Northwestern University, 1950. (Although this is on a specific country it is of great general importance because of its concepts.)

THOMAS, B. E. 'Railways and ports in French West Africa', *Econ. Geog.,* 1957, 1–15.

*Road transport*

HAWKINS, E. K. *Road Transport in Nigeria,* 1958 (see remark on Gould book, above).

1 : 4 million Michelin road map, no. 153 *Africa (North and West).*

*Ports*

HILLING, D. 'The evolution of the major ports of West Africa', *Geogl J.* 1969, 360–78.

HOYLE, B. S. and HILLING, D. eds. *Seaports and Development in Tropical Africa,* Macmillan, 1970.

*Air transport*

REICHMAN, S. *Air Transport in Tropical Africa—a geographical approach,* 2 vols, Paris, Institut de Transport Aérien, 1965.

JONES, D. *The Time Shrinkers,* Rendel, 1971.

## Chapter 10  Population

1. Robert F. Stevenson, *Population and Political Systems in Tropical Africa,* Columbia Univ. Press, 1968, asserts a positive correlation between societies of higher population density and the presence of state organisation.

2. See especially Ester Boserup, *The Conditions of Agricultural Growth: the economics of agrarian change under population pressure,* Allen & Unwin, 1965. Also Akin L. Mabogunje, 'A typology of population pressure on resources in West Africa', in Zelinsky, Kosinski and Prothero eds, *Geography and a Crowding World,* (see references below), for studies of population pressure among the Egba, Ibo and Mossi.

3. See particularly, *Migrants and Malaria,* Longmans, 1965, and 'Population mobility and trypanosomiasis in Africa', *Bulletin of the World Health Organisation,* 1963, 615–26.

4. See especially 'River blindness in Nangodi, Northern Ghana: a hypothesis of cyclical advance and retreat', *Geogrl Rev.* 1966, 398–416, and Charles C. Hughes and John M. Hunter, 'Disease and development in Africa', *Social Science and Medicine,* 1970, 443–93.

5. Hughes and Hunter, *op. cit.,* 469.

## Supplementary references

ADAMS, J. G. U. and CHURCH, R. J. HARRISON. 'The population of West Africa', in Paul F. Griffin, ed., *Geography of Population,* The National Council for Geographic Education, Palo Alto, California, 1969.

BARBOUR, K. M. *Population in Africa: a geographer's approach,* Ibadan, 1963.

BARBOUR, K. M. and PROTHERO, R. M. *Essays on African Population,* Routledge, 1961.

BASS, W. *et al.,* eds. *The Demography of Tropical Africa,* 1970.

BREESE, G., ed. *The City in Newly Developing Countries,* Prentice-Hall, 1969.

CALDWELL, J. C. and OKONJO, C. *The Population of Tropical Africa,* Longmans, 1968.

CLARK, C. *Population Growth and Land Use,* Macmillan, 1967.

HANCE, W. A. *Population, Migration and Urbanization in Africa,* Praeger; Pall Mall Press, 1970.

HUNTER, J. M. 'Ascertaining population carrying capacity under traditional systems of agriculture in developing countries', *Professional Geographer,* 1966, 151–54; and 'Population pressure in a part of the West African savanna', *Ann. Ass. Am. Geogr.* 1967, 101–14.

KAYSER, B. 'La démographie de l'Afrique Occidentale et centrale', *Cah. Outre-mer,* 1965, 73–86.

KOLL, M. *African Urban Development,* Dusseldorf, 1971.

LYSTAD, R. A., ed. *The African World,* Pall Mall Press, 1965. Chapter on Demography.

MABOGUNJE, A. L. *Regional Mobility and Resource Development in West Africa,* Montreal, McGill University, 1972.

MABOGUNJE, A. L. *Urbanization in Nigeria,* University of London Press, 1968 (included here because of its techniques).

MINER, H., ed. *The City in Modern Africa,* Pall Mall Press, 1967.

OMINDE, S. H. and EJIOGU, C. H., eds. *Population Growth and Economic Development in Africa,* Heinemann, 1972.

ORAM, N. *Towns in Africa,* OUP, 1965.

PROTHERO, R. M. 'Characteristics of rural-urban migration and the effect of movements upon the composition of population in rural and urban areas of sub-Saharan Africa' in *World Population Conference 1965,* United Nations, vol. 4, 1967, pp. 523–26.

*Sociological Review,* Special number on Urbanism, July 1959.

STEEL, R. W. 'Land and population in British tropical Africa', *Geography,* 1960, 1–17; 'Problems of population pressure in tropical Africa', *Trans. Inst. Br. Geogr.* **49**, 1970, 1–14.

STEEL, R. W. and PROTHERO, R. M., eds. *Geographers and the Tropics,* Longmans, 1964.

TREWARTHA, G. T. *A Geography of Population: world patterns,* Wiley, 1969.

TREWARTHA, G. T. *The Less-Developed Realm: a geography of its population,* Wiley, 1972.

TREWARTHA, G. T. and ZELINSKY, W. 'Population patterns in tropical Africa', *Ann. Ass. Am. Geogr.* 1954, 135–62.

*Urbananisierung in Afrika,* for German Institute for African Studies, Hamburg, by Africa Verlag, 1971.

WHITE, H. P. and GLEAVE, M. B. *An Economic Geography of West Africa,* 1971, Chs 3 and 10.

ZELINSKY, W., KOSINSKI, L. A. and PROTHERO, R. M. *Geography and a Crowding World,* OUP, 1970.

**Maps**

Cartes Ethno-Demographiques de l'Afrique Occidentale, Dakar, IFAN, 1 : 1 million, with text.

*West African International Atlas,* Organisation of African Unity.

For material on or maps of population in the individuals lands of West Africa, see references for Chapters 12–28.

## Chapter 11 Introduction to the political divisions

Parts of this chapter are based on my *Some Geographical Aspects of West African Development,* 1966, by permission of the London School of Economics and Political Science and G. Bell, and from the 1970 version by permission of the Ohio University Center for International Studies Africa Program, Athens, Ohio, USA.

1. J. D. Fage, *An Atlas of African History,* E. Arnold, 1958, and R. Oliver and J. D. Fage, *A Short History of Africa,* Penguin, 1962.
2. Sir Harry Johnston, *Liberia,* Hutchinson, 1906, vol. 1, pp. 280–96, and R. Earle Anderson, *Liberia—America's African Friend,* North Carolina Press, 1962, pp. 83–95.
3. Statistics are from the United Nations *Demographic Yearbook,* 1971.
4. L. P. Green and T. J. D. Fair, *Development in Africa: a study in regional analysis with special reference to Southern Africa,* Witwatersrand, 1962, p. i. See also Charles A. Fisher, *The Reality of Place,* An Inaugural Lecture, School of Oriental and African Studies (University of London, 1965), pp. 14–19.

**Supplementary references**

*Africa report*

*Africa Research Bulletin* (Political, Social and Cultural Series).

*Africa South of the Sahara,* Europa Publications.

FISHER, C. A., ed. *Essays in Political Geography,* Methuen, 1968, Chs 13–16.

*Notes and references*

HAMDAN, G. 'The political map of the New Africa', *Geogrl Rev.* 1963, 418–39.

HAMDAN, G. 'Capitals of the New Africa', *Econ. Geogr.* 1964, 239–53.

HANCE, W. A. *African Economic Development,* 2nd edn, Praeger; Pall Mall Press, 1967, Chs 6, 8 and 9.

HAZLEWOOD, A., ed. *African Integration and Disintegration: case studies in economic and political union,* OUP for Royal Institute of International Affairs, 1967.

ROBSON, P. *Economic Integration in Africa,* Allen & Unwin, 1968.

SMITH, R. H. T., ed. 'Spatial structure and process in tropical West Africa', *Econ. Geog.,* 1972, 229–355.

WIDSTRAND, C. G. *African Boundary Problems,* Uppsala, 1969.

*International Atlas of West Africa,* Organisation of African Unity, Sheet 42.

## Chapter 12  Senegal

Professor Paul Pélissier, University of Paris and formerly of the University of Dakar, who guided me in Senegal, has made most valuable suggestions concerning this chapter, the most recent in 1971.

1. See C. Camara, 'St Louis Senegal', *Nigerian Geogrl J.,* Dec. 1969, 17–36.
2. See R. Nguyen Van Chi-Bonnardel, *L'Economie maritime et rurale de Kayar: village Sénégalais,* Dakar, IFAN/ORSTOM, 1967; and Eliane Sy, 'Cayar, village de pêcheurs-cultivateurs au Sénégal', *Cah. Outre-mer,* 1965, 342–65.
3. See *La Presqu'île du Cap Vert,* Dakar, IFAN, 1949; and 1 : 20 000 maps with that title published by the Institut Géographique Nationale, Paris, 1966.
4. On Dakar the main references are A. Seck, *Dakar-Métropole Ouest Africaine,* Dakar, IFAN, 1970, and Richard J. Peterec, *Dakar and West African Economic Development,* Columbia Univ. Press, 1967. The Institut Géographique Nationale, Paris, publishes maps on the scales of 1 : 50 000, 1 : 10 000 and 1 : 7 500. On the port the best source is Assane Seck, 'The changing role of the port of Dakar', in B. S. Hoyle and D. Hilling, eds, *Seaports and Development in Tropical Africa,* Macmillan, 1970, pp. 41–56.
5. See *Les Industries du Cap Vert,* Dakar, Institut de Science Economique Appliquée, 1964.
6. See also G. Savonnet, 'Une ville neuve du Sénégal: Thiès', *Cah. Outre-mer,* 1956, 70–93 and *La Ville de Thiès: étude de géographie urbaine,* IFAN, St Louis, Senegal, 1955.
7. P. Pélissier, 'Les Paysans Sérères', *Cah. Outre-mer,* 1953, 105–27.
8. P. Grenier, 'Les Peul du Ferlo', *Cah. Outre-mer,* 1960, 28–58.
9. See P. Pélissier, 'Les Diola: étude sur l'habitat des riziculteurs de Basse-Casamance', *Cah. Outre-mer,* 1958.

10. On this and on cultivation of Senegalese groundnuts generally see Y. Pehaut, 'L'Arachide au Sénégal', *Cah. Outre-mer,* 1961, 5–25.
11. R. Nguyen Van Chi-Bonnardel, 'Les problems de la pêche maritime au Sénégal', *Anns Geogr.* 1969, 25–57.
12. R. Nguyen Van Chi-Bonnardel, 'Circulation, trafic et transports routiers au Sénégal', *Bull. IFAN,* **33**, B, 1971, 693–746.
13. R. Nguyen Van Chi-Bonnardel, 'Sénégal et transports aériens', *Bull. IFAN,* **32**, B, 1970, 927–74.

**Supplementary references**

BOUTILLIER, J. L., *et al. La Moyenne vallée du Sénégal,* Paris, 1962.
CHURCH, R. J. HARRISON. 'Senegal', *Focus,* American Geographical Society, Sept. 1964.
DESCHAMPS, H. *Le Sénégal et la Gambie, Que sais-je?,* Paris, 1964.
LUNEL, A. *Sénégal,* Lausanne, 1967.
PEHAUT, Y. 'Les Problemes économiques du Sénégal, *Cah. Outre-mer,* 1966, 234–72.
PELISSIER, P. *Les Paysans du Sénégal: les civilisations agraires du Cayor à la Casamance,* Fabrègue, Saint-Yrieux, 1966.
*Etudes Sénégalaises,* IFAN, St Louis.
*Travaux du Départment de Géographie de l'Université de Dakar.*

**Maps**
All published by IGN, Paris, unless otherwise stated.

*Topographic*
1 : 10 000 Dakar
1 : 10 000 Cape Verde peninsula.
1 : 20 000 Cape Verde peninsula.
1 : 50 000 Cape Verde peninsula, Senegal valley, Casamance.
1 : 200 000 West Africa.
1 : 500 000 West Africa.

*Roads and tourist*
1 : 200 000 Niokolo–Koba National Park.
1 : 500 000 Roads and tourist information.

*Administrative*
1 : 500 000 Roads, tourist information and administrative areas.
1 : 1 000 000 Administrative areas with areas of Cercles.
1 : 2 000 000 Administrative areas.
1 : 2 500 000 Adminstrative and roads.

## Notes and references

*Geological*
1 : 20 000  Cape Verde peninsula. Service des Mines, Dakar.

*Vegetation*
1 : 200 000  Thiès. ORSTOM, Paris.

*Livestock*
Various scales. Density and movement of livestock, meat consumption, breeds, transhumance, etc. ORSTOM, Paris.

*Population*
Various scales. Demographic and peoples. ORSTOM, Paris.

### Chapter 13    The Gambia: riverine enclave

Dr H. R. Jarrett, formerly resident in the Gambia, very kindly read this chapter.
1. See F. Huxley, 'Exploration in Gambia', *Geogrl Mag.* **22,** 1949, 270–77; and E. Gordon, 'A land use map of Kuntaur in the Gambia', *Geogrl J.* **116,** 1950, 216–17 for detailed land use and soil maps.
2. See H. R. Jarrett, 'Major natural regions of the Gambia', *Scottish Geogrl Mag.* **65,** 1949, 140–44; and 'Geographical regions of the Gambia', *ibid.* **66,** 1950, 163–69.
3. Warrington Yorke, 'The problem of Bathurst', *West African Review,* March 1937, 7.
4. Quoted in Winston S. Churchill, *The Second World War,* vol. 4, *The Hinge of Fate,* Cassell, 1950, p. 662.
5. H. R. Jarrett, 'Population and settlement in the Gambia', *Geogrl Rev.* 1948, 633–36.

### Supplementary references

BOTTING, D. 'Dilemma of Africa's smallest nation', *Geogrl Mag.* **41,** 1969, 659–69.
DESCHAMPS, H. *Le Sénégal et la Gambie, Que sais-je?,* Paris, 1964.
GAILEY, H. A. *A History of the Gambia,* Routledge, 1964.
GRAY, J. M. *A History of the Gambia,* 1940; new edn, Cass, 1966.
HASWELL, M. R. *Economics of Agriculture in a Savannah village,* Colonial Research Studies, no. 8, HMSO, 1953.
RICHARDSON, D. A. R. 'Private enterprise on the River Gambia', *Progress,* 1966, 229–38.
SOUTHORN, LADY. *The Gambia,* Allen & Unwin, 1952.

498

**Maps**
*Topographic*
1 : 50 000  Directorate of Overseas Surveys.
1 : 125 000  Directorate of Overseas Surveys.
1 : 200 000  IGN, Paris.
1 : 500 000  DOS. Also Road Map, Department of Survey, Banjul.
1 : 1 000 000  Directorate of Overseas Surveys.

*Special*
1 : 25 000  Land Use, Directorate of Overseas Surveys.
1 : 50 000  Land Use, Directorate of Overseas Surveys.
1 : 50 000  Oil Palm Areas, Directorate of Overseas Surveys.

*Town plans*
1 : 2 500  Banjul, Fajara and Bakau, Sere Kunda.

## Chapter 14    Mauritania

I am indebted to Monsieur G. J. Duchemin, formerly Director of the
Senegal–Mauritania Centre of the Institut Fondamentale d'Afrique Noire,
for his valuable comments on this chapter and for guiding me in
Mauritania on my first visit.
1. See C. Toupet, 'Nouadhibou (Port Etienne) and the Economic
   Development of Mauritania' in B. S. Hoyle and D. Hilling, eds,
   *Seaports and Development in Tropical Africa,* 1970, 27–40.
2. See also Chapter 7. There are excellent cattle maps of Mauritania and
   Senegal by F. Bonnet-Dupeyron, published by the ORSTOM.

**Supplementary references**
BRIERLEY, T. 'Mauritania', *Geogrl Mag.* **37,** Feb. 1965, 764–65.
GERTEINY, A. G. *Mauritania,* Pall Mall Press, 1968.
HILLING, D. 'Saharan iron ore oasis', *Geogrl Mag.* **41,** 1969, 908–17.
MARBEAU, V. 'Les Mines de fer de Mauritanie (MIFERMA)', *Annls Géogr.* 1965, 175–93.
PUJOS, J. *Croissance économique et impulsion extérieure: Etude sur l'économie mauritanienne,* 1964.
TOUPET, C. 'Orientation bibliographique sur la Mauritanie', *Bull. IFAN,* **21,** 1959, 201–39.
TOUPET, C. 'Mauritanie' in S. P. Chatterjee, ed. 'Developing countries of the world', *Proc.* 21st Inter. Geogrl Congr. 1968, pp. 238–47.
WESTEBBE, R. M. *The Economy of Mauritania,* Praeger; Pall Mall Press, 1972.

**Maps**
All published by IGN, Paris, unless otherwise stated.

*Notes and references*

*Topographic*
1 : 20 000  Kédite Ijil (iron ore area).
1 : 20 000  Nouadhibou (Port Etienne).
1 : 50 000  Senegal valley.
1 : 100 000  Cape Blanc.
1 : 50 000  Senegal valley.
1 : 200 000  West Africa.
1 : 500 000  West Africa.

*Transhumance*
Various scales. ORSTOM, Paris.

*Population*
Various scales. ORSTOM, Paris.

## Chapter 15    Mali: Marxian socialism in an inland state

M. La Cognata of the Ecole Normale Supérieure de Bamako gave me most valuable help for this chapter in 1971, and M. Gérard Brasseur, now of the Office de la Recherche Scientifique et Technique Outre-Mer likewise for the initial version.

1. See M. L. Villien-Rossi, 'Bamako, capitale du Mali', *Bull. IFAN,* **28,** B, 1966, 249–380 and also in *Cah. Outre-mer,* 1963, 379–93.
2. See P. B. Hammond, 'The Niger project: some cultural sources of conflict, in William H. Lewis, ed., *Emerging Africa,* Washington, 1963, pp. 12–28.
3. R. J. Harrison Church, 'Timbuktu', *Geogrl Mag.* **42,** 1970, 683–89.
4. J. Gallais, 'Le paysan dogon', *Cah. Outre-mer,* 1965, 123–43.

**Supplementary references**

BRASSEUR, P.  *Bibliographie Général du Mali,* Dakar, IFAN, 1964.
BRASSEUR, G.  'Le Mali' in S. P. Chatterjee, ed., 'Developing countries of the world', *Proc.* 21st Internat. Geogrl Congr. 1968, pp. 257–64.
CHURCH, R. J. HARRISON.  'Problems and development of the dry zone of West Africa', *Geogrl J.* 1961, 187–204.
DUMONT, R.  *Afrique Noire: développement agricole Réconversion de l'économie agricole,* Guineé, Côte d'Ivoire, Mali, 1962.
GALLAIS, J.  *Le Delta Intérieur du Niger: étude régionale,* 2 vols, Dakar, IFAN, 1967.
GALLAIS, J.  *Le Delta Intérieur du Niger et ses bordures,* Paris, 1967.
JOHNSON, H. G., ed. and part author, *Economic Nationalism in Old and New States,* Allen & Unwin, 1969.
WILDE, J. C. *et al., Agricultural Development in Tropical Africa,* 2 vols, Johns Hopkins Press, 1967.

500

**Maps**
All published by IGN, Paris, unless otherwise stated.
1 : 20 000  Bamako and environs.
1 : 50 000  Bafoulabé area.
1 : 200 000  West Africa.
1 : 500 000  West Africa.
1 : 2 500 000  Mali—general.
1 : 2 500 000  Mali (layer coloured), Moscow, 1964.

## Chapter 16  Upper Volta

I am most grateful to Monsieur le Moal, Director of the former Institut Français d'Afrique Noire at Ouagadougou, who guided me in the Upper Volta and gave helpful advice on this chapter in earlier editions, and to M. Georges Savonnet, Director of Research, ORSTOM, for advice with the latest edition.
1. See Akin L. Mabogunje, 'A typology of population pressure on resources in West Africa', in Zelinsky, Kosinki and Prothero, eds, *Geography and a Crowding World,* OUP, 1970.

**Supplementary references**
DAVEAU, S. 'Les plateaux du Sud-Ouest de la Haute-Volta: Etude géomorphologique', *Travaux du Département de Géographie de l'Université de Dakar,* 1960.
DAVEAU, S. LAMOTTE, M. and ROUGERIE, G. 'Cuirasses et chaines birrimiennes en Haute Volta', *Annls Géogr.* **71,** 460–82.
REMY, G. *Yobri: étude géographique du terroir d'un village gourmantché de Haute Volta,* ORSTOM, 1967.
SAVONNET, G. *Pina,* ORSTOM, 1970, and *Atlas de Haute Volta,* Centre Voltaïque de la Recherche Scientifique, Ouagadougou, 1968.
VAN WETTERE-VERHASSELT, Y. 'Bobo-Dioulasso: le développement d'une ville d'Afrique Occidentale, *Cah. Outre-mer,* 1969, 83–94.
WILDE, J. C., *et al. Agricultural Development in Tropical Africa,* 2 vols, Johns Hopkins Press, 1967.
*Etudes Voltaïques,* Centre Voltaïque de la Recherche Scientifique, Ouagadougou.

**Maps**
All published by IGN, Paris.
1 : 200 000  West Africa.
1 : 500 000  West Africa.
1 : 1 000 000  Road and administrative map of Upper Volta.

*Notes and references*

## Chapter 17   Niger

I was indebted to M. Le Moal, former director of the Institut Français d'Afrique Noire at Ouagadougou, Upper Volta, for valuable criticism of this chapter in earlier editions, and to M. S. Diarra of the University of Dakar for some help in the present edition.
1. For an interesting, though old study of the Tuareg, see F. R. (Lord Rennell of) Rodd, *People of the Veil*, 1926.

### Supplementary references
CHURCH, R. J. HARRISON. 'Niger', *Focus, Am. geogrl Soc.* Sept. 1965.
DONAINT, P. and LANCRENON, F. *Le Niger, Que Sais-je?*, Paris, 1972. *Etudes Nigériennes*, Niamey.

### Maps
All published by IGN, Paris.
1 : 15 000  Niamey, Zinder and Maradi.
1 : 50 000  Niger valley and southern borderlands.
1 : 200 000  West Africa.
1 : 500 000  West Africa.
1 : 1 000 000  Niger.
1 : 2 500 000  Niger—general.
1 : 5 000 000  Niger—administrative.

## Chapter 18   The Portuguese province of Guinea

This chapter is based on material by Professor Orlando Ribiero, Professor of Geography in the University of Lisbon. It has been updated for the latest edition by Professor Raquel Soeiro de Brito, also of the University of Lisbon. I am grateful to both these helpers.

### Supplementary references
GUINARÃES, C. 'O Clima da Guiné Portuguesa', *Boletim Cultural da Guiné Portuguesa*, **14**, no. 55.
HORTA, C. A. P. 'Análise Estrutural e Conjuntural da Economia da Guiné, *Boletim Cultural da Guiné Portuguesa*, **20**, no. 80.
QUINTINO, F. R. 'Os Povos da Guiné', *Boletim Cultural de Guiné Portuguesa*, **22**, nos 85–86, and 96.
RIBEIRO, O. 'Sur quelques traits géographiques de la Guinée Portugaise', *CIAO de Bissau*, 1952; 'L'Amenagement du Terroir en Afrique Occidentale', *Bull. Soc. roy. de Géographie d'Egypte*, **25**, 1953, 165–77.
BRITO, R. S. DE. 'Guiné, Cabo Verde, e S. Tomé e Príncipe; alguns aspectos da Terra e dos Homens', Lisbon, *ISCSPU*, 1966.

TEIXEIRA, A. J. DA S. *Os Solos da Guiné Portuguesa: Carta Geral, Características, Formação e Utilização,* Junta de Investigações do Ultramar, Lisbon, 1962.

TEIXEIRA, J. E. *Geologia da Guiné Portuguesa, Curso da Geologia do Ultramar (JIU),* vol. 1, 1968, pp. 53–104.

TEIXEIRA DA MOTA, A. *Guiné Portuguesa,* 2 vols (Monografias dos Territórios do Ultramar), Agência Geral do Ultramar, Lisbon, 1954. Has English and French resumés.

TENREIRO, F. *Bibliografia da Guiné, Garcia de Orta,* vol. 2, no. 1, 1953, pp. 97–134.

**Maps**

*Atlas de Portugal Ultramarino,* 1947.

1 : 50 000 Ministério do Ultramar is an excellent series.

1 : 500 000 Covers the whole country.

## Chapter 19 Guinea: Marxian socialism in a highland watershed

M. M. Houis, formerly Director of the Institut Français d'Afrique Noire at Conakry, who accompanied me in much of Guinea at great trouble to himself, further assisted me by his criticism of the original chapter. M. Jean Suret-Canale, Chargé de Recherches au Centre Nationale de la Recherche Scientifique, Paris, and formerly in Guinea has given me very great help with the latest version.

1. J. Suret-Canale, 'Le cuirassement des sols en Guinée', *Recherches Africaines,* 1960, 75–76.
2. J. Gallais, 'La riziculture de plaine en Haute-Guinée', *Annls Géogr.* 1959, 207–23.
3. J. Suret-Canale, 'Un exemple de l'industrialisation africaine: Fria', *Annls Géogr.* 1964, 172–88.

**Supplementary references**

CHARLES, B. *Guinée,* Lausanne, 1963.

DUMONT, R. *Afrique Noire: développement agricole. Reconversion de l'économie agricole: Guinée, Côte d'Ivoire, Mali,* 1962.

CHURCH, R. J. HARRISON. 'Guinea', *Focus* (American Geographical Society), March 1967.

SURET-CANALE, J. *La République de Guinée,* 1970.

SWINDELL, K. 'Industrialization in Guinea', *Geography,* 1969, 456–58.

**Maps**

All published by IGN, Paris, unless otherwise stated.

1 : 50 000 Western Guinea.

1 : 200 000 West Africa.

1 : 500 000 West Africa.

1 : 2 000 000 Guinea relief model. Administration Centrale de Géodésie et Cartographie, Prague, 1963. ·

## Chapter 20   Sierra Leone

Dr H. R. Jarrett, formerly at Fourah Bay College, Freetown, criticised the first version of this chapter and one map is his. Dr G. J. Williams, also formerly of that college, gave me great help with the latest version. I am most grateful to both of them.

1. See S. Gregory, *Rainfall over Sierra Leone,* University of Liverpool, Dept. of Geography, Res. Paper no. 2, 1965, which has a bibliography.
2. F. J. Martin, *A Preliminary Survey of the Vegetation of Sierra Leone,* Freetown, Govt Printer, 1938.
3. A. R. Stobbs, *The Soils and Geography of the Boliland Region of Sierra Leone,* Freetown, Government of Sierra Leone, 1963.
4. M. K. Wells, 'The structure and petrology of the Freetown layered basic complex of Sierra Leone', *Overseas Geology and Mineral Resources,* Supplement series 4, 1962.
5. S. Gregory, 'The raised beaches of the peninsular area of Sierra Leone', *Trans. Inst. Br. Geogr.* 1962, 15–22.
6. G. J. Williams, 'The Guma Valley Scheme, Sierra Leone', *Geography,* 1965, 163–66.
7. See Roy Lewis, 'Creoledom revisited', *Geogrl Mag.* **36,** May 1964, 9–19.
8. For example, Graham Greene, *The Heart of the Matter,* Heinemann, 1948. For scientific studies see Christopher Fyfe and Eldred Jones, eds, *Freetown: a symposium,* Sierra Leone University Press, 1968; H. R. Jarrett, 'The port and town of Freetown', *Geography,* 1955, 108–18; 'Recent port and harbour developments at Freetown', *Scottish geogrl Mag.* **71,** 1955, 157–64, and 'Some aspects of the urban geography of Freetown, Sierra Leone, *Geogrl Rev.* 1956, 334–54.
9. On the port, see J. McKay, 'Physical potential and economic reality: the underdevelopment of the port of Freetown', in B. S. Hoyle and D. Hilling, eds, *Seaports and Development in Tropical Africa,* 1970, pp. 57–74.
10. Martin, *op. cit.* pp. 4–5.
11. H. D. Jordan, *Development of Mangrove Swamps Areas in Sierra Leone,* Commission for Technical Cooperation in Africa South of the Sahara, 1963.
12. See K. Swindell, 'Iron ore mining in West Africa: some recent developments in Guinea, Sierra Leone and Liberia', *Econ. Geog.* 1967, 333–46.

13.  See K. Swindell, 'Diamond mining in Sierra Leone', *Tijdschr. v. econ. soc. Geog.* 1966, 96–104.

**Supplementary references**

CLARKE, J. I., ed. *Sierra Leone in Maps,* University of London Press, 2nd edn, 1969.
FYFE, C. *A History of Sierra Leone,* OUP, 1962.
FYFE, C. *Sierra Leone Inheritance,* OUP, 1964.
LEWIS, R. *Sierra Leone,* HMSO, 1954.
PETERSON, J. *Province of Freetown: a history of Sierra Leone, 1787–1870,* Faber, 1969.
PORTER, A. J. *Creoledom,* OUP, 1963.
RANKIN, F. HARRISON. *The White Man's Grave: a visit to Sierra Leone in 1834,* 1836.
RIDDELL, J. B. *The Spatial Dynamics of Modernization in Sierra Leone: structure, diffusion and response,* Evanston, 1971.
SAYLOR, R. G. *The Economic System of Sierra Leone,* Durham, NC, 1967.
VAN DER LAAN, H. L. *The Sierra Leone Diamonds,* OUP, 1965.
WEST, R. *Back to Africa: a history of Sierra Leone and Liberia,* 1971.
WILLIAMS, G. J. 'Sierra Leone stakes its mineral claims', *Geogrl Mag.* 1970, 398–401 and *Bibliography of Sierra Leone, 1925–67,* New York Africana Publishing Corporation, 1971.
*Sierra Leone Geographical Journal,* Freetown.
*Sierra Leone Studies,* Freetown.

**Maps**

*Topographic*
1 : 10 000  Freetown peninsula, DOS.
1 : 50 000  Special sheet: Freetown, DOS.
1 : 50 000  Sierra Leone, DOS.
1 : 250 000  Sierra Leone, US Army Map Service.
1 : 500 000  Sierra Leone, Layer Coloured, GSGS.
1 : 1 000 000  Sierra Leone, DOS.

*Various*
1 : 16 000  Land use of Rhombe.
1 : 40 000  Land use of Ribi, Bumpe and Little Scarcies.
1 : 50 000  Geological maps of Sula mountains, Kangari hills, Gola forest, North Kambui hills.
1 : 50 000  Soil maps of the Bolilands.
1 : 500 000  Chiefdom Boundaries, Agricultural Production and Trade.

1 : 1 000 000 Administrative, Vegetation, Tribal, Geological, Soil, Population, Agricultural Products, Soil Conservation, Land Classification, Population and Fallows, Degraded Areas, Zones of Production, Forest Reserves, Mineral Deposits, Navigable Waterways.

## Chapter 21 Liberia

The first version of this chapter was read by Professor P. W. Porter of the University of Minnesota, who carried out field work on population and land use in Liberia. The latest version has been greatly helped by advice from Professor W. Schulze of the University of Giessen and formerly for many years at the University of Liberia.

1. See W. Schulze, 'The ports of Liberia: economic significance and development problems', in B. S. Hoyle and D. Hilling, eds, *Seaports and Development in Tropical Africa,* Macmillan, 1970, pp. 75–102.
2. R. J. Harrison Church, 'The Firestone Rubber Plantations in Liberia', *Geography,* 1969, 430–37.
3. Schulze, *op. cit.*
4. *Ibid.*

**Supplementary references**

AZIKIWE, B. N. *Liberia in World Politics,* Negro Universities Press, 1970.

BUELL, R. L. *Liberia: a Century of Survival 1847–1947,* Univ. of Pennsylvania Press, 1947.

CLOWER, R. W., DALTON, G., HARWITZ, M. and WALTERS, A. A. *Growth without Development: an Economic Survey of Liberia,* Northwestern Univ. Press, 1966.

GNIELINSKI, STEFAN VON. *Liberia in Maps,* University of London Press, 1972.

HANCE, W. A. *African Economic Development,* Praeger, Pall Mall Press, 1967, Ch. 3.

HOLAS, B. and DEKEYSER, P. *Mission dans l'Est Libérien,* Dakar, IFAN, 1952, has a 50 page bibliography.

HOLSOE, S. E. *A Bibliography on Liberia,* Part 1: Books, Univ. of Delaware, 1971.

JOHNSTON, SIR H. *Liberia,* 1906 (for early data).

MCLAUGHLIN, R. U. *Foreign Investment and Development in Liberia,* Praeger; Pall Mall Press, 1966.

SCHULZE, W. *A New Geography of Liberia,* Longman 1973.

SCHWAB, G. *Tribes of the Liberian Hinterland,* edited with additional material by G. W. Harley, Peabody Museum, vol. 31, 1947.

SOLOMAN, M. D. and D'AZEVEDO, W. L. *A General Bibliography of the Republic of Liberia,* Northwestern Univ. Press, 1962.

**Maps**

1 : 20 000 Monrovia region (11 sheets). Prepared for the Bureau of Surveys, Lands and Titles, Department of Public Works and Utilities, by Hansa Luftbild, Gm.b.H, Munster, 1963.

1 : 125 000 United States Coast and Geodetic Survey, Washington, DC, 1957.

1 : 500 000 United States Coast and Geodetic Survey, Washington, DC, 1957.

1 : 1 000 000 United States Coast and Geodetic Survey, Washington, DC, 1957.

## Chapter 22   The Ivory Coast

I record with deep thanks the help of Professor Gabriel Rougerie, of the University of Paris, formerly of the Institut Français d'Afrique Noire at Abidjan, who guided me in and around that town, and who has made valuable comments upon this chapter; both for the first edition and in 1972.

1. See D. C. Betts, 'The San Pedro project in the Ivory Coast', *Geography*, 1971, 47.
2. See Mireille Bouthier, 'The development of the Port of Abidjan and the economic growth of Ivory Coast', in B. S. Hoyle and D. Hilling, eds, *Seaports and Development in Tropical Africa*, 1970, 103–26.

**Supplementary references**

AMIN, S. *Le Développement du Capitalisme en Côte d'Ivoire*, 1967.

BONNEFONDS, L. 'La transformation du commerce de traite en Côte d'Ivoire depuis la dernière guerre mondiale et l'Independance', *Cah. Outre-mer*, 1968, 395–413.

COULIBALY, S. 'Les Paysans Senoufo de Korhogo', *Cah. Outre-mer*, 1961, 26–59.

DESANTI, D. *Côte d'Ivoire*, Lausanne, 1962.

DIAWARA, M. T. 'The Ivory Coast—birth of a modern state', *Progress*, 1967, 66–70.

DUMONT, R. *Afrique Noire: Développement Agricole. Reconversion de l'économie agricole: Guinée, Côte d'Ivoire, Mali*, 1962.

HILTON, T. E. 'The changing Ivory Coast', *Geography*, 1965, 291–95.

HOLAS, B. *La Côte d'Ivoire*, Abidjan, 1963.

ROUGERIE, G. *La Côte d'Ivoire, Que sais-je?*, Paris, 1972.

SKINNER, S. W. *The Agricultural Economy of the Ivory Coast*, Washington, 1964.

WILDE, J. C., *et al. Agricultural Development in Tropical Africa*, 2 vols, Johns Hopkins Press, 1967.

*Etudes Eburnéennes*, CNRCI, Abidjan.

*Bibliographie de la Côte d'Ivoire*, Bibliothèque Nationale, Abidjan.

**Maps**
All published by IGN, Paris, unless otherwise stated.
1 : 10 000  Abidjan.
1 : 50 000  Southern Ivory Coast.
1 : 200 000  West Africa.
1 : 500 000  West Africa.
1 : 2 500 000  Ivory Coast—general.
1 : 3 000 000  Ivory Coast, Michelin.
*Atlas de Côte d'Ivoire,* ORSTOM, Abidjan.

## Chapter 23   Ghana

Professor E. A. Boateng, now Vice-Chancellor of the University of Cape Coast, Ghana, and Dr H. P. White, University of Salford advised me on the first version of this chapter and Dr George Benneh, University of Ghana, gave me equally generous help with this version.

1. See J. M. Hunter, 'Regional patterns of population growth in Ghana, 1948–60', in J. B. Whittow and P. D. Wood, eds, *Essays in Geography for Austin Miller,* 1965; and Enid R. Forde, *The Population of Ghana,* Northwestern Univ. Press, 1968.
2. See *Portfolio of Ghana Maps,* map 8.
3. See also H. P. Wood, 'Environment and land utilisation on the Accra plains', *Journal of the West African Science Association,* 1954, 46–62; T. E. Hilton, 'The economic development of the south-eastern coastal plains of Ghana', *Trop. Geog.* 1962, 18–31; and 'The settlement pattern of the Accra plains', *Geography,* 1970, 289–306; and Rowena M. Lawson, *The Changing Economy of the Lower Volta, 1954–67,* 1972.
4. White, *op. cit.,* 61.
5. Used in a more restricted sense than Hilton's or White's (*op. cit.*) *Accra Plains* which comprise those parts of (*a*), (*c*) and (*e*) which lie west of the Volta river.
6. See D. Hilling, 'Port development and economic growth: the case of Ghana', in B. S. Hoyle and D. Hilling, eds, *Seaports and Development in Tropical Africa,* 1970.
7. R. J. Harrison Church, 'The achievement of Tema', *Bull. Ghana Geogrl Assoc.,* Jan. 1967.
8. W. E. F. Ward, *A History of Ghana,* Allen & Unwin, 1958 edn, p. 57. An outstanding work is Ioné Acquah, *Accra Survey,* Accra, 1958. R. P. Brand, 'The Spatial Organization of Residential Areas in Accra, Ghana, with particular reference to aspects of modernization', *Econ. Geog.,* 1972, 284–98 and see also R. R. Brand, *A selected bibliography of Accra, Ghana, a West African colonial city,* 2 parts, Monticello, Illinois, 1970 and 1971.
9. An important study is J. M. Hunter and D. F. Hayward, 'Towards a model of scarp retreat and drainage evolution: evidence from

508

Ghana, West Africa', *Geogrl J.* **137**, 51–68.
10. See J. M. Hunter, 'River blindness in Nangodi, Northern Ghana: a hypothesis of cyclical advance and retreat', *Geogrl Rev.* 1966, 398–416.
11. T. E. Hilton, 'Land planning and resettlement in northern Ghana', *Geography*, 1959, 227–40.
12. Ward, *op. cit.*, pp. 54–55.
13. T. E. Bowdich, *Mission from Cape Coast Castle to Ashantee*, 1817, and quoted by R. W. Steel, 'The towns of Ashanti: a geographical study', *C. R. Congr. Internat. Géog.* 1949, 81–93. See also K. A. J. Nyarko, 'The development of Kumasi', *Bull. Ghana geogrl Ass.* **4**, no. 1, 1959, 3–8, and W. Manshard, 'Die Stadt Kumasi', *Erdkunde*, **15**, fig. 3, 1961, 161–80. For maps of Kumasi see *Portfolio of Ghana maps and Geogrl J.* **110**, 162.
14. See D. Hilling, 'Port development and economic growth: the case of Ghana', in B. S. Hoyle and D. Hilling, eds, *Seaports and Development in Tropical Africa*, 1970, pp.    –   .
15. P. Hill, *The Migrant Cocoa Farmers of Southern Ghana: a study in rural capitalism*, CUP, 1963.
16. See G. Benneh, 'Educating peasant farmers towards the twentieth century', **44**, *Geogrl Mag.* Nov. 1971, 97–101.
17. See T. E. Hilton, 'The coastal fisheries of Ghana', *Bull. Ghana geog. Ass.* July 1964, 34–51; 'Ghana fisheries', *The Economist*, 25 Feb. 1967, 742–43.

**Supplementary references**
BOATENG, E. A. *A Geography of Ghana*, CUP, 1965.
BOURRET, F. M. *Ghana: the road to independence*, OUP, 1960.
CLARIDGE, W. W. *A History of the Gold Coast and Ashanti*, 2 vols, Cass, 1964.
FAGE, J. D. *Ghana: a historical interpretation*, 1950.
HILTON, T. E. *Ghana Population Atlas*, Univ. of Ghana; Nelson, 1960.
LA ANYANE, S. *Ghana Agriculture*, 1963.
MANSHARD, W. *Die geographischen Grundlagen der Wirtschaft Ghanas*, Wiesbaden, 1961.
ROUCH, J. *Ghana*, Lausanne, 1964.
WARD, W. E. F. *A History of Ghana*, Allen & Unwin 2nd edn, 1966.
WILLIS, J. B. *Agriculture and Land Use in Ghana*, 1962.
*Economic Survey*, Central Bureau of Statistics, Accra, annual.
*Bulletin of the Ghana Geographical Association*.

**Maps**
*Portfolio of Ghana maps.* Survey Department.

*Topographic*
1 : 50 000  Directorate of Overseas Surveys.
1 : 62 500  Ghana Survey Department.
1 : 125 000 and 1 : 250 000  Ghana Survey Department.
1 : 400 000  General wall map. Ghana Survey Department.
1 : 500 000  Road map. Also Forest Reserves overprinted on road map. Ghana Survey Department.
1 : 750 000  Historical map. Colony and Ashanti since AD 1400. Ghana Survey Department.
1 : 1 Million Layer Coloured General Map. Ghana Survey Department.

*Special and Cadastral*
1 : 5 000  Volta delta and Volta dam site. Directorate of Colonial Surveys.
1 : 1 250, 1 : 6 250 and 1 : 12 500  Town Plans. Ghana Survey Department.
1 : 1 Million Geological Map. Ghana Geological Survey.

## Chapter 24   Togo

M. Gérard Brasseur, once stationed at Lomé, has given me most useful criticism of this chapter, most recently in 1972.

1. On the subject of the divided Ewe see B. W. Hodder, 'The Ewe problem: a reassessment', in Charles A. Fisher, ed., *Essays in Political Geography,* 1968, pp. 271–83, and the present author's *Modern Colonization,* 1951, pp. 118–21. For a study of the Ewe see Madeline Manoukian, *The Ewe-speaking People of Togoland and the Gold Coast,* International African Institute, 1952.

2. *Report by First Visiting Mission of United Nations to French Togoland,* 1950; J. C. Froelich, 'Densité de la population et méthodes de culture chez les Kabré du Nord-Togo', *Co. R. Congr. Internat. Géog.* Lisbon, 1949, vol. 4, 168–80, and 'Généralités sur les Kabré du Nord-Togo', *Bull. IFAN,* 1949, 77–106; H. Enjalbert, 'Paysans noirs: Les Kabré du Nord-Togo', *Cah. Outre-mer,* 1956, 137–80; D. V. Sassoon, 'The Cabrais of Togoland', *Geogrl Mag.* 1950, 339–41; E. Guernier, *Cameroun-Togo* (*Encyclopédie de l'Afrique française*), 1951, p. 428, has a map of the new villages, on p. 426 a general population map of Togo and, on p. 431, an ethnic map.

**Supplementary references**
CORNEVIN, R. *Le Togo, Que sais-je?,* Paris, 1972.
CORNEVIN, R. *Histoire du Togo,* 1969.

**Maps**
All published by IGN, Paris.
1 : 15 000  Lomé.

1 : 50 000  Southern and north-eastern Togo.
1 : 200 000  West Africa.
1 : 500 000  West Africa.
1 : 500 000  Togo roads and tourist map.

## Chapter 25  Dahomey

M. and Mme Brasseur, formerly resident in Dahomey, who gave me great help there, have made me further indebted to them for their comments on this chapter, most recently in 1972.

1.  See P. Brasseur-Marion, 'Porto-Novo' in *Porto-Novo et sa Palmeraie*, Dakar, IFAN, 1953, pp. 7–47.
2.  See A. Mondjannagni, 'Cotonou: some problems of port development in Dahomey', in B. S. Hoyle and D. Hilling, *Seaports and Development in Tropical Africa*, 1970.
3.  On the Porto-Novo oil palm country see G. Brasseur, 'La Palmeraie de Porto-Novo' in *Porto-Novo et sa Palmeraie, op. cit.*

### Supplementary references

CORNEVIN, R. *Dahomey, Que sais-je?*, Paris.
CORNEVIN, R. *Histoire du Dahomey*, Paris, 1962.
PELISSIER, P. 'Les Pays du Bas-Ouémé, *Cah. Outre-mer*, 1962, 204–54, 315–59; 1965, 81–125.
VALLET, J. *Région du Grand Hinvi*, Paris, 1968.
WHITE, H. P. 'Dahomey—the geographical basis of an African State', *Tijdschr. v. econ. soc. Geog.* 1966, 61–68.
*Études Dahoméennes*, IFAN and later IRAD, Porto-Novo.

### Maps

All published by IGN, Paris.
1 : 50 000  Southern, northwestern and northeastern Dahomey.
1 : 200 000  West Africa.
1 : 500 000  West Africa.

## Chapter 26  The Federation of Nigeria

I am indebted to Professors W. B. Morgan and J. C. Pugh, formerly of Ibadan University and now at King's College London, for most helpful criticism of earlier versions of this chapter, and for the latest one to Dr S. A. Agboola of the University of Ife, Mr M. J. Mortimore of Ahmadu Bello University, Zaria, and the staff of the Department of Geography, University of Lagos.

1.  See Barry Floyd, *Eastern Nigeria,* Macmillan, 1969, Ch. 2; Y. Karmon, *A Geography of Settlement in Eastern Nigeria,* Hebrew University, Jerusalem, 1966; W. B. Morgan, 'Settlement patterns of the Eastern

Region of Nigeria, *Nigerian Geogrl J.* 1957, 23–30, and 'The grassland towns of the Eastern Region of Nigeria', *Trans. Inst. Br. Geogr.* 1957, 213–40; R. Mansell Prothero, 'The population of Eastern Nigeria', *Scottish Geogrl Mag.* 1971, 165–70.

2. See N. C. Mitchell, 'Yoruba towns', in K. M. Barbour and R. M. Protherto, eds, *Essays on African Population,* Routledge, 1961, pp. 279–301.
3. See A. L. Mabogunje, 'A typology of population pressure on resources in West Africa', in W. Zelinsky *et al.,* eds, *Geography and a Crowding World,* OUP, 1970, pp. 121–23.
4. J. T. Coppock, 'Agricultural Developments in Nigeria', *J. Trop. Geogr.* **23**, 1966, 1–18.
5. See also B. J. Garnier, *Weather Conditions in Nigeria,* Climatological Research Series, no. 2, Department of Geography, McGill University, Canada, 1967.
6. For additional information on the geographical regions see R. K. Udo, *Geographical Regions of Nigeria,* Heinemann Educational, and the sources noted under individual regions.
7. See J. C. Pugh, 'The Porto-Novo–Badagri Sand Ridge Complex', *Research Notes,* Dept. of Geography, Univ. Coll., Ibadan, no. 3, pp. 3–14, and 'A Classification of the Nigerian Coastline', *J. W. Afr. Sci. Ass.* **1**, Oct. 1954, no. 1, 3–12.
8. On Badagri see B. W. Hodder, 'Badagri—slave port and mission centre', *Nigerian Geogrl J.* Dec. 1962, 75–87, and 'Badagri—one hundred years of change', *Idem,* 1963, 17–30.
9. See Akin L. Mabogunje, *Urbanization in Nigeria,* University of London Press, 1968, Chs 10–11 and 'The evolution and analysis of the retail structure of Lagos', *Econ. Geog.* 1964, 304–23; also, *Report on the Redevelopment of Metropolitan Lagos,* United Nations, 1964, and 1 : 20 000 map of Lagos, Federal Surveys.
10. For this and succeeding divisions of Western Nigeria, I originally drew upon K. M. Buchanan, 'An outline of the geography of the Western Region of Nigeria', *Malayan J. Trop. Geog.* 1953, 9–24 and 'The delimitation of land use regions in a tropical environment —an example from the Western Region of Nigeria', *Geography,* 1953, 303–7.
11. See Rolf Güsten, *Studies in the Staple Food Economy of Western Nigeria,* 1969.
12. On cocoa see R. Galletti, K. D. S. Baldwin and I. O. Dina, *Nigerian Cocoa Farmers: an economic survey of Yoruba farming families,* OUP, 1956.
13. See Camille Camara, 'l'Organisation de l'espace géographique par les villes Yoruba: l'exemple d'Abeokuta', *Annls Géogr.* 1971, 256–87.
14. See Akin L. Mabogunje, *Urbanization in Nigeria,* Chs 8–9, and 'The growth of residential districts in Ibadan, *Geogrl Rev.* 1962, 56–77;

and P. C. Lloyd, A. L. Mabogunje and B. Awe, *The City of Ibadan*, CUP, 1967.

15. See J. T. Coppock, 'Tobacco growing in Nigeria', *Erdkunde,* 1965, 297–306.

16. Further reference should be made to Barry Floyd, *Eastern Nigeria,* Macmillan, 1969.

17. See H. A. Oluwasanmi, *et al., Uboma,* Geographical Publications, 1966; W. B. Morgan, 'Farming practice, settlement pattern and population density in South-Eastern Nigeria', *Geogrl J.* **121,** 1955, 320–33; and R. Udoh, 'Patterns of population distribution and settlement in Eastern Nigeria', *Nigerian Geogrl J.* 1963, 73–88.

18. J. T. Coppock, 'Agricultural developments in Nigeria', *J. Trop. Geog.* 1966, 1–18.

19. I acknowledge my indebtedness to A. T. Grove, *Land Use and Soil Conservation in Parts of Onitsha and Owerri Provinces,* Bulletin no. 21 of the Geological Survey of Nigeria, 1951 and 'Soil erosion and population problems in South-East Nigeria', *Geogrl J.* **117,** 1951, 291–306.

20. C. Daryll Forde, 'Land and labour in a Cross River village, Southern Nigeria', *Geogrl J.* **90,** 24–51, describes a village athwart the ridge east of Afikpo.

21. Grove, *op. cit., Geogrl J.,* 293–5.

22. See also Ch. 3, pp. 52–54, pp. 68–69, and *inter alia,* S. A. Agboola, 'The Middle Belt of Nigeria: the basis of its unity', *Nigerian Geogrl J.* 1961, 41–46; R. A. Pullan, 'The Concept of the Middle Belt in Nigeria: An attempt at a climatic Definition', *Nigerian Geogrl J.* 1962, 39–52; M. B. Gleave and H. P. White, 'The West African Middle Belt', *Geogrl Rev.* 1969, 123–39; M. Mason, 'Population density and "slave raiding" – the case of the middle belt of Nigeria', *J. Afr. Hist.* 1969, 551–64.

23. A mine of information is Max Lock and Partners, *Kaduna 1917, 1967, 2017. A survey and plan of the Capital Territory for the Government of Northern Nigeria,* 1967.

24. For this and other settlement schemes see J. T. Coppock, 'Agricultural developments in Nigeria', *J. Trop. Geog.* 1966, 1–18.

25. See M. J. Mortimore, 'Population densities and rural economies in the Kano close-settled zone, Nigeria' in W. Zelinsky *et al.,* eds, *Geography and a Crowding World,* 1970, 380–88; and A. T. Grove, 'Population densities and agriculture in Northern Nigeria' in K. M. Barbour and R. M. Prothero, eds, *Essays on African Population,* 1961, 115–36.

26. See M. J. Mortimore, ed. *Zaria and its Region,* Occasional Paper no. 4, Nigerian Geographical Association and Department of Geography, Ahmadu Bello University, 1970.

27. See M. J. Mortimore, *Land Use in Kano city and township: A map*

      *on the scale of 1/12 500 with commentary,* Occasional Paper no. 2, Department of Geography, Ahmadu Bello University, Zaria, 1966; *Land and people in the Kano close-settled zone,* Department of Geography, Ahmadu Bello University, Zaria, 1965; also B. W. Trevallion, *Metropolitan Kano, 1960–80,* Pergamon Press, 1966.

28. B. E. Sharwood Smith, *Sokoto Survey 1948,* Gaskiya, Zaria.

29. The post civil war situation is described by S. A. Agboola in 'Nigeria aims at self-sufficiency', *Geogrl Mag.* **44,** Oct. 1971, 43–49.

30. Report on the *Sample Census of Agriculture 1950–51,* Lagos, 1952.

31. See Peter Kilby, *The Nigerian Oil Palm Industry,* 1967.

32. See J. T. Coppock, 'Tobacco growing in Nigeria', *Erdkunde,* 1965, 297–306.

33. See J. S. Oguntoyinbo, 'Rainfall, evaporation and cotton production in Nigeria', *Nigerian Geogrl J.* 1967, 43–55.

34. J. C. Gardiner, *Oilseed Processing in Nigeria,* Lagos, 1953, and *Oilseed Processing in Nigeria: a statement of policy,* Lagos, 1954.

35. A. Melamid, 'The geography of the Nigerian petroleum industry', *Econ. Geog.* 1968, 37–56; L. H. Shatzl, *Petroleum in Nigeria,* 1969; Scott R. Pearson, *Petroleum and the Nigerian Economy,* 1970.

36. See B. W. Hodder, 'Tin mining on the Jos Plateau of Nigeria', *Econ. Geog.* **35,** 109–22; and articles by H. Hake, *West Africa,* 16 23 and 30 Jan. and 6 Feb. 1965.

37. See Fig. 26.14 and P. J. Wagland, 'Kainji and the Niger Dams Project', *Geography,* 1969, 459–63.

38. See Chapter 8 and its bibliography. Also Carl K. Eicher and Carl Liedholm, *Growth and Development of the Nigerian Economy,* Michigan State Univ. Press, 1970; Peter Kilby, *Industrialization in an open economy 1945–66,* 1969; C. C. Onyemelukwe, *Problems of Industrial Planning and Management in Nigeria,* 1966; Alan Sokolski, *The Establishment of Manufacturing in Nigeria,* New York, 1965; F. A. Wells and W. A. Warmington, *Studies in Industrialization: Nigeria and the Cameroons,* OUP, 1962.

39. On Nigerian ports reference should be made to Babafemi Ogundana, 'Patterns and problems of seaport evolution in Nigeria', in B. S. Hoyle and D. Hilling, eds, *Seaports and Development in Tropical Africa,* 1970.

40. See also E. K. Hawkins, *Road Transport in Nigeria,* OUP, 1958.

41. Peter M. Gould, 'Air traffic in Nigeria', *African Studies Bulletin,* **4,** 1961, 21.

**Supplementary references**
*Agriculture in Nigeria,* FAO, 1967.
BUCHANAN, K. M. and PUGH, J. C. *Land and People in Nigeria,* University of London Press, 1959.

BURNS, SIR A. *History of Nigeria,* 7th edn, Allen & Unwin, 1969.
CROWDER, M. *The Story of Nigeria,* 2nd edn, Faber, 1966.
LA ROCHE, H. *Nigéria, Que sais-je?,* 2nd edn, Paris, 1968.
STAPLETON, G. B. *The Wealth of Nigeria,* 2nd edn, OUP, 1967.
*Nigeria* (quarterly).
*Farm and Forest* (quarterly), Ibadan.
*Nigeria Trade Journal* (quarterly).
*Digest of Statistics* (quarterly).
*Nigerian Geographical Journal* (twice yearly).

**Maps**
Survey Departments, Lagos, Ibadan, Benin, Enugu and Kaduna.


*Topographic (all Federal Surveys)*
1 : 50 000.
1 : 62 000.
1 : 100 000.
1 : 125 000.
1 : 250 000.
1 : 500 000.


*Town plans*
1 : 1 200, 1 : 2 400, 1 : 4 800 and 1 : 12 500 for most towns. Also 1 : 20 000
   of Lagos.


*Geological*
1 : 100 000, 1 : 125 000 and 250 000. A few sheets available.
1 : 2 000 000  Nigeria.


*Population*
1 : 750 000  Eastern States.
1 : 1 000 000  Federation of Nigeria.
1 : 1 000 000  Northern Region.


*Various*
1 : 500 000  Mid-Western State. General map.
1 : 750 000  Road map of Western Nigeria.
1 : 750 000  Eastern States. Local Government.
1 : 750 000  Eastern States. Forestry Resources.
25 miles to 1 inch. Road map of Nigeria.
1 : 2 000 000  Northern States. Roads.
1 : 2 000 000  Northern States. Population 1952.

1 : 3 000 000  Northern States. Forests.

1 : 3 000 000  Nigeria of Administrative Areas; Agricultural Products; Communications (Internal); Communications (Rail, Road and River); Educational Facilities; Forest Reserves; Geology and Mineral Deposits; Health Facilities; Industries, Main Agricultural Exports and Locations of Mineral Deposits; Languages and Dialects; Mineral Deposits and Power Resources; Railways and Principal Commodities; Raindays; Rainfall; Rest Houses and Hotels; Soil Map; Telecommunications, Internal—Exchanges and Telephone Routes System; Telecommunications Internal—Telegraph and Radio Trunk Routes; Temperature; Trade (Internal); Tribal.

# Abbreviations used in the references

| | |
|---|---|
| *Ann. Ass. Am. Geogr.* | Annals of the Association of American Geographers |
| *Annls Géogr.* | Annales de Géographie |
| *Bull. IFAN* | Bulletin of IFAN (see below) |
| *Econ. Geog.* | Economic Geography |
| *Econ. Hist. Rev.* | Economic History Review |
| *Cah. Outre-mer* | Les Cahiers d'Outre-Mer |
| CUP | Cambridge University Press |
| *Geogrl J.* | Geographical Journal |
| *Geogrl Mag.* | Geographical Magzine |
| *Geogrl Rev.* | Geographical Review |
| IFAN | Institut Fondamental (formerly Français) d'Afrique Noire |
| IGN | Institut Géographique National, Paris |
| *J. Afr. Hist.* | Journal of African History |
| *J. Trop. Geog.* | Journal of Tropical Geography |
| *J. W. Afr. Sci. Ass.* | Journal of the West African Science Association |
| *Q. Jl roy. met. Soc.* | Quarterly Journal of the Royal Meteorological Society |
| ORSTOM | Office de la Recherche Scientifique et Technique Outre-Mer |
| OUP | Oxford University Press |
| *Scottish Geogrl. Mag.* | Scottish Geographical Magazine |
| *Tijdschr. v. econ. soc. Geog.* | Tijdschrift voor Economische en Sociale Geografie |
| *Trans. Inst. Br. Geogr.* | Transactions of the Institute of British Geographers |

# Index

# Index

The numbers in **heavy type** refer to an important reference. An asterisk(*) indicates that further reference should be made to the same subject under the countries.

## A